Contemporary Organizational Behavior

From Ideas to Action

KIMBERLY D. ELSBACH

University of California, Davis

ANNA B. KAYES

Stevenson University

D. CHRISTOPHER KAYES

The George Washington University

PEARSON

Boston   Columbus   Indianapolis   New York   San Francisco   Amsterdam
Cape Town   Dubai   London   Madrid   Milan   Munich   Paris   Montréal   Toronto
Delhi   Mexico City   São Paulo   Sydney   Hong Kong   Seoul   Singapore   Taipei   Tokyo

Vice President, Business Publishing: Donna Battista
Editor in Chief: Stephanie Wall
Senior Editor: Kris Ellis-Levy
Program Management Lead: Ashley Santora
Program Manager: Sarah Holle
Editorial Assistant: Bernard Ollila
Vice President, Product Marketing: Maggie Moylan
Director of Marketing, Digital Services and Products:
    Jeanette Koskinas
Executive Product Marketing Manager: Anne Fahlgren
Field Marketing Manager: Lenny Raper
Senior Strategic Marketing Manager: Erin Gardner
Project Management Lead: Judy Leale
Project Manager: Ann Pulido
Creative Director: Blair Brown
Senior Art Director/Program Design Lead: Janet Slowik
Interior and Cover Designer: Creative Circle

Cover Image: © Andrea Francolini/Corbis
Procurement Specialist: Carol Melville
VP, Director of Digital Strategy & Assessment:
    Paul Gentile
Manager of Learning Applications: Paul Deluca
Digital Editor: Brian Surette
Digital Studio Manager: Diane Lombardo
Digital Studio Project Manager: Robin Lazrus
Digital Studio Project Manager: Alana Coles
Digital Studio Project Manager: Monique Lawrence
Digital Studio Project Manager: Regina DaSilva
Full-Service Project Management: Valerie Iglar-Mobley/
    Integra-Chicago
Composition: Integra Software Services
Printer/Binder: Courier/Westford
Cover Printer: Courier/Westford
Text Font: 10/12 Minion Pro

BRIEF CONTENTS

CONTENTS

TOPIC SUMMARY 4: PERCEPTION 117

Part 3 Leading and Leadership Processes in Organizations

TOPIC SUMMARY 5: LEADERSHIP 151

TOPIC SUMMARY 6: MOTIVATION 187

TOPIC SUMMARY 7: PERSUASION, INFLUENCE, AND IMPRESSION MANAGEMENT 233

Part 4 Interpersonal Processes in Organizations

SECTION II
Cases 539

SECTION III
Exercises 593

Preface

Contemporary context... essential OB concepts... learning put into action

Overview

Contemporary Organizational Behavior: From Ideas to Action was built on three simple ideas:

1. Build a text around a few key ideas for each topic (rather than an extensive list of terms).
2. Invite recognized Organizational Behavior (OB) experts and thought leaders to write original contributions about how their ideas relate to contemporary organizations. These contributions include, for example, a description of how an OB concept applies to organizations or how it provides a more robust explanation of a concept. Another example of a contribution is relating a stream of research to a key OB idea or an author offering insights on how they teach a particular OB concept in their own class.
3. Create breathtaking case studies and experiential exercises that help students apply the concepts to their own experience with the goal of improving their own understanding of organizational behavior.

With these ideas in mind, *Contemporary Organizational Behavior* provides the first organizational behavior textbook designed specifically for today's learner and instructor. This is not a typical textbook, rather than traditional chapters, the content is broken into three sections: Topics, Cases, and Experiential Exercises. Each Topic contains a short, engaging summary of the central concepts plus two to four authoritative readings from topic experts. The Cases section includes eight real-world case studies from contemporary organizations. The Experiential Exercises section includes 38 exercises that bring concepts to life. Whether undergraduate or graduate students, each section can be tailored to the unique learning needs of each classroom.

Key Features

- Covers 14 key organizational behavior topics.
- Each topic includes a Topic Summary written by the textbook authors and two to four articles authored by an expert on that topic. Rather than having the entire book authored by one scholar (as in traditional texts), students have the opportunity to read the latest thinking in OB in the words of an expert on the topic. The expert contribution section provides students with direct access to the best minds across the full variety of topics in Organizational Behavior.
- Perfect for professors seeking to supplement lectures but who still want theory; also perfect for a 'topical' readings course.
- Can be customized or used as a traditional text complete with case studies, exercises, and online support material.

- The expert contribution section provides students direct access to the best minds and the latest thinking in Organizational Behavior.
- Demonstrates the relevance of research by combining an evidence-based approach to learning with more traditional theories.

This text addresses a critical challenge in management education. Learners enjoy understanding the relevance of ideas *and* seeing the practical implications of ideas. They like to learn, but learning is often outcome oriented and needs to be relevant to present circumstances. Students want to understand the connection among concepts, personal experience, reflection, and action. By putting concepts, theories, and research in a contemporary context, the book shows how students can put abstract ideas into action in an organization

The text is designed for students interested in moving beyond memorization and repetition to critical thinking and application. *Contemporary Organizational Behavior* stands in contrast to many texts. Most traditional texts focus on knowledge acquisition in the form of learning new terms and concepts. This book encourages students to move beyond acquisition of knowledge to applying the concepts. Students must engage in critical thinking, application, and relating concepts to their direct experience. Students are introduced to core OB terms and topics and then asked to engage in interactive exercises that include individual work, teamwork, and class discussion questions. Learning is also applied through case studies and conversations.

The text addresses a common concern expressed by many faculty. Faculty seek relevance without sacrificing expertise or rigor. The content of the book takes students deeper into a topic by offering several readings, which reflect different levels of difficulty. The book helps learners understand the relevance of theory and research for contemporary organizations.

How to Use this Book

Modular Approach

- The text is organized into three sections:
  - Topic Summaries and Expert Contributions—brief overviews of key theory, research, and terms on a given topic are accompanied by original works written by experts in Organizational Behavior that put theory, research, and concepts into a contemporary context.
  - Case Studies—engaging cases written by author Kim Elsbach and other experts.
  - Experiential Exercises—a collection of easy to facilitate exercises to use in class to get your students acclimated to working in groups.
- Adaptable to different levels of experience.
- The unique format allows the instructor two options:
  - The instructor can follow a pre-existing template of topics, or
  - The instructor can create a unique custom text by mixing and matching topic summaries and readings with the case studies and experiential exercises that are just right for your students' level of experience.
- A matrix of case studies and exercises matched to topics provides guidance and suggestions on how to fully utilize the text. The matrices are located in the Preface and in the *Instructor's Manual*. This allows each topic section to engage in the learning cycle: experiencing through exercises, reflecting on individual experience, drawing on theory, and applying through case studies.

How Our Text Helps Students Learn

We designed this text based on the experiential learning model. Key features of the book are linked to the four processes of experiential learning.

Experiential Exercises

Experiential exercises engage students in activities that ignite thinking, spark connections between concepts and experience, and make learning more exciting. Experiential exercises also create new experiences that can serve as the basis for collective reflective.

Experiential exercises can take the form of reflective exercises. Reflective exercises encourage students to take a step back and reflect on prior experiences. The exercises then encourage students to bring experience from outside the classroom and apply these experiences to class concepts. By drawing on experiences from work, social settings, and other direct experiences, students make connections between their own experiences and class concepts.

Topic Summaries and Spotlight on Research

Topic Summaries and **Spotlight on Research** features encourage conceptual learning. The text encourages abstract thinking through topic summaries that introduce key terms, theories, and models. Each topic summary is introduced by a conceptual overview that introduces the topic and integrates key ideas into an overarching framework. Theories, terms, and models no longer serve as simply abstract ideas. Instead, these abstract notions help students frame their experiences in new ways, provide new insights that may lead to personal and professional development, and encourage students to look at situations more holistically.

The **Spotlight on Research** feature helps students understand how evidence-based research in the field of organizational behavior can help them learn. Spotlight on Research highlights an interesting research study and shows students how this research can inform practice. Students develop an appreciation for the value of evidence-based research and see how they can use evidence-based research to support their own thinking and opinions.

Cases, OB at Work, and Expert Contributions

Cases, features such as **OB at Work**, and **Expert Contributions** help students apply learning in new ways. Students can begin to place organizational behavior concepts in context and move the study of organizational behavior from ideas to action.

Cases illustrate concepts and allow students the opportunity to exercise judgment and to improve their understanding of the challenges associated with applying organizational behavior concepts to organizational problems. When cases are used in the classroom, students can gain insight into the perspective of others and begin to understand how context plays a role in applying concepts. Importantly, cases serve as an integrative tool where students can apply concepts that they have learned across different chapters.

OB at Work illustrates how professionals apply organizational behavior concepts in their own careers and workplaces. Each OB at Work segment features an individual and explains how they have turned to OB concepts to help them solve an organizational problem, improve a process, or make sense of a work related situation.

Expert Contributions apply concepts discussed in the topic summary. This unique feature provides students valuable insights into how to apply the latest thinking in OB.

Elements of the Text Mapped into the Experiential Learning Cycle

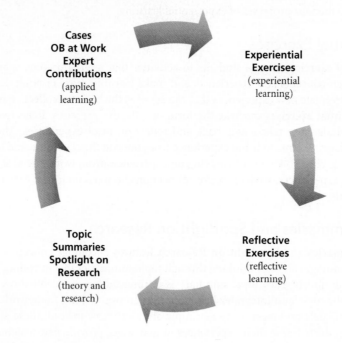

Organization of the Text

Contemporary Organizational Behavior: From Ideas to Action is organized into topic sections, rather than traditional chapters. Each topic section contains a short, engaging summary of the central concepts, and two to four authoritative readings from topic experts. Professors may also assign a real-world case study from a contemporary organization and/or experiential exercises that bring topic concepts to life. This provides the basis for understanding both the underlying theory that explains organizational behavior and how this theory is applied in a contemporary context.

Topic Summary—Each topic summary provides students with a succinct summary of a particular topic in organizational behavior. Each of these topics in organizational behavior could be a separate book! We have consolidated the thinking on this topic and framed it in a way to show you the connection among important ideas. Features in the topic summary include:

> **Learning Objectives**—The learning objectives for each topic are listed in the beginning of the topic summary and are matched within the text. Students can refer to the learning objectives as you study the topic summary.

> **Key Terms**—Key terms are provided at the beginning of each topic summary and are bolded to stand out. After you read the topic summary, students can refer to the terms listed to check their comprehension of the material that they learned. Students can take notes and write down any questions they have to bring up in class discussions or to refer to the course instructor.

OB at Work—Real experiences by workplace professionals are highlighted in this feature. This helps students see the ideas of organizational behavior put into action.

Spotlight on Research—Organizational behavior ideas are based on research that scholars have conducted and published. Oftentimes, scholars will conduct research based on a question that they have about life in organizations. We provide students with an overview of a contemporary research study and discussion questions to frame their thinking.

Expert Contributions—We asked leading scholars in organizational behavior that specialize in various topics to contribute a reading around one or more of their ideas. These ideas have been published in books, peer reviewed journal outlets, and presented at conferences, and are often based on years of research, thinking, and scholarly conversation. They wrote the readings specifically for *Contemporary Organizational Behavior*.

Instructor Resources

At the Instructor Resource Center, www.pearsonhighered.com/irc, instructors can easily register to gain access to a variety of instructor resources available with this text in downloadable format. If assistance is needed, our dedicated technical support team is ready to help with the media supplements that accompany this text. Visit http://247.pearsoned.com for answers to frequently asked questions and toll-free user support phone numbers.

The following supplements are available with this text:

- Instructor's Manual
- Test Bank
- TestGen® Computerized Test Bank
- PowerPoint Presentation

Custom Library

www.pearsonhighered.com/custombusiness

Pearson Custom Business gives you the freedom to create an ideal textbook—with cases to match—that meets your students' needs and your course requirements. Pick the material you'll use—students pay only for the content you choose.

Preview our extensive library online with over 50,000 case studies, articles, and text chapters—and build your perfect book quickly and easily. You can request an evaluation copy to examine before you order. You can make changes if you wish, and there is no cost or obligation—you are in control. Visit www.pearsonhighered.com/custombusiness to learn more.

Student Resources

CourseSmart

CourseSmart eTextbooks were developed for students looking to save the cost on required or recommended textbooks. Students simply select their eText by title or author and purchase immediate access to the content for the duration of the course using any major credit card. With a CourseSmart eText, students can search for specific keywords or page numbers, take notes online, print out reading assignments that incorporate lecture notes, and bookmark important passages for later review. For more information or to purchase a CourseSmart eTextbook, visit www.coursesmart.com.

Our Team

Writing a textbook is a team effort. We would like to thank the many people that contributed to our book, all with a desire to focus on student learning. This includes the professionals that were willing to be interviewed to place their experiences in the context of organizational behavior concepts. This also includes the numerous graduate and undergraduate students who gave us feedback around content, and were willing to participate with topic summaries, readings, case studies, and exercises inside and outside of our classes. We would like to especially thank our colleagues across many colleges and universities who provided guidance, support, feedback and ideas in shaping this text. In particular, colleagues at the Organizational Behavior Teaching Society who helped us refine our ideas, while preserving the focus on learning.

Mohammad Ali, University of Maryland–Eastern Shore

Wendy S. Becker, Shippensburg University, PA

Mark Bing, University of Mississippi, MS

Carl Blencke, University of Central Florida, FL

Nicholas Brockunier, University of Maryland–University College, MD

Judi Brownell, Cornell University, NY

Don Caruth, Texas A&M University, TX

Kalyan Chakravarty, California State University–Northridge, CA

Constance Cook, Governors State University, IL

Kristl Davison, University of Mississippi, MS

Diane Denslow, University of North Florida, FL

Ken Dunegan, Cleveland State, OH

Kim Gower, Virginia Commonwealth University, VA

Andrew Johnson, Santa Clara University, CA

Avan Jassawalla, SUNY Geneseo, NY

Timothy Madigan, Mansfield University, PA

Douglas Mahony, Lehigh University, PA

Laura Martin, Midwestern State University, TX

Carrie Messal, College of Charleston, NC

Jessica Methot, University of Florida, FL

Morgan Milner, Eastern Michigan University, MI

Lorianne Mitchell, Eastern Tennessee University, TN

Dan Morrell, Middle Tennessee State University, TN

Kenneth Murrell, University of West Florida, FL

Sharon Norris, Spring Arbor University, MI

Floyd Ormsbee, Clarkson University, NY

Rhonda Palladi, Georgia State University, GA

Tracy Porter, Cleveland State, OH

Scott A Quatro, Covenant College, GA

Anne Reilly, Loyola University, LA

Katherine Roberson, Southern Illinois University–Edwardsville, IL

Joe Rode, Miami University, FL

Matthew Rodgers, Ohio State University, OH

Ben Rosen, University of North Carolina, NC

Holly Schroth, University of California–Berkley, CA

Leslie Shore, Metropolitan State University, MN

Tony Simons, Cornell University, NY

Randall Sleeth, Virginia Commonwealth University, VA

Kenneth Thompson, DePaul University, IL

Linda Tibbetts, Miami University, FL

Susana Velez-Castrillion, University of Houston, TX

Paula Weber, St Cloud University, MN

The authors would like to acknowledge the hard work of the following professionals for creating the content for the supplements package. Their hard work and commitment is truly appreciated.

Instructor's Manual: Donna Galla, American Public University, Charles Town, WV

PowerPoints: Tracy Porter, Cleveland State University, Cleveland, OH

Test Bank: Laura Martin, Midwestern State University, Wichita Falls, TX

Expert Contributors

Deborah Ancona, Massachusetts Institute of Technology

Neal M. Ashkanasy, University of Queensland

Sigal G. Barsade, University of Pennsylvania

Rabi S. Bhagat, University of Memphis

David Bowen, Thunderbird School of Global Management

David L. Bradford, Stanford University

Jeremy Brees, Florida State University

Henrik Bresman, INSEAD, France

W. Warner Burke, Teachers College, Columbia University

David Caldwell, Santa Clara University

Stacy M. Campbell, Kennesaw State University

W. Keith Campbell, University of Georgia

Michael A. Campion, Purdue University

Michael C. Campion, University of South Carolina

Catherine S. Daus, Southern Illinois University, Edwardsville

Daniel Denison, IMD Business School

D. Keith Denton, Missouri State

Shari Duron, Consultant

Amy C. Edmondson, Harvard Business School

Joyce Ehrlinger, Washington State University

Jan Kees Elsbach, CEP America

Ellen Ensher, Loyola Marymount University

Samantha Fairclough, University of Mississippi

Robert Folger, University of Central Florida

Robert Fulmer, Duke Corporate Education

Jennifer L. Gibbs, Rutgers University

Donald E Gibson, Fairfield University

Cristina B. Gibson, University of Western Australia

Stephen Gilliland, University of Arizona

Thomas Gilovich, Cornell University

Alan M. Glassman, California State University

Rob Goffee, London Business School

Bradley Googins, Boston College

Elisa Grant-Vallone, California State University, San Marcos

Markus Hällgren, Umeå University, Sweden

Laurie Helgoe, Davis and Elkins College

Michael Hogg, Claremont Graduate University

Erika James, Emory University

Sonya Jewell, University of California, Davis

Gareth Jones, IE Business School, Madrid

David A. Kolb, Experience Based Learning Systems, Inc.

Lindsey Kotrba, Denison Consulting

Roy J. Lewicki, The Ohio State University

Jeremy D. Mackey, Florida State University

Michael Marquardt, The George Washington University

Mark J. Martinko, Performance Associates

Richard O. Mason, Southern Methodist University

Roger C. Mayer, North Carolina State University

Philip H. Mirvis, Private Consultant

Troy V. Mumford, Colorado State University

Valerie L. Myers, University of Michigan

Luciara Nardon, Carleton University

Troy R. Nielson, Brigham Young University

Christopher P. Niemiec, University of Rochester

Levi Nieminen, Denison Consulting

Michael A. Roberto, Bryant University

Paul C. Nutt, The Ohio State University

Asha Rao, California State University, East Bay

Michael A. Roberto, Bryant University

Lee Ross, Stanford University

Stuart M. Schmidt, Temple University

Debra L. Shapiro, University of Maryland

Bart Soenens, Gent University

Michael Useem, University of Pennsylvania

Maarten Vansteenkiste, Gent University

Gary R. Weaver, University of Delaware

Bauback Yeganeh, Everidian

Deone Zell, California State University, Northridge

Finally, we would like to acknowledge the tremendous efforts of our editorial team who infused patience and creativity into this process. Kris Ellis-Levy, Senior Editor of Management, partnered with us to realize the vision of the text. As project manager, Ann Pulido kept us on track, along with Sarah Holle, program manager. Our editorial team truly shared our passion for student learning.

– *Kim Elsbach*

– *Anna Kayes*

– *Chris Kayes*

MATRIX OF CASE STUDIES FOR USE WITH TOPIC SECTIONS

CASE TITLE	Introduction to Organizational Behavior	Individual Characteristics	Learning	Perception	Leadership	Motivation
The Case of Apple iPhone 4					X	X
"We Are Global or We Are Nothing": Conflict and Cover-Up at ColequarterMaine						X
EMERGENCY! We Need a Better Compensation System						X
Face Time at TechPoint Software, Inc.			X	X	X	
Whatever Happened to One of the "100 Best Companies to Work For"? A Case Study of Hewlett-Packard	X	X		X	X	X
NASCAR's Drive for Diversity: Can They Reach the Finish Line?			X			X
Perceptions of Leaders Following Public Failures: A Tale of Two Coaches		X		X	X	
Conflict in Santa's Workshop: Learning to Be a Team Player at ToyKing		X				X

MATRIX OF EXERCISES FOR USE WITH TOPIC SECTIONS

EXERCISE TITLE	Introduction to Organizational Behavior	Individual Characteristics	Learning	Perception	Leadership	Motivation
Big Five Celebrity Spotlight		X				
Creating My Brand					X	
My Expat Assignment			X			
How Leaders Effect You					X	X
My Best and Worst Learning Experiences	X		X	X		X
Developing Your Career—Leadership Development in Action	X			X	X	
Development While In College			X	X		
Facts and Opinions			X		X	
Being Positive			X	X		

Persuasion, Influence, and Impression Management	Decision Making	Groups and Teams	Conflict and Negotiation	Diversity and Communication	Culture	Change, Innovation, and Stress	Corporate Social Responsibility, Ethics, and Sustainability
X	X		X		X	X	
X		X		X		X	X
	X	X	X		X	X	X
	X		X		X	X	
X				X	X		
	X	X	X	X	X		
X							X
		X	X	X			X

Persuasion, Influence, and Impression Management	Decision Making	Groups and Teams	Conflict and Negotiation	Diversity and Communication	Culture	Change, Innovation, and Stress	Corporate Social Responsibility, Ethics, and Sustainability
X							X
				X	X		
				X			
			X				
	X						
X				X			

(Continued on next page)

EXERCISE TITLE	Introduction to Organizational Behavior	Individual Characteristics	Learning	Perception	Leadership	Motivation
Force Field Analysis						
Bias and Decision Making				X		
Well-Being at Work						
What Stresses You Out?						X
Laughter Is the Best Medicine		X				
Building My Network–Individual	X	X				
Writing a Team Contract						
Design Your Technology						X
Team Performance Evaluation				X		
Overcoming Resistance						
Employment Branding	X			X		X
OD Techniques at Work						X
A Clash of Cultures						
What's Your University's Culture?						
Find the Artifacts						
Back-to-Back Change						
Social Media Dilemma						
Develop Your Professional Code	X					
Communication Breakdown						
Diversity Rocks		X				
You Can't Handle The Truth				X		
The Ethics of the Climb		X				
Mindmapping	X					
Could I Be a Whistleblower?		X				X
Sustainability Practice at Work						
Who Do I Fire?						
What Are My Values?		X				X
Team Survival Simulation						
Federal Intelligence Simulation In Instructor's Manual					X	

Persuasion, Influence, and Impression Management	Decision Making	Groups and Teams	Conflict and Negotiation	Diversity and Communication	Culture	Change, Innovation, and Stress	Corporate Social Responsibility, Ethics, and Sustainability
	X					X	
	X						
					X	X	
						X	
						X	
X			X	X			
		X		X	X		
						X	
	X	X					
						X	
X				X		X	
				X		X	
					X		
X					X		X
					X		
						X	
X	X						
			X				X
			X	X			
				X			
X				X			X
	X	X					X
		X					
							X
X					X		X
	X		X				
	X	X					
	X	X	X	X			

Section I

Topic Summaries and Expert Contributions

Konstantin Chagin/Shutterstock

1 Introduction to Organizational Behavior

Topic Summary Learning Objectives

1. Describe organizational behavior and its importance.

2. Define the three levels of organizational behavior and the four organizational behavior processes.

3. Describe and provide examples of different types of organizations.

4. Present the skills needed to be effective in contemporary organizations and describe the three learning activities associated with gaining these skills.

5. Apply concepts of organizational behavior to organizations.

Key Terms

applied, p. 7

characteristics of contemporary organizations, p. 8

individual processes, p. 4

interdisciplinary study, p. 6

interpersonal processes, p. 4

interpretive-based learning, p. 9

leading and leadership processes, p. 4

learning activities, p. 9

levels of organizational behavior, p. 3

negative organizational outcomes, p. 7

organization, p. 5

organizational behavior, p. 3

organizational processes, p. 4

performance-based learning, p. 9

positive organizational outcomes, p. 7

practice-based and developmental learning, p. 9

qualitative, p. 6

quantitative, p. 6

situational approach, p. 8

types of contemporary organizations, p. 5

universal approach, p. 8

Introduction to Contemporary Organizational Behavior

1 Describe organizational behavior and its importance.

Organizational behavior (OB) is the study of people and what people think, feel, and do within organizations. People participate in organizations for many different reasons, but in general, organizations facilitate the achievement of goals that could not be achieved by an individual working independently. Working in an organization that is unpleasant can lead to negative consequences on health, well-being, creativity and productivity.[1] On the other hand, many organizational processes can lead to improvements in how people experience organizational life. Most people would rather work in organizations where there is civility, creativity, recognition, and other positive behaviors. Improving how organizations function, building positive organizational environments, and changing negative behavior requires understanding of the highly complex and interrelated processes of organizational behavior.

Figure 1.1 considers three practical challenges faced in organizations and how organizational behavior principles can help to resolve these challenges. For example:

- An employee has an extensive personal network, but still feels unrecognized at work. Developing influence skills may help this employee gain recognition and better leverage her network.

- A team faces a simple, but time critical project, but team members feel that the team is fragmented and not all the members of the team are committed to the project. The team can take time to build cohesion and develop a common purpose to overcome the team's fragmentation.

- An organization has a toxic culture where individuals act in ways that are uncivil and hostile. Increasing communication, improving interpersonal skills, and establishing a culture where positive interactions are rewarded, can help to change the organization's culture.

The three problems outlined here correspond to the **three levels of organizational behavior.** Behavior occurs at three levels—individual, team or group, and organization. In the first example, the employee may rely on individual level organizational behavior processes such as communication, persuasion, and influence. In the second example, teams can receive a boost from team training or a specialized team intervention aimed at clarifying the team's purpose. Finally, an organization with a

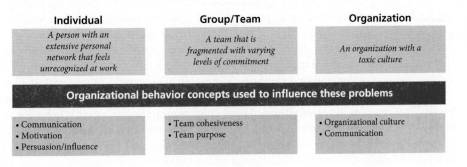

Individual	Group/Team	Organization
A person with an extensive personal network that feels unrecognized at work	*A team that is fragmented with varying levels of commitment*	*An organization with a toxic culture*

Organizational behavior concepts used to influence these problems

• Communication • Motivation • Persuasion/influence	• Team cohesiveness • Team purpose	• Organizational culture • Communication

Figure 1.1
Challenges at Work

Figure 1.2 Topics in Contemporary Organizational Behavior

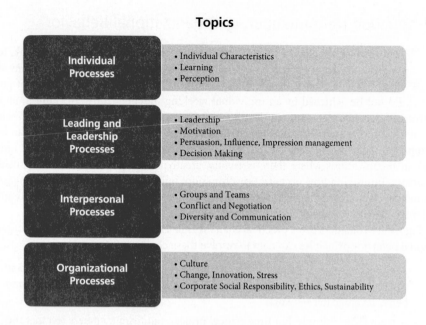

Topics

Individual Processes
- Individual Characteristics
- Learning
- Perception

Leading and Leadership Processes
- Leadership
- Motivation
- Persuasion, Influence, Impression management
- Decision Making

Interpersonal Processes
- Groups and Teams
- Conflict and Negotiation
- Diversity and Communication

Organizational Processes
- Culture
- Change, Innovation, Stress
- Corporate Social Responsibility, Ethics, Sustainability

2 Define the three levels of organizational behavior and the four organizational behavior processes.

toxic culture can change the tone at the organizational level, promoting warmth and civility across various divisions of an organization.[2]

Contemporary Organizational Behavior introduces key organizational behavior terms and provides a deeper look into organizational processes.[3] There are four dynamic organizational processes that shed light on life in contemporary organizations. **Individual processes** describe individual differences in characteristics, learning, and perception. **Leading and leadership processes** describe the factors that impact differences in leadership, motivation, persuasion, influence, impression management, and decision making. **Interpersonal processes** refer to the pattern of interactions among individuals that includes groups and teams, negotiation, and communication and diversity. **Organizational processes** include the ingrained patterns of acting and interacting at the organizational level and cover topics of culture, change, innovation, stress, corporate social responsibility, ethics, and sustainability.

The study of contemporary organizational behavior provides a better understanding of how these organizational processes can improve outcomes for individuals, groups, and organizations by highlighting three critical components. First, a contemporary approach integrates the best and most recent evidence-based research and puts this research into the context of your personal life, work, and participation in organizations. Second, a contemporary approach presents long standing theories and ideas about organizations and shows how these theories and ideas can be helpful in making sense of experiences in organizations. Third, contemporary organizational behavior re-emphasizes the practical nature of organizational behavior as an applied field of study. Organizational behavior does more than explain and describe life in organizations, it is a field of study directed towards change and improvement of organizations and the people in organizations.

What Is an Organization?

An **organization** is where people interact and coordinate in order to achieve a purpose. All organizations share one attribute: organizations require people interacting with one another. However, many different **types of organizations** exist. In fact, researchers have tried for decades to find a definitive classification to explain the various types of organizations, but as soon as a complete list of all types of organizations seems to be identified, a new type of organization emerges. An organization can be a company directed towards making profits or an informal group of students that regularly meet about safety on campus. Even a religious congregation constitutes a type of organization. Essentially, organizations are varied, are formed for different lengths of time and for different purposes. Table 1.1 outlines several types of contemporary organizations.[4] The study of organizational behavior looks at both the similarities and the differences among people and their interactions in organizations.[5]

3 Describe and provide examples of different types of organizations.

Fancy Collection/SuperStock

Table 1.1 Types of Contemporary Organizations

Type of Contemporary Organization	Description	Example
Community of practice	Group of people who share an interest in a topic and interact together on the topic	Associations, international development, education
Hybrid	Form of organization that combines two or more forms. May consist of a team structure embedded in a formal hierarchical structure.	Technology firm, some corporations
Network	An organization with a shared responsibility, equal status among members, and shaped more by the activities of its members than by its hierarchy	Technology firms, craft organizations
Bureaucratic	An organization with specialized roles, and a command and control structure with formal hierarchy	U.S. government agency, armed forces, some corporations
Professional	A public or private organization that consists of people with strong professional norms and similar professions	Healthcare, law, and higher education
Representative democratic	An organization based on the principles of employee autonomy, participation, and even profit-sharing or shared ownership	Credit unions, food-coop

What Is Organizational Behavior?
A Field of Study

Organizational behavior emerged as a distinct field of study in the 1940s. By 1971, organizational behavior had its own division in the prestigious academic organization, The Academy of Management.[6] Research and new ideas have kept pace with the corresponding changes in the workplace and the field of organizational behavior continues to refine its scope. When new issues emerge such as diversity or corporate social responsibility, so too has the study of organizational behavior sought to better understand these issues by drawing on a variety of fields of study and by encompassing complimentary forms of research.

Interdisciplinary

Organizational behavior helps us understand organizations from many different perspectives. For example, economics provides a popular way to understand organizations as a function of supply and demand in a free market. Economics has been highly influential in our perceptions of how organizations function. A closely related approach to understanding organizations comes from the financial perspective, which seeks to understand organizations from the perspective of cash flows, debt, and other financial considerations. In a somewhat related approach, an accounting perspective describes organizations as a series of accounting processes and financial controls and costs. While fields of study such as marketing and strategy largely view organizations as a function of external markets, competitive advantages, and products and services.

Each approach offers insights into how an organization functions and the purpose of the organization; yet, each of these approaches remains incomplete without a comprehensive understanding brought about by the study of organizational behavior. Organizational behavior is an **interdisciplinary study**, which means that it draws from different disciplines in order to understand organizations from multiple perspectives and viewpoints. As an interdisciplinary study, organizational behavior draws from psychology, sociology, anthropology, economics, political science, strategy, management, and even the natural sciences. Early criticisms of organizational behavior included that as a field it borrowed too heavily from other disciplines and did not contribute its own research. The contemporary study of organizational behavior, however, contributes unique insights that are theoretical grounded, based on research, and applied in organizations.

Qualitative and Quantitative Approaches

The distinction between qualitative and quantitative approaches to research is important in the study of organizations. **Qualitative** approaches explore situations and seek a deeper understanding of a situation through the use of detailed methods such as focus groups, interviews, and observation. Qualitative approaches provide deeper and richer understanding of a particular case or situation but this understanding is not necessarily applicable to other situations or to a different context. **Quantitative** approaches, on the other hand, try to predict results and identify factors that are universal. Quantitative approaches rely on surveys and other large-scale data collection techniques. One question to ask yourself as you learn about organizational behavior is whether or not you think certain ideas, studies, or concepts can be applied across all organizations or whether they can only be applied in certain contexts and under certain situations.

Applied

Organizational behavior is an **applied** discipline because it seeks to improve organizations and to make positive impacts on people while solving practical problems that people face in the workplace. It seeks to answer questions, solve problems, and help organizations achieve goals. Although there is agreement that certain outcomes are important, such as job satisfaction, work performance, organizational citizenship behavior (OCB), and effectiveness, no single outcome is universally accepted. Some have argued that different types of organizations should strive for different outcomes. For example, universities should strive to improve the education of students. In contrast, businesses might strive to increase shareholder value through increased revenue growth while a mission driven not-for-profit organization might try to accomplish its mission. Others have argued that organizations should focus on multiple outcomes rather than a single outcome.

Some of the **positive organizational outcomes** that organizations seek to achieve include effectiveness, job satisfaction, organizational commitment, reduced absenteeism, and low turnover intention. For example, organizational behavior researchers offer a connection among interpersonal processes such as support, commitment, and performance. This connection occurs in the workplace for employees as well as in universities for students.[7] If you were to apply organizational behavior principles to your university to achieve positive outcomes, you might encourage a culture of student support that leads to student commitment and ultimately improves student performance in class.[8]

Negative organizational outcomes describe a full range of undesirable behaviors including unethical behavior, sabotage, absenteeism, and incivility. These types of behaviors are what organizational behavior seeks to understand, solve, or prevent.[9] Some

---

How can organizational behavior help you?

- ✔ Learn skills that employers deem critical for the contemporary workplace.
- ✔ Improve your understanding of how organizations function.
- ✔ Identify ways to motivate others.
- ✔ Improve understanding of human behavior.
- ✔ Evaluate and execute different forms of decision making.
- ✔ Garner insights into how you fit into the larger organization.
- ✔ Understand how an organization can help with greater social good and be profitable.
- ✔ Navigate the ethical and performance-based challenges of contemporary organizations.
- ✔ Develop yourself as a person and leader.
- ✔ Improve your overall well being at work and beyond.
- ✔ Understand ways that you contribute to your organization.
- ✔ Solve problems.
- ✔ Match your preferences to learning organizational behavior.

students have asked why employees do bad things, when these bad things result in trillions of dollars of costs annually for organizations and society. Some organizational behavior researchers have argued that simple managerial changes, such as implementing an ethics policy, often fail to prevent bad behavior because many problems faced by organizations involve complex individual processes like emotion and learning.[10] A more complete understanding of unethical behavior at work should encourage you to consider emotions of guilt and shame and how individuals form values. A contemporary approach to organizational behavior focuses on understanding organizations as a set of complex processes that lead to multiple outcomes.

Understanding the Contemporary Organization

Contemporary organizations present many challenges. The rapid pace of change, the complexity of information, and multiple goals place ever increasing demands on organizations. Organizations require continued adaptation in order to function effectively in this environment. How people view the nature of work, how work is accomplished, and how to improve work continues to evolve.[11] Contemporary organizations, despite their many differences, share a few common **characteristics**.[12, 13] These include:

- Pressure to achieve more complex goals
- Emphasis on measurement and data driven decisions
- Greater competition across the organization
- Diminished value on long-term relationships with employees
- Action orientation
- Multicultural membership
- Coordination of work across distance and time
- Unpredictable and ever-changing environment
- Necessity of individual *and* team performance

Even though many people would agree that these characteristics are present in their organization, people continue to disagree about how to respond to these challenges. Some believe that there is always one best way to respond and behave to problems or situations, this is called the **universal approach**. People who take the universal approach believe that one idea or set of tools applies to any situation. The universal approach was popular early in the evolution of the field of organizational behavior. A more contemporary understanding of organizational behavior involves the **situational approach**. The situational approach suggests that problems or situations need to be evaluated in a particular context in order to find the best tool or ideas to respond. An understanding of context improves the ability to understand, describe, and influence behavior in organizations. Once the situation or context for the behavior is understood, then the tools that are necessary to respond effectively can be determined.

As you read and learn about organizational behavior, you may find that some of the ideas or research presented do not support your personal experiences. One reason that your experiences may not match what you are reading about is that organizational behavior often seeks to explain general rules or principles rather than describe specific experiences. This means that concepts and research findings often reflect broader sets of experiences, beyond the experience of a single individual. As you learn new ideas and concepts, you may find yourself questioning your own assumptions and ideas about behavior in the workplace. Understanding organizational behavior through one's own experience is a good starting place, but should be complimented with systematic study and research.

Who Benefits from Organizational Behavior?

All types of organizational members benefit from understanding organizational behavior. Some careers, like human resources, management, and consulting specifically draw on organizational behavior principles. However, knowledge, skills, and principles of organizational behavior can be applied in any career field. Organizational behavior topics and principles are embedded in university curriculum in business schools, medical schools, law schools, engineering schools, and schools of education, to name a few. Nearly all organizations, including the *Fortune* 500 companies, rely on organizational behavior principles for training curriculum for leadership development programs, management decision making, and designing organizational processes.

How Can Organizational Behavior Help You?

A contemporary approach to organizational behavior provides a comprehensive overview of essential organizational behavior concepts and helps you to apply these concepts in practice. Learning and applying organizational behavior concepts is achieved through several different **learning activities**. First, you will learn basic concepts, terms, and theories. A basic understanding of the language associated with organizations facilitates your performance as a student. This is called **performance-based learning** because the outcome of performance-based learning is to recall and demonstrate basic knowledge.

Corresponding to each topic summary are in-depth readings by experts. These expert readings help you to integrate concepts and differentiate among and across ideas, also termed **interpretive-based learning**. Interpretive learning improves your understanding of concepts and ideas by comparing and contrasting them. You should begin to see how the concepts could be applied across different contexts as you develop a deeper understanding of the concepts. Understanding the basic strengths and weaknesses of various concepts is essential to interpretive learning.[14]

Cases studies and exercises further deepen your learning as you learn to apply the concepts in your own life and work. Cases and exercises provide you with the opportunity to experience the concepts firsthand and to interact with others around these concepts. Application of the concepts leads to **practice-based and developmental learning**. Practice-based learning will help you solve behavioral-based problems in the workplace, better understand people's behavior, influence, and apply the concepts in order to meet the challenges of today's changing workplace. Figure 1.3 shows the progressive nature of these learning activities.

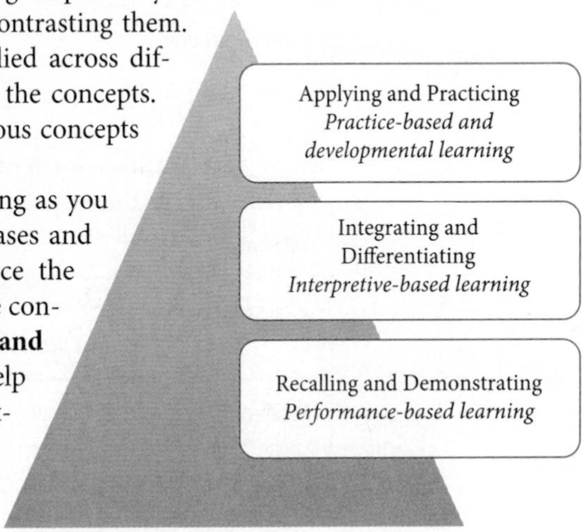

Applying and Practicing
Practice-based and developmental learning

Integrating and Differentiating
Interpretive-based learning

Recalling and Demonstrating
Performance-based learning

Figure 1.3 Learning Activities

4 Present the skills needed to be effective in contemporary organizations and describe the three learning activities associated with gaining these skills.

Skills Necessary in Contemporary Organizations

Navigating contemporary organizations requires more than just learning and applying concepts—success requires learning a combination of emotional, cognitive, and behavioral skills. A survey conducted by the Society for Human Resource Management and the online *Wall Street Journal*[15] identified a list of organizational behavior skills for success in contemporary organizations. A sample of these skills is listed in Table 1.2 below alongside some of the organizational behavior concepts discussed in this book.

Skills are only one factor associated with success. Research also shows that different work preferences are associated with the skills necessary to complete different college majors.[16] For example, accounting and finance students prefer to work with data; information technology students prefer to work with objects; and marketing students prefer to interact verbally. While all studies of preferences have limitations, it may be useful to

Table 1.2 Important Skills Needed and Relevant Contemporary OB Topic

Skills Needed for the Changing Workplace	Relevant Contemporary Organizational Behavior Topic
Adaptability and flexibility	Organizational change, learning, individual characteristics
Problem solving and critical thinking	Individual characteristics, decision making, negotiation, learning
Leadership	Leadership, persuasion, influence and impression management
Professionalism	Individual characteristics, organizational culture, motivation, persuasion, influence, and impression management
Teamwork	Groups and teams, organizational culture, communication and diversity
Communication	Communication, perception, persuasion, influence, and impression management, negotiation, individual characteristics
Innovation	Individual characteristics, leadership, and organizational change and innovation
Diversity	Diversity, learning, organizational culture
Ethics	Corporate social responsibility and ethics, organizational culture, decision making, leadership
Learning	Learning, individual characteristics, perception, motivation
Health and wellness choices	Stress, motivation, individual characteristics

reflect on your own natural preferences and how they impact your learning and engagement within a particular academic course. Similarly, you might find that you have a natural preference for one or more components of learning organizational behavior. For example, if you enjoy teamwork and verbal discussion, you may gravitate towards exercises that involve teamwork and interacting with others. If you prefer data analysis, the expert contributions based on quantitative data might intrigue you. If you enjoy abstract ideas, the topic summaries and readings may be of the most interest to you.

Conclusion

This topic summary will help you understand processes studied by the field of organizational behavior and how improving these processes may lead to improved individuals, groups, and organizations. A contemporary approach to organizational behavior is useful in providing individuals at all levels of an organization a sense of how and why organizations function and why people behave in a particular manner. Organizational behavior topics overlap with important skills that employers identify as most desired in the changing workplace.

OB AT WORK

AVON CEO SHERI McCOY LEADS ORGANIZATIONAL TURNAROUND RELYING ON ORGANIZATIONAL BEHAVIOR PRINCIPLES

Sheri McCoy

5 Apply concepts of organizational behavior to organizations.

Sheri McCoy spent 30 years working in various leadership roles at Johnson & Johnson, working her way to Vice Chairman. At 55 years old, McCoy was surely on track to further success at Johnson & Johnson, but when cosmetics company Avon asked Sheri to take the role of CEO of the $10 billion company, she realized this was the opportunity to revitalize an iconic U.S. cosmetics company.

Avon, one of the largest and most well recognized brands in cosmetics, was experiencing a slump and was looking to reinvigorate its sales and its brand. Under the previous CEO, Avon was unable to achieve its ambitious growth plans. Attempts to rebrand the company's products as luxury goods proved only a partial success. Even though the company's largest sales were in emerging market countries, like Brazil, the company seemed to lack the experience necessary to successfully weather the legal and cultural complexities of many of the emerging markets.

McCoy, a chemical engineer by training, had obtained her MBA and recognized that her success in turning around the company would rely as much on her management skills as her engineering background. The products themselves were well known and successful, but the nuances of transforming a 128-year-old company would require an extreme management makeover. Despite years of growth, the company had failed to invest in modernizing systems, processes, and procedures. With nearly 6 million independent sales representatives around the world, McCoy saw an impressive opportunity to return to the company's history of helping women obtain financial independence as the hallmark of her organizational change strategy. Her four-point plan for returning Avon to prominence draws on many of the basic principles of contemporary organizational behavior.

The first point of her plan identified people as the most important factor for driving change. Identifying dedicated and motivated people, gauging the culture of the company, and spending time with employees was the first step in instituting change. McCoy also emphasizes the importance of identifying the right individuals to lead a change effort. Leading a change effort requires identifying individuals who possess the right skills; these skills include emotional intelligence, the ability to inspire others to accept the change, and the intellectual capacity to see the big picture. However, skills are not the only factor necessary for implementing change, the individual must also have the right 'mindset,' or motivation to accept that the change is necessary. He or she must withstand the challenges ahead through perseverance. Another key attribute for success in the organizational transformation was the ability to listen. McCoy's second point reflects the importance of teamwork in achieving successful change efforts. Teamwork requires understanding how an individual's contribution fits into the larger organizational picture. Organizations work best when they can take advantage of diverse opinions. This creates

(continued)

a healthy tension and better reflects the diversity of stakeholders associated with the contemporary organization.

A third point of organizational change is to create a roadmap that everyone can follow. The roadmap is closely tied to the vision of the company. For Avon, the vision was to "restore the company to its rightful place as an iconic beauty brand with products that customers love and demand..." All stakeholders, employees, investors, customers, and most importantly sales representatives can recite the vision of the company. Importantly, the company's roadmap should communicate a step-by-step plan to achieve this vision.

A fourth key point for managing Avon's turnaround, according to McCoy, rests in assessing the organization's culture. Appreciating the culture and being able to assess the positive aspects of the culture is essential, says McCoy. Despite the positive aspects of the existing culture, certain aspects of any culture can have a negative impact on organizational effectiveness. At Avon, the culture often led to slow decision-making, frequent changes in strategy, and extensive rework.

McCoy relied on these four guiding organizational behavior ideas: people drive change, it takes teamwork, you need to communicate a road map, and culture matters to transform Avon.

Sources: "Avon: The rise and fall of a beauty icon." (2012). April 11. Beth Kowitt. *Fortune.* http://gwtoday.gwu.edu/avon-ceo-sheri-mccoy-talks-turnaround-truths
Sheri McCoy, CEO and Director, Avon Products, Inc. "People Driving Change: Turnaround Management." *Presentation at the George Washington University.* Washington DC. Wednesday March 19, 2014.

SPOTLIGHT ON RESEARCH
Fitting in During the First 90 Days of Employment

How important is the crucial introductory period, the first 90 days of employment, in a new job for long-term performance? Social scientists set out to study the first several months of working and to determine if taking certain actions in these first crucial months can lead to greater productivity or termination for new employees. The study involved identifying factors that lead to employee success and factors that undermine employee success. One study tracked the successes of over 264 new employees over 51 weeks. They also examined various initial social interactions that the employee had and classified these interactions as either providing support to the newcomers or undermining the newcomer. Research on this topic has previously found a connection between the initial social interactions a new employee has in the workplace and later success, but prior studies had only followed the employee through the first 90 days of employment. The current study looked at the first 90 days and beyond.

The study looked at both positive and negative social interactions and the overall impact that these two types of interactions had on new employees over time. The study also factored in any proactive behavior displayed by the new employee. For example,

(continued)

did the new employee seek out support or simply work passively? The study measured social interactions by classifying interactions as either positive or undermining, and interactions with either co-worker or a supervisor. For example, a positive peer social interaction occurs when a helpful peer offers advice or resources to the new employee. In contrast, an undermining supervisor social interaction occurs when a new employee has a particularly hostile conversation with a manager about performance. The first 90 days of employment in any organization include a process of socialization where newcomers are exposed to the organizational culture and the interpersonal interactions that define this culture. These positive or negative interactions may increase or decrease over time. For example, a newcomer could initially experience a lot of positive support from a supervisor, but once the employee establishes his or her own role within the organization, the supervisor might simply choose to ignore the employee.[17]

The researchers concluded that first impressions are important to new employees. Employees should seek out support and positive interactions with both their supervisor and other employees. In fact, thinking ahead, or being proactive, including making suggestions for improvements, getting involved in continuous improvement efforts, initiating new ways of doing work, or increasing efficiency, can lead to better outcomes overall for employees. Initial support led to greater work productivity, social interaction with other employees, and organizational commitment; this was true with both supervisor and peer support.

Undermining of employees increases social withdrawal later in an employee's tenure at the organization and can lead to greater turnover. The fact that undermining behavior had no relationship to termination could occur, because as a new employee experiences undermining behavior, the employee might seek out additional social support elsewhere in the organization. This research does suggest that all interpersonal interactions for new employees are significant, and this significance extends beyond the initial socialization period. It is not enough to only seek out positive support from your supervisor. As a new employee in an organization, it is important for you to gain positive support from peers as well. In addition, once you have become comfortable in the new organization, after the 90-day period, you should continue to seek support. New employees should also be proactive in asking for support and you should seek a work environment where you can easily make requests for support. Overall, the study found that employees who take charge of their career during the first 90 days and beyond, and seek positive support, tend to have better employment outcomes.

Questions for Discussion

1. What have your experiences been as a new employee that you would classify as either a positive or negative interpersonal interaction? Does your experience match what the researchers studied and the conclusions that they reached?

2. What other factors do you think might account for a positive or negative socialization process for newcomers to an organization? If you were going to conduct a study on this topic, what would you include?

Source: Based on the article: John Kammeyer-Mueller, Connie Wanberg, Alex Rubenstein, and Zhaoli Song. (2013). Support, undermining, and newcomer socialization: Fitting in during the first 90 days. *Academy of Management Journal* Vol. 56, No. 4, 1104–1124.

Pairing with this Topic Summary

Suggested Expert Contributions

Challenges of Leadership: The Relevance of Organizational Behavior—David L. Bradford (Stanford University)

How Companies Keep on Winning: A System for Developing Global Leaders—Robert Fulmer (Duke Corporate Education)

Suggested Cases

Case 5: Whatever Happened to One of the "100 Best Companies to Work For"?: A Case Study of Hewlett-Packard

Suggested Exercises

Exercise 5: My Best and Worst Learning Experiences

Exercise 6: Developing Your Career—Learning Development in Action

Exercise 20: Employment Branding

Exercise 27: Developing Your Professional Code

Endnotes

1. Feintzeig, R. (2014). The boss's next demand: Make lots of friends. *Wall Street Journal,* (February 12).
2. Feintzeig, R. (2013). How to disarm a nasty co-worker: Use a smile; hostile work environments cost companies in productivity, creativity; using the 'no venting' rule. *Wall Street Journal* Online (August 27).
3. Brown, K. G., Charlier, S. D., Rynes, S. L., & Hosmanek, A. (2013). What Do We Teach in Organizational Behavior? An Analysis of MBA Syllabi. *Journal of Management Education, 37*: 447–471.
4. Diefenbachm, T., & Sillince, J. A. A. (2011). Formal and informal hierarchy in different types of organization. *Organization Studies, 32*(11): 1515–1537.
5. Gephart, J. P. (2002). Introduction to the Brave New Workplace: Organizational Behavior in the Electronic Age. *Journal of Organizational Behavior, 23*(4): 327–344.
6. Schneider, B. (1985). Organizational Behavior. *Annual Review of Psychology, 36*: 573–611.
7. Heath, C., & Sitkin, S. B. (2001). Big-B versus Big-O: What Is Organizational about Organizational Behavior? *Journal of Organizational Behavior, 22*(1): 43–58.
8. Daily, B. F., Bishop, J. W., & Maynard-Patrick, S. (2013). Practicing What We Teach: Applying Organizational Behavior Theory to Academic Success. *Journal of Managerial Issues, 25*(1): 8-25, 5.
9. Robinson, S. L., & Bennett, R. J. (1995). A Typology of Deviant Workplace Behaviors: A Multidimensional Scaling Study. *Academy Of Management Journal, 38*(2): 555–572.
10. Moore, C., Detert, J. R., Trevino, L. K., Baker, V. L., & Mayer, D. M. (2012). Why Employees Do Bad Things: Moral Disengagement And Unethical Organizational Behavior. *Personnel Psychology*, 65: 1–48.
11. Okhuysen, G., Lepak, D., Ashcraft, K. L., Labianca, G., Smith, V., & Steensma, H. K. (2013). Theories of Work and Working Today. *Academy Of Management Review, 38*(4): 491–502.
12. Kayes, A., Kayes, D. C. (2011). *The Learning Advantage: Six Practices of Learning Directed Leadership*. Basingstoke: Palgrave Macmillan.

13. Kayes, D. C. (2006). *Destructive Goal Pursuit: The Mt. Everest Disaster*. Basingstoke: Palgrave Macmillan.

14. Borredon, L., Deffayet, S., Baker, A. C., & Kolb, D. A. (2011). Enhancing deep learning: Lessons from the introduction of learning teams in management education in France. *Journal of Management Education, 35*(3): 324-350.

15. *Critical Skills Needs and Resources for the Changing Workforce: A Study by the Society for Human Resource Management* and WSJ.com/Careers (June 2008).

16. Gilbert, G. R. , Burnett, M., & Leartsurawat, W. (2010). The Psychological Work Preferences of Business Students. *Journal of Career Assessment,* 18: 189–206.

17. Kammeyer-Mueller, J., Wanberg, C., Rubenstein, A., & Song, Z. (2013). Support, Undermining, and Newcomer Socialization: Fitting in During the First 90 Days. *Academy of Management Journal, 56*(4): 1104–1124.

Challenges of Leadership: The Relevance of Organizational Behavior

David L. Bradford

Stanford University

The Changing World

Few would dispute that today's leaders are facing an increasingly different, difficult, and unknown world.

- Increasing globalization means organizations are faced with new competitors, new markets, and more stringent government regulations.
- Disruptive technologies can destroy industries almost overnight; for example, the video distribution business. Cell phones now replace banks as a way to transfer money within Africa or allow farmers in India to check market prices—freeing them up from the tyranny of middlemen buyers.
- The increasing interdependence of the world's economic systems means that an event in one place impacts others in distant places. A tsunami in Japan disrupts auto production in the United States and Europe. A popular rebellion in northern Africa spikes oil prices. Bankruptcy in Italy could destroy the Euro and cause a world-wide recession.
- Knowledge is becoming obsolete at an astonishing rate. Half of the "facts" that engineering undergraduates learn in their first year will be outdated by the time they graduate.

As the White Rabbit said to Alice, "One has to run fast to stand still." Those who fail to adapt, fall behind. In the first half of the twentieth century, the average length of time that an organization stayed on the *Fortune* 500 list was 60 years; now it is 14. The rapidity of change means that old solutions may no longer resolve new problems or take advantage of new opportunities. Furthermore, the "newness" of a situation can mean that it is impossible to be certain ahead of time what is the right solution. It takes between three and five years (and between four to five billion dollars) to build a new silicon chip fabrication plant; but what will be the chip demand in five years?

These external conditions are forcing a redefinition of the leader's role

1. *The old "Leader–Management" paradigm is dead.* The traditional definition that "Leaders produce change (and are at the top of organizations)" and "Managers (in the middle) produce order" is no longer so simple. Knowledge is now dispersed throughout the organization. It is often those on the front lines, and below the level of management, who are closer to the customer and therefore are more aware of the problems/opportunities and more likely to be familiar with new technology. It is not surprising that many of the leaders of Internet companies are in their 20s and 30s.

2. *Heroic Leadership is passé.* The belief that "The leader is responsible for the overall unit success and the individual employee is responsible for his/her area" doesn't work in today's knowledge economy where information is the product and where everyone contributes to its production. Today, "Everybody is a leader." If knowledge is dispersed throughout the organization, each person has to take leadership in solving problems and seizing opportunities. This often requires producing change (as well as establishing order).

3. *"Leadership goes in three directions."* It is no longer sufficient just to "lead one's direct reports." If one definition of leadership is "taking initiative to achieve organizational goals," then producing significant change means that leaders have to influence sideways and upwards as well as downward. Even to do their job, leaders need others in different departments (or up the organization) for resources, information, and support.

Dilemmas of Leadership

Given that old solutions may not solve new problems and with knowledge spread throughout the organization, it is no longer possible for the leader to have all the answers. This means that one has to rely on others as well for ideas. Furthermore, research shows that when problems are complex and there isn't one expert, group solutions are likely to be superior over individual solutions.

But that poses a dilemma. When do leaders listen to others and when do they use their own judgment? Two historical examples illustrate the issue. When George Washington was besieging the British in Boston, he planned to attack five times and each time he was talked out of it by his generals. In hindsight, it would have been disastrous for him not to listen. On the other hand, Abraham Lincoln discussed the plan with his Cabinet in 1863 to issue the Emancipation Proclamation. To a person they opposed it—which he overruled.

The problem of when to listen and when not to listen is compounded by the fact that today's world is one of constant ambiguity. If the situation is new and the future is uncertain, how can one know what is the right answer? Somebody once defined brilliance as *"Being able to tolerate ambiguity AND do something about it."* Not being able to handle either extreme blocks excellence. The inability to tolerate ambiguity prevents one from "sticking with" the situation and instead rushing to premature (and often false) answers. Staying in ambiguity to collect more information and not acting accordingly leads to *analysis–paralysis.*

The second dilemma is around the limitations of formal authority. In times past, when leaders rose up through the ranks, they had a wealth of previous experience to apply to problems similar to what they had faced before. They knew what was to be done and "giving an order" was sufficient. But today, one needs commitment and initiative from direct reports, not just compliance. Leaders can only "order" the latter, rarely the former.

Furthermore, as noted, those in the middle of the organization have to show leadership, and this requires them to influence peers (both within and outside the department) and make an impression on those above them, including, but not limited to, their immediate supervisor. For these reasons, leaders need the ability to be influential in ways beyond drawing upon their formal authority.

The third dilemma is the relationship between *learning* and *performance.* In the last analysis, it is performance that counted. That is what people are held accountable for. But if change is the constant and the future is unknown, there has to be a process of continuous learning in which learning and performance are inexorably tied. A plan is developed and the first steps are implemented, which allows for data collection to see if the following steps need to be modified.

Learning is not just at the task level, but for individuals and teams as well. In spite of the plethora of executive programs, most learning occurs on the job. But for this to be systematic and not haphazard, several conditions have to exist. Obviously, the first is a willingness when problems arise to do a "root cause analysis" rather than responding defensively and blaming others or external factors. Doing such an examination is more likely when it is structured into the situation. *The Blue Angels,* the Navy stunt flying team, debriefs after each practice with the leader talking first to talk about the mistakes he or she made! How many present leaders are willing to do that?

For leaders (and members) to be willing to take on a learning orientation, there has to be a culture where (prudent) mistakes are seen as learning experiences, not as "career limiting moves." This is especially important for organizations that seek to be innovative. The number of new ideas is correlated with the number of "experiments" that are run. It turns out that the more experiments run, the greater the number of failures. As a scientist learns from an experiment that doesn't work out, so must leaders. Thus, the organizational adage of 'fail early and fail often'.

This adage produces the fourth dilemma of "How are leaders evaluated and how do they evaluate themselves?" In the past, validation came from having the answer, which was likely since change was slow enough (and they stayed in that job long enough) that they had experienced most problems that would or could arise. The evaluation process is compounded when the leader makes a mistake. If the mindset is that leaders should be decisive, have the answer, be (almost always) infallible, then the concern is How will the leader gain members' respect? This external evaluation process is matched by an internal one as well. "How will I know that I am competent if I am in this new situation and I can't provide the right solution?" We discuss the need for transparency, but will self-esteem drop even further if leaders have to admit when they have made a mistake?

New Leadership Competencies Required

These dilemmas demand an entirely new set of competencies in addition to what was required before. This is especially the case for those in the middle of the organization.

- *Leadership (and not just management)* competencies will be needed early in one's career in serving as a department or division leader. This includes being able to articulate a vision and gaining alignment to it.

- *Developing the appropriate culture.* Even though the norms at the division or departmental level need to be *compatible* with the larger organizational culture, they aren't identical. The organization needs to establish the appropriate norms that both maximize performance as well as build a learning culture at the individual, team, and unit level.

- *Change skills as part of the leader's repertoire.* This includes understanding the dynamics of planned change as well as knowing when to use a collaborative approach versus being more direct. Other issues involve knowing how to deal with resistance to change and how to develop allies and build support.
- *Interpersonal and team skills* that now encompass much of what is presently held by organization consultants, but now must be within the skill set of leaders themselves. This includes building a cohesive team, conflict management, and individual development
- *Influence competencies,* especially used to influence those one can't directly control.

In addition to these competencies, there is important internal work that the developing leader needs to do. This raises the question, If one has to be open to the ideas and reactions to others, how then to avoid the trap of listening just to the latest (or loudest)? In addition, if leaders need to be open to feedback, how then to not have the criticism be upending and destructive to one's competence? What is the internal strength that would allow the leader to pick him- or herself up after failure? Answers to these questions require not only a clear set of values, but a high degree of self-understanding and self-acceptance. How can these be learned or do they come from experience and maturity?

The Role of Organization Behavior in Dealing with Leadership Dilemmas

Figure 1 is one way to conceptualize leadership development: *What should I do? Do I have the competencies to achieve that? What is my approach/style to enacting that?*

People hold a wide array of conceptual models of "how the world operates." Whether from previous experience and role models, education, or cultural messages, each person has concepts of *how leaders should act, how teams should operate, how decisions should be made, and how employees should deal with bosses.* These conceptual models help make sense out of the world, both to understand what is going on and what actions to take.

Figure 1

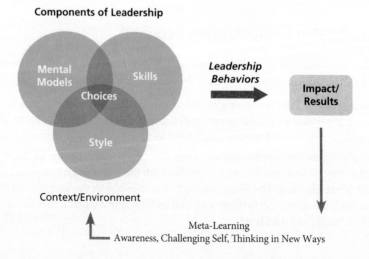

However, when one's models are too limited, leaders either miss what is going on or super-impose a simplistic diagnosis that distorts reality. Either trap prevents handling the complexity that would be needed to be highly effective.

Likewise, people have developed certain competencies in how to solve problems, influence others, and operate in teams. It is one thing to have the correct model and to know what to do and another thing to have the skills to implement the desired action.

Finally, each person has his or her own interpersonal style. Two individuals can be equally competent at raising important issues in meetings, but go about it in different ways. For example, one "sees the glass half-empty" while another sees it as half-full. Some like to focus on new possibilities, others like to focus on bringing decisions to closure. Our style reflects a person's *tendency* to act in a situation; it doesn't determine *how* they have to act. These tendencies can be appropriate in some situations, but can be counter-productive in others. The ability to be direct is an asset in working in some cultures (as in Israel), but may impair effectiveness in others (as in Japan).

These three areas of leadership development (denoted by the three circles in Figure 1) interact with each other. If a person has a limited range of mental models, it is unlikely she or he will develop competencies (or the appropriate style) in implementing other pos-sibilities. And the limitations of one's skill set also impact the mental models one holds and the robustness of the style. Development has to cover all of these three areas.

More choices are available; a) the larger the circles (e.g., the more mental models one holds); b) the greater the set of competencies; c) the more flexible the style; and d) the greater the overlap (e.g., I have the skills and flexibility to implement specific mental models). But further development occurs only upon knowing the impact of one's behavior; has our action had the impact/results that we intended? Only when that is known can there be the meta-learning of increased awareness and thinking in new ways which can further expand the size of the circles and the appropriateness of future actions.

This further development depends on the existence of feedback and one's openness to considering it. Leaders can be proactive in soliciting feedback *or* can send signals that feedback is not wanted. This can be as overt as rejecting the information ("How you are responding is *your* problem") or indirect by indicating that one would be hurt or the rela-tionship damaged if anything but approval was given.

There is a multitude of ways that the study of organization behavior can increase this development. Clearly, the field holds many theories and organizing principles. One way to characterize these is as different pairs of glasses with each pair highlighting a certain phenomenon. However, it is not just "finding the right pair/model for this specific case," but often needing multiple ways of looking at the same situation to see more of the com-plexity and the nuances. Can one shift back and forth among several pairs to determine if this problem is due to the organization's culture, its reward systems, the role demands, or personal needs of the key players? Or to "all of the above?")

Often students are frustrated when they want a solution and the instructor says, "it depends." But one of the outcomes of a careful study of the field is to develop a set of con-tingencies to know what are the major factors that specific actions depends on.

The objective is not just to acquire new mental models, but also to be aware of the implicit assumptions that one presently holds. A case based course can be useful in sur-facing that. In complex cases, there are usually more than one viable solution so the alter-native that a student might present is often based on certain mental models that person holds (as well as the competencies they have and the style that they would use). If built into the learning process is an examination of these personal choices, it can help individuals gain greater self-understanding. Again, it's not an issue of "the right way," but instead, "what are the advantages in my approach and what are the limitations?" And "Are there other options that I might want to consider?"

The Role of Experiential Learning

One of the advantages of the field of organization behavior is that courses often have an experiential component such as role-plays, simulations, or project teams that have a self-examination component. These are especially useful in identifying and developing the *competencies* and *style* areas. Even though cases can help in learning "what should be done," they are limited around implementation. There can be many a slip between knowing what is required and putting that into action. Yes, the boss should be confronted in this situation, *but how are you going to do that?* Setting up situations where students have to behaviorally act out how they would implement their suggestions can provide powerful learning around awareness of competencies and personal style. Furthermore, it provides the opportunity to increase the range of skills practicing alternative approaches.

Providing peer feedback has additional benefits. Learning how to make it behaviorally specific (and not contain attributions of the others motivation or personality) and given in a way to help, not to attack, are crucial management competencies. A related competence is learning how to build conditions where feedback can be easily given. Furthermore, having practice in accepting it on a regular basis makes it a more natural part of the learning process.

If learning is to be continuous throughout one's career, it is important to know how to set up learning environments both for one's self and for others. Even though the classroom differs in some important ways from a company, there are strong similarities in the learning process. In experientially based organization behavior courses that have a strong learning/feedback component, students can acquire the ability to "learn how to learn," meaning, a set of skills that can allow for continuous learning in the future.

Building a Personal "Gyroscope"

Discussed above was the dilemma of how do contemporary leaders, who can't have all the answers but who are still held accountable for results, still be open to others ideas without totally giving way to them? A clear vision and specific strategic and business plans can serve as partial guidelines, but there are still many decisions on *how* to implements those plans. In exploring the assumptions behind one's mental models and seeing the effect of one's behavior, it is possible to gain clarity as to the values behind one's intentions and actions. That clarity on personal values can serve as an important foundation when faced with multiple options and different pressures. This provides a consistency without rigidity, since the same value can be expressed in different ways in different situations.

A related issue is what is the basis of one's self-identify and self-worth? For some, it is the approval of others. Unfortunately, those who have this as the core criteria tend to be poorer leaders because they can't hold to standards if doing something might evoke disapproval from others. For other leaders, it is their track record of success. But failure, rather than being a potential for learning, can become a personally upending experience. Still, others hold on to an image of what they should be. This can come from role models in early life or mental models of "successful leadership." The cost is that this can lead to acting out a presented image that may be at odds with how that person (silently) sees him or herself. That means that even if that behavior leads to success, it can produce the "imposter syndrome" where what was achieved was, "not due to the real me, but to this image that I enacted."

To be able to handle the "slings and arrows of outrageous fortune" one needs both self-understanding and self-acceptance. Picture those inflatable punching dolls that can be knocked off-kilter but have the internal weight (gravitas) to right itself. This, and a clear set of values, provides the personal gyroscope that allows one to handle the ambiguity of today's complex world. It also produces greater authenticity which, we would argue, is a more effective leadership model than trying to portray an image of the perfect leader.

But where can a person test out the scary hypothesis that, "If you knew me, how I really am, I would gain, not lose respect."

In the MBA program at Stanford's Graduate School of Business, the most popular second year elective is Interpersonal Dynamics. In this course, students working in 12-person groups have the ambiguous task of "building a cohesive group where we can learn from each other." Over the term, they start to take the risk of showing more of themselves than they did in the traditional classroom. They test out the hypothesis, "What happens if I admit that I am feeling competitive, a bit insecure, angry at what you said, or envious of your abilities?" What almost universally happens is that, when a climate of safety has been built, this greater authenticity leads to a higher level of acceptance. This can provide a deeper self-acceptance because of the knowledge that others need is not perfection, but our humanness.

This example is not to suggest that this level of openness and vulnerability should be the norm in organizations (although there are a few highly successful teams that operate that way). Interpersonal Dynamics is in an educational setting. The point is that leaders will be better able to handle disapproval and not get knocked over by failure if there is not only a fuller understanding of their own strengths and weaknesses, but an acceptance that they can be flawed and still be an effective leader.

To Conclude

Leadership is not for the fainthearted. One has to deal with an increasingly complex, uncertain world that is making more and more personal demands on those who want to manage. It would be a tall order for organizational behavior courses as part of an undergraduate or MBA program to fully resolve all the dilemmas. Furthermore, there can be no book, no four- or two-year program that can predict all the future challenges. As we have stressed, learning has to be continuous throughout a person's career. The mental models must change as one progresses in an organization or moves to a new field. This demands new competencies and flexibility to fit one's style into different situations.

What the field can provide are the basic tools in "learning how to learn." This includes a willingness to take the risk of experimenting with new behavior and to see experiences as potential learning opportunities. It demands the ability for self-reflection and openness to feedback. Finally, it requires redefining "mistakes." As more than one successful executive has stated, "I have never failed, I have only had learning experiences." Organizational behavior can provide the framework for that rich learning.

How Companies Keep on Winning: A System for Developing Global Leaders

Robert Fulmer

Duke Corporate Education

Over the past decade, I've been involved in seven best practice studies about talent management and human resource management. This research, along with other studies being conducted concurrently, have shown a high degree of innovation designed to address strategic challenges in developing high-performing leaders, including the global "war for talent," increased levels of competition and pressure for change, along with new demographic and generational differences. I've gained valuable insight on how the best companies practice "innovative imitation" to gain competitive advantage from their business and leadership development activities by consistently using strategic, systemic coordination to develop their high potential global leaders.

In this reading I will provide an overview of key insights about how the leading global firms go about developing their potential leaders. I will provide a backdrop from previous research on the subject and an overview of key findings about emerging, innovative best practices from leading firms. Readers should gain an appreciation of the newest concepts in talent management *and* have their appetites whetted to learn more about how these concepts can be used along with appropriately adapted fundamental tools of their discipline. Based on work with some of the world's best firms, I will introduce the "Five A" Model for Strategic Leadership Development that will serve as the integrating template for current or future managers to lead major change efforts.

One of our primary findings is that leaders who keep learning may be the ultimate source of sustainable competitive advantage a firm can possess. With that understanding, many companies are investing in leadership development (programs that help key executives learn leadership skills). In the following sections I will discuss the processes that help transform managers into strong leaders ready for strategic action, and how the best leadership-development organizations design, manage, and deliver world-class programs.

The Strategic Perspective

Perhaps the most significant overall finding to come out of our research is that high-performing firms tie leadership development closely to their business strategies. That is, they engage in leadership training and development because they believe such practices are a part of their long-term strategies for success. The consumer products firm, Johnson & Johnson, for example, revised their performance-management systems (i.e., the systems they use to evaluate and promote managers into leadership positions) to be in line with the leadership qualities suggested by a "leader-of-the-future" workshop. Similarly, Caterpillar used the rollout of a new, fifteen-year corporate strategy program ("Vision 2020") as a leadership development activity and as a means of using "leaders as teachers" to insure buy-in and commitment to the strategy. Finally, General Electric and PepsiCo made leadership assessment part of their overall corporate strategy process.

Increasingly, programs that focus on developing future leaders are seen as a source of competitive advantage. General Electric's former CEO, Jack Welch, described the company's Leadership Development Institute in Crotonville, New York, as a "staging ground for corporate revolutions." General Electric (GE) is so well-known and respected for developing leaders that it has become a hunting ground for headhunters seeking potential CEO's for their clients. A popular Harvard Business School case about the firm's commitment to development (with emphasis on the career and selection of Jeffrey Immelt to replace Welch as CEO) is entitled "GE's Talent Machine: The Making of a CEO."

Hewlett-Packard (HP) is still working to maintain its status as a top high-tech innovator and convince the public and its employees that HP is the hottest "new" high-tech company—without losing the old-time commitment to quality and integrity. As HP has improved leadership development, the company seems to make better business decisions. In our 2010 study, HP was one of the most admired among all technology driven firms.

The Five-A Strategic Model

Pronouncing a strategic vision is not enough to tie leadership development to the company's goals. Our data suggest that there are five critical steps to achieving that end. (See "Making Leadership Development Strategic".) Examples of each step can be found in the corporate leadership programs of benchmark companies. A summary of this model, along with examples from best-practice firms, is provided in Figure I.

Awareness: Developing Multi-Polar Vision

The first step to linking leadership development to firm's strategic vision is develop an awareness of leadership development programs used by other firms. Contemporary leaders must be able to see unique aspects of a firm's internal environment as well as

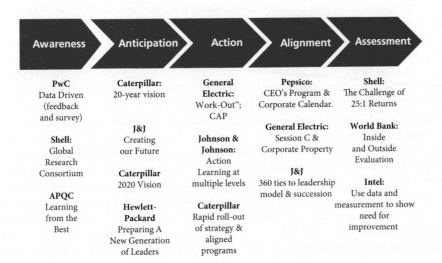

Figure 1 The 5-A Model: Strategic Leadership Development

Awareness	Anticipation	Action	Alignment	Assessment
PwC Data Driven (feedback and survey)	**Caterpillar:** 20-year vision	**General Electric:** Work-Out™; CAP	**Pepsico:** CEO's Program & Corporate Calendar.	**Shell:** The Challenge of 25:1 Returns
Shell: Global Research Consortium	**J&J** Creating our Future	**Johnson & Johnson:** Action Learning at multiple levels	**General Electric:** Session C & Corporate Property	**World Bank:** Inside and Outside Evaluation
APQC Learning from the Best	**Caterpillar** 2020 Vision	**Caterpillar** Rapid roll-out of strategy & aligned programs	**J&J** 360 ties to leadership model & succession	**Intel:** Use data and measurement to show need for improvement
	Hewlett-Packard Preparing A New Generation of Leaders			

gain a mastery of tools, techniques, and practices utilized by other outstanding organizations. For example, firms may utilize the expertise of the American Productivity and Quality Center (APQC), which maintains the world's largest database of benchmarks for real-time performance metrics. APQC can provide instant benchmarks to help firms determine where their organization stands in terms of leadership performance, as well as online tools that compare the company's own data with that provided by peers. In an effort to make best practices widely available, they have sponsored a variety of best practice studies, several of which are reported in this reading (see Benchmarking methodology).

PriceWaterhouseCooper (PwC) uses both internal and external data to determine the learning and development needs of its partners and associates. Internal data come from client-satisfaction and employee-satisfaction surveys, upward communication and analysis of what could be called "450-degree feedback" (from bosses, peers and subordinates, plus client evaluations). PwC uses this information to better understand how its partners are perceived in terms of their technical competence and their responsiveness to clients. External data about new financial and managerial tools or about challenges in the business environment come from market research, business trends and leading-edge thinkers. The firm also works closely with the world's leading developer of custom executive education to administer PwC University offerings for 2000 U.S. partners.

In a similar vein, Shell Oil uses an ongoing conversation with a committee of its managing directors (representing all of Shell's geographic and functional areas) to ensure that its leadership-and-performance program does not simply react to the immediate needs of the business, but is in line with its long-term strategic objectives. Human Resource Development staff members within Shell determine the critical players within each business unit who will go through the program. To gather external perspectives, Shell also has joined the Global Research Consortium, a group of transnational companies that sponsors research on leadership development. The consortium gives its members the opportunity to hear and discuss the latest on leadership and learning.

Anticipation: Seeing and Creating Your Organizations Future

The second step in aligning leadership development with firm strategy is to continually focus on the future of one's firm. Although business cases traditionally focus on the past and best-practice reviews focus on the present, the best leadership-development programs emphasize the future. Top leadership-development companies use anticipatory learning tools: focus groups that explore potential challenges or the impact of emerging technologies; decentralized strategic planning (planning that builds on many organizational levels' imagining of the future); analysis of future scenarios; and the Delphi method (a method of successively developing consensus about decisions). For example, one of the components of Caterpillar's "Leadership Quest" program is having participants work throughout a week-long program to develop a presentation to the CEO about what they thought the strategy of the organization should be in fifteen years. Copies of these presentations are shared with members of Caterpillar's Strategic Planning Committee, which later announced the organization's strategic vision. Perhaps of even greater significance, one month after this announcement, Caterpillar's College of Leadership rolled out a "Leaders as Teachers" program to disseminate the new strategy throughout the organization. Learning sessions designed to achieve alignment across business units and divisions were conducted around the world during the next 30 days. Sessions designed to communicate the vision to all employees around the world were completed within six months. Essentially, all managers at Caterpillar were involved in teaching the essence of the new strategy to their subordinates and helping them to see their role in achieving the strategic goals.

In a similar, but earlier, program, the 600 top leaders at Johnson & Johnson were asked to imagine their organization a decade into the future and to describe what it would look like if they were "totally successful". In contrast to more conventional, top-down strategic planning, this so-called "Merlin Process" had groups throughout the organization describe their ideal of success for the organization. This exercise provided insight and input for senior executives and led to more formal planning sessions. Participants challenged conventional wisdom about the evolution of the health-care industry and focused on defining the actions their divisions could take to create a winning future. An extended scenario was developed from interviews with more than 100 Johnson & Johnson executives in six countries, and from published predictions about the future of health care. Using a modified Delphi approach, participants assessed the probability and impact of 14 hypothetical developments as a means of fine-tuning their vision of the future.

Finally, Hewlett-Packard has historically provided myriad opportunities for emerging leaders to develop and grow. Several years ago, top management recognized that many people who grew up with the founders were retiring and that their immediate successors looked a little too much like one another. They anticipated that, as the company became more global, it would need more diversity of ethnicity and gender. Thus, their vision of the future included the notion of a more diverse set of leaders. In line with this future vision, HP's leadership-development process has become more supportive of diversity goals, provided stretch assignments for the most promising people and making accelerated programs available for individual contributors and first-level managers who demonstrated potential for greater responsibility—with an emphasis on developing a new generation of diverse, global leaders.

Action: Turning Plans into Reality

The third step in the process of aligning leadership development with firm strategy is to turn plans into action. Action, not knowledge, is the goal of best-practice leadership development processes. Best-practice groups bring the world into the classroom, applying real business tools to skill development and using actual corporate challenges as training tools. The concept of "action learning" encourages program participants to develop and implement their own recommendations. Such action learning can, however, be complicated and costly.

At GE, the CEO often chooses the action-learning topics for each of the annual business-management courses and for the executive-development course. Participants in these courses are highly motivated to carry out projects, important as they are to the company's direction. Recommendations made by the participant teams are usually implemented. Students in one management course went to China and developed proposals for GE's operations there. A quality report from an individual in another course led to corporate wide adoption of the Six Sigma initiative (a quality-assurance program designed to eliminate defects from all products). GE also supports what it calls the Change

Acceleration Process (CAP), a systematic attempt to turn managers into professional change agents by disseminating GE's accumulated knowledge about how to initiate, accelerate and secure change. If CAP is successful, people who are comfortable as coaches and facilitators will be the norm at GE.

Similarly, at Johnson & Johnson, the follow up to the "Creating Our Future" exercise emphasized that participants tie ideas to specific business issues through action learning. Johnson & Johnson executives in the different business units "sponsored" this exercise and asked participants to define topic areas where they saw potential for growth. Once a topic was defined, an executive sponsor chose 50 to 130 program participants to perform additional analysis, such as gathering data and interviewing people in the company who might have some relevant insight before attempting to implement suggestions that arose from the exercise.

Alignment: Building Systems for Success in Talent Management

The fourth step in aligning leadership development with corporate strategy is to pay attention to how all "talent management" systems are integrated with corporate strategy. Leading practitioners achieve alignment by insuring that all human resource initiatives are part of an integrated system and are tied directly to the corporate vision/strategy, rather than being a series of individual components. The best companies integrate and align assessment (i.e., performance evaluation), development (i.e., training and education) feedback, coaching and succession planning with corporate strategy.

At Johnson & Johnson, for example, all training functions use 360-degree-feedback evaluations (evaluations that include feedback from superiors, subordinates, and peers) as a part of leadership development. Facilitators assess a multiple-choice, behavioral questionnaire, in which participants rate their performance in many areas and get ratings from supervisors, peers and subordinates. Plans may be made for participants to be coached later or to engage in activities to strengthen weak areas as part of the program

Similarly, General Electric openly ties leadership development to succession planning (i.e., planning for who will replace a leader if he/she leaves or moves to another position). All employees are rated in a nine-block system for the annual "Session C" review. The review includes discussion about people's performance and their adherence to the values in GE's value statement. GE leaders take the view the corporate headquarters "owns" the top 500 people in the company and just "rents them out" to its various business units. In fact, to encourage the sharing of business talent across business units, GE includes a negative variable in its performance appraisals for managers who hold back talented employees. Outstanding business performance and development of leaders go hand in hand.

Finally, PepsiCo's leadership development strategy is grounded in the belief that strong leaders are needed to be successful in the marketplace. This belief is outlined by PepsiCo's two-pronged Human Resource approach, which includes a career growth model for their key employees and a talent management model for leadership development, to ensure that the firm has the right people available for continued success. This two-pronged approach aligns with corporate strategic initiatives, which support the organization's sustainable competitive advantage. The PepsiCo model (Figure 2) shows these components as a part of the annual operating plan. As shown in Figure 2, each stage

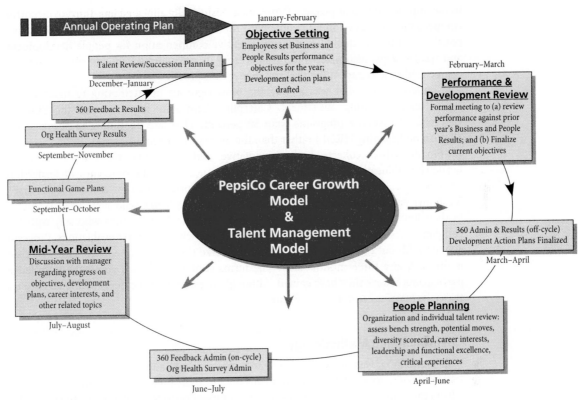

Figure 2 Connecting PepsiCo People Processes

of the planning cycle includes a specific focus on key people issues. Leaders at PepsiCo would be hard-pressed to miss the message that leadership strategy is integral to the overall corporate strategy.

Assessment: the Search for Meaningful, Consistent Measurement

The fifth and final step toward aligning corporate strategy and leadership development is to use relevant modes of measuring leadership performance. As Peter Drucker used to say, "Management should not expect what it does not inspect." The best firms often use business results as the primary means of assessing high-potential talent along with an analysis of multi-rater feedback and employee climate survey. Results delivered by graduates of internal high-potential talent development programs can be productively compared to the results of other employees. Peer group comparisons may be the most direct measure of how high-potential talent development efforts contribute to the bottom line.

For example, in one of Shell's initiatives, a program adds value only if the team project generates revenues at least 25 times greater than the project's cost (a 25:1 Return on Investment). Best-practice organizations always assess the impact of their leadership-development process. PepsiCo has historically allocated one-third of incentive compensation for developing people with the remainder for results. In 2007, the company moved to an equal allocation of incentive compensation for people development and results. Pepsi also utilizes the results from its semi-annual climate survey and 360 degree feedback as part of the performance review process.

Similarly, Caterpillar was among the most rigorous in attempting to measure the return on its learning investment. Caterpillar University has estimated the ROI for Caterpillar University programs were 50 percent. They are beginning to speak about "Return on Learning" (ROL) rather than the more formalized process for ROI.

Finally, Cisco collects both quantitative and qualitative measures. Worldwide Leadership Education has a formal system for measuring the outcomes of leadership development strategy. Examples of metrics include "price range for a one week course," "customer satisfaction scores," "percentage of class graduates who have used learnings in their jobs and had a positive impact," and "percentage of learners who stay with the company." Cisco combines impact research with participants' course evaluations. Program attendees fill out evaluation forms before they take the class, immediately after the class is finished, and three months later. The forms contain questions about the knowledge participants believe they have gained. Although measurement is expensive and sometimes tricky, its benefits cannot be discounted.

Benchmarking Methodology

Benchmarking, was our primary research methodology and involves identifying outstanding practices and processes from any organization anywhere in the world, learning from them and adapting them to a specific company's needs. In phase one, the research team reviewed the literature to identify and then talk with leaders in executive development. At the end of phase one, the study team compiled a list of candidates for potential best-practice partners and a screening report. Sponsors met to review the initial report, select the final best-practice partners and discuss their objectives for the study.

In phase two, sponsors visited best-practice partners for a day, seeking answers to detailed questions about the evolution, design, execution and successes of their leadership programs. The study sought to identify innovative practices and applicable quantitative data, such as budgets, program details and assessment criteria. The deliverables from the project included site-visit summaries, a two-day knowledge-transfer session (in which all the study sponsors and best-practice partners participated) and a final report. Over 100 organizations have participated as sponsors and sent representatives to planning sessions, completed data-gathering surveys and attended or hosted on-site interviews for the studies reported in this reading.

An Executive Primer: Five Steps to Get More From Leadership-Development

Awareness—Make it a point to interview key executives in your firm and others about leadership developments. Insist that the head of HRD or your chief learning officer brief you regularly about the latest thinking on leadership development. Ask other key members of HRD to prepare short summaries of events they attend at corporate expense.

Anticipation—Start your meetings (with managers at all levels) with a request for the most significant trend or prediction that they think will affect your business. Ask them to summarize the most forward-thinking article, book or presentation to help you learn and to get colleagues thinking in anticipatory terms. Be sure that current challenges don't keep you from focusing on the future of your company.

Action—Ask your Human Resource Development team members which business results have originated from your company's educational programs. Discuss the strategic initiatives that need their implementation assistance. Explore how you can use executive learning to make strategic initiatives happen more quickly and effectively.

Alignment—Look at your performance management system (performance appraisals), your succession-planning profiles, your major education and development agendas and feedback from opinion surveys.

Assessment—Evaluate whether your leadership-development activities have been successful. Ask for evidence that programs reflect standards of success when you authorize a budget.

Overall—Think about how you want Human Resource Development, in general, and education, in particular, to support your strategic efforts. How must you change your human-resource profiles so that your company can become what you want it to be?

Bibliographic Sources

R. M. Fulmer, 2011 Top Companies for Leaders, (Hewitt Associates, Fortune and RBL Group); "Do Techies Make Good Leaders," (with Byron Hanson).

R. M. Fulmer, *Wall Street Journal/MIT Sloan Management Review*, Executive Advisor, August 23, 2010.

R. M. Fulmer "Developing Leaders in High Tech Firms: What's Different and What Works," (with Byron Hanson), *People and Strategy*, Octobers, 2010.

R. M. Fulmer and J. Bleak, *The Leadership Investment* (New York: AMACOM, 2007).

R. M. Fulmer, "Developing Strategic Leadership (interview with Marshall Goldsmith*), Business Week*, October 30, 2007.

R. M. Fulmer, "Strategic Human Resource Development," (Houston, TX: APQC, 2006).

R. M. Fulmer, M. Goldsmith, and S. Varghese, "Do You Know Who Your Next CEO Is?" (Washington, D.C.: Human Capital Institute, 2006).

R. M. Fulmer, "Survey of Conference Board CLO Council", 2005; R. J. Kramer, "Developing Global Leaders", (New York: The Conference Board, 2005).

R. M. Fulmer, "Next Generation HR Practices," (Houston, TX: APQC, 2005); *Growing Your Company's Leaders,* (with Jay A. Conger) (New York: AMACOM, 2004.

R. M. Fulmer, "Developing Your Leadership Pipeline," (with Jay A. Conger), *Harvard Business Review*, December, 2003.

R. M. Fulmer, "Developing Leaders: How Winning Companies Keep On Winning," (with Marshall Goldsmith & Phillip Gibbs) *MIT Sloan Management Review*, Fall, 2000.

2 Individual Characteristics

Topic Summary Learning Objectives

1. Define competencies, list the top competencies sought by organizations, and describe the types of and importance of competency models.

2. Describe the importance of emotions in the workplace and different considerations for how emotions operate in organizations.

3. Present the heredity versus environment debate on personality.

4. Contrast the Big Five and Myers-Briggs approaches to personality.

5. Outline attitudes, including self-efficacy, Machiavellianism, locus of control, and self-monitoring, and their role in organizations.

6. Apply concepts of individual characteristics and the impact of these concepts to organizations.

Key Terms

ability, p. 40

attitudes, p. 40

behavior, p. 33

Big Five personality, p. 37

competencies, p. 33

competency models, p. 35

displayed versus felt
  emotions, p. 36

emotions, p. 35

emotional contagion, p. 35

emotional intelligence, p. 36

emotional labor, p. 36

felt versus displayed
  emotions, p. 36

heredity versus
  environment, p. 37

individual differences, p. 33

locus of control, p. 40

Machiavellianism, p. 40

mood, p. 35

Myers-Briggs Type Indicator, p. 38

personality, p. 37

self-efficacy, p. 40

self-monitoring, p. 41

Introduction to Individual Characteristics

This section outlines the individual characteristics associated with individual processes in organizations. The impact of these personal characteristics on what people think, feel, and do is called the study of **individual difference**. Individuals vary in many different ways; one obvious way is physical differences. However, focusing on physical differences supplies only a limited and often biased view of **behavior**. Understanding individual differences is a good start to understanding how individuals will behave in a particular context, but first requires a broader knowledge of the deeper categories of differences. Figure 2.1 summarizes the deeper level individual characteristics. These characteristics include competencies (knowledge, skills, and abilities), emotions, personality, and attitudes.

Competencies: Knowledge, Skills, and Abilities

1 Define competencies, list the top competencies sought by organizations, and describe the types of and importance of competency models.

Competencies describe the knowledge, skills, and abilities necessary for performing different jobs, functions, or tasks.[1] Competencies suggest that individuals differ in the skills they possess and also in how they experience and express emotions. These differences are in turn associated with performance differences. Nearly 96% of organizations routinely measure individual competencies. Organizations also determine what competencies are most important for existing and prospective employees to posses. Below is a list, in order of importance, of the twelve competencies most sought by employers:[2]

1. Critical thinking/problem solving
2. Creativity/innovation
3. Leadership
4. Teamwork/collaboration
5. Written communications (conveying written messages clearly and effectively)
6. Lifelong learning pursuit/self-direction
7. Information technology application
8. Oral communications
9. Ethics/social responsibility

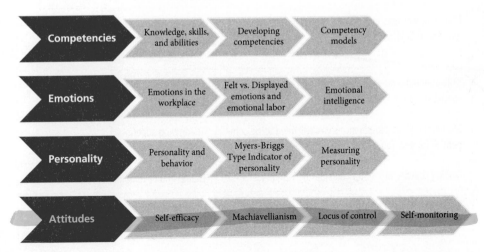

Figure 2.1
Summary of Individual Characteristics

10. Diversity
11. English language (spoken)
12. Writing in English (grammar, spelling, etc.)

Developing Competencies

In many cases, organizations utilize systematic programs to assure that individuals working in the organization are equipped with the right competencies. To achieve this goal, organizations first hire employees whose competencies match the specific job requirements. Once an individual becomes an employee, the organization will further develop the competencies by continually assessing individual performance. Most organizations help employees develop competencies by providing training or guided experiences such as work assignments or job shadowing.

Too often, employees make the mistake of believing that the organization itself is responsible for developing employee competencies, but employees themselves must seek out opportunities to develop competencies. Formal training, practicing new skills in job tasks, on-the-job learning, and seeking out job assignments that lead to growth and development are essential for competency development. Table 2.1 provides a list of common ways that employees and employers can develop competencies.

Table 2.1 Common Ways Employees and Employers Develop Competencies

Common ways that employees can develop their competencies	Common ways employers develop competencies
Following the career development section of news Website	On-the-job skills training
Taking courses	Offering coaching or mentoring programs
Following publications specific to your industry and job	Training courses
Participating in volunteer work	College courses
Following websites and networking with others in your industry or field	Providing resources such as association memberships and access to learning Websites
Skills training programs offered through training specialists or universities	Job rotation and developmental assignments
Monitoring what competencies you will need to be competitive for your job by following job search Websites	Shadowing superiors
Finding coaches or mentors outside the workplace	Leadership development programs
Taking self assessments that highlight strengths and weaknesses	Offering regular seminars and speakers

Competency Models

A **competency model** offers a comprehensive way to identify the groups of competencies associated with organizational performance and involves clusters of competencies. Competency models serve as benchmarks to identify individuals who fit a certain profile, or to identify skills needed by employees within the organization. There are many types of competency models:

- *Organization-wide* models describe competencies that are critical for all employees, across positions and levels of the organization.
- *Function-based* models include competencies that apply to a single business function within the organization, such as marketing.
- *Role-based* models list competencies for a specific role within an organization. They often include behavioral expectations for the role. An example would be the role of leader within a workplace.
- *Job-based* models are developed for a specific job, such as an accounting clerk or a customer service technician.

In some cases, a competency model may be developed for an entire industry or series of career stages and applied across multiple organizations.

Emotions

Emotions in the Workplace

Only recently has the link between emotions and behavior been recognized for both positive and negative outcomes in the workplace.[3] **Emotions** are strong feelings with a short duration. They were often viewed as irrelevant or, even worse, were seen as only disruptive to smooth organizational functioning.[4] Textbooks on organizational behavior often emphasized the negative outcomes of emotion such as anger management, or crying in the workplace. Emotions were only mentioned because managers would need to diffuse workplace emotions and because understanding emotions was necessary to resolve conflict.

This negative view of emotions has changed.[5] There is a growing consensus that emotions play both a positive and negative role in organizations.[6] Emotions underlie all behaviors and are directly linked with behavior. Emotions have a short duration and result from a specific stimulus in the environment. Emotions are distinct from a **mood**, which is broader and lasts longer. It is also important to distinguish between emotions and affect. Affect is a very broad term that encompasses mood and emotions, as described in Table 2.2.[7]

Emotions, mood, and affect can spread in a workplace. This capacity to spread is termed **emotional contagion**. Emotional contagion can be a spillover from inside or outside the workplace. Spillover from a personal or family situation, external to the workplace, could be brought into the work environment. Emotions experienced in the workplace can originate from home, school, work, and social situations.[8]

2 Describe the importance of emotions in the workplace and different considerations for how emotions operate in organizations.

RubberBall/SuperStock

Table 2.2 Emotions, Mood & Behavior

Term	Definition	Characteristic	Example	Behavioral manifestation
Emotion	"A strong feeling"	Short in duration, needs a specific stimulus, typically linked with an action	Fear; anger; sadness; disgust; joy; and love	e.g., anger from a bad performance evaluation could lead to workplace aggression
Mood	"Feelings made up of multiple emotions without a clear onset"	Longer in duration, does not need a specific stimulus; can be classified as positive or negative	Positive, negative	e.g., a supervisor's positive mood is evident during a meeting with her team

Felt versus Displayed Emotions and Emotional Labor

Emotions play an important role because they help in processing information, in making decisions, when working in a group, or when interacting with others. When people recognize and regulate emotions, there can be healthy interactions with others. Working in an organization often requires displaying emotions that are different from what people actually feel. At work, people are required to have two different sets of emotions: one set of emotions that are displayed in the outer world and one set of emotions that are actually felt internally. These two types of emotions are called **displayed and felt emotions**. Felt emotions are the feelings an employee actually feels. Displayed emotions are those emotions that are visible. Employees display different emotions than they actually feel because only some emotions are considered acceptable to display. When there is a wide gap between what an employee actually feels and what is appropriate to display at work, **emotional labor** occurs. Some jobs and some industries require higher degrees of emotional labor. For example, occupations in the service sector such as childcare workers, physicians, and customer service representatives, require higher degrees of emotional labor than do occupations such as accountants, financial analysts, and airline pilots. For example, imagine a customer service representative expressing disgust at a customer's request for a refund. Rather, the customer service representative is expected to express positive emotions such as helpfulness even if he is feeling disgusted at a request.

 ## Emotional Intelligence

The capacity to be aware of one's own emotions and the emotions of others, manage emotions, and respond to emotions in an appropriate way is termed **emotional intelligence**.[9] Emotional intelligence, sometimes called emotional quotient, or EQ, involves being able to recognize and respond to social and emotional situations.[10] Importantly, emotional intelligence as a competency can be developed and changed. Levels of emotional intelligence can differ across individuals. High levels of emotional intelligence have been found to be predictive of high performance in many studies.[11] Emotional intelligence differs from traditional or cognitive intelligence. Traditional intelligence accounts for only a small percentage of success in an organization. It is useful for a baseline or threshold competency, which means that many management and leadership positions require a minimum level of intelligence to be competent at a job, but having a high level of intelligence does not predict whether or not you will be a top performer. Organizations have recognized the connection between emotional intelligence and leadership, and emotional intelligence and job performance. One study estimates that 90% of top performers have high emotional intelligence.[12]

Personality

3 Present the heredity versus environment debate on personality.

Personality refers to a set of individual characteristics that are consistent over time. Personality is a general term that includes emotions, attitudes, perceptions, and behaviors. Experts disagree on whether personality comes from genetics or whether personality is developed over time.[13] The question of whether personality is fixed or changes is important because if you believe that personality is fixed, and that a person will display consistent behavior over time, you will likely interact with that person differently than if you believe that someone can change his or her style. If, on the other hand, you believe that personality changes and develops, you can intervene and change the way you interact with the individual.

The debate on personality involves two viewpoints. The **heredity** perspective states that people are born with a particular set of personality traits and preferences. Proponents of the *heredity* perspective point out that many studies show families and relatives tend to share certain personality characteristics. The heredity perspective points to studies involving twins which tend to find that twins often share similar personalities even when separated at birth. The **environment** perspective supports the notion that personality develops over time and is heavily influenced by the environment. The family and culture in which someone is raised can have a profound impact on their personality, according to this perspective. Different families and national cultures carry belief systems, norms for behaviors, and broad similar patterns of interaction. The environment can also include life experiences. One individual may learn in the workplace to speak up and be loud to sell her ideas to her boss and is rewarded for this behavior. Another individual may learn to be quiet and observe those in authority positions because they are rewarded for this behavior. These experiences would impact how these individuals interact with others over time.

Personality and Behavior

The **Big Five** personality types resulted from extensive studies of a variety of personality characteristics and emerged from an interest in identifying core and enduring personality characteristics.[14] Table 2.3 presents and describes the five dimensions of the Big Five and what each of the dimensions predicts. The Big Five suggests that some individual characteristics are associated with improved performance in organizations. For example, across all occupational groups, high levels of conscientiousness predict positive job performance. Employees who exhibit traits of responsibility, dependability, and perseverance perform higher on job tasks than employees who do not have the same traits.[15] Openness to experience was also predictive of positive learning experiences. That is, employees who were high on the dimension of openness to experience performed well in the classroom or other structured learning experiences. Emotional stability predicted burnout in

Table 2.3 Big Five Personality Dimensions and Workplace Behavior

Dimension	Description	Predicts
Extraversion	Outgoing, sociable, talkative, assertive & active[16]	People are noticed; ability to sell ideas[17]
Agreeableness	Cooperative, good natured, tolerant, & trusting	Cooperation with others, customer service skills
Conscientiousness	Responsible, dependable, achievement focused, & perseverance	Good job performance
Emotional stability	Anxious, worried, depressed, insecure	Emotional exhaustion, burnout[18]
Openness to experience	Curious, flexible, original & intelligent	Predicts creativity and 'trainability'[19]

4 Contrast the Big Five and Myers-Briggs approaches to personality.

stressful situations. If an employee experiences anxiety, worry and depression, they are more likely to experience burnout than employees who do not have these traits in the same situation.

Myers-Briggs Type Indicator of Personality

Perhaps the most widely used measure of personality is the **Myers-Briggs Type Indictor,** or MBTI. The MBTI has been administered to millions of employees and is used in most *Fortune* 500 companies.[20] The MBTI was developed to measure personality based on the work of psychologist Carl Jung. Jung believed in personality type, the idea that personality is based on a specific cluster of different dimensions. MBTI offered a way to widely measure personality along four dimensions. Each dimension is dichotomous, meaning it is built on opposites. The Myer-Briggs types have been linked to career choices, team member interactions, leadership, conflict and quality of intimate relationships. The MBTI measures four dimensions of someone's personality:

Introversion (I)–Extraversion (E)

The Introversion and Extraversion dimension of the MBTI indicates to what extent someone is energized by the internal world or the external world. A student who scored high on the Introversion dimension would be said to have clarity around Introversion as a preference as to how they direct their thoughts. Introverts prefer to think and reflect in their inner world before blurting out ideas. Extraverts on the other hand are energized by the external world and often speak and think at the same time. Oftentimes, Extraverts dominate meetings or social situations. You may be able to observe this behavior in a team project meeting in one of your classes. Do you have team members who are quieter than others? You may be able to guess the personality preferences of these members.

Sensing (S)–Intuiting (N)

The Sensing and Intuiting dimension of the MBTI explains how someone prefers to process information. Sensing types tend to be concrete and detailed and gather data from the five physical senses and the immediate surroundings. Intuitive types, on the other hand, often use their 'gut instinct' or sixth sense to gather information, often with a future orientation. Communication in the workplace about a project between these two different types would consist of someone talking about the 'big picture' (Intuitive type) and someone talking about the specific details (Sensing type). It is difficult to guess how someone prefers to process information, but over time, you may be able to learn other people's preferences with details or with the 'big picture'.

Thinking (T)–Feeling (F)

The Thinking and Feeling dimension of the MBTI describes how someone makes decisions. The Thinking type concentrates on ideas and facts, while the Feeling type focuses on people and harmony when making decisions. Thinking types can focus on facts and remove their personal values from decision making in order to make a decision that is 'fair'. Feeling types often infuse their decisions with their personal values and are sympathetic to the human element in decision making. You may be able to guess people's preferences by paying attention to how much weight someone places on impartial facts when making a decision, versus how much a decision might affect a person.

Judging (J)–Perceiving (P)

Completion of a task is explained by preferences in the Judging and Perceiving dimension. Judging types have a high need for closure in tasks and will push themselves and others to complete tasks on time. Structure and planning characterize Judging types. Perceiving types view deadlines as a bit more flexible and do not have the same need to move immediately to closure. Spontaneity and 'keeping options open' characterize Perceiving types.

Each individual is said to have a preference on each of these four dichotomies. An ENTJ would be someone who has preferences for Extraversion, Intuiting, Thinking, and Judging.[21]

Measuring Personality

The use of personality measurement for job-related decisions (e.g. promotion, selection, job-fit, training opportunities) should be used with caution, because the quality of the method needs to be validated and not contain bias towards any group.

Personality can be measured with three different methods:

1. Personality inventories. Self-report personality inventories, where an individual reports on his or her own preferences, might help some become more aware of their personality preferences and how these impact their leadership style and even career strengths.
2. Projective tests. Projective tests may be used to help someone discover the most suitable workplace fit.
3. Expert interpretation of role-playing activities and interviews. Managers may use role-playing and interviews to help select an applicant for a job based on the right personality fit.

5 Outline attitudes, including self-efficacy, Machiavellianism, locus of control, and self-monitoring, and their role in organizations.

Attitudes

An **attitude** can be attributed to someone based on his or her beliefs, feelings, and actions and is usually subject to change based on experience. To say that personality comes from the environment is to assume that personality can change because it is shaped by external factors. But even if personality is subject to change, it does not change quickly. Attitudes, on the other hand, can change at a more rapid rate. You can think of attitudes as having a cause and effect relationship. Beliefs and feelings create an attitude that results in a behavior.[22] Rather than terming an attitude 'bad' or 'good', it is useful to look at specific attitudes and what behavior results from them. Some specific attitudes relevant to organizational behavior include self-efficacy, Machiavellianism, locus of control and self-monitoring.

Self-efficacy

The confidence that someone experiences relative to a particular task is **self-efficacy**.[23] This differs from self-esteem, which is an attitude of like or dislike of one's self image. One could have high self-esteem and yet at the same time have low self-efficacy around a challenging task. Self-efficacy is subject to change based on the experience with a task. Consider public speaking, for instance. A student could have low self-efficacy around her ability to perform well giving a report in front of a class. After she has had success in her public speaking experiences, her efficacy could increase.

Machiavellianism

Another category to think about with individual differences is the term **Machiavellianism**. This label to describe someone's attitude toward people is based on the character from the essay on power and politics, *The Prince*, written by Niccolo di Bernardo Machiavelli around 1500. The Mach IV scale measures the degree of Machiavellianism—described as the belief that people are objects—the attitude of Machiavellianism and the behaviors of influence and manipulation (High scoring). It might be tempting to use the label as 'bad' when describing the manipulation that accompanies high levels of Machiavellianism. But in some career fields, such as sales, this attitude has translated into high performance.[24]

Locus of Control

The extent to which someone believes that they are in control of their environment is termed **locus of control**.[25] If an individual has a high internal locus of control, they think that they are in control of what happens to them. If a student with a high internal locus of control scored low on a test, he might express dismay that he should have practiced better study habits. If a student with a high external locus of control received a low-test score, she would feel that it was out of her hands and caused by an external factor, like a professor who 'gives' poor grades. The attitudes toward control translate to supervision. Those with a high internal locus of control attitude tend to be more achievement-directed in their work pursuits, while high external locus of control attitudes tend to prefer more directive and hands-on supervision of their work.

Table 2.4 Locus of Control and Employee Beliefs[26]

Employees with an internal locus of control	Employees with an external locus of control
Bad events are caused by mistakes	Bad events are caused by bad luck
Success is caused by effort and hard work	Success is about being in the right place at the right time
Poor grades are caused by lack of effort	Poor grades are handed out and unfair
People can make friends by trying	People like or dislike you, there is little point in trying
High performance evaluations are the result of effort and hard work	High performance evaluations are the result of the boss's whim

Self-monitoring

Self-monitoring is the ability of an individual to adjust her behavior based on the environment in which she operates.[27] High self-monitors have the ability to 'read' a situation and understand what is appropriate behavior in that situation and then display those forms of behavior. High self-monitoring ability has been linked with positive outcomes in the workplace[28] such as promotions, job performance, and leadership.[29] Low self-monitors adjust their behavior based on internal factors, such as beliefs and attitudes, regardless of the environmental context.

Conclusion

Individual characteristics of people help us understand what people think, feel, and do in organizations. People's behavior in the workplace is influenced by competencies, emotions, personality traits, and attitudes. Emotions, shorter and more intense in duration, and moods, longer in duration, govern people's responses in context. Personality is the stable pattern of behavior and internal states. Researchers debate whether individual characteristics are a factor of hereditary or of the environment. Different forms of measurement exist for personality traits. Some personality traits are observable, while others are internal states and are not observable. Patterns of personality traits do not change rapidly, but attitudes are subject to change. Context plays an important role in attitudes as well as other behaviors, influencing reaction and interpretation.

OB AT WORK

OPENNESS, PERSEVERANCE AND CONSCIENTIOUSNESS IN BATTLE: CAPTAIN NATE SELF LEADS ARMY RANGERS IN AFGHANISTAN

Nate Self

Army Captain Nate Self had only a few pieces of information when he was deployed in Afghanistan toward a snowy mountaintop. Within hours of hearing his mission, 25-year-old Captain Self and his team crouched down in the MH-47 helicopter and realized how uncertain their mission was—they might land in the middle of an ongoing operation, or try to salvage a failed mission.

Self and his team would learn more about their mission only after hours of fighting. Unlike conventional forces where there was widespread planning before action, Self's team continually adapted to new information—they had to remain open to new information that could emerge at any point in time. There were nine men, many still teenagers, who had only light arms (handheld machine guns) so that they could get in and out of a situation quickly; they were a Quick Reaction Force (QRF). In addition to the QRF, there were two Air Force rescue jumpers and an eight-person flight crew. "It seemed to me somebody made a pretty big mistake," Self would later recall.[1] The helicopter carrying the team and crew reached 30 feet above the insertion point, but before the helicopter could land they were ambushed by a missile that hit the helicopter, and they were attacked by fire on all sides as they landed and exited the back. His first time in battle tested his ability to be open to new experiences, and adapt quickly.[2] They found cover near an outcropping of rocks that served as a temporary refuge. After a number of attempts, the QRF got through to Joint Special Forces Command (JSOC), sidestepping official protocol; the young Captain Self now reported directly to a two-star general.

6 Apply concepts of individual characteristics and the impact of these concepts to organizations.

Self, always enthusiastic to learn, recalled one of his nights observing at the Command Center and remembered that some of the Predator unmanned vehicles carried guided missiles. He communicated this information to the General and asked if one could be used to hit the enemy bunker. This was a surprising request, because the Predator was the property of the U.S. Central Intelligence Agency and the military had no control over armed Predators. In the end of the battle, the Predator attack destroyed the enemy bunker on the mountaintop, allowing Self and his QRF to recover the body of a fallen Navy SEAL. Self's conscientiousness meant that he was not going to give up, that the responsible and right action was to recover the body of a comrade, Neal Roberts, who was killed in a failed attempt to take the mountain a day before. Nate and his team would persevere in doing the right thing, despite the insurmountable odds they faced. In recovering the body, Self and his team were also able to take control of the mountaintop from enemy forces. This application of organizational behavior concepts to Captain Self's experiences provides an example of the principles of the Big Five personality traits. Specifically, Captain Self exhibits openness to experience and conscientiousness, and helps us understand behavior even in an extremely challenging life or death situation.

Source: Personal interview, Nate Self;
[1]Phillips, S. (Sunday June 26, 2006). Rescue on Roberts Ridge. *Dateline NBC.* Accessed at http://www.msnbc.msn.com/id/1323381.
[2]Self, N. (2008). *Two wars.* Carol Stream, IL: Tyndale.

SPOTLIGHT ON RESEARCH
How CEO Personality Increases Company Income

Can the personality of a company's Chief Executive Officer (CEO) relate to profits? One group of researchers wanted to find out. They turned their expertise to study whether CEO personality might impact the functioning of the top management team and in turn, relate to company income growth.

Prior research had shown a direct link between the top management team (TMT) and a company's success. If the researchers could show that the personality of a CEO could impact the top management team, then in turn how the top management team relates to income growth, they would have evidence that personality has an impact on how a company functions. Personality may have an impact on team functioning because certain personality traits may lead to better team interaction. For example, if a leader displayed a Big Five personality trait of agreeableness, she might facilitate a more agreeable team. The researchers looked at the Big Five personality traits and their relationship to team functioning. In all, they identified 20 different ways that teams function including variables such as how much control the team leader exercised over the group, the degree to which the teams had developed internal factions, and how pessimistic the team may have been.

The researchers faced a limitation in their study of CEO personality and its link to firm effectiveness. They did not have direct access to the CEOs or their management teams. Instead of directly interviewing the CEOs, the team of researchers relied on archival data such as biographies and interviews of the CEOS. They relied on the same types of sources, but not the exact sources to study top management teams to avoid bias in the sources. They developed rigorous selection criteria to make sure other biases such as industry, regulatory environment, or other factors did not play a role in the selection. For each CEO and team, five separate sources were reviewed. In all, the researchers reviewed about 20 pages for each CEO. To determine firm performance, they considered sales, return on investment, and return on assets, but found them all related so the researchers decided to rely on income growth as the best measure of company performance.

The results revealed that indeed, the personality of the CEO was related to both the top management team functioning and firm functioning. Here is what they found:

- CEOs who were high on the Big Five personality trait of conscientiousness were more likely to have teams that were legalistic in their functioning and who displayed a sense of control over their environment.
- CEOs who were high in agreeableness also produced teams with high legalistic functioning but their teams were also high in cohesion and decentralized power.
- CEOs who were high in emotional stability were more likely to lead teams with high cohesion, intellectual flexibility, and leader dominance.
- CEOs who were high on extraversion were perceived to be more dominant, expressing personal opinions.

(continued)

In terms of the relationship between top management team functioning and company income growth, the following relationships were found:

- Top management teams that displayed flexibility, optimism, and cohesiveness were related to income growth.
- In addition, top management teams that took responsible risks were also slightly related to income growth.

The researchers found evidence that their initial hunch proved correct: the personality of a CEO is related to company performance.

Questions for Discussion

1. How important do you think individual personality of the CEO is to the company's performance? Why do you think so?

2. What other individual factors related to the CEO do you think could have an impact on the company's performance? Why do you think so?

*Based on Randall S. Peterson, D. Brent Smith, Paul V. Martorana, & Pamela D. Owens. (2003). The impact of chief executive officer personality on top management team dynamics: One mechanism by which leadership affects organizational performance. *Journal of Applied Psychology, 88,* 5, 795–808.

Pairing with this Topic Summary

Suggested Expert Contributions

Solving the Introvert Problem–Laurie Helgoe (Davis and Elkins College)

Narcissism and Its Role in Organizations–W. Keith Campbell (University of Georgia) and Stacy M. Campbell (Kennesaw State University)

The Importance of Affect at Work–Donald E. Gibson (Fairfield University) and Sigal G. Barsade (University of Pennsylvania)

The Challenge of Managing Emotions in the Workplace –Neal M. Ashkanasy (University of Queensland) and Catherine S. Daus (Southern Illinois University, Edwardsville)

Suggested Cases

Case 5: Whatever Happened to One of the "100 Best Companies to Work For"?: A Case Study of Hewlett-Packard

Case 7: Perceptions of Leaders Following Public Failures: A Tale of Two Coaches

Case 8: Conflict in Santa's Workshop: Learning to Be a Team Player at ToyKing

Suggested Exercises

Exercise 1: Big Five-Celebrity Spotlight

Exercise 7: Development While in College

Exercise 8: Facts and Opinions

Exercise 9: Being Positive

Exercise 14: Laughter Is the Best Medicine

Exercise 15: Building My Network—Individual

Exercise 29: Diversity Rocks

Exercise 31: The Ethics of the Climb

Exercise 33: Could I Be a Whistleblower?

Exercise 36: What Are My Values?

Endnotes

1. *Critical skills needs and resources for the changing workforce: A study by the Society for Human Resource Management* and WSJ.com/Careers (June 2008).
2. Krell, E. (2011). *Competency modeling meets talent management.* Accessed September 8 from SHRM.org.
3. Staw, B.M., Sutton, R.I., & Pelled, L.H. (1994). Employee positive emotion and favorable outcomes at the workplace. *Organization Science, 5*(1): 51–72.
4. Plutchik R. (1994). *The psychology and biology of emotion.* Harper-Collins: New York.
5. Ashkanasy, N.M, and Daus C. S. (2002). Emotion in the workplace: The new challenge for managers. *The Academy of Management Perspectives, 16*(1): 76–86.
6. Ashkanasy, N. M., Zerbe, W., & Hartel, C. E. J. (Eds.). (2002). *Managing emotions in the workplace.* Armonk, NY: M. E. Sharpe.
7. Cosmides, L., & Tooby, J. (2000). Evolutionary psychology and the emotions. In M. Lewis & J. M. Haviland-Jones (Eds.). *Handbook of emotions.* New York: Guilford Press, 91–115.
8. Fisher, C. D., & Ashkanasy, N. M. (2000). Emotions in organizations. *Journal of Organizational Behavior, 21*: 121–234.
9. Ashkanasy, N. M., & Daus, C. S. (2005). Rumors of the death of emotional intelligence in organizational behavior are vastly exaggerated. *Journal of Organizational Behavior, 4*(26): 441.
10. Goleman, D. (1995). *Emotional intelligence: Why it can matter more than IQ.* New York: Bantam Books.
11. Goleman, D., Boyatzis, R., & McKee, A. (2002). *Primal leadership: Realizing the power of emotional intelligence.* Boston: Harvard Business School Press.
12. Available at .www.talentsmart.com.
13. Schacter, D. L., Gilbert, D. T., & Wegner, D. M. (2011). *Psychology. 2*nd *Edition.* New York: Worth Publishers.
14. Barrick, M. R., & Mount, M. K. (1991). The Big Five personality dimensions and job performance: A meta-analysis. *Personnel Psychology, 44*: 1.
15. Baker, A., B., Van Der Zee, K. I., Lewig, K. A., & Dollard, M. F. (2006). The relationship between the Big Five personality factors and burnout: A study among volunteer counselors. *The Journal of Social Psychology, 146*(1): 31-50.
16. Andrew N., Gillian Y., Annette K., & Tania, X. (2012). Predicting the form and direction of work role performance from the big five model of personality traits. *Journal of Organizational Behavior, 33*: 175–192.
17. Goldberg, L. R. (1992). The development of markers for the Big-Five factor structure. *Psychological Assessment, 4*(1): 26-42.
18. Penney, L. M., David, E., & Witt., L. A. (2011). A review of personality and performance: Identifying boundaries, contingencies, and future research directions. *Human Resource Management Review, 21*(4): 297–310,

19. Neal, A., Yeo, G., Koy, A., & Xiao, T. (2012) Predicting the form and direction of work role performance from the big five model of personality traits. *Journal of Organizational Behavior, 33:* 175–192. See also Frei, R. L., & McDaniel, M. A. (1998). Validity of customer service measures in personnel selection: A review of criterion and construct evidence. *Human Performance, 11:* 1–27.

20. CPP website www.cpp.org/about the MBTI.

21. Quenk, N. L., Hammer, A. L., & Majors, M. S. (2001). MBTI® Step II Manual. Mountain View, CA: CPP, Inc.

22. Hogg, M. A., & Vaughn, G. M. (2008). *Social Psychology.* Upper Saddle River: Prentice Hall.

23. Bandura, A. (1997). *Self-efficacy: The exercise of control.* New York: Freeman

24. Jones, D. N., & Paulhus, D. L. (2009). Machiavellianism. In Leary, Mark R. & Hoyle, Rick H. (Eds.). *Handbook of individual differences in social behavior.* New York/London: The Guilford Press, 257–273.

25. Ryon, H. S., & Gleason, M. E. J. (2013). The role of locus of control in daily life. *Personality and Social Psychology Bulletin, 39:* 121-131.

26. Ryon, H. S. & Gleason, M. E. J. (2013).

27. Kilduff, M., & Day, D. V. (1994). Do chameleons get ahead? The effects of self-monitoring on managerial careers. *Academy of Management Journal, 37*(4): 1047–1060.

28. Mehra, A., Kilduff, M., & Brass, D. J. (2001). The social networks of high and low self-monitors: Implications for workplace performance. *Administrative Science Quarterly, 46*(1): 121–146.

29. Dobbins, G. H., Long, W. S., Dedrick, E. J., & Clemons, T. C. (1990). The role of self-monitoring and gender on leader emergence: A laboratory and field study. *Journal of Management, 16(3):* 609–618. See also Duarte, N. T., & Goodson, J. R. (2012). The compensatory role of self-monitoring in performance appraisal. *International Journal of Business and Social Science, 3*(24).

Solving the Introvert Problem

Laurie Helgoe

Davis and Elkins College

> *We have a standard cubicle arrangement. You can see everybody's face in the room of 50 people, so extraverts aren't afraid to shout out whatever comes into their heads.*

> *I don't enjoy the company picnic, summer parties, after-hours happy hour, or the noisy bars. I feel like there's something wrong with me.*

> *At a meeting, I'm thinking what it means theoretically, asking "How is this going to work?" I don't want to sit and talk about it. All the talking becomes interference, noise.*

These comments come from introverts, and these introverts share a problem. Each is out of synch with the work situation described—a situation that seems to work best for the extraverts. To the extent that the American workplace reflects the values of our reward-driven, capitalistic society, squeaky wheels get the grease and introverts have a problem.

Ever since the *Extraversion–Introversion* polarity was identified as one of five factors—the "Big Five"—that best explained personality differences, research on the differences between introverts and extraverts[1] has exploded. This research, along with 50 years of data from the Myers-Briggs Personality Indicator, is giving us a picture—complete with brain topography—of two very different approaches to the world (see Table 1).

According to personality type theory, we all use introversion and extraversion. We just tend to prefer one over the other and use it more often. Sometimes the preference isn't evident until the individual is under stress—the introvert wants to retreat and the extravert wants to talk. Put both together in a room and they both have a problem. Put them together in the workplace, and the problem belongs to the introvert.

And the introvert-at-work problem is not confined to the occasional technical wizard or wallflower that we assume characterizes the introvert. Introverts are an extremely diverse group comprising *half* of the population. (If you want to split hairs, it's a little more than half: the two largest and most recent studies using the Myers-Briggs Type Indicator revealed that introverts make up 51 percent (1998 study) and 57 percent (2001 study) of the U.S. population.)[2]

As an avid fan of the satirical newspaper, *The Onion*, I think some points are best illustrated by legitimizing absurd, but lazily accepted beliefs. It is in this spirit that we list the problems introverts are inflicting on the American workplace. While the opinions expressed in this list do not reflect those of the authors of this book, the research and quotes are real. Names of contributing introverts have been changed.

Problem #1: Introverts Make Extraverts Uncomfortable

There are few things that make an extraverted coworker more uncomfortable than to see an introvert absorbed in his work, content to be alone, quietly generating ideas,

Table 1 Comparing Preferences of Introverts versus Extraverts

Criterion	Introvert	Extravert
Brain and response to external stimulation	**Core processor** External input activates numerous brain regions, especially those associated with reflection, problem-solving and planning.	**Extended Network** External input activates dopamine pathways, drive to engage, and seek rewards in the external world.
Optimal environment	**Quiet and Private** Interruption-free to shut out distractions and allow focus.	**Bustling and Social** Activity and interaction to reduce boredom and stimulate thinking.
Preferred working style	**Personal Laboratory** Gather information, work out solutions privately, and prepare ideas before sharing them.	**Group Effort** Brainstorm with group; bounce ideas back and forth; work on a team; and prepare ideas together.
Enjoyable interactions	**Easy Listening** One-on-one or small; idea-focused group; time to reflect on input and share complete thoughts; social life more private and separate from work.	**Rap Session** Fast-paced; talk freely; doesn't mind interruptions; may compete for airtime; socially inclusive; mix work and social life.
Communication style	**Send and Receive** Get information from presentation or written communication; work with it privately; provide information when ready; written form often preferred.	**Here and Now** Get information informally and when needed, work out solutions while others are present, prefer talking to writing.

crunching numbers or completing reports. Such an exhibit undermines the work that good employees are putting into winning friends and making witty comments.

Don't get me wrong. Extraverts are just as productive as introverts; they just like to mix it up—play a little at work, work a little while socializing after hours. Introverts seem to want to focus on their work while they are at work, and then go home! There are even studies that show that introverts deliberately shut out positive emotional stimuli so they can concentrate on the task at hand. Brian W. Haas and associates looked at reaction time when introverts and extraverts tried to identify the *color* of an emotionally charged word—for example, the word is "joy" and the color of the word is red. Introverts, who were more able to push aside the emotional stimuli and focus on identifying the color had significantly better reaction times than the extraverts.[3] Sure, but where's the joy in that?

The pursuit of happiness is built into our Declaration of Independence *and* into the brains of extraverts. Introverts should really try to be more patriotic, which of course means being more like extraverts. Rather than getting irritated when extraverts try to cheer them up, introverts should appreciate the encouragement. And they could at least meet up with some coworkers to talk about what they're doing rather than barreling ahead and getting so much done on their own. It's not fair and it's not fun. Extraverts like to work in groups and talk things out—and the more the merrier—so even if introverts don't like it, they should be good sports and play along. It's the American way: All for one! Team spirit!

Introverts can be introverts when they get home—after happy hour, of course.

Problem #2: Reflective Types Can't Be Leaders

Good leaders are charismatic, aggressive, and persuasive. They're enthusiastic. They like to take charge and make things happen. In other words, they're extraverts. Introverts can never be leaders because they waste too much time listening, thinking things through, and developing effective plans. Leaders need to be quick and confident, and if they don't have an answer, they should make one up. They won't get anywhere if they are compelled to consider people's input or think before acting. Get ahead or fall behind! Better done than perfect! Better done by an extravert.

Okay, there's always the occasional exception. In a study reported in the *Harvard Business Review*,[4] the extraverted leaders got better results only when the employees were passive. When the employees were proactive, the introverted leaders generated better profits and higher performance, presumably because they used those annoying listening skills and encouraged the employees rather than showing their leadership muscle. Extraverts have really nice-looking leadership muscles. The proactive employees were probably just jealous.

Problem #3: Introverts Lose Because they Don't Schmooze

Everyone knows that to get ahead, you've got to mingle and schmooze and network to win friends and influence people. It's who you know, so the more people you know—the better. And you want to be remembered, so the more you say and the faster you talk—the better. The movers and shakers get there by moving and shaking. It's only logical.

Extraverts are go-getters. They go more and they get more. That's another reason why introverts would benefit by going with the extraverts—to happy hour, for example. But even when they try, introverts fall short of being fully functioning extraverts. Psychologists Maya Santoro and John Zelenski at Carleton University found that introverts who were told to act extraverted showed slower reaction times on subsequent cognitive test than those instructed to act introverted.[5] Introverts can act extraverted and even enjoy it, but they will ultimately be the party-poopers who say they're ready to go home and—how boring—*relax*.

Some introverts will argue that sustained effort is what leads to success, that Bill Gates and Steve Jobs became so successful because they spent a lot of time *away* from people, solving problems and inventing things. Okay, but they're famous. Besides, if introverts just go off and work, they'll run into Problem #1. Extraverts will get uncomfortable.

Yes, there are those introverts who get lucky and get ahead by working hard. Lourdes, an immigrant from Latin America, put herself through community college while working as a waitress. She focused on accounting, earned a position as a CPA at a Big Four firm, became a senior executive, and then president of a mortgage banking company. She had nearly 4,000 employees reporting to her, and now heads up an office for a NYC insurance company. Her success came with remarkably little schmoozing:

> I don't golf. I avoided 99% of the bars, happy hours, and I focused on the technical aspects of work and delivery. I only attended social events when I saw a very specific objective for it. How else would you know anything unless you take time to read it and analyze it? You're not going to pick it up at the bar. You need to put energy into learning and understanding the subject matter.
>
> I'm an immigrant, a woman and a minority. I came to this country with $20 in my pocket, no Ivy League education. I got where I am through sheer effort, long hours. Success—at least the success that matters—comes from substance.

But she does acknowledge that she would do some things differently if she had to start over. A-ha! Let's see what she regrets:

> I would be honest. I would tell people (as I do now), "I'm not going to social hour—it's my quiet time." When you are truthful and show that you are vulnerable, people are less judgmental than if you just don't show up or make an excuse. If I had been able to communicate from a place of knowledge, understanding and empathy, seeing both sides, respecting the need of extraverts to have their social interaction, I would have struggled less with the social demands that come from having a high-profile job.
>
> I also would have been more accommodating of both introverts and extraverts. Introverts can get frustrated with other introverts. They think, "I'm here suffering. How dare you skip out?"
>
> I need to be alone every day for a few hours. It's a biological necessity. Extraverts get energized by going out, and that's fine. I'm now comfortable in my own skin with that.

Well, if you put it that way…

Creating a Workplace that Works—For Everybody

The arguments in the previous section demonstrate the limitations of a one-sided view of what is valuable in the workplace. In the real world, the failed logic underpinning these arguments is not so transparent. Cell phone commercials tell us that being followed by a mob of friends and family is reassuring and that having a huge wireless network is important. Sitcoms are punctuated by intrusions—someone bopping in or stopping by the home or office, no knocking required. We are told to "just do it," and "git r done," and there's no pause in programming to ask what, why, when, or how?

Organizational leaders and consultants can provide that needed pause in the programming. Introverts and extraverts are both subject to—and limited by—assumptions that equate extraversion with success. And the risk of skewering these assumptions, as I have here, is that it leaves us with a fairly hollow caricature of extraversion. It is important to remember that extraverts are not the problem. The assumptions are the problem. Few extraverts identify with an über-extravert, that media-enhanced quick-thinking, fast-talking and wildly entertaining person in the center of the room. And extraverts are diminished when their success is unfairly attributed to advantage or when they feel like the bad guys because they have it easier, or when they deny their preferences to gain favor with introverts.

When introverts or extraverts put energy into questioning, defending, or apologizing for how they're wired—or feeling offended because of the way another person is wired—human resources are depleted and the organization suffers. Instead of trying to force a universal language of the workplace, organizational leaders can optimize their human resources by encouraging a bilingual consciousness. But until introversion becomes a visible, viable, and valued alternative in the workplace, introverts—and extraverts in an introverted mood—will not be fully present until they clock out.

Shutting Off the Program, Tuning In to Personality

Since the publication of my book, *Introvert Power: Why Your Inner Life is Your Hidden Strength*[6], introverts often write to tell me about the moment when they first saw beyond their old programming. The shift may have occurred while they were reading my book or getting feedback from a personality test or when they discovered an article or study that shed new light on the topic. They describe suddenly having words for what they were experiencing, a community of people who share their preferences, and the freedom to, as Lourdes put it, "to just be honest."

But for Lourdes and other introverts who stay tuned in and true to their preferences, shutting off the assumptions that undermine introverts requires commitment. And the workplace is often where this is most difficult.

Personality testing and training, now offered by many organizations, provide a starting point for change. Here are some ways these processes can be enhanced:

1. *Focus in on introversion-extraversion.* In personality training, the introversion–extraversion polarity is discussed as part of a larger constellation of personality characteristics—it's one of the Big Five traits and one of four Myers-Briggs subtypes. This complexity makes personality training interesting and rich, but also limits the opportunity for learning to sink in and arouse change. To get beyond common misunderstandings and culturally supported assumptions regarding introversion and extraversion, it may be necessary to pull this polarity out of the mix and study it as a separate topic.

2. *Engage employees.* Most of us are narcissistic enough to enjoy learning about ourselves, but how we like to learn it will be influenced by how introverted or extraverted we are. Training methods may be steeped in the very biases the training seeks to address. For example, group break-out sessions and open Q&A forums give the *appearance* of engagement, but are approached with dread by most introverts. Engagement cannot be accurately measured by verbal responses alone. Introverts may engage more when listening to a speaker than when participating in a discussion, because the former allows more mental space for reflection. If we stop assuming everyone in the room is an extravert, break-out sessions might include the option of breaking *away* from the group and writing down ideas privately. And instead of applying the same learning model to all, employees could choose among learning tracks such as independent study, seminar participation, or engaging in a group project.

3. *Put assumptions to the test.* Personality testing helps individuals recognize how they tick, what helps them work at their best, and how to work with people who tick differently. But unless existing assumptions are also put to the test, unspoken biases will undermine application of the insights. I've presented a set of common assumptions in this article, and a more extensive list in my book, *Introvert Power: Why Your Inner Life is Your Hidden Strength*, but each workgroup or organization would likely generate its own version. Confidential surveys can help assess: Do employees assume most of their colleagues are extraverts? Do employees assume they are expected to be more extraverted? Do managers assume extraversion is

better for the company? What assumptions are communicated in organization-al literature? Once assumptions are exposed, true communication and change becomes possible.

4. *Facilitate "conversations."* When Lourdes simply and honestly tells her cowork-ers that she's an introvert, gets drained by parties, and is really looking forward to a quiet evening at home, they understand—and many even share similar feelings. Conversations come in many forms, many unspoken, and have the potential to correct or perpetuate assumptions. If, in an effort to be polite, Lourdes apolo-gizes for not being able to make a party, invents excuses, and notes how much she wishes she could come, she perpetuates the assumption that she (and everyone) likes such events. As a part of personality education, employees can create and practice sample dialogue—both written and spoken. For example, the introvert may educate the extravert on why interruptions make her crabby, and the extra-vert can discuss her need for access. Hypothetical conversations allow people to maintain privacy while working out potentially conflict-ridden situations. Co-workers may need only to refer back to a practiced conversation and add, "I'm feeling that way now."

From Problem to Opportunity

The introvert problem discussed in this article only exists when introversion is denied. When introversion is recognized and supported, the problem is transformed into oppor-tunity. Organizations get fully functioning core processors *and* extended networks. And employees get to like their jobs. With or without happy hour.

Endnotes

1. If you think I've misspelled *extravert,* your spellchecker may agree with you. *Extrovert* with an "o" has become more popular outside of academic circles, and is generally given as the primary spelling in dictionaries. *Extravert,* the dictionary's "variant spelling," is used in academic settings and on personality tests, such as the Myers-Briggs Type Indicator (MBTI).
2. For more on these studies, and on the proliferation of erroneous introvert–extravert statistics, see *Introvert Power: Why Your Inner Life is Your Hidden Strength.* By Laurie Helgoe. Naperville, IL: Sourcebooks, 2008.
3. See Haas, B.W., et. al. (2006). "Functional connectivity with the anterior cingulate is associated with extraversion during the emotional Stroop task." *Social Neuroscience, 1*(1), 16-24.
4. See Grant, A. M., Gino, F. & Hofmann, D. A. (2010). "The hidden advantage of quiet bosses." *Harvard Business Review,* Dec 1.
5. See Zelenski, J.M., Santoro, M.S., & Whelan, D.C. (2011). "Would introverts be better off if they acted more like extraverts? Exploring emotional and cognitive consequences of counterdispositional behavior." *Emotion,* Aug 22.
6. See *Introvert Power: Why Your Inner Life is Your Hidden Strength.* By Laurie Helgoe. Naperville, IL: Sourcebooks, 2008.

Narcissism and Its Role in Organizations

W. Keith Campbell
University of Georgia

Stacy M. Campbell
Kennesaw State University

Narcissism, a term used to describe an arrogant, entitled, or grandiose sense of self, is used often in the discussion of behaviors in organizations. Leaders who are greedy, dishonest, self-centered, or vain are described as narcissistic. At the same time, narcissism and entitlement are terms used to describe workers, especially younger ones. Most spectacularly, narcissism is seen in the downfall of many promising leaders and cultural figures. Senator John Edwards derailed his rising political career when news of his "love child" and affair leaked to the press. As Edwards explained his behavior: "In the course of several campaigns, I started to believe that I was special and became increasingly egocentric and narcissistic."[1] A similar explanation was given by Tiger Woods after his numerous affairs were revealed: "I felt that I had worked hard my entire life and deserved to enjoy all the temptations around me. I felt I was entitled."[2] In another set of incidents, a pair of congressmen lost their seats as a result of posting semi-naked pictures of themselves online for admirers to see. These displays of vanity were ultimately self-destructive.

Despite the negative examples of narcissism, it can have many benefits as well. For example, research on U.S. presidents and celebrities alike have found high levels of narcissism in these successful groups.[3, 4] In these cases, narcissism is linked to charisma, the ability to emerge as a leader and the ability (and desire) to perform in the public spotlight. The story we want to tell in this chapter is about the trade-offs that come with narcissism, especially in organizational settings. While narcissism can help an individual rise to the top, narcissism can also lead to his or her own destruction (along with the destruction of those around him or her). We begin, however, with an in-depth look at what we mean by narcissism.

What is Narcissism?

Narcissism is a personality trait that exists across the population of individuals. That is, some individuals have high levels of narcissism and some have low levels, with the average individual somewhere in the middle of the continuum. In research, narcissism is often measured with the narcissistic personality inventory (NPI). The NPI includes items like: "I think I am a special person." "If I ruled the world it would be a much better place." "I like to look at myself in the mirror." And "I am a born leader."[5]

Probably the easiest way to think of narcissism is by breaking it into three parts. The first two parts have to do with how narcissistic individuals see themselves and relate to others. First, narcissistic individuals have a very positive self-concept. That is, they rate themselves more positively than they rate other individuals (e.g., the better than average effect) and also rate themselves more positively than objective measures (e.g., IQ tests) on traits like intelligence, good looks, creativity and social status. Narcissistic individuals can be conceited, entitled, vain, and arrogant at times. Second, narcissistic individuals have interpersonal relationships where emotional warmth, closeness, and caring for others are limited. Narcissistic individuals can be very social, likable, and charming, but their relationships lack a solid foundation of trust and commitment.[6]

The third part of narcissism is in some ways the most interesting. Imagine that you think you are better, smarter, more important, or better looking than you actually are. You would have to structure your life so that you can keep this fantasy going. Furthermore, because you don't have strong caring relationships with other people, you are fine with using others to make you look good. The formal term we use for this process of looking and feeling good is "self-enhancement," and narcissistic individuals are experts at self-enhancement. For example, narcissistic individuals can be materialistic (think throwing the Mercedes keys on the table at lunch or dressing in more glamorous clothing). They might name drop, talk with a loud voice to draw attention to themselves, or turn conversations back to themselves. Narcissistic individuals also look for opportunities to promote themselves, whether it be performing in public or seeking fame. While such self-enhancement can allow people to feel good about themselves and to maintain a positive self view, there is a darker side to self-enhancement as well. Narcissistic individuals can also steal credit from other's successes (or blame others for failures), so that the narcissist looks good. Additionally, when narcissistic individuals get negative feedback (for example, told they are unattractive or failures), this makes them feel threatened and the result is often anger and aggression.

Narcissists' close relationships show many elements of this self-enhancement. In their romantic life, narcissistic individuals are drawn to attractive, high-status potential partners. We often see this in the phenomenon of "trophy spouses." This type of self-enhancement is evident on the Internet. Narcissistic individuals on Facebook post self-promoting and sexy main photos, use self-enhancing self descriptions, and have higher numbers of "friends." This same pattern spills over to personal email addresses, with narcissistic individuals having more self-enhancing and salacious email addresses (for example, 'thehotkingchamp2395').[7]

So, to summarize, with narcissism we see a pattern of behavior designed to enhance the self, often at the expense of others. When the narcissistic individual is successful at this process, he or she will keep her self-esteem up and maintain a positive mood. In contrast, when the self-enhancement efforts go poorly, the narcissistic individual can become angry and depressed.[8]

There are a few other issues involving narcissism that are important to mention. There is also a psychiatric disorder known as Narcissistic Personality Disorder or NPD. NPD is an extreme form of narcissistic personality in which the narcissistic behaviors do significant harm to the individual and/or those around him or her. While narcissistic personality is common, NPD is a relatively rare condition estimated to affect roughly one percent of the population.[9] It is important when discussing narcissism not to use the psychiatric disorder of NPD except when talking about a diagnosed case. Narcissism is something most of us can detect in others, but NPD should only be diagnosed by a trained professional.

Second, there is a distinction between two forms of narcissism, a grandiose form and a vulnerable form. Grandiose narcissism includes traits like assertiveness, confidence, self-esteem, and grandiosity. The more grandiose forms of narcissism are seen commonly in organizational leaders and celebrities. Vulnerable narcissism lacks dominance and assertiveness, but contains entitlement, depression, and low self-esteem. Vulnerable narcissism is seen by clinical psychology and psychotherapists because these individuals will seek psychological treatment for their depression. Here is where the confusion comes in: Individuals can have characteristics of both grandiose and vulnerable narcissism; however, it is not the case that grandiose narcissists are vulnerable "deep down inside." That is, a confident, even cocky, business leader with a wife twenty years his junior and a collection of sports cars probably does not have low self-esteem deep down inside. To the contrary, he probably feels pretty good about himself.[10]

Third, there are gender, age, and cultural differences in narcissism. Overall, men are more narcissistic than women. We find modest differences between men and women on trait narcissism, and much larger difference on NPD, where about three quarters of the diagnoses are of men. Likewise, younger individuals are more narcissistic than older individuals. Part of this probably represents a developmental process where we become less narcissistic as we age.[11] However, some of the differences between younger and older individuals (at least in the United States) is due to cultural changes. College students today, for example, are more narcissistic that those 30 years ago. Today's students also report less empathy, more positive self-views, and higher levels of self-esteem. We should note that there are also cross-cultural differences in narcissism. Narcissism is relatively high in the United States, and is typically lower in Asian cultures.[12]

Narcissism in the Workplace

Narcissism has an influence throughout organizational contexts. We are going to focus on several of these. To begin, however, we would like to suggest that you not think of narcissism as uniquely good or bad, but as a trade-off. Narcissism benefits individuals in the workplace in some contexts, and hurts in others. This is not to say we have a pro-narcissism stance, but that the understanding of narcissism has to have nuance.[12]

One clear example of this trade-off can be seen in the realm of leadership. Table 1 summarizes the costs and benefits of narcissism to leadership. Leadership has been part of the discussion of narcissism going back to the work of Freud. And, indeed, the research shows that narcissism is important to leadership, but not in a simple way. Leadership itself can be divided into two aspects, emergence and effectiveness. Emergence refers to the process by which individuals become leaders, such as through selection, hiring or election; effectiveness refers to the ways in which leaders perform in the leadership role.

Narcissism has a clear benefit to leadership emergence. In groups of strangers in a lab, for example, narcissistic individuals will often emerge as leaders. This same process occurs in business training centers. We also see a link between narcissism and charisma, with narcissistic individuals having high levels of charisma and likability.

But what about effectiveness? We do not find that narcissistic individuals, on average, make effective leaders in the long term. Narcissistic leaders tend to make risky decisions. When these are successful, the rewards for the organization can be large; when these are unsuccessful, however, it can be disastrous. We also find that, at least in lab studies, narcissistic leaders are good at competitive resource extraction. For example, in studies we have looked at willingness to cut down a renewable forest. The narcissistic leaders cut

Table 1 Narcissism and Leadership

Benefits
• Leadership Emergence: Narcissists rise into leadership position more easily than others
• Charisma: Narcissistic leaders can be very charismatic (although not all charismatic leaders are narcissistic)
• Resource Extraction: Narcissistic leaders are good at extracting resources from the environment
• Confidence in Public: Narcissistic leaders are experts at appearing confident in public

Costs
• Risk-taking: Narcissistic leaders are apt to take big public risks, which can put an entire organization in jeopardy
• Failure to Learn from Mistakes: Narcissistic leaders have difficulty learning from their mistakes, and instead like to blame others for their failures
• Ethical Lapses: Narcissistic leaders show poor ethics at times, and narcissism is even linked with white collar crime
• Counterproductive Workplace Behavior: Narcissistic leaders are more likely than others to bully, threaten, or otherwise be uncivil in the workplace

down the forest quickly, which can be seen as positive for the company in the short term. However, the narcissistic leaders destroy the renewable resource more quickly, which is detrimental for the company in the longer term. Narcissistic leaders also have, on average, questionable ethics. That is, their lack of empathy and propensity to exploit others make them more likely to bend the rules when the action will benefit them. Thus, we see a link between narcissism and white collar crime.

Of course, narcissism does not just influence leaders in the workplace. Research shows that narcissism has the potential to influence the performance of many members of the organization. First, narcissism is linked to overconfident decision-making. By that, we mean that narcissistic individuals can be more confident in their own abilities than they should be. In one study, for example, narcissistic individuals were asked to answer a collection of general knowledge questions and then bet on their answers. It turns out the narcissistic individuals were no better than anyone else on the questions, but they were much more confident in their answers. As a result, the narcissistic individuals lost more money on the task than others did. Here is the kicker: Even after their poor performance, the narcissistic individuals still thought they did better than others and would continue to do better in the future. Narcissism also predicts an interesting decision-making phenomenon called "overclaiming." Overclaiming is simply knowing things that do not actually exist. For example, if a narcissistic individual were asked if he had heard of U.S. President Hillston, he would be more likely than others to say yes. Narcissistic individuals like to think they know more than they actually know. Finally, this same pattern of overconfidence can be seen in the stock market investing choices of narcissistic individuals. When selecting stocks, these individuals pick risky stocks—those with high volatility and the potential for gain but also for loss. This research measured stock performance during a bear market. The narcissistic individuals performed more poorly than others in this condition.[14]

As we said though, narcissism is a trade-off. Because of their risk taking, narcissistic individuals will do better in investing than others in a bull market. When the economy is booming, big risks pay off, and narcissistic individuals will take those big risks. Furthermore, narcissistic individuals are better than others at convincing people of their talent. This can be a real benefit in sales. In one study, for example, individuals engaged in a creativity task and then tried to convince others of their creativity. It turns out that narcissistic individual's creativity is not better than other's when judged objectively, but the narcissistic individuals were very skilled at convincing others that their work was highly creative.[15]

Finally, narcissistic individuals can be destructive in the workplace when they feel that they are not able to do what they want. Research has shown that when they experience constraints in the workplace, narcissistic individuals become angry, and this leads to what is technically called "counterproductive work behavior" such as bullying or being aggressive to others.[16] This is part of a more general phenomenon where narcissistic individuals show generally few behaviors in the workplace that are designed to help the organization or team but not actually to help the self[17]. In other words, in addition to being abusive at times in the workplace, narcissistic individuals are not going to be the ones pitching in to make the organization better for everyone. They are typically not team players and in an environment that relies heavily on teamwork like many workplaces, narcissists can decrease productivity, cohesiveness, and the effectiveness of teams. For a narcissist, there is an I in team.

Practical Approaches to Dealing with Narcissism

There a bright side and dark side to narcissism. For example, one can see a successful narcissistic leader who is successful because of risk taking and charisma; but this same person can also have a dark side when he or she is threatened or overcome with feelings of grandiosity.[18] As a result, narcissism is linked to outcomes for the self and the social environment that can be both positive and negative. The challenge is how do we increase the bright side and avoid the dark side of narcissism?

First, we can try to avoid narcissistic individuals altogether. There is a bias in many situations, especially when picking leaders, to like and judge narcissistic individuals as competent. Narcissists have the charisma, confidence, and likability that help them excel in interviews. The key, however, is to be aware of this bias. One suggestion is to take a very careful look at individuals' past workplace behavior before selecting them. In particular, look for instances of interpersonal problems or poor ethics that might betray issues of narcissism.

Second, if you work with narcissistic individuals, you need to be careful regarding the risks, particularly the counterproductive work behavior and ethical problems. One way to address this is with careful measurement and feedback of individuals, so that any issues can be picked up quickly. It is more challenging, however, if you work for someone who is narcissistic. Our advice in this case is to keep careful records of your interactions and be careful to avoid overt conflict as this may lead to retaliation by your narcissistic manager. Another solution is just to get out of the situation, although often that is not possible.

Third, the self-promoting, outgoing behavior and the desire to be the center of attention that is common among narcissists can certainly be beneficial in some situations, like performing in public, energizing a group of subordinates, or meeting and influencing new stakeholders. One suggestion is to use more narcissistic members of your organization in these specific roles where their narcissism may benefit their performance. Another suggestion directed to all individuals is to keep the ability to self-enhance as a "tool in your toolbox." Self-promotion is something that almost everyone needs to do in this culture. The trick is not to let this limited self-promotion turn into narcissism.

Finally, an increasing number of business school students, compared to non-business students, are showing a tendency towards narcissism.[19] This is troubling for organizations recruiting these individuals out of business school. This is a topic that business schools need to address, either in their selection process, or in their training. For example, training in ethics would be very important in a group with elevated narcissism.

Conclusion

Narcissism is a trait linked to grandiosity and entitlement that has a range of consequences in the workplace. Narcissism is a trade-off. It is primarily a destructive force, but has some benefits as well. We need to learn to control expressions of narcissism in the workplace (and in ourselves). There are some contexts where narcissism will give us a competitive advantage (like performing in public), but most if the time it will serve to harm those around us.

Endnotes

1. The Late John Edwards. *New York Daily News.* (2008). Accessed August 9, 2008, at http://articles.nydailynews.com/2008-08-09/news/17903677_1_honest-man-veep-job-john-edwards (viewed 9/1/2011)
2. Tiger Woods: I felt I deserved to enjoy all the temptations. I was wrong. *The Sunday Times* by James Bone. Accessed February 20, 2010, at http://www.timesonline.co.uk/tol/sport/golf/article7034369.ece (viewed 9/1/2011)
3. Deluga, R. J. (1997). Relationship among American presidential charismatic leadership, narcissism, and rated performance. *Leadership Quarterly, 8,* 49–65.
4. Young, S. M., & Pinsky, D. (2006). Narcissism and celebrity. *Journal of Research in Personality,* 40, 463–471.
5. Raskin, R. & Terry, H. (1988). A Principle-Components Analysis of the Narcissistic Personality Inventory and Further Evidence of Its Construct Validity. *Journal of Personality and Social Psychology,* 54, 890–902.
6. Morf, C. C., & Rhodewalt, F. (2001). Unraveling the paradoxes of narcissism: A dynamic self-regulatory processing model. *Psychological Inquiry, 12,* 177–196.
7. For a review, see Campbell, W. K., & Green, J. D. (2007). Narcissism and interpersonal self-regulation. In J. V. Wood, A. Tesser, & J. G. Holmes (Eds.). *Self and Relationships.* New York: Psychology Press, 73–94.
8. Miller, J. D., Campbell, W. K., & Pilkonis, P. A. (2007). Narcissistic Personality Disorder: Relations with distress and functional impairment. *Comprehensive Psychiatry, 170–177.*
9. American Psychiatric Association. (2000). *Diagnostic and Statistical Manual of Mental Disorders,* (4th ed., text revision). Washington, DC: American Psychiatric Association.
10. Miller, J. D., Hoffman, B. J., Gaughan, E. T., Gentile, B., Maples, J. & Campbell, W. K. (2011). Grandiose and vulnerable narcissism: A nomological network analysis. *Journal of Personality,* 79, 1013–1042.

11. Foster, J. D., Campbell, W. K., & Twenge, J. M. 2003. Individual differences in narcissism: Inflated self-views across the lifespan and around the world. *Journal of Research in Personality, 37,* 469–486.

12. For a review, see Twenge, J. M., Campbell, W. K. (2009). *The narcissism epidemic: Living in the age of entitlement.* New York: Free Press.

13. For a review, see Campbell, W. K. & Campbell, S. M. (2009). On the Self-regulatory dynamics created by the peculiar benefits and costs of narcissism: A Contextual Reinforcement Model and examination of leadership. *Self & Identity,* 8, 214–232.

14. Foster, J. D., Reidy, D. E., Misra, T. A., & Goff, J. S. (2011). Narcissism and stock market investing: Correlates and consequences of cocksure investing. *Personality and Individual Differences, 50,* 816–821.

15. Goncalo, J. A., Flynn, F. J., & Kim, S. H. (2010). Are Two Narcissists Better Than One? The Link Between Narcissism, Perceived Creativity, and Creative Performance. *Personality and Social Psychology Bulletin, 36,* 1484–1495.

16. Penney, L. M., & Spector, P. E. (2002). Narcissism and counterproductive work behavior: Do bigger egos mean bigger problems? *International Journal of Selection and Assessment, 10,* 126–134.

17. Judge, T. A., LePine, J. A., & Rich, B. L. (2006). Loving yourself abundantly: Relationship of the narcissistic personality to self and other perceptions of workplace deviance, leadership, and task and contextual performance. *Journal of Applied Psychology, 91,* 762–776.

18. Hogan, R., & Hogan, J. (2001). Assessing leadership: A view from the dark side. *International Journal of Selection and Assessment,* 9, 40–51.

19. Bergman, J. Z., Westerman, J. W., & Daly, J. P. (2010). Narcissism in management education. *Academy of Management Learning & Education,* 9, 119–131.

The Importance of Affect at Work

Donald E. Gibson
Fairfield University

Sigal G. Barsade
University of Pennsylvania

Introduction

Workplaces are emotional; at work, people feel fear at impending deadlines, frustration with inadequate resources, joy in a competitive win, annoyance at a preening co-worker, or compassion for a friend laid off. In today's workplace, taking account of employee emotions is now considered essential for managers. This was not always the case. For decades, until the early 1990s, business managers didn't emphasize employee emotions, and organizational behavior research tended to discount emotions as an area for serious research. Managerial decision-making, for example, was long regarded as a primarily cognitive, rational process in which the decision maker's feelings could only detract from an effective assessment of organizational choices. This perspective was based on a conceptual division between "reason" and "emotion", suggesting that at work, people should be focused on rational aspects such as task performance, operating efficiencies, and objective data analysis rather than emotional aspects such as the happiness, anger, love, and sadness they may feel in response to what happens to them at work.

Recent research in management and psychology, however, is showing just how wrong this view is. Emotions are a critical factor in successful workplace performance.[1] Employees cannot leave their emotions at home, and more importantly, managers shouldn't want them to. Strong feelings are present at any time work issues are confronted that matter to us and our organizational performance. The current research provides substantial evidence of how emotions influence managerial actions in a range of areas including decision making, task performance, leadership, teamwork, and negotiation. After defining what is mean by "affect," next examine each of these areas below.

Defining "Affect"

Given the complexity of human emotions, it's important, first, to define what the term "affect" means. "Affect" is an umbrella term that includes three general components: dispositional or trait affect, emotions, and moods. Dispositional affect refers to personality traits representing a relatively stable, long-term, underlying tendency to experience negative and positive moods and emotions over time and across situations.[2] Emotions are affective states that include physiological reactions and action sequences triggered by stimuli having meaning for individuals.[3] Emotions can be described in terms of their intensity—high or low—and their valence—pleasant or unpleasant—and are of very short duration. Moods are more diffuse, less intense, last longer than emotions, and generally have no clear cause. In contrast to mood, emotions are sometimes labeled "discrete" because they are focused on a specific target or cause, such as the desire to approach objects in anger or to avoid them in fear.

One way of conceptualizing the vast range of emotions one can feel and the different words used to describe these feelings is to think of them as a circle, or "circumplex" of affective descriptors varying in terms of *energy* and *pleasantness* (see Figure 1). This depiction shows, for example, that people can vary in terms of being high positive affect (PA), meaning they tend to be positive, enthusiastic and energetic in many work situations, versus low PA, meaning they tend to be sad, depressed, or lethargic. People also vary to the degree they are high negative affect (NA), tending to be nervous, tense, and stressed, versus low NA, being serene, relaxed and contented.

As a manager, the ability to "read" and comprehend employees' emotional responses and tendencies is clearly important. A manager needs to understand when the team he or she is leading is feeling stressed and needs to have issues addressed, or how to handle particular team members they know will get defensive and angry when provided with negative feedback. Managers also need to understand their own emotional responses and how they are likely to respond to work situations that can be anxiety-provoking, annoying, or energizing. These abilities are grouped under the concept of "emotional intelligence".[4]

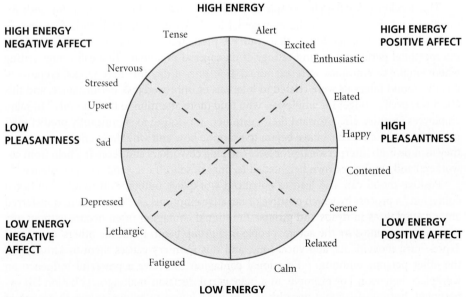

Figure 1 The Circumplex Model of Affect

Source: Based on Barsade & Gibson, 2007, adapted from Feldman Barrett, L & Russell, J.A. (1998). Independence and bipolarity in the structure of current affect. Journal of Personality and Social Psychology, 74(4), 967-984 and Larsen, R.J & Diener, E. (1992). Promises and problems with the circumplex model of emotion. In M. S. Clark (Ed.), *Emotion. Review of personality and social psychology, No. 13.* (pp. 25–59). Thousand Oaks, CA: Sage Publications, Inc.

Research on Affect

Drawing on these conceptualizations of affect and new research methods, researchers are providing a clearer picture of how affect influences important work processes—showing how the emotional sides of people that were previously thought of as "touchy–feely" are actually critical to bottom-line results. This research suggests that workers' emotions, when adequately understood and managed, actually assist, rather than detract from, their ability to get the job done.

Affect and Performance

The intuitive notion that more satisfied workers would make more productive workers was the focus of substantial research throughout the twentieth century, but the results, surprisingly, were not very compelling. Simply finding out that people were "satisfied" (or not) with their jobs was not very highly related to how productive they were.[5] However, using more specific measures of emotions, such as those outlined above, led to more compelling findings: specifically, happy (not just "satisfied") workers tend to be more productive workers in a wide variety of settings. For example, an individual's tendency to experience positive emotions and moods is associated with more positive supervisory evaluations, higher income, increased sales performance, lower turnover and absenteeism, enhanced negotiating ability, and behavior that goes "above and beyond the call of duty" for the organization.[6]

This tendency for happier people to perform better on the job is true for both individual contributors and at the managerial level. An experimental study focusing on managerial performance found that trait PA predicted decision-making effectiveness, interpersonal performance, and ratings of managerial potential.[7] In a call center setting where employee emotions were examined 4–5 times a day for three weeks, employees' positive mood intervals were related to intervals of improved task performance, and this effect was even stronger for employees who paid more attention to their moods.[8] In sales, employees' positive affect toward their customers was found to significantly predict sales performance.[9] Researchers have begun to examine how and why these effects occur, and they include both interpersonal processes (helping coworkers and receiving help from coworkers) and employees' own heightened feelings of self-efficacy and task persistence.[10]

Positive mood can also lead to enhanced workplace outcomes through "emotional contagion," a process by which positive or negative emotions are "caught" and transferred among employees in dyads and groups. Emotional contagion often occurs without any conscious awareness by the actors; people in a group begin to mimic others' emotional expressions, movements, and vocal tone, and this mimicry causes them to actually *feel* the other person's emotion.[11] Emotional contagion can have a powerful influence on workplace behavior. For example, in a managerial decision-making/negotiation lab experiment, both positive and negative moods were found to be contagious in groups of people, with positive mood contagion leading to greater cooperation, less conflict, and higher perceptions of performance than in groups with negative mood contagion.[12] Emotional contagion is especially important in sales settings; one study of coffee shop interactions found that the strength of employees' smiles predicted that of customers' smiles during the purchase encounter, and also predicted customers' satisfaction with the encounter.[13]

Affect in Decision Making and Creativity

Two critical managerial tasks are making decisions among alternatives and generating new ideas and strategies through creative processes. In both of these areas, studies are showing the positive impact of positive traits and moods. In decision making, it was initially theorized that individuals in a positive mood were inclined toward more superficial decision making, while a negative mood should promote more careful, effortful decision processes. However, while under some circumstances negative mood has been shown to lead to better decision making, the preponderance of evidence shows that positive moods lead individuals to better, more flexible and efficient decision making, including decision making requiring more careful, systematic, and thorough processing.[14] One study in a hospital setting, for example, found that doctors who were induced with a positive mood (simply by giving them a gift of candy) came to correct diagnoses of a simulated case more quickly than those with no positive mood induction, and were less likely to incorrectly anchor on an erroneous hypothesis.[15] Just being aware of one's emotions can also lead to better decision making. In a stock investment simulation examining investors who rated their feelings and made investment decisions for 20 business days, those investors who were better able to identify their feelings had more intense feelings, and had better stock performance.[16]

Similarly, in studies examining the influence of affect on creativity, findings generally support an effect for positive traits and moods leading to enhanced creativity. In the laboratory, extensive research has linked individuals in positive moods with more flexible thinking, enhanced problem-solving ability, and more divergent responses than individuals in negative moods.[17] In the workplace, one longitudinal study found that in creative daily work during a project, there was a strong linear relationship between greater positive mood and creativity, such that positive moods were an antecedent to creative thought, but not the opposite.[18]

Why do positive states possibly lead to enhanced creativity? One theory is that positive affect leads to a state in which more cognitive material—that is, more variety in the kinds of ideas that come to mind—is available for processing. Then, once those thoughts are available, positive affect leads to a more complex, flexible way of thinking, making it more likely that the person will make use of the ideas that are available and will see a way to bring these diverse thoughts together in creating a new idea.[19]

Affect in Leadership and Teams

The process of leading teams in organizations is fraught with emotions—from the emotions leaders feel and express to their teams to the feelings team members have toward their leader and each other. Leaders must be effective at regulating their own emotional responses—for example, by being upbeat even when the team is stressed and facing challenging circumstances—and must also be adept at managing the emotions of others—for example, by empathizing with a team member who is struggling with change. To consider this aspect of emotion regulation, think of a leader you consider very effective. This person might hold a formal leadership position in politics or business, such as a president or CEO, or be a leader of a team you are in. What makes him or her effective? Quite likely it is his or her ability to articulate goals for you and the team, connect with you emotionally, give you an ideal to follow that you can be passionate about, and appeal to your shared values. This leader is also likely adept at "reading" the emotions of team members to see whether they are motivated to achieve the team's goals and committed to his or her vision. Effective leaders need to be effective managers of emotions.

Given the findings discussed so far on the influence of positive affect on work outcomes, one would expect, and indeed find, that the trait contributes to leader effectiveness. One study found in a simulated managerial setting that high positive affect MBA students were rated by their peers and outside observers as being better leaders.[20] In a lab study, leaders in positive versus negative moods led groups who performed better in their task, expended less unnecessary effort, and exhibited more coordination in completing the task.[21] In a retail setting, groups with branch managers who experienced more positive affect at work had both more positive group mood and higher quality customer service ratings than groups led by branch managers who felt less positive moods.[22]

Leaders do not always express positive emotions, however; their expressions of negative emotions can have an impact as well. You may have been part of an athletic team and felt the heat of a coach's anger; that emotion served to motivate you and your teammates to perform at a higher level. This use of anger is seen in the workplace as well.[23] Displays of negative emotions can focus followers' attention on situations that need attention, such as discrimination or fairness[24], and can encourage a group to exert more effort to complete a task.[25] However, negative emotions come with risk, as people can react badly to others' anger, fear, and the like. It's likely that the effectiveness of leaders' emotions depends on the traits, expectations, and attitudes of the followers they lead. One study found that group members with higher levels of agreeableness (members who pay attention to and accommodate the needs of others) performed better when their leader expressed happiness, whereas teams composed of participants with lower levels of agreeableness performed better when their leader expressed anger.[26]

The implication of these studies is that leaders tend to have a strong influence on the emotions felt and expressed by the group. Leaders, sometimes consciously and sometimes unconsciously, set the emotional "tone" for the group through their emotional expressions, which can be "caught" by followers through emotional contagion. Effective leaders manage group emotions by understanding how their group is likely to respond to challenging situations and obstacles and providing emotional support—or the sanction of negative emotional energy—to help the group cope effectively with the situation.[27]

What Does this Mean for Managers in Organizations?

Should leaders and managers always express positive, upbeat emotions? Is this what the research on workplace affect is telling you? The story is more complicated than that, of course. What the research indicates is that in terms of motivating performance, managers are well-advised to emphasize the positive aspects of the situation, drawing on their own positive emotions to generate positive emotions in others. However, this tendency to be optimistic and outgoing needs to be combined with an ability to recognize and "read" other peoples' emotions. In other words, the best managers are not those who are just happy all the time. Rather, the best managers are those who pay attention to what their group of employees is feeling and respond appropriately to their employees' emotional needs. That may mean being encouraging and upbeat; it may, at times, mean displaying anger to show how important an issue—like discriminatory behavior or unfair use of resources—really is.

The findings on affect, decision making, and creativity suggest that if managers would like to foster creativity in work teams they should encourage teams to work on their emotional sides as well as their technical sides. As some innovative corporate teams are finding, they should consider engaging in fun activities before they are called on to address an important problem creatively. Teams who have fun together, who laugh more than they bicker, are more likely to adapt to changing situations and devise clever answers to critical organizational dilemmas.

If managers want to address the bottom line, they should follow this rule: Rather than trying to shut down employee emotions under the assumption that they will only get in the way of productivity, the enlightened manager needs to understand his or her own emotions and the emotions of other people. This is the idea of the emotionally intelligent manager. This manager will have a competitive advantage in the workplace as he or she will understand that emotions are information and will be able to use all the cognitive and emotional signals the environment offers to contribute to effective decision making and management. In addition, the message for managers from cutting-edge research is mostly that going to work feeling upbeat and positive can have a demonstrable impact on the people around you, the groups you work with, and ultimately, your effectiveness. Achieving this happiness at work, of course, may not be easy. It may mean looking at the people around you in new ways so that you can see the positive, rather than the negative, aspects in others. It may mean choosing more carefully when you wish to express your irritation. It may mean saving your anger until it really counts. Yes, workplaces are emotional because they consist of people who have emotions. What effective managers do is understand this fact and use that knowledge to enhance their own and the group's productivity.

Endnotes

1. Barsade, S. G., & Gibson, D. E. (2007). Why does affect matter in organizations? *Academy of Management Perspectives, 21(1)*, 36–59.
2. Watson, D., & Clark, L. A. (1984). Negative affectivity: The disposition to experience aversive emotional states. *Psychological Bulletin, 96*, 465–490.
3. Frijda, N. H. (1986). *The emotions*. Cambridge, New York: Cambridge University Press.
4. Salovey, P., & Mayer, J. (1990). Emotional intelligence. *Imagination, Cognition and Personality, 9*, 185–211.
5. Brief, A. P., & Weiss, H. M. (2002). Organizational behavior: Affect in the workplace. *Annual Review of Psychology, 53*, 279–307.
6. Kaplan, S., Bradley, J. C., Luchman, J. N., & Haynes, D. (2009). On the role of positive and negative affectivity in job performance: A meta-analytic investigation. *Journal of Applied Psychology, 94(1)*, 162–176. Lyubomirsky, S., King, L., & Diener, E. (2005). The benefits of frequent positive affect. Does happiness lead to success? *Psychological Bulletin, 131*, 803–855. Staw, B. M., Sutton, R. I., & Pelled, L. H. (1994). Employee positive emotion and favorable outcomes at the workplace. *Organization Science, 5(1)*, 51–71. Thoresen, C. J., Kaplan, S. A., & Barsky, A. P. (2003). The affective underpinnings of job perceptions and attitudes: A meta-analytic review and integration. *Psychological Bulletin, 129(6)*, 914–945.
7. Staw, B. M., & Barsade, S. G. (1993). Affect and managerial performance: A test of the sadder-but-wiser vs. happier-and-smarter hypothesis. *Administrative Science Quarterly, 38(2)*, 304–331.
8. Miner, A. G., & Glomb, T. M. (2010). State mood, task performance, and behavior at work: A within-persons approach. *Organizational Behavior and Human Decision Processes, 112(1)*, 43–57.

9. Sharma, A., & Levy, M. (2003). Salespeople's affect toward customers: Why should it be important for retailers? *Journal of Business Research, 56(7)*, 523–528.

10. Tsai, W., Chen, C., & Liu, H. (2007). Test of a model linking employee positive moods and task performance. *Journal of Applied Psychology, 92(6)*, 1570–1583.

11. Hatfield, E., Cacioppo, J. T., & Rapson, R. L. (1994). *Emotional Contagion*. New York, NY: Cambridge University Press.

12. Barsade, S. G. (2002). The ripple effect: Emotional contagion and its influence on group behavior. *Administrative Science Quarterly, 47(4)*, 644–675.

13. Barger, P., & Grandey, A. (2006). Service with a smile and encounter satisfaction: Emotional contagion and appraisal mechanisms. *Academy of Management Journal, 49(6)*, 1229–1238.

14. Isen, A. M. (2008). Some ways in which positive affect influences decision making and problem solving. In M. Lewis, J. M. Haviland-Jones & Barrett, L. F. (Eds.), *Handbook of Emotions* (3rd ed.), 548–573. New York, NY: Guilford Press. Lyubomirsky, S., King, L., & Diener, E. (2005). The benefits of frequent positive affect. Does happiness lead to success? *Psychological Bulletin, 131*, 803–855. Staw, B. M., & Barsade, S. G. (1993). Affect and managerial performance: A test of the sadder-but-wiser vs. happier-and-smarter hypothesis. *Administrative Science Quarterly, 38(2)*, 304–331.

15. Estrada, C. A., Isen, A. M., & Young, M. J. (1997). Positive affect facilitates integration of information and decreases anchoring in reasoning among physicians. *Organizational Behavior and Human Decision Processes, 72(1)*, 117–135.

16. Seo, M., & Barrett, L. F. (2007). Being emotional during decision making—good or bad? An empirical investigation. *Academy of Management Journal, 50*, 923–940.

17. Isen, A. M. (2008). Some ways in which positive affect influences decision making and problem solving. In M. Lewis, J. M. Haviland-Jones & Barrett, L. F. (Eds.), *Handbook of Emotions* (3rd ed.), 548–573. New York, NY: Guilford Press.

18. Amabile, T. M., Barsade, S. G., Mueller, J. S., & Staw, B. M. (2005). Affect and creativity at work. *Administrative Science Quarterly, 50*, 367–403.

19. Fredrickson, B. L. (2001). The role of positive emotions in positive psychology: The *broaden-and-build* theory of positive emotions. *American Psychologist, 56(3)*, 218–226.

20. Staw, B. M., & Barsade, S. G. (1993). Affect and managerial performance: A test of the sadder-but-wiser vs. happier-and-smarter hypothesis. *Administrative Science Quarterly, 38(2)*, 304–331.

21. Sy, T., Côté, S., & Saavedra, R. (2005). The contagious leader: Impact of the leader's mood on the mood of group members, group affective tone, and group processes. *Journal of Applied Psychology, 90(2)*, 295–305.

22. George, J. M. (1995). Leader positive mood and group performance: The case of customer service. *Journal of Applied Social Psychology, 25(9)*, 778–794.

23. Gibson, D. E., Schweitzer, M., Callister, R. R., & Gray, B. (2009). The influence of anger expressions on outcomes in organizations. *Negotiation and Conflict Management Research, 2*, 236–262.

24. George, J. M. (2000). Emotions and leadership: The role of emotional intelligence. Human *Relations, 53(8)*, 1027–1055.

25. Sy, T., Côté, S., & Saavedra, R. (2005). The contagious leader: Impact of the leader's mood on the mood of group members, group affective tone, and group processes. *Journal of Applied Psychology, 90(2)*, 295–305.

26. Van Kleef, G. A., Homan, A. C., Beersma, B., & van Knippenberg, D. (2010). On angry leaders and agreeable followers: How leaders' emotions and followers' personalities shape motivation and team performance. *Psychological Science, 21(12)*, 1827–1834.

27. Johnson, S. K. (2008). I second that emotion: Effects of emotional contagion and affect at work on leader and follower outcomes. *The Leadership Quarterly, 19(1)*, 1–19.

The Challenge of Managing Emotions in the Workplace

Neal M. Ashkanasy

University of Queensland

Catherine S. Daus

Southern Illinois University, Edwardsville

Raul Alvarez is an e-commerce sales clerk for a large, internet-based sun-protection products organization. He is good at his job and always remains pleasant, no matter how difficult clients become. Today, however, despite wishing his clients a "good day," Raul is having anything but. It began even before he logged on remotely for work. One of his children had awakened ill, and Raul needed to take care of her. Then, Raul had internet connection problems. Once he logged on, he received an email from his boss criticizing Raul's lack of timeliness in completing his reports. Later, Raul had to deal with an irate customer of one of his colleagues (who was on vacation), upset because the special order she had paid extra for and was promised would arrive in time for her vacation did not, in fact, arrive in time. All day, Raul had trouble balancing caring for his child and keeping up with his work. To top it off, Raul's supervisor called to criticize Raul's performance, even though Raul had managed to please every customer. At the end of the interminable day, Raul had 'had it,' and was seriously considering quitting. He usually stayed logged on after his official work time to finalize paperwork, but today he was in too much of a bad mood, so he logged off immediately at 5:00. Raul intentionally did not notate his co-worker's accounts so that his co-worker would have to spend extra time straightening them out. Raul felt it was his 'just desserts' for leaving him in a lurch with the irate customer.

The scenario above unfortunately illustrates an all-too-common day at work for many of us, with its typical frustrations and daily hassles. Most people can recall a similarly hassled day and the effect that it had on them. Indeed, the story is riddled with emotional content. How did Raul manage to stay pleasant with clients under the circumstances? Why was his supervisor so insensitive? Why did such minor occurrences lead Raul to behave so erratically by the end of the day? Will Raul's bad mood affect his performance for the rest of the week? We address these questions in this chapter, and attempt to provide answers, based on recent research into emotion and its effect in the workplace.

Emotions in the workplace have gained prominence from both an academic standpoint and a practical, applied standpoint. In the last decade, the number of both popular and academic conferences, workshops, books and articles (including special issues of academic journals) on emotions is astounding and has catapulted emotions into the mainstream of organizational behavior. Emotional intelligence, popularly introduced in 1995 by Daniel Goleman's *Emotional intelligence: Why it can matter more than IQ,* particularly continues to be a 'hot topic' in organizations today.[1] At around the same time that popular interest in emotions in organizations was stimulated, academics were also becoming interested in the wider topic of emotions in the workplace.[2] In 2002, peering into our 'emotions in the workplace magic ball,' we predicted that "the issue of emotions in the workplace is shaping up as one of the principal areas of development in management thought and practice in the 2000s."[3] We aim to show why we were dead on with our prediction.

Core Concepts

In several recent writings, we developed a comprehensive organizing framework for emotion research in organizations (Figure 1).[4] The framework is built around five levels of emotion research, beginning with the most micro, individual-level perspective, and culminating in the most macro, organization-wide level. In this reading, we focus on the three lowest levels. At Level 1, the *within-person level*, we refer to the day-to-day and moment-to-moment fluctuations in emotion the employees experience at work, where *affective events* are the key drivers of behavior. At Level 2, which focuses on individual

Figure 1 The 5-Level Model of Emotion in Organizations.
Source: Adapted from Ashkanasy and Humphrey, 2011a.

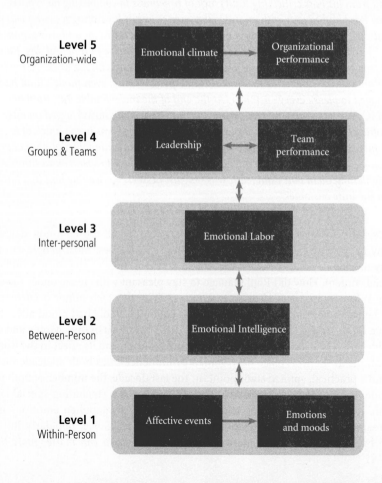

Level 5 — Organization-wide: Emotional climate → Organizational performance

Level 4 — Groups & Teams: Leadership ↔ Team performance

Level 3 — Inter-personal: Emotional Labor

Level 2 — Between-Person: Emotional Intelligence

Level 1 — Within-Person: Affective events → Emotions and moods differences *between-persons*, we deal with the idea of *emotional intelligence*. Finally, at Level 3, where *interpersonal* processes are the focus of attention, we focus on the notion of *emotional labor*, which typifies the dynamic nature of emotion processes that occurs back-and-forth between persons.

Affective Events Theory

Affective Events Theory (AET) is an approach to understanding how our emotions impact our worklife.[5] AET, at its core, integrates a strong emphasis on emotion states and traits as influencing employee attitudes and behaviors/outcomes. Further, according to this theory, it is often the small, everyday hassles or events like Raul experienced that influence the way we process job-relevant information, and think and feel about our jobs, employers, and colleagues. In the last decade and a half since AET was first published, research has solidified support for AET's main tenets.[6]

In particular, research has underscored the *cumulative* nature of hassles; it seems that people at work are capable of dealing with infrequent occurrences, even when these are relatively intense, particularly if they are buffered by uplifting events such as sincere compliments, positive job feedback, or support by friends, family, and colleagues.[7] Thus, the situation becomes much worse if there is an unrelenting series of negative events. Early studies examining AET and the proposed linkages in AET, notably those showing that daily mood significantly impacts overall job satisfaction,[8] have continued AET and its core principles.[9]

Emotional Intelligence

Do you consider yourself someone who is good at 'reading people'? If so, you are not in the minority; many people overestimate their own social, emotional, or intellectual skills.[10] On the other hand, not as many people are as good at this skill as they think they are. So we may ask, "But how could this be an *objective* notion? Isn't it inherently a *subjective* concept?" You might be surprised to know that it isn't. The construct called emotional intelligence includes emotion-related skills, and research has definitively shown that some people are better at it than others. Let us explain.

After two decades of peer-reviewed academic publications, esteemed psychologists and researchers John Mayer, Peter Salovey, and David Caruso[11] have established and legitimized emotional intelligence concept and theory, and paved the way for researchers in any domain, including organizational behavior, to test it accurately.[12] The Mayer and Salovey model of emotional intelligence is today recognized as the "gold standard"[13] and includes four "branches: (1) ability to perceive emotions, (2) ability to assimilate emotions in thought (thinking and feeling), (3) ability to understand emotions and their effects, and (4) ability to manage emotions in self and others.

Researchers used a sophisticated approach called a "meta-analysis," where the results of many studies are aggregated to provide a broad consensual picture, and reported that emotional intelligence can indeed predict job performance above and beyond cognitive ability and personality for many types of jobs.[14] This result applies especially for jobs that are high in emotional requirements, especially when employees need to control their emotions in the service on their job.[15] Other research has shown that emotional intelligence is particularly important in predicting job performance for employees who do not score so high in classical cognitive intelligence.[16]

Emotional Labor

Have you ever come home from your job to find yourself simply emotionally exhausted? It may have been a particularly busy, demanding day, but likely, such days were rife with social interactions, like Raul's. If you can relate to this scenario, you will appreciate the concept of *emotional labor.*

Although emotions and managing emotions in the workplace have always been inherently at the core of management practice and development, research specifically on emotions in organizational settings is relatively recent, and has been advancing rapidly in the last two decades. The earliest such examination focused on emotional labor, which we include as our third and final theoretical exploration. The stage for emotional labor was set in 1983 when Arlie Hochschild published her seminal work *The Managed Heart.*[17] This book became a bestseller and established the idea of *emotional labor,* or the act of managing emotion at work. Drawing from a series of observations and interviews with flight attendants and bill collectors, Hochschild described the emotionally draining process of managing emotions in the service of a job or organization.[18]

Early research on emotional labor centered on customer service jobs, but research has also established it as a stress factor in many jobs.[19] In an early exploration of the organizational impact of emotional labor, it was[20] demonstrated that employees in service settings are expected, by both the company and their customers, to be positive and, when they really are, this positively affects the customers' perceptions through what is called emotional contagion (i.e., the *customer* "*catches*" the positive mood and thus rates service more positively).[21]

Extensive research has also clearly established that emotional labor can be particularly detrimental to the employee performing the labor, and can take its toll both psychologically and physically.[22] Employees may bottle up feelings of frustration, resentment, and anger, which are not appropriate (like Raul) to express. These feelings result, in part, from the constant requirement of employees to monitor their negative emotions, and especially to express positive ones.[23]

Why Do Emotions Matter in the Workplace?

Affective Events Theory

Ultimately, the emotional build-up from events can profoundly affect our behaviors and eventually our organization's effectiveness. AET thus carries an important message: *Emotions in organizational settings and the events that cause them are critical to be aware of, even if they appear to be relatively minor.* The sorts of hassles that generate negative emotions include interactions with supervisors, peers, subordinates, and customers. As you are no doubt aware, the hassles experienced by Raul Alvarez are not uncommon in today's high-performance workplaces. By the same token, uplifts in workplace settings can come from the same sources as the hassles and can buffer much of the stress from negative events and hassles. For managers, it is critical to be aware of the emotional climate, stimulated by workplace events, that their employees are required to behave in. Further, support from an empathic supervisor can go a long way towards countering the effects of workplace hassles.[24]

Emotional Intelligence

As the research we reviewed earlier suggests, the individual difference of emotional intelligence can have a large impact on individuals and organizational behavior functions. Maybe Raul usually exhibits high emotional intelligence skills and as a result is cooperative and works well with his cohort group, but, because of his awful experiences on this day, he chooses not to (or cannot) act so positively (as AET would predict).

This also has implications for Raul's boss. Leadership is one area where emotional intelligence and emotional labor has been shown to be important.[25] Emotional intelligence abilities not only predict who tends to emerge as leaders, but also who is *more effective* as a leader.[26] Thus, an emotionally intelligent leader should be able to recognize when employees are struggling to deal with their emotions, and then to intervene in an empathetic way that will help employees like Raul to carry out their job and not to become so distressed. Leaders do more than just manage, they can become "transformational" and inspire and arouse their followers emotionally. Followers, thus inspired, "become committed to the leader's vision and, ultimately, to the organization" (p. 81). [27] This is referred to as "leading with emotional labor" (p. 363).[28]

All of the evidence, then, would seem to imply that training in emotional intelligence abilities would be helpful for managers in organizations.[29] With reference to our opening vignette and the "branches" of emotional intelligence[30] things would have been much better had Raul's boss *perceived* that Raul was particularly upset by having to deal with his colleagues' mistake, and *understood* Raul's situation. Taking a *thinking and feeling* approach, Raul's boss could then have decided to *manage* the situation, possibly by a decision to withhold negative performance feedback for the moment, knowing that this may escalate Raul's negative feelings. He could then follow up by showing empathy and support, so that Raul would feel energized and proud to be a part of the boss's team.

Emotional Labor

Referring again to our opening vignette, we find that Raul Alvarez suffered negative effects arising from job role expectations conveyed from at least four different sources: the boss, customers, co-workers, and himself. Many occupations, especially service jobs, are characterized by strong norms and/or expectations regarding displays of emotion.[31] Explicit norms may be embedded in recruitment strategies or included in job descriptions, and can be seen everywhere. Have you ever seen a marquis for a fast-food restaurant posting such a message: "Now Hiring Smiling Faces"? Implicit norms can affect how employees are socialized into the organization's culture; how jobs are valued, with service jobs traditionally devalued; and even the means by which raises and/or rewards are distributed. Wait staff who stay on after their shift is over at a restaurant to have a few drinks with co-workers is a common example of implicit socialization processes. It is during such times that employees, particularly new ones, learn 'the dirt' on the restaurant's culture: which boss is to be avoided if possible; what gets one in trouble or rewarded, etc. Further, some organizations blatantly attempt to use reward systems to encourage emotional norms they wish employees to display. For example *Kmart* gives *K Dollars* to employees "caught" being nice to customers or to "secret shoppers," and *Best Buy* gives employees smiley-face stickers to put on their nametags to represent particularly good customer service.

As we illustrated in our earlier review of the emotional labor research, these processes can be problematic both for the organization as well as for the employees. From the organization's perspective, we know that customers' perceptions of service and the employees' attitudes are crucial: Positive attitudes expressed by employees impact customers favorably, and negative attitudes can similarly engender unfavorable impressions, and these can directly impact the 'bottom line' of an organization. When employees are seen by customers to be rude, or they behave inappropriately towards customers, an organization may lose in many ways. Not only may a direct sale be lost, but future sales from both the offended customer as well as everyone she tells about her horrid experience could also be lost; you might think of these as "contagion losses," much as "contagion gains" has been described as positive possible outcomes from employees expressing positive emotions effectively.[32] In sum, it has become clear that successful management of emotional labor by employees plays a critical role in the process of customer retention, recovery, and even "delight".[33]

No less important, however, are the potential negative influences on the individual employees who labor emotionally. Recall your own feelings on days you felt worn out from work. If unchecked, or not given a healthy expressive outlet, such processes can lead to a syndrome of emotional exhaustion and burnout. Emotional labor requirements can lead to emotional exhaustion and even health issues.[34]

Ideas in Action

Based on the foregoing discussion, we identify five recommendations for creating a healthy and positive emotional climate in organizations.[35]

The first of these is to *build an emotion focus into the organization's culture from the outset.* For too long, managers have tended to dismiss the emotional side of work life. For these managers, the workplace is no place for employee emotions, and employees are expected to "leave their emotional selves at home." Based on what we know today, nothing could be further from the truth. Employees are first and foremost members of species *homo sapiens*, and therefore to ignore the emotional side of behavior makes no sense.[36] Indeed, research has shown that emotions are an essential component of human decision making.[37]

The second recommendation is for *managers to assess and then to understand the emotional impact of jobs on employees.* As we discussed with respect to emotional labor, some jobs hold the potential to result in deep emotional effects; not only for employees, but on customers and clients. Employees who must engage in emotional labor can suffer considerably, and these effects can results in lifelong health issues.[38]

Our third recommendation is to *hire employees who fit in to the emotionally healthy organization, and fire those that don't.* Organizations can become toxic for employees, especially when employees and their managers have no understanding of how to handle the deleterious effects of emotion in workplace settings.[39] Employees in this category generate effective events that then can flow through the whole organization. For example, toxic leaders result in negative team member behaviors that ultimately translate throughout the organization, often resulting in a negative evaluation of the leader's performance.[40]

Fourth, we recommend that organizational leaders *strive to create and to maintain a positive and friendly emotional climate through modeling and provision of appropriate rewards and compensation systems.* Emotions at every level of organizing contribute to a healthy emotional climate.[41] In particular, and based on AET, positive affective events serve cumulatively to engender a positive attitude in organizations.[42]

Finally, we recommend that *organizational managers provide resources to train employees and their supervisors in emotional intelligence skills and healthy emotional expression.* One of the basic tenets of emotional intelligence is that it is amenable to improvement though training.[43] Moreover, research has shown that training employees in emotional intelligence has direct benefits in terms of health and well-being.[44]

Conclusions

In this chapter, we have argued that managing emotions in the workplace is both an imperative and a challenge for managers. Gone are the days when organizational managers can choose to dismiss emotions as "something we don't do around here." Recognizing and dealing with emotions in the workplace appropriately is now seen to be a central tenet of effective management. We discussed in detail the three most fundamental levels: (1) the day-to-day and moment-to-moment fluctuations experienced by employees as a result of "affective events"; (2) individual differences in employees' and managers' emotional intelligence; and (3) the need to manage emotion expression and the effects this has on employee health and well-being.

Arising from this, we made five recommendations for engendering a healthy and positive workplace environment. They are (1) to build an emotion focus into the organization's culture; (2) to understand the emotional impact of jobs on employees; (3) to hire and fire on the basis of fit with the emotionally healthy organization; (4) to design reward and compensation systems that encourage a positive and friendly emotional climate; and (5) to train employees and their supervisors in emotional intelligence skills and healthy emotional expression. We conclude that managers who adopt these five recommendations are going to be best equipped to meet the challenges of today's dynamic and exciting workplace environments.

Endnotes

1. Goleman, D. (1995). *Emotional Intelligence: Why it can matter more than IQ.* NY: Bantam Books.
2. Ashkanasy, N. M., & Daus, C. S. (2005). Rumors of the death of emotional intelligence in organizational behavior are vastly exaggerated. *Journal of Organizational Behavior, 26,* 441–452.
3. Ashkanasy, N. M., & Daus, C. S. (2002). Emotion in the workplace: The new challenge for managers. *Academy of Management Executive, 16(1),* 76–86.
4. Ashkanasy, N. M. (2003a). Emotions in organizations: A multilevel perspective. In F. Dansereau and F. J. Yammarino (Eds.). *Research in multi-level issues* (2), Oxford, UK: Elsevier/JAI Press, 9–54. Ashkanasy, N. M. (2003b). Emotions at multiple levels: An integration. In F. Dansereau and F. J. Yammarino (Eds.). *Research in multi-level issues* (2).

Oxford, UK: Elsevier/JAI Press, 71–81. Ashkanasy, N. M., & Humphrey, R. H. (2011a). Current research on emotion in organizations. *Emotion Review, 3*, 214–224.

5. Weiss, H. M. & Cropanzano, R. (1996). Affective Events Theory: A theoretical discussion of the structure, causes and consequences of affective experiences at work. In L. L. Cummings & B. M. Staw (Eds.). *Research in Organizational Behavior*. Westport, CT: JAI Press, 1–74.

6. Weiss, H. M., & and Beal, D. J. (2005). Reflections on affective events theory. In N. M. Ashkanasy, W. J. Zerbe, & C. E. J. Härtel (Eds.). *Research on emotion in organizations*. Oxford, UK: Elsevier/JAI Press, 1–22.

7. Grzywacz, J. G., & Marks, N. F. 2000. Reconceptualizing the work-family interface: An ecological perspective on the correlates of positive and negative spill over between work and family. *Journal of Occupational Health Psychology, 5*: 111–126.

8. Fisher, C. D., & Noble, C. S. (2004). A within-person examination of correlates of performance and emotions while working. *Human Performance, 17*, 145–168.

9. Fuller, J. A., Stanton, J. M., Fisher, G. G., Spitzmüller, C., Russell, S. S., & Smith, P. C. (2003). A lengthy look at the daily grind: Time series analysis of events, mood, stress, and satisfaction. *Journal of Applied Psychology, 88*, 1019–1033. Ilies, R., & Judge, T. A. (2002). Understanding the dynamic relationship between personality, mood, and job satisfaction: A field experience sampling study. *Organizational Behavior and Human Decision Processes, 89*, 1119–1139. Judge, T. A., & Ilies, R. (2004). Affect and job satisfaction: A study of their relationship at work and at home. *Journal of Applied Psychology, 89*, 661–673. Pirola-Merlo, A., Härtel, C., Mann, L., & Hirst, G. (2002). How leaders influence the impact of affective events on team climate and performance in R&D teams. *Leadership Quarterly, 13*, 561–581. Wegge, J., van Dick, R., Fisher, G. K., West, M. A., & Dawson, J. F. (2006). A test of basic assumptions of affective events theory (AET) in call centre work. *British Journal of Management, 17*, 237–254.

10. Dunning, D., Johnson, K., Ehrlinger, J. & Kruger, J. (2003). Why people fail to recognize their own incompetence. *Current Directions in Psychological Science, 12(3)*, 83–87. Kruger, J & Dunning, D. (1999). Unskilled and unaware of it: How difficulties in recognizing one's own incompetence lead to inflated self-assessments. *Journal of Personality and Social Psychology, 77(6)*, 1121–1134.

11. Mayer, J., & Salovey, P. (1997). What is emotional intelligence? In P. Salovey & D. Sluyter (Eds.). *Emotional development and emotional intelligence: Implications for Educators*. New York, NY: Basic Books, 3–31.Mayer, J. D., Salovey, P., & Caruso, D. R. (2002). *Mayer-Salovey-Caruso Emotional Intelligence Test (MSCEIT) users manual*. Toronto, Canada: MHS Publishers.Mayer, J., Salovey, P., & Caruso, D. R. (2004). Emotional intelligence: Theory, findings, and implications. *Psychological Inquiry, 15*, 197–215. Mayer, J., Salovey, P., & Caruso, D. R. (2008). Emotional intelligence: New ability or eclectic traits? *American Psychologist, 63*, 503–517.Mayer, J. D., Salovey, P., Caruso, D. R., & Sitarenios, G. (2001). Emotional intelligence as a standard intelligence. *Emotion, 1*, 232–242. Mayer, J. D., Salovey, P., Caruso, D. R., & Sitarenios, G. (2003). Measuring emotional intelligence with the MSCEIT V2.0. *Emotion, 3*, 97–105.

12. Mayer, J., & Salovey, P. (1997). What is emotional intelligence? In P. Salovey & D. Sluyter (Eds.). *Emotional development and emotional intelligence: Implications for Educators*. New York, NY: Basic Books, 3–31. Mayer, J. D., Salovey, P., & Caruso, D. R. (2002). *Mayer-Salovey-Caruso Emotional Intelligence Test (MSCEIT) users manual*. Toronto, Canada: MHS Publishers.Mayer, J., Salovey, P., & Caruso, D. R. (2004). Emotional intelligence: Theory, findings, and implications. *Psychological Inquiry, 15*, 197–215. Mayer, J., Salovey, P., & Caruso, D. R. (2008). Emotional intelligence: New ability or eclectic traits? *American Psychologist, 63*, 503–517. Mayer, J. D., Salovey, P., Caruso, D. R., & Sitarenios, G. (2001). Emotional

intelligence as a standard intelligence. *Emotion, 1,* 232–242. Mayer, J. D., Salovey, P., Caruso, D. R., & Sitarenios, G. (2003). Measuring emotional intelligence with the MSCEIT V2.0. *Emotion, 3,* 97–105. Salovey, P., & Mayer, J. D. (1990). Emotional intelligence. *Imagination, Cognition and Personality,* 9, 185–211.

13. Jordan, P. J., Dasborough, M. T., Daus, C. S., & Ashkanasy, N. M. (2010). A call to context. *Industrial and Organizational Psychology: Perspectives on Science and Practice, 3,* 145–148.

14. Joseph, D. L., & Newman, D. A. (2010). Emotional intelligence: An integrative meta-analysis and cascading model. *Journal of Applied Psychology, 95,* 54–78. O'Boyle, E. H., Jr., Humphrey, R. H., Pollack, J. M., Hawver, T. H., & Story, P. A. (2010. The relation between emotional intelligence and job performance: A meta-analysis. *Journal of Organizational Behavior, 32,* 788-818.

15. Joseph, D. L., & Newman, D. A. (2010). Emotional intelligence: An integrative meta-analysis and cascading model. *Journal of Applied Psychology, 95,* 54–78.

16. Côté, S. & Miners, C. T. H. (2006). Emotional intelligence, Cognitive intelligence, and job performance. *Administrative Science Quarterly.*

17. Hochschild, A. R. (1983). *The managed heart: Commercialization of human feeling.* Berkeley, CA: University of California Press.

18. Hochschild, A. R. (1983). *The managed heart: Commercialization of human feeling.* Berkeley, CA: University of California Press.

19. Diefendorff, J. M., Richard, E. M., & Yang, J. X. (2008). Linking emotion regulation strategies to affective events and negative emotions at work. *Journal of Vocational Behavior, 73,* 498–508. Mann, S. (1997). Emotional labour in organizations, *Leadership & Organization Development Journal, 18,* 4–12.

20. Pugh, D. S. (2001). Service with a smile: Emotional contagion in the service encounter. *Academy of Management Journal, 44,* 1018–1027.

21. Hatfield, E., Cacioppo, J., & Rapson, R. L. (1992). Emotional contagion, in Clark, M.S. (Ed.), *Review of personality and social psychology: Emotion and social behavior.* Newbury Park, CA: Sage, 151–77.

22. Bono, J. E., & Vey, M. A. (2007). Personality and emotional performance: Extraversion, neuroticism, and self-monitoring. *Journal of Occupational Health Psychology, 12,* 177–192. Judge, T. A., Woolf, E. F., & Hurst, C. (2009). Is emotional labor more difficult for some than for others? A multilevel, experience sampling study. *Personnel Psychology, 62,* 57–88.

23. Grandey, A. A. (2000). Emotional regulation in the workplace: A new way to conceptualize emotional labor. *Journal of Occupational Health Psychology, 5,* 95–110.

24. Ashkanasy, N. M., Härtel, C. E. J., & Zerbe, W.J. (2002). What are the management tools that come of this? In N. M. Ashkanasy, W. Zerbe, & C. E. J. Härtel (Eds.). *Managing emotions in the workplace.* Armonk, NY: ME Sharpe, 285–296. Scott, B. A., Colquitt, J. A., Paddock, E. L., & Judge, T. A. (2010). A daily investigation of the role of manager empathy on employee well-being. *Organizational Behavior and Human Decision Processes, 113,* 127–140.

25. Ashkanasy, N. M., & Humphrey, R. H. (2011b). A multi-level view of leadership and emotions: Leading with emotional labor. In A. Bryman, D. Collinson, K. Grint, B. Jackson, & M. Uhl-Bien (Eds.). *Sage handbook of leadership.* London, UK: Sage, 363-377.

26. Côté, S., Lopes, P. N., Salovey, P. & Miners,C. T. H. (2010). Emotional intelligence and leadership emergence in small groups. *The Leadership Quarterly, 21(3), 496*–508. Walter, F., Cole, M. S., & Humphrey, R. H. (2011). Emotional intelligence: Sine qua non of leadership or folderol? *The Academy of Management Perspectives, 25,* 45–59. Kerr, R., Garvin, J., Heaton, N., & Boyle, E. (2006). Emotional intelligence and leadership effectiveness. *Leadership & Organization Development Journal, 27,* 265–279. Rosete, D., & Ciarrochi, J. (2005).

Emotional intelligence and its relationship to workplace performance outcomes of leadership effectiveness. *Leadership and Organization Development Journal*, 26, 388–399.

27. Ashkanasy, N. M., & Daus, C. S. (2002). Emotion in the workplace: The new challenge for managers. *Academy of Management Executive, 16(1)*, 76–86.

28. Ashkanasy, N. M., & Humphrey, R. H. (2011a). Current research on emotion in organizations. *Emotion Review*, 3, 214–224. Ashkanasy, N. M., & Humphrey, R. H. (2011b). A multi-level view of leadership and emotions: Leading with emotional labor. In A. Bryman, D. Collinson, K. Grint, B. Jackson, & M. Uhl-Bien (Eds.). *Sage handbook of leadership*. London, UK: Sage, 363-377.

29. Ashkanasy, N. M., & Humphrey, R. H. (2011a). Current research on emotion in organizations. *Emotion Review*, 3, 214–224. Ashkanasy, N. M., & Humphrey, R. H. (2011b). A multi-level view of leadership and emotions: Leading with emotional labor. In A. Bryman, D. Collinson, K. Grint, B. Jackson, & M. Uhl-Bien (Eds.). *Sage handbook of leadership*. London, UK: Sage, 363-377. Daus, C. S. & Cage, T. G. (2008). Learning to face emotional intelligence: Training and workplace applications. In Ashkanasy & Cooper (Eds.). *Research Companion to Emotion in Organizations*. Northampton, MA: Edward Elgar Publishing Limited, 245–262. Groves, K., McEnrue, M. P., & Shen, W. (2008). Developing and measuring the *emotional intelligence of leaders. Journal of Management Development*, 27, 225–250.

30. Mayer, J., & Salovey, P. (1997). What is emotional intelligence? In P. Salovey & D. Sluyter (Eds.). *Emotional development and emotional intelligence: Implications for Educators*. New York, NY: Basic Books, 3–31.

31. Diefendorff, J. M., & Greguras, G. J. (2009). Contextualizing emotional display rules: Examining the roles of targets and discrete emotions in shaping display rule perceptions. *Journal of Management*, 35, 880–898.

32. Rafaeli, A. & Sutton, R. I. (1987). The expression of emotion as part of the work role. *Academy of Management Review, 12,* 23–37.

33. Oliver, R. L., Rust, R. T., & Varki, S. (1997). Customer delight: Foundations, findings, and managerial insight. *Journal of Retailing, 73*, 311-336.

34. Diefendorff, J. M., & Greguras, G. J. (2009). Contextualizing emotional display rules: Examining the roles of targets and discrete emotions in shaping display rule perceptions. *Journal of Management*, 35, 880–898. Grandey, A. A. (2000). Emotional regulation in the workplace: A new way to conceptualize emotional labor. *Journal of Occupational Health Psychology, 5*, 95–110. Mann, S. (1997). Emotional labour in organizations, *Leadership & Organization Development Journal, 18*, 4–12.

35. Härtel, C. E. J., & Ashkanasy, N. M. (2010). Healthy Human Cultures as Positive Work Environments. In N. M. Ashkanasy, C. E. P. Wilderom, & M. F. Peterson (Eds.). *The Handbook of Culture and Climate, Second Edition*. Thousand Oaks, CA: Sage, 85-100.

36. Ashkanasy, N. M., & Humphrey, R. H. (2011b). A multi-level view of leadership and emotions: Leading with emotional labor. In A. Bryman, D. Collinson, K. Grint, B. Jackson, & M. Uhl-Bien (Eds.). *Sage handbook of leadership*. London, UK: Sage, 363-377.

37. Damasio, A. R. (1994). *Descartes' error: Emotion, reason, and the human brain*. New York: Putnam.

38. Grandey, A. A. (2000). Emotional regulation in the workplace: A new way to conceptualize emotional labor. *Journal of Occupational Health Psychology, 5*, 95–110.

39. Frost, P. J. (2003). *Toxic emotions at work: How compassionate mangers handle pain and conflict*. Boston, Massachusetts: Harvard Business School Publishing.

40. Dasborough, M. T., Ashkanasy, N. M., Tee, E. E. J., & Tse, H. H. M. (2009). What goes around comes around: How meso-level negative emotional contagion can ultimately determine organizational attitudes toward leaders. *The Leadership Quarterly, 20,* 571–585.

41. Ashkanasy, N. M. (2003a). Emotions in organizations: A multilevel perspective. In F. Dansereau and F. J. Yammarino (Eds.). *Research in multi-level issues* (2), Oxford, UK: Elsevier/JAI Press, 9–54. Ashkanasy, N. M. (2003b). Emotions at multiple levels: An integration. In F. Dansereau and F. J. Yammarino (Eds.). *Research in multi-level issues* (2). Oxford, UK: Elsevier/JAI Press, 71–81. Ashkanasy, N. M., & Humphrey, R. H. (2011a). Current research on emotion in organizations. *Emotion Review, 3,* 214–224.

42. Ashkanasy, N. M., & Ashton-James, C. E. (2007). Positive emotion in organizations: A multi-level framework. In C. L. Cooper & D. Nelson (Eds.). *Positive organizational behavior.* Chichester, UK: John Wiley and Sons, 57–73.

43. Mayer, J., & Salovey, P. (1997). What is emotional intelligence? In P. Salovey & D. Sluyter (Eds.). *Emotional development and emotional intelligence: Implications for Educators.* New York, NY: Basic Books, 3–31.

44. Slaski, M., & Cartwright, S. (2003). Emotional intelligence training and its implications for stress, health and performance. *Stress and Health, 19,* 233–23.

3 Learning

Topic Summary Learning Objectives

1. Recognize behavioral, cognitive, and social approaches to learning, and describe their differences and limitations.

2. Explain the experiential learning process and the four learning styles.

3. Describe the action learning process.

4. Identify multiple intelligences, expertise, learning orientation, and flexibility.

5. Describe the importance of cognitive complexity for learning.

6. Apply concepts of learning to organizations.

Key terms

action learning, p. 83	expertise, p. 85	modeling, p. 80
classical conditioning, p. 79	intelligence, p. 84	multiple intelligences, p. 84
cognitive complexity, p. 85	learning, p. 79	operant conditioning, p. 80
deliberate practice, p. 85	learning cycle, p. 81	performance goal orientation, p. 85
developmental opportunities, p. 89	learning flexibility, p. 85	reinforcement theory, p. 80
efficacy, p. 80	learning goal orientation, p. 85	social learning, p. 80
experiential learning, p. 81	learning styles, p. 82	

Introduction to Learning

When people think about learning, they often think about sitting in a classroom, studying for an exam, or memorizing terms for a course. But, learning takes place both in and out of the classroom. In fact, until recently, learning was defined as a specific change in behavior or thinking. Researchers now recognize that learning is a much more complex process than simply a change in behavior or cognition. People learn in many situations and throughout their lives. Organizations rely on learning to solve problems, innovate, and manage processes. Today, **learning** is defined as the act of gathering, generating, processing, and acting on knowledge.[1] This topic summary focuses primarily on individual learning. It reviews three approaches to learning, describes important processes of learning, and looks at relevant issues in learning—including multiple intelligences, expertise, learning orientation, flexibility, and complexity (see Table 3.1).

Approaches to Learning

To understand how learning operates in contemporary organizations, it is important to know the variety of ways that people learn. This topic summary begins with a review of three well-known approaches to learning. These include the behavioral, cognitive, and social approaches.

1 Recognize behavioral, cognitive, and social approaches to learning, and describe their differences and limitations.

Behavioral Learning

Early research defined learning in limited terms – as a change in behavior. Learning involved a change in behavior that occurred as individuals responded to various rewards and punishments. Over time, these rewards and punishments changed or modified behavior. Russian psychologist Ivan Pavlov, made famous by his dogs and their response to stimuli, introduced a process known as **classical conditioning**. In his experiments, he trained dogs to salivate (behavior response) by ringing a bell (stimulus) and then giving them food (reward). Over time, Pavlov removed the food reward, but the dogs continued to salivate at the sound of the bell. He had successfully modified the behavior of the dogs

Table 3.1 Summary of Learning

Approaches to Learning	Learning Processes	Issues in Learning
• Behavioral • Cognitive • Social	• Experiential learning and the learning cycle • Learning style • Action learning	• Intelligence and multiple intelligences • Expertise • Learning orientation • Flexibility • Cognitive complexity

so that they salivated, even without the presence of the actual reward in the form of food. This behavioral modification occurred because the dogs learned to associate the sound of the bell with the food.[2]

Later, controversial Harvard psychologist B.F. Skinner introduced operant conditioning, further adapting this stimulus, reward, and response connection in humans.[3] **Operant conditioning** occurred when Skinner introduced certain, predetermined positive rewards. With operant conditioning, learning is reinforced through repetition and the resulting positive consequences of performing certain behaviors. He found that over time, producing rewards increased the frequency of certain behaviors. For example, smiling at a baby can produce laughter and encourages good behavior from the child. On the other hand, by introducing punishments, or negative consequences, Skinner could decrease the frequency of other behaviors. These findings paved the way for **reinforcement theory** and its application to organizational practices—such as pay-for-performance systems where organizations use incentives to entice certain behaviors by rewarding these behaviors.[4]

Enticing behavior through rewards proved easy when the desired behavior was simple and confined to an experimental laboratory, but this approach was not necessarily effective in helping people learn in work organizations. Introducing rewards and punishments does little to induce learning when a situation calls for critical thinking or creativity. Also, many consider it unethical to apply these techniques, first developed on animals, to humans. Further, behavioral learning may be able to change behaviors in certain circumstances, but it doesn't explain why people might change their behavior in other situations.

Cognitive Learning

Cognitive learning perspectives emerged in response to some of the limitations of behavior based learning. With the cognitive approach, learning is viewed as a mental process, not simply as a reaction to external stimulation. The cognitive approach seeks to develop a more complete picture of the learning process by mapping the mental processes that occur as a person learns new things. In this view, learning involves developing mental representations of the world. These mental representations, often called, *maps, mental-models,* or *schemas,* provide a mental picture of how individuals perceive, process, and act upon stimuli from the environment. Learning involves not only building these representations in the first place, but also updating them based on new information. The cognitive approach considers behavioral changes as a form of learning, but seeks a more complete picture of learning by including mental processes involved in learning in addition to behavioral changes that occur.[5]

Social Learning

Social-based approaches to learning consider more fully the function of social circumstances and the environment on learning.[6] **Social learning** describes how meaning is transmitted from one person to another.[7] When a person observes others, thoughtfully considering their actions, and then repeats these actions—this is called **modeling**. Modeling, then, is the process of learning that occurs through observation and imitation. **Efficacy**, also called *self-efficacy*, describes the sense of self-determination that emerges as a person observes others, and the sense of confidence that emerges as the person performs the task independently.[8] Efficacy becomes essential as the learner must not only

Robert Daly/Getty Images

observe the task, but must also feel a sense of confidence in his own ability to perform the task. Research generally supports the importance of efficacy for successful learning in both individuals and groups.[9]

Learning Processes

The prior section introduced three important approaches to learning in individuals. This section describes two process of learning in organizations. Experiential learning describes a comprehensive approach to how people learn from experience in organizations. This section also explains how individuals develop unique preferences for learning and in turn exhibit one of four types of learning style. Finally, action learning presents a process for improving how teams learn.

Experiential Learning

Experience-based learning describes learning as a process that occurs primarily through generating new experiences. Experience, not goals, incentives or outcomes, is the basis of learning. Experiential learning has been particularly influential because it describes the kind of learning that most often occurs in organizations.[10] The **experiential learning** process is illustrated in the four-phase process of learning from experience, called the **learning cycle** (see Figure 3.1).[11] Learning begins when a person engages with the world. This invokes a concrete experience, which involves feelings, emotions, and direct experiences. Learning activities related to concrete experience include trying something new, engaging in situations that create emotions, and generating new experiences.

The second phase of learning from experience occurs from the process of reflective observation. Reflective observation includes reflecting on the initial learning experience,

2 Explain the experiential learning process and the four learning styles.

Figure 3.1 The
Experiential Learning
Cycle

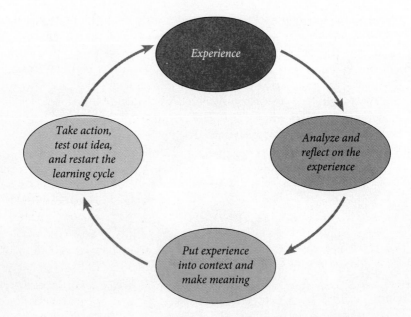

gathering new information about it, looking at the experience from different viewpoints, and making sense of the experience. Learning activities associated with reflective observation include taking in new information, taking time to consider a situation more fully, and discussing the situation with others.

Abstract conceptualization, the third phase of learning from experience, involves creating meaning from the experience by developing a theory or thinking about the learning process in an abstract manner. Activities related to abstract conceptualization involve reading and research, developing models, or creating new meaning from a situation.

And last, the active experimentation phase involves taking action. Learning occurs as a person becomes involved in testing out the plans that were already formulated and testing these ideas in the organization. Active experimentation might include learning a new skill, trying an activity, or testing something out. Taken together, these four phases of experience, reflection, conceptualization, and action constitute an experiential learning cycle.[12]

Learning Style

Experiential learning is closely linked to the concept of learning style. **Learning style** describes a person's preference for learning in one or more of the four learning phases of the learning cycle. Although as many as nine different learning styles have been identified, four styles are considered here.[13]

- The ***creating learning style*** describes a person who likes to brainstorm, try out new things, generate new ideas, and be creative. People with the creating learning style often have difficulty finishing projects or carrying out ideas because they become overwhelmed or bored quickly. Because this person often enjoys introducing new ideas that may not be practical, this is often referred to as the *diverging learning style*. Research shows that people in the creating learning style prefer jobs such as advertising, social work, and working with people.

- The **planning learning style** involves people who prefer to put things together, create new models, and know that ideas are coherent and well thought out. People with the planning learning style are often impractical and more interested in the conceptual interest of something than its' practical value. This is often called the *assimilating learning style* because this type of person likes to learn by bringing together seemingly unrelated concepts into an integrated model. Research shows that people with this learning style gravitate to jobs that involve basic research, analysis, or academic work.

- The **deciding learning style** describes the type of person who likes to put ideas into action. People with the planning style like to solve problems, are practical in approaching situations, and like to make decisions. The problems that this type of person may encounter include solving problems that don't exist and applying the wrong solution to a problem. The style is often called *converging* because this type of person enjoys learning by bringing abstract ideas into practice. People with the deciding learning style often show strengths in professions like accounting, engineering, and medical work.

- The **acting learning style** involves people who enjoy implementing work, engaging directly with people, and accomplishing goals. This type of person likes to create checklists to accomplish tasks, likes coming to closure on activities, and actively engaging with others. The limitations of the acting learning style is that people often take action without first considering alternatives, complete tasks before they are perfected, and become impatient with what they consider to be long, drawn-out decisions. This is often called the *accommodating learning style* due to the fact that people who prefer to learn in this fashion are good at helping reach agreement and focus seemingly divergent activities. People with the acting learning style often specialize in careers that involve dealing with people and taking action, such as human resources, general management, teaching, and sales.

Learning style not only plays an important part in describing your preferences for learning and the career you choose, it also plays an important role in problem solving. When problem solving, a team might consider matching a person's learning style to the particular task the team is set to perform. For example, a person with an acting style might be the person to set deadlines and make sure the team is working toward completion of the task. A person with the deciding learning style might be responsible for implementing key parts of the plan, a person with the planning style might focus on developing the plan, and the person with a creating style might take responsibility for developing multiple ideas for solving the problem.

Action Learning

3 Describe the action learning process.

Action learning is another technique that guides a team from problem generation through solution implementation. Action learning occurs when a team actively seeks to work through a problem faced by an organization, while at the same time, learning about teamwork. Action learning also provides a means for teams to identify an underlying cause of problems and to generate multiple possible solutions. Action learning involves several well-defined steps. Team members describe the problem, reframe the problem to see what elements need further clarification, and work to describe the problem from multiple perspectives. Importantly, action-learning projects also involve an implementation step where the team puts what they have learned into action. Although action learning often involves a formal coach, many times, members of an action-learning team coach one another and function without a formal leader.[14]

Learning in the Contemporary Organization

As organizations become increasingly complex, learning takes on greater importance. Learning provides not only a starting point for improving performance and effectiveness in organizations, but helps those in the organization manage complexity. To understand the role that learning plays in the contemporary organization, this section begins with a discussion of the differences between learning and intelligence. The next section describes how expertise is developed, and finally the role of learning flexibility, orientation, and cognitive complexity is discussed.

4 Identify multiple intelligences, expertise, learning orientation, and flexibility.

Intelligence and Multiple Intelligences

Intelligence describes a general cognitive ability or intellect. Research shows intelligence accounts for only 25 percent of success in management and leadership positions. Many people consider intelligence a threshold competency, which means that many management and leadership positions require a minimum level of intelligence to be competent at a job, but having a high level of intelligence does not predict whether or not you will be a top performer. Since standard measures do not account for success above and beyond a baseline of intelligence required for a job position, researchers have focused on developing a more complete picture of intelligence and its role in organizational success. The SAT was originally designed to measure innate ability, or intelligence, and was even designed along the same structure as an IQ test. More recently, the College Board, the administrators of the test, points out that it currently does not measure innate ability. In the case of the SAT, one pivotal study found that the test just measures how fast someone processes information and does not predict success factors such as graduation or even GPA.[15]

It becomes tempting to think of learning as the same thing as intelligence. Intelligence, however, remains relatively fixed throughout one's lifespan. On the other hand, ongoing learning is necessary in order to function in an organization. The necessary skills for success change as a person takes on different responsibilities in an organization. Early in one's career, performance results from high degrees of technical knowledge, while later in one's career, skills that involve working with people typically become more important.[16]

Alternatives to traditional measures of both intelligence and learning consider a broader range of capabilities. Howard Gardner, for example, developed a systematic alternative to traditional measures of intelligence. In contrast to traditional intelligence, which only considers cognitive capabilities, Gardner identified seven forms of intelligence, which he termed **multiple intelligence.**

- Verbal intelligence involves expressing ideas in words or symbols.
- Mathematical intelligence involves using abstract symbol and patterns such as math or science.
- Visual intelligence includes understanding and handling reality with lines, shapes, size, and space.

- Bodily/kinesthetic intelligence involves knowing and feeling things that the body senses through contact, emotions, and movement.
- Musical–rhythmic intelligence involves understanding through sound or rhythm.
- Interpersonal intelligence involves understanding people and relationships through intimacy, friendship, and bonding.
- Intrapersonal intelligence involves understanding your own feelings and motivations through reflection, self-awareness, and self-evaluation.[17]

Expertise

Another consideration is how individuals develop expertise. **Expertise** is demonstrated through consistent above-average performance. The expert makes good decisions more quickly than others in a particular field, holds greater content knowledge and vocabulary, makes decisions based on general principles rather than idiosyncratic information, but remains flexible in how they apply these principles. Expertise develops as a person engages in **deliberate practice**, a concentrated effort to learn a task that is directed or designed by someone with knowledge of the task. Researchers systematically reviewed the notebooks and journals of experts and found that to develop expertise requires a deliberate practice session nearly every day for about four hours a day, conducted over nearly 10 years of time. In total, developing expertise may require a total of 10,000 or more hours of deliberate practice. Research on expertise and performance provides an interesting basis to study learning in organizations, but so far it has not been applied directly to leaders or managers in organizations.[18]

Learning Orientation and Flexibility

Another important consideration is learning orientation. There are two learning orientations: orientation toward learning goals and orientation toward performance goals.[19] A **learning goal orientation** occurs when an individual focuses on developing or attaining a certain competency. Learning goal orientation leads to taking more risks, embracing failures, and trying new things. A person with a learning goal orientation is open to new experiences even if she is not met with ultimate success. On the other hand, a person with a performance goal orientation is more likely to focus on achieving success by demonstrating a particular competency. A **performance goal orientation** results in avoiding challenges, fear of risk taking, and seeking approval.

Learning flexibility is similar to learning orientation, but flexibility describes the willingness and ability of a person to move from relying on specialized knowledge to a more complex and universal understanding of a situation. Learning flexibility is necessary for more advanced learning and essential for those who want to act at the strategic level of an organization. An individual with learning flexibility will display the ability to utilize different forms of learning and adapt to new learning situations more easily than a person with lower learning flexibility.[20]

Cognitive Complexity and Its Implications for Learning

5 Describe the importance of cognitive complexity for learning.

Cognitive complexity is another aspect of learning. **Cognitive complexity** describes a series of progressive steps where each new step is marked by an increase in the ability to process information in a more complex, and therefore, more complete way. A person with a high degree of cognitive complexity demonstrates the ability to process large amounts of information and to assess that information from various perspectives. Cognitive complexity involves developing two abilities: differentiation and integration. Differentiation involves finding differences between two seemingly similar ideas. Integration involves finding similarities between two seemingly different ideas. With the movement to higher levels of cognitive complexity, a person improves the ability to manage multiple goals or respond to a diverse set of stakeholders. In contemporary organizations, where information processing and complex knowledge are a requirement for success, improved cognitive complexity among organizational members can improve an organization's capability to perform.

Dr. Phillip Tetlock's model of cognitive complexity describes how people gather and process information at different levels of complexity. He demonstrates through his research how the cognitive complexity of leaders such as former United States Presidents Bill Clinton, Jimmy Carter, and George W. Bush, as well as Winston Churchill, led them to make certain decisions. This model has been applied to Supreme Court judicial cases, and policy decisions, as well as decision making in business.[21]

Conclusion

This topic summary has outlined key issues in learning in addition to providing a look at some of the foundational theories of learning. It reviews three approaches to learning, describes processes of learning, and looks at relevant issues of learning in organizations. This topic summary describes not only how learning occurs in a classroom and in the workplace, but also emphasizes the importance of learning for all aspects of life, including expertise, multiple intelligences, and cognitive complexity.

OB AT WORK

CEO ALAN WILSON LEADS McCORMICK SPICE BY BUILDING CORPORATE IDENTITY THROUGH LEARNING

Alan Wilson

You **might have tried chipotle** (pronounced chee-pawt-le), the smoke-dried chili pepper spice that has become a popular flavor the world over. If you have enjoyed this flavor or simply know about it, you have to thank, in part, Alan Wilson and his team at McCormick. As the CEO of McCormick, the world's largest spice company, Wilson and his team helped turn chipotle, a spice mixture first used by the Incas in Peru in the fourteenth and fifteenth centuries, into a popular contemporary flavor. The growth in popularity of chipotle food stands is a telling example of how Wilson reinforces the identity of McCormick as a thought leader in the world of flavor.

McCormick's role as a thought leader means not simply identifying flavor trends, but helping to define them. This requires taking deliberate steps to measure current trends and then *learning* how to influence their future direction. To this end, each year McCormick convenes an expert panel that consists of top chefs from around the globe. The result of this effort is the *McCormick Flavor Forecast*. The Forecast presents a mix of the top spices, herbs, and other flavors that are likely to get the attention of restaurants, consumers, and food writers. Ever wonder how the chef decided to mix cumin and sofrito on your baked chicken? That combination appeared on the 2012 Flavor Forecast. Contemplating why pumpkin spice pops up everywhere in the fall? Check out the Flavor Forecast Holiday edition.

6 Apply concepts of learning to organizations.

The flavor forecast not only captures trends, it also entices foodies to try new things, which in turn reinforces the importance McCormick as the source for flavor.

Since 2002, the forecast has identified growing trends in flavor. What flavor did the first Forecast capture in 2002? You guessed it—chipotle! By helping to establish flavor trends like chipotle, efforts like the Flavor Forecast reaffirm the company's influence as the leading source of flavor.

Wilson learned to capture, shape, and preserve aspects of an organization's identity over the course of his career. His degree in public relations and communications taught him the importance of communicating a clear and engaging identity to the public. Then, while observing generals as an officer in the United States Army, he learned lessons for leading in a complex organization. After years working at a major consumer goods company learning business analytics, he joined McCormick to apply his unique experience to the spice business.

Wilson became CEO of McCormick in 2008. He now heads a multi-billion dollar company that operates in some of the most remote areas of the world. Leading a global company, Wilson appreciates the importance of projecting an identity that is consistent with the company's values. A focus on core values creates consistency, an enduring quality to the company's identity. "We try to use a common language around the world, this helps bring out our culture, but underlying it all, is a passion for flavor," he proudly states. "It's hard to work at McCormick without being a foodie!" he explains with enthusiasm. The

(continued)

culture and identity at McCormick helps everyone in the organization understand how they contribute to the overall mission.

Wilson recognizes the challenges of leading a company with global influence. One challenge requires maintaining sensitivity to local tastes while continuing to influence global flavor trends. "There are challenges to shaping impressions," Wilson notes, "especially when managing across different cultures throughout the world. Flavor is local. When someone introduces you to their culture, one of the first things they do is to introduce you to their food." Operating effectively in this environment requires sensitivity to the uniqueness of these local practices. For example, in the French culture, there is an emphasis on the senses, the quality of the flavor, and the herbs rather than spices. Respecting these local traditions becomes important to maintaining and growing the company's reputation. For example, rather than emphasizing only the McCormick name in France, the company purchased a flavor company that was already established and had an identity in the marketplace.

Since a good portion of McCormick's products is sourced from developing countries, the company retains a sense of familiarity and openness to different parts of the world. This is also a key element of the company's identity. "We've been sourcing from within a few degrees of the equator for over 100 years," Wilson remarks. "This has produced a sense of respect and understanding for emerging markets." The company is also proud of its pioneering work in encouraging sustainable practices. As far back as the early 1970s, McCormick saw sustainability as an important part of what it does as a company, realizing early on, that an important connection exists between its own identity and that of other employers. If they don't have suppliers, they don't have products to sell. To ensure continuity, McCormick has worked with spice farmers around the world to improve handling of materials and encouraging economic development in areas where they source their raw materials.

Building and sustaining an identity through techniques like the Flavor Forecast may appear to be simple marketing tactics, but organizational behavior concepts help illustrate how learning identity is more than a marketing tool. Identity is at the core of how an organization views its role in the world. Wilson helps shape and secure McCormick's core identity as a thought leader on flavor, as a company that thrives in under-developed parts of the world, and as a forward thinker on sustainability.

Source: Interview with Alan Wilson.

SPOTLIGHT ON RESEARCH
Acquiring Leadership Skills Requires the Right Assignment and Openness Towards Learning

One of the great debates among organizational behavior researchers involves the following question: How do organizations develop better managers and leaders? Some believe that leadership emerges as an employee takes on new responsibilities, develops a better understanding by taking on new roles within the organization, and at the same time, is provided strong support from managers, professional coaches, and peers. Others believe that individual orientation and willingness to grow and learn accounts for the most effective leadership development. At its core, the debate comes down to a long-standing argument about which is more important for developing leaders—individual characteristics, such as motivation, learning orientation, or personality; or environmental characteristics such as support and opportunity. A group of researchers applied scientific rigor to answer this debate.

Researchers surveyed 215 junior leader/managers and their supervisors to learn what predicted success. The researcher wanted to know not just what the managers themselves thought about their learning, but how the supervisors viewed the learning of these managers as well. The researchers were particularly interested in two factors that prior research had shown to be related to learning: One factor was learning orientation. In other words, when a manager interested in taking chances and developing new skills (high learning orientation) or when a manager is more interested in showing off her competence and capabilities by avoiding situations that might lead to failure (low learning orientation). The second factor involved the nature of the job assignment. For example, what role did having the right job, position, or experiences have in shaping leaders. The study drew on prior research to identify 10 different types of job assignments based on how well they led to developmental opportunities. **Developmental opportunities** provide the basis for learning, improving skills, and growing as a professional.

Does the job require the employee to do the following?

- Take on new and unfamiliar challenges
- Develop new directions for the organization
- Address problems inherited by the manager
- Manage people problems

Does the assignment involve the following?

- High stakes
- Broad scale and scope
- Influencing others even without formal authority
- Handling pressure from outside the department
- Managing a diverse workforce
- Working across cultures

After surveying both the managers and their supervisors, the researchers found an answer to the question about which counts more, factors related to the leader or factors associated with the environment: it takes a little of both.

The research found that junior employees in highly developmental assignments were more likely to be rated as highly competent by their managers. Competency was measured in terms of business knowledge, courage to take a stand, bringing out the best in people, acting with integrity, commitment to success, and insightfulness. Prior promotions had no effect so people weren't in these assignments simply because they had performed better in their prior positions. The study showed that having assignments that were developmental in nature, not simply having more responsibility, proved key for developing leaders. Further, employees with high learning orientation (as opposed to those ranked high on performance orientation) were also ranked as more competent. The conclusion: those junior employees who had both a high learning

(continued)

orientation and had access to highly developmental assignments were seen as more competent by their managers. In the end, evidence shows that leaders who have both a high orientation toward learning and the right developmental assignments are seen as the most competent leaders.

Questions for Discussion

1. Why is learning so important for employees in the workplace?

2. How would you apply this research to your own workplace? What practices do you think are important? Why do you think so?

*This spotlight on research is based on the article: Dragoni, L., Tesluk, P. E., Russell, J. E. A., & Oh, In-Sue. (2009). Understanding managerial development: Integrating developmental assignments, learning orientation, and access to developmental opportunities in predicting managerial competencies. *Academy of Management Journal, 52*, 4, 731–743.

Pairing with this Topic Summary

Suggested Expert Contributions

Action Learning—Michael Marquardt (The George Washington University)

Deliberate Experiential Learning: Mastering the Art of Learning from Experience
—David A. Kolb (Experience Based Learning Systems, Inc.) and Bauback Yeganeh (Everidian)

Learning-Directed Leadership in a Changing World
—Anna B. Kayes (Stevenson University) and D. Christopher Kayes
(The George Washington University)

Suggested Cases

Case 4: Face Time at TechPoint Software, Inc.

Case 6: NASCAR's Drive for Diversity: Can They Reach the Finish Line?

Suggested Exercises

Exercise 3: My Expat Assignment

Exercise 5: My Best and Worst Learning Experiences

Exercise 7: Development While Still in College

Exercise 9: Being Positive

Endnotes

1. Kayes, D. C., & Kayes, A. B. (2007). Learning. In J. Bailey & S. Clegg (Eds.).*International encyclopedia of organization studies*. Thousand Oaks, CA: Sage. See also Bailey, J., & Kayes, D. C. (2005). Learning, individual. In N. Iicholson, P. G. Audia, & M. M. Pillutla (Eds.). *The Blackwell encyclopedia of management (2)* XI, 213–215. London, UK: Blackwell.
2. Pavlov, I. F. (1927/1960). *Conditioned reflexes. New* York: Dover Press.
3. Skinner, B. F. (1938). *The behavior of organisms.* New York: Appleton-Century-Crofts.
4. Komaki, J. L., Collins, R. L., & Penn, P. (1982). The role of performance antecedents and consequences in work motivation. *Journal of Applied Psychology, 67*(3): 334–340.

5. Piaget, J. (1926/1952). *The language and thought of the child.* London: Routledge.

6. Newman, B. M., & Newman, P. R. (1999). *Development through life: A psychosocial approach. 7th Edition.* The Ohio State University. New York: Wadsworth.

7. Bandura, A. (1989). Regulation of cognitive processes through perceived self-efficacy.*Developmental Psychology, 25(5):* 729–735.

8. Bandura, A. (1986). *Social foundations of thought and action: A social cognitive theory.*Englewood Cliffs, NJ: Prentice Hall.

9. Stajkovic, A. D., & Luthans, F. (2003). Behavioral management and task performance in organizations: Conceptual background meta-analysis and test of alternative models.*Personnel Psychology, 56(1):* 155–92. See also Stajkovic, A. D., Luthans, F., (1998). Self-efficacy and work-related performance: A meta-analysis. *Psychological Bulletin, 124(2):* 240–261.

10. Raelin, J. A. (1997). A model of work-based learning. *Organization Science,* 8(6): 563–578.

11. Kolb, D. A. (1984). *Experiential learning.* Prentice Hall. See also Dewey, J.*Experience and education.* New York: Macmillan, 1938.

12. Kolb (1984).

13. Kolb, A. Y., & Kolb, D. A. (2005). Learning styles and learning spaces: Enhancing experiential learning in higher education. *Academy of Management Learning and Education, 4(2):*193–212.

14. Marquardt, M. J. (1999). *Action learning in action.* Palo-Alto: Davies-Black.

15. Hiss, W. C., & Franks, V. W. (2014). Defining promise: Optional standardized testing policies in American college and university admissions. *National Association for College Admission Counseling.* Available at: http://www.nacacnet.org/research/research-data/nacac-research/Documents/DefiningPromise.pdf.

16. Mumford, M. D., Zaccaro, S. J., Connelly, M. S., & Marks, M. A. (2000). Leadership skills: Conclusions and future directions. *The Leadership Quarterly,* 11(1): 155–170.

17. Gardner, H. (1985). *Frames of mind: The theory of multiple intelligences.* New York: Basic Books.

18. Ericsson, K. A. & Lehmann, A. C. (1996). Experts and exceptional performance: Evidence of maximal adaptation to task constraints. *Annual Review of Psychology, 47,* 273–305.

19. Seijts, G. H., Latham, G. P., Tasa, K., & Latham, B. W. (2004). Goal setting and goal orientation: An integration of two different yet related literatures. *Academy of Management Journal, 47(2):* 227-239.

20. Sharma, G., & Kolb, D. A. (2010). The learning flexibility index: Assessing contextual flexibility in learning style. In S. Rayner & E. Cools (Eds.). *Style differences in cognition, learning, and management: theory, research, and practice.* (Routledge Studies in Management and Society). London: Routledge, pp. 60-77.

21. Suedfeld, P., Tetlock, P.E., & Streufert, S. (1992). Conceptual/integrative complexity. In C. Smith (Ed.). *Handbook of thematic content analysis.* New York: Cambridge University Press, pp. 393–401. See also Tetlock, P.E., & Tyler, A. (1996). Winston Churchill's cognitive and rhetorical style: The debates over Nazi intentions and self-government for India. *Political Psychology, 17,* 149–170. Reprinted in H. Gyorgy (1998). (Ed.). *Historical and political psychology.* Budapest: Osiris Publishing House/Malden, MA: Blackwell. See also Tetlock, P. E. (1985). Integrative complexity of American and Soviet foreign policy rhetoric: A time-series analysis. *Journal of Personality and Social Psychology, 49(6):* 1565–1585.

Action Learning

Michael Marquardt

The George Washington University

Action learning has quickly emerged as a tool used by organizations for solving their critical and complex problems. It has concurrently become a primary methodology utilized by companies around the world for developing leaders, building teams, and transforming corporate culture. Action learning programs have become instrumental in creating thousands of new products and services, saving billions of dollars, reducing production and delivery times, expanding customer bases, improving service quality, and positively changing organizational cultures.[1]

Recent surveys by the American Society for Training and Development indicate that two-thirds of executive leadership programs in the United States use action learning. A 2009 study by the Corporate Executive Board noted that 77 percent of learning executives identified action learning as the top driver of leadership bench strength. *Businessweek* identified action learning as the "latest and fastest growing organizational tool for leadership development."[2]

Necessary Components to Optimize the Power and Success of Action Learning

Since Reg Revans first introduced action learning in the coal mines of Wales and England in the 1940s, there have been multiple variations of action learning.[3] However, all forms of action learning share the elements of real people resolving and taking action on real problems in real time, and learning while doing. Action learning programs that optimize both the power and action of action learning has six components:

1. A Problem (project, challenge, opportunity, issue or task)

Action learning centers around a problem, project, challenge, issue, or task of high importance to an individual, team and/or organization. It should provide opportunities for the group to generate learning opportunities; to build knowledge; and to develop individual, team, and organizational skills. Groups may focus on a single problem of the organization or multiple problems introduced by individual group members.

2. An Action Learning Group or Team

The core entity in action learning is the action learning group (also called a *set* or *team*). The group is ideally composed of four to eight individuals who examine an organizational problem that has no easily identifiable solution. The group should have diversity of background and experience, so as to acquire various perspectives and encourage fresh viewpoints. Depending upon the action learning problem, groups may be volunteers or may be appointed; they may come from various functions or departments, may include individuals from other organizations or professions, and may involve suppliers as well as customers.

3. A Process that Emphasizes Insightful Questioning and Reflective Listening

Action learning emphasizes questions and reflection above statements and opinions. By focusing on the right questions rather than the right answers, action learning focuses on what one does not know as well as on what one does know. Action learning tackles problems through a process of first asking questions to clarify the exact nature of the problem, then reflecting and identifying possible solutions, and only then taking action. The focus is on questions, since great solutions are contained within the seeds of great questions. Questions build group dialogue and cohesiveness, generate innovative and systems thinking, and enhance learning results.

4. Taking Action on the Problem

Action learning requires the group to be able to take action on the problem on which it is working. Members of the action learning group must have the power to take action themselves or be assured that their recommendations will be implemented, barring any significant change in the environment or the group's obvious lack of essential information. If the group only makes recommendations, it loses its energy, creativity, and commitment. There is no real meaningful or practical learning until action is taken and reflected upon. One is never sure an idea or plan will be effective until it has been implemented. Action enhances learning because it provides a basis and anchor for the critical dimension of reflection. The *action* of action learning begins with taking steps to reframe the problem and determining the goal, and only then determining strategies and taking action.

5. A Commitment to Learning

Solving an organizational problem provides immediate short-term benefits to the company. The greater, longer-term, multiplier benefit is the learning gained by each group member (as well as the group as a whole), and how this learning is applied on a systems-wide basis throughout the organization. Thus, the learning that occurs in action learning has greater value strategically for the organization than only the immediate tactical advantage of early problem correction. Accordingly, action learning places as much emphasis on the learning and development of individuals and the team as it does on the solving of problems. The smarter the group becomes, the quicker and better will be the quality of its decision making and action taking.

6. An Action Learning Coach or Facilitator

Coaching is necessary for the group to focus on the important aspects of the process (i.e., the learning) as well as the urgent aspect (resolving the problem). The action learning coach helps the team members reflect both on what they are learning and how they are solving problems. Through questions, the coach enables group members to reflect on how they can improve their work as a team and how they can better solve the problem.

The learning coach also helps the team focus on what they are achieving, what they are finding difficult, what processes they are employing, and the implications of these processes. The coaching role may be rotated among members of the group, or it may be a person assigned to that role throughout the duration of the group's existence. More and more organizations are utilizing a skilled, trained coach to serve in this role.[4]

Multiple-Problem and Single-Problem Action Learning Groups

Action learning groups may be formed for the purpose of handling either a single problem or several problems. In the *single-problem group*, all the group members focus all of their energies on solving that problem. In this type of action learning, both the membership and the problem are determined by the organization. The primary purpose of the group is to solve the problem proposed to them by the organization. The group may disband after handling just one problem, or may continue for a longer, indefinite period of time and work on a series of challenges submitted to them by the organization. Membership in the action learning groups is determined by the organization based upon the type of problem and the aims of the programs.

For example, if the organization is seeking to create networks across certain business units, members from those units will be appointed. If the development of high potential leaders is the goal, then such leaders will be placed in these action learning programs. If the issue is more focused, then participants may be selected according to their interests, experience, and/or knowledge. In some in-company action learning programs, individuals may be allowed to volunteer, but the organization reserves the right to confirm or not confirm the final composition of an action learning group.

In *multiple-problem sets* (also referred to as *open-group* or *classic* action learning or action learning *circles*), each individual member brings his or her problem/task/project to the group for their fellow members to help solve. The members self-select to join the group, and support and assist each other on the problems that they bring. During each action learning session, each member is allocated time for the group to work on his or her problem. Thus, a six-member group that meets for three hours would devote approximately 30 minutes to each person's problem.

In open-group action learning, the members may meet on a monthly basis for a few months or a few years. Open-group action learning is usually voluntary, and has more limited funding. Thus, the groups often meet on their own time, and rotate the coaching role among themselves. Over a period of time, new members may join as older members withdraw. The members are usually representatives from a variety of organizations, as well as independent consultants and people who are no longer in the workplace.[5]

Overview of the Stages of Action Learning

There are many different forms of action learning. Action learning groups may meet one time or several times over a few days or over several months, may handle one or many problems, may meet for short periods or long periods. However, action learning generally operates along the following stages and procedures:

Formation of group—The group may be volunteer or appointed, and may be working on a single organizational problem or each other's individual problems. The group may have a predetermined amount of time and sessions or may determine these aspects at the first meeting.

Presentation of problem or task to group—The problem (or problems, if a multi-problem group) is briefly presented to the group. Members ask questions to gather more information about the problem or task.

Reframing the problem—After a series of questions, the group, often with the guidance of the action learning coach, will reach a consensus as to the most critical and important problem that the group should work on and establish the crux of the problem, which may differ from the original presented problem.

Determining goals—Once the key problem or issue has been identified, the group searches for the goal, the achievement of which would solve the reframed problem for the long term with positive rather than negative consequences on the individual, team, or organization.

Developing action strategies—Much of the time and energy of the group will be spent on identifying and pilot-testing possible action strategies. Like the preceding stages of action learning, strategies are developed via the reflective inquiry and dialogue modes.

Taking action—Between action learning sessions, the group as a whole (as well as individual members) collect information, identity status of support, and implement the strategies developed and agreed to by the group.

Capturing learnings—Throughout and at any point during the session, the action learning coach may intervene to ask the group members questions that will enable them to reflect on their performance and to find ways to improve their performance as a group.

Example of an Action Learning Program

An international financial firm has decided to use action learning as the methodology for handling a critical organizational challenge as well as for developing their high-potential leaders. Six managers from different departments are chosen to be members of the action learning group. Prior to the commencement of the action learning, they are asked to identify the specific leadership competencies that they seek to improve during their participation in the action learning sessions. The challenge assigned to the six managers is to develop a global strategy for the manufacturing division of the company, reporting their recommendations to the executive council within three months. The firm decides to utilize an external action learning coach to work with the group. The action learning group meets one day a week for three months, during which time the goals are clearly established, strategies developed and pilot-tested, and actions recommended. At the end of each session, the action learning coach assists the group members in reflecting on the application and development of the competencies they have chosen to develop. During each session, learnings and knowledge that can be applied to the team and to the financial firm are also targeted. After a period of three months, the group presents to the executive council its recommendations as well as its individual, team, and organizational learnings. The executive council, following some questions and minor modifications, accepts the proposed strategies and assigns the team the responsibility for coordinating and implementing the proposed strategies and action plan.

Applications of Action Learning

Action learning is used to accomplish the following five objectives: (1) solve problems, (2) develop leaders, (3) build teams, (4) create learning organizations, and (5) increase individuals' professional skills.

1. Problem-Solving

Action learning begins with and builds around solving problems—the more complex and the more urgent, the better suited is action learning. The dynamic interactive process used in action learning allows the group to see problems in new ways and to gain fresh perspectives on how to resolve them. Questioning from multiple perspectives creates solid systems thinking in which the group sees the whole rather than parts, relationships rather than linear cause–effect patterns, underlying structures rather than events, and profiles of changes rather than snapshots. The action learning process enables the group to look for underlying causes and leveraged actions, rather than symptoms and short-term solutions. Action learning examines both macro and micro views so as to discover when and how to best implement the proposed actions. As a result of its fresh approach to problem-solving, action learning generates "breakthrough" insights, solutions, and effective strategies.[6]

2. Leadership Development

Most leadership development programs, whether corporate or academic, have been ineffective and expensive.[7] The weakness of traditional leadership development programs are caused by a number of factors, most notably: (a) teachers rather than practitioners are the purveyors of knowledge; (b) a separation exists between the learning and action; (c) very little learning get transferred to the workplace; (d) the business environment is changing so fast that the knowledge gained from the programs are too slow and inadequate; and (e) there is an absence of reflective thinking in the education process.[8] Typical executive development programs provide little of the social and interpersonal aspects of the organizations, and tend to focus on tactical rather than strategic leadership.

Action learning differs from normal leadership training in that its "primary objective" is to ask appropriate questions in conditions of risk, rather than to find answers that have already been precisely defined by others, and that do not allow for ambiguous responses because the examiners have all the approved answers.[9] Action learning does not isolate any dimension from the context in which managers work; rather, it develops the whole leader for the whole organization. What leaders learn and how they learn cannot be dissociated from one another, for how one learns necessarily influences what one learns.[10]

Traditional leadership programs that use case studies are like learning how to steer a boat by looking out the stern. Examining what happened yesterday will not drive change or make a company competitive. Today, success factors keep changing, and no company can stay on top by doing what it used to do. In action learning, we have the opportunity to grow as leaders, because we are reflecting on what is urgent and important to us and when our assumptions are challenged. McGill and Beatty point out how action learning provides managers the opportunity to take "appropriate levels of responsibility in discovering how to develop themselves" (p. 37).[11]

3. Building Teams

Action learning teams are extremely cohesive and high-performing. They become more effective every time they meet, because the action learning process focuses on how individually and collectively teams can become smarter and faster. A "teamthink and teamlearn" capability steadily emerges. The group shares clear responsibility and accountability on real problems causing a need for deliberative team unity and success.

The process of ongoing questioning and shared learning builds powerful caring and cohesion among the members. Developing consensus around problems and goals develops clearness of task, strong communications, collaboration, and commitment, during which powerful team synergy and learning emerge.

4. Creating Learning Organizations

A learning organization is constructed around four primary subsystems: (a) increased learning skills and capacities; (b) a transformed organizational culture and structure; (c) an involvement of the entire business chain in the learning process; and (d) enhanced capability to manage knowledge. Members of action learning groups transfer their experiences and new capabilities to their organizations in a number of ways.

- First, action learning groups themselves are mini-learning organizations and model perfectly what a learning organization is and how it should operate.
- Action learning groups seek to learn continuously from all their actions and interactions. They adapt quickly to external and internal environmental changes.
- Learning and knowledge are continuously captured and transferred to other parts of the organization that could benefit from these experiences.
- Individuals who participate in action learning groups appreciate the tremendous benefits of questions and reflection in helping them to continuously improve when they return to their respective jobs. They are better learners, as well as better leaders.
- As the action learning members resume their day-to-day activities, their new mindsets and skills gradually impact the entire organization, resulting in a culture more likely to learn continuously, to reward learning, and to connect learning to all business activities.[12]

5. Individual Professional Growth and Development

Weinstein notes that participants in action learning achieve learning at three different levels: (1) understanding something intellectually, (2) applying a newly acquired skill, and (3) experiencing and thereby undergoing an inner development that touches on beliefs and attitudes and leads to personal development.[13] Action learning is particularly effective at this third level since it provides the opportunity for internal dissonance, while the problem and/or action may provide the external trigger. In action learning we become more aware of our blind spots and weaknesses, as well as our strengths, and we receive the feedback and help that we have requested.

Action learning generates tremendous personal, intellectual, psychological, and social growth. Butterfield, Gold, and Willis note how action learning participants experience "breakthrough learning" when they became aware of the need to reach beyond their conscious beliefs and to challenge their assumptions about their present worldviews.[14]

This readiness to change and grow is a prerequisite for development. Some of the specific skills and abilities developed for those participating in action learning include:

- critical reflection skills, which are key to *transformative* learning for the individual[15]
- inquiry and questioning abilities, where the individual can do more than just advocate and push personal opinions

- systems thinking, so that individuals begin to see things in a less linear, less accurate fashion
- ability to adapt and change
- active listening skills and greater self-awareness
- empathy, the capacity to connect with others
- problem-solving and strategy-selection skills
- presentation and facilitation skills

Action learning has also been utilized as a highly valuable tool for examining and advancing one's personal career. For example, job seekers have effectively used action learning to help them better understand themselves, their career goals, their strengths, and the best resources for locating and landing a job.

Conclusion

Although it is a deceptively simple process involving six components and two ground rules, its amazing power is based upon the interweaving and interconnectedness of numerous theories and principles from the disciplines such as education, management, physics, sociology, systems thinking, political science, and economics.[16] The power, speed, and ease in which action learning can be implemented has resulted in its rapid rise as one of the top methods for leadership development, team building, organizational transformation, as well as for complex problem solving.

Endnotes

1. Marquardt, M. (1999). Action learning in action. Palo Alto, CA: Davies-Black. Marquardt, M., S. Leonard, A. Freedman, & C. Hill. (2009). Action learning for developing leaders and organizations. Washington, DC: APA Press. Boshyk, Y. and L. Dilworth. (2010). Action learning and its applications. Houndmill, Hampshire: Palgrave Macmillan. Pedler, M. (Ed.). (2011). Action learning in practice, (4th ed.). Aldershot, England: Gower.
2. Corporate Executive Board. (2009). What drives leadership bench strength? Learning and Development Roundtable Email sent to all members. Washington, DC: Corporate Executive Board. Byrnes, N. (2005). Star search. How to recruit, train and how on to great people. Business Week, 40, 71.
3. Marsick, V., & O'Neil, J. (1999). The many faces of action learning. Management Learning, 30(2),159–177. York, L., O'Neil, J., & Marsick, V. (Eds.). (1999). Action learning: Successful strategies Cho, Y., & Egan, T. (2010). The State of the Art of Action Learning Research Advances in Developing Human Resources 12(2), 163–180.
4. Coughlan, P., & Coghlan, D. (2011). Collaborative strategic improvement through network action learning. Cheltenham: Edward Elgar Publishing. Marquardt, M. (2011). Optimizing the power of action learning. (2nd ed.). Palo Alto, CA: Davies-Black.
5. Marquardt, M. (2011).
6. Marquardt, M., & Yeo, R. (2011). Break-through Problem Solving with Action Learning. Stanford University Press.
7. Pfeffer. K., & Fong, C. (2002). The end of business schools: Less success than meet the eye. Academy of Management Learning and Education 1(1), 78–95.

8. McNulty, N., & Canty, G. (1995). Proof of the pudding. Journal of Management Development, 14(1), 53–66.

9. Revans, R. (1982). The ABCs of action learning. Bromley, U.K.: Chartwell-Brat.

10. Dilworth, L. (1998). Action learning in a nutshell. Performance Improvement Quarterly, 11, (1), 28–43.

11. McGill, I., & Beaty, L. (1995). Action learning. London: Kogan Page, p. 37.

12. Marquardt, M. (2000). Action learning and leadership. The Learning Organization, 7 (5), 233–240.

13. Weinstein, K. (1995). Action learning: A journey in discovery and development. London: HarperCollins.

14. Butterfield, S., Gold, K., & Willis, V. (1998). Creating a systematic framework for the transfer of learning from an action learning experience. Academy of HRD Proceedings, 490–496.

15. Mezirow, J. (1991). Transformative dimensions of adult learning. San Francisco: Jossey-Bass.

16. Marquardt, M. (2011).

Deliberate Experiential Learning: Mastering the Art of Learning from Experience

David A. Kolb

Experience Based Learning Systems, Inc.

Bauback Yeganeh

Everidian

> *Learn*
> *As though you will live forever.*
>
> *Live*
> *As though you will die tomorrow.*
> —John Wooden

The ancient Chinese curse, "May you live in interesting times," might well apply to all of us living today in the rapidly changing and expanding global community. Every day we face new challenges and opportunities at work and in our personal lives. At work there are technological innovations, expanding multi-cultural market opportunities and new organizational forms that demand greater personal responsibility and higher quality and productivity. Our personal lives have grown far more complex with increasing responsibility to manage our financial, health, and personal affairs.

To survive and thrive in these "interesting times" individuals are called upon to adapt and learn in ways that are unprecedented in human history. For many years now there has been an increasing emphasis on continuing lifelong learning and on the promotion of learning in education. The emphasis has shifted from teaching to learning[1] with learner centered educational policies and curricula focused on learning how to learn. Central to this change is a focus on the responsibility of the individual for managing and directing his or her own learning. Expertise at learning has become the key capability necessary for survival, success, and fulfillment.

Learning can have magical transformative powers. It opens new doors and pathways, expanding our world and capabilities. It literally can change who we are by creating new professional and personal identities. Learning is intrinsically rewarding and empowering, bringing new avenues of experience and new realms of mastery. In a very real sense, you are what you learn. We suggest an approach to living that puts learning first and foremost, an approach that we call "the learning way." The learning way is about approaching life experiences with a learning attitude. It involves a deep trust in one's own experience and a healthy skepticism about received knowledge. It requires the perspective of quiet reflection and a passionate commitment to action in the face of uncertainty. The learning way is not the easiest way to approach life but in the long run it is the wisest. Other ways of living tempt us with immediate gratification at our peril. The way of dogma, the way of denial, the way of addiction, the way of submission and the way of habit; all offer relief from uncertainty and pain at the cost of entrapment on a path that winds out of our control. The learning way requires deliberate effort to create new knowledge in the face of uncertainty and failure; but opens the way to new, broader and deeper horizons of experience.

Yet, many of us live our daily lives making little or no conscious effort to learn from our experiences. We tend to assume that effective learning happens automatically and have given little thought to how we learn or how we might improve our learning capability. Yet research in many areas has shown that experience alone does not produce much learning. Research on automaticity helps to explain this by suggesting that many of the activities of our daily lives are conducted on "automatic pilot" without conscious awareness and intention.[2] The shift from automatic pilot to deliberate learning leads to the learning way—a way of living that puts learning at the forefront of one's life. Learning from experience is at the center of the learning way, and Experiential Learning Theory broadens our understanding of these ideas.

Learning from Experience

Philosopher John Dewey, one of the founding scholars of experiential learning, recognized that experience alone did not produce learning. He emphasized that learning involved "that reconstruction or reorganization of experience that adds to the meaning of that experience and which increases ability to direct the course of subsequent experience" (74).[3] He argued that it was necessary to reflect on experience in order to draw out the meaning in it and to use that meaning as a guide in future experiences. He observed that the reflective process seemed to be initiated only when we are 'stuck' with a problem or difficulty or 'struck' by the strangeness of something outside of our usual experience.[4]

Following Dewey, Experiential Learning Theory (ELT)[5] describes how experience is transformed into learning through a cycle of learning involving experiencing, reflecting, thinking, and acting. ELT defines learning as "the process whereby knowledge is created through the transformation of experience. Knowledge results from the combination of grasping and transforming experience" (41).[6] The ELT model portrays two opposing modes of *grasping* experience—Concrete Experience (CE) and Abstract Conceptualization (AC)—and two opposing modes of *transforming* experience—Reflective Observation (RO) and Active Experimentation (AE). Learning from experience is a process of constructing knowledge that involves a creative tension among these four learning modes. This process is portrayed as an idealized learning cycle or spiral where the learner "touches all the bases"—experiencing, reflecting, thinking, and acting—in a recursive process that is responsive to the learning situation and what is being learned. Immediate *concrete experiences (experiencing)* are the basis for observations and *reflections*. These reflections are assimilated and distilled into *abstract concepts (thinking)* from which new implications for action can be drawn. These implications can be *actively tested* and serve as guides in creating new experiences (See Figure 1).

We will show how the experiential learning model can be used to approach learning in a deliberate way, increasing learning effectiveness by understanding how we learn from our experiences and our own unique style of learning. Deliberate strategies and practices for mastering the process of learning from experience will be outlined. Our approach to deliberate experiential learning draws on theories in three areas; meta-cognition,[7] mindfulness[8] and studies of expert learning called deliberate practice.[9]

Figure 1 The
Experiential Learning
Cycle

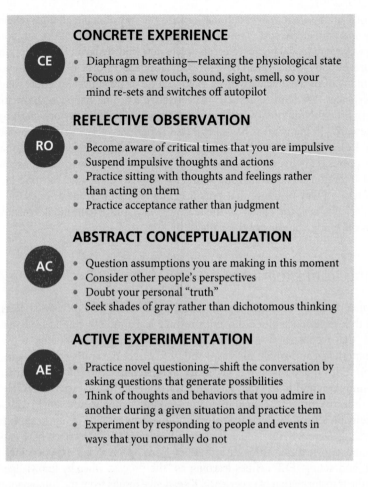

CONCRETE EXPERIENCE

CE
- Diaphragm breathing—relaxing the physiological state
- Focus on a new touch, sound, sight, smell, so your mind re-sets and switches off autopilot

REFLECTIVE OBSERVATION

RO
- Become aware of critical times that you are impulsive
- Suspend impulsive thoughts and actions
- Practice sitting with thoughts and feelings rather than acting on them
- Practice acceptance rather than judgment

ABSTRACT CONCEPTUALIZATION

AC
- Question assumptions you are making in this moment
- Consider other people's perspectives
- Doubt your personal "truth"
- Seek shades of gray rather than dichotomous thinking

ACTIVE EXPERIMENTATION

AE
- Practice novel questioning—shift the conversation by asking questions that generate possibilities
- Think of thoughts and behaviors that you admire in another during a given situation and practice them
- Experiment by responding to people and events in ways that you normally do not

Meta-cognition—Understanding Yourself as a Learner

In the late 1970s, Flavell introduced the concept of meta-cognition.[10] He divided meta-cognitive knowledge into three sub-categories: 1) knowledge of person variables refers to general knowledge about how human beings learn and process information, as well as individual knowledge of one's own learning processes, 2) task variables include knowledge about the nature of the task and what it will require of the individual, 3) knowledge about strategy variables include knowledge about ways to improve learning as well as conditional knowledge about when and where it is appropriate to use such strategies.

By using the experiential learning model, learners can better understand the learning process, themselves as learners and the appropriate use of learning strategies based on the learning task and environment. When individuals engaged in the process of learning by reflective monitoring of the learning process they are going through, they can begin to understand important aspects of learning: how they move through each stage of the learning cycle, the way their unique learning style fits with how they are being taught, and the learning demands of what is being taught. This comparison results in strategies for action that can be applied in their ongoing learning process.

Develop a Learning Identity

A key aspect of learning is a person's beliefs about themselves, particularly their views about their ability to learn. At the extreme, if a person does not believe that they can learn, they won't. Learning requires conscious attention, effort, and "time on task". These activities are a waste of time to someone who does not believe that they have the ability to learn. On the other hand, there are many successful individuals who attribute their achievements to a learning attitude. Oprah Winfrey for example has said, "I am a woman in process. I'm just trying like everybody else. I try to take every conflict, every experience, and learn from it. Life is never dull."

One's self-identity is deeply held. One is likely to defend against experiences that contradict this identity. For the vast majority of us our self-identity is a mix of fixed and learning beliefs. We may feel that we are good at learning some things like sports and not good at others like mathematics. Every success or failure can trigger a reassessment of one's learning ability. Figure 2 depicts one's self-identity as balancing characteristics that reinforce a fixed self and a learning self. Fixed-self factors threatened by the successes of others shift the balance to the fixed self. Factors associated with the learning self tip the balance toward becoming a learner.

In Figure 2 we suggest several practical steps for developing a positive meta-cognitive learning identity.

Trust your experience. Place experience at the center of your learning process, making it the focal point of your choices and decisions. This does not mean that you shouldn't learn from experts or the experience of others since this advice is also part of your experience. The key is to own your choices and validate them in your experience. When you do this you take charge of your learning and your life.

Trust the learning process. Avoid an excessive focus on the outcomes of immediate performance and focus instead on the longer term recursive process of learning by

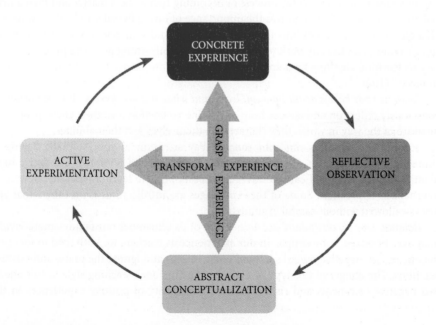

Figure 2 Becoming a Learner

tracking your performance progress over time. Rarely is a single performance test a matter of life and death, and to treat it as such only reinforces a fixed identity. Every performance is an occasion for learning and improvement in future performances.

Redefine your relationship to failure. No one likes to fail but failure is an inevitable part of doing something new. Thomas Edison provided a role model for the learning response to failure when he said "Failure is the most important ingredient for success." James Dyson, the inventor of the Dyson vacuum cleaner and founder of Dyson, Inc, sees Edison as a role model saying he "...achieved great success through repeated failure. His 10,000 failures pale in comparison to his 1093 U.S. patents. Each one of Edison's inventions, from the Dictaphone to the light bulb came from his inability to give up" (28).[11]

Failures can also help focus your priorities and life path on your talents and strengths. In her commencement address to the 2008 graduates of Harvard University, J. K. Rowling described the low period in her life after graduation, which was marked by failure on every front, and talked about its benefits as leaving her with a new sense of focus on the only type of work that was important to her. She reflected in her address that if she had not failed, that she never would have had the energy and motivation to spend her time writing, an area where she truly belonged. Failure, she found, created a sense of freedom to focus on her area of expertise.[12]

Let go of strong emotional responses in order to learn from failure. Failures, losses, and mistakes provoke inevitable emotional responses. Yet it is important to learn to regulate emotional reactions that block learning and feed into a fixed identity. Golfers who slam their club and curse themselves and the game after a bad shot lose the opportunity to coolly analyze their mistake and plan for corrections on the next hole. An effective way to deal with the emotions that follow judging oneself a failure is to breathe calmly and intentionally while accepting the current moment as it is. This enables a clearer mind with which to move forward.

Risk losing. Joel Waitzkin in *The art of learning* provides a handbook of his metacognitive learning based on his process of becoming first a chess master and then a martial arts champion. He emphasizes the importance of losing in order to learn how to win. "If a big, strong guy comes into a martial arts studio and someone pushes him, he wants to resist and push the guy back to prove that he is a big strong guy. The problem is that he isn't learning anything by doing this. In order to grow, he needs to give up his current mindset." (107).[13]

Reassess your beliefs about how you learn and what you are good at. It is important to consciously reflect on and choose how you define yourself as a learner. Often people are unaware of the way in which they characterize themselves and their abilities.

Monitor the messages you send yourself. Pay attention to your self-talk. Saying to yourself, "I am stupid." or, "I am no good at ..." matters and reinforces a negative fixed identity; just as saying, "I can do this" reinforces a positive learning identity. Beware of internalized oppression. Some of these messages are introjections from others that you have swallowed without careful examination.

Balance your success/failure accounts. Most of us remember our failures more vividly than our successes. For example, in our experience as teachers we both tend to focus on the one or two negative remarks in our course ratings and ignore the praise and positive reactions. The danger of this type of focus is adjusting one's teaching style to suit one or two negative comments and risking losing the majority of positive experiences in the room. A deeper danger is that such a focus will negatively shape longer-term thoughts and behaviors about oneself.[14] Sometimes it is useful to make an inventory of learning strengths and successes to balance your accounts.

Learning style

In addition to believing in ourselves as learners, it is also important to understand how it is that we learn best, our learning style. An understanding of one's unique learning preferences and capabilities, and the match between these and the demands of learning tasks, can increase learning effectiveness. It can suggest why performance is not optimal and suggest strategies for improvement, as well as help explain why some topics and courses are interesting and others are painful. It can also help explain why some develop a non-learning self-identity. Our most gratifying experiences in teaching individuals about their learning style have been when they come up and say, "My whole life I thought I was stupid because I didn't do well in school. Now I realize that it is just because I learn in a different way than schools teach."

One way to gain meta-cognitive understanding of how we learn is to take the Kolb Learning Style Inventory (KLSI). Those who use the KLSI[15] to assess their learning style often decide that they wish to develop their capacity to engage in one or more of the four learning modes, experiencing (CE), reflecting (RO), thinking (AC) and acting (AE). In some cases this is based on a desire to develop a weak mode in their learning style. In others it may be to increase capability in a mode that is particularly important for their learning tasks. Because of the dialectic relationships among the learning modes, containing the inhibiting effects of opposing learning modes can be as effective in getting into a mode as actively trying to express it. Overall learning effectiveness is improved when individuals are highly skilled in engaging all four modes of the learning cycle.

Mindful Experiential Learning

Mindfulness is one special form of meta-cognition that is especially effective for enhancing learning from experience. Mindfulness is an age old set of practices used to overcome the tendency to "sleep walk" automatically through our lives. In recent times, these practices have been accepted into mainstream psychology, social psychology, and medicine. Empirical studies are now finding statistical support for what many have known for two millennia: that practicing mindfulness enhances mental and physical health, creativity, and contextual learning.

William James, the originator of the theory of experience on which ELT is based, stated, "no state once gone can recur and be identical with what it was before" (155).[16] The mind often neglects the rich context available for observation. Instead, it automatically labels stimuli based on limited exposure and moves on to the next stimulus to under-observe. Labeling experiences as fun, boring, sad, happy, urgent, relaxed, and so on are also often based in automatically categorizing experience, rather than being fully present in the unique context of every moment. For James, everything begins and ends in the continuous flux and flow of experience. This emphasis on immediate direct sensual experience is exactly the focus of the here and now experience that characterizes mindfulness.

James emphasized the importance of attention, as he noted—"My experience is what I agree to attend to." (403).[17] This also is a central element of mindfulness.

The practices of mindfulness are aimed at helping the individual: 1) focus on present and direct experience, 2) be intentionally aware and attentive, and 3) accept life as an emergent process of change. Our research on mindfulness and experiential learning[18] suggests that the practice of mindfulness can help individuals learn from experience by enhancing presence and intentional attention.

A review of the mindfulness literature defines presence, intense, and present-moment consciousness, as the "active ingredient" in mindfulness practices in every tradition.[19] Attending to the present moment serves to quiet the mind; reducing automatic, habitual patterns of thinking and responding. Presence enhances Concrete Experience and allows the learning cycle to begin. In a sense, we cannot learn from experience if we do not first *have* an experience, and often habitual automatic processes do not allow direst experiencing in the moment to occur.

Intentional attention—the process of being aware about what we are attending to—is, as James says—the process that creates our experience. Mindfulness becomes important when we consider *how* we choose to process and learn from the events in our lives. By intentionally guiding the learning process and paying attention to how we are going through the phases of the learning cycle, we make ourselves through learning. How and what we learn determines the way we process the possibilities of each new emerging experience, which in turn determines the range of choices and decisions we see. The choices and decisions we make to some extent determine the events we live through, and these events influence our future choices. Thus, we create ourselves through the choices of the actual occasions we live through. For many, this learning style choice is relatively unconscious, an auto-pilot program for learning. Mindfulness can put the control of our learning and our life back in our hands.

Deliberate Practice—Becoming an Expert Learner

We all know that learning involves repeated practice. However, time spent practicing does not necessarily lead to learning and improved performance. Going to the practice range and hitting bucket after bucket of balls doesn't necessarily improve your game, and in fact, may make it worse by ingraining bad habits. Expert performance research teaches a great deal about learning from practice.[20] The good news from this work is that greatness, for the most part, is not a function of innate talent; it is learned from experience. The not-so-good news is that it involves long-term commitment (10 years or 10,000 hours for many top experts) and a particular kind of practice that is hard work, called deliberate practice.

The basic techniques of deliberate practice are useful for improving our ability to learn from experience. Essentially deliberate practice involves intense, concentrated, repeated performance that is compared against an ideal or "correct" model of the performance. It requires feedback that compares the actual performance against the ideal to identify "errors" that are corrected in subsequent performance attempts. In this sense, deliberate practice can be seen as mindful, experiential learning—focused reflection on a concrete performance experience that is analyzed against a meta-cognitive ideal model to improve future action in a recurring cycle of learning. Learning relationships can be of great help in deliberate practice by providing expert models, feedback, and support for the focused effort required.

We have created a practical model (Figure 3) from meta-cognition mindfulness and deliberate practice work to identify practices that can be used to develop the capacity to engage in one or more of the four modes of the learning cycle. The specific mindfulness practices can improve one's ability to fully engage specific experiential learning modes and more fully engage the total process of learning from experience. Keep in mind that the key to being deliberate when learning is intentionality, as opposed to being on auto-pilot in any of the phases.

Conclusion

Understanding yourself as a learner can help you cultivate deliberate experiential learning practices to become more intentional about how you think and behave in a given learning environment. In order to be more aware of learning processes, learn-

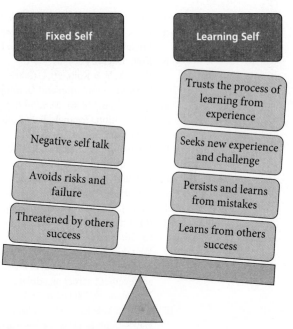

Figure 3 Deliberate Experiential Learning Practices
Source: Yeganeh and Kolb, 2009.

ers must find unique ways to engage in routines of momentary awareness. Regular practices can help create anchor points for learners to check in on thoughts and behaviors and assess the degree to which they are being intentional in learning situations. Finally, we encourage learners not to be discouraged when facing difficulty in starting a deliberate experiential learning practice. It may be best to try one or two specific learning practices, and go from there. Anything more can be overwhelming and may actually inhibit progress. As techniques are mastered, additional methods can be added. In this reading, we have provided deliberate experiential learning practices that can improve the quality of learning in the four modes of experiential learning. These can be adapted to coaching processes, employee development programs, dialogue sessions, cultivating emotional intelligence, daily meeting practices, and much more. We have presented new research and practical approaches to deliberate experiential learning in organizations. We encourage others to develop innovative ways to deliberate experiential learning in organizations and to share the results through articles and presentations so that one day it becomes the norm. We believe it is needed more now than ever before.

Endnotes

1. Boyatzis, Cowen, & Kolb, D. A. (1991). Reflections on curriculum innovations in higher education: The new Weatherhead MBA program. In R. Sims and S. Sims (Eds). *Managing institutions of higher education in the 21st Century.* Westwood, CT: Greenwood Press.
2. Bargh, J. A., & Chartrand, T. L. (1999). The unbearable automaticity of being. *American Psychologist, 54*(7), 462–479.
3. Dewey, J. (1944). *Democracy and Education.* NY: Free Press.

4. Dewey, J. (1910). *How we think.* Boston, MA: D.C. Heath.

5. Kolb, D. (1984). *Experiential learning: Experience as the source of learning and development.* Englewood Cliffs, N.J.: Prentice Hall.

6. Kolb, D. (1984).

7. Kolb, A. Y. & Kolb, D. A. (2009). The learning way: Méta-cognitive aspects of experiential learning. Simulation and Gaming: An Interdisciplinary Journal. 40(3): 297-327.

8. Yeganeh, B. (2006). *Mindful Experiential Learning.* Case Western Reserve University Dissertation. Yeganeh, B. & Kolb, D. A. (2009). Mindfulness and experiential learning. *OD Practitioner* 41(3): 8–14.

9. Ericsson K. A., Krampe, R. T., & Tesch-Römer, C. (1993). The role of deliberate practice in the acquisition of expert performance. *Psychological Review* 100: 363–406.

10. Flavell, J. H. (1979). Meta-cognition and cognitive monitoring. *American Psychologist.* 34(10): 906–911.

11. Yang, J. (2008). My latest product launch was a failure. How do I move on? *Fortune* July 7, 28.

12. Rowling, J. K. (2008). A stripping away of the inessential. *Harvard Magazine.* July–August, 55–56.

13. Waitzkin, J. (2007). *The art of learning: A journey in the pursuit of excellence.* N.Y.: Free Press.

14. Blackwell, Trzesniewski, & Dweck. (2007). Implicit theories of intelligence predict achievement across an adolescent transition: A longitudinal study and an intervention. *Child Development.* 78(1):246-263.

15. Kolb, A. Y. & Kolb, D. A. (2011). The Kolb Learning Style Inventory-Version 4.0 Boston, MA: Hay Resources Direct. www.learningfromexperience.com

16. James, W. (1890). The Principles of Psychology. New York: Henry Holt and Company.

17. James, W. (1890).

18. Yeganeh, B. (2006).

19. Lyddy, C. J. (2010). Mindfulness' active ingredient: The state of presence. CWRU Department of Organizational Behavior Working Paper.

20. Baron, R. A. & Henry, R. A. (2010). How entrepreneurs acquire the capacity to excel: Insights from research on expert performance. *Strategic Entrepreneurship Journal.* 4: 49–65. Ericsson K. A. (2006). The influence of experience and deliberate practice on the development of superior expert performance. In *The Cambridge Handbook of Expertise and Expert Performance*, Ericsson KA, Charness N, Hoffman R, Feltovich J (Eds.). Cambridge University Press: New York; 683–703. Ericsson, K. A. & Charness, L. (1994). Expert performance: Its structure and acquisition. *American Psychologist, 49*(8): 725–747. Ericsson K. A., Krampe, R. T., & Tesch-Römer, C. (1993).

Learning-Directed Leadership in a Changing World

Anna B. Kayes
Stevenson University

D. Christopher Kayes
The George Washington University

This article introduces and explains how learning-directed leadership provides a unique approach to leadership based on how leaders learn and facilitate learning in others. Learning directed leadership describes how leaders manage and make sense of complex, dynamic, and novel organizational situations. This article emphasizes the importance of learning as the basis for leadership. Learning is the basis for leading change and continuous improvement in organizations and it is among the top competencies that predict effective leadership. We provide two examples of learning directed leadership—a process change in a large group of hospitals that resulted in preventing nearly 2,000 infections, and a consulting firm where learning competencies were highly related to success.

Novel, complex, and dynamic organizations present a unique challenge to leaders. Increasing amounts of information and the demands of technology create a situation where data is readily available, but where knowledge is difficult to create. The extensive amount of information available to leaders has been referred to as "big data" and the consequence that result when leaders try to manage the information has been called "data exhaustion."[1] Leaders face a situation where an overdependence on technology runs rampant, increasing the ease of access and quantity of information, without the ability to make sense of it. Compounding the problem of access and quantity of information, is the rapid rate of disruptive change in organizations. For example, a 2007 study sponsored by the American Management Association reported that 82 percent of organizations surveyed thought the pace of change had increased in the previous five years, and that at least one major disruptive change had occurred that had affected their organization in the last year.[2]

Table 1 provides a quick list of the demands faced by today's leaders, based on the work of James Reason, a scholar who studies learning and failure in high-risk situations.[3] Where James Reason may have been concerned with high-risk organizational situations, this list describes characteristics of almost any organization today. In fact, contemporary leaders in business organizations share many of the same challenges faced by high-stress, and high-consequence positions such as pilots, surgery teams, and military quick reaction forces.

Table 1   Characteristics of a Complex Leadership Environment

Characteristic	Definition
An uncertain, dynamic environment	Change is rapid, and few situational variables are absolutely clear.
Many different sources of information	Diversity of data exists, both internal and external in the workplace; employees are constantly connected through technology to rapidly changing information.
Shifting, ill-defined, or competing goals	Goals change rapidly, and there is little agreement about task or process clarity and desired outcomes. Goals may conflict with other priorities and objectives even within the same organization.
Need to respond to rapidly changing situation	Situational variables change rapidly and must be accurately identified and addressed.
High stakes	Consequences are great for any errors.
Multiple people with different priorities and agendas	Purposes of individuals differ from that of the group. Various stakeholders internal and external to the organization hold onto competing priorities and agendas.

Source: Based on Reason, 1995.

The Shift from Traditional to Learning-Directed Leadership

It is no wonder that leaders who operate in an environment with one or more of these characteristics require learning-directed leadership. Because, operating in this volatile context requires leadership with the ability to adapt, make sense of experiences, and respond appropriately. It is important to note that learning directed leadership describes a process, not a formal position. When referring to 'leaders', we are not referencing managers in organizations, although managers may be leaders. *We advocate that anyone in an organization has the capacity to exercise leadership, and in particular has the capacity to exercise learning directed leadership.*

Learning directed leadership shifts the focus of how leaders operate, and the skills required to do so. Traditional approaches to leadership focus on power, influence, and position as the sources of leadership. Where these are important factors, today they prove less important in a complex and dynamic world where disruptive change is considered normal, and leadership requires quick adaptation, and sensemaking. Sensemaking is where meaning is made out of people's experiences. That is, having experience is not enough, it is the skill to reflect on the experience and make sense out of the experience in the context of a rapidly changing situation that is important. Learning results from the reflection on the experience, not simply the experience itself. Leaders working in the world of "big data" engage learning in addition to traditional leadership tools to institute change. Knowledge rather than only power, coordination rather than just influence tactics, and expertise rather than position—these are the shifts taking place in leadership. Whereas, traditional forms of power are tied to one's position within an organization or access to organizational resources, learning-directed leaders see continual learning as their primary advantage, not the hoarding of power and resources. At their core, learning-directed leaders work to be open to new information, stand ready to revise past assessments of a situation, cultivate knowledge, and build new expertise along the way.[4]

Leadership requires a shift in understanding about how leaders view the nature of problems, how problems are solved, and who solves the problems. The process of learning directed leadership starts with recognizing the nature of a problem and distinguishing between ill-structured and well-structured problems. Well-structured problems require time, patience, and persistence. Given enough time and resources, leaders can always solve well-structured problems. An example of a well-structured problem is reducing a budget by 15 percent. On the other hand, determining a new strategic direction in a fast-changing marketplace is an ill-structured problem. In addition, with an ill-structured problem, there might not be one solution and the solution that is adopted, might need to be updated rapidly or even changed altogether once new information is obtained. Tackling an ill-structured problem is not the work of just one person who sits at the top of the organizational hierarchy, but rather requires the involvement of many individuals embedded throughout the organization.

Traditional leaders often focus their time and attention on well-structured problems. Learning-directed leaders, on the other hand, are equipped to solve ill-structured problems. No matter how much time, persistence, and patience a leader invests, the problem and even the cause of the problem can never be fully understood, and people will never fully agree on one right decision. In fact, there is not always a single best solution for an ill-structured problem. Figure 1 represents the shift in thinking required for a leader to be successful in this context. The shift, although difficult, is essential for leading, as an example from the medical profession illustrates.

Eliminating Infections in Critical Care Medicine

Thousands of central line catheters are inserted or replaced around the country each day. Central line catheters serve several functions. They dispense medications or fluids and can be used to measure blood volume. In the most trying cases, a central line catheter

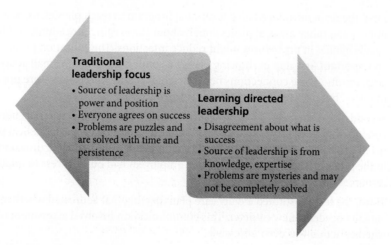

Figure 1 Moving from Traditional to Learning-Directed Leadership

can save a life or limit pain after it is inserted into veins in the neck, groin, or chest. Inserting one of these devices is a routine medical procedure. Unfortunately, every year, an estimated 80,000 patients contract an infection that could have been avoided. Many patients, sadly, estimated between 30,000 and 50,000, die as a result of these infections.[5]

At first glance, the procedures involved in changing a central line catheter appear simple and routine. After all, this is a procedure that is performed thousands of times each day in hospitals. But learning to *change an existing procedure* is much more difficult. Improving the process of inserting or changing central line catheters has proven particularly challenging over the years. Learning to change a well-established procedure, like the process of changing central line catheters, involves monitoring hundreds of pieces of information, complex coordination, and overcoming deeply ingrained cultural barriers.[6]

One of the reasons that central line catheters lead to so many problems is the very nature of the process itself—and the limitations of human learning. A medical professional may care for hundreds of patients a month, and since the human mind is only capable of remembering a limited amount of data at any one time, keeping track of each and every catheter change, and each task associated with each change will quickly lead to data exhaustion. The mind simply cannot remember whether a particular task was completed with the existing patient or with an earlier patient. Further, many professionals do not have direct access to the correct supplies. Changing a catheter may prove to be a challenge because resources must be obtained from different locations, which requires additional information as to where the right resource is located and available. Adding to the problem, changing and inserting a catheter requires communication and coordination among various professionals.

A team of physicians assembled with the objective of finding a way to improve the way that central line catheters were changed and monitored. This group hoped to lower the injury and death rate of patients who required catheters. The team was led by Dr. Peter Pronovost of the Department of Anesthesiology and Critical Care Medicine at the Johns Hopkins Hospital. The team approached the problem by first assembling and interpreting research from a range of fields. Then they explored the best way to put these practices into action.[7] They began by reviewing prior research on catheter-related infections and related topics. From this research, they identified five practices that showed promise in limiting infection.

- First, the team introduced an educational program to teach physicians, residents, nurses, and other medical professionals about the existing procedures and how small changes in procedures might reduce infections. The education program was an important first step in showing people a connection between small actions and large results. These connections between small actions and results were not always intuitive, but over time, practitioners learned to trust them.

- Second, the team created a central cart that centralized all the materials needed to conduct the procedure with a greater degree of safety. In the past, medical personnel might have to search for the proper equipment, losing valuable time and focus in the process. This step made sure that employees had quick access to quality resources.

- Third, the team instituted a daily care plan meeting that addressed whether patients needed a new catheter. This communication involved assessment of whether action was even necessary.

- Fourth, and most important, the team implemented a checklist procedure, adopted from preflight checklists used by airline flight crews. The process, led by the bedside nurse, ensured proper and safe changing procedures for each new catheter. This process compensated for the data exhaustion effect inherent in such a routine and simple task. The steps on the checklist were clear, concise, concrete, and easy for everyone to understand their meaning. For example, when inserting a catheter, the professionals were to wash their hands; clean the patient's skin with a disinfectant; wear a cap and gown, and use a surgical drape; insert the catheter through parts of the body other than the groin; and remove any unnecessary catheters. The checklist ensured that each catheter change was logged and followed, creating a paper trail for each new professional to follow.

- Fifth, the team created a new protocol for enforcing the guidelines. Nurses would be allowed to stop the process if any care provider failed to follow the guidelines as stated on the checklist.

The team achieved a remarkable success rate that garnered international attention. Researchers estimated that, when adopted in 50 intensive care units in Michigan, the procedure might have prevented 2,000 infections, reaching an infection rate near zero.[8] The new procedure proved so successful, statistically it was more effective than giving the patients antibiotics. Learning occurred because the checklist process facilitated people's behavioral change by improving coordination. The common checklist improved how individuals communicated and tracked patient activity and increased the capacity of healthcare workers to process and monitor large amounts of data by creating a consistent process of documentation. The success of the central line catheter change initiative sheds light on five ways that learning directed leadership can help manage aspects of big data and data exhaustion.

Increasing Awareness

An organization wide effort increased awareness of a system wide problem. Increasing people's awareness of a system wide problem meant that people within the organization came to understand that there was a need to learn that the organization in its current state did not have the right process in place. When a new process was introduced, the new process in turn improved the capacity of individuals to sift through, and monitor large amounts of data. They did so by creating a consistent process of documentation. A simple checklist improved effectiveness, showing that even routine processes can present an opportunity for learning.

Learning from Past Experience

One reason that the intervention proved so successful was that it relied on a comprehensive review of existing knowledge. The researchers did not start from scratch, designing their own studies of the problem. Rather, they sifted through years of studies, in diverse fields from medicine to flight crew operations. They did not limit their learning from solutions only proposed from medical journals, they sought out knowledge from many different areas. They identified ways to put these research findings into action, and make the abstract ideas implementable. But they went further by seeking out best practices and identified what practices were cursory and which were absolutely central to success.

Much of the success could be attributed to the fact that these techniques had been used before, and only the most successful processes were adopted.

Facilitating Behavior Change

Learning facilitates behavioral change by improving coordination. The common checklist improved how individuals communicated and tracked patient activity and care. Those responsible for changing the catheters were no longer performing the task alone, but were now changing the catheters in concert with others in the organization. The checklist created a common log that was accessed by all the health care professionals providing care for the patient. The greater coordination created what researchers refer to as transactive memory—a process where learning and memory and behavior is coordinated across individuals.[9] Transactive memory has three characteristics.

First, team members believe in the *credibility* of the information shared by other members, effectively *coordinating* actions. Second, coordination means that information moves across and between individuals in a way that contributes to the team's overall performance. The catheter-safety program encourages coordination by helping teams establish a common set of procedures that guide action. Third, the process improves coordination among a group of *specialized* professionals. Organizations manage complexity by distributing labor across different groups through the organization. Nurses, physicians, and residents each perform a specific duty. This division of labor helps the organization but creates challenges for coordination. Learning occurs when team members understand, respect, and utilize the unique expertise of these diverse roles. The catheter safety program provides evidence that when learning becomes a daily practice, it improves performance.

Improving Judgment

In addition to creating awareness, learning from past experience, and making incremental changes to behavior, lessons from catheter safety checklists point to the importance of improving professional judgment. The checklist implementation process marks an important shift from institutionalizing organization-wide policies to allowing experienced professionals to exercise judgment. For example, the development and implementation of a checklist is not abstract but part of the daily routine of professionals. For certain, implementation requires a coordinated effort at all levels of the organization, including strong support from management, but ultimately, the change occurs at the most direct levels of patient care, not policy enacted from above in the hierarchy. The program success results from the learning that occurs as professionals exercise autonomy and judgment unencumbered by overly burdensome institutional rules.

The link among professional judgment, learning, and improving professional judgment is important. In a 1986 study, Vimla Patel and his colleagues found that experienced physicians saw medical situations in a more holistic and complete way than did residents. Residents had limited professional judgment compared with experienced physicians. In other words, physicians relied on a greater source of data, including patient histories and lifestyle data to make a diagnosis. In non-routine cases, experts rely on "flexible reasoning" to generate alternatives, revise hypotheses, and develop meaningful courses of action. Judgment and similarly, learning, require adapting, looking at a broad range of information, challenging, and understanding context.[10]

Breaking Down Hierarchy

The cornerstone of the catheter-safety program can be found in the introduction and use of a common checklist. However, from a learning standpoint, the checklist itself serves simply to facilitate a larger learning process that occurs. The process facilitates the break-down of traditional organizational and professional hierarchies. The checklist requires that every person involved in the catheter process use the checklist—title, positional power, and hierarchy do not matter as much as the checklist process matters.

Medicine's adoption of checklists builds on a legacy established by commercial pilots. Studies of numerous air tragedies and near misses have revealed that all too often, dysfunctional power dynamics among the flight crews contributed to the disaster. Overly authoritarian cockpit captains ignored the insights and warnings of co-pilots, leading to a crash or near miss. The checklist serves to neutralize traditional forms of power, such as rank or profession, because authority no longer rests in the rank of individuals, but in their knowledge, and this paves the way for learning. Nurses and residents gain the authority to stop a procedure if it doesn't conform to guidelines. They do not have to wait for the doctor in charge to point out an error, anyone is empowered to point out an error.

Each of these five processes underscores the importance of learning in improving organizational effectiveness. The initial experiment for catheter safety has been adopted by other hospitals around the United States. It stands as a remarkable example of learning in organizations, and how learning and adaptation is important for leaders. We can't emphasize enough that the learning from such an effort occurs on two levels. The first level is the learning that occurs from engaging in the process of building the procedure. The second level of learning occurs as an outcome of the continued engagement in the process itself. The catheter safety program provides a powerful example of how leaders rely on learning to achieve results. Learning directed leadership requires developing the skills necessary to learn and infuse learning in others.

Learning-Directed Leadership in Consulting Firms

Leaders in a variety of industries realize the benefits of learning directed leadership.[11] One study involved a professional services firm with more than 3,000 partners world-wide. The study analyzed the scores of about 30 of the organization's top partners using a 360-degree feedback process where peers, subordinates, and supervisor ranked each partner. A 360-degree feedback process asks specific stakeholders that know the top part-ner, to provide specific reactions on strengths and weaknesses of the skills of the partner. The feedback forms a complete circle based on the hierarchy relative to the partner—supervisor, peers, subordinates. Each partner also completed the survey which measured traditional leadership skills as well as skills associated with learning. Two of the most highly correlated metrics were the partner's scores on valuing learning and facilitating learning in others. In other words, there was a strong relationship between the top per-forming partners on the skills of valuing learning and facilitating learning in others and their performance. The more a senior partner demonstrated these learning competen-cies, the more successful they became. Leaders in all professions, not just the medical and consulting professions require learning in order to meet the demands placed on them in the world of big data.

Conclusion

Learning directed leadership is essential for leading in today's complex, novel, and dynamic organizational environment. Learning directed leadership puts learning, not performance alone, at the center of the leader's world. Learning requires a variety of skills and starts with understanding the demands of ill-structured problems. Learning directed leadership can lead to significant improvements in organizational functioning by increasing awareness of opportunities for organizational change and coordination, improving judgment, and overall lowering the burden brought about by the complex, dynamic, and novel environment.

Endnotes

1. *The Economist,* (2010). "Data, data everywhere. A special report on managing information," February 27.
2. American Management Association. (2007). *How to build a high performance organization.*
3. Reason, J. (1995). Safety in the operating theatre—Part 2: Human error and organizational failure, *Current Anesthesia and Critical Care, 6.*
4. Mills, T. M. (1967). *The Sociology of Small Groups.* Prentice-Hall.
5. Landro, L. (2010). Building team spirit: Nurses hesitate to challenge doctors even when doctors are ordering the wrong drug or operating on the wrong limb, *Wall Street Journal Online,* February 16.
6. Kayes, A., & Kayes, D. C. (2011). *The learning advantage: Six practices of learning-directed leadership.* Palgrave Macmillan.
7. Pronovost, P., & Vohr, E. (2010). *Safe patients, smart hospitals: How one doctor's checklist can help us change health care from the inside out.* Hudson Street Press.
8. Landro, 2010.
9. Wegner, T. G., & Wegner, D. M. (1995). "Transactive memory," in A. S. R. Manstead & M. Hewstone (Eds.). The Blackwell Encyclopedia of Social Psychology, Blackwell.
10. Patel, V. L., Groen, G. J., & Frederiksen, C. H. (1986). Differences between students and physicians in memory for clinical cases, *Medical Education, 20.*
11. Boyatzis, R. E. (2006). Using tipping points of emotional intelligence and cognitive competencies to predict financial performance of leaders, *Psicothema, 18.*

4 Perception

Topic Summary Learning Objectives

1. Recognize the role of perception in shaping people's beliefs and behavior.

2. Explain what factors impact individual perception.

3. Describe some common biases and problems with perception.

4. Explore levels of attribution.

5. Outline the process of critical reflection to minimize perceptual errors.

6. Apply concepts of perception to organizations.

Key Terms

attribution, p. 121

bias blind spot, p. 122

consensus, p. 122

consistency, p. 122

critical reflection, p. 123

distinctiveness, p. 122

halo effect, p. 121

heuristics, p. 118

hindsight bias, p. 119

horns effect, p. 121

Implicit Associations Test (IAT), p. 120

in-group favoritism, p. 121

intergroup level attribution, p. 121

interpersonal level attribution, p. 121

intrapersonal level attribution, p. 121

novelty, p. 118

organizational level attribution p. 121

perception, p. 118

selective perception, p. 119

self-fulfilling prophecy, p. 121

self-serving bias, p. 122

stereotype, p. 120

Introduction to Perception

Perception is the process of taking in, interpreting, and taking actions based on information that is obtained from the environment. Perceptions are important because they determine what constitutes reality for individuals—information is filtered through frameworks based upon current knowledge and past experience. These frameworks become reality.[1] This section summarizes perception and its origins. It considers factors that help to shape what is perceived and examines limitations brought about by the process of perception. Figure 4.1 illustrates a framework of perceptions and biases reviewed in this topic summary.

1 Recognize the role of perception in shaping people's beliefs and behavior.

What Is Perception?

Perception involves selecting a subset of sensory information. By selecting and processing only a limited amount of information, what is perceived as reality also becomes limited. Individuals differ in how they filter information, what information they pay attention to and how they prioritize the significance of information, thus two people can interpret the same situation differently.[2] Perception is not to be confused with a heuristic. **Heuristics** are rules by which people make decisions, whereas perception is the process of taking in and acting on raw data in an environment. Heuristics are closely related to perceptions because both involve relying on incomplete information that leads to incomplete judgments and actions. A key difference between heuristics and perceptions lies in their underlying purpose. In rational and behavioral decision-making processes, heuristics are always limiting. Heuristics may describe how a manager makes less than optimal decisions. Perceptions, on the other hand, are often viewed as a normal consequence of making decisions in the face of a complex environment. Heuristics and perceptions also emerge from distinct disciplines. The study of heuristics focuses primarily on making economic based decisions—essentially optimizing economic value and yielding the highest profit.[3] The study of perceptions, on the other hand, emerges from psychology and sociology and is generally concerned with behavior—with little or no consideration for the economic value of that behavior. A better understanding, however, of what factors influence perception and common limitations of perception will help improve decision- making processes in organizations.

2 Explain what factors impact individual perception.

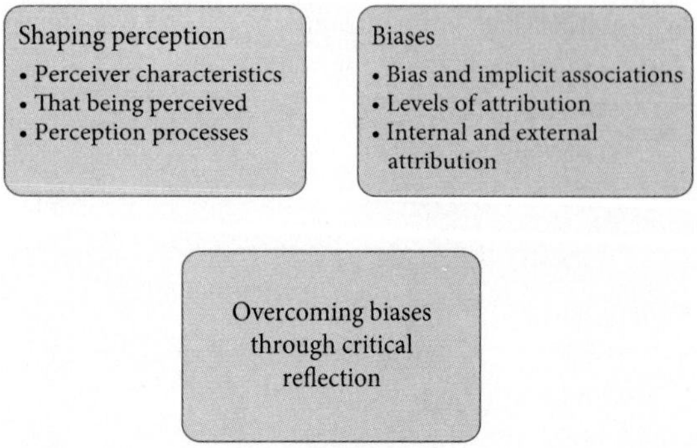

Shaping perception
- Perceiver characteristics
- That being perceived
- Perception processes

Biases
- Bias and implicit associations
- Levels of attribution
- Internal and external attribution

Overcoming biases
through critical
reflection

Figure 4.1 Summary Framework of Perceptions and Biases

Where Does It Come From?

Perception begins with the particular characteristics of the perceiver. Experience, knowledge base, values, emotions, motivation, and even personality of the perceiver shape what information is recognized and how that information is prioritized, organized, interpreted, and acted upon.

That Being Perceived

Perception is also based upon what is being perceived. Novelty and the environmental context play a part in perception. **Novelty** describes what is new or different to us—for example, when you meet someone for the first time. Researchers have found that you make judgments about a person's trustworthiness, competence, aggressiveness, and likability within the first tenth of a second.[4] These 'first impressions' are astonishingly reliable in predicting how people will feel about each other months later. Not only is perception shaped by this first encounter, the initial perception shapes lasting perception too. Another factor shaping perception is distinctiveness. When information is different, it is more likely to be noticed. For example, if someone is dressed casually in a formal office, or an argument in a meeting is very intense, the perceiver is more likely to take notice. Size also plays a role in perception, as a larger-sized object is more likely to be noticed. The large office of a colleague, for example, would stand out. The nature of the environment, whether something occurs at work or a social setting also impacts perception. Imagine someone approaches you and asks you out on a date. You would perceive this action quite differently if it occurred in your boss's office than if it occurred at your local coffee shop.

The Process of Perception

The process by which people perceive has limitations. So much information and stimuli exist in your environment that you cannot possibly recognize and sort through it all. In order to overcome this limitation, people select and retrieve small bits of information. The information is then organized and interpreted. People then make sense of the information by identifying or creating patterns, even when no actual pattern exists. For example, you might notice that meetings tend to run longer on Mondays when it rains, but you fail to account for all the meetings that run longer on other days when it is sunny. The limitations that occur during the process of perception lead to common biases.

Common Limitations and Biases

3 Describe some common biases and problems with perception.

Selective perception describes the process where information and its recall becomes consistent with people's values and experiences while information that disconfirms people values and experience is ignored.[5] Selective perception explains how people experience and remember differently. Selective perception highlights individual differences in the perception process. Early studies of selective perception identified biases in perception of fault in penalties at a Dartmouth and Princeton football game. After a football game, where both Dartmouth and Princeton racked up a number of penalties, two researchers interviewed students at both schools. Interestingly, students at Dartmouth overwhelmingly remembered instances from the game where Princeton players committed penalties, whereas students from Princeton remembered Dartmouth's violations.[6] In another example of selective perception, people in general report that media coverage of their preferred presidential candidate is hostile and biased while not perceiving the same level of hostility and bias coverage of the opposing candidate.

A specific instance of selective perception is hindsight bias. **Hindsight bias** occurs when an individual perceives that the likelihood of an event has increased after the fact, or in hindsight. After an event has occurred, people may selectively perceive the outcome was inevitable, by exaggerating factors that would have caused it.[7] People mistakenly believe that they knew the outcome of the event after it has happened by looking at the steps that led up to the event. For example, a friend calls you and tells you he just landed a job from the company that he had interviewed just a few weeks before. You declare and believe that 'I knew it all along!' even through in reality you had expressed doubts earlier in the week that your friend would likely never hear back from that company.

Fancy Collection/SuperStock

Another limitation with perception occurs through stereotyping. A **stereotype** involves determining that someone holds certain traits based on a category. For example, you might engage in stereotyping by assuming that because someone is tall that they must play basketball. Tall people (category) = skilled in basketball (trait people assign to this category). Stereotyping occurs due to limitations in the ability to process data. Because the perceptual process can be flawed by nature, people need to simplify processes by using shortcuts, like pre-sorting people into categories. These categories are often applied to groups that do not fit the default group in society. For example, in China, Chinese men are unlikely to be stereotyped, but in the United States, Chinese men are likely to be stereotyped.[8]

Bias and Implicit Associations

The Implicit Associations Test (IAT) was developed by researchers interested in studying stereotyping by measuring the unconscious attitudes and beliefs that people hold about different groups.[9] The measure of unconscious attitudes and beliefs includes categories such as race, age, gender, attitudes towards gender roles in science and at work, and sexual orientation. The male dominance of musicians in symphonies in the 1970's illustrates unconscious association. In the early 1970s there were few women in major symphony orchestras. There was a widely held belief that men were the most talented of the world's top virtuosos. A number of orchestras experimented with auditions where the musician auditioning for the role sat behind a screen so as not to be visible to the hiring committee. What is interesting is that the auditioning change was not instituted because of the suspicion of gender bias, but was instituted to make sure the hiring committee was not biased in favor of the students of a few prominent teachers and schools. Surprisingly, this change in how auditions were conducted was a leading factor that resulted in a doubling of women hired by major symphony orchestras. It turns out that males on average show no more natural musical talent than women. The phenomenon of male dominance in symphony orchestras was explained by a culture that rewards and encourages male talent, not by natural talent.[10]

Stereotyping also occurs when you show preference to a group that shares the same characteristics as you. Researchers Banaji and Greenwald report that it is surprising that 75 percent of males who take the IAT on the dimension of gender and career associate males with work roles and females with family roles. More shocking is the bias of women, where 80 percent report an association between male with work and female with family. Bias can also exist when a member of one group gives a preference to another member of the same group. A hiring manager who has a child in a Cub Scout troop may give preference in the interview process to an applicant whose child is in the same Cub Scout troop. This **in-group favoritism**, giving preferential treatment to a member of your group, is a form of bias that can be unfair or harmful, even if unintended.[11]

When people form a general impression of someone based on one favorable or less than favorable characteristic, there is the halo or horns effect. The **halo effect** occurs when a person has one positive characteristic and this effects all other perceptions of the person. For example, you meet someone who is friendly (positive), and you determine that he or she must also be a good leader, good with finances, ethical, and a good member of society. The **horns effect** occurs when a person has one negative characteristic and this effects all other perceptions of the person. When interviewing a candidate for a job, a manager discovers that the candidate has sweaty hands. This negative characteristic leads the manager to determine that the person is untrustworthy, unethical, and that he or she would be a poor performer at work.[12]

Another perceptual limitation occurs when someone's expectations influence another person to act consistently with those expectations.[13] This process is called **self-fulfilling prophecy**. For example, consider a professor who expects that everyone in her management class will score high on the final exam and expects the class to contribute wise and interesting comments to class discussions. The expectation forms her behavior towards her students— she might listen intently to student comments and praise and reward their brilliance. This behavior in turn reflects positively on the students and increases the self-confidence of students ("I am brilliant in class!"). In turn, the students become more willing and motivated to contribute their best thoughts. The professor then takes notice of the students' willingness and motivation, which further reinforces her perception that students are wise and interesting during class discussions. As in the case with the professor just described, self-fulfilling prophecy can lead to positive outcomes when the expectation is positive. Researchers Banazi and Greenwald point out that Asian stereotypes may motivate Asian Americans to apply themselves to their academics, earn scholarships, and eventually achieve successful careers in engineering and medicine. This stereotype, then, becomes a self-fulfilling prophecy.

4 Explore levels of attribution.

The process of **attribution** describes how blame or credit is attributed to someone for an event, whether or not they had anything to do with it.[14] For example, the weather reporter on the local news channel might be blamed for bad storms, even when the newscaster did not cause the weather. Viewers attribute the bad storms to the newscaster, even when rationally there is no connection.[15] Attributions can occur at the intrapersonal, interpersonal, intergroup, and even organizational levels as shown in Figure 4.2. At the **intrapersonal level,** you would assign blame or credit to yourself. The **interpersonal level** of attribution occurs when blame or credit is attributed to another person with whom you interact. The **intergroup level** means that you would attribute responsibility to another work group. For example, a sales team might attribute poor sales numbers to the manufacturing team, claiming they are more interested in existing products than in new product development. The **organizational level** describes

Intrapersonal attribution

Interpersonal attribution

Intergroup attribution

Organizational attribution

Figure 4.2 Levels of Attribution

what occurs when members or sub-groups in the organization assign credit or blame to the organization.[16] For example, organizational leaders may attribute poor organizational performance to all the employees in the organization when there may be other factors, such as entry of new competitors. Researchers have even found that managers attribute high or low organizational commitment to employees who opt for flexible work practices.[17] These managers attribute high organizational commitment to employees when they think employees are involved in flexible work practices in order to be more productive, but attribute low organizational commitment to employees when they think employees are using flexible work practices to better accommodate their personal lives.

The process of attribution can be considered along two dimensions—internal and external as shown in Figure 4.3. Blame or credit can be assigned based on internal factors or external factors, where internal factors are within the person's direct control, and external factors occur in the environment.[18] If someone is late for work, you might attribute laziness, an internal factor, to the behavior. On the other hand, if someone is late for work, you might attribute bad traffic, an external factor, to the behavior. Why would people think one person is lazy when they are late and think another person must have been stuck in traffic? The three categories that determine internal or external attribution are: **consensus**, **distinctiveness**, and **consistency**:[19]

- Consensus occurs when behavior is analyzed as being just like other people's behavior in the same situation or different than other people's behavior (e.g., everyone else was late that same day).
- Distinctiveness occurs when behavior is analyzed as often occurring in other situations or seldom occurring in other situations (e.g., someone that is late to work often is late to meetings, late with handing in work, etc.)
- Consistency occurs when the behavior is analyzed as being similar or dissimilar over time (e.g., this person is always late to work).

Figure 4.3 Factors Causing Internal or External Attributions

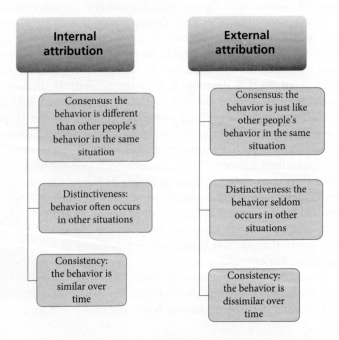

Internal attribution

Consensus: the behavior is different than other people's behavior in the same situation

Distinctiveness: behavior often occurs in other situations

Consistency: the behavior is similar over time

External attribution

Consensus: the behavior is just like other people's behavior in the same situation

Distinctiveness: the behavior seldom occurs in other situations

Consistency: the behavior is dissimilar over time

Self-serving bias is a more specific attribution, where people take credit for personal success but deny responsibility for failure.[20] People are motivated to protect and even enhance their self-esteem through this process. Researchers have even found that employees credit themselves for good performance at work, divorced people blame the ex-spouse for the failed marriage, and athletes often credit themselves when they win.

Another individual bias occurs when people underestimate the role that bias plays in their own decisions, but overestimate the role that bias plays in other people's decisions. This combination is called the **bias blind spot**, and describes the tendency for people to ignore their own bias, while recognizing or exaggerating bias in others.[21]

What Are Some Organizational Applications for Perception?

A variety of individual and organizational applications for perception exist. Bias can play a part in human resource decisions including promotions, performance appraisals,[22] flexible work practices,[23] pay, hiring,[24] and terminations.[25] Perception and attribution may explain why some individuals in the workplace are viewed as 'leaders' and why others are not viewed as 'leaders'. Impression management in the workplace, or actively working at placing ourselves in the most positive light in a given situation, is connected with perceptual processes.

Managing the Process of Perception at Work

Researchers Fooke and Gardner present a process that encourages people in the workplace to think and reflect more deeply on perceptions and how these perceptions may be distorted.[26] The starting point for managing the perceptual process is questioning the assumptions that went into the initial observation. This process is called **critical reflection**, or the analysis of the validity of your assumptions, knowledge, understanding, and beliefs. This process involves four stages. Applying critical reflection to organizational actions encourages the reduction of perceptual distortion and minimizes bias in important human resource decisions such as hiring, performance management, leadership selection, and decision making as described in Table 4.1.

5 Outline the process of critical reflection to minimize perceptual errors.

Table 4.1 Stages of Critical Reflection

Question to Ask Yourself	Description of Stage	Example in Action
What happened and what do I believe caused it?	Identifying the • assumptions or beliefs that led to your thoughts and actions; • underlying values and impact of these values; and • past experiences that impact my beliefs.	A human resource manager is asked to conduct a sexual harassment investigation and he starts with an initial assumption about the supervisor who is accused. He reflects on his personal values of fairness and respect, and his past experiences as a human resource manager making decisions in difficult situations. The employee alleging harassment has perceived that a workplace compliment was inappropriate.

(continued)

Table 4.1 Continued

Question to Ask Yourself	Description of Stage	Example in Action
Why did it happen and what do I and others think caused it to happen?	Analyzing the validity of these beliefs in terms of • how they relate to your experiences; • the experiences of others, such as team members, employees, or other stakeholders; and • your current context. This is where you seek out other points of view that might differ from your own point of view and compare your own conclusions. You would identify perceptions that you formed from fact and perceptions that you formed from assumptions.	He questions his own assumption about the supervisor's behavior by gathering witness statements and conducting a thorough investigation that involves a number of stakeholders, including an interview with the supervisor and the employee who brought the allegation.
What is my new understanding of what happened? What did I learn?	Determining • a new interpretation of an experience; • event; or • decision. There is no one right answer, but reflecting on different possibilities and what was learned from this process.	The human resource manager re-reads his notes from all of the stakeholder interviews and reflects on the importance of training to define what is in fact sexual harassment in the workplace and how to manage and prevent it. He notes that he has learned to be even more detailed in his training workshops to explain different examples of harassment. He understands that the supervisor in question had complimented the shoe selection of one of her employees and this was the cause of the harassment complaint.
What will I do differently now and in the future?	Aligning • Future behaviors and actions with this new set of beliefs. Identify areas that need to be changed and put this into action in the future.	The human resource manager communicates the results of his investigation to the employee alleging harassment and to the supervisor. He then revises the policy manual to better address these issues and develops a training class that includes material on issuing compliments in the workplace.

Conclusion

The process of perception provides important considerations for understanding contemporary organizational behavior. Although limitations and biases in the perceptual process often lead to poor conclusions, these perceptual processes can help people in organizations make decisions. Perceptual shortcuts occur often in contemporary organizations where novelty and information threaten to overload decision making. Because of the biases that perceptual processes create, the perceptual process is by nature limited. The perceptual process can be managed more effectively through the use of critical reflection.

OB AT WORK

SUZY GANZ HELPS PEOPLE AND ORGANIZATIONS SHAPE PERCEPTIONS THROUGH EMBROIDERED PRODUCTS

Suzy Ganz's plans didn't include working for a manufacturing business on the top of her career list when she graduated from the Wharton School of business. After receiving her MBA, she spent a few years working on Wall Street. Now, as the CEO of Lion Brothers, she helps over 1600 companies worldwide shape their image by designing, manufacturing, and delivering apparel identity and insignia. Suzy weaves together many of the concepts she learned in her organizational behavior courses. For example, she understands that the identity of a company is tied to the culture in which it operates and that change must be considered along with continuity. This means promoting rapid innovation and new technology, while honoring the tradecraft and history of her manufacturing firm. Working on Wall Street and running a manufacturing firm in the United States require many of the same skills. This means demonstrating the value of integrity and connecting the concept of integrity to employee work. Promoting a sense of stewardship towards customers encourages employees to do the right thing and to do good work that makes a difference to customers.

6 Apply concepts of perception to organizations.

Lion Brothers is in the business of emblems—symbols of people and organizations that shape perceptions. For example, Lion Brothers produces emblems for the Super Bowl, Boy Scouts, Girl Scouts, and many professional and college sports teams. The company has produced emblems for military uniforms for every major U.S. military campaign in the last century. Lion even has the distinction of having crafted the first emblem to land on the moon. Specifically, Lion Brothers worked closely with NASA to design and manufacture the insignia worn by the astronauts of Apollo 11, the first to land on the moon. These emblems, or symbols, are a part of U.S. history and often stir strong emotions in those who wear these emblems and those who observe these emblems.

In order for Lion Brothers to thrive in today's competitive, international manufacturing markets, it has to continue to embrace the innovative spirit that was part of the company's founding. In order to compete with inexpensive foreign competition, innovation has been key. One of the innovations that Lion Brothers executed under Suzy's collaborative leadership was with the Girl Scouts of America *Make Your Own Badge* program. Shrinking manufacturing innovation to a 'quantity of one' was a way that Lion Brothers could directly impact an individual Girl Scout, a Girl Scout troop, a pack, and even an entire social network. With the support and technical guidance of Lion Brothers, the Girl Scouts are able to provide a girl scout with the tools to make her own badge, tell her own story, and create a badge of her. A Girl Scout might typically prescribed achievements in camping or even financial literacy. These badges are already manufactured and produced in mass quantities. Each Girl Scout can customize her own badge and receive a physical badge to wear and a digital badge for sharing through social media. Lion Brothers was able to connect their organizational identity of craftsmanship with their new role in innovation to shape the identity of the young

(continued)

leaders of the future. The badge allows the girl to tell her own story and name her own badge. The importance of how people perceive themselves and express themselves is a starting point for employees of Lion Brothers to think about how they can marry the rich tradition of 'best in craft' with the needs of their stakeholders. When employees understand the needs of their customers, they work tirelessly and efficiently to execute a challenge.

Similarly, when Nike won the contract to be the partner for the NFL, Lion became the provider of choice for apparel identity and insignia. Lion delivered with a new technologically advanced way to print products for NFL jerseys at an unprecedented speed. Recognizing that perceptions are shaped one patch at a time, Suzy understands whether it is allowing a single Girl Scout to design her own patch or rapidly designing patches for a sports team, perception matters in business. By employing organizational behavior concepts, CEO Suzy Ganz's collaborative leadership style brings together stakeholders and employees to create a workplace culture where employees identify with the necessity of innovation, while still preserving the heritage of manufacturing craftsmanship.

Source: http://forgirls.girlscouts.org/make-your-own-badge-site-launches/
http://forgirls.girlscouts.org/make-your-own-badge-site-launches/

SPOTLIGHT ON RESEARCH
Self-Attribution Bias in Corporate Executives

Self-attribution bias can be measured in chief executive officer (CEO) statements about company financial performance, research suggests. Self-attribution bias is where someone takes credit for good performance, but bad performance is blamed on external factors. In the CEO study, CEO's attribute good financial performance to their own success as leaders, and bad performance to market conditions. Researchers obtained transcripts of CEO interviews that were conducted on CNN over a period of approximately nine years. Also collected were the turnover statistics of these same CEO's to determine whether they were terminated, resigned voluntarily, or were still employed. The assumption that the researchers wanted to measure with turnover data is that CEO's with self-attribution bias are also overconfident and wasteful of firm money, and probably terminated at a higher rate than CEO's who do not engage in self-attribution bias. Viewership statistics were retrieved to find out the impact of viewership on CEO actions. Financial data, including stock price data and accounting data, was also gathered. Self-attribution was measured by coding the transcript speech in order to look for words like 'I,' or words like 'economy,' 'competitor,' or even 'them.' The words were carefully counted in each sentence to measure how frequently CEO's would attribute good firm performance to themselves and how frequently CEO's would attribute bad firm performance to others or to general conditions, such as the economy.

From the evidence gathered and analyzed, the researcher found a number of interesting results. First, CEO's do engage in self-attribution bias, and in turn are more likely to be fired when they continually over attribute firm performance to their own ability. Self-attribution bias can also be described in terms of overconfidence—that is, CEO's who engage frequently in this type of bias are also overconfident. Stock market investors do not like statements of self-attribution bias, and when the CEO is fired, the stock market response is usually extremely positive, increasing significantly. Shareholders seem to respond favorably to a merger or acquisition, especially after the interview of mildly or moderately overconfident CEOs. Shareholders generally do not welcome acquisitions or mergers from the extremely overconfident CEO. Viewership impacted a CEO's actions after the interview. Where viewership was high, the CEO was more likely to move to a larger, publically traded company in a different industry. The research team speculates, in conclusion, that a minor or moderately overconfident CEO has a positive result for the company, but an excessively overconfident CEO who engages in routine self-attribution bias has negative results for a firm.

Questions for Discussion

1. What implications do you think these findings have for other managers in an organization who engage in self-attribution bias?

2. How would you encourage a top manager in an organization to not engage in self-attribution bias?

3. What additional information would you have gathered or explored if you were a researcher exploring this topic?

Based on an article by Kim, Y. (2013). Self-Attribution bias of the CEO: Evidence from CEO interviews on CNBC. *Journal of Banking and Finance, 37*, 2472–2489.

Pairing with this Topic Summary

Suggested Expert Contributions

Hurricane Katrina: A Case Study in Attribution Biases—Mark J. Martinko (Performance Associates), Jeremy Brees (Florida State University), and Jeremy D. Mackey (Florida State University)

The Bias Blind Spot and Its Implications—Lee Ross (Stanford University), Joyce Ehrlinger (Washington State University), and Thomas Gilovich (Cornell University)

Social Identity: How We Define Ourselves By Our Groups—Michael Hogg (Claremont Graduate University)

Suggested Cases

Case 4: FaceTime at TechPoint Software, Inc.

Case 5: Whatever Happened to One of the "100 Best Companies to Work For"?: A Case Study of Hewlett-Packard

Case 7: Perceptions of Leaders Following Public Failures: A Tale of Two Coaches

Suggested Exercises

Exercise 5: My Best and Worst Learning Experiences

Exercise 6: Developing Your Career—Leadership in Action

Exercise 8: Facts and Opinions

Exercise 11: Bias and Decision Making

Exercise 18: Team Performance Evaluation

Exercise 20: Employment Branding

Exercise 30: You Can't Handle The Truth

Endnotes

1. Fernberger, S. W. (1941). Perception. *Psychological Bulletin, 38*(6): 432–468.
2. Pronin, E. (2006). Perception and misperception of bias in human judgment. *Trends in Cognitive Science, 11*, 37–42.
3. Arrow, Kenneth J. (1986). Rationality of self and others in an economic system. In R. M. Hogarth & M. W. Reder (Eds.). *Rational choice: The contrast between economics and psychology.* Chicago, IL: University of Chicago Press, 201–215.
4. Willis, J, & Todorov, A. (2006). First impressions: Making up your mind after a 100-ms exposure to a face. *Psychological Science, 17*(7): 592–598.
5. Beyer, J. M., Chattopadhyay, P., George, E., Glick, W. H., Ogilvie, D., & Pugliese, D. (1997). The Selective Perception of Managers Revisited. *Academy of Management, 40*(3): 716–737.
6. Hastorf, A. H., & Cantril, H. (1954). They Saw a Game: A Case Study. *Journal of Abnormal and Social Psychology, 49*(1): 129–134
7. Nestler, S., & von Collani, G. (2008). Hindsight bias, conjunctive explanations and causal attribution. *Social Cognition, 26*(4)(08): 482–493.
8. Banaji, M. R., & Greenwald, A. G. (2013). *Blindspot: Hidden bias of good people.* Delacorte Press.
9. Banaji, M. R. & Greenwald, A. G. (2013).
10. Banaji, M. R. & Greenwald, A. G. (2013).
11. Banaji, M. R. & Greenwald, A. G. (2013).
12. Nisbett, R. E., & Wilson, T. D. (1977). The halo effect: Evidence for unconscious alteration of judgments. *Journal of Personality and Social Psychology, 35*(4): 250–256.
13. Fiedler, K., Walther, E., Freytag, P., & Plessner, H. (2002). Judgment Biases in a Simulated Classroom—A Cognitive–Environmental Approach. *Organizational Behavior and Human Decision Processes, 88*(1): 527–561.
14. Harvey, J. H., Town, J. P., & Yarkin, K. L. (1981). How fundamental is 'the fundamental attribution error'? *Journal of Personality and Social Psychology, 40*(2): 346–349.
15. Forgas, J. P., & Locke, J. (2005). Affective influences on causal inferences: the effects of mood on attributions for positive and negative interpersonal episodes. *Cognition and Emotion, 19(7)*: 1071–1081.
16. Silvester, J., & Chapman, A. J. (1997). Asking "why?" in the workplace: Causal attributions and organizational behavior. *Journal of Organizational Behavior, 18*, 1–14.
17. Leslie, L. M., Manchester, C. F., Park, T., & Mehng, S. (2012). Flexible Work Practices: A Source of Career Premiums or Penalties? *Academy of Management Journal, 55*(6): 1407–1428.

18. Carroll, J. J. (1998). Evaluations of risk: Do organizational or individual biases prevail? *Academy of Management Perspectives, 12*(4): 129–130.

19. Oghojafor, B. E. A., Olayemi, O. O., Oluwatula, O. O., & Okonji, P. S. (2012). Attribution theory and strategic decisions on organizational success factors. *Journal of Management and Strategy, 3*(1): 32.

20. Coleman, M. D. (2011). Emotion and the self-serving bias. *Current Psychology: A Journal for Diverse Perspectives on Diverse Psychological Issues, 30*(4): 345–354.

21. Pronin, E. (2006).

22. Sidle, S. (2009). Explaining performance in annual reports: Are American or Japanese executives more self-serving? *Academy of Management Perspectives, 23*(1): 81–82.

23. Leslie, L. M., Manchester, C. F., Park, T., & Mehng, S. (2012).

24. Denrell, J. (2005). Selection bias and the perils of benchmarking. *Harvard Business Review, 83*(4): 114–119.

25. Sronce, R., & McKinley, W. (2006). Perceptions of organizational downsizing. *Journal of Leadership & Organizational Studies, 12*(4): 89–108.

26. Fook, J., & Gardner, F. (2007). *Practicing Critical Reflection: A Resource Handbook.* Maidenhead: Open University Press.

Hurricane Katrina: A Case Study in Attributional Biases

Mark J. Martinko
Performance Associates

Jeremy Brees
Florida State University

Jeremy D. Mackey
Florida State University

The nation looked on in disbelief as Hurricane Katrina swept through New Orleans in August 2005. Almost more troubling than the destruction was the lack of leadership willing to assume responsibility and take control of the situation. New Orleans' Mayor Ray Nagin blamed other government officials while the Governor of Louisiana, Kathleen Blanco, blamed Nagin's poor planning. At the same time, Michael Brown, the Director of the Federal Emergency Management Agency (FEMA), blamed the poor government response on the bickering between Governor Blanco and Mayor Nagin. President George Bush acknowledged some responsibility, but ultimately blamed the system. The media portrayed these officials as incompetent and focused on their unwillingness to accept blame and aid the citizens in the Superdome and Convention Center, who needed food and water.

The purpose of this reading is to show how the actor–observer bias explains divergent perceptions of responsibility after Hurricane Katrina. First, we define and explain this bias. Then we illustrate this bias with examples from the Hurricane Katrina disaster. Finally, we will offer strategies for reducing the negative impacts of this bias.

The Actor-Observer Bias

An actor is a person behaving or performing and is the focus of the attention of the observer. The actor–observer bias asserts that actors are biased towards crediting or blaming external causes for their successes and failures while observers are biased towards focusing on the internal characteristics of actors. A primary cause of this bias is the difference in the focus of attention between actors and observers. Actors primarily focus on their environment because that is what they literally see. On the other hand, observers often concentrate on the actors' behaviors resulting in the tendency to use actors' dispositions to explain their actions.

The actor–observer bias is prevalent throughout virtually all cultures and can be readily observed in a multitude of contexts. Considering the actions of government officials following Hurricane Katrina will help us further illustrate this point.

Hurricane Katrina: A Case Study in Attributional Biases

Below we illustrate how the actor–observer bias played out in the Hurricane Katrina disaster by detailing how the actors deflected blame by attributing their failures to the situation while the media was biased toward blaming the failures on the characteristics of the actors.

Mayor Ray Nagin as an Actor

Mayor Ray Nagin called for a last-minute voluntary evacuation of New Orleans on Saturday, August 27, 2005 despite much earlier warnings of the severity of the impending hurricane. Nagin blamed his delayed reaction on a host of factors, including businesses failing to shut down and a lack of state and federal assistance. In addition, he attributed his failure to help people in the Superdome and Convention Center on situational factors and other people, thereby neglecting to take responsibility for his own mistakes.

Mayor Ray Nagin from the Observer's Perspective

The actor–observer bias would predict that the media (observers) would blame the dispositional factors of Mayor Nagin (actor) for the failure of the citizens of New Orleans to evacuate and for the lack of a timely rescue effort. That is exactly what happened.

For example, Douglas Brinkley described Nagin as "a very lame, ineffectual, wrong-headed mayor for this time," and even suggested that some of Nagin's failures were "criminal." Congressional investigations were equally harsh, suggesting that Nagin conducted an "incomplete evacuation" that led to "deaths, thousands of dangerous rescues, and horrible conditions for those who remained."

The reaction of the media and Congressional investigations to Mayor Nagin's actions provides a clear example of the effects of the actor–observer bias. Nagin (the actor) blamed situational factors and the media and Congressional investigations (observers) blamed Nagin's flawed personality characteristics and lack of effort.

Governor Kathleen Blanco as an Actor

Louisiana Governor Kathleen Blanco also failed to assume responsibility for the aftermath of Hurricane Katrina. Blanco believed that "the blame game can get in the way of protective efforts" and that the political talking heads "know not of what they speak," illustrating that she did not accept responsibility for the state's untimely response to Hurricane Katrina. Blanco went as far as to claim that her biggest mistake was "believing the promises of FEMA." She often placed blame on FEMA's slow response and Nagin's ineffective evacuation plan.

Governor Kathleen Blanco from the Observer's Perspective

As observers, the news media and Congressional investigations tended to blame Blanco's personal characteristics for Louisiana's slow and ineffective response to the aftermath of Hurricane Katrina. Republican committee member Christopher Shays was especially displeased with Blanco's unwillingness to order a mandatory evacuation of New Orleans, going as far as to say to her, "It should have been mandatory...the fact that you don't recognize that is more troubling to me than I can express."

Criticism of Blanco ranged from White House representatives claiming that she was "unorganized and indecisive" to New Orleans residents suggesting she was "incompetent," a "buffoon," and even saying outright, "She's an idiot." Thus, observers often attributed Louisiana's slow and ineffective response to the personal characteristics of Governor Blanco and her repeated unwillingness to accept responsibility by blaming other people and the situation.

Michael Brown as an Actor

Michael Brown, the director of FEMA, provided a compelling display of actor bias when he repeatedly attributed blame for the aftermath of Hurricane Katrina to state and local officials. Brown stated, "I told them we needed help—to order a mandatory evacuation." After his resignation, Brown continued to speak of the "dysfunctional" relationship between Nagin and Blanco, citing his inability to persuade them to work together as his "most serious mistake." Brown also attributed responsibility for FEMA's lack of response capabilities to budget issues and shortages of qualified personnel. According to Brown, "We [FEMA] put that money in our budget request and it was removed by Homeland Security officials." In a *New York Times* article, Brown said, "Don't blame me." These examples illustrate the actor bias as Brown deflected personal blame by blaming other people and the situation.

Michael Brown from the Observer's Perspective

The accounts of observers, such as the news media and congressional investigators, offer a very different assessment of Michael Brown's responsibility for the inadequate response to the disaster. Observers laid a disproportionate portion of the blame on the personal characteristics of Michael Brown as opposed to the challenging circumstances created by the hurricane and the other actors.

Brown was criticized by Republicans and Democrats during hearings in Washington D.C. Representative Kay Granger (R-TX) told Brown, "I don't know how you can sleep at night. You lost the battle." Representative Gene Taylor blamed Brown personally saying, "You get an F-minus in my book." The news media also leveled blame on Brown. The editor of the *New Orleans Times-Picayune* stated, "The top officials at FEMA should be fired." These observers heaped blame on Brown, reinforcing the notion that observers exhibit a strong tendency to blame failures on actor characteristics and deemphasize situational factors.

President George Bush as an Actor

President Bush also demonstrated the actor bias. When interviewed by Diane Sawyer from ABC, Bush deflected blame by attributing the problems in New Orleans to uncontrollable circumstances by stating "I hope people don't play politics during this period of time...this is a natural disaster, the likes of which our country may have never seen before." Long after Katrina's landfall, the Bush administration continued its efforts to deflect blame by stating the hurricane "was not a normal hurricane and the normal disaster relief system was not equal to it." These statements appear to have been designed to shift blame from personal to situational factors.

President George Bush from the Observer's Perspective

Media coverage of the Katrina disaster repeatedly blamed the personal characteristics of President Bush rather than acknowledging possible situational explanations, as predicted by the actor–observer bias. Columnist Charles Krauthammer stated that president Bush was "late, slow, and simply out of tune with the urgency and magnitude of the disaster" in his September 9, 2005 *Washington Post* article. Similar criticism came from Aline Kaplan in a letter to the editor, stating, "He said the wrong things in the wrong tone of voice. He demonstrated consistently the wrong emotions…he let the American people down."

Criticisms and attributions of personal blame for President Bush also came from senators and other politicians. Sen. Kent Conrad blamed Bush, saying, "It is hard to say, but it is true: There was a failure by [Bush] to meet the responsibility here." Not all media coverage laid blame squarely on President Bush, though. FOX News' Bill O'Reilly said, "He [Bush] was lethargic. That was his mistake. Maybe he's exhausted." Despite this less critical news coverage, the actor–observer bias still remained, because the explanations for President Bush's actions were still focused on his personal characteristics instead of situational explanations. These examples once again demonstrate observers' tendencies to attribute negative events to actors' personal characteristics, as well as actors' tendencies to focus on situational factors.

Reviewing the Aftermath of Hurricane Katrina

We will now discuss the consequences of the actor–observer bias and offer suggestions for reducing the negative consequences of this bias.

Consequences of Attributional Biases

There are several key consequences of the actor–observer bias. One consequence is that actors often receive more credit or blame than they deserve. Thus, actors may be rewarded or punished to undeserved levels when they experience successes and failures. We saw in the Hurricane Katrina example that observers tended to criticize public actors for their failure to assist the residents of New Orleans despite situations that were often beyond the actors' control. Because of observer biases, public officials and high-profile executives are often turned into scapegoats and fired even when they have been confronted with circumstances beyond their control.

A second problem that occurs is that because observers focus on their leaders, they oftentimes fail to see their own culpability for failures. Thus, in many ways, many of the people of New Orleans who failed to evacuate were part of the problems that they were blaming on their leaders. This evasion of responsibility also likely results in observers' failing to take proactive steps to resolve their situations.

Finally, biases by both observers and actors cloud each party's ability to diagnose the causes of their problems. In the case of Katrina, more objective analyses of the problems by both observers and actors would likely have facilitated more effective and timely resolution of the many problems that occurred.

Strategies for Overcoming Attributional Biases

The following strategies can be used to reduce the negative effects of the actor–observer bias by encouraging more balanced attributions, which may lessen the differences between the perspectives of actors and observers.

Experience

Experience and knowledge can lessen the effects of biases. Research indicates that leaders with more experience and knowledge of their members' job environments rate their members' behaviors more positively and objectively, thus reducing their observer biases. The news media often uses this strategy by employing experts to provide perspective when tragedies occur. In the case of Katrina, it appears that biases may have been exacerbated since it appears that many of the public officials responsible for addressing the disaster had little experience.

Task Interdependence

Research indicates that leaders are more lenient with their evaluations of members when outcomes depend on the performance of both members and leaders. One of the major problems in the Hurricane Katrina disaster is that it appears that local, state, and federal governments did not recognize their interdependencies and defended their territories. Coordination between departments and divisions prior to disasters that emphasizes interdependencies is likely to reduce perceptual differences when unexpected events occur.

Impression Management: Accounts and Apologies

Accounts and apologies can be useful impression management techniques when members are evaluated by their leaders. Accounts serve as explanations for actions and situational constraints. Apologies serve to acknowledge wrongdoing. Research suggests that leaders give more favorable evaluations when members explain the reasons for their poor performances. Apologies work best when they are perceived by leaders as sincere and a promise to not repeat the behavior is included. Thus, if Nagin, Blanco, Brown, or Bush had explained the reasons why they made the decisions they did, admitted that they made mistakes, and given sincere apologies accompanied by assurances that they would not repeat their mistakes, the news media, as well as other observers, would likely have been less scathing in their reviews.

Pictures

Verbal and visual pictures can help observers better understand why decisions were made in certain ways. If actors provide observers with detailed, accurate descriptions of situational factors, then observers are more likely to be less biased in their attributions. Observers who viewed pictures of New Orleans in newspapers after the hurricane were much more likely to realize that no single person or small group of people could be held responsible for the aftermath of Hurricane Katrina.

Increasing Physical and Psychological Closeness

Physically and psychologically close actors and observers are likely to have some level of appreciation for each other's perspective. This is often achieved in the workplace by leaders' observing members and sharing tasks with them. For example, Japanese managers are generally encouraged to spend two weeks each year doing entry-level jobs. If observers were able to identify more with Nagin, Blanco, Brown, and/or Bush, then their criticisms might have been less harsh.

Attribution Training

Attribution training refers to the idea that individuals are able to actively manage attributional biases when made aware of them. Oftentimes, simple awareness is a successful first step in developing more objective attributions. In part, this book chapter is designed as an informal tool to train individuals. More formalized methods, such as clinical feedback, also facilitate awareness of personal biases and their influences. Within the aftermath of Hurricane Katrina, awareness of observer biases could have helped major actors anticipate public reactions. Awareness of observer biases could have also helped observers to be less critical of the actors.

Providing Information

The actor–observer bias may be partially overcome by providing the other party with the relevant information needed for them to make more objective attributions. All of the major actors and observers within the Hurricane Katrina disaster could have benefited from talking to interviewers and making more transparent the information they all had access to at the time of the disaster.

Accessing Information

Limited information is partially responsible for the actor–observer bias. Thus, it is especially important that actors take steps to ensure they have access to all the relevant information from which to make decisions. Important government leaders often remain insulated from pertinent information because their handlers or support staff members filter outside information. Thus, it is possible that some of the actors in the Katrina disaster were making decisions without all of the necessary information.

360-degree Feedback

More data points from various perspectives can lead to more objective attributions. Using 360-degree feedback is a way of avoiding biases. The news media can avoid observer biases by reporting news from multiple perspectives, using point and counterpoint perspectives. In the wake of Hurricane Katrina, major actors probably did themselves a disservice by not being more available to the media to share their perspectives.

The Illusion of Control

Public figures and leaders are often given more credit or blame than they objectively deserve. In some cases, leaders can take advantage of this. For example, President Clinton, in his 1992 presidential bid against George Bush, framed his core campaign message around the economy. By saying "It's the economy, stupid," Clinton was able to attach blame for the poor U.S. economy to Bush and subsequently received credit when the economy rebounded after his election. This happened despite the fact that neither president really had much control over the success or failure of an economy.

Conclusion

The actor–observer bias was used in this reading to examine the question of why there were differences in perceptions of responsibility and blame following Hurricane Katrina. We believe the actor–observer construct offers an explanatory framework for illustrating why different parties, depending on where they stand, attribute failure so differently. Moreover, we suggest that if both observers and actors were made more aware of their attributional biases in such situations, some differences in perceptions could be managed. In addition, these parties could arrive at more objective and balanced attributions for these, or similar, outcomes. Our analysis of the actor–observer bias highlights the importance of carefully considering your interpretation of your own behaviors and words, as well as the behaviors and words of others. While it remains unlikely these biases will be eliminated all together, we are hopeful that a more explicit understanding of actor and observer dynamics can help avoid the negative consequences of these biases.

Endnotes
Selected References

Information on attribution theory and the actor–observer bias can be found in Dr. Mark Martinko's book *Thinking Like a Winner: A Guide to High Performance Leadership* (Tallahassee, FL: Gulf Coast Publishing, 2002). Quotes and accounts from Mayor Ray Nagin, Governor Kathleen Blanco, FEMA Director Michael Brown, and President George Bush can be found in the news media, including but not limited to: the *Seattle Times,* the *Times-Picayune,* CBS' Sixty Minutes, the *New York Times, Atlanta Journal Constitution, The Independent, Science Notebook,* the *St. Petersburg Times,* the *Southeast Missourian,* the *Boston Globe,* the *Vancouver Sun,* the *Los Angeles Times,* the *Hartford Courant,* and the *Final Report of the Select Bipartisan Committee to Investigate the Preparation For and Response to Hurricane Katrina.*
This reading is based on an earlier article in *Organizational Dynamics.* Please review the *Organizational Dynamics* article for a complete list of resources: Martinko, M. J., Breaux, D. M., Martinez, A. D., Summers, J., & Harvey, P. (2009). "Hurricane Katrina and attributions of responsibility." *Organizational Dynamics, 38*(1): 52–63.

The Bias Blind Spot and Its Implications

Lee Ross
Stanford University

Joyce Ehrlinger
Washington State University

Thomas Gilovich
Cornell University

Everyday events often prompt us to assess the objectivity of opinions and judgments—our own, those of our friends and colleagues, and those of jurists, political leaders, and advocates for interest groups.

- Was our decision to promote a favored employee influenced by a desire to nurture a friendship or was it the result of an even-handed evaluation of her qualifications?

- Was the television pundit's bleak assessment of national healthcare influenced by the political leanings of the network's owners or was it a fair evaluation of the proposals on the table?

- Was a presidential decision to go to war a reflection of cool-headed assessments of national interest or the result of ideological blindness, unwarranted optimism, or personal anger?

- Are our assessments of whether our own or others' judgments are biased the product of our personal biases?

A wealth of evidence suggests that people's judgments are not, in fact, objective, but subject to a number of cognitive and motivational biases.[1] For example, individuals consistently rate themselves above average across a variety of domains,[2] take credit for their successes but explain away their failures,[3] and believe that most others share their deeply held beliefs when, in fact, they don't.[4] Most people also believe that they are more moral[5] and less self-interested[6] than others. On top of all of these biases, people suffer from a "bias blind spot," or the conviction that their own judgments are less susceptible to bias than the judgments of others.[7]

In this reading, we focus on this *bias blind spot*, and discuss its causes and consequences. We first introduce the concept of "naïve realism" and its relevance to perceptions of bias in the self versus others. We suggest that one source of the bias blind spot is reliance on introspection, and show that people view personal connections to an issue as a source of bias in others but enlightenment in the self. Moving forward, we show how the bias blind spot can impede the resolution of conflicts in organizations and beyond.

Naïve Realism and Bias

We argue that unwarranted faith in one's own personal objectivity follows naturally from the stance of "naïve realism," or the tacit belief that one's own judgments and understandings of the world are direct and unmediated reflections of objective reality or "the way things are".[8] In other words, naïve realism is the belief that one's own perception of the world is correct and accurate. A corollary of such beliefs is the notion that judgments that *differ* from one's own are inaccurate or incorrect. Thus, people often perceive that people who hold judgments different from their own are either uninformed, unintelligent, lazy, irrational, or motivated to see only what they want to see.[9] For example, some members of a political party (e.g., Democrats) believe that the media is biased against "their side" on specific controversial issues and in overall political coverage.[10] Stephen Colbert jokingly referred to this tendency when he proclaimed that "reality has a well-known liberal bias".[11] No doubt, liberals would find this a more accurate parody of conservative views than would conservatives.

Naïve realism and its corollaries, we suggest, are apt to exert considerable influence on the decisions, preferences, and priorities of managers and employees within organizations. For example, a manager's decisions will reflect his or her perception of what is "realistic" with respect to which projects are most worthy of resources, which employees are most deserving of being promoted, and what project goals and timelines are reasonable. That said, others in the organization will each have their own naïve realist perceptions of what is "realistic" and, to the degree that those perceptions do not match those of the manager, conflict is likely to arise. The manager's promotion and resource allocation choices will be seen by those who disagree as biased by self-interest or the temptation to play favorites. The manager, in turn, is apt to view complaints by advocates of non-funded projects and non-promoted employees as reflections of self-interested bias on the part of the disgruntled employees.

Strategies for Assessing Bias

Research shows that both managers and employees use one of two strategies to determine whether a given judgment is a product of bias.[12] First, both groups may consult their own theories of bias. That is, people are aware that human beings are motivated to seek pleasure and avoid pain, that they give heavy weight to their own needs and preferences, and that they have an arsenal of psychological defense mechanisms at their disposal. This strategy leads people to suspect bias when they see others express self-serving beliefs. Second, people know that their co-workers are inclined to see matters through the prism of their ideology, political stance, and culture. This awareness, in turn, leads people to suspect bias whenever they hear someone express a belief that is obviously congruent with the claimant's worldview.

As a result of these two strategies, a claim that a contested electoral outcome was fair, a procedure for counting votes appropriate, or a judicial decision wise may be viewed as biased when the claim is made by someone whose interests were served by the outcome, and/or by someone whose worldview was congruent with the claim. For example, say we know a trained psychologist (i.e., someone whose worldview is aligned with the notion that scientific methods are superior for understanding human behavior) who is attempting to influence a foundation to give her a research grant to study drug addiction, instead of giving it to a religious group that is also interested in understanding drug addiction (i.e., she has a self-interest in their decision). If this psychologist makes the claim that "psychologists are better able to help us understand human behavior than are religious clergy," we may suspect this statement is based on bias because we know that (a) she may benefit from any decision based on this claim, and (b) her worldview is aligned with this claim.

By contrast, people tend to rely on a different strategy for detecting bias in themselves. Managers and employees look within themselves to determine whether they felt the pull of bias when they made a judgment or claim. This type of introspection is a good strategy for detecting bias only to the degree that the bias leaves some detectable trace. Introspection is typically viewed as something akin to an archeological exploration, in which true information about one's decisions, motives, and personality can be uncovered if one just digs deep enough. Research suggests, however, that this view of introspection is not accurate.[13] Many of the processes that bias our judgments and decisions occur outside of conscious awareness and, as such, leave no trace of their operation.[14] In fact, introspection is likely to lead to the conviction that one's assessments are relatively free of distorting influences[15] and even that one acted *in spite* of one's preferences, not because of them. At the same time, we take other people's claims that their decisions were made objectively with a grain of salt. Simply stated, people are quick to infer self-interested bias on the part of their superiors, peers, and subordinates in the organization, but are reluctant to infer the same things about themselves.[16] Moreover, people are quite aware that people are capable of deceiving themselves and others about the degree to which their judgments and decisions have been free from bias, but apparently, do not recognize this about themselves.

The only instances in which people are likely to concede that their judgments may be biased are when they are talking about judgment *in general* (i.e., they may agree that bias is a human condition that affects most people). Yet, when asked about bias related to any *specific* judgment they have made, these same individuals will be much less likely to acknowledge the effects of bias.

This effect was demonstrated in a study by Joyce Erlinger. In this study, one group of undergraduate college students was asked to make their own predictions about a number of possible events (e.g., receiving an attractive job offer before graduation), while a different group was asked to consider a set of predictions about these same events supposedly made by a specific other student. Participants were then asked to rate the degree to which the predictions they had just considered might be influenced by *a desire to make accurate, honest assessments* versus *a desire to think positive events likely and negative events unlikely to happen*. As predicted, participants in the study thought that their own predictions were less biased than those of the other student, and that their own predictions about *specific* outcomes were less subject to bias than generalized assessments they might make (see Figure 1).

Figure 1 Perceived Bias in Predictions of the Future

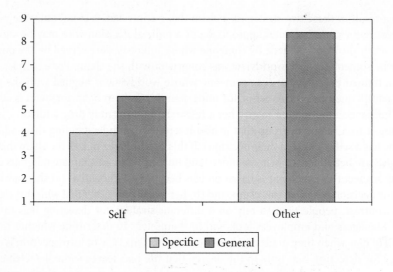

Personal Connection as a Source of Enlightenment or Bias

Naïve realism leads people to be convinced that they are relatively objective and free of distorting biases, but it need not entail the belief that one is a dispassionate observer who brings nothing personal to the task of interpreting issues and events. Everyday experience teaches us that our personal experiences and identities have an impact on our views. Managers, for example know that their perceptions regarding an appropriate project timeline are, in part, a product of the experiences they have had as managers. Similarly, in advocating for federal funding for stem cell research, Congressman Dick Gephardt spoke of caring for his elderly mother and insisted that "unless you've gone through something, you really don't understand it."[17]

More recently, Republican Mayor of San Diego, Jerry Sanders, testified in court that his personal connections to gay and lesbian family and friends gave him an enlightened perspective on the importance of legalizing gay and lesbian marriage. Indeed, Sanders credited his personal connections for correcting what he described as an unconscious, anti-gay bias that impacted his previous political stance. As a result, Sanders reversed prior political commitments and lent his full support to the cause of legalizing gay marriage. Gephardt and Sanders thus not only acknowledged their personal connections, they cited them as essential sources of information rather than sources of bias. In contrast, Maggie Gallagher of the National Organization for Marriage, viewed Sanders' personal connections as a distorting influence on his view of the issue. In response to Sanders' testimony, Gallagher said, "He gave a moving testimony in court today about how much he loves his lesbian daughter...Politicians are not elected to advance the views and values of their families."[18]

Ehrlinger, et al. (2005) conducted a second set of studies to determine whether people acknowledge that personal connections influence perceptions but show an asymmetry in their beliefs about the impact of such connections on the self versus others. In particular, the researchers wanted to know whether introspection leads people to believe that their own personal connections to a given issue provide them with unusual insight and understanding. At the same time, do they see others' connections as a source of self-serving bias that should be guarded against in making decisions?

In one study, they surveyed Jewish, Arab, and Muslim individuals following the collapse of the Israeli-Palestinian peace process that resulted in a spike in violence. Participants were asked to indicate whether their own status, or that of members of the other relevant community, had been a source of illumination or bias in evaluating issues relevant to the conflict. As predicted, participants viewed their own status as more enlightening and less biasing than the status of those on the opposing side. Indeed, in absolute terms, Arab and Muslim participants viewed their own personal connections to the issue as a significant source of enlightenment. Jewish participants (most of whom were born in the United States and thus perhaps less personally involved in the crisis than the Arab/Muslim participants) did not consider their own connection to the issue to be particularly enlightening, but they also did not see it as a source of bias (see Figure 2).

A second study examined students' assessments of bias on the part of individuals—themselves and other students—with respect to two campus issues. Minority and Caucasian students were asked about the impact that racial identity might have on views regarding affirmative action in university admissions. In addition, varsity and intramural athletes were asked how varsity or non-varsity athletic status might influence views about whether a new weight training room should be reserved for the exclusive use of varsity athletes.

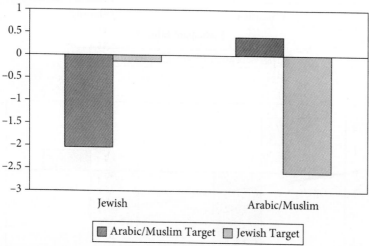

Figure 2 Perceptions of the Degree to Which One's Ethnic or Religious Status Offers an Enlightened as Opposed to Biased Perspective on Issues Related to the Conflict in the Middle East

Note: Zero represents the midpoint of the scale in Figures 2 and 3, such that positive numbers represent a belief that one's perspective is more enlightened by a personal connection and negative numbers represent a belief that a personal connection leads to a biased perspective on the issue in question.

Once again, participants showed the predicted asymmetry in judgments of whether personal connections provided enlightenment or led to bias. Caucasian students thought that ethnicity would bias views about affirmative action policies more for racial minority students than for fellow Caucasians. The opposite was true of minority students, who thought a student's ethnicity would lead to more bias for Caucasian than fellow minority students. Moreover, in absolute terms, minority students thought that a fellow minority student's ethnicity would serve as a significant source of enlightenment rather than bias, whereas Caucasian students thought that the absence of such an identity was a source of slightly more enlightenment than bias. The same pattern was in evidence in student athletes' assessments of bias and enlightened understanding about the use of an exclusive weight room (see Figure 3).

Figure 3a

Perceptions of the Degree to Which One's Ethnicity Offers an Enlightened as Opposed to a Biased Perspective on Attitudes about Affirmative Action

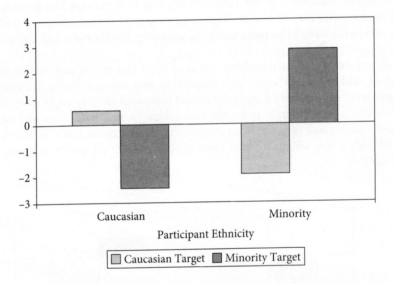

Figure 3b

Perceptions of the Degree to Which One's Athletic Status Offers an Enlightened as Opposed to a Biased Perspective on Allocation of Athletic Space

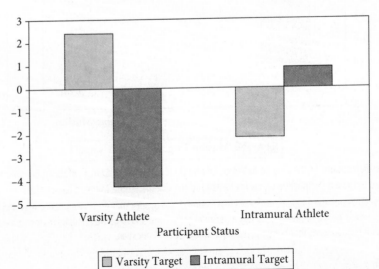

Implications for Conflict Management

This blindspot with respect to one's own biases, but not the biases of others, has important implications for our understanding of interpersonal and intergroup conflict. If people rely on theories about bias when evaluating the views of another party, but rely on introspection to detect discernible traces of bias in their own views, efforts to resolve disagreements are apt to meet with frustration. If the disagreement is accompanied by hatred and the conviction that the other party seeks to prevail rather than reach an acceptable compromise, the question of bias becomes secondary. The assumption will be that the other party sees the conflict through the prism of self-interest, its general dislike of "our side," or its misguided ideology. Managers and their employees, for example, will expand little effort in trying to truly understand the perspective of those on the other side of an issue and, as a result, will show little interest in meetings or discussions designed to resolve conflict.

But even if there is no assumption of intractable ill-will and the conflicting parties believe agreement is possible, the road to a mutually satisfactory solution is bound to be a difficult one and the process of seeking that agreement is apt to engender ill-will and distrust. Evidence from laboratory experiments[19] as well as real-world experiences in peace building through citizen dialogue in Northern Ireland and in the Middle East[20] suggest that enlightened and good-hearted people on both sides of such conflicts are often willing, even eager, to meet with their counterparts. But that willingness is predicated on the assumption that once one explains to the other side how things "really are"—that is, once one corrects the other side's "misconceptions" about history, motives, conceptions of justice, etc.—those on the other side will be willing to make the kinds of concessions they vowed they would never make.

Rarely, if ever, do the antagonists come to the discussions expressing the hope that doing so will "clear up *my own* misconceptions," or "prompt *me* to see the wisdom of making heretofore unacceptable concessions." Some are optimistic that an agreement can be reached; some are wary and regard the process as a test—one that will reveal whether the other side is "serious" about agreement (that is, open to being persuaded) or merely posturing (in which case it would be valuable to discover this and not waste time or effort in fruitless further exchanges). In both cases, however, the dialogue is bound to be frustrating. It can seem that those on the other side are stubbornly clinging to their claims and convictions despite one's efforts to enlighten them with one's own wisdom. People on both sides are likely to assume that they are being reasonable, candid, and objective, and therefore that the other side's intransigence reflects closed-mindedness and an unwillingness or inability to overcome their biases. Experience suggests that people who have disagreements within organizations similarly show little interest in "being set straight" and are inclined to attribute resistance by those on the "other side" to closed-mindedness or some other failing.

Although full agreement on the issues that divide conflicting parties is often elusive, such "public peace processes" can be valuable. Often the parties discover that, on matters not directly involved with the conflict, those on the other side share their own aspirations and frustrations in pursuit of living meaningful lives, raising healthy children, expanding professional opportunities, and developing peaceful communities. In the course of such discussions, "theories" about those on the other side, particularly theories that stereotype and dehumanize them, can sometimes yield to experience.

Summary

In summary, research on the bias blind spot tells us that people are aware of bias in judgments, but that they believe that this bias applies mostly to other people. By contrast, when assessing their own, specific judgments (e.g., about the fairness of a grading policy, or the right candidate to back in an election), people tend to perceive that they are unbiased, and that their view of the world is accurate. Moreover, when they perceive that a personal connection or experience has affected their judgments, most people tend to view this effect as "enlightenment" (i.e., something that improves the accuracy of their judgment) rather than bias.

An important consequence of this bias blind spot for organizations and their members is that conflicts between groups with opposing worldviews and self-interests may be difficult to resolve. It is not enough that these groups come together and listen to each other's perspectives. The members of these groups must also be willing to acknowledge that their own beliefs may be biased. To the extent that such acknowledgement is possible, the bias blind spot bias may be overcome.

Endnotes

1. Gilovich, T. (1991). *How we know what isn't so: The fallibility of human reason in everyday life*. New York, NY: The Free Press; Kunda, Z. (1990). The case for motivated reasoning. *Psychological Bulletin,108*, 480–498; Nisbett, R.E., & Ross, L. (1980). *Human inference: Strategies and shortcomings of social judgment*. Englewood Cliffs, NJ: Prentice Hall, Inc.

2. Alicke, M. D., Klotz, M. L., Breitenbecher, D. L., Yurak, T. J., & Vredenburg, D. S. (1995). Personal contact, individuation, and the better-than-average effect. *Journal of Personality and Social Psychology, 68,* 804–825; Dunning, D., Meyerowitz, J. A., & Holzberg, A. D. (1989). Ambiguity and self-evaluation: The role of idiosyncratic trait definitions in self-serving assessments of ability. *Journal of Personality and Social Psychology, 57,* 1082–1090.

3. Miller, D. T., & Ross, M. (1975). Self-serving biases in the attribution of causality: Fact or fiction? *Psychological Bulletin, 82,* 213–225; Whitley, B. E., & Frieze, I. H. (1985). Children's causal attributions for success and failure in achievement settings: A meta-analysis. *Journal of Educational Psychology, 77,* 608–616.

4. Lord, C. G., Ross, L., & Lepper, M. R. (1979). Biased assimilation and attitude polarization: The effects of prior theories on subsequently considered evidence. *Journal of Personality and Social Psychology, 37,* 2098–2109.

5. Epley, N., & Dunning, D. (2000). Feeling 'holier than thou': Are self-serving assessments produced by errors in self- or social prediction? *Journal of Personality and Social Psychology, 79,* 861–875.

6. Miller, D. T, & Ratner, R. K. (1998). The disparity between the actual and assumed power of self-interest. *Journal of Personality and Social Psychology, 74,* 53–62.

7. Pronin, E., Gilovich, T., & Ross, L. (2004). Objectivity in the eye of the beholder: Divergent perceptions of bias in self versus others. *Psychological Review, 111,* 781–799; Pronin, E., Lin, D. Y., & Ross, L. (2002). The bias blind spot: Perceptions of bias in self versus others. *Personality and Social Psychology Bulletin, 28,* 369–381; See also Armor, D. A. (1999). The illusion of objectivity: A bias in the perception of freedom from bias. *Dissertation Abstracts International: Section B: The Sciences and Engineering, 59,* 5163; Friedrich, J. (1996). On seeing oneself as less self-serving than others: The ultimate self-serving bias? *Teaching of Psychology, 23,* 107–109.

8. Ross, L. & Ward, A. (1996). Naïve realism in everyday life: Implications for social conflict and misunderstanding. In T. Brown, E. Reed, & E. Turiel (Eds.). *Values and knowledge*. Hillsdale, NJ: Erlbaum, 103–135.

9. Pronin et al, 2004

10. Vallone, R. P. Ross, L. & Lepper, M. R. The hostile media phenomenon: Biased perception and perceptions of media bias in coverage of the Beirut Massacre. *Journal of Personality and Social Psychology*, 1985, *49*, 577–585.

11. C-SPAN. (Producer). (2006, April 29). 2006 White House Correspondents' Dinner. [Video file] Retrieved from http://www.c-spanvideo.org/program/192243-1.

12. Ehrlinger, J, Gilovich, T & Ross, L. (2005). Peering into the bias blind spot: People's assessment of bias in themselves and others. *Personality and Social Psychology Bulletin, 31*, 680–692; Pronin et al, 2004.

13. Nisbett, R. E., & Wilson, T. D. (1977). Telling more than we can know: Verbal reports on mental processes. *Psychological Review, 84,* 231–259; Wilson, T.D., & Brekke, N. (1994). Mental contamination and mental correction: Unwanted influences on judgments and evaluations. *Psychological Bulletin, 116,* 117–142.

14. Wilson, T. D. (2002). *Strangers to ourselves: Discovering the Adaptive Unconscious*. Cambridge, MA: Harvard University Press.

15. Ehrlinger et al, 2005; Pronin, E. & Kugler, M.B. (2007). Valuing thoughts, ignoring behavior: The introspection illusion as a source of the bias blind spot. *Journal of Experimental Social Psychology, 43,* 565–578.

16. Kruger & Gilovich, 1999; Miller & Ratner, 1998; Pronin et al, 2004.

17. Solomon, J. (2001, August 15). Family crisis shifts politics. *USA Today*.

18. Gallagher, M. (2010, January 19). San Diego Mayor Sanders: The Reason Prop 8 Happened. [NOM Web log post] Retrieved from http://nomblog.com/697/.

19. Goplen, J. Fay, A. F., & Ehrlinger, J. (2011). If you only knew: How naïve realism contributes to overconfidence in persuasive abilities. *Manuscript in Preparation*, Florida State University.

20. Bland, B., Powell, B. & Ross, L. (2005). Building a peace constituency for the achievement and implementation of a peace agreement in the Middle East. In M. Fitzduff & C. Stout (Eds.). *Peacemaking and Public Policy, (1),* New York: Praeger; Bland, B., Powell, B. & Ross, L. (2011). Understanding and overcoming barriers to agreements that restore human rights. In R. Goodman, D. Jinks, & A. K. Woods (Eds.). *Understanding social action, promoting human rights*, Oxford University Press, City; Ross, L. (2011). Perspectives on disagreement and dispute resolution: Lessons from the lab and the real world. In E. Shafir (Ed.). *The behavioral foundations of public policy*. Princeton University & Russell Sage Foundation Press, Princeton, NJ.

Social Identity: How We Define Ourselves By Our Groups

Michael Hogg

Claremont Graduate University

Most people have a repertoire of different ways to conceive of themselves—that is, they have many different *identities* that define their self-concepts. Some of these identities may be described as *personal identities*, which are definitions and evaluations of oneself in terms of idiosyncratic personal attributes (e.g., witty, shy), and/or personal relationships (e.g., X's friend, Y's spouse). Other of these identities are defined as *social identities*, which are definitions and evaluations of oneself in terms of the attributes of specific groups one belongs to (e.g., women, University X students, architects). So, if you ask me "who are you?" and I answer, "I'm a social psychologist," you might reasonably assume that my social identity is defined, in part, by the group "social psychologists" along with the attributes that characterize that group (e.g., scholarly, interested in group behavior). It would also be reasonable to assume that I perceive myself as defined by my affiliation with the group "social psychologists" more than by my affiliation with other groups to which I may belong, but didn't mention, such as "parents" or "Californians." That is, by mentioning the group "social psychologists" first and foremost in answer the question "who are you?", I indicated what part of my self-concept was most important to me (at least at that moment).

In the following sections I describe why people are motivated to acquire social identities, how social identities are cognitively developed, and some of the consequences (both positive and negative) of maintaining social identities. These insights come from decades of research in social psychology and help to explain how we define ourselves by our groups.[1]

Motivations for Social Identities

There are two primary motivations for defining oneself through one's groups: (1) the need to enhance one's self-esteem, and (2) the need to reduce uncertainty about oneself and one's world.

First, humans have been shown to have a strong desire to maintain a favorable self-concept. Thus, according to the *self-esteem hypothesis,* individuals are motivated to define themselves through social identities that reflect positively on them, in terms of status or positive distinctiveness. As a result, individuals are more likely to identify with positively viewed groups or groups that have a higher relative status in a community or industry.[2] For example, if a student has a choice of introducing himself to his girlfriend's parents as a member of the "Model Airplane Club" on campus or a member of the "Business Entrepreneurs Society", he may choose the latter as a means of enhancing his self-esteem, as well as his status in the eyes of his girlfriend's parents.

A second motivation for social identification is related to uncertainty reduction.[3] In addition to motives for self-esteem enhancement, humans appear to have a basic need to reduce feelings of uncertainty about themselves, their social world, and their place within it—they like to know who they are and how to behave, and who others are and how they might behave. Because social identity ties self-definition and behavior to groups that describe and prescribe behavior (more about this later), it reduces uncertainty about who we are and about how we and others will behave. Some groups are better suited to uncertainty reduction than others—specifically groups that are simple, unambiguous, and clearly defined (e.g., the Army). Under conditions of more extreme uncertainty this process may be taken further. People may zealously identify with groups that are "extremist"—such as cults. Such groups have homogeneous attitudes, values, and membership, inflexible customs and carefully policed boundaries, and orthodox and ideological belief systems. They are intolerant and suspicious of outsiders and of internal dissent and criticism, and are rigidly and hierarchically structured, often with strong autocratic leadership.

Building Blocks of Social Identities

The building blocks of social identity include group *prototypes* and *stereotypes*. People mentally represent the groups that may define their social identities in terms of *prototypes*—fuzzy sets of interrelated attributes (behaviors, attitudes, customs, dress, and so forth) that capture similarities within groups and differences between groups. One way to think of a group prototype is what comes immediately to mind if, for example, I were to say to you "French" or "librarian". In the former case, you may think of groups of people who are well-dressed and drink wine with every meal. In the latter case, you may think of groups of people with glasses who are shy and introverted. Individuals who possess all of the characteristics of a prototype (e.g., a librarian who is introverted, wears glasses, and is soft-spoken), are seen as more "prototypical" of their group than individuals who have only some of these characteristics (e.g., a librarian who wears glasses but is extroverted). Yet, the simple act of categorizing a person as a group member often leads us to perceive that person in terms of the group's prototype. Thus, rather than "seeing" your local librarians as idiosyncratic individuals, you see them as embodiments of the prototype for librarians. In this way they become *depersonalized*.

When we perceive groups that we do not belong to (what are called "outgroups"), our group prototypes may become *stereotypes*. Stereotypes are overgeneralizations about members of a group, such that we perceive all group members as having the same characteristics (e.g., all librarians are shy and wear glasses). Because we have less contact with members of outgroups, we are unlikely to encounter high variation in outgroup members (e.g., because we are not in contact with many librarians, we may not encounter librarians who are extroverted and have 20/20 vision). As a result, we are more likely to view outgroup members in terms of stereotypes than we are to view members of our own groups (our "ingroups") in terms of stereotypes. The reduction in stereotyped perceptions for groups with which we have extensive contact (and therefore, more varied experience) is called the *contact hypothesis*.[4]

Although less likely than with outgroups, it is possible to view ourselves and our ingroups via group stereotypes. When we do this, we are said to have "self-stereotyped"— (i.e., viewed ourselves and all members of our ingroups as possessing the same traits and characteristics). Such self-stereotyping may be motivated by individual needs or desires to be accepted by a group with which we seek membership (e.g., a first-year teacher at a grade school may adopt stereotypical behaviors and perceptions to convince himself and other, more senior, teachers at the school that he is one of their group).

Consequences of Social Identities

Our social identities have important implications for our lives and work. In particular, they affect us by (1) motivating group–normative behavior, and (2) influencing our liking/disliking of others. These consequences may be both positive and negative.

Group Normative Behavior

When we define ourselves in terms of group prototypes, we prescribe group-appropriate ways to think, feel and behave. In this way, our social identities not only transform our self-conceptions, they may also motivate group-normative behavior. Group members often feel compelled to adhere to standards, adopt attitudes, and behave in ways that are normative for their group.[5]

A potential downside to such group normative behavior is that group members may police their own and other members' behaviors so strictly that poor decisions get made. A classic example of this pitfall is called *groupthink*.[6] In groups with very strong norms and very strongly identifying members (i.e., individuals whose social identities are centrally defined by their membership in the group), opinions that run counter to the majority may be discounted, external opinions may be blocked out, and individual members may self-censor their own doubts in order to maintain harmony and consistency in group ideology and behavior. Yet, these same outcomes may prevent group members from considering important alternatives or from seeing potentially dangerous results associated with their existing assumptions. Famous examples of groupthink that have previously been identified include the disastrous Bay of Pigs Invasion under President John F. Kennedy, and more recently, the decision to go to war in Iraq based on faulty decision making about the existence of weapons of mass destruction under President George W. Bush.

Because it is critical to know what the identity-defining group norms are, people are highly motivated to obtain reliable information about them. There are many sources of such information, and people in groups tend to spend substantial time talking about what the group's normative attributes and actions.[7] Members can also observe fellow members' behavior, or construct a norm that contrasts with the behavior of outgroup members or deviant/marginal ingroup members. However, the most reliable information is almost always gleaned from the identity-consistent behavior of people who are known to be generally prototypical members of the group. Members pay very close attention to these people and infer from their behavior what is contextually group normative and thus, self-defining.

This idea underpins the *social identity theory of leadership*.[8] In visible groups, prototypical members occupy a leadership role, and prototypical leaders are more effective than non-prototypical leaders. People look to these people to provide reliable information about their identity as group members. They do this because prototypical leaders are assumed to be "one of us": highly identified members who are trusted because they are unlikely to behave in ways that jeopardize the group. It is this trust that paradoxically allows prototypical leaders to be normatively innovative, which is a key transformational function of effective leadership. People are prepared to follow their lead even if initially the direction they are taking the group seems odd. Of course, blindly following a leader who appears prototypical may also be a recipe for disaster if that leader has no other qualifications with which to lead.

Liking and Disliking of Others

Social identities may also affect our feelings toward others by indicating, through group prototypes, who is most similar to us. In particular, the more "ingroup–prototypical" others are (i.e., the more similar they are to the prototype for our ingroup), the more we like them. This is because we are typically "ethnocentric" in evaluating our own group and its prototype more favorably than outgroups and their prototypes. *Ethnocentrism* is the belief that all things related to the self (like one's ingroup) are superior to all things unrelated to the self (like outgroups). Furthermore, because within one's ingroup there is usually agreement over prototypicality, prototypical members are liked by all—they are "popular". Likewise, less prototypical members are "unpopular" and can be marginalized as undesirable group deviants. Outgroup members are, of course, very un-prototypical of the ingroup and so are liked less than all ingroup members. The negative side of these consequences is that decision makers (e.g., a hiring manager at a software company) may favor those who are most prototypical of their ingroup while disregarding other, more relevant information (e.g., the person's education, past job experience, skills, and abilities).

Our liking of others is also affected by the extent to which a person is seen as threatening to the integrity of one's ingroup.[9] People who espouse beliefs or engage in behaviors that are non-normative of the ingroup are disliked more if they are ingroup than outgroup members, and particularly if they are ingroup members who lean towards rather than away from the outgroup. Such ingroup deviants are considered "black sheep"—those who are particularly threatening to one's social identity because they create uncertainty about what it means to be an ingroup member. Thus, the Republican senator who espouses a liberal ideology and agrees with many of the tenets of the Democratic Party may be disliked more than any other senator (including all Democratic senators) by other Republican senators because she threatens the existing belief system that defines what it means to be a Republican. The downside of this consequence is, obviously, that group members who try to take the group in a new (and possibly positive) direction may be shunned by the group. As a result, groups may miss out on creative new ideas and become stuck in old and unproductive ways.

Conclusion

Groups provide people with social identities—a significant aspect of their self-concepts. These social identities are typically defined by group prototypes. In turn, group members may internalize and conform to group norms, support the group's leaders, especially if they are prototypical, and support others who exhibit behaviors and attitudes that are prototypical of the group. On the downside, social identities may lead group members to become deaf to internal dissent, hostile towards external criticism, likely to blindly follow leaders who appear prototypical of the group, and predisoposed to disfavor those who appear unprototypical of the group. Understanding the power of social identities, thus, is important to understanding, explaining, and managing one's social life.

Endnotes

1. Abrams, D., & Hogg, M.A., (1999). *Social Identity and Social Cognition*. Oxford, UK: Blackwell.
2. Hogg M.A., Terry, D.J., (2000). Social identity and self-categorization processes in organizational contexts. *Academy of Management Review*, 25:121–140.
3. For example, see Pinto, I. R., Marques, J. M., Levine, J. M., & Abrams, D. (2010). Membership status and subjective group dynamics: Who triggers the black sheep effect? *Journal of Personality and Social Psychology*, *99,* 107–119.
4. Allport, G. W., (1954). *The nature of prejudice*. Cambridge, MA: Perseus Books.
5. Leonardelli, G. J., Pickett, C. L., & Brewer, M. B. (2010). Optimal distinctiveness theory: A framework for social identity, social cognition and intergroup relations. In M. P. Zanna (Ed.). *Advances in experimental social psychology*, Vol. 43, 65–115. San Diego, CA: Elsevier.
6. Janis, I.L. (1972). *Victims of Groupthink*, Boston: Houghton-Mifflin.
7. Hogg, M. A., (2007). Uncertainty-identity theory. In M. P. Zanna (Ed.). *Advances in experimental social psychology*, *Vol. 39,* 69–126. San Diego, CA: Academic Press.
8. Hogg, M. A., & Smith, J. R., (2007). Attitudes in social context: A social identity perspective. *European Review of Social Psychology*, 18, 89N131.
9. Haslam, S. A. (2004). Psychology in organisations: The social identity approach (2nd ed.). London: Sage.

5 Leadership

Topic Summary Learning Objectives

1. Identify the factors of leadership—the leaders, those being led, and the context.

2. Explain the differences between leadership and management.

3. Describe the trait, behavioral, situational, LMX, and charismatic approaches to leadership.

4. Compare and contrast transformational with transactional leadership and describe different approaches to transformational leadership.

5. List the contemporary issues in leadership and why they are important.

6. Apply the concepts of leadership to organizations.

Key Terms

authentic leadership, p. 158	interpersonal behaviors, p. 153	situational leadership approach, p. 153
bureaucratic leadership, p. 156	leader–member exchange, p. 157	styles of leadership, p. 153
charisma, p. 154	leadership, p. 152	task behaviors, p. 153
charismatic leadership, p. 155	leadership grid, p. 153	traits, p. 152
dark side, p. 158	path–goal theory, p. 154	transactional leadership, p. 156
demagogue, p. 158	quid pro quo, p. 156	transformational leadership, p. 155
follower attribution, p. 155	shared leadership, p. 158	

1 Identify the factors of leadership—the leaders, those being led, and the context.

Introduction to Leadership

Leadership describes the process, whereby a leader enlists others to help achieve a change, vision, or goal.[1] This topic summary shows how contemporary approaches to leadership build on earlier theories and regard leadership as a process of influence, communication, and inspiration. The contemporary study of leadership concerns itself with three primary factors:

1. traits and behaviors of the leader. Behaviors can further be divided into interpersonal and task-related behaviors.
2. those being led, which include the interactions between the leader and the follower, and
3. context, situation, or contingencies that shapes leadership.

These three factors interact to provide a comprehensive picture of the leadership process (see Figure 5.1).

2 Explain the differences between leadership and management.

Leaders versus Managers

The first consideration is to understand the distinction between leadership and management. Leadership involves activities such as increasing organizational flexibility, helping others understand the most important things to get done, producing change, communicating, and inspiring.[2] Managing, on the other hand, involves creating order and efficiency, establishing plans, and allocating resources.[3] Management is typically associated with a formal position in an organization, but leadership can be demonstrated by anyone, regardless of one's position. As long as the person has the capacity to influence, inspire, or carry out change through others they are considered a leader.

The Leader

Early approaches to leadership focused almost exclusively on the leader as a person. Two primary facets of the leader proved important: the leader's traits and the leader's behaviors.

Traits

Traits describe attributes of the leader. They include intelligence, and may also include personality and even physical traits. Over 300 different traits have been associated with leadership.[4] Several traits have gained attention because recent studies show a correlation between these traits and leadership. For example, research has shown that people in organizations attribute qualities of leadership to people with personality factors such as extraversion,[5] physical characteristics such as height and weight,[6] and cognitive ability. But, possessing these traits does not translate into leadership effectiveness. Despite the findings of this research, a single trait has yet to be conclusive.

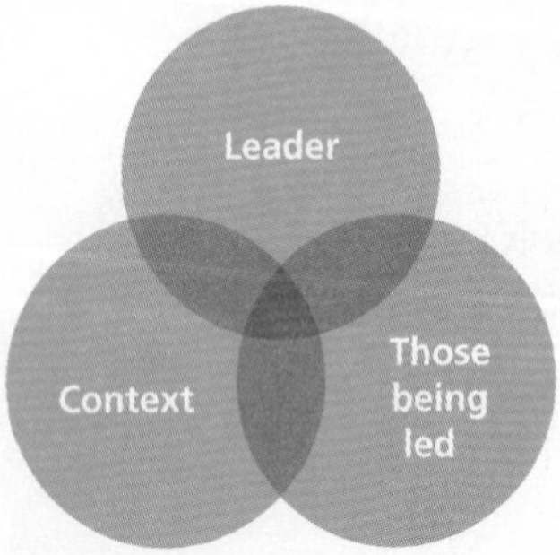

Behaviors

Many researchers have downplayed the role of traits and instead focused on behavioral facets of leadership. In contrast to the trait approach, the behavioral approach focuses on what leaders do and how they act. Actions, accordingly,

Figure 5.1 Three Factors that Define Leadership

Leadership Grid

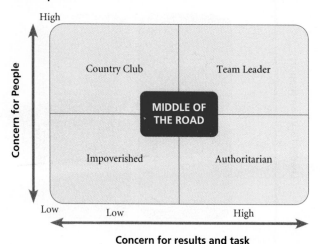

Figure 5.2
Leadership as a
Function of Concern
for People and Task

are thought to form the basis of leadership. In contrast to traits, which are typically factors with which a leader is born, behaviors are learned. Thus, more contemporary approaches emphasize facets of a leader that are learned behaviors, and thus, focus their research on the specific skills a leader needs in order to be effective. Researchers have identified two types of behaviors that are critical for leadership: **task behaviors**, or those behaviors associated with performing a particular task, and **interpersonal behaviors**, or those behaviors related to people.[7]

3 Describe the trait, behavioral, situational, LMX, and charismatic approaches to leadership.

Blake and Mouton's **leadership grid** shows how leaders vary in their level of concern for either people or task.[8] The leadership grid describes five different **styles of leadership** based on the degree to which a leader shows concern for people or a task (see Figure 5.2):

- The Country Club style of leader shows high concern for people, but fails to focus on task.
- The Impoverished style of leader shows concern for neither people nor for task.
- The Authoritarian style of leader shows high concern for task but little or no concern for people.
- The Team Leader style shows concern for both people and task.
- Finally, the Middle of the Road leadership style shows a limited, but by no means high, concern for both people and task.

Some researchers suggest that by themselves, leadership traits and behaviors fail to distinguish leaders from non-leaders.

Context, Situation, and Resources

Others focus on the context, situation, and resources associated with leadership. This perspective focuses on how leaders change their behaviors or learn new skills as they encounter different circumstances. The **situational leadership** approach suggests that successful leaders shift their behaviors to address different situations as they arise. For

Figure 5.3

Situational Model
of Leadership

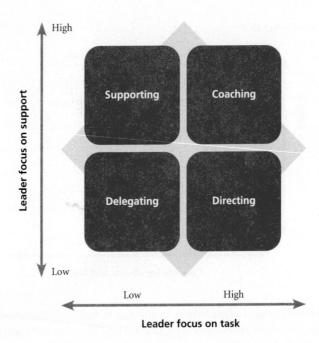

example, a leader might shift between a concern for a task and a concern for a person (people) depending on what an organization needs at any one time. Hersey and Blanchard's model of situational leadership (see Figure 5.3) has gained popularity, particularly among those who provide leadership training in organizations.[9] Their model describes how leaders shift their behavior based on the motivation and competence level of the follower. The leader adjusts the degree of support or direction given to each follower based on an assessment of the follower's motivation and competence on a task. For example, if the follower is highly motivated and highly skilled, the leader will be low in both support and direction, allowing the follower to determine his or her own direction on the task. If, on the other hand, the follower is in need of development, then the leader will provide specific direction on how to perform the task. The leader may also demonstrate coaching and supporting behaviors as the follower becomes more autonomous and learns to function independently.

Access to resources is another factor linked to leadership. The nature of the organization, the specific task, and the type of occupation should be considered. House's **path–goal theory** argues that leaders provide the right context for work when there is: 1) rewards for work performed, 2) a clear path to achieve goals, and 3) the right resources necessary to reach goals.[10] Path–goal theory suggests that access to external resources may be more important in determining leadership success than the capability of the individual leader.

The specific *context* of leadership is also important. Social instability, for example, is offered as a determinant of leadership. Sociologist Max Weber offered that during times of great social instability, such as times of change or crisis, a special type of leader was likely to emerge.[11] He believed that in times of social instability, followers were likely to seek out a 'charismatic' leader. The term **Charisma** comes from ancient Greek. It translates as 'divinely inspired gift.' Charismatic leaders hold an unmistakable appeal

Visions of America/SuperStock

to followers. Followers find charismatic leaders inspiring, interesting, and hold them in high regard. Charismatic leaders often evoke strong emotions in their followers. Charisma is usually understood as a trait of the leader, but some have offered a different view of **charismatic leadership**. In this view, charisma is a behavior and therefore charisma is a skill that can be learned in order to gain the attention and loyalty of followers.[12] For example, charismatic leaders articulate an appealing vision, take personal risk to achieve the vision, show sensitivity to the environment and to followers so that the needs of the followers are addressed. Charismatic leaders often display unconventional behavior as well.[13]

Those Being Led

Followers also play an important role in understanding leadership. For example, followers might attribute a sense of 'greatness' or charisma to the leader. According to a line of thinking called **follower attribution**, leaders emerge because they fulfill a psychological need for followers. In times of social instability, for example, followers may turn to a leader in order to reduce feelings of confusion or fear. Followers may also turn to a leader because they believe the leader will help the followers achieve a goal or establish a compelling vision of the future. The needs and goals of the follower become even more important in discussions of transformational leadership, as discussed next.

Transformational Leadership

4 Compare and contrast transformational with transactional leadership and describe different approaches to transformational leadership.

Transformational leadership makes a distinction between two types of leaders. A transformational leader obtains followers by building trust and a sense of loyalty between the leader and follower. The transformational leader seeks positive outcomes and invites others to share in the vision, and appeals to the moral values of the follower in an attempt to raise their consciousness about ethical issues. Ultimately, the transformational leader inspires a following by encouraging achievement of a higher purpose. In contrast, a **transactional leader** simply appeals to the self-interests of the followers as the leader offers the follower something tangible in exchange for loyalty. Transactional leaders offer a true **quid pro quo**, or 'something in exchange for something' mentality. For example, a transactional political leader may try to motivate voters by appealing to their self-interest and offering to lower taxes for a particular group. In contrast, the transformational political leader would appeal to a deep sense of patriotism.

Much of the work on transformational leadership began with James McGregor Burns. He studied political leaders and believed that leadership could only be understood by looking at the relationship between the follower and the leader.[14] According to Burns, a transformational leader is a person who

> "looks for potential motivators in followers, seeks to satisfy higher needs, and engages the full person of the follower. The result...is a relationship of mutual stimulation and evaluation that converts followers into leaders and may convert leaders into moral agents." (p. 4)

Rather than appealing to exchange and self-interest like the transactional leader, the transformational leader seeks out the higher-level motivations of the follower. The ultimate goal of the transformational leader is to change the status quo, improve the moral capacity of the individual follower, and in the process, transform the culture. In addition to the transformational and transactional leader, Burns also identified a third type—the bureaucratic leader. The **bureaucratic leader** is a person who motivates followers by appealing to legitimate authority bestowed by an institution or by appealing to rules and traditions.

Although Burn's original study focused mainly on political leaders, transformational leadership applies to business leadership as well. Bernie Bass built on Burn's idea and applied the notion of transformational leadership to other types of leaders.[15] Professors Warren Bennis and Burt Nanus concluded that all kinds of leaders, especially business leaders, might demonstrate transformational qualities. Transformational leadership involves the skills of:

- *Managing attention* by creating a sense of focus and direction related to the clarity or purpose for the organization.
- *Communicating* their mission in a way that is accessible or understandable to followers.
- *Gaining the trust* of followers in the organization by showing consistency between their message and their actions and how they treat various individuals within the organization.
- *Showing respect* and care about the situation of the follower.
- *Taking risks* because they are unafraid of failures that might occur when trying different things.
- *Creating new ways* of doing things and new things to do rather than relying on traditions.[16]

Kouzes and Posner studied transformational leadership by collecting data from thousands of leaders within organizations. They identified several factors that lead to successful leadership. These factors include:

- *Challenging the process* by searching for opportunities, experimenting, and taking risks.
- *Inspiring a shared vision* by envisioning the future and by enlisting others in the vision.
- *Enabling others to act* by fostering collaboration and strengthening others involvement.
- *Serving as role models* by setting examples and achieving small wins and by encouraging the heart by recognizing contributions and celebrating accomplishments.[17]

Leader–Member Exchange

Transformational leadership helps us understand the relationship among leaders, those being led, and the context. **Leader–member exchange** is another approach that emphasizes the importance of this relationship.[18] Leader–member exchange, or LMX, describes the importance of a strong interpersonal relationship between the leader and a select group of followers. Trust develops between the leader and these privileged followers. But, those followers who are not in this select group will not share in this deep trust and often miss out on access to information and other resources.

Contemporary Issues in Leadership

Contemporary studies of leadership identify how formal leadership theories might be applied to more contemporary issues in organizations. Issues include globalization, ethics and corporate social responsibility, and diversity and gender.

5 List the contemporary issues in leadership and why they are important.

Globalization

After reviewing how leadership differs across many different cultures, Robert House and his colleagues concluded that different cultural situations demand different skills, roles, and experiences from a leader. Cultures differ on several key dimensions including:

- the degree of assertiveness that is acceptable
- time-orientation towards either the future or the past
- gender equality
- orientation toward humaneness
- institutionalism
- performance
- power and uncertainty[19]

From a cross-cultural perspective, many of the traits and behaviors associated with leadership may not be as relevant across different cultures. Despite the growing importance of China and other Asian countries, the study of leadership has yet to fully consider how concepts found in Asian culture might impact leadership. For example, the concept of interpersonal favors (ren-qing) and reciprocation which is represented by the saying that if someone brings you a drop of water, you reciprocate with a spring. Likewise, social conventions like face-saving behaviors (mian-zi) and social networks (guanxi) are not recognized in Western leadership theory.[20]

Ethics and Corporate Social Responsibility

Concerns are growing about the abuse of power by leaders, inappropriate behavior in organizations including corruption, and incidents of leaders realizing personal gains at the expense of followers. These and other problems put ethical concerns of leadership at the forefront of contemporary leadership studies.

Ethical approaches to leadership build on the notion of integrity and the belief that leaders must be more conscious of their own values, the values of society, and the individual follower. **Authentic leadership** offers an approach that emphasizes ethics and integrity. At the same time, it de-emphasizes the importance of power. Authentic leaders demonstrate congruence between their values and their actions, hold clear knowledge of their own values, and rely on these values when leading. Also, authentic leaders surround themselves with others who share these same values. The authentic leader shows transparency and communicates her true values, which in turn generates trust between the leader and the follower.[21]

Contemporary leadership studies have also focused on exposing the negative outcomes of some types of leadership.[22] Due to the potential destructive aspects of leading, some have referred to this as the dark side of leadership. The **dark side** emerges when a leader appeals to fear or prejudice in order to gain followers. Leaders who draw on negative emotions are referred to as **demagogues**. A demagogue espouses a vision that reflects personal need rather than the larger goal or issue at hand, often exaggerates their self-description and manipulates their audience by stereotyping others. Cult leaders such as Jim Jones are considered demagogues because their motives are selfish and destructive. In the case of Jim Jones, as a religious leader, he was selfish and engaged himself in many of the behaviors that he condemned in others. He eventually killed nearly all of his church members.

Diversity and Gender

The early study of leadership remained preoccupied with men and masculine traits related to leadership. In fact, early studies of leadership often referred to the 'great man' theories of leadership. Contemporary leadership studies, however, have finally begun to account for issues associated with women and diversity when considering leadership. Women now represent 23 percent of CEOs in the private and public sector and nearly 20 percent of the United States Congress are women. Yet, some have argued that women must meet different social expectations than men and thus, women face different leadership challenges. For example, women may be expected to take charge and command, just like a man in a leadership role. At the same time, a female leader may be expected to show warmth and understanding, characteristics typically associated with women.[23] Perspectives like **shared leadership**, which consider what happens when leadership responsibilities are shared among multiple leaders, may provide insights into different ways of leading.[24] In addition to trying to understand difference in culture and gender, leadership studies have turned to study unique environments, like a trauma center, that represent a continually changing and contemporary work environment. In this context, the work that is performed ranges from routine and even boring to novel and intense. Studying leadership in different contexts may lead to improved understanding of how leadership skills differ based on the particular context.

Conclusion

Leadership describes the process whereby a leader influences followers to help achieve something important to the organization. This topic summary shows how contemporary approaches to leadership build on earlier theories and regard leadership as a process that considers followers and context. Contemporary approaches to leadership emphasize elements of a leader that are learned behavior, and leadership research focuses on the specific skills a leader needs in order to be effective and the context that this occurs.

OB AT WORK
LEADERSHIP IN CRITICAL-CARE MEDICINE

David Stockwell

Dr. **David Stockwell** relies on his knowledge of organizational behavior to ensure the best delivery of medical care. As the Medical Director of the Pediatric Intensive Care unit at the Children's National Medical Center, he observes physicians and other medical personnel on a daily basis. He realizes that leadership plays an important role in how doctors and nurses carry out their daily patient visits, often called 'rounds', interact with patients and their relatives, and administer medical care. The best physicians, he explains, set clear task goals, engage with both patients and other medical professionals, and establish an environment of learning. Convincing other physicians that leadership plays an important part in their success requires more than just casual observation.

Like most physicians in the United States, Dr. Stockwell received expert training in medicine and has spent most of his adult life learning how to provide the best care possible through proper diagnosis and treatment, but Dr. Stockwell saw that most physicians received little or no training in leadership. This lack of training in leadership may lead to problems including poor patient care, failure to achieve daily goals, and generally poor 'bedside manner'.

6 Apply the concepts of leadership to organizations.

In order to improve the leadership of medical personnel on his unit, Dr. Stockwell developed a program based on organizational behavior and leadership principles. First, Dr. Stockwell became familiar with general leadership theories. Several important leadership theories stood out for him. Transactional and transformational leadership helped him understand how physicians needed to focus on both the emotional and the medical aspects of patient care. Context factors in leadership helped David realize the importance of building a culture safe for identifying and talking about errors. To further his knowledge, Dr. Stockwell returned to school and earned an MBA where he learned about the role of motivation, teams, and personality in medicine. With his new knowledge of organizational behavior and leadership, he developed a list of skills that were important for leading in the Critical Care Unit, which are summarized in the following table:

Leadership Skills for Physicians in a Pediatric Intensive Care Unit*

- Understands and acknowledges the importance of teamwork
- Communicates goals and expectations
- Acknowledges errors and mistakes, including those of the leader
- Recognizes and addresses conflicts on the team
- Encourages team members take on responsibilities
- Helps manage stress and time pressures
- Encourages learning
- Identifies goals and set high standards

(continued)

Dr. Stockwell found that concepts from leadership helped improve medical care on his unit. Leadership skills proved to be an important part of successful patient care. Physicians who demonstrated the highest levels of leadership showed better performance on two activities: achieving daily patient care goals and doing so in a timely manner. Drawing on his newly acquired knowledge of organizational behavior concepts, Dr. Stockwell continues to teach his fellow physicians and other medical professionals on his unit the importance of leadership in the highly specialized work of medical care.

SPOTLIGHT ON RESEARCH
The Impact of Unconventional Leader Behavior on Organizational Creativity

People often become attracted to leaders because of their peculiar use of words, gestures, or the unconventional stances they take on issues. Researchers have long known that unconventional behavior of this sort fascinates some followers. Some researchers argue that charismatic leaders gain influence over followers due to the unconventional behavior they display and the compelling ideas they communicate.

Followers may find this kind of behavior interesting, but researchers wanted to understand what unconventional behavior demonstrated by leaders might mean to organizations. For example, did followers become more motivated, perform their jobs better, or did they show more creativity when engaged with a charismatic leader? Students at one university received a first-hand opportunity to find out how the unconventional behavior of leaders might improve creativity.

One group of students came to class and their instructors used conventional tools to conduct the course. Their instructor sat in a chair near the students, spoke to students in a normal way, and in every other element of behavior appeared uncontroversial. A second group of students experienced something markedly different. The instructor gave course instructions on the back of t-shirts that students were asked to wear, often stood on a chair, and confirmed correct answers on an exam by handing out scratch and sniff stickers. Rather than write on the board in front of the classroom, the instructor wrote student comments on socks and hung them from a clothesline strung across the classroom.

These students took part in an exercise to better understand if unconventional behavior demonstrated by a leader, in this case, a course instructor, would improve creativity. A group of outside observers who knew nothing about the task rated the creativity of each individual and each group. The result of the study revealed that, under some circumstances, the group exposed to the unconventional leader behavior demonstrated higher levels of creativity. This study revealed additional insights as well. Creativity only increased if the students also perceived the instructor as a role

(continued)

model. In addition, when groups of students already had a high degree of motivation for creativity, their exposure to an unconventional leader increased group cohesion, the emotional sense of belonging to the group. The study lends credence to the notion that unconventional behavior, demonstrated by leaders, can indeed increase the performance outcomes of followers.

Questions for Discussion

1. How might you and your classmates react if your instructor acted in such an unconventional way?

2. What limits to unconventional behavior might there be? For example, are there certain behaviors, as demonstrated by instructors that might actually decrease creativity?

3. What unconventional behavior have you observed in the workplace? In other settings? Was it effective? Why do you think so?

*Based on the article by Jaussi, K. S., & S. D. D. Dionne (2003). "Leading for creativity: The role of unconventional leader behavior." *Leadership Quarterly*, 14, 475–498.

Pairing with this Topic Summary

Suggested Expert Contributions

The Ups and Downs of Leading People—Michael Useem
(University of Pennsylvania)

Crisis Leadership: The New Norm for Effectively Leading Organizations—Erika James
(Emory University)

Why Should Anyone Be Led by You?—Rob Goffee (London Business School) and Gareth Jones (IE Business School, Madrid)

Suggested Cases

Case 1: The Case of Apple iPhone 4

Case 4: FaceTime at TechPoint Software, Inc.

Case 5: Whatever Happened to One of the "100 Best Companies to Work For"?: A Case Study of Hewlett-Packard
Case 7: Perceptions of Leaders Following Public Failures: A Tale of Two Coaches

Suggested Exercises

Exercise 2: Creating My Brand

Exercise 4: How Leaders Effect You

Exercise 6: Developing Your Career—Leadership Development in Action

Exercise 38: FIS Simulation

Endnotes

1. Yukl, G. (2010). *Leadership in organizations* (7th ed.). Upper Saddle River: Pearson Prentice Hall.
2. Kotter, J. P. (1990). *A force for change: How leadership differs from management.* New York: Free Press.
3. Bennis, W. G. (1959). Leadership theory and administrative behavior: The problem of authority. *Administrative Science Quarterly, 4,* 259–260.
4. Stodgill, R. M. (1948). Personal factors associated with leadership: A survey of the literature. *Journal of Psychology, 25,* 35–71.
5. Judge, T. A., Bono, J. E. Ilies, R., & M. W., Gerhardt. (2002). Personality and leadership: A qualitative and quantitative review. *Journal of Applied Psychology,* August, 765–780.
6. Judge, T. A., & Cable, D. M. (2004). The effect of physical height on workplace success and income: Preliminary test of a theoretical model. *Journal of Applied Psychology, 89,* 3, 428–441. Judge, T. A., & Cable, D. M. (2010). When it comes to pay, do the thin win? The effect of weight on pay for men and women. *Journal of Applied Psychology, 96,* 95–112.
7. Bales, R. F. (1950). A set of categories for the analysis of small group interaction. *American Sociological Review, 15,* 257–263. Benne, K. D., & Sheats, P. (1948). Functional roles of group members. *Journal of Social Issues, 2,* 42–47.
8. Blake, R. R., & Mouton, J. S. (1964). *The managerial grid.* Houston: Gulf Publishing. Fiedler, F. 1967. *A theory of leadership effectiveness.* New York: McGraw-Hill.
9. Hersey, P., & Blanchard, K. H. (1984). *The management of organizational behavior* (4th ed.). Englewood Cliffs: Prentice Hall.
10. House, R. J. (1971). A path–goal theory of leader effectiveness. *Administrative Science Quarterly, 15,* 321–339.
11. Weber, M. (1947). *The theory of social and economic organizations.* Translated by T. Parsons. New York: Free Press.
12. House, R. J. (1977). A 1976 theory of charismatic leadership. In J. g. Hunt & L. L. Larson (Eds.) *Leadership: The cutting edge.* Carbondale: Southern Illinois University Press, 189–207.
13. Conger, J. A. (1989). *The charismatic leader: Behind the mystique of exceptional leadership.* San Francisco, CA: Jossey-Bass. Conger, J. A., & Kanungo, R. (1987). Toward a behavioral theory of charismatic leadership in organizational settings. *Academy of Management Review, 12,* 637–647.
14. Burns, J. M. (1978). *Leadership.* New York: Harper & Row.
15. Bass, B. M., & Steidlmeier, P. (1999). Ethics, character, and authentic transformational leadership. *Leadership Quarterly, 10,* 181–217. Bass, B. M., & Avolio, B. (1990). *Multifactor leadership questionnaire.* Palo Alto, CA: Consulting Psychologists Press.
16. Bennis, W. G., & Nanus, B. (1985). *Leaders: The strategies for taking charge.* New York: Harper & Row.
17. Kouzes, J. M., & Posner, B. Z. (1995). *The leadership challenge: How to keep getting extraordinary things done in organizations* (2nd ed.). San Francisco: Jossey-Bass.
18. Graen, G. B. & Uhl-Bien, M. (1995). Relationship-based approaches to leadership: Development of leader-member exchange (LMX) theory of leadership over 25 years: Applying a multi-level multi-domain approach. *Leadership Quarterly, 6,* 219–247.
19. House, R. L., Hanges, P. J., Javidan, Dorfman, P. W., Gupta, V. (2004). *Culture, leadership and organizations.* Thousand Oaks, CA: Sage.
20. Chin, J. L. (2010). (Ed). Special issue: Diversity and leadership. *American Psychologist, 65,* 3, 149–225.

21. Avolio, B. J., & Gardner, W. L. (2005). Authentic leadership development: Getting to the root of positive forms of leadership. *The Leadership Quarterly, 16,* 3, 315–338. George, B. (2004.) *Authentic leadership.* Thousand Oaks, CA: Jossey-Bass. See also Greenleaf, R. K. (2003). *The servant–leader within: A transformative path.* New York: Paulist Press.

22. Kellerman, B. (2004). *Bad leadership.* Cambridge, MA: Harvard Business School Press. Maccoby, M. (2000). Narcissistic leaders: The incredible pros, the inevitable cons. *Harvard Business Review,* Jan. Offermann, L. R. (2004). When followers become toxic. *Harvard Business Review.* January 55–60.

23. Chin, J. L. (2010). (Ed.). Special issue: Diversity and leadership. *American Psychologist, 65,* 3, 149–225.

24. Sims, H. P., Faraj, S., & Yun, S. (2009). When should a leader be directive or empowering? How to develop your own situational theory of leadership. *Business Horizons, 52,* 149–152. O'Toole, J., Galbraith, J., and Lawler, E. E. (2002). When two (or more) heads are better than one: The promise and pitfalls of shared leadership. *California Management Review, 44,* 4. Pearce, C. L., & Conger, J. A. (2002). *Shared leadership.* Thousand Oaks: Sage

The Ups and Downs of Leading People

Michael Useem

University of Pennsylvania

Leadership is a matter of mobilizing those who report to you. Whether a community, cause, or a company, it means mustering those below for higher purpose. Or at least that is a common definition of what it means to lead other people.

Yet that downward focus obscures moments when a manager can apply much the same skill set to making a difference in the upward direction, persuading a boss to think more strategically or change course before it is too late. It is not a matter of undermining authority or eroding power of those above. Rather, upward leadership means stepping in when a manager's superiors would benefit from additional guidance in ways that benefit the enterprise, regardless of personal payoff.

Leading up is not the same as managing up, a vital but separate aspect of career management. Leading up means influencing those in positions of superior power. Most everybody prefers the good graces of a good boss, of being seen as a diligent worker and team player. The title of a classic article by John Gabarro and John Kotter perfectly captures the essence of this career enabler: "Managing Your Boss," and successfully doing so requires, in their view, appreciating the boss's blind spots, works pressures, and personal predilections. The creative steps for doing so are many, nearly five dozen in the subtitle of one self-help manual: *59 Ways to Build a Career-Advancing Relationship with Your Boss.*[1]

Other volumes proffer advice for the related challenge of simply coping with a bad boss: *When Smart People Work for Dumb Bosses: How to Survive in a Crazy and Dysfunctional Workplace*, offers one book. Another title: *I Hate My Boss!: How to Survive and Get Ahead When Your Boss is A Tyrant, Control Freak, or Just Plain Nuts!*[2]

Leading up is a different calling—one that places enterprise purpose above parochial interest. It entails offering up strategic advice, better products, or early warnings—and doing so regardless of the benefits or costs to the upward leader.

Leading up is a two-pronged affair, requiring leadership in two opposed directions at the same time. It is a matter of stepping into a breach when nobody above you is doing so. And it is also a matter of drawing the best from those below you before you step off a cliff yourself.

Leading up is not always invited or welcomed. Many managers have worked for a superior who managed ever detail, ruled without a strategy, or faulted everything and praised nobody. In such a situation, upward leadership can be risky, futile, or even fatal.

Even when it is appreciated, upward leadership is not a natural skill set any more than are the capacities that define downward leadership. But like all leadership abilities, it can be learned through study, experience, and feedback. Building on this premise, the business-school faculty on which I serve requires that all of our 2,500 undergraduate students and 2,000 MBA students successfully complete a course on leadership. Everybody can improve their leadership for both directions, we believe, and as a primer for the upward direction, I offer four accounts of those who have led up—or failed to do so when they should have.[3]

If you have not had occasion to lead in any substantial way, it is nonetheless likely that you will have an opportunity to do so from time to time in your community, where you work, or maybe even in a social cause or political campaign. In anticipation of such a moment, mastering the art of leading others—not only reporting to you but also of those to whom you report—can be an important step.

A good way to explore and test the ideas that follow is to try them out with individuals whose leadership you look up to, whether a sports coach, religious leader, public official, or work supervisor. In doing so, however, it is important to be cautious, since although some leaders welcome guidance from below, others can be resentful or even threatened. The exercise of upward leadership is thus undertaken with good purpose, but also careful consideration.

The Cost of Not Leading Up

Samsung Group is Korea's largest conglomerate, making everything from ships and steel to mobile phones and semiconductors. Unlike domestic rival Hyundai, another diversified giant, however, Samsung does not produce automobiles, though not for the lack of trying.

The chairman of Samsung Group, Lee Kun Hee, decided in 1994 that his company should enter into the auto market, and he directed $13 billion at the effort, targeting the production of 1.5 million vehicles by 2010. Though car making was already a crowded and over-supplied industry, with too many sellers vying for too few buyers, the ambitious Samsung chairman was an auto enthusiast and fan of his plan.

Yet, less than a year after the first cars rolled off its production line, Samsung Motors sold off its assets to French car manufacturer, Renault, and exited the auto making business. Lee was even forced to reach into his own family fortune for $2 billion to meet the demands of Samsung's unhappy creditors. His own subordinates had opposed the auto investment to begin with, but they had opted to suffer in silence, evidently reluctant to bring their reservations up to the powerful chieftain. Had they done so, even if very unwelcome advice at the time, it would have certainly saved the company, its investors, and the chairman himself from a very costly mistake.

The human cost of failing to take vital news up the chain was ever more starkly evident in the wake of the sudden surfacing of USS Greeneville, a nuclear submarine, off the coast of Hawaii on February 9, 2001. Commander Scott D. Waddle had been demonstrating the submarine's capabilities to sixteen civilian visitors on board that day, and after an abbreviated periscope inspection of the surface, the Greeneville shot to the surface, unaware that a Japanese training ship for high school students, the Ehime Maru, was by chance at precisely the same spot. The training ship sunk within minutes of its ramming, killing five crew members and four high school students.

A subsequent investigation revealed that the commander's subordinates had been concerned that he was rushing too quickly through the demonstration of the emergency maneuver. The submarine's second ranking officer, for instance, harbored private doubts about the commander's pace, and while he "was thinking these things," an investigator concluded, "he did not articulate them to the commanding officer." And that was because the commander, in the words of the investigator, "doesn't get a lot of corrective input from subordinates because he's very busy giving directions and the ship has experienced a lot of success when he does."

For cash losses stemming from the failure of upward leadership, few disasters come close to that experienced by AIG Financial Products (AIGFP). Its parent, American International Group (AIG), had been founded in Shanghai in 1919, and by 2008 it employed more than

115,000, serviced 74 million customers, generated $110 billion in revenue, and managed assets of $860 billion. It had become one of the 30 blue-chip stocks that define the Dow Jones Industrial Average, and it ranked among the 20 largest publicly traded companies worldwide.

AIG had launched its London-based AIG Financial Products in 1987 to insure complex and risky financial products, such as bundles of subprime home mortgages. At its peak, fewer than 400 employees at AIGFP managed an insurance portfolio of $1.6 trillion, the equivalent of more than half the GDP of France, and in doing so they produced 17 percent of the parent's operating income. The average employee earned more than $1 million annually, and confidence and optimism predictably prevailed. AIGFP's president, Joseph Cassano, reported, "It is hard for us, without being flippant, to even see a scenario within any kind of realm of reason that would see us losing one dollar in any of those transactions."

Despite the sanguine view at the top, by 2008, AIGFP's mid-level managers had become increasingly alarmed about the systemic risks that had built-up in the sub-prime home mortgage market, defaults of which their division had been massively insuring against. But warning signs did not travel well up the hierarchy. Cassano, in the words of one observer, had a "real talent for bullying people who doubted him," and the division had become, in the words of one of its traders, "a dictatorship." Another employee reported that "the fear level was so high that when we had these morning meetings you presented what you did not to upset him." Still another said, "the way you dealt with Joe was to start everything by saying, 'you're right, Joe.'"[4]

With failures in the subprime home mortgage rapidly spreading in 2008, Lehman collapsed on September 15 in part because of them. AIGFP's leadership, and that of its parent, proved unprepared to face the resulting downdraft—despite ample warnings that would have come up from the middle ranks had they been tolerated. The parent company collapsed a day later, brought down by the enormous losses of AIGFP. AIG was in the red by $61 billion by the end of the year, the largest annual shortfall in corporate history, and the United States ultimately injected more than $170 billion and took control to save the firm from bankruptcy.

The sources of the failures of those in the middle to lead up were diverse. In the case of Samsung, it was partly a product of a CEO style that did not encourage upward warnings when a direction looked faulty. In the case of the USS Greeneville, it was partially attributable to the commander's prior successes that discouraged upward warnings about his own shortcomings. And in the case of AIGFP, it was due in no small part to its president's brow-beating of subordinates.

Whatever the sources, the consequences of the upward leadership failures were enormous. For Samsung, billions of dollars in lost investment; for the Greeneville, nine lives; and for AIG, the firm's collapse. With the benefit of hindsight, the Samsung chairman, Greeneville commander, and AIG chief executive would certainly have preferred that their subordinates had compelled them to lead in a different direction.

What It Takes

From witnessing the costs of not leading up and then seeking to understand its absence, it is evident that upward leadership requires a combination of courage and perseverance: courage to challenge superiors before their intent or ignorance can cause a disaster; perseverance for the determination to inform and convince superiors despite their continuing inertia or resistance.

Turned upside down, upward leadership also requires downward encouragement, and that is to embolden people below to speak up and inform their superiors what they need to know, to fill in for the superiors' shortcomings when future success is threatened or know when a different direction is better. Such a mindset is built, not born, and for that, managers who regularly insist that more junior staff examine proposals and challenge their judgment help create a culture of upward leadership. Asking those of lesser rank to say what they candidly think and consistently complimenting them for doing so are among the small measures that can make a big difference.

Risk and Reward

The stark costs of the failures of upward leadership can be matched by the special benefits when it works well. For an affirmative illustration of upward leadership that ultimately served the national interest, consider the upward leadership of U.S. Trade Representative, Charlene Barshefsky.

A Washington-based lawyer, after graduating seventh in her law-school class at Catholic University, Barshefsky had been invited to join the new administration of President Bill Clinton in 1993 as an international trade official. She had been equivocal, even paralyzed, over whether to accept the invitation until driving to work one morning, when a passing car displayed a license plate with "Go4It." Upon reaching the office that morning, she did.

Chinese officials in 1995 had reiterated a long-standing interest in becoming a member of the World Trade Organization, the Geneva-based agency that sets the rules for international movement of goods and services. Membership had its privileges: country exports are boosted, but it also required responsibility, including openness and fairness in trade. Barshefsky warned at a Beijing press conference that "China cannot expect the American people to support new agreements if existing agreements are not enforced" for the protection of intellectual property and related issues, and she outlined an arduous "road-map" for the Chinese to follow if they hoped to gain U.S. support in their bid for WTO membership.

Barshefsky realized that opening trade with China would be an arduous path for the United States as well. It was not a front-burner for her president, but she believed a swift normalization of trade with China was unequivocally in the interests of the country that Bill Clinton had sworn to protect, even though his own political party contained many who were strongly opposed to free trade. For Barshefsky's, the driving principle was one of economic growth and improved security, in her words pursuing "Roosevelt's overarching vision that countries that send goods across borders don't send armies." She believed in a "bringing together of nations that were adversaries, an opening of the trading system to help ensure peace, stability, and prosperity," and that would constitute "policy making at its best for the broadest good."

Upward leadership requires one's own development of a vision and then helping one's superior to appreciate and act on it. It entails not just intellectually applauding the vision but also personally resolving to making it a reality. On both fronts, Barshefsky was ahead of the curve. She needed little instruction from the president to appreciate what the future would look like with China's incorporation into the global economy.

As Barshefsky began the arduous process of negotiating with the Chinese government, led by premier Zhu Rongji, she opened a parallel campaign with the U.S. constituencies most affected. She met with business associations and trade unions, she talked with official supporters and political detractors, and her staff painstakingly reviewed hundreds of letters received from members of Congress, organized labor, trade associations, and business firms.

Zhu signaled his readiness to make the necessary concessions to complete the deal, and he departed for Washington to confirm the accord. President Clinton had signaled his readiness to receive him: "If China is willing to play by the global rules of trade," he declared, "it would be an inexplicable mistake for the United States to say no." Yet, when the Chinese premier arrived at the White House in 1999, President Clinton was not yet ready to play. He faced intense resistance from his own party and wavered between approval and rejection. Behind closed doors, Charlene Barshefsky argued that the agreement be signed, but others cautioned Clinton against the prospect of a fight with his own political constituency whose support he otherwise needed.

The president concluded that the timing was not right, and on the very day of the Chinese premier's arrival in the capital, Clinton told the premier that the deal would have to wait. Stunned and humiliated, Zhu overtly expressed his displeasure: "Surely the American side realizes that the time has come to end negotiations which have already gone on for 13 years."

Not surprisingly, Barshefsky found herself in a cross-fire of recriminations. "Barshefsky cut one of the strongest trade deals the U.S. has ever negotiated," wrote the *Wall Street Journal*, but she "couldn't sell it to her most important client, Clinton." Even the Chinese premier chided her, saying that the United States "made public many documents and said we had agreed to them, but in fact we have not agreed."

To get negotiations back on track, Barshefsky turned to her Chinese counterpart in Washington to lock down what had already been agreed upon, and pushed for a statement that confirmed the progress to date. "I had to keep the deal together," she recalled. "To lose what we had when we were so close to getting it done would have been tragic."

Undercut by a superior who she had thought was ready for the agreement and then widely criticized for arranging the Chinese visit that went nowhere, Barshefsky's immediate response was to go back to business and full steam ahead. She appreciated that upward leadership on behalf of large causes will encounter significant setbacks, and without missing a beat, she plunged ahead in the mission she knew was too worthy for anything less. Barshefsky was soon back in Beijing to jump start the negotiations. Her relentless pursuit of the goal, whatever the inconsistency from above, would finally and fully pay off for her president and the country when the two sides signed a final agreement in Beijing in late 1999.

Still, Congressional approval was not assured, and Barshefsky threw herself into persuading Capitol Hill to vote for the pact as she entered into Congressional arm twisting at its best. She also sought to build public support, seeing it as essential if the president were to secure the votes he needed. She helped secure the backing of 42 state governors, 149 prominent economists, and 200 chief executives. The House of Representatives voted 237 to 197 for the measure, and then the Senate by a vote of 83 to 15. The legislation normalized trade with China, signaling the greatest change in U.S. relations with the country since president Nixon's historic visit in 1972.

A White House official observed, "This thing didn't get done because of happenstance." A "helluva lot of things went into getting it done," and at the forefront was the upward leadership of Charlene Barshefsky. Without several years of dogged pursuit of an agreement, and without her appreciation for the fact that the president would only back it and Congress would only approve it if she negotiated a deal they needed and then persuaded them of that simple truth, it may never have gotten done.

Courage to Lead Up

A common element among those who successfully lead up is a driving urge to make things happen on high, and an unflinching willingness to take charge when not fully in command.

The exercise of upward leadership has been made easier by contemporary expectations in many companies that managers learn not just from their superiors but from all points of the compass. The phrase "360-degree feedback" has come to mean a manager's annual task of gathering reaction from direct subordinates and immediate bosses. So it is with leading up: instead of just motivating those below, managers should look to muster those above. And conversely, superiors need listen to those below.

Once established, a company-wide emphasis on leading upwards serves as a kind of inertial guidance system, continually reminding everybody that they are obliged to stand up without the need for superiors to ask them to do so.

Eight Principles for Leading Up

For the Person Leading Up	For the Person Who Seeks Upward Leadership from Those Below
Confidence: Building a boss's confidence in you depends on giving him or her your confidence and complete commitment to the enterprise.	*Convey Your Intent:* For upward leadership from those below, convey your vision and strategy through repeated expression of and consistent adherence to them.
Clear-Minded: The more uncertain your superiors are about achieving a goal, the more clear-minded you must be in formulating and executing a strategy for reaching the goal.	*Listen to Subordinates:* Stay tuned to what subordinates are saying since they may appreciate the moment's risks and opportunities better than yourself.
Communicate: An effective upward relationship with a boss requires an open two-way flow of information and support.	*Use their Advice:* Subordinates will offer their best advice if you consistently hear, value, and make use of it.
Courage: Persistence often pays but it requires resilience to stay on a path that is likely to entail frequent setbacks and resistance.	*Virtuous Circle:* Downward and upward leadership reinforce one another, and if you are effective in one, it fortifies the other.

Further Reading

John Baldoni, *Lead Your Boss: The Subtle Art of Managing Up*, Amacom, 2009.

Jim Collins, *Good to Great: Why Some Companies Make the Leap…and Others Don't*, Harper-Collins, 2001.

Michael Useem, *Leading Up: How to Lead Your Boss So You Both Win*, Crown Business, 2001.

Michael Useem, *The Leader's Checklist*, Wharton Digital Press, 2011.

Endnotes

1. John J. Gabarro and John P. Kotter, "Managing Your Boss," *Harvard Business Review*, May–June, 1993; Michael Dobson and Deborah Singer Dobson, *Managing Up: 59 Ways to Build a Career-Advancing Relationship with Your Boss*, Amacom, 2000.
2. William Lundin and Kathleen Lundin, *When Smart People Work for Dumb Bosses: How to Survive in a Crazy and Dysfunctional Workplace*, McGraw-Hill, 1999; Bob Weinstein, *I Hate My Boss!: How to Survive and Get Ahead When Your Boss is A Tyrant, Control Freak, or Just Plain Nuts!* McGraw-Hill, 1997.
3. These accounts are drawn from Michael Useem, *Leading Up*, Crown Business, 2001, and Michael Useem, "Developing Leadership to Avert and Mitigate Disasters," in Howard Kunreuther and Michael Useem (Eds.)., *Learning from Catastrophes: Strategies for Reaction and Response*, Pearson, 2010. Sources for the accounts (including personal interviews) and the quoted materials are reported in these volumes.
4. Michael Lewis, "The Man Who Crashed the World," *Vanity Fair*, August, 2009.

Crisis Leadership: The New Norm for Effectively Leading Organizations

Erika James

Emory University

The dawn of the twenty-first century has proven to be a remarkable time for business-related crises around the world. Coming out of 2000 and the potential threat of the Year 2000 technological challenge (Y2K or millennium bug), businesses progressed through a series of financial scandals and meltdowns (including Enron, Worldcom, Lehman Brothers, and Merrill Lynch) and other catastrophes. To date, the century has been peppered with natural disasters (e.g., Hurricane Sandy in 2012, the Japanese tsunami in 2011, Haiti earthquake in 2010, and the 2005 Hurricane Katrina along the gulf coast of the United States), and by what many consider to be potentially the most severe environmental tragedy in history—the British Petroleum (BP) off-shore oil rig explosion in the Gulf of Mexico that killed 11 workers and caused extensive damage to marine and wildlife, as well as to the economic vitality of the region. The decade was further marked by labor disputes, and other employee crises (e.g., Wal-Mart's class action sex discrimination) and product recalls (e.g., Firestone and Toyota). In addition to this sampling of business crises there were the litany of personal crises that have adversely affected individual careers (e.g., Tiger Woods, Martha Stewart, former U.S. senator and one-time presidential candidate John Edwards). Moreover, we expect new crises to manifest with the proliferation of social media.[1]

The consequences to a firm's reputation as a result of a crisis can be severe. Yet it is often the case that the mishandling of a crisis, not always the crisis event itself, is what leads to the most sobering consequences for a firm and its leadership. Consider the 2010 oil spill in the Gulf of Mexico after the BP offshore oil drill exploded. Almost a year later, there is little visible environmental damage to the gulf coast, and many businesses are slowly returning to pre-spill conditions. Yet, what continues to exist in the public's memory are the missteps made by the BP leadership. One prominent blunder was related to communication with stakeholders, which was deemed insensitive to the victims. Another problem was with the perceived slow response time to the leak at the outset of the crisis. Perhaps even more importantly, however, were the potential mistakes by BP even before the explosion—mistakes associated with safety, for example, that oil industry experts believe may have contributed to the explosion and subsequent leak. The costs of BP's mishandling of the crisis were numerous, including a severe dip in the firm's reputation, increased regulatory scrutiny, and considerable financial implications in the form of legal fees, reimbursements, and clean-up expenses.

Background on Crisis

Crisis management includes: 1) the definition of crisis, 2) crisis typologies, and 3) the crisis-management process.

Defining Crisis. The notion of a business crisis was initially referred to as a type of strategic issue that has the potential to lead to negative organizational outcomes in the absence of an intervention.[2] Strategic issues were thought to differ from non-strategic issues because they are accompanied by time pressure and ambiguity. The more important, immediate, and uncertain the issue, the more likely it is to be characterized by a firm as a threat or crisis.[3] In more recent years, researchers added to the characterization of crisis by suggesting that it is a high-impact, low-probability event that threatens the security and well being of the public, and is often ambiguous in cause, effect, and means of resolution.[4] Finally, James and Wooten (p. 142) defined crisis as "any emotionally charged situation that, once it becomes public, invites negative stakeholder reaction and therefore has the potential to threaten the financial well being, reputation, or survival of the firm or some portion thereof."[5]

Consistent with each of the definitions described above is the idea that crises are rare events. Unlike a run-of-the-mill business problem, a true crisis event is something that is encountered infrequently, and as such, managers do not have a boiler-plate strategy for dealing with it. In addition, each of the aforementioned definitions alludes to crises being significant events. The potential adverse impact is severe, and, in the most extreme case, can lead to the demise of the organization. Finally, crises take a toll on individuals or groups that have a stake in the organization. Typical stakeholders include consumers, employees, neighboring communities, and even the natural environment.[6] In some cases, the effects of a crisis have consequences for people beyond local geographic boundaries and can affect stakeholders remotely, as was the case when the Chernobyl nuclear plant in Ukraine exploded, releasing radioactive material into the atmosphere that spread across country borders in the USSR and Europe.

Crisis Typologies. Although crises have some common features, there is no singular type of crisis event. As a result, scholars have devoted considerable attention to categorizing crises in meaningful ways. The benefit for doing so is that typologies can offer insight into how different organizational threats develop,[7] how stakeholders may be affected, and most importantly how to identify appropriate management responses.[8] Among the most basic crisis typologies are those that are dichotomous. For example, crises can be *sudden* or *smoldering* in nature. Sudden crises are those unexpected events that disrupt daily operations. Natural disasters and acts of terrorism are two forms of sudden crises. Smoldering crises, conversely, are those events that start out as small, internal problems within a firm, become public to stakeholders, and eventually escalate to crisis status as a result of inattention by management. According to the Institute for Crisis Management, nearly three-quarters of all business crises fall into the smoldering category and include such crises as: mismanagement, labor disputes, fraud, and class action lawsuits.[9] As organizations continue to increase in complexity, so too do the crisis types to which they may be vulnerable. Thus, in the evolution of the study of crisis and crisis management, organizational scholars have increasingly argued for and developed more sophisticated crisis typologies and engaged in more fine-grained analysis of crisis events.

Crisis Management Process. Whether a crisis is sudden or smoldering, the management of it is a process that unfolds over time. There are five typical stages of a business crisis.[10] These phases provide insight into effective management practices during times of crisis.[11] Phase 1 is called the *signal detection* phase because it is during this stage where crisis managers have the opportunity to heed warning signs that signal a crisis may be imminent. For various reasons, including the illusion of invulnerability, many managers fail to recognize the warnings and fail to act in ways that could prevent the crisis or reduce its adverse impact. Phase 2, *preparation and prevention*, is characterized by intentional planning activities intended to anticipate and avoid crises at the outset. Phase 3, or *damage control* and crisis containment, is enacted once a crisis event has occurred. Here, a manager's responsibility is to develop and execute a strategy for ending the crisis and limiting its scope and impact on stakeholders. Finally, in phase 4, the objective is *business recovery*, or getting the organization back to status quo.

Understanding these phases of a business crisis is a necessary precursor to developing the leadership competency to be a leader of organizations. However, research that only emphasizes these phases, or that seeks to focus only on developing more crisis typologies, is limiting. Rather, I argue that the challenge of managing crises is increasingly becoming a leadership responsibility and as such needs to be more closely aligned with the leadership literature. Understanding crisis phases and typologies, therefore, serve as a backdrop to the next section where I specifically discuss leadership in times of crisis.

Crisis Leadership: What Leaders Do

So what differentiates firms that successfully maneuver through a crisis, and thrive in its aftermath, from those that merely survive and return to status quo? One important answer is the *leadership* displayed throughout the crisis handling process. As described by James and Wooten, crisis leadership is the ability to take a broad and long-term view of the organization and its stakeholders so as not to be blinded by a need to react and be defensive.[12] Crisis Leadership is also about tapping into creativity, in oneself or in others, in such a way as to use the crisis as a starting point for making the organization better off after the crisis than it was before.[13] Yet too often, crisis leadership is mistaken for a series of reactive decisions and strategic communication. Even worse is when leaders deem a crisis to be over merely because the acute stage of the problem has been addressed. To be clear, the tactical aspects of crisis response, including crisis communication and damage control, are an important and necessary part of crisis management. But true leadership during crisis entails something so much more than these management activities.[14] As James and Wooten articulated, there are key aspects of crisis leadership, several of which are described below.

Building Trust. In order to achieve the proverbial opportunity from crisis, it is incumbent upon leaders to engage in the difficult process of building a foundation of trust with an organization's internal and external stakeholders. Without trust, organizational decision making and strategy implementation are doomed to fail because: 1) employees need to feel safe in their work environments, 2) customers need to have faith in the products or services rendered by organizations with which they do business, and 3) business partners require cooperative intentions and mutually beneficial work arrangements. To build trust, leaders need to communicate openly, honestly, and often.[15] Although sharing information is paramount, some leaders fear that it will be perceived as a sign of weakness because access to information is power. Yet, giving away power and allowing oneself as a leader to be vulnerable is precisely the behavior that fosters trust in the workplace and ensures that internal and external stakeholders will be by your side during difficult times. Leaders then use that foundation to prepare their organizations for difficult times, to contain crises when they occur, and to actively learn from crisis situations for the purposes of creating positive organizational change and innovation.

Perhaps no other crisis conjures up the centrality of trust more than the now infamous case of the Johnson & Johnson (J&J) Tylenol crisis. The pharmaceutical giant had built a reputation of being one of the most trusted brands in the world, and the firm's credo exemplified their commitment to establishing trust with all their stakeholders.[16] In 1982 the company was rocked by a crisis when bottles of its flagship product, Tylenol, had been laced with poison and killed seven people. Fear among consumers was wide spread, yet, to pull the product from store shelves all over the country would have been costly to the firm. J & J realized, however, that the cost of the firm's reputation was far more expensive than the cost to temporarily pull the product. The company was guided by its commitment to stakeholders and was able to restore public trust in its brand despite circumstances that would have severely strained many other firms.

Taking Courageous Action. The ability to take courageous action is another important leadership competency during crisis. However, during these trying times is when it is often most difficult to be courageous and take risks. There is so much ambiguity associated with a crisis and its impending outcomes that managers often attempt to counter that risk by becoming extra conservative in their response to it.[17] Effective crisis leaders will embrace the opportunity to think and act big, yet responsibly. This often entails making decisions and adopting behavior that is counter-intuitive or that goes beyond what might be mandated by the situation.

The now infamous plane landing of US Airways Flight 1549, by Captain Sullenberger demonstrates a leader taking courageous action. Shortly after the flight departed New York's LaGuardia airport, the plane hit a flock of birds which disabled both of the jet's engines. The plane would have to make an emergency landing despite there being two airports in the vicinity. Sullneberger's assessment was that the plane would not make it to either destination. Rather than become paralyzed by fear he made the courageous decision to attempt a landing in the Hudson River despite his having no first-hand experience with water landings. The decision paid off and everyone, passengers and crew, walked away from the accident.

Learning from Crisis. Just as building trusting relationships and taking courageous action with stakeholders is an important pre-crisis leadership responsibility, adopting a learning stance is an important post-crisis leadership objective.[18] The field of medicine offers a relevant analogy. When a patient is severely injured and risks bleeding to death, doctors generally apply a tourniquet. When the bleeding stops, it is customary to loosen the tourniquet. Without additional attention to subsequent healing, however, the wound never completely mends. Furthermore, in the absence of understanding the factors leading up to the injury, the person remains vulnerable to injuries in the future. The same logic applies to organizational crises. If leaders fail to appropriately "dress the wound" left by the crisis event, or fail to engage in a root cause analysis to understand why the crisis occurred or what the organization could have done differently to prevent its escalation, then they leave themselves vulnerable to repeat threats.

Organizations learn from either their own previous mistakes or from the mistakes of others, as was the case when a newspaper headline read the "Georgia Power Learns from Coca-Cola Bias Suit: Utility's Response Shows Lessons Gleaned from Soft Drink Giant's Actions."[19] On the heels of a public and costly class action discrimination lawsuit by the Coca-Cola Company in Atlanta, GA, Georgia Power, also located in Atlanta, seemingly took stock of the mistakes made by Coca-Cola in their handling of the lawsuit. In light of that learning, Georgia Power favorably altered its course for managing it's own discrimination-related crisis and was rewarded with positive media attention, which can easily translate into positive reputational benefits.[20]

Ideas in Action: Benefits of Crisis Leadership

Whereas crisis management is about the tactical aspects of responding to crisis (e.g., crisis communication and damage control), as I have outlined above, crisis leadership entails a more holistic set of behaviors. Furthermore, crisis leadership is a mindset accompanied by those behaviors. The mindset is essentially one in which all things are possible and a belief that even in times of crisis, people and organizations can emerge better off after a crisis than before. As shown in Figure 1, there are two key opportunities to be reaped from crisis. The first is the opportunity to reduce the frequency, likelihood, or impact of future negative events. If, for example, in managing a crisis, leaders eliminate conditions that detract from their firm's ability to compete, or if they make changes that make future crises less likely to recur, then they are better off as a result of having experienced the crisis. On the other hand, opportunity may be realized if organizations can enhance the frequency, likelihood, or impact of future positive events. Leaders who are able to introduce changes into the organization's culture, systems, processes, products, or services that have the effect of enhancing firm performance are more inclined to yield good outcomes for the firm and its stakeholders.

Figure 1 Crisis Leadership Behaviors and Organizational Outcomes

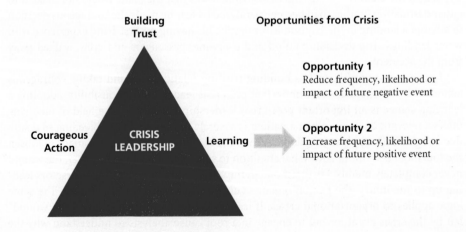

Building Trust

Opportunities from Crisis

Courageous Action

CRISIS LEADERSHIP

Learning

Opportunity 1
Reduce frequency, likelihood or impact of future negative event

Opportunity 2
Increase frequency, likelihood or impact of future positive event

Conclusion

On the surface, the hallmarks of effective crisis leadership are applicable under any leadership circumstance, so highlighting leadership in the context of a crisis may seem unnecessary. While there is some truth to this assertion, there are unique features of leadership during times of crisis that warrant special attention. First, leaders in crisis are often forced to operate under heightened visibility and publicity. The public nature of these situations can foster anxiety that may adversely affect behavior and performance.[21] Second, during crisis a leader's fight or flight response is activated which can also result in suboptimal (e.g., less strategic and thoughtful) decision-making, restrict information processing, and constrict control within an organization such that power and influence becomes concentrated with the most senior-level decision makers.[22] Finally, because crises are unpleasant to deal with, leaders desire for them to reach resolution quickly. In the process of "efficient" crisis management, however, leaders may circumvent sound business practices and engage in behavior that is deceptive or unethical—the antithesis of crisis leadership. However, by consciously being attuned to the big picture of a crisis and the opportunities for innovation that can be created as a result of some crises, organizations may be positioned to reap numerous benefits. This article highlights important leadership competencies to help leaders transition from crisis management to crisis leadership.

Endnotes

1. Pearson, C. Roux-Dufort, C. Clair, J. (2007). *International Handbook of Organizational Crisis Management*. New York: Sage.
2. Dutton, J. E. (1986). The processing of crisis and non-crisis strategic issues. *Journal of Management Studies*, 23 (5), 501–517.
3. Billings, R. S., Milburn, T. W., & Schaalman, ML. (1980). A model of crisis perception: A theoretical empirical analysis. *Administrative Science Quarterly*, 25: 300–316.
4. Pearson, C. Roux-Dufort, C. Clair, J. (2007).
5. James, E.H. & Wooten, L.P. (2005). Leadership as (Un)usual: How to Display Competence in Times of Crisis. *Organizational Dynamics*, 34(2), 141–152.
6. Mitroff, I., Pearson, C. & Shrivastava, P. (1988). Conceptual and empirical issues in the development of a general theory of crisis management. *Technological Forecasting and Social Change*, 33, 83–107.
7. Gundel, S. (2005). Towards a new typology of crises. *Journal of Contingencies and Crisis Management*, 13(3), 106–115.
8. Pearson, C. & Mitroff, I. (1993). From crisis prone to crisis prepared: A framework for crisis management. *Academy of Management Executive*, 7(10), 48–59.
9. James, E.H. & Wooten, L.P. (2005).
10. Pearson, C. & Mitroff, I. (1993).
11. James, E.H. & Wooten, L.P. (2005).
12. James, E.H. & Wooten, L. P. (2010). *Leading Under Pressure: From Surviving to Thriving Before, During, and After a Crisis*. New York: Routledge Press.
13. Brockner, J. B. & James, E. H. (2008). Toward an understanding of when executives see crisis as opportunity. *Journal of Applied Behavioral Science*, 44(1): 94–115.

14. James, E.H. & Wooten, L.P. (2005). Brockner, J. B. & James, E. H. (2008).
15. Mishra, A. (1996). Organizational response to crisis: The centrality of trust. In, R. Kramer and T. Thomas (Eds.), *Trust in Organizations* (261–287). Newbury Park, CA: Sage.
16. James, E.H. & Wooten, L. P. (2010).
17. Staw, B, M., Sandelands L. E.m & Dutton, J. E. (1981). Threat-rigidity effects in organizational behavior: A multilevel analysis. *Administrative Science Quarterly*, 26, 501–524
18. Brockner, J. B. & James, E. H. (2008). James, E.H. & Wooten, L. P. (2010).
19. Quinn, M. (2000). Ga Power learns from Coca-Cola bias suit cases similar: Utility's response shows lessons gleaned from soft drink giant's actions. *Atlanta Journal-Constitution, p. F1.*
20. James, E.H. & Wooten, L.P. (2005).
21. Eysenck, M. W., Derakshan, N., Santo, R. & Calvo, M. G. (2007). Anxiety and cognitive performance: Attentional control theory. *Emotion*, 7(20): 336–353.
22. Staw, B, M., Sandelands L. E.m & Dutton, J. E. (1981). Threat-rigidity effects in organizational behavior: A multilevel analysis. *Administrative Science Quarterly*, 26, 501–524

Why Should Anyone Be Led By You?

Rob Goffee
London Business School

Gareth Jones
IE Business School, Madrid

Leadership isn't easy. This seems an obvious statement. But much of the literature and the media frenzy surrounding leaders and leadership suggests that leadership is effortlessly attained or effective leadership can be explained by a list of desirable attributes. It cannot.

The success of the many leaders we have worked with and interviewed over the past two decades stems from active engagement in a complex series of carefully cultivated relationships—often in very different contexts. Leaders who nurture these relationships and master different contexts are able to help their organizations achieve a clearly identified higher purpose. Those who get it wrong are often derailed. The high rates of CEO turnover that have attracted interest over recent years are proof that the risks of leadership can be great.

Walking on the high wire is a powerful metaphor for the work of leaders. The reality is that with their eyes on the prize, leaders have to be constantly aware of the potential price of leadership. As a leader you are involved in a balancing act in five key areas:

- Knowing and showing yourself—enough
- Taking personal risks
- Reading—and rewriting—the context
- Managing social distance
- Communicating with care

If you ever want to silence a room full of restive executives, drop the tone of your voice and quietly ask them 'Why should anyone be led by you?' You'll get silence—it's a hard question.

Leadership: An Overview of Past Research

People have been talking about leadership at least since the time of Plato. But in organizations all over the world—in dinosaur conglomerates and new-economy start-ups alike—the same complaint emerges: we don't have enough leadership. We have to ask ourselves, 'Why are we so obsessed with leadership?'

One answer is that there is a crisis of belief in the modern world that has its roots in the rationalist revolution of the eighteenth century. During the Enlightenment, philosophers claimed that through the application of reason alone, people could control their destiny. This marked an incredibly optimistic turn in world history. In the nineteenth century, two beliefs stemmed from this rationalist notion: a belief in progress and a belief in the perfectibility of man. This produced an even more optimistic world view than before. It wasn't until the end of the nineteenth century, with the writings first of Sigmund

Freud and later of Max Weber, that this ideology was challenged. These two thinkers questioned Western man's belief in rationality and progress. The current quest for leadership is a direct consequence of their work.

The founder of psychoanalysis, Freud theorized that beneath the surface of the rational mind was the unconscious. He supposed that the unconscious was responsible for a considerable proportion of human behavior. Weber, the leading critic of Marx and a brilliant sociologist, also explored the limits of reason. Indeed, for him, the most destructive force operating in institutions was something he called technical rationality—that is, rationality without morality.

For Weber, technical rationality was embodied in one particular organizational form— the bureaucracy. Bureaucracies, he said, were frightening not for their inefficiencies but for their efficiencies and their capacity to dehumanize people. Weber believed that the only power that could resist bureaucratization was charismatic leadership. But even this has a very mixed record in the twentieth century. Although there have been inspirational and transformational wartime leaders, there have also been charismatic leaders like Hitler, Stalin, and Mao Tse-tung who committed horrendous atrocities.

By the twentieth century, there was much skepticism about the power of reason and man's ability to progress continuously. Thus, for both pragmatic and philosophic reasons, an intense interest in the concept of leadership began to develop. It also became clear that effective leadership had a big positive impact on performance. In the 1920s, the first serious behavioral science started. The first leadership theory—trait theory—attempted to identify the common characteristics of effective leaders. To that end, leaders were weighed and measured and subjected to a battery of psychological tests. But no one could identify what effective leaders had in common. Trait theory fell into disfavor soon after expensive studies concluded that effective leaders were either above-average height or below.

Trait theory was replaced by style theory in the 1930s, primarily in the United States. One particular style of leadership was singled out as having the most potential. It was a hail–fellow–well–met democratic style of leadership, and thousands of American executives were sent to training courses to learn how to behave this way. There was only one drawback. The theory was essentially capturing the spirit of FDR's America—open, democratic, and meritocratic. And so when McCarthyism and the Cold War followed the New Deal, a completely new style was required. Suddenly, everyone was encouraged to behave like a Cold War warrior! The poor executive was completely confused.

Recent leadership thinking is dominated by contingency theory, which says that leadership is dependent on a particular situation. That's fundamentally true, but given that there are endless contingencies in life, there are endless varieties of leadership. Once again, the beleaguered executive looking for a model to help him is hopelessly lost.

For this article, we ransacked all the leadership theories to come up with the five essential leadership qualities. Like Weber, we look at leadership that is primarily antibureaucratic and charismatic (knowing and showing yourself enough). From trait theory, we derived the qualities of personal risks and individual differences. Unlike the original trait theorists, however, we do not believe that all leaders have the same weaknesses; our research only showed that all leaders expose some flaws. Managing social distance grew out of style theory, which looked at different kinds of relationships between leaders and their followers. Finally, context theory set the stage for needing to read the situation—and to rewrite it through careful communication.

Knowing and Showing Yourself—Enough

Leadership is personal. It is unlikely that you will be able to inspire, arouse, excite, or motivate people unless you can show them who you are, what you stand for, and what you can and cannot do.

Inspirational leaders capture what is unique about themselves—and use it, skillfully. Consider Sir Martin Sorrell, leader of the world's largest communications services company, WPP. Sorrell runs an organization full of creative talent. Creative people are notoriously difficult to lead or even manage but are critical to WPP's success.

Sorrell is a bundle of energy. He is opinionated, forthright, and clever. Over a sustained period he has applied these talents to build a formidable global business. And over the years he has also learned to use some of his personal differences as a leader. Ask his colleagues about Sorrell and a fairly consistent picture emerges.

First they will tell you of his legendarily rapid response to e-mails—whenever, wherever. It's not unusual, for example, for Sorrell to spend a working week in the United States but remain on U.K. time for those he works with in London. All of Sorrell's colleagues have access to him. His message is clear: I am available. You are important. As he told us, "If someone contacts you, there's a reason. It's got nothing to do with the hierarchy. It doesn't matter if they're not a big person. There's nothing more frustrating than a voice-mail and then nothing back. We're in a service business."

But this is not the only difference he communicates. "I am seen as the boring, workaholic accountant and as a micromanager," he told us. "But I take it as a compliment rather than an insult. Involvement is important. You've got to know what's going on." Anyone receiving a visit from Sorrell can expect some tough one-to-one questioning—on the numbers as well as the creative side of the business. Sorrell's difference reminds people that, central though creativity is, WPP is a creative business.

Sorrell is not the most introspective character in the world—he is far too busy for that. But he knows enough about what works for him in a particular context. He uses his leadership differences—accessibility, close involvement in business detail, restlessness—to balance the creative side. These leadership assets are a foil for, on the one hand, the hierarchy and complacency that can strangle large, successful businesses and, on the other, unrestrained generation of new ideas, which can lead creative organizations to lose business focus.

To show people who you are requires a degree of self-knowledge (or at least self-awareness) as well as self-disclosure. One without the other is hopeless. So to be yourself, you must know yourself and show yourself—enough.

Taking Personal Risks

Showing yourself as a leader always involves risks, and the risks are personal. Leaders must always be willing to commit themselves—knowing that they can be undone.

Charles de Gaulle poignantly observed of those who aspired to lead, "The price they have to pay for leadership is unceasing self-discipline, the constant taking of risks, and perpetual inner struggle...whence that vague sense of melancholy which hangs about the skirts of majesty."

Because they really care about the purpose of the organization, effective leaders reveal themselves—what they care about, why they care about it, and how they believe the organization can achieve its stated goals.

Leadership is not an end in itself. It is for a purpose—feeding the world, curing cancer, making great music widely available or selling lots of BMWs. Leaders feel this deep involvement with the purpose of their organizations. It's one of the reasons that they can tap into deep reservoirs of energy.

But there is also an element of detachment that enables authentic leaders to monitor and adjust their own effectiveness. For example, effective leaders reveal weakness. In doing so they give their followers a chance to help and encourage them to reveal their own. The revelation of weakness humanizes the leader. Initially we suspect that the revelation of weakness is unknowing. But once leaders begin to recognize the impact of displays of fallibility, self-awareness increases—and with it the option to modify their behavior, if only in small ways.

Effective leaders care enough to reveal their authentic selves. This doesn't mean that they show everything. They can be slightly enigmatic and followers respond to this by being curious to know more about them.

This combination of caring involvement and detachment based on self-knowledge is what we call 'tough empathy.' It means leaders don't lose sight of their overarching purpose. They give people what they need rather than what they want. People and task are integrated in the enactment of leadership.

Reading—and Rewriting—the Context

The exercise of leadership is contextual. Always. Effective leaders understand that there are no universals, no guaranteed ways of ensuring leadership impact. On the contrary, they practice and hone their context-reading skills and realistically appraise their ability to rewrite that context.

Being sensitive to context, being able to detect the way the wind is blowing, is as essential for any leader as it is for a high-wire walker. Authentic leaders have good, sometimes excellent, situation-sensing capabilities.

Franz Humer, the Chairman of Roche and Diageo, is a classic sensor. He is highly accomplished in detecting shifts in climate and ambience; he can read subtle cues and sense underlying currents of opinion that can elude less perceptive people. Humer says he developed this skill as a tour guide in his mid-twenties when he was responsible for groups of 100 or more. "There was no salary, only tips," he explains. "Pretty soon, I knew how to hone in on particular groups. Eventually, I could predict within 100 percent how much I could earn from any particular group." Indeed, great sensors can easily gauge unexpressed feelings; they can accurately judge whether relationships are working or not. The process is complex, and as anyone who has ever encountered it knows, the results are impressive.

Effective situation sensing involves three separate but related skills. The first is made up of observational and cognitive skills. Leaders see and sense what's going on in their organizations—and then use their cognitive skills to interpret these observations. They know when team morale is shaky or when complacency needs to be challenged. They collect information, seemingly through osmosis, and use it to understand the context in which they are aspiring to lead.

The second element involves behavioral and adaptive skills. Having observed and understood the situation, effective leaders adjust their behavior. They adapt without ever losing their sense of self. For leaders, this behavioral element of situation sensing involves the self-conscious use of social skills to maximize leadership impact in a particular context.

Think of Mayor Rudy Giuliani of New York. During the traumatic hours and days immediately following 9/11, Giuliani sensed that as a leader he needed to be out on the streets, with the people. He tuned in to the context. At a time of terrible anguish, Mayor Giuliani gave New Yorkers a sense of pride in themselves and their city that helped them cope.

The final element of effective situation sensing is that leaders use their own behavior to change the situation. Leaders are not passive recipients of the context. On the contrary, they work with their followers to socially construct an alternative reality. This is what differentiates those who merely react to situations from those who have the capacity to transform them.

Leaders know that situation sensing is important. They also know that it becomes more critical as you move up organizational hierarchies. Elevation brings with it increasingly sanitized information—filtered through the eyes and ears of others who may have a view about what the leader should know. Effective leaders know this and take steps to ensure they remain connected to the action, sensitive to the ever-changing context.

Managing Social Distance

Effective leaders are able to evoke high levels of emotional response, loyalty, and affection. Remember emotions are major sources of energy at work. The fully rational human being is emotional—emotions are not the froth on the cappuccino, they are the coffee. Leaders empathize with those they lead, step into their shoes, and get close to them. Yet they also seem able to communicate a sense of edge, to remind people of the job at hand and the purpose of the collective endeavor. In doing so, they move skillfully from closeness to distance and back again. They are able to get close to their followers, yet paradoxically they keep their distance. The underlying concept of social distance comes from the work of Georg Simmel's writing in the early decades of the twentieth century. He uses it to measure the degree of intimacy between individuals.

Skillful management of social distance is becoming even more important for leaders. Hierarchies, for example, are becoming flatter. Hierarchies have always been much more than structural devices. They have also been sources of meaning for people. Moving through stable hierarchies gave the illusion of becoming more of a leader.

Those days are gone. Leaders now need distance to establish perspective—to see the big things that may shape the future of the organization—and closeness to know what is really going on inside their business.

A sense of closeness delivers two important benefits. First, it enables leaders to know and understand their followers—a vital prerequisite for effective leadership. Second, closeness enables followers to know more of their leaders. By being close we show who we are. It offers a context for disclosure—of weakness as well as strength.

Of most significance here is that social distance enables leaders to handle performance issues. Distance can be used to signal that a different kind of conversation is about to start. It is also useful for leaders to be able to stand back and focus on the larger strategic purposes of the organization without being distracted by personal ties. If those who aspire to leadership can't do closeness they never really find out what's going on and if they can't do distance they shy away from confronting performance issues.

Communicating with Care

It is commonplace to read that effective leaders are good communicators. They are, but there is more to it. Skillful leaders make sure they use the right mode of communication. This requires a fine appreciation of the message, the context, and the people you wish to communicate with, as well as of your own personal strengths and weaknesses.

Clearly, context is important. The mistake many leaders make is to assume that followers can be engaged primarily through rational analysis and straightforward assertion of the facts. But this approach, on its own, is rarely successful in energizing others.

To properly engage others, leaders need to construct a compelling narrative. Effective leaders bring their case alive through rich examples, personal experiences, analogies, and stories.

Why are these devices so powerful as means for leadership communication? There are several reasons. First, a convincing story is a means of engaging others. It presents a puzzle that must be solved, a challenge that must be overcome—a quest, if you will. And stories are effective because ultimately they allow others to draw their own conclusions.

Second, well-chosen use of personal experiences can help followers identify with leaders. Personal anecdotes and experience are an important means of reducing social distance—and revealing authentic biography. By using familiar episodes or contexts from daily life, leaders are often able to connect with others on the basis of shared experience.

Third, by personalizing their communications—through anecdotes, analogies, and humor, for example—leaders are able to reveal more of who they are. And the more leaders reveal their own emotions (skillfully) the more they evoke an emotional reaction in others.

Jack Welch, the celebrated former CEO of General Electric, used this technique to connect with people, frequently recalling stories from his childhood and early adult life to illustrate key messages.

Time and again leaders face the difficult question of pace and timing. In a socially networked world, with performance pressures increasing, many business leaders in particular feel driven to show their impact faster and faster. Effective leaders sense situations, articulate and communicate fast—before Twitter does it for them.

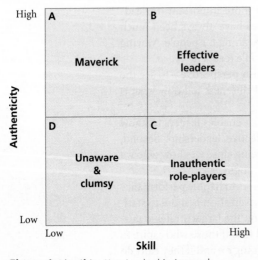

Figure 1 Identifying Your Leadership Approach

Ideas into Action

In our Harvard Business Review article "Why Should Anyone Be Led By You?" the concluding injunction is clear if you wish to be a more effective leader you should, Be Yourself—More—With Skill.

It is a beguilingly simple message that of course involves more than seems the case. We are really concerned with measuring two variables: authenticity—the extent to which individuals both know and selectively show their true self; and skill—the extent to which individuals deploy themselves in situationally appropriate ways. These variables are represented in the simple matrix reproduced below (Figure 1). We ask people to consider three questions: Where are you in the matrix now? Where do you want to get to? And what do you need to work on in order to get there? In box B, individuals combine skill and authenticity to produce effective leadership. In box A, individuals have a profound sense of who they are, what made them and what values they stand for. However, they lack the skills to make adequate use of their leadership assets. They fail to read context, to communicate in a compelling way and to use social distance appropriately with their followers. In box C, we find individuals who exhibit considerable interpersonal skills but who lack a strong sense of self. Their followers may feel that they are being manipulated. In box D, we find the clumsy individuals so successfully satirized in television's *The Office*.

The matrix helps but it also conceals some significant differences between the two variables. Measuring improvements in leadership skills is easier. You can use repeated 360-degree feedback to give us a sense of how people's leadership skills are developing. In general, the results are encouraging. Individuals can learn relationship skills, situational skills, and communication skills which improve their leadership impact. The power of this technique rests upon the notion that you can't be a leader without followers. Their perceptions matter. If the feedback says that you're not a great team leader—then you aren't. We are operating in an area where, in so far as things are defined as "real", then they are "real" in their consequences.

The other variable—authenticity—is much harder to measure. How can we know whether individuals have really come to know and show themselves? Do we sometimes confuse effective leadership with skillful roleplaying? There are no easy answers to these difficult questions. We stress that leadership development is not an event but a process, arguably lifelong.

Conclusion

Effective leaders, therefore, combine the expression of authenticity and the deployment of skill. Difficult? Yes. However, we are constantly and pleasantly surprised by the ways in which leaders in a wide variety of context bring meaning and performance to organizations. They provide purpose and excitement. They balance authenticity with skill—and they can make a big difference.

Appendix 1: Leadership Differences and Minorities

Our view is that leadership rests upon the expression of authentic personal differences. However, minority groups often have negative stereotypical differences projected on to them.

Gender differences can be used to either a positive or negative effect. Women, in particular, are prone to being stereotyped according to differences—albeit usually not the ones that they would choose. Partly this is because there are fewer women than men in management positions. According to research in social psychology, if a group's representation falls below 20 percent in a given society, then it's going to be subjected to stereotyping whether it likes it or not. For women, this may mean being typecast as a "helper," "nurturer," or "seductress"—roles that may prevent them from defining their own differences.

In earlier research, we discovered that some women try to avoid this dynamic by disappearing. They try to make themselves invisible. They wear clothes that disguise their bodies; they try to blend in with men by talking tough. That's certainly one way to avoid negative stereotyping, but the problem is that it reduces a woman's chances of being seen as a potential leader. She's not promoting her real self and differences. Another response to negative stereotyping is to collectively resist it—for example, by mounting a campaign that promotes the rights, opportunities, and even the number of women in the workplace. But on a day-to-day basis, survival is often all women have time for, therefore making it difficult for them to organize themselves formally.

A third response that emerged in our research was that women play into stereotyping to personal advantage. Some woman, for example, knowingly play the role of "nurturer" at work, but they do it with such wit and skill that they are able to benefit from it. The cost of such a strategy? It furthers harmful stereotypes and continues to limit opportunities for other women to communicate their genuine personal differences.

Appendix 2: Four Popular Myths About Leadership

We can all be leaders

Not true. Some people don't have the self-knowledge or the authenticity necessary for leadership. In addition, individuals must also want to be leaders, but many employees are not interested in shouldering that responsibility. Others prefer to devote more time to their private lives than to their work.

Leaders deliver business results

Not always. If results were an outcome of good leadership, picking leaders would be straightforward. In every case, the best strategy would be to go for people in companies with the best results. But clearly, it's not that simple. Businesses that dominate markets can often do very well—at least for a period—with competent management rather than great leadership. Equally, some well-led businesses do not necessarily produce results, particularly in the short term.

People who get to the top are leaders

Not necessarily. One of the most common misperceptions is that people in senior positions are leaders. But people who make it to the top may have done so because of political acumen, not necessarily because of leadership ability. What's more, leaders are found all over the organization, from the executive suite to the shop floor. By definition, leaders are simply people who have followers, and hierarchism or position doesn't have much to do with that. Effective military organizations like the U.S. Navy have long realized the importance of developing leaders throughout the organization.

Leaders are great coaches

Rarely. There is an unrealistic expectation that good leaders ought to be good coaches. But that thinking assumes that a single person can both inspire others and impart skills. Of course, it's possible that great leaders may also be great coaches, but we see that only occasionally. More typical are leaders like Steve Jobs whose distinctive strengths lie in their ability to excite others through their vision rather than through their coaching talents.

6 Motivation

Topic Summary Learning Objectives

1. Recognize the importance of internal, social, and organizational factors associated with motivation in organizations.

2. Compare motivation theories based on internal factors.

3. Identify theories based on social factors.

4. Describe how organizational factors, job characteristics, and managerial beliefs can impact motivation.

5. Apply the concepts of motivation to organizations.

Key Terms

cognitive evaluation theory, p. 190

equity theory, p. 191

existence, relatedness, and growth (ERG), p. 189

expectancy theory, p. 191

flow, p. 192

hierarchy of needs, p. 188

hygiene factors, p. 193

job characteristics, p. 194

justice: distributive, procedural, interpersonal, informational, p. 192

motivators, p. 193

needs for: affiliation, achievement, power, p. 189

optimal experience, p. 192

self-determination theory, p. 191

talent management, p. 196

Theory X and Theory Y, p. 194

two-factor theory (or motivator–hygiene theory), p. 193

1 Recognize the importance of internal, social, and organizational factors associated with motivation in organizations.

Introduction to Motivation

Motivation describes the effort and persistence exerted by individuals as they work through specific tasks. Organizations rely on motivated employees to accomplish work, improve productivity, build exciting work environments, and achieve organizational goals. Researchers have long debated which theories accurately predict what motivates behavior in organizations. Many well-recognized theories of motivation exist, but not all these theories have been confirmed by research. Despite the lack of research support, many motivation theories persist because organizations find these theories helpful when trying to motivate organizational members. Organizations should consider three primary factors when motivating employees: factors internal to the individual, factors related to the social interaction among employees, and factors related to the organization and the job itself. (see Figure 6.1).

2 Compare motivation theories based on internal factors.

Internal factors
Physiological and Psychological Needs

The study of human motivation has often focused on factors associated with the individual. According to human motivation expert Abraham Maslow, motivation consisted of a series of progressively higher needs.[1] According to Maslow's explanation, motivation occurs when people try to satisfy their unmet needs. Maslow explained two general categories of needs. Lower needs focused on factors that could only be satisfied externally, such as physiological and safety needs. Higher needs, like social belonging and acceptance, self-esteem, and self-actualization were satisfied through individual activity. Self-actualization, the highest form of motivation, involved achieving one's full potential as a person, determining one's own direction and purpose, and reaching self-defined success. Maslow believed that all humans should focus on self-actualization.

For Maslow, needs were described as progressive or a **hierarchy of needs**, where each lower level need had to be fulfilled before a higher need could be achieved. An individual can only progress to the next stage of motivation after a lower need has been satisfied. For example, an individual could not pursue self-actualization until lower needs like social belonging had been met. Similarly, social belonging could not be achieved until lower needs like physiological and safety needs were met first (see Figure 6.2).

Maslow's depiction of motivation persists in organizations, despite the fact that there is little or no evidence to support its major claims. Research, as well as individual experience, suggests that individuals can, in fact, pursue higher needs even when lower needs are not satisfied, contrary to Maslow's model. For example, when an artist is not making any

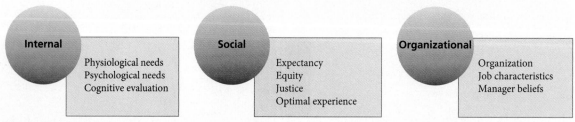

Figure 6.1 Key Factors Associated with Motivating Employees

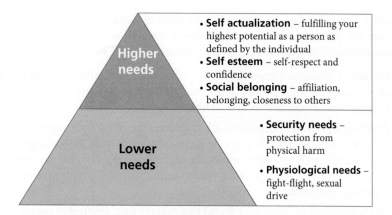

Figure 6.2
Maslow's Hierarchy
of Needs

money for food (physiological needs), and yet is trying to be the best he can be in writing music (self actualization). Research and personal experience support that individual motivation is not simply a progression through a series of increasingly higher level needs.

Clay Alderfer realized that much of Maslow's work is helpful to organizations, even if, in its entirety, the hierarchy of needs approach failed to fully explain motivation. Alderfer preserved the basic idea of Maslow's theory, but with a slight modification. Alderfer believed that people not only progressed up the hierarchy, but that they could also 'regress' down the hierarchy. In addition, fulfillment of all levels of needs could be pursued at any one time; thus, Alderfer believed that motivation was not necessarily hierarchical. Alderfer described three dimensions of motivation: **existence, relatedness,** and **growth**, what he termed *ERG* theory of motivation.[2] Both the ERG and the hierarchy of needs approach emphasize categories of human motivators; however, Alderfer believed that individuals seek to fulfill multiple needs simultaneously.

Like Maslow and Alderfer, psychologist David McClelland characterized motivation as a process of fulfilling individual needs. McClelland believed that needs were a factor of individual psychological states and that each individual displayed a dominant psychological need.[3] His research found that one of three psychological needs predominates in individuals: the need for affiliation, achievement, or power.

1. **Need for Affiliation**
   The need for affiliation includes the need for close interpersonal relationships and belonging, mutual understanding, and security in relationships.

2. **Need for Achievement**
   The need for achievement involves the need for accomplishment, seeking to create new and better contributions, setting goals of moderate difficulty that are achievable, and striving to do things better.

3. **Need for Power**
   The need for power involves the need to influence others and control one's direct environment, which includes two sub-factors.

   Socialized power—used to improve a group to which one belongs for the betterment of others (working for a client or organization), which is generally seen as positive.

   Personalized power—personal dominance, controlling others, and ostentatious display of successful power acquisitions—generally characterized as negative.

While a person might be motivated by all three of these needs to some degree, each person has one predominant need. McClelland's research revealed some insightful patterns about motivation among managers in organizations.

- The power-motivated manager is more concerned with influence than taking all the credit for success; thus, power-motivated managers are often perceived as being more consistent in their actions.

- By taking a personal interest in each employee, the affiliation-oriented manager may appear to be applying inconsistent standards. By seeking to maintain harmony amongst employees, the affiliation-motivated manager shows reluctance to engage in necessary conflict associated with making unpopular decisions.

- McClelland and his associates found that achievement-motivated people often excel at certain tasks, such as sales, but may not make the best managers. The achievement-motivated manager's need for goal attainment encourages the manager to take personal credit for accomplishments rather than celebrating successes as a team. Thus, the achievement-motivated manager is less likely to involve or inspire others. Further, she may be afraid to delegate and has a tendency to micromanage. Those who are achievement motivated tend to focus on their own individual goals, and not those of the organization. They seek short-term feedback on their own performance, but are less apt to give feedback to others who may need to know about progress.

In his work in hierarchical organizations with clear lines of authority, McClelland found that the best managers scored as much as 70 percent higher on 'power motivation' than managers with a 'need to be liked'. Several reasons may explain why power-motivated managers are labeled the 'best' managers. Power-motivated managers direct behavior toward institutional, not necessarily individual, accomplishments, and do not have a strong need to be liked as individuals; thus, they easily delegate and make unpopular, although seemingly fair, decisions.

In contemporary organizations where individuals are encouraged to work as a team or to work independently, those who are motivated through affiliation needs or through achievement needs may be seen as better managers. Further, power motivation may be a key factor for emerging leaders, but as leaders gain greater authority in an organization, achievement motivation may be more important for job success.[4]

Cognitive Evaluation Theory

Where McClelland focused on people's needs for power, affiliation, and achievement, cognitive evaluation theory explains motivation as based on people's needs for competence and control. **Cognitive evaluation** theory says that the introduction of rewards, such as pay, actually creates a situation where the motivation and thus the effort a person puts into a task decreases.[5] When people are intrinsically or internally motivated to perform work, they feel a sense of personal accomplishment and competence, become excited by their contribution, and even experience work as fun. Once rewards are introduced, like pay, recognition, or some other incentive, the activity becomes less motivating. The activity actually begins to feel more like a burden. Cognitive evaluation theory explains that when incentives and rewards are introduced, a person begins to experience a loss of control over the task. This occurs as the rewards that were once intrinsic shift to rewards that are extrinsic. The approach describes how tasks can increase motivation when an individual exercises autonomy, control, and discretion over how and when the task is performed. Pressure to perform overshadows the qualities of the task that were once motivating. Cognitive evaluation falls under the heading of **self-determination theory** which describes how individuals have a need for autonomy, competence, and relatedness. Some factors, such as external rewards have the opposite effect intended and actually can reduce someone's motivation, while other factors such a social support, competence, and intrinsic rewards support motivation.[6] Next, we consider motivation based on social factors.

Social Factors

Social factors associated with motivation involve expectations, social perceptions, and interpersonal dynamics. Expectations serve as an important form of motivation. According to **expectancy theory**, employees will exert effort at a task to the degree that they believe that effort will result in improved performance, which in turn will result in something of value.[7] A simple formula for expectancy theory is:

3 Identify theories based on social factors.

$$\text{Effort} \rightarrow \text{performance} \rightarrow \text{reward}$$

When an individual effort results in increased performance, it should lead to greater rewards. When this chain of events fails to emerge, individuals will begin to feel less motivated and therefore put in less effort. For example, if an employee increases effort and performance increases, but no rewards follow, an employee may feel that their expectations have not been met. This also means that if a reward follows effort, that an individual has to perceive that the reward is valuable. If an employee increases effort and performance increases, and the employee is rewarded with something that they do not perceive as valuable, they may also feel that their expectations have not been met.

Equity theory describes a psychological process where people compare the efforts put into a task and the rewards they receive with others. The other individual that is referenced is called the referent comparison. The theory holds that an individual believes that the effort she puts into a task and the reward she receives should be comparable to the effort and reward experienced by another as illustrated in the following equation.

$$\frac{\text{My effort}}{\text{My reward}} = \frac{\text{other effort}}{\text{other reward}}$$

Equity theory describes the amount of equity that people perceive in their environment. For example, an individual might say, "If the rewards I receive are less than the rewards someone else receives, and I perceive we both put in the same effort, then I may become less motivated to continue at my current level of effort."[8]

Perceived Justice

Some argue that motivation is a factor of social perceptions, specifically perceived justice in organizations. Justice describes whether employees perceive that the organization is fair or not. In particular, employees will be motivated to the degree that they perceive that rewards are distributed fairly, that procedures for allocating resources are fair, that people are treated fairly, and that information is shared within the organization. Relative to motivation, the more that employees view their organization as fair along these dimensions, the more likely they are to see the organization as fair overall, and thus feel connected to the organization. There are four dimensions of perceived justice:[9]

- **Distributive justice** describes fairness in how rewards and resources are distributed across an organization.
- **Procedural justice** describes fairness in how decisions are reached and how outcomes are determined.
- **Interpersonal justice** describes fairness in how people interact and are treated.
- **Informational justice** describes fairness in what information is used and communicated within the organization.

Optimal Experience

Another stream of research associated with motivation is the study of **optimal experience**, more commonly called flow.[10] **Flow** describes the process where a person becomes completely engaged in the activity at hand. When experiencing flow, an activity feels effortless and a person feels mastery over the task. One's attention is focused directly on meeting a very specific and achievable goal. Conditions to experience flow include:

- Perceived challenge that stretches but does not exceed someone's skill set
- Clear goals and immediate and continued feedback

Flirt/SuperStock

People often explain flow activities as among their best moments, when time stood still or tension and indecision disappeared. Most people can recall at least one flow experience in their life, which may include participation in athletic activities, competitive games like chess, or perhaps a work activity where one has developed a specific expertise.

Flow experiences emerge when an individual is challenged by the task but has acquired enough skills to be adequate at accomplishing the task: a mountain climber challenged by a new route up the mountain, a student learning a new skill, or a surgeon conducting a challenging procedure. Flow is likely to be experienced when skill and challenge are compatible and the activity requires complete mental and sometimes physical attention. Building optimal experiences requires a social context where individuals are constantly challenged and developing new skills (see Figure 6.3).

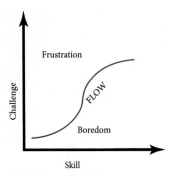

Figure 6.3 Optimal Experience

Organizational Factors
Organization Characteristics

In addition to social factors described above, researchers have considered the importance of organizational and job characteristics in motivation. One of the most widely recognized approaches to motivation lies in the work of Fredrick Herzberg's **two-factor theory**, also called motivator–hygiene theory. Herzberg described motivation along two dimensions.[11] One dimension included **hygiene factors** such as pay, working conditions, quality of supervisor, and organizational policies. Although hygiene factors served to motivate,

4 Describe how organizational factors, job characteristics, and managerial beliefs can impact motivation.

their motivational power was short lived. In order for hygiene factors to motivate employees, an organization needed to create a constant stream of new improvements in these factors. For example, pay raises, new office furniture, or a policy change would only keep employees from becoming dissatisfied with their work. Simply put, hygiene factors kept employees from becoming dissatisfied with their work, but did not motivate employees to work harder. Instead of the focus on hygiene factors, Herzberg recommended that organizations focus on **motivators** such as improving opportunities for advancement, recognition, and self-development. Sustained motivation could only occur from improvement in these areas (see Figure 6.4).

Job Characteristics

One approach to improve motivation is to change or improve the characteristics of the task that employees perform. The

Lead to satisfaction (motivators)
Achievement
Recognition
Work design and nature of work
Responsibility
Advancement
Growth

Lead to dissatisfaction (hygiene factors)
Supervision
Relationship with supervisor
Working conditions
Salary
Relationships with peers
Personal life
Relationship with subordinate
Status
Security

Figure 6.4 Hygiene versus Motivators

job characteristics model describes how the nature of the job itself can be motivating. Hackman and Oldham describe **job characteristics** that motivate work behavior.[12] Job characteristics that improve motivation include:

- *Skill Variety* Skill variety allows organizational members to engage multiple skills and abilities in a challenging environment.
- *Task Identity* Task identity occurs when an organizational member works on the job from start to finish, takes a personal interest in starting and completing various tasks, and holds a strong sense of ownership.
- *Task Significance* Task significance is when work performed by a member of the organization makes a positive and substantial impact on the organization, society, or group. When skill variety, task identity, and task significance are present in a job, a member experiences work as more meaningful, which in turn leads to intrinsic motivation.
- *Autonomy* Autonomy occurs when organizational members can complete the task without significant oversight or interruption from their boss, other workers, or regulators. Autonomy contributes to feelings of personal responsibility.
- *Feedback* Feedback is when organizational members receive regular input and evaluation on their performance, which creates increased knowledge of a member's results (see Figure 6.5).

While the job characteristics approach considers the nature and the structure of work tasks, managers' beliefs about employees also impact motivation.

Manager Beliefs

Management expert Douglas McGregor captured the distinction between internal and external forms of motivation with his classic Theory X and Theory Y approach. Theory X managers focus on external rewards while Theory Y managers focus on internal rewards. How a manager views others in the organization determines which mechanisms a manager will choose to motivate those in the organization. Some managers believe in **Theory X**. Theory X describes the assumptions that people are basically lazy, need to be motivated, and will not work hard if left to their own devices. Managers who hold to **Theory Y**, on the other hand, actively encourage others in the organization to work

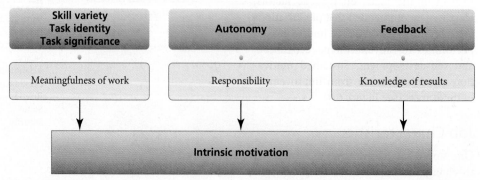

Figure 6.5 Job Characteristics Model

independently because they believe that employees are fundamentally self-directed and capable. In contrast to Theory X managers, managers who believe in Theory Y think that people are basically good, intrinsically motivated, and are eager to work.[13]

Theory X holds negative assumptions about the nature of people such as:

1. Employees are basically lazy and will attempt to avoid work when possible.
2. Employees must be coerced and controlled.
3. Employees will avoid responsibilities when possible.
4. Employees place security needs over other needs and dislike change.

Theory Y holds more positive assumptions about the capacity of people. It says that:

1. Work is as natural as play.
2. People will demonstrate direction and self-control when they are committed.
3. The average person can accept and seeks responsibility.
4. Decision making should be widely dispersed throughout the organization.

Contemporary Application

Most or all of the approaches to motivation discussed so far emerged between 1940 and into the mid-1980s. The fact that these theories emerged in prior decades often prompts students who are studying motivation to ask about the contemporary relevance of these theories. After all, most theories of motivation were developed to address cultures in Western Europe and the United States. Many of the approaches sought to improve motivation in manufacturing or production organizations that flourished in Western economies during the period. For example, Herzberg developed his two-factor theory to address inequalities he observed between the ways that organizations tried to motivate executives versus frontline employees. When organizations sought to motivate executives, they often focused on motivators, but when attempting to motivate frontline employees, they relied on hygiene factors. Herzberg wanted to make the process of motivation more democratic within organizations by introducing motivators to all employees.

Many of the formal efforts in contemporary organizations to motivate employees rely on applying the theories summarized here. In fact, organizations spend billions of dollars each year trying to motivate employees. Organizational approaches to motivation can be summarized as

1. External (extrinsic) rewards and includes salary, gifts, bonuses, and other incentives. An organization may send a motivated employee a gift basket, free food, golf clubs, a certificate acknowledging good work, or even a trip to a spa.
2. Internal (intrinsic) rewards. This approach relies on helping employees identify and enhance their natural capacity for motivation. Organizations that are trying to address internal motivation, might offer employees a session with a leadership coach, or an opportunity to allocate a percent of their work time to a project of their choice.

Human Resource Systems

Human resource systems can be powerful tools that have the capacity to motivate organizational members. These systems include compensation, benefits, performance management, formal and informal recognition programs, non-financial rewards programs, and training and career development systems. Talent management is a specific approach that capitalizes on human resource systems to support an organization's strategy.

Talent Management

Many contemporary organizations seek to engage both internal and external forces through an approach to motivation called **talent management**. Talent management programs seek to integrate various human resource and motivational efforts that exist across an organization into a comprehensive organizational strategy. Talent management programs differ across organizations, but most of these programs encompass a few key characteristics.

Talent management programs engage organizational members at each step of their employment and include efforts at attraction and selection, retention, and development. Talent management efforts begin while a person is still a candidate for employment and the effort continues throughout a career. The organization purposefully offers growth, development, and challenging opportunities to develop new skills, set goals, and have new work experiences. Talent management efforts include employment-branding efforts designed to promote the unique benefits of working at an organization. Consumer products company Johnson and Johnson, for example, promotes the benefits of working for a large organization that has a small company feel by showing how the company values personal relationships and the needs of individual employees. The U.S. Army and their successful employment branding campaign "Be All You Can Be", advertises the benefits of self-improvement and development that occur through the Army's comprehensive training programs. Employment branding efforts help the organization to attract and retain employees and create a sense of identity, affiliation, and belonging for organizational members.

Incentive systems designed to meet the employee and organizational goals are central to talent management efforts. Organizations spend considerable time and effort developing compensation programs designed to motivate, retain, and attract talent. The best talent management programs involve both direct compensation like pay and bonuses, but also include indirect financial compensation, like healthcare benefits, life insurance, stock options, and retirement benefits. Other indirect non-financial benefits, such as training, are also important.

Training strategies are designed to motivate employees by identifying unique challenges for employees at different stages of their careers. So members manage their careers based on life stage. For example, while younger employees are often motivated by opportunity and salary, employees with families and other outside responsibilities may seek out opportunities for flexibility or less travel.

Conclusion

Organizations rely on theories of motivation to guide their motivation efforts. Motivation can be explained by examining internal factors, social factors, and organizational factors. Internal factors include physiological, psychological, and cognitive approaches to motivation. Social factors are explained through expectancy, equity, justice, and flow theories. Organizational factors can be viewed through the lens of organization and job characteristics, Theory X and Y, and human resource talent management efforts. Traditional theories are often adapted to address contemporary organizational issues.

OB AT WORK

NICOLE SAPIO PROMOTES MOTIVATION THROUGH MISSION AT THE AMERICAN HEART ASSOCIATION

Nicole Sapio

As a leader in an organization whose mission is to build healthier lives—free of cardiovascular diseases and stroke—Nicole Sapio has the opportunity to apply organizational behavior concepts not just to motivate others and boost employee productivity, but also to actually save lives. In the role of Executive Vice President at the American Heart Association's Great Rivers Affiliate, Nicole works with many different stakeholders ranging from employees to volunteers and supporters. This widespread reach allows for meaningful impact because of the critical nature of the American Heart Association mission and the depth and breadth of stakeholders that value and participate in this mission.

Nicole's interest in workplace motivation and productivity influenced her decision to study how employees learn about goals, are motivated or not motivated by goals, and how goals impact strategy. This study, as part of her doctoral work, carries over into her work practices at the American Heart Association. As a leader in a mission-centric organization, Nicole understands that goals are essential to accomplishing work, but that there are also important things to consider when setting and managing goals. This is especially relevant in an organization that includes many volunteers and stakeholders.

5 Apply the concepts of motivation to organizations.

In traditional organizations, there are a variety of tools that managers can use to motivate their employees, such as bonuses, pay raises, or performance evaluations. These tools are primarily extrinsic or external in nature, designed to motivate people as they seek a reward or seek to avoid negative consequences. Nicole also believes in tapping into the intrinsic, or internal, factors. For example, when working with board members or volunteers, Nicole notes that, "the key to success is for these important individuals to be committed to the mission and dedicated to the success of the American Heart Association".

Nicole motivates external stakeholders by ensuring alignment and communicating clearly and consistently across different stakeholder groups. This is central to tapping into the intrinsic factors, such as individual values or personal goals that individuals hold for themselves and their desire to be involved in a mission-centric organization. In order to implement the mission strategies and related goals of the American Heart Association, the staff (team) connects every day with many individuals who share in the desire to build healthier lives, free of heart disease and stroke. Nicole's academic research found that communication about strategy and related goals was critical to achieving and maintaining alignment in organizations. Internal and external communications in various shapes and forms—newsletters, town hall gatherings, reporting mechanisms, and other vehicles—is a cornerstone of motivating successfully through mission. Communicating about the mission of the organization and the specific work being undertaken to accomplish the mission, and connecting an individual's internal motivations to the work of the organization, is the centerpiece.

(continued)

For internal stakeholders (employees), being mission-centric is again a critical component—spending time understanding why someone chooses to work at a mission-centric organization, encouraging employees to express their personal commitment to the mission and communicating details about the important work of the organization. Within this work there are goals set to support strategy.

One of the key tenets that Nicole focuses on in managing goals within the organization is recognizing the reciprocal nature of goal-setting—meaning that organizational-level strategy and individual involvement in goal-setting are equally important. Nicole's academic research bore this out as well. Harnessing the power of this top-down/bottom-up interaction is central to successfully managing goals. In practice, this means being clear and concise about organizational-level strategy, supported by two primary elements: a goal-setting process at the individual level that involves feedback loops, and communication tools that continuously educate about strategy details and progress and facilitate alignment. Communication is also important to tapping into the intrinsic motivators related to the organization's mission.

The first element, involving employees' setting their own goals within the framework of organizational strategy and ensuring fit with strategy-level goals that drive the mission, is essential. An example is creating processes that support this idea, such as having a goal-setting system that involves various feedback loops before goals are finalized. Then, reinforcing those goals consistently through frequent communication is necessary. One of the key reasons of importance Nicole recognized, both through her academic research and in her leadership experience, is that many organizational (external) and personal (internal) factors influence goals, even once those goals are formally set through a process as previously described. This is where communication as a practice comes in again, to consistently discuss, reinforce, and re-align goals and individuals in organizations. In a mission-centric organization, the internal, or intrinsic, factors are very important, tapping into the personal motivation to come to work every day on behalf of a shared mission.

Source: Interview with Nicole Sapio, 2014.

SPOTLIGHT ON RESEARCH
What Do People Prefer In a Job? Exploring Intrinsic and Extrinsic Motivation at Work

Social scientists have been trying to solve the mystery of motivation for decades. Few topics have received as much attention and research over the years. One study sought to identify what aspects of a job people most prefer because an understanding of job preferences would shed light on what aspects of a job might be motivating for employees. Further, the study sought to find if there were individual differences in job preferences. For example, did people report different preferences based on gender, age, or industry?

The study looked at surveys collected from nearly 7,000 workers in the U.K. across different industries and regions. They asked these people to rank their job preferences on 15 different intrinsic and extrinsic job characteristics. Results are shown in the table below:

Extrinsic Factors	Ranking
Good promotion prospects	13
Good pay	7
A secure job	2
Convenient hours of work	10
Choice in your hours of work	12
Good fringe benefits	14
Good training provisions	11
Intrinsic Factors	
Good relations with your supervisor/manager	5
A job where you can use your initiative	6
Work you like doing	1
The opportunity to use your abilities	4
An easy workload	15
Good physical conditions	8
A lot of variety of work	9
Friendly people to work with	3

Researchers also found some interesting statistical differences among preferences based on gender, age, marital status, and whether the employees were public or private sector workers.

Males were less interested than females in extrinsic job factors including job security, convenience, choice of working hours, and training opportunities. Males were also less interested than females in intrinsic job attributes like good relations with a supervisor, good working conditions, friendly employees, and liking the work. However, males were more interested than females in a job where they could best utilize their abilities.

Older employees (between ages 46 and 65) were less interested than younger employees in promotion prospects, and they were also less concerned than younger employees about good pay and job security. But, older workers did place a high value on the choice of hours. In addition, married workers, or those living together, placed a higher importance than single workers on a choice of flexible work hours. In contrast, single employees preferred a good paying job, promotion prospects, and job security.

There were also some differences to note in whether the employees worked in the public or private sector. Public sector employees were more interested than private sector employees in job security, good hours, and access to training.

The researchers conclude that there is an important link between specific job characteristics and job preferences and that these preferences differ among individuals. This research suggests that managers should consider these preferences when assigning work to employees, interviewing applicants, and attempting to find ways to motivate individuals and teams.

Questions for Discussion

1. How might you explain some of the demographic differences relative to motivation? (e.g. gender, age, etc.) Why do you think this?

2. How would you apply this research to your workplace? What should managers consider about motivation differences?

---

*Based on the article by John Sutherland (2012). "Job attribute preferences: who prefers what?" *Employee Relations, 34, 2,* 193–221. Data adapted from Felstead, A., Gallie, D., Green, F., and Zhou, Y. 2007. "Skills at work", 1986–2006, ESRC Centre on Skills, knowledge and organizational performance (SCOPE), Cardiff and Oxford.

Pairing with this Topic Summary

Suggested Expert Contributions

Creating a Happy, Stress-Free Workplace: It's a Matter of Perspective—D. Keith Denton (Missouri State)

Moving Beyond the American Dream: How Intrinsic and Extrinsic Aspirations Relate to Psychological, Social, and Physical Health—Chris Niemiec (University of Rochester), Bart Soenens (Gent University), and Maarten Vansteenkiste (Gent University)

High-Tech, High-Touch Tension: Trends in Human Resource Management—Troy R. Nielson (Brigham Young University), Ellen Ensher (Loyola Marymount University), and Elisa Grant-Vallone (California State University, San Marcos)

Trade-Offs in Using Pay for Performance—Kimberly D. Elsbach (University of California, Davis)

Suggested Cases

Case 1: The Case of Apple iPhone 4

Case 2: "We Are Global or We Are Nothing": Conflict and Cover-Up at ColequarterMaine

Case 3: EMERGENCY! We Need a Better Compensation System

Case 5: Whatever Happened to One of the "100 Best Companies to Work For"?:
A Case Study of Hewlett-Packard

Case 6: NASCAR's Drive for Diversity: Can They Reach the Finish Line?

Case 8: Conflict in Santa's Workshop: Learning to Be a Team Player at ToyKing

Suggested Exercises

Exercise 4: How Leaders Effect You

Exercise 5: My Best and Worst Learning Experience

Exercise 13: What Stresses You Out?

Exercise 17: Design Your Technology

Exercise 21: OD Techniques at Work

Exercise 33: Could I Be a Whistleblower?

Exercise 36: What Are My Values?

Endnotes

1. Maslow, A. H., (1954). *Motivation and personality.* New York: Harper & Row.
2. Alderfer, C. P. (1972). *Existence, relatedness, and growth.* New York: Free Press.
3. McClelland, D. C. (1961). *The achievement society.* New York: Van Nostrand Reinhold.
4. McClelland, D. C., & Burnham, D. H. (1995). Power: The great motivator. *Harvard Business Review.* Jan/Feb, 73, 1, 126–139; McClelland, D. C. "Power motivation in traditional and emerging roles." *HayGroup.* Video available online at:http://www.haygroup.com/ww/media/details.aspx?id=1583&c=3
5. Deci, E. L. (1975). *Intrinsic motivation.* New York: Plenum.
6. Deci, E. L., & Ryan, R. (2002). *Handbook of self-determination research.* Rochester, NY: University of Rochester Press.
7. Herzberg, F. (1959). *The motivation to work.* New York: John Wiley and Sons; Herzberg, F. I., (1987). One more time: How do you motivation people? *Harvard Business Review,* Sep/Oct, 65, 5, 109–120.
8. Hackman, J. R., & Oldham, G. R. (1980). *Work redesign.* Reading, MA: Addison-Wesley.
9. Vroom, V. H. (1964). *Work and Motivation.* New York: Wiley, 1964.
10. Adams, J. S. & Rosenbaum, W. B. (1962). The relationship of worker productivity to cognitive dissonance and wage inequalities. *Journal of Applied Psychology, 46,* 161–164.
11. Greenberg, J. (1995). *The quest for justice on the job: Essays and experiments.* Thousand Oaks, CA: Sage; Folger, R., & Cropanzano, R. (1998). *Organizational justice and human resource management.* Thousand Oaks, CA: Sage. Colquitt, J. A., & Greenberg, J. (2003). Organizational justice: A fair assessment of the state of the literature. In J. Greenberg (Ed.), *Organizational Behavior: The state of the science.* (2nd Ed.). Mahwah, NY: Erlbaum.
12. Csikszentmihaly, M. (1997). *Finding Flow: The psychology of engagement with everyday life.* New York: Basic Books.
13. McGregor, D. (2005). *The Human Side of Enterprise.* Annotated Edition. New York: McGraw-Hill.

Creating a Happy, Stress-Free Workplace: It's a Matter of Perspective

D. Keith Denton

Missouri State

Keeping a little perspective can be good for your attitude. True, it might not be the best of times to be looking for a job with less wage growth and near-record unemployment levels, many might see it as a time of less opportunity, but comparatively speaking, we've got it pretty good.

The Good Ol' Days

If you were looking for a job a little over a hundred years ago, the key question was not about simply finding work but about finding work you would enjoy. A key question you might reasonably be asked then is, "Do you expect to die on your job?" Today, a reasonable question would be, "Do you expect to work enough to be able to feed your family?"

The type of work during your grandparents' or great-grandparents' time was also different. You would not worry about promotion opportunities or relocation, you were just satisfied to have a job. Work in the early twentieth century was mostly the hard labor kind that made you an "old" person by 50.

The statistics and stories in the late nineteenth century and early twentieth century are eye-opening. The simple fact was <u>if</u> you could get a job, you would probably work there until you died. In 1880, 58 percent of men 75 years and older worked, and they were the lucky ones. Today, in the United States, it's only about 8 percent, and they are the unlucky ones. You could forget working 40 hours a week or having weekends off. Sunday was, at best, a day of rest, not recreation. It was dangerous work. From 1880 to 1890, 35,000 workers died and well over a half a million were injured at work—every year!

These past times, to today's college students, might seem like another world, but fortunately some of the folks from these times are around to share their experiences. Meet Mr. Bill Thom, born in 1920. He is a walking history lesson. He actually lived through the "Great Depression," not our recent "Great Recession." He immigrated to the United States with his family from Scotland and was a teenager during the Great Depression.

It was a different world—people did not lock their doors and did not relocate for jobs. There were few automobiles and just as few roads—no computers, no television. He remembers how work was in the 1930s. If you were lucky enough to work, you only worked a little bit. If you had a job, you only worked a day and off two or three. That's fine for a college student who supplements his or her parent's tuition payments, but not if you're trying to feed a family. He worked for Public Works (WPA) for $.25 an hour, shoveling shale to make roads.

Work Ethic

People of a bygone era, like Mr. Thom, valued work in and of itself. He says being polite and respectful was a way of life, "We always used Mr., Mrs., or Sir, thank you, and please when speaking to people." Today, he says it seems those looking for work want it to be fun and don't want to be bored. Research supports his conclusions. Let's travel back in time just a generation or two ago to your parents' time. In 1975, almost half or 48 percent of those surveyed by the National Opinion Research Center rated work as "the important thing" in their life versus 36 percent who voted for leisure as most important. By the year 2000, those numbers had reversed, with 45 percent choosing leisure and only 34 percent choosing work as "the most important thing".[1]

But you don't have to go back to your parents', grandparents', or great-grandparents' time to see differences in how people perceive happiness and work. While recently teaching in China, I walked to work one morning and saw a Chinese man already sitting on the side of a sidewalk selling sandals. That evening as I was leaving, particularly late, I noticed he was still there trying to sell sandals. I asked, "How is business?" He said, "So-so." I asked him if he enjoyed his work. He looked at me in a curious way and said, "In life all you need is a place to live, something to do, and enough to eat." He had something to do, something to eat, and a place to stay. It was not about keeping up with trends or the Joneses, nor about greed, lust, or envy. It was enough; happiness comes from within, not the job.

I Hate My Life

Meanwhile, back in the United States, clinical depression is up to ten times more common today than just two generations ago.[2] It is a different time with different expectations about life and work. In the 1930s, Bill Thom, or in today's world, that nameless Chinese man, was not worried about depression. The only thing Bill Thom was worried about was survival with a big "D", as in Great Depression, not a little "d", as in not being happy.

There is an increasing body of evidence that shows there is no significant relationship between how much you earn, in terms of money or sandals, and whether you feel good about life. Grumpy people are grumps for some other reason, and it's not how much you earn or how you earn it.

Worry, stress, and pessimism are not new things. Workers were increasingly less satisfied even before the most recent economic crisis. Employees were giving dismal ratings for work policies on promotions, bonuses, and training. Even relationships with co-workers, which normally ranks as the most enjoyable part of a person's job, had dipped.[3] So, what's going on? Are we simply becoming a nation of whiners? Is it all about instant gratification and self-absorption?

"Worry, Worry, Trouble, and Toil"

In 2003, a poll by *Money* asked their subscribers about their level of worry about political and economic issues facing the United States. While grade school kids were playing computer games and attending soccer and baseball practice, parents were worried and stressed.

At that time, gas was cheap, SUVs were all the rage, houses had two-car garages, and families were taking vacations, but worry and anxiety were still there. Fifty-five percent of *Money* respondents said they were "extremely worried" (that's more than half) and another 39 percent said they were "somewhat worried".[4] Ah, those good ol' days of '03—not 1903, but 2003.

Happiness is not about material things. As Bill Thom can attest, materially we are better off. Graph out American life since World War II (your great-grandparents' time) and you will find every line involving money and material things has soared upward due to inflation. Inflation-adjusted income per American has almost tripled. Take a look at a typical graph of these types of distribution seen below.[5]

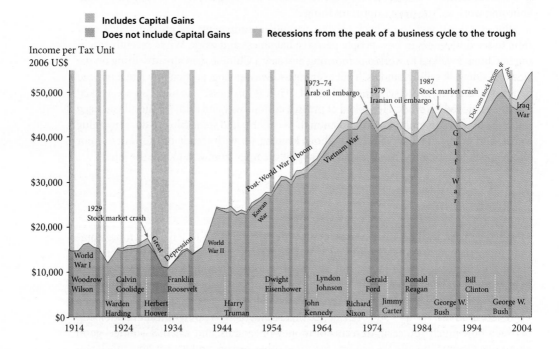

The trend line is strong and upward. We got it pretty good. Not too long ago, a two-car garage was a goal, not a three-car garage. iPhones, the Internet, and personal electronics did not exist in your parents' time. Everything, including spending and earning, has trended up, but charts of American happiness have flat lined since World War II.

Are You Happy?

Polls by the National Opinion Research Center, as far back as 1950, show about one third of Americans describe themselves as "very happy." Periodically, that same institute has consistently collected the same information. Here's the surprising thing: the percentage of "very happy" people has stayed the same for over 60 years. But, other data over that same period has not stayed the same for those with the little "d"—depression. Charts of incidents of depression since 1950 show clinical depression is three to ten times more common today than just two generations ago. Obviously, it's not about money.

When a *Time* magazine poll asked people about their source of happiness, money ranked fourteenth out of over twenty items. Excluding the Great Depression, you will find about five to ten percent of Americans are unemployed. Unemployment can make you unhappy, even depressed. Study after study has shown absolutely no correlation between money and happiness. Other factors in your life are the true drivers of happiness. Primarily issues like family satisfaction, friendships, relationships, and self-esteem determine happiness. Often, materialistic goals, like increasing your income and buying bigger cars and homes can actually cause people to give up those things that make them happier.[6]

Psychologist Martin Seligmen of the University of Pennsylvania says people mistakenly think expensive purchases are "shortcuts" to well-being. The body of evidence of research shows there is no significant relationship between how much you earn and whether you are satisfied with life. A *Time* poll showed that happiness increased as income rose to $50,000 (medium income for U.S. household is $43,000). After that, more money did not affect happiness. Even *Forbes'* top 400 wealthiest people were only the tiniest bit happier than the general public. Even wealthy people can be jealous of others wealthier than they.[7]

It is obvious to people like Bill Thom and the Chinese gentleman that having something to do—a job—is a blessing. Too often people expect jobs to give them emotional satisfaction, not just a paycheck. Managers must remember that employee happiness and optimism generally come from inside a person, not inside the job. It is "fool's gold" to continually strive to create happy employees. Decade after decade shows that about one third of people are generally "very happy." It is better performance, training, coaching, recognition, and performance feedback that should be the focus.[8] Those most satisfied with their jobs are not necessarily the highest performers. If employees are happy, there shouldn't be a need for change.[9]

Inequity as a Dissatisfier

Most Americans, during the life of Bill Thom and probably your grandparents' time, lived in small towns or urban areas where living conditions for most people were equal. Rapid growth of the top 5 percent of households produced a sizeable group of people who were noticeably better off than most of the middle class. Research demonstrates that nations with equal levels of income, like Scandinavian countries, have higher well-being than in nations like the United States, where wealth is unevenly distributed. Interestingly, polls show that Americans believe that whatever their income level, they feel they need more to live well.[10]

Obviously, it is difficult to be happy if you do not have a job or if you are worried your job is in jeopardy. But anyone, managers or employees, who expects their job to be their primary source of satisfaction and happiness is going to be disappointed. There is, however, something leaders can do beyond reducing inequity on the job.

Managing Optimism

Research shows that optimism toward life can extend your lifespan. A study from Wageningen University in The Netherlands asked 999 elderly Dutch men and women their agreement with the statement, "I still have many goals to strive for." Agreement with this statement was highly predictive for longevity. Nine years after the survey, the death rates for optimistic men were 63 percent lower than their less optimistic peers. Women's optimism reduced their death rate by 35 percent.[11]

Here, also, is a bit of good news for managers. Another study showed pessimistic college students randomly assigned to optimism workshops had fewer visits to their school's health clinics and lower rates of depression and anxiety than those who did not take the class. Robert Colligan, professor emeritus of psychology at Mayo Clinic, says positive self talk can also be helpful. He points out that a student who makes a bad grade should replace "I'll probably fail all my other courses, too" with "I'll do better next semester."[12]

Research demonstrates that introverts are just not as happy as extroverts, although this viewpoint is debatable. Professor Fleeson asked 50 undergraduates to act assertive and energetic, and then rate their emotions. He then repeated the experiment but asked them to act shy and passive. The neat thing was simply _acting_ extroverted resulted in higher levels of happiness and fun.[13] Fleeson's work in the _Journal of Personality and Social Psychology_ tells us that happiness is something we all can achieve.

Greg Easterbrook's research clearly shows that people who are grateful, optimistic, and forgiving have better lives, are happier, and have higher incomes. Ed Diener, a psychologist at the University of Illinois, also collected data on this subject. If you positively evaluate your well-being, you will on average have a stronger immune system, a better marriage, and be able to better cope with difficulties.[14]

Easterbrook notes that Freud said unhappiness is a default condition. It takes less effort to be unhappy than to be happy. Lazy people can always find some reason to feel unhappy and complain. It takes real effort to focus on a happy, optimistic outlook, but the benefits are pretty dramatic. Dilip Jeste showed that those who think they are aging well are not necessarily the healthiest ones. Optimism and the ability to cope were found to be more important to successful aging than traditional measures of wellness and health. It is attitude, not physical health, that is the best predictor of successful aging. One study even showed that people who had described themselves as highly optimistic a decade earlier actually had lower rates of death from cardiovascular disease than did pessimistic people.[15]

Doing Your Part

Perhaps as much as half of one's potential for happiness is inherited, like our tendency toward optimism or shyness. A sizeable percent of happiness comes from having strong marriages, family ties, friendships, spirituality, and self-esteem. But managers can help by reducing stress and worry. True leaders do not prey on people's worries, fears, or negative feelings. It is a leader's responsibility to help cultivate positive emotions and to help employees to not be so self-absorbed. Encourage volunteering and taking credit for good events and discourage placing too much blame on themselves; it is not an easy task.

Abraham Lincoln is reported to have said that most people are as happy as they make up their minds to be. Research supports that conclusion. One of the more interesting studies was when researchers compared three groups – lottery winners, average people, and those who had accidents that rendered them paraplegic. The jaw-dropping conclusion was that paraplegic people were the happiest. It seems that over time, they were able to look at the world from a happier perspective despite their difficulties.[16] Things you say to yourself and others do impact your mood and others' moods.

Negative words and even thoughts trigger stress chemicals. Stop harsh criticism of yourself and others. Keep positive thoughts. Be generous because it seems that the act of creating happiness creates it for both the giver and receiver.[17]

Conclusion

It is clear to any leader or aspiring manager that you should recruit, test, train, and favor your more optimistic and extroverted people. A happy disposition can make up for a lot in terms of skill and working conditions. When possible, recruit those who are less materially focused.

But remember, only about one-third of us fit into the "very happy" group. Managers can still help control how the other two-thirds feel by establishing a better work environment. Focus on creating an atmosphere where people are respectful to others in the workplace. Place a premium on honesty and trustworthiness. A positive work attitude is most important. Someone who has an attitude that "life sucks" and "I hate this job," is going to be unhappy. What's more, they will make people around them unhappy. Positive attitudes, though, like negative ones, can be infectious to others.

But the best advice for any leader looking to create a happier, less stressed work environment is to be a good role model. As Stein says, define good behavior and what character is expected at work. A survey of 1,000 United States workers by Saratoga Institute listed "positive work relations" as the top factor that makes employees more likely to stay with their employers. Courtesies go a long way toward creating that positive supportive workplace.[18] Be considerate, fill up the copier, printer, and coffee pot. Return e-mails. Turn down the volume on your CD or radio. Practice personal integrity. Expect and demonstrate attendance, timeliness, and work place courtesy so everyone can find their happy place.

Endnotes

1. Samuelson, R. J. (2001). Indifferent to Inequality. *Newsweek*, 137(19), 45.
2. Morris, H. J. (2001). Happiness Explained. *U. S. News and World Report*, 31(8).
3. Caudron, S. (2001). The Myth of Job Happiness. *Workforce*, 80(4), 32.
4. Gertner, J. (2003). What Are We Afraid Of? *Money*, 32(5), 80.
5. http://visualizingeconomics.com/blog/2008/05/04/average-income-in-the-united-states-1913-2006
6. Caudron, S. (2001).
7. Easterbrook, Greg. (2005). The Real Truth about Money. *Time*, 165(3), A-32-A34.
8. Caudron, S. (2001).
9. Raphael, Todd. (2002). Happiness May Be Overrated. Workforce, 81(5), 80.
10. Easterbrook, G. (2005).
11. De Keukelaere, L. (2006). Optimism Prolongs Life. *Scientific American Mind*, 17, 7-7.
12. De Keukelaere, L. (2006).
13. Becker, A. (2003). Don't Worry, Be Extroverted. *Psychology Today*, 36(3), 14.
14. www.livescience.com/humanbiology/060227_happiness_keep.html.
15. www.livescience.com/humanbiology/051212_aging_happy.html.
16. Becker, A. (2003).
17. O'Donnell, E. (2003). How To Find True Happiness. *Natural Health*, 33(6), 58.
18. Lerner, D. (2008). What Does Research Tell Us About Depression, Job Performance, And Work Productivity? *Journal of Occupational and Environmental Medicine*, 50(4), 401–410.

Moving Beyond the American Dream: How Intrinsic and Extrinsic Aspirations Relate to Psychological, Social, and Physical Health

Christopher P. Niemiec
University of Rochester

Bart Soenens
Gent University

Maarten Vansteenkiste
Gent University

Work has a strong and pervasive influence on the lives of most adults. Beyond occupying a substantial portion of their waking hours,[1] work-related activities facilitate individuals' establishing and developing a personal identity[2] and accumulating evidence—suggesting a variety of factors can affect employees' performance and wellness on the job.[3] Indeed, while at work, some employees experience opportunities to cultivate deep and mutually supportive relationships with others; to strive for excellence; to gain a sense of accomplishment; and to initiate and direct tasks that are personally relevant and valued. All too often, though, employees experience alienation, incompetence, and coercion vis-à-vis their supervisors and co-workers. Whereas the former set of opportunities is associated with satisfaction, engagement, dedication, and performance, the latter is associated with emotional exhaustion, work–family conflict, burnout, absenteeism, and turnover intention.[4] Such findings underscore the profound and diverse influence of socio-contextual factors on employees' health and functioning.

It is also important to consider whether personal factors affect employees' performance and wellness at work. To facilitate such a discussion, consider the following sketches of two hypothetical individuals. Juliette is in her late 30s, has been married for seven years, and has two young children. She has been employed in a mid-sized corporation for nine years and has risen steadily up the corporate ladder. As a result of her success, Juliette and her family enjoy a very comfortable standard of living and, in many ways, epitomize the American dream. So too with Marie, who also is in her late 30s, is married with children, and has enjoyed success in the same mid-sized corporation as Juliette. In fact, the only difference between Juliette and Marie is the value orientation that shapes each of their life's path. Juliette places strong importance on coming to know and accept who she really is, on having good friends on whom she can depend, on working for the betterment of society, and on being physically healthy. Marie, in contrast, places strong importance on having expensive possessions, on being admired by many people, and on having others comment often about how attractive she looks. From a psychological perspective, it is interesting to ponder whether Juliette and Marie may experience varied levels of psychological, social, and physical health as a function of the different types of values that organize and direct their behavior. As well, it is important to consider whether there are divergent consequences associated with attainment of these different types of values.

In this article, we use self-determination theory to guide a discussion of research on value orientations, which inform the development and pursuit of life goals (or aspirations) that organize and direct behavior over extended periods of time. Value orientations are considered to be relatively stable, motivationally relevant factors that, in the work domain, may contribute to the psychological, social, and physical health of employees. Self-determination theory (SDT) is an approach to human motivation and personality in social contexts that recognizes the importance of value orientations in people's lives.[5] With its meta-theoretical roots grounded in organismic philosophy, SDT posits that not all aspirations will contribute to well-being even when attained, a position that diverges from most contemporary goal theorists.[6] From the perspective of SDT, it is important to consider the different types of life goals that people pursue and (sometimes) attain, and to examine whether these aspirations are differentially associated with full functioning and organismic wellness.[7]

SDT distinguishes two different types of aspirations based on their associations with satisfaction of the basic psychological needs for autonomy, competence, and relatedness.[8] This distinction began with the work of researchers Kasser and Ryan, who found evidence for the existence of two general categories of life goals.[9] One factor, which was labeled *intrinsic*, included values for personal growth, community contribution, close relationships, and physical health, whereas a second factor, which was labeled *extrinsic*, included values for the accumulation of wealth and material possessions, social recognition and fame, and having an appealing image. The intrinsic factor was so labeled because its goals are expressive of humans' organismic growth tendency and are theorized to be conducive to satisfaction of basic psychological needs. The extrinsic factor, in contrast, was so labeled because its goals reflect an "outward" orientation[10] toward obtaining external indicators of worth and are theorized to be unassociated with basic psychological need satisfaction.[11] Importantly, evidence for the distinction between intrinsic and extrinsic aspirations has been obtained among diverse cultural groups throughout the world.[12] Table 1 provides a

Table 1 Description of and Sample Items for Intrinsic and Extrinsic Aspirations

Intrinsic Aspirations	
Description	Intrinsic aspirations are expressive of humans' organismic growth tendency
Aspirations and sample items	**Personal growth:** To grow and learn new things **Community contribution:** To help others improve their lives **Close relationships:** To have deep, enduring relationships **Physical health:** To be physically healthy
Extrinsic Aspirations	
Description	Extrinsic aspirations reflect an "outward" orientation toward obtaining external indicators of worth
Aspirations and sample items	**Money:** To be a wealthy person **Fame:** To be admired by many people **Appealing image:** To achieve the look I've been after

brief description of intrinsic and extrinsic aspirations, as well as sample items for the values that constitute these two general categories of life goals.

Intrinsic and Extrinsic Aspirations

An important agenda for research in SDT on life goals has been to examine the relation of pursuing intrinsic and extrinsic aspirations to psychological, social, and physical health. Using both college students and adults, Kasser and Ryan found that those who place strong importance on intrinsic (relative to extrinsic) aspirations report higher levels of positive affect, self-actualization, and vitality, as well as lower levels of depression, narcissism, and physical symptoms.[13] Similar findings have been reported in countries as diverse as Russia,[14] South Korea,[15] and Germany,[16] as well as in the domains of exercise[17] and health care.[18] Importantly, such correlations generalize beyond psychological health, as adolescents who place strong importance on extrinsic (relative to intrinsic) aspirations report higher levels of risky behaviors[19] and bulimic symptoms.[20]

More germane to our focus on organizational behavior, evidence suggests that the goals people pursue affect both their attitudes toward others and their interpersonal behaviors. For instance, those who place strong importance on extrinsic (relative to intrinsic) aspirations also endorse attitudes aligned with social dominance and racial prejudice;[21] report less empathy;[22] and score higher on Machiavellianism, an interpersonal orientation involving manipulation of others.[23] Such attitudes toward others are associated with non-optimal interpersonal behaviors, as researchers also found that those who place strong importance on extrinsic (relative to intrinsic) aspirations report higher levels of acquisitiveness and greed, yet produce *less* profit for their group in a "Tragedy of the Commons" dilemma.[24] In contrast, those who place strong importance on intrinsic (relative to extrinsic) aspirations not only report higher levels of subjective well-being but also report higher levels of ecologically responsible behavior.[25] To summarize, the pursuit of intrinsic aspirations for personal development, meaningful affiliation, and physical health (as opposed to the pursuit of extrinsic aspirations for money, fame, and an appealing image) is conducive to health and wellness, as well as to adaptive interpersonal attitudes and behaviors, and ultimately contributes to "the bottom line" (profit) in a simulated resource-management game.

Recent research has examined holding intrinsic and extrinsic values in the work domain *per se*. Using a sample of unemployed individuals, researchers found that those who hold an intrinsic (relative to extrinsic) work value orientation report higher levels of flexibility around issues of training and pay.[26] Similarly, Belgian employees who hold an extrinsic (relative to intrinsic) work value orientation report lower levels of job dedication, job vitality, and job satisfaction, as well as higher levels of emotional exhaustion and turnover intention.[27] Importantly, and in line with SDT, employees' basic psychological need satisfaction explained a statistically significant proportion of each of the associations between work value orientations and work-related functioning. Therefore, part of the reason that holding an extrinsic work value orientation undermines optimal functioning is that such values thwart satisfaction of the basic psychological needs for autonomy, competence, and relatedness at work. Similar findings have been reported from outside of SDT. For instance, those who place strong importance on materialism report lower levels of satisfaction with their jobs and their careers.[28] Unfortunately, such adverse correlates are not limited to work-related experiences, as those who place strong importance on materialism report higher levels of work–family conflict.[29] It is likely that the pursuit of intrinsic goals would be associated with cooperation and organizational citizenship, whereas the pursuit of extrinsic goals would be associated with individualism, competition, and unethical behavior. Such hypotheses await additional empirical inquiry.

Critical Accounts of the SDT Perspective on Aspirations

As alluded to above, most contemporary goal theorists[30] suggest that attainment of valued goals, regardless of their content, is conducive to psychological, social, and physical health. In contrast, SDT argues that because the pursuit and attainment of intrinsic (but not extrinsic) aspirations are associated with basic psychological need satisfaction, it is primarily when people attain intrinsic (rather than extrinsic) goals that they will experience full functioning and organismic wellness. A few studies have provided support for this hypothesis. For instance, one study found that those who attain intrinsic (relative to extrinsic) aspirations report higher levels of self-esteem, vitality, self-actualization, and quality of interpersonal relationships, as well as lower levels of depression and anxiety, whereas attainment of extrinsic (relative to intrinsic) aspirations is unrelated to psychological health.[31] This hypothesis was also extended to a sample of senior citizens and found that attainment of intrinsic (relative to extrinsic) aspirations is associated with higher levels of well-being, ego integrity, and death acceptance, as well as lower levels of ill-being, despair, and death anxiety, whereas attainment of extrinsic (relative to intrinsic) aspirations is associated with higher levels of despair and lower levels of death acceptance.[32] To obtain a longitudinal perspective on this hypothesis, researchers Niemiec, Ryan, and Deci[33] followed recent graduates from one to two years post-college, an important period of transition during which young adults seek to establish a career path and develop an identity.[34] In line with SDT, results showed that attainment of intrinsic aspirations is associated with higher levels of well-being and lower levels of ill-being, whereas attainment of extrinsic aspirations is unrelated to well-being and actually contributes to higher levels of ill-being.

Such findings offer an important qualification to the general expectancy-value theory[35] view that attainment of any valued goal is conducive to health and wellness. Yet it is also possible that these results reflect an artifact of the samples from which data were drawn, rather than a generalizable psychological phenomenon. One argument, for instance, is that the association between life goals and well-being is a function of the type of values that are emphasized by the environment in which goal pursuits occur.[36] Such an environmental-match perspective would suggest that the pursuit and attainment of extrinsic (relative to intrinsic) aspirations should facilitate psychological health in contexts (such as business schools and organizations) that emphasize the importance of money, fame, and image. In contrast, SDT argues that regardless of the values that are emphasized within an environment, only those goal pursuits and attainments that allow for satisfaction of basic psychological needs are expected to promote health and wellness, and research has supported this hypothesis. In a sample of business students in Singapore, those who place strong importance on materialistic pursuits report lower levels of self-actualization, vitality, and general happiness, as well as higher levels of anxiety, physical symptoms, and time spent unhappy.[37] To provide additional support for this hypothesis, researchers examined aspiration pursuits using a sample of Belgian students who were majoring in business or studying to become teachers.[38] Results showed that those who place strong importance on intrinsic (relative to extrinsic) aspirations report lower levels of substance use and internal distress, as well as higher levels of well-being. Importantly, these associations were not moderated by the program of study in which the students were enrolled.

Conclusion

In this article, we used SDT to guide a discussion of research on the relation of intrinsic and extrinsic aspirations to psychological, social, and physical health. Table 2 provides a brief overview of outcomes associated with the pursuit of intrinsic (relative to extrinsic) aspirations, and Table 3 provides a brief summary of the key points from this review. A growing body of evidence suggests that the pursuit and attainment of intrinsic (relative to extrinsic) aspirations facilitate optimal functioning and wellness, and similar dynamics have been shown in the work domain. Thus, we encourage employees to pursue intrinsic (rather than extrinsic) aspirations, and we implore managers to create need-supportive conditions that are conducive to such pursuits. To do so, managers can relate from the employees' perspective, encourage self-initiation and choice, create optimal challenges, give informational feedback, provide a rationale for requested actions, and minimize use of controlling language. In fact, past research has shown that such a style has a positive impact on employees' work-related experience.[39]

Table 2 Overview of Outcomes Associated with Pursuit of Intrinsic (Relative to Extrinsic) Aspirations

		Psychological Health	Social Health	Physical Health
Life Aspirations	Higher levels of:	Subjective well-being Self-actualization Vitality	Pro-ecological behaviors	
	Lower levels of:	Depression Narcissism Anxiety	Social dominance Racial prejudice Machiavellianism Acquisitiveness	Risky behaviors Bulimic symptoms
Work Aspirations	Higher levels of:	Job dedication Job vitality Job satisfaction		
	Lower levels of:	Emotional exhaustion Turnover intention	Work–family conflict	

Table 3 Summary of Key Points

Summary of Key Points
1. Life goals (or aspirations) organize and direct behavior over extended periods of time.
2. Some people place strong importance on intrinsic aspirations for personal growth, community contribution, close relationships, and physical health. Other people place strong importance on extrinsic aspirations for money, fame, and an appealing image.
3. The pursuit of intrinsic (relative to extrinsic) aspirations is conducive to psychological, social, and physical health.
4. The pursuit of extrinsic (relative to intrinsic) aspirations among employees and business students does *not* yield well-being benefits despite the apparent person–environment match.
5. The attainment of intrinsic (but *not* extrinsic) aspirations is conducive to psychological, social, and physical health.

Endnotes

1. U.S. Bureau of Labor Statistics (2011). *American Time Use Survey—2010 Results*. Available online at http://www.bls.gov/news.release/pdf/atus.pdf.
2. Doherty, M. (2009). When the working day is through: The end of work as identity? *Work, Employment and Society, 23*, 84–101.
3. Schaufeli, W. B., Bakker, A. B., & Van Rhenen, W. (2009). How changes in job demands and resources predict burnout, work engagement, and sickness absenteeism. *Journal of Organizational Behavior, 30*, 893–917.
4. Gagné, M., & Deci, E. L. (2005). Self-determination theory and work motivation. *Journal of Organizational Behavior, 26*, 331-362.
5. Deci, E. L., & Ryan, R. M. (2008). Facilitating optimal motivation and psychological well-being across life's domains. *Canadian Psychology, 49*, 14–23.
6. Locke, E. A., & Latham, G. P. (1990). *A theory of goal setting and task performance*. Englewood Cliffs, NJ: Prentice Hall.
7. Niemiec, C. P., & Ryan, R. M. (2013). What makes for a life well lived? Autonomy and its relation to full functioning and organismic wellness. In I. Boniwell & S. David (Eds.), *Oxford handbook of happiness*. Oxford: Oxford University Press.
8. Ryan, R. M., Sheldon, K. M., Kasser, T., & Deci, E. L. (1996). All goals are not created equal: An organismic perspective on the nature of goals and their regulation. In P. M. Gollwitzer & J. A. Bargh (Eds.), *The psychology of action: Linking cognition and motivation to behavior*. New York: Guilford Press, 7–26
9. Kasser, T., & Ryan, R. M. (1996). Further examining the American dream: Differential correlates of intrinsic and extrinsic goals. *Personality and Social Psychology Bulletin, 22*, 280–287.
10. Williams, G. C., Cox, E. M., Hedberg, V. A., & Deci, E. L. (2000). Extrinsic life goals and health-risk behaviors in adolescents. *Journal of Applied Social Psychology, 30*, 1756–1771.
11. Kasser, T. (2002). *The high price of materialism*. London, UK: The MIT Press.
12. Grouzet, F. M. E., Kasser, T., Ahuvia, A., Dols, J. M. F., Kim, Y., Lau, S., et al. (2005). The structure of goals across 15 cultures. *Journal of Personality and Social Psychology, 89*, 800–816.
13. Kasser, T., & Ryan, R. M. (1996).

14. Ryan, R. M., Chirkov, V. I., Little, T. D., Sheldon, K. M., Timoshina, E., & Deci, E. L. (1999). The American dream in Russia: Extrinsic aspirations and well-being in two cultures. *Personality and Social Psychology Bulletin, 25*, 1509–1524.

15. Kim, Y., Kasser, T., & Lee, H. (2003). Self-concept, aspirations, and well-being in South Korea and the United States. *The Journal of Social Psychology, 143*, 277–290.

16. Schmuck, P., Kasser, T., & Ryan, R. M. (2000). Intrinsic and extrinsic goals: Their structure and relationship to well-being in German and U.S. college students. *Social Indicators Research, 50*, 225–241.

17. Sebire, S. J., Standage, M., & Vansteenkiste, M. (2009). Examining intrinsic versus extrinsic exercise goals: Cognitive, affective, and behavioral outcomes. *Journal of Sport and Exercise Psychology, 31*, 189–210.

18. Niemiec, C. P., Ryan, R. M., Deci, E. L., & Williams, G. C. (2009). Aspiring to physical health: The role of aspirations for physical health in facilitating long-term tobacco abstinence. *Patient Education and Counseling, 74*, 250-257.

19. Williams, G. C., Cox, E. M., Hedberg, V. A., & Deci, E. L. (2000).

20. Verstuyf, J., Vansteenkiste, M., & Soenens, B. (2012). Eating regulation and bulimic symptoms: The differential correlates of health-focused and appearance-focused eating regulation. *Body Image, 9*, 108–117.

21. Duriez, B., Vansteenkiste, M., Soenens, B., & De Witte, H. (2007). The social costs of extrinsic relative to intrinsic goal pursuits: Their relation with social dominance and racial and ethnic prejudice. *Journal of Personality, 75*, 757–782.

22. Sheldon, K. M., & Kasser, T. (1995). Coherence and congruence: Two aspects of personality integration. *Journal of Personality and Social Psychology, 68*, 531–543.

23. McHoskey, J. W. (1999). Machiavellianism, intrinsic versus extrinsic goals, and social interest: A self-determination theory analysis. *Motivation and Emotion, 23*, 267–283.

24. Sheldon, K. M., & McGregor, H. A. (2000). Extrinsic value orientation and 'the tragedy of the commons'. *Journal of Personality, 68*, 383–411.

25. Brown, K. W., & Kasser, T. (2005). Are psychological and ecological well-being compatible? The role of values, mindfulness, and lifestyle. *Social Indicators Research, 74*, 349–368.

26. Van den Broeck, A., Vansteenkiste, M., Lens, W., & De Witte, H. (2010). Unemployed individuals' work values and job flexibility: An explanation from expectancy-value theory and self-determination theory. *Applied Psychology: An International Review, 59*, 296–317. Van den Broeck, A., Vansteenkiste, M., De Witte, H., Soenens, B., & Lens, W. (2010). Capturing autonomy, competence, and relatedness at work: Construction and initial validation of the Work-related Basic Need Satisfaction scale. *Journal of Occupational and Organizational Psychology, 83*, 981–1002.

27. Vansteenkiste, M., Neyrinck, B., Niemiec, C. P., Soenens, B., de Witte, H., & Van den Broeck, A. (2007). On the relations among work value orientations, psychological need satisfaction and job outcomes: A self-determination theory approach. *Journal of Occupational and Organizational Psychology, 80*, 251–277.

28. Deckop, J. R., Jurkiewicz, C. L., & Giacalone, R. A. (2010). Effects of materialism on work-related personal well-being. *Human Relations, 63*, 1007–1030.

29. Promislo, M. D., Deckop, J. R., Giacalone, R. A., & Jurkiewicz, C. L. (2010). Valuing money more than people: The effects of materialism on work–family conflict. *Journal of Occupational and Organizational Psychology, 83*, 935–953.

30. Locke, E. A., & Latham, G. P. (1990).

31. Kasser, T., & Ryan, R. M. (2001). Be careful what you wish for: Optimal functioning and the relative attainment of intrinsic and extrinsic goals. In P. Schmuck & K. M. Sheldon (Eds.), *Life goals and well-being: Towards a positive psychology of human striving.* Seattle: Hogrefe & Huber Publishers, 116–131.

32. Van Hiel, A., & Vansteenkiste, M. (2009). Ambitions fulfilled? The effects of intrinsic and extrinsic goal attainment on older adults' ego-integrity and death attitudes. *International Journal of Aging and Human Development, 68,* 27–51.

33. Niemiec, C. P., Ryan, R. M., & Deci, E. L. (2009). The path taken: Consequences of attaining intrinsic and extrinsic aspirations in post-college life. *Journal of Research in Personality, 43,* 291–306.

34. Adams, G. R., & Marshall, S. K. (1996). A developmental social psychology of identity: Understanding the person-in-context. *Journal of Adolescence, 19,* 429–442.

35. Vroom, V. H. (1964). *Work and motivation.* New York: John Wiley & Sons.

36. Sagiv, L., & Schwartz, S. H. (2000). Value priorities and subjective well-being: Direct relations and congruity effects. *European Journal of Social Psychology, 30,* 177–198.

37. Kasser, T., & Ahuvia, A. (2002). Materialistic values and well-being in business students. *European Journal of Social Psychology, 32,* 137–146.

38. Vansteenkiste, M., Duriez, B., Simons, J., & Soenens, B. (2006). Materialistic values and well-being among business students: Further evidence of their detrimental effect. *Journal of Applied Social Psychology, 36,* 2892–2908.

39. Deci, E. L., Connell, J. P., & Ryan, R. M. (1989). Self-determination in a work organization. *Journal of Applied Psychology, 74,* 580–590.

High-Tech, High-Touch Tension: Trends in Human Resource Management

Troy R. Nielson
Brigham Young University

Ellen Ensher
Loyola Marymount University

Elisa Grant-Vallone
California State University, San Marcos

> *A manager called me for advice. One of her employees*
> *had called in sick but posted pictures on Facebook of himself*
> *having a great time in Disneyland on his "sick" day.*
> —Anonymous Human Resources Manager

> *I got into HR because I love people. But it is kind of scary because I can go*
> *to work and not see people, because of technology. Just a few years ago,*
> *people would come in to HR on payday—now we have lost those moments.*
> *I have to make sure to walk the floor just to put the people connection*
> *back into my job. We have to be careful to not take*
> *the human out of human resources.*
> —Anonymous Human Resources Manager

Technology can enable us to know a great deal about employees, such as a "sick" day off in Disneyland. However, it can also prevent us from interacting with employees as routine opportunities for interaction, like picking up a paycheck, become obsolete. The tension between delivering high-touch Human Resource Management (HRM) in a world that is increasingly high tech is one of the greatest challenges facing HRM.[1] This tension suggests a number of interesting new trends that we will explore next.

According to Internet World Statistics, the number of people connected to the Internet has increased from nearly 361 million in 2000 to over 2 billion as of March 2011.[2] The global connectivity of employees will continue to have important implications for organizations in general, and Human Resource Management in particular. The potential cost savings to organizations that effectively use technology and the Internet in their HR functions is compelling. For example, the use of technology in training and development contributed positively to the bottom line for many organizations, like IBM, which generated over $284 million dollars in cost savings due to eLearning, and saved over $35 million from its HR department's online expense system.[3]

Because of the importance of HRM to organizational success, we examine the unique challenges and opportunities related to balancing the tension between high tech and high touch. We examine the trends related to HR and technology through the lens of three major HR activities: 1) Recruiting, 2) Renewing, and 3) Relating to employees.

How We Know What We Know

Our data were collected in two ways. First, we examined a wide variety of articles and books from academia and the popular press and identified the major ways that the Internet and technology has affected HR processes. Second, we conducted in-depth interviews with 10 experienced HR professionals to find out about their direct experiences with HR and technology. (See Table 1 at the end of this article for more detailed information about our 10 HR professionals). From these interviews and the archival data, we identified and analyzed key trends, important takeaways, and discussion points for students to consider.

Recruiting Employees

"In the not-so-distant past, recruiters and staffing managers pored through resumes, posted on job boards, and hosted expensive job fairs in top markets to find candidates and fill jobs. Now, they might interact with social network site users by posting a challenging technical question, then contact individuals who provide the best answers to discuss a potential job."[4]

Table 1 Interview Participants

Participant	Industry	Title
Gerald	Entertainment	Director, Diversity Development
Jana	Entertainment	Manager, Human Resources
Amanda	Retail	Manager, Human Resources
Dylan	Healthcare	Vice President, Learning and Development
Brad	Consumer Goods	Vice President, Human Resources
Penny	Online Gifting	Senior Vice President, Human Resources
Pam	Mining & Metals	Global Reporting and Information Manager
Krist	Construction	Vice President, Human Resources
Sarah	Retail	Human Resources Manager
Kathy	Computer software	Human Resources Director

Given the high unemployment rates of the past few years (around 9–10% from 2009–2011) and emphasis on acquiring the best talent from such a large pool, recruitment has played an even more critical role than in the past.[5] HR professionals have been adopting online recruitment tools at a rapid rate. Today, we would be hard pressed to find a company that does not use online tools for employee recruitment and selection. Technology still enables recruiting to be done faster at lower costs, and with access to a broader base of talent. So, what has changed in recent years that has affected the recruitment of new employees? Students will not be surprised by the answer—the rise of social media.

Based on the interviews and recent articles, two primary themes emerged about the impact of social media on recruiting. First, LinkedIn and Facebook are the most prominently used social media applications for recruiting-related activities. Second, as the use of these recruiting channels has increased, reliance on online job boards has decreased. As helpful as these tools are for recruitment, we also note some important considerations.

SHRM (Society for Human Resource Management) recently reported that the percentage of companies that use social networking websites in their recruiting efforts rose from 34 to 56 percent in the past three years.[6] *Fortune* magazine put it even more emphatically for job seekers: "Facebook is for fun. Tweets have a short shelf life. If you're serious about managing your career, the only social site that really matters is LinkedIn."[7] The HR professionals we interviewed (with one exception) all use LinkedIn; most also use Facebook, and Twitter is not used much yet for recruiting purposes. Consider the following quotes from two of our interviewees:

- "The ability to use social media became a key differentiator when we were assessing applicant tracking systems. We chose a platform that allowed us to more easily reach out to passive job searchers via social media applications as well as one that better leveraged our internal talent's built-in social networks." (Penny, SVP of HR)

- "We tweet, we post, we have a group on LinkedIn, we send weekly lists of openings internally and externally; our ATS [Applicant Tracking System] has capacity to forward openings to friends and for employees to make referrals." (Pam, Global Reporting and Information Manager)

Both quotes suggest company efforts to more proactively create relationships with prospective employees, especially with friends of current employees. Not everything about LinkedIn and Facebook is good news for organizations. LinkedIn makes it easier for headhunters to connect with star performers at specific companies and to entice them to leave for other companies. Another issue raised by one of our interview respondents was that concerns about an applicant's professionalism surfaced because of content on that applicant's Facebook page. He added that so far, such problems were the exception, not the rule (Brad, VP of HR).

A second theme is that as social media usage becomes more prominent in recruiting, a company's website becomes increasingly important and the use of job boards like Monster.com and Careerbuilder.com becomes less important. Multiple interviewees commented that they have reduced their reliance on job boards. None mentioned an increase in using such recruiting channels. The social media sites leverage the social networks of individuals who already have a connection with the company—current employees, former employees, and customers. A related implication of this shift is that a company's website, particularly for those seeking employment, deserves even greater attention. One interviewee commented that all jobs posted on social media applications linked prospective applicants to the company jobs web page (Jana, HR Manager). As another HR leader stated, "We have also increased our focus on our career site and our Web presence knowing that it has become very important to candidates in their job search." (Penny, SVP of HR).

HR professionals continue to face recruiting challenges in light of these changes. First, the potential for resume overload and keeping up with the speed of social media recruiting can be daunting. Google, one of the most popular tech companies to work for, receives over 150,000 resumes per month, and the company claims to read all them.[8] Second, companies need to continue to innovate the process of selection (choosing the best individuals for a given position from among a larger pool of job applicants). In larger companies, the process of screening applicants' resumes is typically a collaborative process between HR and an applicant tracking system. Google illustrates innovative approaches to employee selection. Google has developed an extensive survey that all job applicants are required to fill out. The answers to this survey are fed into an algorithm that grades each candidate on how well they would fit into the company culture. Additionally, the software system developed by Google for tracking their job candidates allows employees to share comments about each applicant as that individual's resume moves through each step of the recruiting process.[9] Using pre-employment online assessments can provide unbiased comparable data for managers, but companies must be careful as biased tests or privacy breaches can be grounds for discrimination lawsuits.[10]

Renewing Employees

Looking ahead to 2015, it is clear that the field of training and development is at a crossroads. Traditional training and development functions are close to being overtaken by newly accessible, just-in-time learning that professionals and departments can easily attain. There is also a significant need for training and development to take a more strategic role in defining and developing the next generation of leaders.[11]

Organizations renew their employees' knowledge, skills, and abilities primarily through training and career development processes. Training and development is an important expenditure for most organizations. Approximately five billion dollars per year is spent on the training and development of employees in U.S. organizations.[12] It is not surprising that organizations commit significant financial resources to training. PricewaterhouseCoopers found that 26 percent of private companies cited the lack of skilled workers as a potential barrier to future company growth.[13] Even in lean economic times, organizations recognize the pressing need to renew the skills of their employees.

As the need for training and development increases, many companies have found that technology and the Internet provide a lower cost solution in the guise of online training or e-learning. Cost reductions for online training pertain to several major categories of expenditures including: a) direct costs of travel and indirect opportunity costs of time away from job, b) production of training materials, c) maintenance costs for content updates and course refreshers. In addition to cost reduction, online training also offers a number of important advantages: it helps the employee learn faster, and in some cases, better; delivers learning free of the limitations of time and geography; and tracks and evaluates the effectiveness of the training more effectively.[14]

Although many companies use some form of online training, two vexing problems remain with this medium that highlight the tension between the prevalence of high tech with the remaining importance of high touch. As HR Manager Amanda noted, "We are a people company so although online training is convenient, many employees still prefer to learn face-to-face." First, people enjoy classroom learning not only because of what they learn, but because of the social aspects and bonding that occurs in a face-to-face environment. Second, face-to-face learning is perceived by many HR professionals as resulting in greater retention, or learning stickiness, as compared to e-learning.

To increase the effectiveness of online training, there has been an influx of creative and sophisticated technologies including the use of games, 3-D simulations, and mobile apps. Currently, 70% of organizations use video games, and by 2013, the usage of video games in employee training and development is expected to increase to 80 percent[15] Diverse companies—including Cisco, Sodexo, Federal Express, UPS, and the U.S. Army—all use customized video games in their training of their employees. Video games are popular with training participants because they are fun, creative, and interactive. Moreover, research indicates that the ramification of training can help employees build important business skills, such as critical thinking and decision making, and may aid in retention.[16] 3-D technologies are also growing in usage and popularity as a training and communication tool for employee development. 3-D virtual platforms are Internet-based, multi-user environments where employees create avatars to represent themselves. The largest and most well known 3-D virtual platform is Second Life—created to develop knowledge both in educational and organizational settings. Virtual training is beneficial to increase team-building communication, conflict resolution, and team development. Organizations such as IBM hold conferences in Second Life and have found large savings, of approximately $250,000, in comparison to a real-world event. 3-D training can also be customized for organizations. For example, the Hilton Garden Inn provided a 3-D customer service simulation using the Playstation PSP. In this 3-D simulation, hotel employees interacted with virtual guests to increase their customer service skills.[17]

Simulations not only help employees learn but also provide assessment data about common mistakes made in a gaming situation so that action can be taken before they become real-life mistakes. One of the positive aspects of the high-tech approach to employee development is the ability to track and develop accountability for employee growth. Krist (VP of HR) indicated that "Talent Development is all tracked via a Learning Management System (LMS). Via the LMS, all training courses are offered and progress is tracked along with 360-degree performance appraisals, employee opinion surveys, and personality profiles." The results are then be interpreted and communicated to employees via a personalized high-touch approach.

In fact, employee communication has seen several innovations that highlight the tension between high-tech and high-touch in organizations. One growing trend is the development of internal social media, such as customized, organizational Facebook pages. These pages can be a tremendous tool for networking, knowledge sharing, and social interactions. In addition, organizations such as Triple Creek are providing online platforms for mentoring activities.

However, employees are able to create their own career development opportunities through the use of technology. Networking technologies such as Facebook, LinkedIn,

Twitter, and the blogosphere have transformed the way employees network. Social media allows employees to develop their own personal brands and engage existing contacts and create new ones. For example, there are numerous online mentoring programs available, such as MentorNet, to enable individuals to connect with others in their profession.

Although the high-tech approach technology has led to important innovations in employee training and development, employees still crave the high-touch personalized approach to learning. Organizations need to provide unique learning styles for employees to engage in renewal. Renewal might be about offering employees opportunities for continued education or providing entertaining activities for employees to unwind and relieve stress. When students search for a job, they need to consider whether the prospective employer offers renewal and if this fits their needs.

Relating to Employees

"While the decision to post videos, pictures, thoughts, experiences and observations to a social networking site is personal, a single act can create far reaching ethical consequences for individuals as well as organizations. Therefore it is important for executives to be mindful of the implications and to elevate the discussion about the risks associated with it to highest levels of leadership."[18]

Over the last decade, technological advances have transformed the nature of relationships within the workplace. Interviews with employees showed several common themes. Issues of trust, privacy, and employee safety have become increasingly salient for HR professionals. Concerns related to balancing work–family and an "always connected" mentality are also increasingly relevant.

Not long ago, the main concerns with technology were related to ergonomic issues and strain from computer use. While these concerns are still valid, HR professionals today grapple with more complex issues, such as distracted employees (e.g., texting while driving and social media during business hours) and employee sabotage. Policies addressing these issues need to be clear. The 2008 California train crash that killed 25 people due to the operator's texting brought these issues to the forefront. In October 2010, the Occupational Health and Safety Administration (OSHA) sent a clear statement to employers that it is "the responsibility and legal obligation to create and maintain a safe and healthful workplace that would include having a clear, unequivocal and enforced policy against the hazard of texting while driving."[19] This concern was echoed by the HR professionals: "The use of electronic resources while driving has created a whole new area of liability" (Kathy, HR Director). How employees spend time in the workplace is also a concern. The inappropriate use of email, the Internet, and social media are not only waste company-paid time but could create legal issues as well. One HR professional explained, "With the new cell phones that are really just small computers, every employee has access to everything—just as if an employee brought their desktop computer to work" (Kathy, HR Director). Whether or not to monitor employee use continues to be a debate within organizations. Indeed, the greatest challenge for managers seems to be finding the right balance of permissiveness and scrutiny. One HR manager explains, "In HR, we walk a tightrope between privacy and employee protection issues" (Krist, VP of HR).

Not surprisingly, the employee–employer relationship between has been significantly influenced by the rise of social media over the last 10 years. Social media can be a distraction for employees, but information posted by an employee can harm a company's reputation or its intellectual property. According to a recent Deloitte survey, 74 percent of employees believe it is easy to damage a company's reputation on a social media site while 5 percent of employees felt that employees' social networking sites were "none of an employer's business."[20] However, poor choices made by employees can have severe consequences for organizations. For example, an interviewee from the entertainment industry explained, "There are situations where employees go to a movie (that their organization produced) and then post negative information about it. What do we do? This is a gray area in HR" (Jana, HR Manager).

Court cases highlight some of the concerns associated with increased use of social media. For example, Lisa Fried-Grodin describes one of these incidents in an article in the *New Jersey Law Journal.* Two employees set up a password-protected MySpace account for employees to rant about their employer and management. After management found out and obtained the password, the two employees were terminated. The employees filed a lawsuit against the employer and ultimately won the case.[21] Is it ethical to rant about one's boss or employer online? Is it legal? These are issues that HR professionals are addressing today. On one hand, employers have a clear responsibility to protect employee privacy, but on the other hand, need to trust their employees to not sabotage the organization.

In addition to trust and privacy issues between the organization and employees, technology transforms the way that colleagues interact. Mobile technology creates a smaller world where it is incredibly easy to connect to people; however, the ease of connecting from any location may simultaneously lead to deteriorating relationships between employees. For example, a recent organizational practice called "hoteling" is when employees do not have a permanent workspace but simply reserve a space for the days they will be in the office. Some of the HR professionals interviewed expressed concerned with how the increased use of online communication changes the culture of organizations and limits day-to-day conversations. The ease of connecting remotely makes life easier in many ways, but also reduces "real time" interactions that are critical to interpersonal relationships and teamwork.

Technology produces a similar tension when it comes to work–family balance. The opportunity to connect 24/7 provides employees with tremendous flexibility and can ease work–family conflicts, but may simultaneously blur the boundaries between work, home, and play, and could eventually contribute to heightened stress. Even with these concerns, telecommuting continues to be an important organizational trend. According to SHRM, 55 percent of organizations offer at least part-time telecommuting to their employees and 17 percent offer a full-time telecommuting option.[22] As one interviewee explained, "We have several employees who have skills and experience that we need to be successful in the marketplace who do not want to relocate their families. In the past, they would have had to relocate or not work for us; now we have the ability to allow them to continue to work in their home state and contribute to the success of the company…they are connected to the cloud environment" (Kathy, HR Director). The increased technology that allows employees to work remotely and provide more opportunity to balance work and home activities may also create stress from the feeling of always being connected.

Takeaways and Discussion Points

Technology and social media have drastically changed the way business is conducted. It is imperative that organizations establish polices and address issues with employees in a clear manner. A strong policy includes language that prohibits employees from making disparaging remarks about the organization or other employees, prohibits employees from disclosing confidential information, makes it clear that the organization is monitoring online activity, and trains employees on appropriate and inappropriate use. Another key implication is that the tension between high-tech and high-touch has increased in the past decade. It is essential for both company leaders and employees to review organizational routines, practices, and culture for imbalances between automation and humanization. Finally, technology puts more of the onus for career advancement and success on the shoulders of the employee. Technology makes it easier for companies to proactively attract talent—it also makes it easier for talented employees to proactively leave.

Questions for Reflection

- Employers will often check an applicant's Facebook page and LinkedIn profile (as well as doing a Google search) once that person reaches a certain stage in the hiring process—what "brand message" do these pages communicate to prospective employers about the employee?
- How does technology influence your ability to balance professional and personal demands? How can employers use technology to help balance the work–life conflict?
- If you were an HR manager, to what extent would you recommend that employee usage of company technology resources be monitored? Why?
- How can you use technology to better take charge of your career development?

Endnotes

1. Naisbitt, J., Naisbitt, N., & Philips, D. (1999). *High Tech High Touch and Our Accelerated Search for Meaning.* London: Nicholas Brealey Publishing.
2. World internet usage statistics sews and world population stats. (n.d.). *Internet World Stats - Usage and Population Statistics.* Retrieved June 15, 2011, from http://www .internetworldstats.com
3. Blomberg,J., Forbes, N., & Stanford, P.. (2005). IBM's on demand workplace: the integrating platform for work at ib. Proceedings of the IBM's on demand workplace, http://www .thefutureofwork.net/assets/IBM_intro_March_9_05.pdf
4. Babcock, P. (2010). Recruiting strategies for social media. Retrieved July 28 from http://www.shrm.org/hrdisciplines/staffingmanagement/Articles/Pages/ RecruitingStrategiesforSocialMedia.aspx
5. Bureau of Labor Statistics Data. (n.d.). *Databases, tables & calculators by subject.* Retrieved June 15, 2011, from http://data.bls.gov/timeseries/LNS14
6. SHRM Research Spotlight. (2011). *HR Magazine, page 11.*
7. Hempel, J. (2010). How LinkedIn will fire up your career. *Fortune.*

8. Kopytoff, V. (2005). How Google woos the best and brightest. *San Francisco Bay Area — News, Sports, Business, Entertainment, Classifieds: SFGate.* Retrieved June 15, 2011, from http://www.sfgate.com/cgi-bin/article.cgi?f=/c/a/2005/12/18/GOOGLE.TMP

9. Hansell, S. (2007). Google answer to filling jobs is an algorithm. *The New York Times - Breaking News, World News & Multimedia.* Retrieved June 15, 2011, from http://www.nytimes.com/2007/01/03/technology/03google.html?_r=1&oref=slogin.

10. Baer, B. (2010). Pros & Cons of Personality Testing for Employment. *eHow | How to Videos, Articles & More - Trusted Advice for the Curious Life | eHow.com.* Retrieved June 15, 2011, from http://www.ehow.com/list_6887288_pros-cons-personality-testing-employment.html.

11. Goodman, N. (2011). Planning for the Future. *Training Magazine.* Retrieved from http://www.trainingmag.com/article/planning-future.

12. Noe, Raymond. (2010). *Employee Training and Development.* New York: McGraw Hill Publishing.

13. Private Companies See Strong U.S. Economy. (2011). *The Business Journal.* Retrieved June 15, 2011, from http://business-journal.com/private-companies-see-strong-us-economy-p19310-1.htm.

14. Noe, R. (2010). *Employee Training and Development.* New York: McGraw Hill Publishing.

15. Lorenz, M. (2010). Virtually Awesome: How Smart Companies Use Video Games To Recruit, Retain Employees. *Career Builder.* Retrieved from http://thehiringsite.careerbuilder.com/2010/03/04/businesses-embrace-video-gameserious-business-benefits-of-video-games/.

16. See Levitz, J. (2010). UPS Thinks Out of the Box on Driver Training. *The Wall Street Journal.* Retrieved from http://finance.yahoo.com/career-work/article/109258/usps-thinks-out-of-the-box?mod=career-leadership; Ripin, A.J. (2011). A New Day for Corporate Learning. *Training Magazine.* Retrieved from http://www.trainingmag.com/article/new-day-corporate-learning.

17. See Helweg-Larsen, E. (2011). Business Simulations: Begin with the End in Mind. *Training Magazine.* Retrieved from http://www.trainingmag.com/article/business-simulations-begin-end-mind; Jankowski, Mark. (2011). A New Revolution in Online Training. *Training Magazine.* Retrieved from http://www.trainingmag.com/article/new-revolution-online-training.

18. Deloitte, LLP. (2009). "Social networking and reputational risk in the workplace." *Ethics & the Workplace Survey.*

19. http://osha.gov/distracted-driving/index.html.

20. Deloitte, LLP. (2009). "Social networking and reputational risk in the workplace." *Ethics & the Workplace Survey.*

21. Fried-Grodin, L. (2010). Do's and Don'ts of Monitoring the Activities of Employees on Social Networking Sites. *New Jersey Law Journal, 202,* 109.

22. Meinert, D. (2011). Make Telecommuting Pay Off. *HR Magazine, Volume 56 (6);* (www.SHRM.org/publications/hrmagazine/Editorial Content/2011/0611).

Trade-Offs in Using Pay for Performance

Kimberly D. Elsbach

University of California, Davis

In a recent scholarly review, Barry Gerhart, Sara Rynes, and Ingrid Smithey Fulmer examined the extensive research on what in organizations is called "merit-based pay" or "pay for performance."[1] *Pay for performance* typically refers to compensation plans in which one's pay is based on a measurement of one's performance (which contrast with traditional salary plans, in which a person is paid a set amount regardless of actual performance). In this article, I provide a concise summary of the major findings described by researchers and relate those findings to social psychological research. Specifically, I summarize findings about the primary ways that pay for performance plans (1) affect employees and organizations, (2) measure performance, and (3) reward performance. These insights are displayed in Table 1.

Table 1 Dimensions of Pay for Performance Compensation Plans

How Pay for Performance Plans Affect Employees and Organizations
1. Motivating individuals —enhancing employee self-esteem through rewards for performance —reducing employee uncertainty by making clear what performance is valued —enhancing employee's sense of control by showing how outcomes are related to effort 2. Influencing workforce composition —employees who dislike plans may choose to leave —"forced distribution" plans may remove even some high performing employees
How Pay for Performance Plans Measure Employee Performance
1. Subjective performance measures —qualitative evaluations of performance quality, which may be biased and may be hard to get raters to separate employees on these measures 2. Objective performance measures —quantitative evaluations of performance quantity and quality, which don't typically measure all aspects of job, only those that can be "quantified"

(continued)

Table 1 Continued

How Pay for Performance Plans Reward Employee Performance
1. Base salary plus individual merit pay 　—most common but also subject to bias 　—may cause competition and ill-will among employees for top rewards 　—has greatest effect on pay through effects on long-term promotions 2. Base salary plus collective merit pay 　—reduces competition for top rewards by basing rewards on total group performance 　—may lead to "free-riding" by employees who gain rewards off the work of others 　—works best in small firms where "free-riding" problems are less likely 3. Base salary plus small group rewards 　—reduce free-riding problems found with large collective pay plans 　—encourage group collaboration and teamwork

How Pay for Performance Plans Affect Employees and Organizations

Significant psychological research suggests that pay for performance plans affect employees in two primary ways: (1) by motivating individuals through needs satisfaction, and (2) by altering the composition of the work force in organizations.

Pay for Performance as an Individual Motivator. All pay plans are designed to motivate employees by providing a valued outcome (i.e., pay). Pay is valued, at a basic level, because it helps people satisfy essential needs for food, housing, safety, comfort.[2] Yet, beyond these essential needs, individuals in most organizations are motivated by a set of higher-level human needs, including needs for self-esteem enhancement, uncertainty reduction, and control. Thus, one way that pay for performance plans may affect employees is by satisfying these higher-level human needs.

Self-esteem enhancement is a human need to perceive oneself as positively distinct and socially valued.[3] Because pay for performance plans may distinguish individuals as high-performers and high-earners, they help individuals to meet needs for self-esteem enhancement, especially if high performers are recognized publicly.[4] On the downside, pay for performance plans may also distinguish low-performers and low-earners who may then suffer threats to their self-esteem. As discussed below in the section on "workforce composition," employees may react to such threats by reducing their effort at work, or leaving the organization altogether.

Uncertainty reduction is also recognized as a human need, and is described as a need to "reduce uncertainty about one's world and one's place in it."[5] By clearly linking pay to specific performance outcomes, pay for performance plans may reduce uncertainty about what behaviors are valued and desired in organizations. In turn, individuals may be motivated to enact these desired behaviors (e.g., working hard for performance rewards) as a means of validating that they belong in the organization—thus, further reducing uncertainty about their place in the world. Of course, if the pay for performance plans do not clearly link outcomes to performance (e.g., sometimes superior performance is overlooked, or not recognized), then uncertainty reduction will not occur. In cases where employees perceive that pay is not tightly linked to performance, there will be calls to replace pay for performance plans with more traditional salaried pay.[6]

Finally, humans have been shown to possess a *need for control* over their lives and futures.[7] Pay for performance plans may provide a type of control by allowing individuals to influence their future pay and status through their own effort and performance. To the extent that individuals can control their performance (i.e., they work in jobs where they are able to work more effectively merely by applying more effort), they may exercise great control over these important outcomes. By contrast, in jobs where performance is influenced by factors outside of one's control (e.g., poor decisions by top managers or unpredictable fluctuations in the economic environment), the control incentives of pay for performance plans may be much weaker.

In sum, there are a number of human needs that may motivate individual employees to work harder and more effectively if that effort is perceived to effect the satisfaction of those needs. Perhaps as a result of these motivations, researchers have found that pay for performance plans exert a significant incentive effect on productivity. In fact, such plans have been shown to increase individual productivity up to 30 percent over traditional salaried compensation plans.[8] Yet, as noted above, these positive effects may not occur in all situations, and in some cases, the opposite effect (e.g., lowered productivity) may occur.

Pay for Performance as an Influence on Workforce Composition. A second way that pay for performance plans may affect employees and their organizations is by leading individuals to join or leave workforces based on their ability and desire to perform well under a given plan. Researchers have labeled these effects on workforce composition "sorting effects."[9] Pay for performance plans may achieve sorting effects through *self-selection* (i.e., only employees who wish to work under such plans will join or remain with an organization), or through *managerial discretion* (i.e., managers may hire and fire employees based on their ability to perform well under a plan). Because these processes (i.e., self-selection and managerial discretion) often lead to a workforce that is well suited to working in a pay for performance environment, they are typically associated with improvements in productivity. In some cases, up to a 50 percent of the productivity increases associated with pay for performance plans has come from changes in workforce composition.[10]

Research has shown that high achievers (e.g., college students with high GPAs) are more likely than lower achievers to value pay for performance plans, especially those that measure and reward individual performance.[11] Further, people with high needs for achievement and low risk aversion have been shown to be most attracted to jobs with pay for performance plans.[12] Given these findings, an organization that uses pay for performance plans may, over time, acquire a workforce that has a relatively high performance level overall. Yet, this effect may have a downside. If pay for performance plans are designed in ways that require that some performers to be rated "high" and others to be rated "low"—what are called *"forced distribution plans"*—then even employees who are relatively high performers, compared to most in their field, may be rated as "low performers" in their organization. These low ratings have been shown to hurt morale because they are perceived as unfair.[13]

How Pay for Performance Plans Measure Employee Performance

According to Gerhart, Rynes, and Smithey Fulmer, there are two primary ways that performance is measured in pay for performance plans. First, performance may be measured subjectively based on observations and evaluations of employee behavior (e.g., ratings of "leadership quality," "citizenship," or "team effectiveness" by supervisors, peers, or subordinates). Second, performance may be measured objectively based on quantitative measures of output (e.g., sales, contracts signed, patients seen).

Subjective performance measures are often used when employee output is hard to measure quantitatively or objectively (e.g., when evaluating creative workers, such as graphic designers who are coming up with ideas for an advertising campaign), or when output may be sporadic or only occur after long periods of work (e.g., when evaluating researchers who are developing a new cancer drug). In these cases, it may be difficult, if not impossible, to "count" the output of workers over a relatively short period of time (i.e., counting the output of a grade school teacher over the course of a week), making objective and quantitative measures a poor fit for evaluation. Subjective measures, by contrast, can be devised to measure qualitative output (e.g., how well a teacher teaches) and can be designed to measure almost any behavior that is desired (e.g., citizenship behaviors such as helping out co-workers or doing work above and beyond one's job description).

On the downside, subjective measures are, well, subjective. They are prone to any number of human biases and are only as good as the information used as input. For example, if I evaluate a 5th grade teacher by attending one of his classes, I may just happen to evaluate a particularly poorly executed class. To really get a good sense of the teacher, I would need to attend many of his classes, which is often not feasible. I might also attend to only the negative comments or behavior in the class (it is well-established that negative information is more salient and remembered than is positive information),[14] and thus, obtain a poor impression of the teacher's effectiveness. Finally, I might just not like the teacher very much for personal reasons (e.g., he may belong to a different political party than I do, making him less likeable than teachers who are more similar to me).[15] As a result of these biases, as well as different levels of skill and ability in making observations of particular behaviors, researchers have found large differences in ratings of an individual across different observers when using subjective measures.[16] Recognition that such differences exist across raters may lead employees to perceive subjective measures as unfair and prone to political manipulation (e.g., complaints that only the boss's "favorite" employees are rated highly).

An additional challenge of using subjective measures is getting raters to use them to differentiate employees when it counts. If subjective measures provide high differentiation across employees (i.e., some are rated high, some middle, and some low) and those measures become publicly known and are used to affect actual pay bonuses, they may hurt relationships between the low- and even middle-rated employees and their rater (e.g. their supervisor). Similarly, if subjective measures are based on evaluations by one's peers (e.g., members of one's project team or department), then poor evaluations may undermine group collegiality. As a result, researchers have found that when subjective evaluations are used, evaluators resist making large differentiations across employees and thus, most employees are rated highly and receive similar overall ratings.[17] In turn, the ratings lose their ability to provide strong boosts to self-esteem for highly-rated employees (i.e., because all employees are rated high).

Objective performance measures, by contrast, are often used when output can be measured quantitatively and objectively (e.g., sales volume per month, patients seen per week). While such measures do not apply in many jobs, when they do apply, objective measures are often touted as a means of "fairly" compensating employees based on the work they actually do.

Problems arise, however, because objective measures do not, typically, measure all aspects of a job. So, while a physician may be compensated based on the number of patients she sees in her clinic per week, she is not compensated for the quality (or lack of quality) with which she cares for patients. Further, she may not be compensated for other aspects of her job, such as advising co-workers, mentoring medical residents, or providing administrative support by serving on committees. Finally, she may not feel she is compensated fairly for work she does in a group. For example, she may feel that she does most of the work when working on team of physicians in the trauma department. Yet, each member of the trauma team is each credited with an equal share of the patients seen each shift.

In response to these perceived inequities, the physician may feel she is unfairly compensated for the work she does. Her morale may suffer and she may leave her job. Alternatively, she may decide to stop engaging in any activities that are not measured and compensated, and thus, her organization may lose her valuable and needed skills.[18] Still another possible response is that she may strategically alter her work routines so that she gains the most from the performance plan, at the expense of her patients and co-workers. For example, she could try to see only minor ailments in her clinic and see them for a maximum of 10 minutes each, thus increasing her number of patients seen, while pushing the more difficult patients on to the shoulders of her colleagues and reducing the care of the patients she does see.

How Pay for Performance Plans Reward Performance

While objective and subjective measures of performance make up the components of most pay for performance plans, they are typically only one part of an employee's total compensation plan. Often, pay for performance is combined with salary or hourly pay in a compensation package, in addition, the pay for performance dimension of a compensation plan may be rewarded on an individual, group, or organizational basis. In this last section of the paper, I will describe some of the most common types of compensation plans that involve pay for performance.

Base Salary Plus Individual Merit Pay. The most common pay for performance plan, by far, is merit pay. When using merit pay, an individual's base salary is increased (usually on an annual basis) based on an individual performance measure (either subjective or objective). Because high achievers prefer individual performance measures and pay for performance plans, these plans tend to be popular with these types of employees, and have been shown to increase productivity.[19]

Yet merit pay plans do have their problems. For example, to the extent that merit ratings are based on subjective measures, they may be subject to all of the biases discussed above, and in turn, perceived as unfair by employees who are not highly rated. Also, as noted earlier, these plans often do not provide significant differences in pay across employees because raters do not wish to cause ill will among subordinates or disharmony among peers by rewarding them with highly disparate amounts of pay.[20] An additional problem with merit pay systems may arise when forced distribution systems are used. In these cases, only a small proportion (e.g., 10%) of workers may receive the highest rating. As a result, employees may be engage in competitive behavior (and reduce cooperative behavior) to obtain the highest ratings.

Where merit ratings appear to have the greatest effect is on promotions and long-term workforce composition because merit ratings provide a strong signal about the relative performance of an employee compared to peers, even if the effects on actual pay are small. For example, in one study, a 1-point difference in performance ratings on a 4-point performance scale translated into a 48 percent difference in promotions over a 6-year period.[21] Because promotions lead to much greater differences in pay than do annual bonuses, this effect of merit pay can lead to substantial differences in pay over time.

Base Salary Plus Collective Merit Pay. To avoid the difficulties with individual merit pay systems (e.g., low variance in ratings, possible bias in ratings, and competition among employees) and to motivate employees to "think like business owners," many organizations have implemented pay for performance plans that reward employees based on the performance of larger groups or collectives (e.g., business units, or the entire organization). These plans come in different forms such as *gain sharing* (rewards based on facility performance), *profit sharing* (rewards based on profits at the business unit or organization level), and *stock sharing* (rewards based on the performance of company stock). A characteristic of most collective merit pay plans is that they impose a risk on employees because pay may go up or down based on the performance of the collective. As a result, employees may demand a higher base salary to off-set the risk associated with these plans. In fact, researchers have found that overall labor costs are higher in organizations with profit-sharing plans.[22]

In terms of effects, research shows that collective merit pay plans produce a modest improvement in overall performance, especially in employee-managed firms.[23] Yet, an important moderating factor affecting this improvement is the size of the firm. Small firms (i.e., those with a few hundred workers) have shown the greatest improvements, while larger firms (i.e., those with several hundred to over a thousand employees) have shown small to negligible improvements.[24] This outcome may result from the fact that in larger firms, individual employees perceive their efforts will have little effect on the overall performance of the firm, and thus are less motivated to increase their own productivity.

Base Salary Plus Small Group Reward Systems. Similar to collective merit pay plans, individuals may be rewarded, in part, based on the performance of small teams of which they are members. These plans allow individual employees to have significant influence over the performance (and thus rewards) of the group, alleviating some of the problems with the large collective merit plans. At the same time, they encourage team members to work collaboratively, as their bonus pay depends on the group's overall performance, rather than their individual performance. There is less research on these types of plans than there is for individual and large collective merit plans. Yet there is some evidence that these plans can improve productivity. In particular, plans that reward group members, after each member or the entire team surpasses a pre-determined goal, appear effective in getting team members to work collaboratively and motivating high performers to help out lower performers.[25]

Conclusion

Overall, the research and findings about pay for performance plans suggest that there is no one right plan for all firms and employees. Instead, the research shows a number of trade-offs that need to be considered when constructing a compensation plan that involves pay for performance. Among these trade-offs are the ability of such plans to meet human needs, positively effect workforce composition, accurately measure desired outputs, and motivate desired behaviors by individuals and groups. Considering these trade-offs should be the first step by managers attempting to incorporate pay for performance in their compensation plans.

Endnotes

1. Gerhart, B., Rynes, S. L., & Smithey Fulmer, I. (2009). Pay and performance: Individuals, groups, and executives. *The Academy of Management Annals, 3*, 231–315.
2. Pittman, T. S., & Ziegler, K. R. (2007). Basic human needs. In A.W. Kruglanski and E.T. Higgins, (Eds.) *Social Psychology: Handbook of Basic Principles*, 473–489.
3. Baumeister, R. F. (1998). *The self*. In D. T. Gilbert, S. T. Fiske, & G. Lindzey (Eds.), *The Handbook of Social Psychology, Fourth Edition*. Boston: McGraw-Hill, 680–740.
4. ibid.
5. Hogg, M. A. (2007). Uncertainty-identity theory. In M. P. Zanna (Ed.), *Advances in experimental social psychology, (39)*, 69–126. San Diego, CA: Academic Press.
6. Gerhart, B. (2001). Balancing results and behaviors in pay for performance plans. In C. Fay (Ed.), *The Executive Handbook of Compensation*. New York: Free Press, 214–237.
7. Baumeister, R.F. (1998). The self. In D. T. Gilbert, S. T. Fiske, & G. Lindzey (Eds.), *The Handbook of Social Psychology, Fourth Edition*. Boston: McGraw-Hill, 680–740.
8. Locke, E.A., Feren, D.B., McCaleb, V.M., Shaw, K.N., & Denny, A.T. (1980). The relative effectiveness of four methods of motivating employee performance. In K.D. Duncan, M.M. Gruenberg, & D. Wallis (Eds.), *Changes in Working Live*. New York: Wiley, 363–388.
9. Gerhart, B., & Milkovich, G. T. (1992). Employee compensation: Research and practice. In M.D. Nunnette, & L.M. Hough (Eds.). *Handbook of Industrial & Organizational Psychology, (2nd Ed)*. Palo Alto, CA: Consulting Psychologists Press, Inc, 481–569.
10. Lazear, E. (2000). Performance pay and productivity. *American Economic Review*, 90, 1346–1361.
11. Trank, C. Q., Rynes, S. L., & Bretz, R. D., Jr. (2002). Attracting applicants in the war for talent: Differences in preferences among high achievers. *Journal of Business and Psychology*, 16, 331–345.
12. Turban, D. B., & Keon, T. L. (1993). Organizational attractiveness: An interactionist perspective. *Journal of Applied Psychology*, 78, 184–193. See Cable, D. M., & Judge, T. A. (1994). Pay preferences and jobs search decisions: A person-organization fit perspective. *Personnel Psychology*, 47, 317–348.

13. Gerhart, B., Rynes, S. L., & Smithey Fulmer, I. (2009). Pay and performance: Individuals, groups, and executives. *The Academy of Management Annals, 3,* 231–315.

14. Baumeister, R. F., Bratslavsky, E., Finkenauer, C., & Vohs, K. D. (2001). Bad is stronger than good. *Review of General Psychology,* 5, 323–370.

15. Cialdini, R. B. (2006). *Influence: The Psychology of Persuasion.* New York: Harper Business.

16. Viswesvaran, C., Ones, D. S., & Schmidt, F. L. (1996). Comparative analysis of the reliability of job performance ratings. *Journal of Applied Psychology,* 81, 557–574.

17. Henemen, R. L. (1992). *Merit Pay: Linking Pay Increases to Performance Ratings.* Reading, MA: Addison-Wesley.

18. Milgrom, P., & Roberts, J. (1992). *Economics, Organization and Management.* Englewood Cliffs, NJ: Prentice Hall.

19. Henemen, R.L. (1992). *Merit Pay: Linking Pay Increases to Performance Ratings.* Reading, MA: Addison-Wesley.

20. Murphy, K. R., & Cleveland, J. N. (1995). *Understanding Performance Appraisal: Social, Organizational, and Goal-Based Perspectives.* Thousand Oaks, CA: Sage.

21. Gerhart, B., & Milkovich, G. T. (1989). Salaries, salary growth, and promotions of men and women in a large, private firm. In R. Michael, H. Hartmann & B. O'Farrell (Eds.). *Pay Equity: Empirical Inquiries.* Washington, DC: National Academy Press, 23–43.

22. Kim, S. (1998). Does profit sharing increase firms' profits? *Journal of Labor Research,* 19, 351–370.

23. Doucouliagos, C. (1995). Worker participation and productivity in labor-managed and participatory capitalist firms; A meta-analysis. *Industrial and Labor Relations Review,* 49, 58–77.

24. Kruse, D. L. (1993). *Profit-Sharing: Does it Make a Difference?* Kalamazoo, MI: Upjohn Institute for Employment Research.

25. Katz, B (2001). Getting the most out of your team. *Harvard Business Review,* 79, 22.

7 Persuasion, Influence, and Impression Management

Topic Summary Learning Objectives

1. Recognize the use of persuasion and discuss the different types of persuasion tactics.

2. Describe sources of social power and their origin.

3. Explain impression management.

4. Differentiate the factors that influence choice on power and persuasion combination.

5. Apply concepts of persuasion, influence, and impression management in organizations.

Key Terms

authority, p. 241	impression management, p. 241	reciprocal liking, p. 235
autonomy, p. 239		reciprocity, p. 241
availability heuristic, p. 238	liking, p. 235	relevance, p. 241
consistency, p. 237	organizational politics, p. 234	scarcity, p. 238
experience, p. 240		schema, p. 237
expertise, p. 239	personal attractiveness, p. 241	social power, p. 238
formal authority, p. 241	persuasion tactics, p. 234	social proof, p. 236

Introduction to Persuasion, Influence, and Impression Management

People use purposeful techniques in the workplace for many reasons including attempts to change people's behavior, sell ideas, gain resources, or shape impressions. These techniques, termed **persuasion tactics**, may be used to wield influence in social contexts such as negotiations, distribution of organizational resources like salary or time off, or even in workload distribution in group projects. The tactics that people choose to use are based on a variety of bases of power of which they have access. Six common persuasion tactics are a starting point to understand this behavior.[1] Organizational researchers have identified primary sources of social power, along with several sub-types of each source.[2] These tactics and sources of power may be combined to maximize their effects on influence. The use of influence can be viewed as a form of **organizational politics**, which is any behavior by people in organizations, based on social power and designed to get one's way. Figure 7.1 provides an overview of persuasion and power tactics discussed in this topic summary.

Tactics of Persuasion

In a widely used framework of persuasion by Robert Cialdini, there are six common persuasion tactics that individuals use to encourage others to say "yes" to their requests.[3] These tactics have been shown to be effective as a *means of exerting influence* in a wide variety of contexts—ranging from children hoping to delay their bedtime, employees negotiating the price of a sales contract, students attempting to change a grade, to U.S. Presidents trying to persuade their constituents to support their decision to go to war. According to research, each of these persuasion tactics works by getting the individuals who are targets of persuasion to forego careful evaluation and logical analysis of requests in favor of more mindless compliance.[4] Such compliance is gained because the targets of persuasion:

1. rely on *cognitive biases or heuristics*, which are shorthand decision-making rules or assumptions, are

2. motivated by *human needs*, needs to be liked or respected as a means of self-esteem enhancement, or

3. give in to the *pressure of social norms,* which are widely agreed-upon customs, such as showing deference to superiors, because doing so helps them to feel secure and part of a group.[5] These tactics are summarized in Table 7.1.

Figure 7.1
Summary of Persuasion and Power Tactics in Organizations

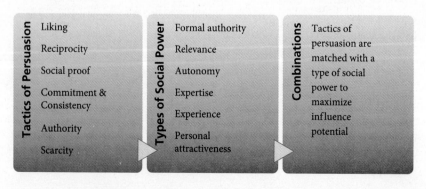

Tactics of Persuasion	Types of Social Power	Combinations
Liking	Formal authority	Tactics of persuasion are matched with a type of social power to maximize influence potential
Reciprocity	Relevance	
Social proof	Autonomy	
Commitment & Consistency	Expertise	
Authority	Experience	
Scarcity	Personal attractiveness	

Table 7.1 Common Persuasion Tactics

Persuasion Tactic	How It Works
Liking	We are more likely to say "yes" to requests of people we like because we desire their approval to enhance our self-esteem, and we assume that people who are likable possess other desirable traits, such as intelligence.
Reciprocity	We feel obligated to repay favors or acts in-kind because it is a social norm.
Social Proof	We look to others to determine appropriate behavior in ambiguous situations because we assume that what the majority is doing is appropriate. Also conforming to the majority helps us feel secure and part of a social group.
Commitment and Consistency	We feel pressure to act consistently with previously stated opinions, beliefs, and behaviors because inconsistency is seen as a character flaw in many societies. Consistency with previously demonstrated beliefs also helps us to reduce uncertainty about the right way to behave and think.
Authority	We mindlessly comply with requests from those displaying trappings of authority because this is a social norm. Also, we have schemas of what authority figures look like and we mindlessly comply with the requests of people fitting those schemas.
Scarcity	We value something more if it is portrayed as scarce because we weigh potential losses heavily in decision making and we can easily recall examples of scarce and valuable things (e.g., diamonds).

Liking

Liking is a form of persuasion that impacts people's beliefs and behaviors. Why do online retailers ask you to "like us" on Facebook or other social media sites? It's free advertising, of course, but more than that, it demonstrates to your Facebook friends that you endorse the retailer's products. In essence, it's as if you were asking your friends to buy their products. This is a very effective way to convince people to buy products (i.e., having their friends endorse the product) and is the basis for the "Liking" persuasion tactic. That is, we are more likely to say "yes" to the requests of people we like. In addition to our friends, research shows that we tend to like people who are physically attractive, who are similar to us in attitudes and characteristics, and who flatter and compliment us.[6]

The reason the liking tactic works is explained by both human needs and heuristics. First, humans possess a general need for self-esteem enhancement, which may be met by gaining the liking or respect of others.[7] Further, people tend to like those who like them, a phenomenon called **reciprocal liking**.[8] So if someone is nice to you and acts like he or she likes you, you may feel better about yourself and you may like him or her in turn. As a consequence, you may agree to his or her requests. Second, people are prone to a cognitive bias called the *halo effect* which leads them to assume that people who are attractive and likeable will have other desirable traits as well, such as intelligence and wisdom.[9] So if we like someone, we may also assume that they are wise and intelligent and that we would do well to go along with their requests or follow their commands.

Reciprocity

In many societies it is a social norm to repay favors or acts in kind. So if a colleague helps you finish a project at work by staying late one day, it is assumed that you will do the same for him if he asks in the future. Likewise, if you help your roommate move into a new apartment, you may assume that she will help you move as well. Even if a person does a favor for you that you don't necessarily want or ask for (e.g., a charitable organization sends you free address labels in the mail), you may feel obligated to repay this "favor" by donating some money to the charity. This is how the tactic of **reciprocity** works: a persuader does you a favor (that you may or may not want or ask for), and then asks for a specific favor in return (which you feel obligated to agree to). Many times the only way to repay the favor is through an act that has far more value than that of the original favor (e.g., I send you a dollar in the mail with a survey, and you fill out the 20 page survey and return it to me because it is the only way to repay me—even though your time is worth much more than a dollar). This tactic works for the simple reason that people do not like to feel like they owe something to another person. This social norm of reciprocity is powerful because it is consistently demonstrated and confirmed in many societies.[10] As noted earlier, such social norms drive behavior because conforming to them allows individuals to feel secure and part of a larger social group.[11]

Social Proof

It is not uncommon for people to find themselves in situations where the appropriate way to act is not obvious or known to them. For example, if you are attending your first church service in a small American town, and you see the congregation begin to pass around an offering plate for donations, you may not know what to do. But you would quickly come to understand that you should put cash into the plate, and also get an idea about how much to donate by watching all of the other churchgoers around you. In a similar manner, if a salesperson is trying to get you to pay more for the "safety package" on your new minivan, you may not know if specific safety features (e.g., fog lights, back-up cameras, driver alarms) are necessary. However, if the salesman shows you that the respected *Parents* magazine has recommended these safety features for all minivan drivers with children, you may "decide" that purchasing the safety package is the right thing to do. This is how the tactic of **social proof** works: in an ambiguous situation where appropriate action is not readily apparent, we look to others to tell us what we should do. Even if those "others" are merely recommendations from experts, or someone is telling us that "everyone is doing it."

The tactic of social proof works for at least two reasons. First, as noted earlier, conforming to social norms allows individuals to feel more secure because they are part of a larger group. Second, people often use social proof as a heuristic to determine what is appropriate because they don't have time or motivation to carefully consider their particular situation, and it is easier to assume that what most people are doing must be the right thing to do. This kind of thinking can lead to outcomes that are more negative than merely buying an unwanted safety package for a minivan. Past studies have shown that social proof was responsible for peoples' unresponsiveness when a neighbor was shouting for help during a stabbing (i.e., they all assumed that the crisis had been attended to since no one was responding).[12]

Commitment and Consistency

Like the norm of reciprocity, the norm of consistency is strongly rooted in many cultures and societies. With **consistency**, people are expected to behave with publicly stated or demonstrated beliefs, opinions, and values—especially if those beliefs, opinions, or values are given voluntarily, without coercion or compensation. In contrast, to behave inconsistently (e.g., to vote against a policy after previously claiming support for it), is seen as "wishy-washy" and a sign that a person lacks integrity. Former Senator John Kerry was famously called a "flip-flopper" during his 2004 presidential campaign because he changed his stance on the U.S. war in Iraq.[13]

In addition to conforming to normative pressures, we may behave consistently with previously stated or demonstrated beliefs because doing so helps us to meet human needs for uncertainty reduction. *Uncertainty reduction* is the need to reduce uncertainty about our world and our place in it.[14] Acting consistently helps to justify and reinforce our earlier behaviors and statements. In this way, consistency reduces our uncertainty about the right way to behave. By contrast, inconsistent behavior creates uncertainty about the right way to think and act, and causes us stress and anxiety.

As an influence tactic, the norm of consistency may be used effectively if a persuader can remind a person of previous public commitments he or she has made that are consistent with a current request. For example, if I want you to contribute to my "Save our Schools" fundraiser, and you appear hesitant to do so, I may remind you that you voted in favor of a school improvement plan last year, or that you said that "education is the most important investment we can make in our future" at a cocktail party last month. By reminding you of these public commitments in support of education, I can make the important point how not donating to my fundraiser would be an inconsistent act on your part. This tactic can even be effective if public commitments are made in a nonverbal manner. For example, if you visit a college campus to determine if you want to attend that institution, you may buy a sweatshirt with the college name and logo on it. After several months of wearing the sweatshirt, you may start to feel obligated to attend that institution. Why? Because you have been publicly displaying your commitment to the school every time you wear the college logo!

Authority

The tactic of **authority** simply involves displaying the trappings and behaviors of those in power—including the dress, accessories, demeanor, and language typically associated with powerful roles. For example, a student may attempt to convince her classmates to follow her suggestions for a group project by acting as an authority figure through her language and demeanor when she speaks confidently and uses technical jargon. Similarly, a rookie consultant may attempt to convince his clients that he is worth the six-figure fee his company is charging by using language, dress, and "inside stories" that make him look like a seasoned veteran.[15]

The tactic of authority works in the same ways that social proof works: through the power of social norms and the mindlessness of heuristic thinking. First, we follow the requests of those displaying the trappings of authority because other people do, since it is a social norm. People do this in real life and in movies, television, and books. In organizations, there is an assumption that a person who looks like they have authority, deserves authority, because most people treat the person as an authority. Second, most of us have been conditioned, from a young age, to automatically equate authority with a specific type of look and demeanor. That is, we have a **schema**, or a mental image, of what an authority figure will look and act like. When we see someone who fits this schema, we are likely to mindlessly assume they are an authority figure because this is cognitively easier than carefully determining if they are, in fact, an authority. Unfortunately, this type of mindless obedience to figures of authority may be used to convince people to carry out undesirable acts such as hazing and bullying that they would clearly have rejected if they had more carefully considered the legitimacy of a persuader's authority.

Scarcity

The tactic of **scarcity** is used to get people to overvalue and over-desire a specific outcome by portraying it as scarce. For example, if a car buyer is ambivalent about purchasing a new sports car, the car dealer may increase the buyer's desire for the car merely by telling him that the car is the only one left on the lot. Organizations selling training workshops will often announce that space is limited and only a few seats remain for registration. In both of these cases, creating a sense that the outcome is also rare increases the value of an already desired outcome. This effect occurs, in part, because of a cognitive bias that leads people to weigh potential losses more heavily than potential gains when making decisions.[16] People are averse to losing things—even if what is lost is merely the *opportunity* to obtain an outcome. An additional cognitive heuristic that leads people to value things more if they are portrayed as scarce is the **availability heuristic**, which is the notion that we think that something is more important or more worthy if we can easily recall similar examples.[17] Because we can easily recall examples of scarce and valuable things, we think that the association of scarce and valuable must be a worthy one.

2 Describe sources of social power and their origin.

Sources of Social Power

Social power is an individual's *ability to influence others*—in other words, his or her ability to effectively use the persuasion tactics described previously. Social power can come from two primary sources: 1) *positional sources* that are assigned to a person by legitimate authorities, and 2) *personal sources* that are earned by a person's own experience, education, and personal characteristics.[18] Each of these primary sources of social power has a number of types. These types are summarized in Table 7.2.

Formal Authority

A first type of positional power—**formal authority**—provides power through assigned titles, ranks, privileges, and responsibilities. A person with formal authority typically has control over scarce and valued resources such as pay and budget, as well as the ability to approve or cancel projects, hire and fire personnel, and override the decisions of those with less authority. Formal authority provides a clear chain of command, and is useful in organizations that rely on hierarchy and structure to guide the actions of a large and dispersed workforce.

Relevance

Relevance is a second type of positional power and refers to a person's importance to achieve collective goals. For example, in a research university setting, faculty members who teach and publish research may have great relevance, because teaching and research are the primary goals in that type of institution. As a result, faculty members may have

Table 7.2 Sources of Social Power

Source of Positional Power	How It Works
Formal Authority	Assigned control over resources and decision making gives one power
Relevance	Assigned role that is important to achieving goals gives one power
Autonomy	Assigned ability to act independently gives one power
Source of Personal Power	**How It Works**
Expertise	Scarce knowledge and skills relevant to goals gives one power
Experience	Past experience relevant to goals gives one power
Personal Attractiveness	Physical attractiveness, likability and charisma gives one power

great power over decisions at the University because faculty input and support for decisions is seen as critical to the success of those decisions. Relevance can shift, however, as the environment changes. For example, during finals week at the university, the teaching assistants, who are typically graduate students who are paid to grade exams, may be more relevant than faculty to the goals of the institution. If these teaching assistants go on strike during finals week, they may then exercise great power over decision making.

Autonomy

Autonomy involves having independence and discretion over decisions in a particular area. Autonomy is typically associated with a specific job description or role and is a third type of positional power. When decisions in their area need to be made, a person with autonomy can exercise great power because he or she needs no outside approval for making choices. For example, an administrative assistant to a CEO may not have great formal authority in the company, but he may be given autonomy for keeping the CEO's schedule and making decisions about moving around appointments. Anyone desiring to meet with the CEO needs the administrative assistant's help to get on the CEO's calendar. This provides the administrative assistant with great power in the area of "CEO access."

Expertise

Expertise is a type of personal power because it depends not on holding a title, rank, or role, but on having accumulated a specific type of knowledge or competence. Individuals with expertise have power because they can provide critical input to decision making. A college student starting out at an entry-level position may lack a lot of position-based power, but may have an up-to-date skill set on social media and have personal power. People in organizations do not need to have positional power in order to have personal power. Expertise is often gained through education and experience over time, a source of power in its own right, discussed next.

Trevor Lush/Purestock/SuperStock

Experience

Experience and track record are considered personal sources of power because events in the real world often unfold much differently than would be predicted by theoretical models. Thus, merely having knowledge of a subject area such as marketing or advertising is not the same as having experience in running a real-world project in that area. For example if someone had managed a national television campaign for a new beverage, they would have personal power based on experience. Having experienced events first-hand provides a type of intuition about what might happen in a given context. Further, knowing that a person has had this type of experience provides that person with a reputation for knowing what to do and increases others' confidence in that person. Both of these attributes (i.e., intuition and reputation for knowing what to do) provide the experienced group member with social power.

Personal Attractiveness

A final type of personal power is **personal attractiveness**—including physical attractiveness, as well as charisma and likability. As noted earlier, because of the "halo effect," people who are attractive and well liked are perceived to have other positive traits, such as ethicality, intelligence, and trustworthiness. These traits provide an attractive person with power because they are associated with our schemas of leadership.

Choosing to Influence

People in organizations make choices to influence based on many different factors. Three to consider are the objectives they want to achieve, the impression they want to convey, and the nature of their influence target. This choice impacts the combination of persuasion tactics and sources of power.

Impression Management

3 Explain impression management.

The choice that people in organizations make about exerting influence includes three main factors. First, the individual should begin by identifying the objective that they want to achieve. For example, does someone wants to influence an outcome for a personal benefit or do they want to exert influence for an organizational benefit? If the leader of a project team wants to apply persuasion tactics in order to encourage his team members to finish a report early, this would benefit the organization. In contrast, if a leader of a project team wants to apply persuasion tactics to receive an individual performance bonus for running the project, this would be a personal benefit. The second involves the impression they want to make. **Impression management** is the process of controlling the influence process in order to impact the ideas that are formed about a person, an idea, or an event. A project manager may seek to control the perception of her leadership as being collaborative. Finally, considerations of the target of influence are useful. These considerations include if the target is an individual, a team, or an entire organization. Also, considerations can involve the level of power the target holds relative to the influencer. A project manager may assess her target is her boss—someone who has more positional power then she does, or her target may be a peer in another department—someone with equivalent positional power.

The Influence Choice Checklist

✔ What outcome do I hope to achieve?
✔ Is this outcome important enough for me to exert influence?
✔ What impression do I want to convey to others?
✔ Who is my target of influence?
✔ What sources of power do I have relative to this target and in this situation?
✔ What combination of persuasion tactic and power would be most effective at achieving my objective while managing impressions?
✔ What if I am unsuccessful, what is my second choice of persuasion tactic and source of power?

Combinations of Tactics and Power

4 Differentiate the factors that influence choice on power and persuasion combination.

While all of the persuasion tactics and sources of power can be used on their own, to influence others, a closer look suggests that there are some complimentary combinations of these two dimensions of influence that may maximize their effectiveness. For example, a person with power that emanates from **formal authority**, where she holds the formal title of "manager" and controls many important resources such as project funding. She may be better able to use the tactic of **authority** by convincing others to comply with her requests by dressing and acting like a top executive than a person whose source of power emanates from **personal attractiveness**. This is because the trappings of authority may come across as more credible if the person displaying them also has a formal title or rank to legitimate his or her authority. Similarly, a manager who is in a position of **relevance** regarding one of your goals in that he can approve your project, may help you to achieve that goal, and then later, may use the norm of **reciprocity** to get you to comply with one of his requests. Thus, his relevance power may allow him to more effectively use reciprocity as an influence tactic.

Table 7.3 Maximizing Influence By Combining Persuasion Tactics with Sources of Power

Power/Persuasion	Combination and How Combination Works
Formal Authority/Authority	Formal titles and ranks make it easier for a persuader to put on trappings of authority and gain mindless compliance from others through the tactic of authority.
Relevance/Reciprocity	Persuaders in positions relevant to achieving our goals may help us achieve those goals, and then use the norm of reciprocity to get us to comply with their later requests.
Autonomy/Scarcity	Persuaders who have autonomy over decision making may convince us that they, alone, can give us access to desired resources, thus, making those resources appear even more scarce and valuable.
Expertise/Commitment & Consistency	Persuaders who have expertise in a given domain may be able to convince us (because of their expertise) that their requests are consistent with ideologies or beliefs that are held and previously committed to.
Experience/Social Proof	Past experience may allow persuaders to speak with credibility about social norms in a given arena (because of their first-hand experience with social norms in that area) and then convince others to comply with those norms through the tactic of social proof.
Personal Attractiveness/Liking	Persuaders who are attractive are known to be more likable and may have an easier time using liking to get us to agree to their requests.

A number of these combinations are described in Table 7.3 above. You may think of many other ways that sources of power and tactics of persuasion may be used to accomplish various objectives.

Conclusion

The process of social influence provides us with a better understanding of organizational politics. Many different tactics exist. This section summarizes the two main components of interpersonal influence: persuasion tactics and sources of power. Effectively applying these components to wield influence involves understanding how they work on their own, as well as how they may be combined to maximize someone's impact. The choice around tactic and power combinations rests on the objectives to be achieved, the impressions that people want to manage and the nature of the target of influence.

OB AT WORK

JOSH PAVANO LEVERAGES SOCIAL INFLUENCE TO EFFECT CLEAN WATER IN UGANDA

Josh Pavano

On a consulting abroad trip to Uganda, MBA student, Josh Pavano, never thought the experience would fundamentally alter his purpose in his life and his work. On this trip, he observed children in Uganda carrying large buckets of dirty water—water that could cause disease or even death. Josh experienced first hand, how a lack of clean water, a global crisis according to the World Health Organization for 1.5 billion people, became a very real and local problem. Josh learned about the connection between water and health, education, poverty, and quality of life for women and children. Now, Josh leverages his knowledge and experience to promote his purpose—bringing clean water to sub Saharan Africa. "In order to promote my purpose, I needed to involve others and connect a community of people who shared a vision of what it would be like for children to have access to clean water."

5 Apply concepts of persuasion, influence, and impression management in organizations.

He created Jonas Umbrellas to raise funding for this important social cause. This company provides a symbol that is easily connected with the mission of clean water—the umbrella. Josh describes it as 'fashion with a purpose'. "Stay Dry. Give Water. Make a Difference" is a statement that reflects the mission of Jonas Umbrellas and immediately connects consumers with the clean water cause. Drop in the Bucket and Jonas Umbrellas formed a collaborative effort. The organizations agreed to provide funding for one clean water well at a school in Africa for every 3000 umbrellas sold. Once one of their uniquely designed patterns sells out, the pattern is retired and a well is funded. Each of these wells provides clean water for 1,000 families. Consumers can purchase an umbrella and are given the choice to remain connected to the cause for clean water through participating in crowd funding or by following pictures, videos, a blog, and even a chance to win a trip to visit the children that benefit from Jonas Umbrellas. This allows consumers to join a community of like-minded people that want to save lives through clean water.

Organizational behavior principles help Josh in his work by promoting the importance of clean water in Uganda. As Josh knows, social influence can change people's emotions, beliefs, opinions, and behaviors. The passion that Josh and his team bring to this cause is contagious to others, "*I often get asked why give back, why try and solve an unsolvable problem? To me it has always been about making a difference in just one person's life. It isn't about me or Jonas, it is about the one girl who has to miss school and walk 5 Km everyday to gather dirty water for her family. It's about the little boy who can't eat because he got sick from the only water he had available. It's about providing someone with a chance to make their life and their family's life better.*" When people understand the scope of the water problem and believe that others deserve something as fundamental as clean water to prevent disease and death and have an opportunity to take action in a small but significant way, they act. Josh noted that, "I want to influence others to care and become a piece of the puzzle that will address the water crisis. We are all a part of the global community and we can make a difference."

Source: Personal interview www.jonasumbrellas.com

SPOTLIGHT ON RESEARCH
Influencing Others through 'Flirting' at Work

Researchers were interested in how those in organizations use sexual suggestions such as flirting in the workplace, as a means to exert purposeful influence. The dominance of sexual-based work issues surfaces in current news stories and academic research. Many of these work issues include topics like dating in the workplace, sexual harassment, or sexy clothing at work. Dating relationships at work describes mutual and consensual workplace romances. Sexual harassment, on the other hand, is the request for sexual favors or other verbal or nonverbal sexual behavior that creates a hostile work environment. There have been reports of employees fired for wearing clothing that were too sexy for the workplace or who were denied promotion for being sexy. These areas of 'sex in the workplace' are often discussed and published with the assumption that there is some form of disruption to work productivity.

Another category of sexuality in organizations is termed 'strategic sexual performances'. This includes activities—such as flirting—which are not sexual harassment and are not occurring in a dating relationship. That is, expressions of sexuality are used purposefully to gain social influence in the workplace. More specifically, these performances are any behavior that contains a sexual intent or content by participants or observers. The behavior is strategic in that it is designed with intent to influence someone's behavior or attitude in order to achieve a desired outcome. For example, an employee might flirt with his boss in order to obtain permission to leave early from work. These strategic sexual performances are a form of ingratiation, with the specific intent to: 1) make the target feel better about herself, 2) appear to be helpful, or 3) self-presentation designed to make the target feel better about the influencer. The sexual orientation of the influencer impacts the selection of the target and the selection of the strategic sexual performance behavior. So, males could exhibit ingratiatory behavior directed at males or females, and females could exhibit ingratiatory behavior directed at males or females. The researchers found examples of people who have openly admitted to blatant flirting and ego enhancement of those in power in an organization. These tactics are used with the purpose of career advancement. After all, workplaces are a context for competition among people for scarce resources, rewards, and promotions and sexual performance tactics are an attempt to influence.

Questions for Discussion

1. What is your reaction to this article? Have you observed this type of behavior at work?

2. Why do you think people attempt ingratiation in the form of a 'strategic sexual performance' at work?

3. What are other forms of ingratiation that you have observed that are more or less effective than a 'strategic sexual performance'?

Based on the article: Watkins, M. B., Smith, A. N., and Aquino, K. (2013). The Use and Consequences of Strategic Sexual Performances ACAD MANAGE PERSPECT August 2013 27:173-186; published ahead of print June 18, 2013, doi:10.5465/amp.2010.0109

Pairing with this Topic Summary

Suggested Expert Contributions

Impressing Up: Objectives, Tactics, and Results of Upward Influence—Asha Rao (California State University, East Bay) and Stuart M. Schmidt (Temple University)

How You Look to Others: Understanding and Managing How Others Perceive You —Kimberly D. Elsbach (University of California, Davis)

On Being Trustworthy—Roger C. Mayer (North Carolina State University)

Suggested Cases

Case 1: The Case of Apple iPhone 4

Case 2: "We Are Global or We Are Nothing": Conflict and Cover-Up at ColequarterMaine

Case 5: Whatever Happened to One of the "100 Best Companies to Work For"?: A Case Study of Hewlett-Packard

Case 7: Perceptions of Leaders Following Public Failures: A Tale of Two Coaches

Suggested Exercises

Exercise 2: Creating My Brand

Exercise 9: Being Positive

Exercise 15: Building my Network—Individual

Exercise 20: Employment Branding

Exercise 23: What's Your University's Culture?

Exercise 26: Social Media Dilemma

Exercise 30: You Can't Handle the Truth

Exercise 34: Sustainability Practices at Work

Endnotes

1. Cialdini, R. (2008). *Influence: Science and Practice,* 5th Edition. New York: Pearson.
2. Whetten, D.A., & Cameron, K.S. (2010). *Developing Management Skills,* 8th Edition. New York: Pearson.
3. Cialdini, R. (2008). *Influence: Science and Practice,* 5th Edition. New York: Pearson.
4. Milgram, S. (1974). *Obedience to authority.* New York: Harper Row.
5. Gilovich, T., Griffin, D., & Kahneman, D. (Eds.) (2002). *Heuristics and Biases: The Psychology of Intuitive Judgment.* Cambridge, UK: Cambridge University Press. Also see: Terry, D.J., & Hogg, M.A. (2000). *Attitudes, Behavior, and Social Context: The Role of Norms and Group Membership,* Mahwah, NJ: Lawrence-Erlbaum.
6. Cialdini, R. (2008). Influence: Science and Practice, 5th Edition. New York: Pearson.
7. Baumeister, R.F. (Ed.) (1999). *The Self in Social Psychology.* Philadelphia, PA: Psychology Press.
8. Lowe, C.A.; & Goldstein, J.W. (1970). Reciprocal liking and attributions of ability: Mediating effects of perceived intent and personal involvement. *Journal of Personality and Social Psychology,* 16(2): 291–297.

9. Dion, K., Berscheid, E., & Walster, E., (1972). What is beautiful is good. *Journal of Personality and Social Psychology, 24*, 285–90.
10. Cialdini, R., (2008). Influence: Science and Practice, 5th Edition. New York: Pearson.
11. Terry, D.J., & Hogg, M.A., (2000). *Attitudes, Behavior, and Social Context: The Role of Norms and Group Membership.* Mahwah, NJ: Lawrence-Erlbaum.
12. Cialdini, R., (2008). *Influence: Science and Practice,* 5th Edition. New York: Pearson.
13. Cialdini, R. (2008). *Influence: Science and Practice,* 5th Edition. New York: Pearson.
14. Hogg, M.A., & Terry, D.J., (2000). Social identity and self-categorization processes in organizational contexts. *Academy of Management Review, 25*, 121–140.
15. Ibarra, H., 1999. Provisional Selves: Experimenting with Image and Identity in Professional Adaptation. Administrative Science Quarterly, 44, 764–791.
16. Tversky, A., & Kahneman, D., (1981). The framing of decisions and the psychology of choice. *Science, 211*, 453–458.
17. Tversky, A., & Kahneman, D. (1973). Availability: A heuristic for judging frequency and probability. *Cognitive Psychology, 5*, 207–233.
18. Whetten, D.A., & Cameron, K.S. (2010). *Developing Management Skills,* 8th Edition, New York: Pearson.

Impressing Up: Objectives, Tactics and Results of Upward Influence

Asha Rao
California State University, East Bay

Stuart M. Schmidt
Temple University

> *All the world's a stage,*
> *And all the men and women merely players:*
> *They have their exits and their entrances;*
> *And one man in his time plays many parts*
> —William Shakespeare,
> *All the world's a stage*
> (from *As You Like It 2/7*)

Introduction

Anita wants a raise in her upcoming review cycle and is trying to understand how to get it. She has made a concerted effort to be nice to her boss, complementing her on various issues. She has been at work on time in her publishing firm and does all her work on time. Still, she is concerned that it is not enough to be rated in the top ten percent of employees and get a hefty raise. Anita feels her boss likes her, but she isn't sure she has made a strong enough impression.

Stephan is frustrated with the way things are going at work. He has aggressively gone after new clients for his law firm, has been a "rainmaker" in the practice, driven himself really hard and also driven his peers (perhaps a bit too hard!). However, Stephan feels that he doesn't get his due from his boss for being so aggressive and tenacious, and doesn't know how to make the right impression to be promoted to partner.

In workplaces, employees can become dependent on immediate supervisors for promotions, compensation, and quality of work life. Therefore, like Anita and Stephan, we want our bosses to think well of us. Subordinates often wonder how to impress their superiors in terms of competence, trustworthiness, and amiability. The answer lies in understanding the role of upward influence in impression management.[1]

What impressions do employees look to create? What are their objectives in influencing upward? What tactics work best with supervisors? What results can be expected? In the following sections, we will answer these questions as we discuss impression management and the upward influence process. This process incorporates objectives, power, tactics, the resulting impressions created, and the results of having created those impressions. We have developed this process primarily, on the basis of our studies of American, Australian, and British private and public sector organizations.

Research on Upward Influence in Impression Management

Impression management refers to the process by which people seek to control the reactions of others to their images (e.g., how they are perceived in terms of their "leadership ability" or "trustworthiness"). This area is both a popular topic in academic research and the self-help press. The latter is replete with websites, books, articles, and columnists' tips on how to impress your boss to get your way. While acknowledging a plethora of goals in impression management (e.g. to appear competent or dangerous) prior research has focused on one main motive—how to get your boss to like you. The assumption here is that liking, or attraction, forms the basis for most positive evaluations, which leads to rewards at work. Consequently, the tactics people use in impression management have primarily, been forms of "ingratiation" (e.g., paying compliments to others, or doing favors to make oneself more likable to others).

Yet, there is more to impression management than ingratiation. If we look more carefully at the theoretical foundations of impression management, we can better understand how a variety of influence tactics are used to affect how others perceive us. In particular, we can understand how and why upward influence tactics affect those who are in superior power positions. Researchers increasingly focus on upward influence tactics of people across the globe in China, United States, Australia, Japan, and some European nations.

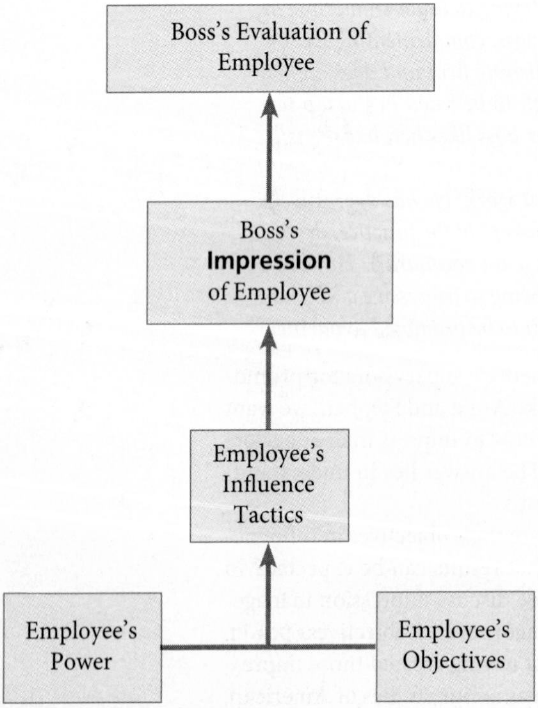

Figure 1 Process of Influencing Upward

Setting the Stage

Shakespeare had it right. *All the world is indeed a stage*—especially the workplace. This concept has developed over time, while researchers have developed a comprehensive impression management model where employees are described as actors on a stage, performing to their audience.[2] Within that setting, employees have to make conscious, tactical choices to stage their character to create the right impression with their audience. In upward impression management, supervisors and the organizational hierarchy are our audience. There are four key elements here of impression management: determining objectives in impression management; the construction of impressions using social influence tactics; understanding the organizational context in which they will be enacted; and finally, affecting the perceptions of your target, (i.e. the boss you seek to influence). These linked steps form the process illustrated in Figure 1.

Why We Court Favor with the Boss

Organizations are staffed by human decision makers who are subjectively rational and swayed by emotions and selective perceptions.[3] Objective criteria for good

Table 1 Objectives for Influencing the Boss

Objectives	Example
Personal	
Receive favorable evaluation	Obtain good to excellent on performance appraisals for general performance or specific projects
Gain compensation, benefits	Change my schedule; increase my pay and/or benefits
Help with own work	Lighten my workload; assistance with completion of projects
Workplace	
Boss accepts my ideas	Have innovative ideas accepted by the boss
Get more responsibility	Be given challenging assignments and be responsible for important work
Manager works better	Get manager to fully complete assignments as anticipated and expected
Give work to boss	Be innovative—may create more work for the boss who has to obtain resources and implement changes

*Listed in order of popularity within the "personal" and "workplace" categories.

performance and promotions are often lacking in today's team-based "service" driven workplace. Therefore, social and emotional skills become increasingly important when determining one's status in organizational hierarchies. In today's times, bosses place more emphasis on performance evaluations, personal contributions, and professional development more than ever.

The main goal in impression management is for an employee to be perceived favorably by their manager. Prior research has identified characteristics that managers watch for: appearing competent, pitiful, morally worthy, or even dangerous.[4] Seven sought-after objectives are listed in Table 1.[5]

Personal objectives include getting good performance appraisals on overall performance or specific projects, getting rewards in the form of compensation and benefits, and getting some help with workload. Employees seek the workplace objectives of gaining more responsibility and authority, and gaining a supervisor's acceptance of ideas. These objectives also include expecting their manager to be fair and serve as a resource—meaning the manager may need to garner resources for a project to succeed.

Do We Have Power to Influence the Boss?

Power provides the potential for exercising upward influence, without it, it is hard to influence up in managing one's image. Power enables choices among tactics.

Where does power come from? In traditional organizational hierarchies, subordinates tend to have less power than management. However, the more value that

Table 2 Employee's Power

Employee Has More Power if the Organization Has:	Employee Has Less Power if the Organization Has:
Few Rules and Regulations (Low Formalization)	Many Rules and Regulations (High Formalization)
Few Standard Operating Procedures (Low Routinization)	Many Standard Operating Procedures (High Routinization)
Innovative Culture (Values Change)	Non-Innovative Culture (Discourages Change)

employees add to workplaces and organizations, the greater their power. Power lies in multiple areas of the workplace with contextual factors providing opportunities for upward influence. There are three contextual characteristics of workplaces that matter: the lack of rules governing the workplace (formalization), the absence of "standard operating procedures" (routinization), and the presence of an innovative culture, where change and new ideas are encouraged and valued. These workplace characteristics facilitate building employee power, which then permits employess flexibility in using upward influence tactics. Table 2 illustrates these three contextual characteristics of workplaces.

Employees have more power to influence their superiors in organizations where there is less formalization and routinization of tasks, and the presence of an innovative culture. This type of environment allows employees more freedom to use a range of influence tactics because employee behavior is less constrained on the whole. By contrast, in more formal structured environments where there are extensive standard operating procedures that constrain employees to a specific set of behaviors, it is harder for lower-status employees to influence higher-status managers.

What Do We Do? How Do We Play Our Role?

An image is constructed by modifying the audience's perception. Prior research has focused on self-presentation by individual actors to create the sought after impression.[6] Such individual self-presentation tactics include supplication (i.e., demonstrating weakness), intimidation (i.e., demonstrating strength), ingratiation (i.e., demonstrating likeability), and self-handicapping (i.e., demonstrating a handicap or disadvantage). A more comprehensive repertoire of influence tactics include *other* actors on the organizational stage. These tactics, described in Table 3, were identified in prior research on social influence and are listed below in order of their popularity.

Reason—an employee uses facts, figures, and data to support logical arguments. Reason is a powerful tactic that helps create an image of competence, professionalism, and expertise. However, this tactic requires extensive planning, real expertise, and preparation.

Table 3 Tactics Used to Influence Upward*

Tactics	Actions
Reason	Providing information and logical arguments to support a request. Example: "I explained the reasons for my request."
Use of Allies	Bringing other people together to pressure my boss. Example: "My colleagues spoke to my boss for me."
Friendliness	Creating a good impression by being thoughtful, friendly, and using flattery to create goodwill. Example: "I smiled and acted very friendly."
Bargaining	Offering to make an exchange and negotiate. Example: "If you help me now, I'll help you next time."
Assertiveness	Being direct, forceful, and persistent. Example: "I persisted in requesting a purchase order."
Use of Higher Authority	Involving higher levels in the organization to help provide pressure. Example: "I obtained the support of higher-ups."

*Tactics listed in order of popularity for influencing upward

Use of Allies—an employee brings in others to apply pressure in influencing-up. Rather than acting alone, many voices speak together. However, there is the danger of creating an impression of a conspiracy or "ganging-up", which could lead to a negative impression.

Friendliness—an employee uses flattery, praise, and creates goodwill. This is the stereotypic impression management strategy related to ingratiation. Friendliness may involve the other actors if one considers those actors' reactions to ingratiation before deciding which behaviors to continue and which to discontinue (i.e., continue flattery only if it seems to be effective in increasing one's likeability with a specific other). Despite its popularity, over-reliance on this tactic can easily lead others to question one's motives and competence. Indeed, English has a rich vocabulary of terms to describe overly obsequious upward ingratiators (e.g., "fawner", "bootlicker", and "yes man" are among the more polite terms).

Bargaining—an employee offers to negotiate and make trades for mutual advantage. This tactic creates obligations and one needs to have resources to trade.

Assertiveness—an employee takes a hard line and is direct, forceful, demanding, and persistent. This is similar to "intimidation". This tactic may involve other actors if one considers the relative power of others when deciding how direct and forceful to be (i.e., one can be more forceful with those one step above oneself, than with those three steps above oneself) . While being persistent can be advantageous, there is the danger of creating an impression of being pushy and difficult.

Use of Higher Authority—an employee looks for powerful players in the organizational hierarchy for support to bring pressure. Although it may be effective in the short run, this tactic undermines relationships and creates an impression of inadequacy.

Connecting the Dots, Choosing the Right Tactics

The tactics you choose should relate to your objectives and your contextual power. To reach personal objectives, such as time off or a raise, *friendliness* may prove to be a more effective tactic than *assertiveness*. However, in seeking workplace objectives, there is often an implied legitimacy for giving an impression of persistence and professionalism. In these situations, using tactics such as *bargaining, reason, assertiveness,* and *higher authority* may prove to be more effective. Forming *allies* is a smart tactic for either set of objectives—workplace or personal—if used carefully. While there is "power in numbers," one may be seen as "ganging up."

Earlier discussions suggest that you have less power in a formalized, routinized, low-innovation environment. In such situations using a tactic like *friendliness* may allow employees to form allies, and thus, extend their influence. In innovative contexts, by contrast, even employees low on the hierarchy can develop power through their criticality in organizational performance. In these situations, using tactics such as *assertiveness, reason,* and *bargaining* become feasible.

Are We Successful? Does the Audience Applaud?

According to our research, the impressions managers formed of subordinates, as a result of the specific upward influence tactics used, showed *friendliness* to be most effective in creating impressions of amiability. In the opening example, then, Anita's tactic of being nice to her boss was definitely a good idea. However, she may need to balance this *friendliness* with another tactic, such as *reason*, which helps create an impression of competence. Although *friendliness* is necessary for being seen as amiable, *reason* is important for creating the impression of competence.

Literature has focused on positive rather than negative impressions, so we also performed research, to see if potentially unintended negative impressions result from the tactics used by subordinates. When subordinates came across as tenacious negotiators who used a fair amount of *assertiveness,* but little *friendliness* and *reason,* managers perceived them as disagreeable and gave them poor performance appraisals. Stephan, in our earlier example, may face problems because though he is highly competent and delivers results, he may be antagonizing important people in the process and creating a negative image with his boss. There are costs associated with influence, so pairing up *assertiveness* and *bargaining* with *reason* and *friendliness* is most effective in influencing up.

Tactics can blend together to form impressions. The managerial audience pieces together all the 'parts' that the subordinate actor plays. Although managers perceive forming *allies* as friendly, it can take on a negative image when combined with *assertiveness* and *bargaining.*

Ideas in Action

Determine your goals and match tactics. Are you seeking personal or workplace outcomes? If they are personal, then research points in the direction of *friendliness*. Being positive, friendly, and engaging will be helpful. For objectives that are workplace related, you have a greater range of tactics available to choose from such as *reason, allies, higher authority, assertiveness* and *bargaining.*

Assess your power. While it may appear that you have less power because you are lower on the ladder than your boss, think through the context and see where you can tap into workplace sources to exercise influence. Increasing your power allows you to use a wider range of tactics than if you have little power. Power gives you choices. Do you have skills or knowledge that give you power in innovative situations?

Use a range of tactics. Do not sing with just one note. Instead, play a symphony where you blend a range of tactics. For instance, *reason* alone is dry, *assertiveness* alone is too aggressive, and *friendliness* alone may stroke a false note of ingratiation. However, together, we find that FAR (*friendliness, assertiveness* and *reason*) make for a powerful alliance of tactics that are used successfully.

Be cautious in the tactics you combine because the whole is greater than the sum of its parts. Some play well together, like FAR, but forming allies can transform from good to bad when combined with assertiveness and bargaining—where working through your allies becomes a hostile, "ganging up" move.

Conclusion

All actors on the organizational stage try to make a good impression with their upward audience. In doing so, they can access a range of influence to form the images they seek to create. Prior research has tended to focus on ingratiation as a key strategy, while recent research indicates that a range of tactics is available depending on the desired objectives. Different tactics are recommended for personal vs. workplace objectives and in non-innovative firms. People should also combine their tactics since their audience views them holistically to form positive or negative images of their subordinates.

Endnotes

1. E. Goffman. (1959). *The presentation of self in everyday life.* Garden City, NY: Anchor Publishing.
2. W. I Gardiner and M. J. Martinko. (1988). Impression management: An observational study linking audience characteristics with verbal self presentation, *Academy of Management Journal (31),* 42–65.
3. J. G. March and H. A. Simon. (1958). *Organizations.* New York, NY:Wiley and Sons.
4. E. E. Jones and T. S. Pittman. (1980). Towards a general theory of strategic self presentation, in J. Suls. (Eds.). *Psychological perspectives of the self,* 231–262. Hillsdale, NJ: Erlbaum.
5. A, Rao, S. M. Schmidt and L. H. Murray. (1995). Upward impression management: Goals, influence strategies and consequences, *Human Relations (48)*2, 147–167.
6. Gardiner and Martinko. (1988). *Academy of Management Journal.*

How You Look to Others: Understanding and Managing How Others Perceive You

Kimberly D. Elsbach

University of California, Davis

Have you ever been evaluated negatively by a supervisor or teacher when you thought you were performing well? Have you ever been surprised when a teammate decided that someone else should take over the leader role even though you thought you would be perfect for the task? Have you ever heard that another person at work questioned whether you were capable of handling a new task assignment that you thought you could handle easily?

It turns out these surprising, and often inaccurate, perceptions of us by our peers and superiors are common in work and school contexts, and often lead to undesirable consequences.[1] Incorrect perceptions of us by coworkers or teammates may lead to friction in work groups and poor performance in tasks that require collaboration. Misperceptions of our skills and abilities may mean we are evaluated unfairly or assigned an undesirable task. Avoiding and undoing these unwanted consequences requires more than awareness that misperceptions occur, it requires an understanding of what leads to misperception in the first place.

In this article, I will discuss some of the underlying psychological process that may lead others to view you differently than you view yourself. I will then discuss how you may use this understanding to influence how others see you.

The Psychology of How People See You

Psychologists have identified two primary categories of perceptual processes that influence how observers perceive you: (1) motivated processes, and (2) automatic processes (See Table 1). *Motivated processes* occur when observers' own wants and needs affect what they see. For example, because your supervisor wants to feel good about herself, she may form a negative view of you if you criticize her. In this case, your supervisor doesn't necessarily intend to perceive you negatively, but her negative evaluation is motivated by her desire to preserve her own self-esteem. By contrast, automatic perception processes occur when observers' daily routines and vantage points affect what they see, often in an unconscious way. For example, because your professor only sees you when you're in the classroom (and thus, doesn't see that you were up all night with a sick friend), she may view your lack of class participation as an indication that you don't care about the class, rather than a temporary consequence of your lack of sleep. In this case, your professor is probably unaware that she is viewing you in negatively biased way, it is just a consequence of her vantage point (i.e., only seeing you in class). Understanding both motivated and automatic perceptual processes are the first steps in managing how others see you.

Table 1 Psychological Processes Affecting How People See You

Perceptual Process	How People See You
Motivated Perceptions	Desires for self-enhancement may lead observers to view similar others in positive ways and dissimilar others in negative ways. Desires for positive—distinctiveness may lead observers to view dissimilar others in stereotypic and unfavorable ways.
Automatic Perceptions	Everyday experiences may lead observers to develop "schemas" and stereotypes of appropriate and legitimate characteristics for specific roles (e.g., leaders). Salient cues in the immediate environment may determine which categories an observer assigns and evaluates us (e.g., one's gender will be salient and will be evaluated based on stereotypes).

Motivated Perceptions: How Observers' Wants and Needs Affect How They Perceive Others

An important motive in guiding our perceptions of others is the need for self-enhancement.[2] *Self-enhancement motives* include desires to view oneself as generally positive (e.g., see oneself as a generally "good" person), positive in a distinct manner (e.g., see oneself as a "good athlete"), and positive relative to others (e.g., see oneself as the "best athlete in my school"). Because we seek to see ourselves positively, we may be biased in our assessments of others because our assessments of others have bearing on our own self-evaluations. These tendencies are the basis for *social identity theories* of self-perception.[3]

In some cases, for example, self-enhancement motives may affect our perceptions of others because we see members of our own group as a reflection of ourselves. By contrast, we tend to see members of competing groups as different (or even opposites) of ourselves. Thus, if I have the same job title and rank as a colleague and think that I will be perceived as similar in ability as that colleague (and perhaps, categorized in the same group as that colleague), self-enhancement motives may cause me to evaluate my colleague more positively because his or her positive evaluation is also a reflection of my own value and worth. If, by contrast, I believe that I am in competition with my colleague, I may evaluate him or her more negatively because that negative evaluation will increase my relative status and value compared to my colleague. In this manner, researchers have found that when participants in a competitive task were told that a new acquaintance was going to be their partner in the task, those participants viewed the acquaintance as having higher ability and greater intelligence than a new acquaintance that was portrayed as being an opponent in the same task.[4] These findings suggest that if we view coworkers as competitors, we may evaluate them negatively, while if we view them as collaborators, we may evaluate them positively.

In other cases, we may have *positively distinct* images that we wish to maintain in work or social settings. For example, researchers have shown that medical residents in different specialties (e.g., surgery or radiology) seek to maintain the positive and distinctive identities of their respective specialties (e.g., surgery residents perceive that they have the toughest training and are the most complete doctors among all specialties).[5] As a result, these researchers found that surgery residents perceived residents in other specialties in negative and contrasting ways as a means of increasing the positive-distinctiveness of their own specialty and of maintaining a positive comparison relative to others.[6] For example, some surgery residents viewed radiology as an "easy" specialty and perceived radiologists as merely "technicians" rather than "true physicians." Such stereotypic and *contrasting perceptions* helped surgery residents to preserve their own distinctive and positive self-perceptions as "the most complete doctors."

Automatic Perceptions: How Observers' Daily Routines Affect How They Perceive Others

In contrast to motivated perceptions, *automatic perceptions* are driven by salient and dominant environmental cues that unconsciously influence what we perceive as acceptable and normal.[7] In some cases, these cues of acceptable and normative behavior result from our everyday experiences. If, for example, we routinely see the same types of attributes related to a given role (e.g., the mass media commonly depicts "leaders" as older, white males who are non-emotional in their speech and interactions) we may come to think of those collections of cues (what are called *"schemas"*) every time we encounter a person who occupies that role.[8] In other words, a specific schema of a leader (i.e., a person who is older, white, male and non-emotional) may become *"chronically-accessible"* in our minds because we encounter that schema repeatedly in our everyday experience.[9] In turn, these kinds of chronically-accessible schemas guide, unconsciously, our evaluations of people who claim the role of leader. Thus, we may negatively evaluate a woman who acts emotionally in delivering a speech because she does not fit our schema of a "typical" or "legitimate" leader.

In other cases, the cues that become salient and dominant in our evaluations of others are triggered by something in our immediate environment. For example, if "Sue" is the only woman in her workgroup of electrical engineers, her gender may be what is salient when the group performs a peer evaluation. As a result, she may be evaluated negatively because stereotypes of women as poor at math and science may be triggered by her gender. If by contrast, she is the sole engineer in a cross-functional work group that includes employees in design, marketing, and sales, Sue may be evaluated positively because stereotypes of engineers as intelligent and capable may be triggered by her professional background. Psychologists have found that such cueing of stereotypes and evaluations happens when different aspects of a person's identity are made salient because they contrast with others in their environment.[10]

Managing How People See You

While the previous discussion suggests misperceptions are likely to occur and may lead to negative evaluations by observers, it also provides the understanding necessary to help us prevent, or at least minimize, misperceptions by observers in our work and social lives. In particular, the insights provided above point to *categorizations* as a central cognitive mechanism involved in biased perceptions of others. Categorizations are defined as how we understand a thing by viewing it as similar or distinct from other things (e.g., is a vase a piece of furniture or a piece of art?).[11] Research on motivated and automatic perception suggests that if, and how, an observer categorizes a person has important implications for how they are perceived.[12] For instance, research on motivated perception suggests that categorizing a person as an "opponent" or "competitor" leads observers to evaluate that person more negatively, while categorizing a person as "partner" or "teammate" leads to more positive evaluations of that person.[13] Psychologists often refer to such categories of people with which we are distinct or dissimilar as "out-groups," while they refer to categories of similar others "in-groups."[14] As shown in the medical residents example, surgery residents perceived other medical specialties (e.g., radiology) as out-groups and sought to maintain positively distinct perceptions in comparison to those out-groups.

At the same time, research on automatic perception suggests that categorizing a person into a group with well-established schemas or stereotypes is likely to lead to automatic evaluations of that person in line with those schemas and stereotypes.[15] Thus, if one is categorized as a member of the group "leaders", then one may be attributed stereotypic characteristics of leaders. Some of those characteristics may be positive (e.g., a "leader" may be attributed the characteristics of "high status" and "competence"), while others may be negative (e.g., a "leader" may also be attributed the characteristics of "arrogance" and "inaccessibility").

Together, these insights about categorization and perception may help us to design behavioral and verbal tactics that promote positive and desired perceptions of ourselves. Three of these tactics include: (1) self-categorizations that indicate one is an in-group member with observers, (2) behavioral and physical displays that indicate desired categorizations, and (3) categorizations of our evaluators that increase their own self-esteem (see Table 2).

Self-Categorization as an In-Group Member

Rather than hoping for an accurate or desired categorization by observers, individuals may ensure such categorizations by claiming them for themselves. That is, we may *self-categorize* ourselves so that we occupy categories associated with desired perceptions.

Table 2 Using Categorization to Manage How People See You

Categorization Tactics	How They Effect How People See You
Self-Categorizations as In-group Members	Self-categorizing oneself as an "in-group" member with observers may lead observers to evaluate us more positively as a means of protecting self-esteem.
Behavioral/Physical Displays that Signal Desired Categorizations for Ourselves	Behavioral and physical displays that align ourselves with well-known prototypes or schemas for roles or professions may lead observers to automatically evaluate us in-line with them.
Categorizing Our Evaluators in Positive Ways	Those who evaluate us in positive ways to enhance their self-esteem and reduce their motivation to self-enhance through negative categorizations.

In particular, if we categorize ourselves in ways that show we occupy the same groups as observers (i.e., we are in-group members with observers), we are likely to elicit more careful and individuated evaluations (and less stereotypic evaluations) by observers. Because many stereotypic evaluations are negative, such a strategy may reduce the chance that we are viewed in negative ways.

In this manner, psychologists found that, when observers—who were working on a problem-solving task—evaluated the performance of a second participant, they were more likely to evaluate the second participant in stereotypic and competitive ways if that participant was described as belonging to an out-group (i.e., a group who used a different problem-solving style than the observer), than an in-group (i.e., a group who used the same problem-solving style as the observer).[16] In this case, the participant's use of self-categorizations to show that he/she was an in-group member with an observer appeared to reduce that observer's use of negative, out-group stereotypes to evaluate that participant.

Based on these findings, when leading a team, categorizing oneself as a "coach" or "team leader" (instead of a "supervisor" or "boss") may be advantageous because it indicates that one is "on the same side" as the other team members (i.e., an in-group member) and may lead to more individualized and positive evaluations of one's behaviors by those team members, while producing less stereotypical and negative evaluations (i.e., evaluations of "bosses" as "arrogant" and "inaccessible"). Similarly, if a new employee self-categorizes herself as an in-group member with important colleagues or coworkers (e.g., by introducing herself as a "team member") she may gain more individualized and positive evaluations from those colleagues.

Behavioral and Physical Displays that Signal Desired Categorizations

Another way to signal desired categorizations is through *behavioral and physical displays* (e.g., dress and display of office mementoes) that make clear the categories to which one belongs. These types of signals lead observers to categorize us according to well-known schemas or prototypes, and in turn, to evaluate us in terms of those schemas or prototypes. For example, researchers have found that newly-hired employees of professional service firms, such as consulting and investment banking firms, may adopt language and behaviors (e.g., telling stories of past consulting experiences and using appropriate lingo) that signal that they are legitimate members of the profession (and thus deserving of their high fees), even though they are, in fact, new to the profession.[17]

I found confirmation of this perceptual process in a study of Hollywood screenwriters who were pitching television shows and movie scripts to producers.[18] In particular, I found that screenwriters who, through their interpersonal behavior and appearance, appeared to fit well-known prototypes, or stereotypes of screenwriters (e.g., "artistic" types who were introverted and nervous and unkempt, but had highly unusual ideas and passion for them, or highly organized and well-groomed "showrunners" who knew all of the logistics and budget issues to consider in a television series or feature film) were more likely to be perceived as creative than screenwriters who did not fit one of these prototypes.

In addition to these types of individuating traits and behaviors, people may signal desired categorizations through more general, but frequent behaviors that place them into a favorable group. For example I found, in research study of corporate office workers, that employees who engaged in the repeated behavior of "being seen at work" (also called "passive face time"), were perceived by supervisors as more dependable/reliable and committed/dedicated than employees who did not engage in this behavior.[19] Further, I found that these perceptions were made unconsciously and automatically. Like the study of Hollywood screenwriters, these attributions may have resulted because the frequent behavior of "being seen at work" signaled a broad prototype of the dedicated and committed worker, and thus, led observers to categorize individuals according to these prototypes.

Categorizing Our Perceivers and Evaluators in Positive Ways

The last tactic that may be used to reduce the chances that our perceivers evaluate us unfairly and unfavorably is *other-categorization* (i.e., categorizing our perceivers). Researchers have found that merely reminding an evaluator of a recent success or a positive attribute that they possess (e.g., reminding them they are "top tier" in a specific area of expertise) may enhance the evaluator's self-esteem and reduce the likelihood that he/she will make negative evaluations of others.[20] In such cases, evaluators may be less motivated to self-enhance (because they have just been self-enhanced by your comment on their success), and less likely to need to increase their own status by negatively evaluating others. These positive effects of compliments on evaluators may explain the extensive research findings showing ingratiation and flattery (e.g., giving compliments or doing favors) to be effective means of improving one's performance appraisals.[21]

Conclusion

Being judged poorly by others is an everyday experience that most of us don't think about consciously. This article suggests that understanding how we may be negatively evaluated by others, via categorizations, may help us to avoid making the wrong impression when it counts. Further, it suggests that categorization tactics may be a useful means of portraying ourselves (and our evaluators) in ways that lead to positive and desired impressions.

Endnotes

1. Malloy, T. E., & Albright, L. (1990). Interpersonal perception in a social context. *Journal of Personality and Social Psychology, 58*, 419–428.
2. Baumeister, R.F., & Tice, D.M., 1985. Self-esteem and responses to success and failure: Subsequent performance and intrinsic motivation, *Journal of Personality. 53*, 450–467.
3. Hogg, M. A., & Abrams, D. (1988). *Social identification: A social psychology of intergroup relations and group processes.* London: Routledge.
4. Klein, W. M., & Kunda, Z. (1992). Motivated person perception: Constructing justifications for desired beliefs. *Journal of Experimental Social Psychology, 28*, 145–168.
5. Pratt, J. G., Rockmann, K. W., and Kaufman, J. B. (2006). Constructing professional identity: The role of work and identity learning cycles in the customization of identity among medical residents. *Academy of Management Journal, 49*, 235–262.
6. Alicke, M. D., & Guenther, C. L. (2011). *Self-enhancement and self-protection in social judgment.* In Alicke, M. D. & Sedikides, C., (Eds .). *Handbook of Self-Enhancement and Self-Protection,* 174–191. New York, Guildford Press.

7. Macrae, C. N., & Bodenhausen, G.V. (2001). "Social cognition: Categorical person perception." *British Journal of Psychology, 92*: 239–255.
8. Fiske, S., & Taylor, S. (1991). *Social Cognition.* New York: McGraw-Hill.
9. Medin, D. L., Lynch, E. B., Coley, J. D., & Atran, S. (1997). "Categorization and reasoning among tree experts: Do all roads lead to Rome?" *Cognitive Psychology, 32,* 49–96.
10. Pittinksy et al.
11. McGarty, C. (1999). *Categorization in Social Psychology.* London: Sage Publications.
12. Macrae, C. N., & Bodenhausen, G. V. (2000). "Social cognition: Thinking categorically about others." *Annual Review of Psychology, 51,* 93–120.
13. Klein, W. M., & Kunda, Z. (1992). "Motivated person perception: Constructing justifications for desired beliefs." *Journal of Experimental Social Psychology, 28,* 145–168.
14. Fiske, S., & Taylor, S. (1991). *Social Cognition.* New York: McGraw-Hill.
15. Quinn, K. A., & Macrae, C. N. (2005). "Categorizing others: The dynamics of person construal." *Journal of Personality and Social Psychology, 88,* 467–479.
16. Reynolds, K. J., & Oakes, P. J., (2000). "Variability in Impression Formation: Investigating the Role of Motivation, Capacity, and the Categorization Process." *Personality and Social Psychology Bulletin, 26,* 355–373.
17. Ibarra, H., (1999). "Provisional selves: Experimenting with image and identity in professional adaptation." *Administrative Science Quarterly, 44,* 764–791.
18. Elsbach, K. D., (2003). "How to pitch a brilliant idea." *Harvard Business Review, 81,* 117–123.
19. Elsbach, K. D., Cable, D. M., & Sherman, J. W. (2010). "How passive 'face time' affects perceptions of employees: Evidence of spontaneous trait inference." *Human Relations, 63,* 735–760.
20. Baumeister, R.F., & Tice, D.M., 1985.
21. Ferris, G. R., Judge, T. A., Rowland, K. M., & Fitzgibbons, D. E. (1994). "Subordinate influence and the performance evaluation process: Test of a model." *Organizational Behavior and Human Decision Processes, 58,* 101–135.

On Being Trustworthy

Roger C. Mayer

North Carolina State University

Organizations are comprised of people who work together to accomplish goals. As an employee, you need others to accomplish their tasks, competently and ethically, so that you can get your work done. In short, you need to trust them. Trust is a commonly used and emotionally loaded word, and different people mean different things when they claim to "trust" someone at work. In this article, I will first discuss the meaning of "trust." I will then consider how it affects the workplace if employees do not trust each other. Lastly, I will discuss what employees can do to make themselves more trustworthy to others.

Scholars in the organizational sciences have studied trust since the 1950s. Based on these studies, the most prominent definition of interpersonal trust is a *willingness to be vulnerable to another party who cannot be monitored or controlled.* If you are willing to be vulnerable to someone, you are willing to take a risk at that person's hands; you are willing to allow them to have influence over things that matter to you. Everyone has their own reasons for deciding how much to trust someone else in the workplace or in life. Still, there are strong patterns that have been identified when deciding if someone is trustworthy. Fortunately, there are things you can do to understand these patterns, and by focusing on them, there are ways that you can become more trustworthy in the eyes of others.

Why Does Trust Matter?

Why should you care about how much others at work trust you? We all know it feels better to be around people we trust and that it is uncomfortable to have to work with someone we distrust. Is trust just a "feel good" phenomenon? Research shows trust in the workplace is not just about feeling good, or about employees being happy with their jobs. Trust does this, but it does much more.

When people in the workplace trust each other, it changes the basic way they interact with each together, which can change their outcomes, both individually and collectively. People communicate more openly when they trust the party with whom they are communicating (e.g., they share more information that could potentially be held against them). Trust is particularly important if the communicator has made a mistake, or thinks he or she *may* have made a mistake. If the communicator is concerned about culpability for a mistake, trust allows her or him to share information that can fix a problem or improve a process in the organization. If trust is lacking, the communicator will tend to withhold the very information that can best fix the mistake or improve the situation. When employees trust upper-management, they are more willing to get behind organizational change efforts. If trust is lacking, employees resist change. Management has a more difficult time implementing strategic decisions when employees resist change. One of the most robust outcomes of trust in the workplace is that employees who trust engage in more organizational citizenship behaviors, i.e., they help one another more and do more things outside of their formal job description.

Foundations of Trustworthiness

As previously noted, there is no formula for trusting others in the workplace. Nevertheless, research has found there are three issues that tend to drive how trustworthy employees deem others to be: the person's ability, integrity, and benevolence.

Ability

The best way to prove trustworthiness is the ability to perform your job. *Ability* is the skills and competencies in a particular domain that allow employees to accomplish tasks. As an employee, you are expected to contribute a set of skills to the team. You are employed because you are expected to accomplish a set of tasks. Executing your responsibilities competently provides a solid basis for your manager, as well as others in the company, to give you the freedom to get your job done without being constantly monitored.

To be deemed trustworthy by others, you need to perform your job well. Learn the duties expected of your position, and commit yourself to continuous personal improvement at the required skills. Don't accept "meets requirements," but always look to improve. In addition to your manager, your peers can give you feedback on areas where you can improve. Don't be afraid to ask them for feedback. On the other end of the spectrum, observe how people who are marginal in their job skills affect the organization. These people may cause their coworkers to work harder at their jobs to overcome the lack of trustworthiness they engender.

The judgment of how much ability someone has is not limited to a narrow, myopic definition bounded by the person's job description. While that provides an important foundation, more is often expected. You need to demonstrate on a continuing basis that you understand how your work affects others. Whose performance is affected if your work is not done well? Whose job is made easier if you do a particularly good job? This wider view of your ability goes beyond the boundaries of your organization. How well do you understand the industry and what your company needs to do well to compete effectively in its industry? Such "big picture" considerations strengthen your credibility as being capable, both as a subordinate and as a peer. They strengthen the case that you know how to prioritize your efforts toward the most important objectives.

One of the arenas that is nearly universally needed is the ability to work well with and to positively influence others. While you may be technically competent at your job, developing strong interpersonal skills also contributes to both your job performance and the perception that others hold that trust in your abilities.

Integrity

We live in an era where infamous breaches of integrity have unfortunately, become all too commonplace. Like trust, integrity means different things to different people. For our purposes, *integrity* is the perception that a party adheres to a set of values that the perceiver finds acceptable. The scandals at such corporations at Enron and WorldCom, and the more recent Ponzi scheme perpetrated by Bernie Madoff, provide appalling reminders that not everyone in the business world behaves consistently with high moral standards. These scandals led to losses of investors' life savings, security, and careers for many people, and cost others years in prison, and even life itself.

While these scandals are clearly memorable, more mundane breaches of integrity are commonplace in most workplaces. Padding expense reports or helping yourself to office supplies, while they may seem innocuous and commonplace, send signals about your values to others. Stretching the truth about your contribution to a project may seem like normal impression management to you, but can be seen by others as signals of low integrity. For many people, such breaches of integrity are fed by rationalizations such as "everybody does this," "nobody will know," or "it doesn't matter" in order to justify their own unethical behavior. From a perspective of becoming more trustworthy to others, however, nothing could be further from the truth. Other people look at the behaviors they see you engage in to make judgments about your integrity. Often you are aware when they can see what you are doing—but not always. Sometimes others hear about you from third parties, or believe they can infer your integrity from actions they believe you have taken.

So far I've discussed things that can damage your trustworthiness by tarnishing your integrity. But what can you do to strengthen your integrity, and therefore your trustworthiness in others' eyes? An important piece of this is how acceptable your values are to those around you. Take a look at your company's stated values. While often sketchy, they may provide some foundation for values that you share with coworkers. Certainly if your behavior is inconsistent with company values, it would not be surprising to learn that others at work have concerns with your integrity.

There are some rules of thumb for making ethical decisions that are also valuable for building your integrity. One recommends that you ask yourself how you would like to see your actions described on the front page of the newspaper, particularly if they were written up by someone who didn't care for you. Taking this perspective helps you to realize how your integrity, reflected in your actions, could be seen by others—without the filter of self-justifying rationalizations on your part.

You've probably heard the expression "walk the talk." Doing what you say you'll do, and acting consistently with the values you profess, are important to having others judge you as having integrity. If you pick and choose when you'll actually follow lofty values that you profess, others are likely to react negatively to the inconsistencies in your behavior. Inconsistency in how you enact your professed values leaves others room to wonder what your values *really* are. For example, saying you are a team player, but taking care of yourself instead of the team's needs is likely to be noticed by your coworkers, and will likely be seen as a lack of integrity.

Word about the way you treat others gets around. This is particularly true in this information age of social networking. Expect that what you do to one, you do to all. If, for example, you do not keep information confidential that should be kept confidential, it is not only the injured party who will be irate. If you take unfair advantage of a coworker, it suggests to other coworkers that they could be next. Expect that others will find out what you've done, and make negative judgments about your integrity.

Finally, it's important to note that research suggests that perceptions of integrity may be the most stable of the three trustworthiness factors (i.e., ability, integrity, and benevolence), and others' perceptions of your integrity are affected more by the lowest-integrity behavior they see from you (or think they see from you) than by the highest-integrity behavior that they attribute to you. These findings explain in part why ex-convicts have such a difficult time finding employment: others are hesitant to believe that an ex-con can truly reform, even after prolonged good behavior.

Benevolence

The third and final issue that has a large effect on people's judgments of trustworthiness is benevolence. This refers to the perception that *someone else believes you have their best interests at heart*. In this context, it does not refer to treating all other people in a positive way—that would influence others' assessment of your integrity. Rather, benevolence is individualistic: it deals with how much a *specific other person believes* you have his or her best interests at heart. Does the other person think you would go out of your way to help him/her out? At issue for benevolence are the relationships you develop with others.

There is much written about how to develop positive relationships with others. One classic book on this area is Dale Carnegie's *How to Win Friends and Influence People*. It provides a lot of ideas beyond those touched on here. The important thing for benevolence is that others get a clear, unambiguous message that you care about their interests. Some of the issues brought up here may seem obvious, but are worth your careful consideration to identify any possible weaknesses on your part.

To build the level of benevolence others perceive in you, it is important that you take time to interact with others. In an attempt to focus on doing their jobs, many employees closet themselves away at work. While paying attention to performing is a good thing, it is important to strike a balance between focusing on your own work and building relationships with others. To deem you trustworthy, people need to know you will be there for them in their time of need. They are more likely to be comfortable that they know how you will respond if they know you, and have a developed relationship with you. While getting to know others, pay attention to what they need. What are things on which they could use help from you? Are there ways that you can help them out and cover for them? When others have problems, deadlines, or other pressing needs, step up and help—even when you are not asked. It sends a signal that you care about them. The better you know a person, the more effectively you can understand what her or his interests are and how you can help to serve them.

As a manager, you have control over resources that your subordinates need. You also have influence over their opportunities. As a manager, pay attention to developmental needs and desires of your subordinates. There is an easy but often overlooked way to figure out where they'd like their careers to go: *ask them*. Take the time to discuss where they'd like to be in a few years, and help them get there. Assign them tasks and projects that will allow them to develop the skills and experiences that will qualify them for the position they would like. It sends a signal that they are more than just a tool for you to get your job done, but that you want to make sure their needs are met. The payoff for you is that they will recognize your loyalty to them as individuals, and will be more likely to reciprocate your efforts.

Becoming More Trustworthy

The examples provided above were selected to highlight the origins of one of the three main factors of trustworthiness (i.e., ability, integrity, and benevolence), and what you might do to increase how you are perceived on that factor. There are many others that are likely to affect more than one of these factors. A few will be considered here.

The way you use available power to get things accomplished has been recognized to influence others' trust in you since the late 1950s. This early work suggests there are five core bases of how much power one has. *Reward power* gives someone the ability to influence others because they desire the rewards that can be given. *Coercive power* is based on the unpleasant outcomes someone can administer for failure to comply with their wishes. *Legitimate power* derives from the willingness to do as someone asks because of internalized expectations based on the person's role. (I have yet to find any student from any culture in the world who was not raised to believe that students should do what their teacher asks). *Expert power* is influence derived from the expectation that doing what the influencer says will lead to improved performance or outcomes—simply put, following because the person knows what they are talking about and can therefore be helpful. Finally, *referent power* comes from the follower's desire to be more similar to the influencer, or want to be perceived positively by the person who has power.

Using legitimate power (e.g., "Do it because I'm the boss") does not help you become more trustworthy. It might get the work done that you seek, but does nothing to increase perceptions of your ability, integrity, or benevolence. While using coercive power might make you seem to have higher ability, this is likely to be more than offset by decreasing perceptions of your benevolence and integrity. Using reward power might be expected to increase your trustworthiness, but can be seen as a weak fallback strategy for getting things done. If you run out of rewards to give (e.g., budget is depleted), this basis for accomplishing goals evaporates. The two bases that show the most promise for building trustworthiness are expert and referent power. Using expert power to influence others reinforces the perception of your ability. Referent power relies on building the relationship, which reinforces benevolence.

Finally, there are two related topics to consider. Firstly, actions speak louder than words. Anyone can claim to be worthy of others' trust. Those who *show consistently over time* that they have strong ability, have integrity in all their dealings, and show genuine concern for those around them are likely to be the most trustworthy in others' eyes. Perhaps most important in the quest to become more trustworthy is that you need to *be genuine*. "Acting like" you care about others, or that you have integrity, will surely be seen through in the long run. No matter what excuses you proffer, weaknesses in your skills will eventually become evident. The final challenge is not to "appear" to be trustworthy, but to focus your efforts on becoming as strong as possible on ability, integrity, and benevolence.

8 Decision Making

Topic Summary Learning Objectives

1. Describe programmed and non-programmed decision making.

2. Recognize the six-step process of rational decision making.

3. Describe the behavioral economic-based decision making approach to overcoming bias and errors.

4. Identify the organizational psychology-based approach to decision making.

5. Discuss the importance of the five activities in natural decision making.

6. Apply concepts of decision making to organizations.

Key Terms

behavioral economic-based decision making, p. 269

bounded rationality, p. 271

certainty, p. 268

decision making, p. 267

garbage can approach, p. 271

heuristic, p. 270

intuition, p. 272

mental accounting, p. 269

naturalistic decision making, p. 271

non-programmed decisions, p. 267

organizational psychology-based decision making, p. 271

perfect information, p. 268

probability, p. 268

problem framing, p. 269

programmed decisions, p. 267

prototypes, p. 272

rational decision making, p. 268

satisficing, p. 271

sensemaking, p. 272

uncertainty, p. 268

Introduction to Decision Making

1 Describe programmed and non-programmed decision making.

Decision making describes how individuals and organizations choose among different alternatives and identify the best solution to a problem. Organizations face two types of decisions: programmed and non-programmed. **Programmed** decisions are characterized by routine decision-making situations where actions have clearly identifiable and often predictable outcomes. Organizations engage in programmed decisions on a regular basis and have established procedures and metrics for decision making. **Non-programmed** decisions require new methods and procedures, often involve highly complex, and non-routine problems. In non-programmed decision making, the relationship between decisions and their expected outcomes remains unclear.[1] While many decisions in organizations involve programmed decisions, like determining budgets, hiring personnel, and production decisions, a growing number of decisions in organizations are non-programmed. For example, forecasting future income streams, establishing strategy, and dealing with changing customer demands have become non-programmed decisions in many organizations.

Rational Decision Making

This topic summary explores four approaches to decision making and their limitations. Figure 8.1 summarizes the four approaches to decision making and the key concepts associated with each form of decision making.

1. *Rational decision making* is the systematic weighing of options to maximize desired outcomes by estimating the probabilities of various outcomes.[2]

2. *Behavioral economic-based decision making* focuses on how incentives and psychological biases may interfere with rational decision making and cause decision makers to make less than optimal decisions.[3]

3. *Organizational psychology-based decision making* also includes the systematic weighing of options, but in addition, considers the role of emotions, politics, and practical considerations which impact outcomes.[4]

4. *Naturalistic decision making* describes the process where decision makers rely on a quick assessment of a situation and draw on experience and intuition to determine a course of action. In naturalistic decision making, emotions and prior experience play a key part in making effective decisions.[5]

Rational	Behavioral Economics	Organizational Psychology	Naturalistic
• Perfect and objective information • Probability • Uncertainty	• Mental accounting • Framing • Heuristics	• Bounded rationality • Satisficing • Garbage cans	• Experience • Intuition • Sensemaking

Figure 8.1

Approaches to Decision Making

Rational decision making describes the process by which individual decision makers systematically weigh various choices by calculating the probability of success for each choice. Much of the research on rational decision making has focused on investment decisions and how investors make decisions, but the rational approach has also been applied to organizational behavior. Rational decision making relies on two key beliefs about what constitutes the best decisions.

First, decision makers must be objective, which means the decision maker eliminates, as much as possible, emotional, perceptual, and other psychological biases. Because emotions and bias can interfere with the decision-making process, decision makers turn to systematic tools like mathematics, statistical models, and other quantitative measures in order to make the best decisions.

Second, decision makers must have access to perfect information. Perfect information means the decision maker has access to all the necessary and accurate information to make a decision. When all relevant, necessary, and accurate information is at the disposal of the decision makers, they are said to have **perfect information**. The less perfect the information, the less objective the decision maker, and in turn the more likely the decision will be less than optimal. The more a decision maker deviates from being rational and objective, the less desirable the decision. The rational decision-making process is based on the ability of the decision maker to calculate the mathematical probabilities of various outcomes.[6]

Probability and Uncertainty

Probability is central to rational decision making. **Probability** is a mathematical formulation that seeks to predict the **certainty** that an event will occur. Rational decision making instructs decision makers to rely on probability to determine which choice has a higher probability of success. Probabilities can range between 1 and 0. A probability of 1 means that an event is 100 percent certain to occur, whereas a probability of 0 means there is no chance an event will occur. For example, when a person tosses a coin, the probably that it will land on heads is nearly 50 percent. Meaning the person flipping the coin has a .50 probability that the event, landing on heads, will occur. As situations become more complex, probability becomes more difficult to predict. **Uncertainty** simply means that nearly every possible outcome, is to some degree, unknown.

Advocates of the rational decision making approach, namely economists like Milton Friedman, do not ignore the fact that not all decisions are rational. Rather, they argue that, taken as a whole, the system itself acts in a rational manner. These economists believe that, not each and every decision is rational, but the net outcome of all decisions is likely to be rational.

2 Recognize the six-step process of rational decision making.

Improved Decision Making: The Six Steps of Rational Decision Making

Rational decision making emphasizes the systematic gathering and processing of information to improve the quality of the decisions. This six-step process is representative of the rational decision making process.

1. *Identify the problem or opportunity*—clearly state the problem to be solved.
2. *Identify criteria of decision*—determine what outcomes are being sought and identify measures that will determine success.
3. *Identify alternatives*—identify alternative courses of action.

4. *Allocate weights*—allocate weights to each alternative by determining how well it fits the criteria for decision making.

5. *Evaluate alternatives*—evaluate each alternative.

6. *Select best alternatives*—select the best alternative among the choices identified.[7]

When people follow these six steps, they are following the rational decision-making process. However, in many cases, people will not be able to conform to this process because they face constraints and hold certain biases. The purely rational basis of decision making has been challenged because it fails to account for the importance of emotions and perceptions in making decisions.

Behavioral Economic-Based Decision Making

The **behavioral economic-based decision making** approach offers a response to the limitations of the rationalist approach to decision making described in the previous section. Nobel prize-winning economists Daniel Kahneman and Daniel Tversky developed a behavioral-based approach to explain how people deviate from rational decision making. People may not be fully rational in how they make decisions, but they deviate in systematic and predictable ways.[8] Their work has spurred an entire stream of research called behavioral economics.[9] The behavioral economics approach describes how people actually make decisions. Similar to the rational approach, much of the research on behavioral economics has focused on investment decisions, but the behavioral approach has relied on techniques from psychology to investigate these decisions.

Behavioral economics blends contemporary psychology with decision-making research to expose the specific mental tricks that individuals perform when faced with difficult choices. Economist Richard Thaler coined the term **mental accounting** to refer to the mental tricks that individuals employ when making financial and business decisions.[10] For example, when investing, individuals tend to overemphasize the investments that increase in value and overlook investments that lose value. Mental accounting tricks like these distort an investor's perception of overall gains and losses. Mental accounting is one way individual decision making is influenced by psychological processes.

Another way that decision making in practice can deviate from rational decision making occurs through **problem framing** which explains how a situation is framed, or presented, will impact the choices made by decision makers.[11] Problem framing shows one of the ways that decision makers deviate from rational behavior: decision makers seem unable to accurately and consistently calculate probabilities because they are preoccupied with how a problem is framed. When faced with a choice, individuals tend to choose problems framed as 'positive' or 'gains' over choices framed as 'negative' or 'losses'. For example, consider that you are the manager of a company that employs 6,000 people at three different manufacturing plants. You are faced with the choice to either:

a. save two of the three plants that will result in the loss of 4,000 jobs, or

b. close one of three plants that will save 2,000 jobs

In this decision, slightly modified from the original research, the individual decision makers were more likely to choose 'saving' 2,000 jobs over 'eliminating' 4,000 jobs, even though both decisions result in the same outcome (a loss of 4,000 jobs, closing 1 plant versus retaining two plants and retaining 2,000 jobs).[12]

3 Describe the behavioral economic-based decision making approach to overcoming bias and errors.

Improved Decision Making: Overcoming Bias and Errors

The behavioral economics-based approach consistently shows that in many cases, people fail to make rational decisions; instead, the actual process by which people make decisions is fraught with bias, subject to interpretation, and based on perceptual errors. Researchers continue to find new ways for decision makers to take shortcuts in the rational decision-making process in order to facilitate easier decision making. Researchers call these shortcuts **heuristics**. Here are some of the most common heuristics:

- *Overconfidence* describes the situation when an individual has a higher assessment of a positive outcome in a situation than is warranted by reading facts or evidence in the case. With overconfidence bias, individuals tend to put too much weight on their own opinion or perspective at the expense of data. The result is that people tend to overestimate the probability of a successful outcome.

- *Anchoring* occurs when the decision maker relies too heavily on one single characteristic of a decision rather than equally weighing other, perhaps more relevant characteristics. For example, a person estimates a future stock price based on the price paid for the stock rather than its future potential return. In this case, the original price serves as a reference point rather than more important information, such as potential net income of the company.

- *Confirmation* describes how individuals seek information that confirms or reinforces existing beliefs or opinions. In confirmation bias, individuals fail to adapt or integrate new information or fail to update their decision based on new or contradicting information. An example of confirmation bias occurs when an investor makes a judgment about the future return of a stock, conducts research that confirms the initial judgment, but tends to ignore any information that might contradict the initial judgment.

- *Gambler's fallacy* states that in many cases, individuals believe that luck is on their side rather than recognizing the randomness of events. For example, a person flips a coin three times. After the coin lands on heads three times in a row, they conclude that heads is more likely to occur in future tosses, failing to recognize that the probability of each toss is always the same.

- *Availability* describes how individuals seek out readily accessible information when making a decision rather than seeking information that may be difficult or expensive to access. For example, college admission offices rely on a few pieces of readily available data when deciding whether or not to admit a student. Because admissions offices have easy access to SAT scores and high school grades, they may be more likely to rely on this data rather than considering other factors that are not readily available through transcripts, like individual motivation and openness to experiences.

- *Hindsight* bias occurs when a person changes their viewpoint, opinion, or reassesses a situation based on new information, but say that they held the first position all along. This explains why hindsight bias is often called the 'I knew it all along syndrome'.[13]

In the next two sections, we explore how organizational psychology and naturalistic decision making approaches take into account some of the challenges of decision making in contemporary organizations.

Organizational Psychology-Based Decision Making

4 Identify the organizational psychology-based approach to decision making.

Organizational psychology-based decision making, is most concerned with the context of decision making. For example, organizational psychology approaches to decision making suggest that in most cases, decision makers cannot rely on perfect information. Because the cost, both in terms of time, money, and other resources is so great, decision makers never obtain perfect information. Instead, decision makers encounter **bounded rationality**, the process where decision makers are forced to act, but must rely on limited information and time constraints when making a decision. The idea of bounded rationality suggests that perfect rationality and objectivity sought by rational decision makers is never fully achieved, but that decision making is always bounded by certain practical constraints. For example, a manager is unable to calculate the probability that hiring a particular candidate will result in higher performance than another candidate, so she relies on other factors to make a decision, including the candidate's prior job performance. This approach emphasizes that decision makers can never fully rely on complete objectivity to guide the decision making process. Making a decision that is not based on perfect information and pure objectivity is called **satisficing**. Satisficing results in making a decision that is 'good enough' to solve the immediate problem at hand, but not necessarily the best decision that is possible.

Since most decisions are based on less than perfect information and because decision makers draw conclusions that are not purely objective, the organizational psychology-based approach is often referred to as the **garbage can** model of decision making. Influential theorist James March describes decision making in organizations as "a collection of choices looking for problems, issues, and feelings looking for decision situations in which they might be aired, solutions looking for issues to which they might be the answer, and decision makers looking for work."[14] March describes decision making as a process that is not always systematic, but rather, is more like a "garbage can into which various problems and solutions are dumped by participants." Decisions arise in organizations as groups of individual decision makers weigh goals and agendas, past organizational practices, available resources, and current incentives. To characterize decision making as a garbage can implies that decision making in most cases is not the systemic and rational process described by the rational decision-making models. Rather, decision making is infused with emotions, politics, and other non-rational factors.

Naturalistic Decision Making

In some cases, the decision maker, faced with time and resource constraints, has only one realistic option. Most decision-making environments involve unforeseen or unpredictable consequences making certainty hard to come by and risk difficult to estimate.[15] Accurate probabilities may be difficult to compute due to the complex and dynamic nature of the variables involved. Time and resource constraints limit the ability of decision makers to gather all the relevant information before making a decision. **Naturalistic decision making** describes how managers, teams, and organizations make decisions in

Renault Philippe/Hemis.fr/SuperStock

natural settings. The first research on naturalistic decision making studied firefighters to understand how fire crew chiefs reacted during fires. Fire chiefs and other emergency management commanders in high stakes environments must take quick action; decision makers cannot make decisions by systematically weighing different choices. Rather, they make decisions by drawing on past experiences. The research revealed fire chiefs did not follow the rules set out by rational decision-making research; rather, fire chiefs drew on years of experience with fires to assess the situation at hand.

In naturalistic settings, people do not weigh a series of choices and decipher probabilities of success for each choice. These activities are time consuming and do not yield useful results. Imagine calculating the probability of successfully rescuing someone trapped in a burning building prior to deciding whether or not to enter! Rather than weighing various options, as the rational decision-making process would suggest, the fire chiefs were more likely to identify one single course of action and follow it through.[16]

Naturalistic decision making describes how decision makers draw on their experience, assess a situation, and then determine a single, best course of action from the available data.[17] Decision makers scan their environment for relevant information, then they classify the situation based on a **prototype**, an imagined version of the situation that the decision maker has previously encountered. This especially applies in time-sensitive and complex environments where choices cannot be methodically weighted or probabilities calculated. All of this is to say that decision makers rely on **intuition**, the process of assessing a situation, identifying problems or opportunities, and knowing what action to take, even when the decision maker cannot consciously describe the situation. Intuition often involves an immediate emotional and cognitive reaction.

An approach closely related to naturalistic decision making is called **sensemaking**. Although not categorized as a decision making approach per se, sensemaking describes the process of how people gather information, make judgments, and then take action.[18] This describes how people are prone to look retrospectively to make sense of what occurred. Sensemaking offers an alternative viewpoint to rational decision making because decision makers often take action, even when they do not have a rational justification. Decision making is better described as justification for actions that have no rational basis, which calls to mind an old phrase used in organizations: 'Managers aren't rational people, they are people who rationalize.'

Improved Decision Making: Assessing the Environment and Building Expertise

5 Discuss the importance of the five activities in natural decision making.

To improve decision making, the naturalistic approach advises decision makers to focus their attention on five activities.

- First, the decision makers should always be thinking about how to avoid failure. Being preoccupied with failure helps decision makers identify potential areas where decisions can go wrong.

- Second, decision makers should be reluctant to simplify interpretations of decisions. With complex decisions, the decision maker considers a variety of potential variables, not ruling out seemingly unimportant variables simply because they cannot explain potential outcomes at the moment.

- Third, decision makers need to exhibit sensitivity to operations. Because many decisions are good in theory, but in practice prove less than satisfactory, decision makers need to focus on implementing the operation.

- Fourth, decision makers should focus on resilience, that is, understand and have mechanisms in place if decisions fail. Some suggest that about half of decisions fail, so decision makers need to be prepared to respond when decisions do not go as planned.

- Finally, decision makers should put less emphasis on organizational decision making structures and more emphasis on training decision makers who have expertise to look at a situation in its entirety.[19]

These five factors help decision makers understand the decision-making environment and to equip them with the tools necessary to handle the unexpected. The naturalistic decision-making process is particularly valuable in improving decisions in non-programmed decision contexts. When making a decision, individuals should consider that most decisions are made not from the rational weighing of decisions, but from the deeply rooted beliefs and biases of the decision maker.[20]

Conclusion

The four approaches to decision making in organizations—rational, behavioral economics, organizational psychology, and naturalistic—illustrate the benefits and limitations of decision making. When making a decision, decision makers need to consider if a decision is a programmed or a non-programmed decision and take advantage of what research has revealed about effective decision making.

OB AT WORK
DARRELL DARNELL RELIES ON MULTIPLE FORMS OF DECISION MAKING TO GAUGE RISK

Darrell Darnell

Darrell Darnell is the head of safety and security for a major university located in the Washington, DC. He arrives at work before dawn and retreats to an office where he reviews a list of possible threats and challenges, revisits the latest local and international news, monitors the local weather forecast, and plans his meetings with numerous stakeholders. Early hours, reams of information, and uncertainty are not unusual in contemporary organizations. Darnell spends his day predicting and reporting something that he cannot always directly see. Darnell relies on multiple forms of decision making to understand the latest threat patterns and predict the school's future direction. Even more important, he has developed a network throughout the university that collects, monitors, assesses, and reports specific threats.

6 Apply concepts of decision making to organizations.

How does Darnell predict a threat without always seeing it directly? He draws on multiple sources of data and combines hard facts with years of judgment gained through experience. He spends his mornings pulling data from various computers, seeking multiple data points, and tracking reports that may come in from various public safety and private sector organizations. He relies, to some degree, on the latest decision making technology available. But even with the latest technology, fastest computers, and various advisory networks, Darnell cannot rely solely on rational decision-making models. For example, even something as seemingly predictable as the weather takes judgment that cannot be measured by rational models.

Think about being the person who determines the deciding factor if school is going to be canceled or not due to the weather. "Even the most advanced computer systems contain certain biases, rely on certain types of modeling that may not be appropriate for certain conditions, or simply don't account for all the necessary variables," reports Darnell. "Further, most of the models are static, they don't update often enough based on incoming information. I need a more rapid update cycle. Besides, models may be effective at determining regional trends, but what I do often requires predicting weather patterns in specific neighborhoods. The models don't often do that."

Instead of relying solely on computer simulations to predict events, Darnell makes measured decisions about risk from his 20 years of experience. Over the years, he has learned the limitations of following computer-automated rational models. "The models do not take into account specifics of a situation," he says, "for example, many risk models do not take into accountant the unique situation my university faces being located in a major metropolitan area in Washington, D.C. And models cannot predict human behavior—the key variable in any situation." Most general approaches to security do not account for the fact that his university has a unique location, but his experience tells him he needs to account for this when assessing risk. Someday, computer programs may be able to account for every factor that predicts risk. Perhaps computers may even be more

(continued)

effective at predicting risks, such as weather, in geographic areas as small as a neighborhood. However, it is unlikely that these computers will ever outsmart the decisions of people. Organizations will continue to rely on people like Darnell to make sense of different computer-generated models and to understand the unique 'personality' of each potential risk, and threat. Predicting what might unfold in a future situation is just as much an art as it is a science, and relies on the judgment of the decision maker.

If describing and predicting the risk is not complicated enough, Darnell must also consider how he presents information to internal and external constituents. As one of the most visible administrators in his university, it is important that he communicate directly with the students, parents, and broader community about sensitive issues, such as crime. Simply reporting decisions is not enough; how the information is presented or framed is important as well. With the variety of information people are exposed to each day, Darnell needs to be concise, informative, and conscious of how his audience will perceive the information.

For example, a phrase like 'there is a 30% chance of a storm tomorrow' he knows holds a very specific, scientific meaning. Most individuals are not concerned with an abstract probability, explains Darnell, "Students want to know if classes are going to be canceled or delayed due to the weather so they can plan." A probability is not informative enough in many cases. Also, how a risk is framed can have an effect. If Darnell classifies a risk as being "small," that means something completely different to people than when he says he assesses something as being likely "safe." Experience has taught him that people tend to hear things based on emotions rather than consider the pure rational aspects of stating a probability.

For Darnell, being an effective decision maker is not only about understanding probabilities or reading computer models, it is about performing a public service that affects lives on a daily basis. Darnell continues to rely on a combination of experience, judgment, and rational modeling to describe and predict risks.

Source: Personal interview with Darrell Darnell.

SPOTLIGHT ON RESEARCH
Do Emotions Help or Hinder Decision Making?

Organizational decision making involves timely decisions based on available information. Researchers agree that emotions play a role in decision making, however, the debate continues as to whether emotions can help or hinder decision making. One group of researchers hypothesized that while emotions played an important role, one could argue "whether affective feelings are functional or dysfunctional for decision making is largely dependent upon how people experience those feelings and what they do about them during decision making" (p. 923).

The researchers believed a few distinct aspects of emotions proved important. First, prior research helped explain how people experience emotions differently. Emotions may either be experienced deeply or not at all, depending on the individual and the situation.

(continued)

In other words, the experience of emotions differs across individuals. Second, they found that not all emotions induce the same biases. Negative emotions, like anger, produced different results than positive emotions, like happiness. Further, how a decision maker handles various emotions determines how those emotions relate to decision making. Said another way, the type and intensity of the emotion, as well as the way that a person regulates that emotion, determines the impact of the emotion on decision-making effectiveness. Researchers believed that the more intense the emotion, and the more the person was able to recognize and regulate the emotion, the greater the effect it would have on decision making.

Researchers turned to a stock market simulation to test the role of emotions on making investment decisions. The participants in the study played a simulated stock market game on the Internet. Study participants, or investors as they were, received a fictional $10,000 to invest across 12 different local companies. First, for 20 days, investors made daily investment decisions based on actual stock market prices. They had access to additional information typically employed by investment professionals to make stock purchase decisions. Investors then reported their particular emotions each day after making the decisions. The survey tapped into a broad range of emotions, from unpleasant emotions like anger, disappointment, and frustration to pleasant feelings like calm, happiness, and interest. The study logged 22 different emotions in all. Next, before logging out of the simulation, investors briefly explained their investment decisions.

Researchers used standard investment risk measures to observe investor decisions. Successful investment decisions were measured by a combination of short- and long-term performance measures, while considering a few additional factors, like investment experience and age, as well. Interestingly, more experienced investors actually made weaker decisions over less experienced decision makers!

This negative result related to decision making success wasn't the only interesting finding. Researchers found that "those who experienced their feelings with greater intensity during decision making—achieved higher decision making" (p. 933–934). The study found that investors who understood their emotions (rather than ignored them) and took subsequent action to regulate their emotions, performed better. In addition, the study found that investors were more likely to recognize and regulate negative emotions over positive emotions. In the final analysis, negative emotions contributed to better decision making but found positive emotions had no measurable impact.

One conclusion drawn from the study is emotions aid in decision making, especially when emotions are felt strongly. Awareness of one's own emotions may help the decision maker understand their possible decision-making errors or heuristics. Only when the decision maker is aware of the emotion can he or she take action to regulate the emotions and possibly avoid the onset of errors. A second conclusion shows decision makers may be more willing to regulate negative feelings rather than positive feelings. Positive emotions may lead to poor decisions when not regulated, for example, overconfidence may lead them to be more confident in a decision than is warranted.

Some have suggested that managers focused too quickly on positive emotions such as engagement, optimism, and confidence. Thus, the best decision maker could avoid errors brought about by negative emotions, but are less likely to overcome limitations brought about by positive emotions. To improve decision making, organizations can emphasize that emotional awareness, expression, and regulation positively impact decision making, so conventional wisdom, such as relying on purely rational decisions, stripped of emotions may do more harm than good. Indeed, this research shows that greater emotional awareness improves, not detracts, from decision making.

Questions for Discussion

1. Why are emotions important in the workplace? Do you agree or disagree with what the authors found in their study? Why?

2. How might you apply this research in the workplace?

Source: Based on Seo, M. G., Feldman Barrett, L. (2007). Being emotional during decision making—good or bad? An empirical investigation. *Academy of Management Journal, 50*, 4, 923–940.

Pairing with this Topic Summary

Suggested Expert Contributions

Leading Decision-Making Processes—Michael A. Roberto (Bryant University)

On Best-Practice Decision Making—Paul C. Nutt (The Ohio State University)

How Temporary Organizations Promote Dysfunctional Goal Pursuit: The Case of the 1996 Mount Everest Disaster
— Kimberly D. Elsbach (University of California, Davis) and Markus Hällgren (Umeå University, Sweden)

Suggested Cases

Case 1: The Case of Apple iPhone 4

Case 3: EMERGENCY! We Need a Better Compensation System

Case 4: Face Time at TechPoint Software, Inc.

Case 6: NASCAR's Drive for Diversity: Can They Reach the Finish Line?

Suggested Exercises

Exercise 8: Facts and Opinions

Exercise 10: Force Field Analysis

Exercise 11: Bias and Decision Making

Exercise 18: Team Performance Evaluation

Exercise 26: Social Media Dilemma

Exercise 31: The Ethics of the Climb

Exercise 35: Who Do I Fire?

Exercise 37: Team Survival Simulation

Exercise 38: FIS Simulation

Endnotes

1. Simon, H. A. (1977). *The new science of management decision*. Englewood Cliffs, NJ: Prentice Hall.
2. Simon, H. A. (1976). *Administrative Behavior: A study of decision-making processes in Administrative Organizations*. New York: Free Press.
3. Kahneman, D., Slovic, & P., Tversky. A. (1982). *Judgment under uncertainty: Heuristics and biases*. Cambridge University Press.
4. March, J. G. & Simon, H. A. (1958). *Organizations*. New York: Wiley; Cyert, R. M., March, J. G., (1963). *A behavioral theory of the firm*. Englewood Cliffs, NJ: Prentice Hall.
5. Klein, G. (1999). *Sources of power*. MIT Press; Weick, K. E. (1993). The collapse of sensemaking in organizations: The Mann Gulch Disaster. *Administrative Science Quarterly, 38*, 628–652.
6. Simon, H. A. (1976).
7. Simon, H. A. (1977).
8. Kahneman, D., & Tversky, A. (1979). Prospect theory: An analysis of decisions under risk. *Econometrica, 47*, 2, 263–291.
9. Becker, G. S., & Murphy, (2001). *Social economics: Market behavior in a social environment*. Cambridge, MA: Harvard University Press. Akerloff, G., & Shiller, R. (2010). *Animal spirits: How human psychology drives the economy, and why it matters for global capitalism*. Princeton, NJ: Princeton University Press.
10. Thaler, R. H. (1999). Mental accounting matters. *Journal of Behavioral Decision Making, 12*, 3, 183–206.
11. Problem adopted from Bazerman, M. (1998). *Judgment in managerial decision making* (4th Ed.) 48. New York: John Wiley.
12. Berg, N., & Gigerenzer, G. (2010). As-If Behavioral Economics: Neoclassical Economics in Disguise? *History of Economic Ideas, 18*, 1, 133–166; Harford, T. (2011). Why We Do What We Do: Behavioral economics under attack. *Financial Times*. Posted Sunday, Jan. 30, (2011), at 7:00 AM ET.
13. Biases are described in Gilovich T., Griffin D., & Kahneman, D. (Eds). *Heuristics and Biases: The Psychology of Intuitive Judgment*. Cambridge University Press. See also Agans, R. P., & Shaffer, L. S. 1994. The Hindsight Bias: The Role of the Availability Heuristic and Perceived Risk. *Basic and Applied Social Psychology, 15*, 4, 439–449. Hindsight bias is described in Fischoff, B., & Beyth, R. (1975). "I knew it would happen" Remembered probabilities of once-future things. *Organizational Behaviour and Human Performance*. 13, 1–16
14. Cohen, M. D., & March, J. G. (1974). *Leadership and Ambiguity: The American College President*, 81. New York: McGraw-Hill.. Cited in Minor, J. B. (2002). *Organizational Behavior: Foundations, theories, and analysis* 640–641. New York: Oxford University Press.
15. March, J, (1994). *A primer on decision making: How decisions happen*. New York: Free Press.
16. Klein, (1999).
17. Klein, G. (2008). Naturalistic Decision making. *Human Factors: The Journal of the Human Factors and Ergonomics Society, 50*, 3, 456–460.
18. Weick, K. E. 1993. *Sensemaking in organizations*. Thousand Oaks, CA: Sage.
19. Weick, K, E., & Sutcliffe, K. M. (2001). *Managing the unexpected: Assuring High Performance in an Age of complexity*. San Francisco: Jossey-Bass.
20. Ariely, D. (2010). *Predictably Irrational, Revised and Expanded Edition: The Hidden Forces That Shape Our Decisions*. New York: Harper Perennial.

Leading Decision Making Processes

Michael A. Roberto

Bryant University

When an organization makes a poor decision, people wonder how it could have happened. What was management thinking? How could they have been so stupid? Consider a few major events over the past two decades. How could BP and its partners have made a series of choices that led to the catastrophic 2010 oil spill in the Gulf of Mexico? How could NASA have downplayed the threat from the foam strike that occurred during the January, 2003 launch of the Columbia space shuttle? Why did Daimler acquire Chrysler in 1998, destroying so much shareholder value in the process?

When considering these failures, we often envision a moment in time when senior executives gathered to make an important choice. We think of decision making as an event of crucial importance. However, decisions typically don't occur at one moment in time, in just one person's head, or at one team meeting. Decision-making processes involve many people. These processes stop and start, get sidetracked at times, and take place across multiple units and levels of an organization. In James Bryan Quinn's research, he reported that an executive once told him, "When I was younger, I always conceived of a room where all these [strategic] concepts were worked out for the whole company. Later, I didn't find any such room."[1] Indeed, many conversations take place "off-line" during one-on-one meetings and other informal gatherings (at the water cooler or the coffee bar, for instance). In many cases, decisions don't really occur in formal meetings—instead, those sessions simply serve as an opportunity for a team to ratify a decision that has already been made.

Managers can have a hard time pinning down precisely when they chose a particular course of action. In describing a major strategic choice, a defense industry executive once told me, "The decision to do this didn't come in November of 1996, it didn't come in February of 1997, it didn't come in May of 1997. You know, there was a concept, and the concept evolved."[2] In short, decision making is not simply an event that takes place in the corner office—it is a dynamic process. A lack of intelligence often doesn't explain why leaders fail to make the right call; politics, emotion, and personality clashes often prove to be a team's downfall instead.[3]

When making decisions, many leaders focus first and foremost on the task at hand—on the content of the decision. They ask themselves the question: "What course of action should I choose?" They focus on finding the right solution. However, leaders should step back and first ask themselves a different question: "How should I go about making this decision?" They should focus on the *process*, not just the outcome. As leaders, they have the opportunity to shape the decision-making process by creating the conditions that enable a team to function effectively.[4] Moreover, they can design and lead a process that fosters better critical thinking and a more candid dialogue. In short, successful leaders *decide how to decide* before jumping in to try to solve a problem.

Deciding How to Decide

Consider an example of how one leader decided how to decide. In 1961, President John F. Kennedy chose to support a group of rebels who hoped to invade Cuba and overthrow Fidel Castro. The Bay of Pigs Invasion proved a complete failure. Afterward, Kennedy asked his advisers, "How could I have been so stupid to let them go ahead?".[5] Scholars later described this flawed decision as a classic example of groupthink. Irving Janis described *groupthink* as the powerful pressure for conformity that arises in groups. Put another way, people sometimes go along to get along. Groupthink leads to a premature convergence upon a single alternative; individuals often hold back if they have a different point of view.[6]

Fortunately, Kennedy and his advisers reflected upon the Bay of Pigs failure and devised a new approach to making high-stakes choices in the future. During the Cuban Missile Crisis, Kennedy assembled a team to determine a course of action—but directed the group to engage in a different kind of decision-making process. Kennedy chose not to attend a number of key meetings; he wanted to create an atmosphere in which his advisers could feel free to speak candidly. Kennedy directed each adviser to consider the "policy problem as a whole, rather than approaching the issues in the traditional bureaucratic way whereby each man confines his remarks to the special aspects in which he considers himself to be an expert and avoids arguing about issues on which others present are supposedly more expert than he".[7] He wanted them to behave as "skeptical generalists" rather than simply representing their department or agency's interests. Put simply, the President asked them to look at the "big picture." From time to time, Kennedy invited lower-level officials and outside experts to present their information and ideas, wanting to make sure he had access to fresh perspectives.

The team split into subgroups, instead of meeting as a whole, to develop and debate two alternative courses of action. One subgroup outlined the plan for a military air strike, while the other put forth a proposal for a naval blockade on Cuba. They then sketched out the President's speech to the nation under each scenario, and finally exchanged white papers and developed detailed critiques of one another's proposals. Each subgroup refined its proposal based on the feedback from the others. Finally, Robert Kennedy and Theodore Sorensen, two of the President's closest confidantes, played the role of devil's advocates. They surfaced and challenged key assumptions, pointed out flaws of each plan, and uncovered hidden risks.

President Kennedy learned from the Bay of Pigs failure how to proceed in the Cuban Missile Crisis by recognizing that he had not considered the details of the CIA's plan. In the Cuban Missile Crisis, Kennedy shaped and influenced how that decision process unfolded. He designed a process that encouraged a vigorous debate, welcomed dissenting views, and promoted the careful evaluation of multiple alternatives. Even though he did not take part in key meetings with his advisers, he remained firmly in control of the decision-making process, and in so doing, put himself in a position to receive the best information and advice before having to make a final choice.

Making a decision entails four key design choices (see Figure 1). First, leaders must consider the *composition* of the team that will be involved in the decision-making process—who has relevant knowledge and expertise and how will they be involved? These people may not be members of the executive team. For example, a leader may want to invite junior-level experts with unbiased opinions. Second, leaders must shape the *context*

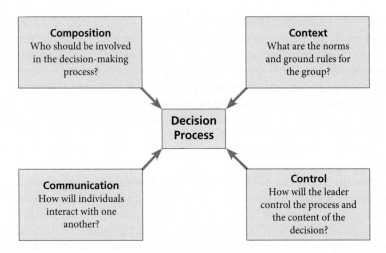

Figure 1 Deciding How to Decide

of the decision process. They could ask team members to adhere to certain ground rules during meetings. For instance, they might ask people to refrain from electronic devices, side conversations, checking social media, or from interrupting others when they speak. Third, leaders must focus on how individuals and subgroups will *communicate* with one another. Will subgroups and devil's advocates be used to foster dialogue and debate? Will people put proposals in writing? How and when will meetings take place? Finally, leaders must consider how they will *control* the decision-making process? Will they be present at all key meetings or will they choose not attend certain sessions to encourage candid dialogue among key advisers? Perhaps most importantly, how will the leader make the final call and then communicate the rationale of the decision to all key parties involved? Choosing how to decide involves addressing these questions at the outset, before an organization begins deliberating. Leaders improve the odds of a sound decision if they can design and shape a high-quality decision-making process.

The Attributes of a Quality Decision Process

As a leader chooses how to decide, what type of process should they strive to create? What are the characteristics of a high-quality decision-making process? Good processes means simultaneously cultivating constructive *conflict* and building management *consensus*. Vigorous debate leads to the generation of multiple alternatives, the surfacing and probing of crucial assumptions, and the examination of hidden risks. Conflict leads to critical thinking, thereby improving the odds of choosing the right plan. However, conflict alone does not lead to good results. For an organization to perform well, it must not only choose wisely, but also implement those decisions in an effective and timely manner.

Leaders must build *consensus* during the decision-making process to improve the odds of a smooth implementation of their plans. Consensus does not mean unanimity by interested parties. It does not mean that teams, rather than leaders, make decisions. Consensus means that people have accepted the final decision, despite the fact that they may not agree with certain parts of the plan. Consensus has two critical components: a high level of commitment to cooperate in the implementation process and a strong, shared understanding of the rationale for the decision.[8] Commitment and understanding insure that people are moving in the same direction during the implementation process, and they will persevere in the face of obstacles. During a decision-making process, leaders must expect debate with the need to build shared commitment and understanding.

Unfortunately, many decision-making processes lack sufficient dissent and debate. People do not feel comfortable speaking up at times. The problem often begins with the leader, who has not created a safe climate within the team. In a safe climate, people feel comfortable asking questions, offering a different view, and admitting mistakes. In an unsafe climate, people worry about how others will treat them if they challenge the conventional wisdom, admit an error, or question the leader.[9]

Consider the culture at NASA before the Columbia shuttle accident. As former astronaut James Bagian explained, "At senior levels, during the 1990s, dissent was not tolerated, and therefore, people learned if you wanted to survive in the organization, you had to keep your mouth shut."[10] Rodney Rocha, a NASA engineer, had serious concerns about the foam strike that occurred during launch. He formed an ad-hoc team to analyze the risk and pressed his superiors for more data. However, he did not speak up at a crucial Mission Management Team meeting at which senior managers concluded that no safety-of-flight risk existed. When asked why he did not speak up during that meeting, he said, "I couldn't do it. I'm too low down...and she's [Linda Ham, Mission Management Team leader] way up here."[11]

Andrew Grove, former Chairman and CEO of Intel, once wrote that, "Debates are like the process through which a photographer sharpens the contrast when developing a print. The clearer images that result permit management to make a more informed—and more likely correct—call."[12] Leaders can encourage debate through a variety of techniques. For instance, they can break a team into subgroups to generate and debate options, or they can assign individuals to serve as devil's advocates—as President Kennedy did during the Cuban Missile Crisis. Business leaders also can ask individuals to role play competitors. A role play exercise often encourages people to think differently about a firm's strategy. For instance, when a leading aerospace firm made a crucial decision in the late 1990s, a group role played how rivals might team up to compete with them on a key military program. The exercise generated a lively debate, exposed flaws in their plans, and helped them make a better decision. One executive explained, "We actually had someone role play the other alliance that was forming, and they did a competitive assessment of us, just like a football team. You know, you scrimmage using the other guy's plays. The results portrayed the other alliance's view of us, and it was very revealing."[13]

Keeping Conflict Constructive

While debates can be good for teams, conflict becomes dysfunctional at times. Leaders must remember that conflict comes in two forms: cognitive and affective.[14] Cognitive conflict involves debates about the issues. It means that we disagree on how to accomplish a particular goal or task. Affective conflict involves personal friction, personality clashes, and emotional outbursts. It often means people attack each other personally rather than sticking to the facts. Cognitive conflict leads to higher quality decisions, but affective conflict often has bad consequences. It can impede a group's ability to work together moving forward, making implementation a challenging endeavor.

What can a leader do to minimize interpersonal conflict? Before deliberations begin, leaders should establish ground rules that foster constructive dialogue—clarifying the roles that particular individuals will play during the decision-making process. Leaders also should help individuals understand and respect the fact that their colleagues may have different ways of analyzing problems. After a contentious debate, leaders can help a group reflect upon their experience and learn how to work together more effectively in the future.

During the deliberations, a leader can use a variety of techniques to break an impasse and get the conversation moving in a positive direction. For instance, a leader can ask curious, non-threatening questions to reframe an issue when emotions begin to flare. As negotiation expert William Ury has said, "The most obvious way to direct the other side's attention toward the problem is to tell them about it. But making assertions can easily arouse their resistance. The better approach is to ask questions."[15] Unfortunately, people often focus on advocating their position during a heated debate rather than trying to understand others' thinking. The same arguments get repeated—people stop trying to learn; they just want to win. Leaders can shift a group out of pure advocacy mode by asking questions that help people discover one another's goals, assumptions, and logic.

Asking participants to revisit key facts and assumptions proves very useful at times. Leaders should strive to get people to step back from the positions that they have taken, and help them discover precisely how and why they disagree. Probing underlying assumptions sometimes leads to entire new lines of inquiry and new data gathering. Sometimes, revisiting underlying facts and assumptions helps people find common ground. Gaining agreement on a crucial assumption, for example, can serve as a launching point for the resolution of other differences. Leaders should look for these small "win" opportunities because they create positive momentum, demonstrate that opposing parties can work together constructively, and build trust.[16]

Finally, leaders sometimes can ask people to step into others' shoes to help keep conflict constructive. At New Leaders for New Schools, a non-profit agency dedicated to improving education, the executive team disagreed about the strategy during the early days of the organization. As individuals debated two options, one executive worried that the opposing camps might get very upset with one another and have a hard time compromising at all. He proposed that the group favoring Option A should take some time to develop a memo outlining why Option B would be best for the organization. The group favoring Option B devised a memo outlining the arguments for Option A. This simple swap helped each group understand the other side better, and they managed to work constructively together to resolve their differences moving forward.[17]

Building Consensus

How do leaders build shared commitment and understanding? They must strive to create a fair process. What do we mean by that? Research shows that individuals do not only care about the outcome of a decision. They care about how the decision was made. They are much more likely to commit to cooperate in its implementation if they perceive the decision-making process to be fair.[18] Some managers equate fairness with "voice" (i.e., giving everyone a chance to air their views and ideas). However, fair process means more than letting people express their views. People want to feel that their views have been *considered in a genuine manner*. They dislike being presented with a fait accompli. If individuals perceive that a leader has already made up his or her mind before deliberations begin, they tend to become unhappy and feel their opinions were disregarded.

What can leaders do to enhance perceived fairness in the decision-making process? They must consider everyone's proposals and ideas in a genuine way. In other words, leaders must pay close attention to the proposals put forth by their subordinates and demonstrate that they have offered others an authentic opportunity to influence the final decision.[19]

What techniques can leaders employ to demonstrate they are truly listening to others' ideas? First, leaders must provide an overview of their plan to make a decision—a process roadmap. Second, they should refrain from stating their initial position. Alternatively, an initial outline of their view could be provided but make it clear you are open to other perspectives and options. Third, leaders must engage in active listening. They should ask clarifying questions, avoid interrupting others, and take detailed notes as people express their views. Leaders should summarize what they have heard and repeat it back to the group to ensure that they have understood key arguments accurately. Finally, leaders should explain the rationale for their decisions. They should explain the criteria used for selecting the decision among various alternatives and should describe how and why they incorporated others' input. They might also explain why they may have chosen not to follow particular input. These steps all make the process more fair, and as a result, increase shared buy-in for key decisions.

Questions, Not Answers

Peter Drucker, author and educator, once said, "The most common source of mistakes in management decisions is the emphasis on finding the right answer rather than the right question."[20] For leaders to be successful, they must ask the difficult, probing questions to gather all the important facts and opinions before making a decision. Sometimes, leaders will not even recognize all the right questions to ask, so their advisers may need to question one another in a constructive manner. For this reason, leaders should not simply focus on the content of a decision—they must consider how to design a high quality decision-making process, in which their advisers can engage in a vigorous give-and-take discussion. Leaders must work hard to keep that conflict constructive, as well as to show that they are truly listening to others' views. Throughout the decision-making process, leaders should keep in mind the advice of Cyrus the Great, who once described the goals of all good decision makers: "Diversity in counsel, unity in command."

Endnotes

1. Quinn, J. B. (1980). *Strategies for Change*. Homewood, IL: Irwin, pp. 13.
2. Roberto, M., Edmondson, A., & Bohmer, R. (2005). *Columbia's Final Mission*. Harvard Business School Multi-Media Case Study No. 305–032, pp.14.
3. Garvin, D., & Roberto, M. (2001). "What you don't know about making decisions." *Harvard Business Review*. 79(8): 108–116.
4. Hackman, J. R. (2002). *Leading Teams: Setting the Stage for Great Performances*. Boston: Harvard Business Press.

5. Sorensen, T. (1966). *Kennedy*. New York: Bantam, pp.346.
6. Janis, I. (1982). *Groupthink: Psychological Studies of Policy Decisions and Fiascoes* (2nd Ed.). Boston: Houghton Mifflin.
7. Janis, I. (1982). *Groupthink: Psychological Studies of Policy Decisions and Fiascoes* (2nd Ed.). Boston: Houghton Mifflin, pp. 141.
8. Wooldridge B., & Floyd, S. (1990). "The strategy process, middle management involvement, and organizational performance." *Strategic Management Journal*, 11: 231–241.
9. Edmondson, A. (1999). "Psychological safety and learning behavior in work teams." *Administrative Science Quarterly*. 44.
10. Roberto, M., Edmondson, A., & Bohmer, R. (2005). *Columbia's Final Mission*. Harvard Business School Multi-Media Case Study No. 305–032.
11. ABC News. (2003). "Final Mission." *Primetime Live*.
12. Grove, A. (1996). *Only the paranoid survive: How to exploit the crisis points that challenge every company.* New York: Currency-Doubleday, pp.116.
13. Roberto, M. (1995). *Why Great Leaders Don't Take Yes for An Answer.* Upper Saddle River, NJ: Wharton School Publishing, pp. 96.
14. Amason, A. (1996). "Distinguishing the effects of functional and dysfunctional conflict on strategic decision making." *Academy of Management Journal, 39*(1).
15. Ury, W. (1993). *Getting past no: Negotiating your way from confrontation to cooperation.* New York: Bantam Books, pp. 80.
16. Weick, K. (1984). "Small wins: Redefining the scale of social problems." *American Psychologist, 39*(1): 40–49.
17. Roberto, M. (1995). *Why Great Leaders Don't Take Yes for An Answer.* Upper Saddle River, NJ: Wharton School Publishing.
18. Lind, A., & Tyler, T. (1988). *The social psychology of procedural justice.* New York: Plenum Press; Kim, W., & Mauborgne, R. (1997). "Fair process: Managing in the knowledge economy." *Harvard Business Review*, 75(4): 65–75.
19. Korsgaard, M., Schweiger, D., & Sapienza, H. (1995). "Building commitment, attachment, and trust in strategic decision-making teams: The role of procedural justice." *Academy of Management Journal, 38*(1), 60–84.
20. Drucker, P. (1954). *The practice of management,* 351. New York: Harper Row, pp. 351.

On Best-Practice Decision Making

Paul C. Nutt

The Ohio State University

Introduction

This reading focuses on a series of studies that examined how organizational leaders make decisions and their successes.[1] More than four hundred decisions were studied—many carried out by first-rate managers in well-run companies. For each decision, practices used by the decision maker were documented, as well as key situational indicators and results. Decision-making practices were correlated with results realized, accounting for situational factors, to make practice appraisals. A first-hand account of events provided insight on why some practices work and others fail.

Failure occurred in half of the decisions studied, suggesting that failed decisions are a common-place event in organizations.[2]—in both the best and brightest as well as the more novice manager, working in both highly regarded and struggling organizations. Some of the decisions were discarded before an implementation attempt and some after a concerted effort; in both instances no benefits were realized. Motivated by the wasted resources and forgone benefits, whereas ways to improve matters were sought. Findings suggest that decision makers were not at the mercy of changes in customer tastes, financials, draconian regulations, or other situational factors that erect barriers and pose difficulties. Best practice was found to produce good results regardless of the situation being confronted.

Best practices are highlighted and failure-prone practices uncovered, illustrating each decision, such as selecting a location for EuroDisney; recalling apple juice at BeechNut; the Pinto at Ford; marketing infant formula to third-world countries by Nestlé; and building a new International Airport in Denver, Colorado. To fully appreciate the discussion that follows, review Table 1 for a summary of each decision as well as a summary of events that preceded and followed the pivotal decision.

Table 1 Illustrative Decisions and Key Events

Description	Key Events
EuroDisney Walt Disney had long-standing fascination with Europe and hoped for a presence there. Soon after a park opened in Tokyo to record crowds, Eisner, the current CEO, set out to realize "Walt's dream." Two hundred sites were considered, quickly narrowing possibilities in Spain and France. The French government provided considerable financial bait, offsetting the negatives of weather and the French sour disposition. Unfortunately, at the park opening, Eisner was pelted with Brie cheese. French intellectuals called the park Euro-dismal. The fiascos continued—correcting errors at record numbers made in the last park while failing to anticipate current issues. The Anaheim project failed to develop able land around the park. Orlando had plenty of land but underestimated hotel demand. In Tokyo, officials failed to secure royalties for Disney characters. The French debacle seemed to overcome all this by getting cheap land at bargain prices and government subsidies. Eisner underestimated short train ride from Paris, arguably one of *the* travel destinations—as a result, hotel occupancy was at 37%. Demand was influenced by costs and limitations imposed by Disney on picnicking and alcohol. Europeans wanted to see Americana in America, if at all, and not in France. Losses reached $1 million a day, ending Eisner's dream as a miracle worker.	• Realize "Walt's dream" • Tokyo Disneyland creates success • Commitment to land, hotel space, and royalties • Location in France • Cut ticket pricing • Allow alcohol • Permit picnicking
BeechNut's Apple Juice BeechNut, in its hundred-year history, had evolved into a mainstream baby food producer by portraying an image of producing all natural baby food. After the company was acquired by Nestle, officials were told to improve profitability. As part of this effort, BeechNut sought a less expensive apple juice supplier and obtained a contract with Universal Juice (UJ) at 25% below market. The Research and Development Director, Jerome J. LiCari, became concerned with the price so he visited their facility and found 55-gallon vats, but no mixing facilities. Samples were sent to a laboratory that found the ingredients to be unnatural, likely containing syrup additives. The information was presented to BeechNut's CEO, who dismissed the concerns and forced LiCari out. Processing Apples Inc. (PAI), a cooperative representing apple growers, hired an investigator who reported that Universal Juice (UJ) did not purchase apples. PAI officials met with BeechNut top management, asking them to join a lawsuit against Universal Juice. They refused. Company officials stalled to unload $3.5 million in inventory to developing countries—violating international law. Subsequently, LiCari heard of top management's deceptions reported BeechNut to the FDA, who then forced BeechNut to terminate "apple juice" sales and prosecuted its top managers for criminal wrongdoing. The CEO and COO were fined and jailed. The incident cost the company over $25 million.	• Purchase at 25% below market from Universal Juice • PAI suspicions or LaCari's warnings ignored • LiCari fired • Not join PAI lawsuit against Universal Juice • Dispose of $3.5 million in inventory • Discovered by FDA

(continued)

Table 1 Continued

Description	Key Events
Nestlé's Infant Formula Infant formula was developed in the 1930s as a substitute for breast milk. Nestlé experienced strong sales of formula until the market saturated and the birth rate fell. In an attempt to boost sales, infant formula was sold in third-world countries with an aggressive marketing, but the company soon gained $300 million in sales. This increase provoked critics to voice concerns. A report called the "Baby Killer" claimed infant formula misuse was the direct cause of infant deaths. Nestlé's unaffordable prices (50 percent of a family's income) coaxed mothers in poverty-stricken areas to stretch their supply by diluting it. Nestlé responded by contending that new mothers unable to provide breast milk, supplement it a superior solution—animal milk mixed with water and mashed roots. Company officials refused to change their advertising, contending that ads coaxing the use of infant formula were just business and that they could not be accountable for product misuse caused by poverty. The controversy grew until the World Health Organization took note of a report called "Nestlé Kills Babies" and called for a suspension of third-world sales. A worldwide boycott ensued. Nestlé officials covered up the effects of the boycott, refusing to revamp the controversial marketing practices and continued to promote third-world sales for seven more years. Nestlé chose to fight the boycott until its industry association called for the adoption of an "ethical marketing plan" for infant products by infant-formula producing companies. Nestlé officials never fully adopted the code, believing they were unjustly attacked by critics with an agenda.	• Infant formula marketed to developing countries • Response to "Baby Killer" report • Assume critics have self-interest • Continue third-world marketing • Boycott initiated • Sue activist groups and fight the boycott
The Ford Pinto Ford's recall blunders have a long history. The Pinto, with its exploding gas tanks, arguably heads the list. The safety of the car was in doubt from the beginning when crash tests found 8 of 11 cars failed. The three that did not fail had the gas tanks fixed. Company officials rejected an offered fix of $2.35 a vehicle, $137 million in total. They decided it was too expensive because the cost of a fix exceeded the cost of paying the injured and their families, estimated at near $50 million for injury compensation and car value (as shown in court documents). Ford officials argued that a low-cost car could not be expected to perform perfectly; there was risk to owning one. Safety standards surpassed those in place when the car was manufactured. Company officials trotted out their motto of a "two-thousand pound car to two-thousand dollars" to resist a recall. A tragic accident occurred when three college girls in a Pinto had the gas tank explode, killing all inside. Lawsuits ensued, which made public Ford's economic reasons for not recalling the Pinto. The company dodged a huge loss in court with a technicality but company reputation was damaged for decades, contributing to the current sorry state of the U.S. auto industry.	• Gas tank test data • Dismiss the NHTSA investigation • Stifle employee concerns • Cover up of test data and misrepresent frequency of problem • Cost–benefit data • No recall • Fatal accident, vehicles recalled

Table 1 Continued

Description	Key Events
Denver International Airport (DIA) The inadequacies of Stapleton, Denver's airport, the sixth busiest airport in the country, included too close and too short runways—posing safety concerns and limiting flights in inclement weather. Pena, in his candidacy for mayor of Denver, saw an opportunity, calling for a new airport instead of a planned renovation. Ballot initiatives proved controversial, but after years of effort, the Denver International Airport was approved. Pena hardly aimed low, spearheading a state-of-the-art facility with a dramatic mix of architecture and technology, located more than an hour's drive from the city on land owned by his family. Contracts were arranged for Pena's family and friends to do key work and costs were misrepresented to make the project seem feasible. This increased airport financing cost when its bond rating approached the junk designation. Technology was faulty, leading to long delays for bags and inter-airport transport. Travelers grumbled about the delays and costs to get to Denver. The DIA's opening was delayed five times. The project came in at $4.9 billion, well over budget, which more than doubled the cost per passenger.	• Legal problems in Stapleton expansion plan • Pena runs on new airport platform city and country endorse new airport • Continental and United stop paying • New airport • DIA site annexed by county • Critics call for a vote—airport approved • Opening delayed five times

Pivotal decision is shown in bold. Cases based on: Nutt, P. C. (2002). *Why Decisions Fail*, San Francisco, CA: Berrett-Koehler.

Avoiding Traps with Best Practices

Traps arise when decision makers apply failure-prone practices, prompting failed decisions by[3] making claims without research, ignoring interests and valuable input, offering ambiguous directions, misusing evaluations, overlooking or ignoring ethical questions, and failing to learn. Decision makers in the EuroDisney, Ford, BeechNut, Nestlé, and DIA cases each make use of one or more of these failure-prone practices. Table 2 summarizes the traps and best practices that can dodge the traps. The discussion that follows demonstrates each trap and best practices, illustrating each with the decisions in Table 1.

Perform Due Diligence before Believing the Claims of Those in Power

Decisions commence when a stakeholder makes a claim about something that requires attention and seeks an endorsement.[4] The claim specifies what the stakeholder believes a decision is about (i.e., its arena of action). A trap is set when decision makers embrace such a claim to appease powerful stakeholders or cater to interests they represent, without uncovering other claims.[5]

   Eisner claimed that Walt's dream demanded a park in Europe while economics called for the location near Paris offered by the French (Table 1); Pena claimed a new airport was needed; Ford officials believed the Pinto had an acceptable level of safety; BeechNut officials claimed people bought their product so it has value in the market place. And Nestlé officials claimed their marketing practices could not cause infant deaths. Note how

Table 2 Traps in Group Decision Making

Failure Prone Practice	Trap	Best Practice
Believe the claims of those in power without due diligence to confirm those claims	Trapped by selecting a claim according to the influence of the claimant	Reconcile the claims of all stakeholders
Use power and/or persuasion to implement decisions	Trapped by social and political forces stirred up by a claimant	Use participation or intervention to implement decisions
Assume that ambiguous aims will result in desired results	Trapped by ambiguous or argumentative aims.	Make aims clear
Consider few alternatives that provide only minor modifications of existing practices	Trapped by limited search and no innovation.	Use resources to conduct search and promote innovation.
Apply defensive evaluations to justify favored alternative (that is often linked to an ambiguous goal)	Trapped by defending ideas and failing to document benefits and risks in realizing such benefits.	Document benefits and risks of several alternatives.
Overlook or downplay ethical issues	Trapped by treating an impending decisions as ethically neutral.	Uncover the values prompting ethical positions and align them with the values of critics to explore potential arenas of action and remedies.
Tolerate no failure	Trapped by perverse incentive of guaranteed success that encourages cover-ups	Show that some failure is inevitable and that blame is useless.

the claim has, or allows one to infer, a remedy. Eisner dictated the Paris location; Nestlé rejected any change in their marketing practices; Ford officials resisted a recall; Pena endorsed a new airport over a rehab of Stapleton; and BeechNut officials refused to join the PAI lawsuit. In each case, the course of actions was seen as timely and pragmatic by decision makers. As a result, there was no attempt to analyze the claim, to uncover competing claims, or to make the concerns behind each claim explicit—although gathering this kind of intelligence is often recommended.[6] Instead, influential supporters made a claim actionable.[7]

A claim selected in this way often leads to failure. Did BeechNut or Ford officials understand the concerns of insiders and other key players when they rebuffed a recall? No one asked about LiCari's motives or how BeechNut's parent company (Nestlé) would react to doing business with a dishonest supplier? Answers may have steered management away from dumping bogus apple juice on unsuspecting customers. By dismissing concerns about its marketing practices, Nestlé discouraged their staff from seeking ways to redesign advertising, such as calling attention to dangerous breast milk substitutes. Ford's top management was taken aback by the chorus of criticism from industry observers. When Eisner announced EuroDisney at a press conference he was pelted with Brie cheese. The fiascos occurred because claims ignored key concerns, posing questions about decision maker's motivations.[8]

Without clarity about concerns, the arena of action (the marketing plan, resisting a recall, a new airport) becomes suspect.[9] Was the EuroDisney decision about its location, the wisdom of a park in Europe, or investing in a park compared to another venture? Was Nestlé's decision about protecting a product, a marketing approach, or safe product use? Were the BeechNut and Ford decisions about limiting liability or protecting company image? Was the DIA decision about serving the flying public's interests' or bolstering Pena's campaign for mayor?

Failure is reduced when the arena of action embraces the claims (and concerns) of key stakeholders. This may include key company insiders as well as unions, suppliers, stockholders, creditors, customers, current and future alliance partners; supportive sister organizations, competitors, communities in which an organization operates, environmental groups, and the general public. Uncovering the concerns behind the claims of each constituency enhances decision maker credibility and mobilizes support. Stakeholders who see how decision maker arguments support an arena of action are more apt to be supportive. Momentum is created as word spreads to others with interests.[10] This also broadens the decision maker's views, suggesting other arenas of action and their comparative merits.[11]

Deal with Interests and Interest Groups Through Participative Decision Making

In failed decisions, position power was often applied to implement decisions. Implementing in this way requires either an edict (do this) or persuasion (do this because). Both are failure prone because interests stirred up by the decision are ignored.[12] Eisner and Pena's implementation approaches had the appearance of an edict. Edicts were also used by Ford officials to resist reports about the Pinto's safety hazards, by BeechNut top managers to reject joining the PAI lawsuit, and by Nestlé officials in refusing to alter their marketing approach. In each case, the edict provoked opposition. Even unaffected parties were found to resist edicts because they do not like being forced into a pre-determined set of actions. When using an edict, the best one can hope for is indifference.[13] Using an edict produces resentment and token compliance in the powerless and battles from others. Research shows that edict implementations failed in two of three decisions.

Persuasion requires that interested parties be open to rational arguments.[14] Had Nestlé officials meet with their critics, they may have exposed the biased contentions of key critics and avoided the seven year boycott. Pena and Eisner used the media to promote their airport and park and as outcomes suggest, such persuasion had no effect on interested parties with something to lose. Ford officials were not moved by the arguments insiders offered about Pinto safety.[15] Persuasion was not enough to coax BeechNut into joining the PAI lawsuit—failing in one of two implementation attempts.

When an edict failed, decision makers often resorted to persuasion; attempting to explain why a preferred course of action had merit.[16] Both Eisner and Pena tried persuasion after an edict provoked opposition. Eisner acted surprised as to what set off the French media. The company's plan to prohibit alcohol and picnicking as well as expensive admissions costs had created issues for potential customers. The media picked up on this as well as the financial concessions offered by the French government and concluded the park was a bad idea, leading to Eisner's disastrous press conference. Persuasion often appears to draw on tainted arguments when it follows an edict.

Social and political issues arise from the interests of key players inside and outside of the organization. They are apt to oppose a decision if these interests seem threatened.[17] To deal with interests, implementation should begin early in a decision making effort. If power can be shared, teams can be created by involving insiders and/or outsiders with key interests.[18] This promotes a disclosure of concerns as well as ownership of a conclusion. Another approach, *intervention*, demonstrates the need to act. Current performance is documented and credible performance norms identified. Using this information, key parties are shown the importance of the decision by collecting and managing interests along the way. Best practice uses participation when interested parties are localized, such as Eisner asking staffers for their opinion on how to use retained earnings, Nestlé officials asking insiders for the best way to exploit a potentially lucrative market, or Pena asking his subordinates for pros and cons of the new and rehab airport options. Best practice applies networking when dealing with influential outsiders, such as Pena meeting with United and Continental or community factions to identify interests and preferences or Nestlé dealing with the WHO and other influential interest groups.

Make Clear Expected Results and Delay Decisions Until Aims Are Agreed-Upon

Expected results were vague, misleading, or disputed in failed decisions.[19] This confused key players and squandered resources as remedies were sought. Using economic benefits to justify the Denver International Airport was misleading, if not an outright misrepresentation (Table 1). Major building efforts often oversell plans with bloated and unrealistic expectations, in the case in Denver. Ambiguous directions were also linked to failure. Realizing "Walt's Dream" appeared to be Eisner's aim, but this was never fully explained. Insiders motivated to make a profit found it hard to justify a theme park in Europe, or perhaps anywhere. People at Ford, confronted with ambiguity, inferred an aim from the Pinto's mission: A 2000-pound car for $2000 and a "safety doesn't sell" mindset. BeechNut decision makers did not make the needs for "cost control" (imposed by the parent company) clear to insiders—who failed to appreciate what was motivating top managers. Clarifying aims initially eliminates misunderstandings. Had BeechNut officials asked insiders to look for ways to offset inventory losses, insiders would be empowered to offer options, such as cost cutting or revenue enhancers. By keeping the aims imposed by their parent under wraps, BeechNut officials denied themselves access to such ideas.

In other failed decisions, decision makers embrace a quick fix, inferring desired results for its seeming benefits. Subordinates often view such benefits differently, forming differing impressions about desired results. Misunderstandings arise as courses of action were offered to deal with idiosyncratic notions of an expected result. The merits of alternatives are debated, not the assumed results prompting them. The ensuing dispute become a key source of conflict in decision making.[20]

To avoid this trap, decisions need to be agreed upon by all parties. This requires a move from thinking about solutions to thinking about expected results. Eisner sought a park in France—the solution was clear but the aim obscure. Consider profit, market presence, and image. Actions that produce profit, enhance image, and grow a market would be quite different. Lacking clarity in expected results, insiders had a hard time understanding what Eisner was up to and how to help. Best practice helps clarify aim before the search is attempted.

Consider Many Alternatives in Decision Making

Four out of 10 decisions were found to consider only one alternative and just one of 10 decisions was innovative. Pena latched onto a new airport to promote his mayoral campaign; Nestlé officials were determined to continue their marketing practices; Eisner was committed to a park in Europe; and Ford and BeechNut rejected recalls. When a remedy was plucked from a claim or derived from existing practices, no search was attempted. Nearly one-third of the decisions studied adopted the quick fix found in a ready-made plan, making search pointless.[21]

The allure of current business practices also limited search.[22] One in five decisions derived a remedy from minor adaptations of current business practices. Because past use suggested a field test, such an adaptation appeared to be cost-effective.[23] The business plan for EuroDisney was derived from the previous parks and, as observers note, was always one park behind. The Anaheim project failed to secure land surrounding the park and missed out on lucrative hotel revenues, which was rectified in the Orlando project. Tokyo had land commitments but failed to secure copyright agreements for the Disney characters. The EuroDisney plan secured land and copyrights but failed to consider potential park visitor's reactions to overnight stays, ticket pricing, alcohol policies, and no picnicking. As a result, ticket sales and hotel occupancy were less than half of forecasts.

Both claim-inferred remedies and adaptations of current practices discouraged search and stifled innovation, which set a search trap. This trap was sprung so often that just one in five decision makers conducted a formal search and only one in 10 sought innovative ideas. To dodge the search trap, make a commitment to uncover several options and at least one with innovative features. A search can be conducted using repeated solicitation, integrated benchmarking, and innovation. Repetitive solicitation sends a request for proposal (RFP) to vendors, when needs seem clear, and to consultants, when needs seem vague or uncertain, asking for ideas that meet specifications. Decision makers learn from the proposals and conduct a new search with more understanding of recent developments. Integrated benchmarking visits successful organizations to get ideas. Practices and procedures with a good fit to the adopting organization are identified and integrated to form a plan. A custom-made remedy requires innovation, which offer "first mover" advantages.[24] Multiple options were found to be both efficient and effective. Research shows the time to search is no greater than when a single alternative is uncovered and that the benefits realized more than justify the costs of search.

Document the Benefits and Risks of All Alternatives

Evaluation always follows a quick fix.[25] Decision makers strike a defensive posture, attempting to justify their favored course of action. After all is said and done, more resources are consumed in defensive evaluations than in all other decision-making activities combined. Eisner was eager to fund evaluations of the French deal to determine potential profits from projections of ticket sales, concessions, and hotel stays, but spent nothing on asking hard questions about other ways to make money. Pena knew the cost of the new airport but made no attempt to compare the cost and benefits of a new airport with rehabilitation options. BeechNut knew the cost of the inventory slated for disposal but did not pay attention to the warning signs. Ford knew the cost of a recall compared to projected litigation costs but made no attempt to assess the cost of negative public relations. Little was spent on finding less costly ways to fix the Pinto's gas tank until a vehicle recall was forced on them. The money spent on defending such ideas with defensive evaluations could have been better spent on seeking new ones.

Defensive evaluations are possible only if aims are ambiguous. Lacking clarity in the expected results, an *idea champion* can slant evaluations toward one-sided information collection and testimonials. Pena contended the DIA would create business opportunities for the greater Denver area and collected information and testimonials accordingly. Defensive evaluations find what the idea champion expects to find—offering shallow findings and predicable conclusions.[26] Bloated estimates and unrealistic forecasts often result, such as cost estimates for the DIA and forecasts of ticket sales and hotel occupancy for EuroDisney. The information collected is tailored to support what the decision maker wants to do, or must do, to satisfy others. Even when decision makers have the organization's interests at heart, such evaluations appear self-serving. More evaluations are mounted to deal with suspicions, prompting more doubts and more evaluations. This cycle of suspicion and evaluation grows until huge sums are spent, setting the evaluation trap.

To dodge the evaluation trap, collect information about the benefits of alternatives called for by expected results, as well as the risk of each. This kind of evaluation will be feasible only if expected results are clear. This makes defensive evaluations, carried out to support pet ideas, untenable. When expected results are clear, the only justifiable evaluation is to document the benefits of alternatives, and the likelihood of realizing them. In the BeechNut decision, an aim to minimize losses suggests an evaluation of disposal and no disposal options, which would call for determining possible losses inherent in selling the inventory to compare with inventory disposal costs, and the risk of each.[27]

Confront Ethical Questions

How a preferred course of action is viewed by observers often poses ethical questions.[28] When Ford officials stonewalled a Pinto recall, insiders were alarmed. Nestle management refused to alter its marketing approach, provoking consumer advocates to raise concerns. Pena brushed aside the DIA's cost and distance from its service area, prompting media scrutiny. BeechNut officials hid their motives for refusing to join the PAI lawsuit, which lead to a key manager's resignation. Eisner embraced the French deal without thinking about how a park would be seen by potential patrons. In each case, a proposed course of action posed ethical questions to insiders and outsiders. Opposition materialized when such questions were ignored.

Misunderstood values set an ethical trap. Automotive industry observers, such as the NHTSA and Mother Jones, believed a "profit drives principle" value was followed by Ford when officials refused to recall the Pinto. Ford officials saw the NHTSA, and other critics, as having their own agenda, validating their mission by dramatizing minor incidents.

BeechNut saw inventory disposal as unrealistic, given cost cutting pressures. To make this point, BeechNut officials postured to look like a victim, ignoring the prospect of being seen as a villain, should their actions be disclosed. Nestlé saw its marketing plan as pragmatic—while others termed them a "baby killer," contending it had no purpose other than making the company a lot of money. The values of critics and company officials were not apparent to one another. The ethical trap was sprung when decision makers did not examine the values motivating concerns and dismissed the questions posed—prompting whistleblowing by insiders and building contentious relationships with outsiders. Those who oppose an action are enticed to boycott products, as in the Nestlé case, and insiders are motivated to leak or to engage in whistleblowing, as in the BeechNut case. Even if such actions are avoided, there was a loss of trust that tainted future dealings, as in the Pinto and DIA decisions.

The values behind "ethical positions" allow decision makers to shift discourse from the lowest to the highest denominator. Ethical questions are resolved when actions appear to embrace common values held by key stakeholders. To achieve this, create forums for ethical questions voiced, allowing a forum for a decision maker to look for values behind the positions of a critic. If such values can be affirmed it is often possible to make minor modifications in a claim or a preferred course of action and have it endorsed. Had Nestlé officials affirmed the values of the groups that claimed their marketing was killing babies, they would have cut the ground from under them. Nestlé could have endorsed the values of human life and demonstrated how safe use of their product saves lives by discouraging the breast milk substitutes being consumed in third-world countries. A marketing plan stressing safe product use is apt to be endorsed by the WHO and other credible bodies, which would stymie their most vocal opponents. If this fails—offer mediation. Nestlé officials could have held town meetings to expose what critics were saying, looking for unwarranted contentions that could be countered. This would demonstrate a willingness to hear out critics, which would boost legitimacy. Companies with mediation win lawsuits involving whistleblowing. Companies without it lose them.

Promote a Culture of Learning Instead of Intolerance of Failure

Learning identifies decision making practices to avoid, and those to embrace. Learning is thwarted when organizational leaders insist on success. Because decisions fail more often than leaders realize, decision makers are motivated to conceal their practices.[29] This conceals information essential for learning. Eisner expressed surprise when EuroDisney revenues were far below projections, but revealed little about the flawed analyses. Ford officials claimed they were startled by litigation that followed a fatal crash with a Pinto, but said nothing about the gas tank tests. BeechNut said little about their contract with UJ. Pena singled out targets for blame and made design changes to justify the airport's ballooning cost. Nestlé ignored questions about product marketing practices.

To conceal, decision makers offset bad news with good news to sidetrack threatening questions. The cover-up is two tiered: the distorted good news and the creation of misleading information. The deception is "undiscussable."[30] There must be a cover-up to cover ones tracks. Actions that become undiscussable produce knowledge gaps required to understand why a decision failed. Ford officials presented the Pinto as a bargain and said nothing about its safety—again, actions taken to cover up safety concerns became undiscussable. Pena extolled the virtues of a new airport and said noting about cost overruns, design flaws, and the difficulties imposed on air travelers. Eisner signed off on EuroDisney promotions as losses piled up due to low attendance and few overnight stays. The lack of due diligence about cultural expectations and hotel use were undiscussable. Nestlé officials called attention to sales and brushed aside concerns about how their product was being used. Their approach to product safety became undiscussable. At BeechNut, top managers used arguments about acceptance in the market place to delay the PAI and allow time to dispose of the inventory—their motives were undiscussable.

The culprit here is a *perverse incentive* that requires success when some failure is inevitable. This makes it difficult for anyone involved in a decision to come forward with insights into what happened and why as decision makers in the cases take defensive action, saying nothing about practices and actions that contributed to failure. Such information is essential for learning, even it the task was a failure. To eliminate a perverse incentive, organizational leaders must demonstrate that it no longer applies. Leaders must show that they understand some failure is inevitable and that the organization's only interest is to determine what does and does not work, not to assign blame. After a "guaranteed success" perverse incentive is rooted out, a quest to uncover failure-prone practices becomes possible.

Lessons for Decision Making

We discussed the key principles and practices for successful decision making. A key principle was staying "issue centered".[31] using an exploratory mindset. Cooperrider and Srivastra[32] use the notion of a "mystery" to make this point. A decision does not pose a problem to be solved but a mystery to be embraced. The urge to "fix" something is at odds with the mystery, which calls for skillful questioning to get to the bottom of the issue.

A claim that captures the fancy of a protagonist is but one part of the puzzle. A superficial diagnosis of such a claim runs considerable risk of failing to find concerns that merit attention. Pause in the claim reconciliation stage with open meetings and other forums in which stakeholders representing various points of view indicate what they know about the situation. Have others gather to listen. Challenged those listening to reflect, seeking to make sense of what is heard. Ask participants to look for what is most appreciated and what has given life to the issue before doing anything else.

A pause to reflect suggests an openness in which answers are revealed and wisdom gained. Delbecq[33] suggests a posture of "indifference." The indifference is directed toward the action to take, not whether action is needed. Commitments are deferred to reflect, seeking insights. Judgment is suspended to gain understanding. To do so, decision makers must let go of desires for a quick fix. Dispel the urge to calm the chaos, stem the clamor for answers, relax the tension, and the many other pressures for rapid action. Realize that quick fixes are often motivated by fear, greed, or a lust for power. These anxieties are often present but usually exaggerated. Fears get amplified and greed and power needs remain unfulfilled because the quick fix is overrated. The recommended contemplation sets aside the quick fix until the true reasons for acting materialize and insights can emerge.

To preserve freedom of choice, decision makers listen and avoid hasty actions. A rush to judgment is also provoked by fear, greed, or needs for power. Confront each. Position "in the decision," accepting the uncertainty of not knowing what is best, agreeing not to screen out messages, and engaging in reflective listening. Adopt a coaching role by initiating exploratory dialogues with many stakeholders. This requires one to give up directing events, using prerogatives of power and control. Look for relevant interests and how competing interests can be reconciled.

As the decisions illustrate, the pressure to act can be intense. Pausing to reflect in the face of such pressure is difficult. When challenged to act remind others of the alternative. Ask them to recall the last time someone quickly found a way to "fix the problem with (fill in the blank)." Ask how many meetings were called <u>after</u> the fix? How many of the quick fix solutions turned out to be bad ideas? How many required retrofits? And, how long did all this take? Who got blamed and what did all that blame accomplish? Ask the critic to visualize the chaos, the squandered energy, and the smoldering resentment. Ask if it seems wise to spend some time to pause and reflect today to avoid all this chaos tomorrow? To avoid all this, stay issue-centered by uncovering and exploring claims and the concerns that prompt them. Such an investment today pays dividends tomorrow.

Endnotes

1. Nutt, P.C. (2002), *Why Decisions Fail*, San Francisco, CA.: Berrett-Koehler.
2. Nutt, P.C. (2010), "Building an Action Theory of Decision Making" in (Nutt, P.C. and Wilson D.C., Eds.) *Handbook of Decision Making*, Oxford, UK: Wiley-Blackwell Ltd.
3. The research methods are described in Appendix I of Nutt, *Why Decision Fail*.
4. Cyert, R.M. and March, J.G. (1963), *Behavioral Theory of the Firm*, Englewood Cliffs, NJ: Prentice-Hall.
5. Nutt, P.C. (1999), "Surprising but True: Half of Organizational Decisions Fail", *Academy of Management Executive*, 13 (4), 75–90.
6. Simon, H.A. (1977), *The New Science of Management Decisions*, Englewood Cliffs, N.J.: Prentice Hall (revised edition).
7. Also supported by work cited in: Cyert, R.M. and March, J.G. (1963), *Behavioral Theory of the Firm*, Englewood Cliffs, NJ: Prentice-Hall; Pfeffer, J. (1992), *Managing with Power: Politics and Influence in Organizations*, Boston, MA: Harvard University Press; Pfeffer, J., and Salancik (1974), "Organizational Decision Making as a Political Process: The Case of a University Budget," *Administrative Science Quarterly*, 19, 135–151.
8. March, J.G. (1994), *A Primer on Decision Making: How Decisions Happen*, New York: Free Press and Starbuck, W.H. (1983), "Organizations as Action Generators," *American Sociological Review*, 48, 91–102.
9. Pounds, W. (1969). "The process of problem finding," *Industrial Management Review*. Fall, 1–19.
10. Confirming conclusions offered by: Coch, L. and French, Jr., J.R. (1948), "Overcoming Resistance to Change," *Human Relations*, 1, 512–532; Cray, D., Mallory, G.B., Butler, R.J., Hickson, D.J., and Wilson, D.C. (1988), "Sporadic, Fluid, and Constricted Processes: Three Types of Strategic Decisions in Organizations," *Journal of Management Studies*, 26 (1), 13–40; Beyer, J. M., and Trice, H. M. (1982). "The utilization process: a conceptual framework and synthesis of empirical findings," *Administrative Science Quarterly*, 27 (4/5), 591–622.

11. Cooperrider, D, and Srivastva, R. (1987), "Appreciative Inquiry in Organizational Life" in *Research in Organizational Change and Development,* JAI, Vol. 1. and Kolb, D. (1983), "Problem Management: Learning from Experience," in S., Srivastra (ed.), *The Executive Mind*, San Francisco, CA: Jossey Bass, 109–143.

12. More detail on these finding can be found in Nutt, P.C. (1986), "The Tactics of Implementation," *Academy of Management Journal*, 29 (2), 230–261. and in Nutt, P.C. (1998), "Leverage, Resistance, and the Success of Implementation Approaches." *Journal of Management Studies*, 35 (2), 3–240.

13. French, J. and Raven, B. (1959), "The Bases of Social Power," in (D. Cartwright, ed.), *Studies in Social Power*, Ann Arbor, MI: Institute for Social Research.

14. Quinn, J. B. (1980). *Strategies for Change: Logical Incrementalism.* Homewood, IL: Dow Jones-Irwin. and Huysmans, J. (1970), *The Implementation of Operations Research*, New York: Wiley.

15. Denhardt, J. (2000), *Business, Institutions, and Ethics*, Oxford: Oxford University Press. Argyris, C., and Schon, D. (1978), *Organization Learning: A Theory of Action Perspective*, Reading, Mass.: Addison-Westley.

16. Churchman, C.W. (1975), "Theories of Implementation," in (R.L. Schultz and D.P. Slevin), *Implementing Operations Research/Management Science*, New York: Elsevier.

17. Interests are discussed in: Hickson, D., Butler, R., Gray, D., Mallory, G., and Wilson, D. (1986). *Top Decisions: Strategic Decision-Making in Organizations.* San Francisco, CA: Jossey Bass. and in Rodrigues, S. and Hickson, D. (1995). "Success in Decision-making: Different Organizations, Different Reasons for Success". *Journal of Management Studies.* 32 (5) 654–679.

18. More discussion of teams being used to manage interests can be found in: Downs, A. (1967), *Inside Bureaucracy*, Boston, MA: Little & Brown. and in Eisenhardt, K. (1989), "Making Fast Decisions in High Velocity Environments," *Academy of Management Journal*, 32, 543–576.

19. Nutt, P.C. (1993), "The Identification of Solution Ideas during Organizational Decision Making," *Management Science*, 39 (9), 1071–1085.

20. Nutt, P.C. (1989), *Making Tough Decisions*, San Francisco, CA: Jossey Bass.

21. Nutt, P.C. (2004), "Expanding Search During Strategic Decision Making", *Academy of Management Executive*, 18 (4), 13–28.

22. The dangers of limiting search are also considered in Pettigrew, A., (1985), *The Awaking Giant*, New York: Blackwell. and in Van de Ven, A., Polley, D.E., Garud, R., and Venkataraman, S. (1999), *The Innovation Journey*, New York: Oxford University Press.

23. Hart, G. and Bogan, A. (1993), *The Baldrich Prize*, New York: McGraw-Hill.

24. For discussions of first move advantages see: Damanpour, F. (1991), "Organizational Innovation and Preference: The Problem of Organizational Lab," *Administrative Science Quarterly*, 29, 392–409, Germunden, H. and Hauschildt, J. (1985), Number of Alternatives and Efficiency of Different Types of Management Decisions, *European Journal of Operational Research*, 22(2), 178–190, and Nadler, G. and Chandon, W. (2003), *Ask the Right Questions*, Los Angeles: Center For Breakthrough Thinking Press.

25. Further information on the dangers of misused evaluations consult: Mintzberg, H., Raisinghani, D. and Theoret, A. (1976), "The Structure of Unstructured Decisions," *Administrative Science Quarterly*, 21 (2), 246–275. and Langley, A., Mintzberg, H., Pitcher, P., Posada, E., and Macary, J. (1997), "Opening Up Decision-Making: The View from the black Stool," *Organization Science*, 6 (3), 260–279.

26. Defensive evaluations were also used in: McKie, D. (1973), A *Sadly Mismanaged Affair: The Political History of the Third London Airport*, London: Croon Helm.; Brunsson, N. (1982), "The Irrationality of Action and Action Rationality: Decisions, Ideologies, and Organization Action," *Journal of Management Studies*, 19, 29–44. and Pinfield, L. (1986), "A Field Evaluation of Perspectives on Organizational Decision Making," *Administrative Science Quarterly*, 31, 365–388.

27. Ways to formulate and analyze the impact of risk can be found in Nutt, P.C. (1989), *Making Tough Decisions*, San Francisco, CA: Jossey Bass. and Nutt, P.C. (2002), *Why Decisions Fail*, San Francisco, Calif.: Berrett-Koehler.

28. Ethics are considered in a slightly different manner in Bardaracco, J.L. (1997), *Defining Moments: How Managers Must Choose Between Right and Right*. Cambridge, Mass.: Harvard University Press. and Johnson, M. (1993), *Moral Imagination*, Chicago, University of Chicago Press.

29. Nutt, "Surprising but True: Half of Organizational Decisions Fail."

30. Discussability is described more fully in Argyris, C., Putnam, R., and Smith, D.M. (1987), *Action Science*, San Francisco, Calif.: Jossey-Bass.

31. Delbecq, A.L. (1989), "Sustaining Innovation as an America Competitive Advantage, " College Park. Md. Institute of Urban Studies, University of Maryland.

32. Cooperrider, D, and Srivastva, R. (1987), "Appreciative Inquiry in Organizational Life" in *Research in Organizational Change and Development*, JAI, Vol. 1.

33. Delbecq, "Sustaining Innovation as an America Competitive Advantage."

How Temporary Organizations Promote Dysfunctional Goal Pursuit: The Case of the 1996 Mount Everest Disaster

Kimberly D. Elsbach
University of California, Davis

Markus Hällgren
Umeå University, Sweden

"In the context of the altitude, the setting, I'm reasonably comfortable." Hall answered, doing his best not to alarm her. (Rob Hall, dying at Mount Everest, over a satellite phone to his pregnant wife) (Krakauer, 1997: 234)

Prior to becoming stranded in the Death Zone (above 8000 meters), Rob Hall and others served as expedition leaders and guides to clients striving to the summit of Mount Everest. The reasons for being stranded have been described as a case of escalating commitment to a failing course of action.[1] This mean a process in which resources are continually poured into an obviously failing project despite evidence that such investments are not improving the outcome.[2] This process occurs, for example, when work continues on development of a software program despite feedback that the chosen design will not work, or in the Everest case, when climbers continue, or are pushed to continue toward the summit, despite feeling extreme fatigue, encountering dangerous weather, missing deadlines along the way to reaching the summit, and eventually ending with the death of eight climbers. In traditional organizations, escalating commitment is found to contribute to continued support for money-losing ventures.[3]

As we will explain below, this escalating behavior may have resulted, at least in part, from the fact that the expedition team was a "temporary organization" (i.e., an organization that is constructed to meet a specific goal but is disbanded once the goal was achieved), that became focused, single-mindedly, on achieving a pre-defined goal.[4] In traditional industries, temporary organizations might include movie film crews or corporate project groups (i.e., collectives that are designed to complete a single, pre-defined project by a set date and are disbanded once that goal is achieved). In guided mountaineering companies, reaching the summit and back alive is the goal of an expedition (i.e., the temporary organization), which is constructed from climbers, guides, and Sherpas (those who carry gear, food, and often break trail), and is disbanded after the team returns to base camp.

In the case of the Mount Everest disaster, we will explain how the pre-defined goal of reaching the summit led members of two climbing teams to make poor decisions and to escalate their commitment to this failing course of action. We then use this case to illustrate how leaders of temporary organizations may avoid disastrous decisions by minimizing their propensity toward dysfunctional goal pursuit.

Temporary Organizations and Dysfunctional Goal Pursuit

Temporary organizations are usually defined by both time and goals. First, *time is a significant factor* because of the assumption that the organization will dissolve at some point—when resources end, when the goal is reached, or when the deadline is met. In contrast to permanent organizations where long-term survival and superior performance are the main concerns,[5] temporary organizations are constantly focused on time, and in particular, how much time they have to work with before they meet their deadline. This understanding of time as a feature that results in the end of work *creates an action-oriented type of organization that is focused on task execution* in which *reaching the goal is its raison d'être (reason for being)*.

In addition, the nature of goals in temporary organizations is often distinct from the nature of goals in permanent organizations. Permanent organizations typically have significant time to develop goals, as well as a long history of past goal development to consider, prior to attempting to achieve them. As a result, in permanent organizations, goals are relatively well-developed and clear prior to launching projects to achieve them. By contrast, in temporary organizations, *goals often become clearer within a short time frame as their attainment becomes closer*. Take, for example, a movie film project. Such projects often have loosely defined end goals, even if there is a clear script in hand. As filming progresses and the story develops in the minds of the director and actors, the end goal becomes clearer.[6] Thus, the end goal may not be clearly understood until very near the end of the project.

The combination of focusing on time and goal achievement and on the potential emergent nature of end goals helps explain why temporary organizations may produce escalating commitment. Specifically, these dimensions of temporary organizations may cause leaders to: (1) associate their own personal value and success with achievement of pre-determined and advertised goals, (2) limit their consideration of alternative courses of action not associated with a pre-determined goal, and (3) resist alterations to goal definitions as they approach what they perceive to be the "end" of the project. These three processes of "dysfunctional goal pursuit" in the context of the Mount Everest disaster are described next and will illustrate how they contributed to leaders' escalating commitment to a failing course of action.

Leaders Strongly Associate with Pre-defined Goals

Temporary organizations, such as a project team constructed to design a new tablet computer, often predetermine and communicate specific goals in highly visible ways (e.g., through organizational advertising and promotional materials). Meanwhile the organizational leader (often a project manager) is identified as personally responsible for achieving those goals. The success or failure of the project is thus tightly linked to one person and could influence the career path of that individual.[7] If the project is a success, the leader may receive accolades that promote his or her career, but if the project is a failure, the leader's career could take a negative turn. The tight linking of goal achievement to leader success means individual leaders may take unusual risks to achieve a pre-determined goal, or choose to continue to pursue a goal even when there is evidence that success has a low-probability—which was the scenario on Mount Everest.

Prior to the Mount Everest disaster, there had been a growing commercialization of guided mountaineering companies that helped clients climb, often otherwise unattainable mountains such as Mount Everest, for a fee. One of these companies in the early 1990s was 'Adventure Consultants' founded by guide Rob Hall and (the late) Gary Ball. In 1996, the commercial mountaineering competition among companies became even fiercer with the founding of the charismatic guide, Scott Fischer's, company 'Mountain Madness'.

In the spring of 1996, both Hall's and Fischer's companies launched expeditions to climb Mount Everest. Fischer's expedition consisted of three guides, eight clients, and seven climbing Sherpas, in addition to non-climbing personnel stationed at the base camp (positioned low on the mountain where the expedition began). Three of the clients had attempted the climb before and failed, for the other five it was the first attempt at a summit over 8000 meters. Hall's team had a similar level of experience and consisted of three guides, eight clients, and eight climbing Sherpas. Several of the climbers on Hall's team had the goal of being the "firsts"—for example, one was attempting to be the first Scandinavian woman to summit Mount Everest while another was trying to be the first climber to summit the seven highest peaks on seven different continents. The guides on both expeditions were accomplished mountaineers, as were the Sherpas, who had collectively achieved many successful summits of Mt. Everest and other demanding 8000-meter peaks.

For Hall, that year meant defending and improving his market position from previous years (in terms of summit–client ratio, 1995 had been unsuccessful). For Fischer, as a first-year entrepreneur, it meant positioning his company as Hall's main competitor for clients and ensuring a steady flow of income in future years. For both leaders, then, a successful year was defined as getting as many climbers to the summit of Mount Everest as possible (a goal that was supported by the climbers themselves). Achieving that goal would allow Hall and Fischer to finance future commercial climbs with clients and to finance their own climbs without clients. This goal would also enhance both leaders' careers and their firms' reputations. The focus on their goal of summiting clients was further accentuated by technological developments that allowed for continuous media coverage of the expeditions, including the Internet forum *Outside Online* (www.outsideonline.com) as well as climbers on the expedition providing media coverage for *NBC Interactive Media* (Sandy Hall Pittman) and for the periodical *Outside Magazine* (Jon Krakauer).

Together, these factors made the goal of getting all clients to the summit of Mount Everest highly visible and tightly linked to the expedition leaders. As a result, when weather conditions worsened and their teams fell behind in their climbing attempts, both Hall and Fischer continued to push clients toward the summit. Perhaps if they had not been so visibly linked to the single goal of summiting, Hall and Fischer may have felt less pressure to achieve this goal in the context of the poor weather conditions.

At the same time, this association of the pre-defined goal of summiting was only one of the aspects of the expedition that contributed to their escalating commitment. A second aspect, described below, is that alternative goals (i.e., other than getting all clients to the summit) were not considered at the outset or during the course of the expedition.

Initial Goals Lock Activities to One Alternative

The longer into a temporary organization project execution, the more resources are consumed.[8] What is usually not considered is that the longer into a project timeline, less alternative paths there are to consider. This outcome often begins in the beginning with the dismissal of alternatives. In the tablet computer development project, for example, resources may be allocated to allow for different options at the start of the project (e.g., whether or not to include a separate keyboard). This initial limitation locks the considered actions into a situation where alternative paths, having been rejected in the beginning, are less likely to reoccur later in the project. As a result, leaders make only small alterations to the design at later stages of a project and have difficulty abandoning completely, the single alternative in which they have invested, and are left with no choice but to move forward.

In the 1996 expeditions, every decision by the leaders at the beginning of the expedition was associated with rejection of alternative goals that may have been considered later (e.g., summiting with only some of the climbers). For example, when the expedition started, it was decided that pushing for the summit would have to happen at a specified time given there was only a short weather window available for summit attempts around the 1st of May. Because of the large number of expeditions on the mountain that year, it was decided that Hall and Fischer would make the first attempt with the other expeditions following some days after. Once they initiated their summit push, the prediction of poor weather in the coming days, the high number of other climbers on the mountain waiting to attempt summits, declining resources, and the energy levels of their expedition climbers effectively cancelled any future attempts for Hall and Fischer. Summiting at this one time became the only alternative they had, with no other options considered or planned for. Thus, when Hall and Fischer did not progress as quickly as planned and encountered bad weather high on the mountain, they could not consider turning back. Turning back would have meant planning for extra days on the mountain and perhaps, an additional summit attempt. Neither Hall's nor Fischer's plans had included these alternatives.

As a result, both expeditions started the summit push around midnight on May 1, 1996. Ideally, this would have allowed the climbers to summit around the relatively safe time window of noon to 2 P.M. Yet, the weather conditions became worse as the climb progressed, and eventually, two of Fischer's and five of Hall's clients turned around before or during the final summit push. Not considering this course of action as an alternative, Hall "was profoundly disappointed that five of his eight clients had packed it in."[9] Hall and Fischer both continued their pursuit of their pre-defined goal and summited at 3:40 P.M., long after the "safe" summit window.

These findings show how Hall and Fischer became fixated on a single goal, and how their early planning based on this single goal made it difficult, if not impossible, to consider alternative courses of action later on. In the next section, we describe a final, and related aspect of temporary organizations that further contributed to the leaders' inability to change direction late in the expeditions (i.e., the non-negotiable nature of pre-determined goals as reaching them becomes closer).

Goals Become Non-Negotiable as We Get Closer to Achieving Them

In temporary organizations, the focus on time increases devotion to a pre-defined goal as achieving that goal gets closer. In addition, the closer the leaders get to reaching the goal, the easier the goal is to clearly define and the harder it is to negotiate what the results are—further locking the activities into one interpretation. In the tablet computer project example, it may be necessary to delay goal definition, rather than choosing one solution immediately, because project leaders don't know how things will work until they try them in a prototype. As the project proceeds, however, the most viable outcome becomes clearer and all resources are directed toward meeting that specific goal. At the same time, it becomes harder to argue for alternative goals since they are less clearly defined. With that, even more pressure follows to succeed in reaching the specified goal.

At Mount Everest, this lock-in effect was evident. Leaders became fixated on reaching the summit the closer to it they climbed. The summit represented a clearly defined goal and other options (i.e., turning around sometime before reaching the summit) were less clearly defined.

Ironically, only a few days prior to Hall and Fischer's fateful summit attempts, another climber, Göran Kropp, attempted to summit solo. He turned around only 350 feet, or sixty minutes, before the summit because he considered himself too tired to make a safe descent. Fischer's comment at the time was: "To turn around that close to the summit…that showed incredibly good judgment."[10] This comment showed how much easier it was for Fischer to consider alternative options when he was not in the midst of his own expedition, with his own goals looming ahead in a clear way.

After having reached the summit, many of the extremely tired climbers (guides and clients) of Hall's and Fischer's expeditions ran out of bottled oxygen. At the same time, darkness fell and weather deteriorated to storm conditions, and the climbers soon found themselves in whiteout conditions where they had no idea in what direction to go—and the cold was getting worse. The climbers were thus effectively caught in the storm above the highest camp without any shelter. At the end, 8 of 33 climbers that made a summit attempt, died during the descent from Mount Everest.

Summary: Dysfunctional Goal Pursuit and Escalating Commitment

Our previous discussion shows how three dimensions of dysfunctional goal pursuit (i.e., having leaders associate strongly with a pre-defined goal, having initial goals limit consideration of alternatives, and having goals become difficult to negotiate as they become closer to being achieved) may be common in temporary organizations. In turn, these dimensions can lead to disastrous escalation of commitment, as shown in the Mount Everest case. These ideas are summarized in Table 1.

Table 1 How Dysfunctional Goal Pursuit Occurs in Temporary Organizations

Dimensions of Dysfunctional Goal Pursuit	Influence from temporary organization	Example from Mount Everest
Leaders associate with the goal	The organization makes the goal highly visible, and thus, achievement of the goal becomes strongly linked to the success of leaders and their careers.	The leaders owned the guiding company; the company advertised their goal achievement success; media coverage contributed to visibility
Initial goals lock activities to one alternative	The need to achieve a goal in short time focuses attention on one alternative, and other alternatives are rejected and not planned for from the start.	The decision to push for the summit at one particular time made it impossible to plan for alternative goals, such as making later attempts.
The clearer the goal, the harder to negotiate its success	The closer goal attainment becomes, the more important that particular goal becomes in defining the success of the organization, and the harder it becomes to alter the goal.	As the summit approached, there was no room for negotiation about reaching it as a goal.

What Can Be Done?

Since the features of temporary organizations promote dysfunctional goal pursuit and escalating commitment, it may be hard to avoid these processes when working in such an organization. Still, there are ways of minimizing escalating commitment, even in temporary organizations. Before elaborating on some of these ways, it is important to mention that escalating commitment is usually identified in unsuccessful organizations. Where the same behavior results in a positive outcome, it is celebrated. Moreover, there are different reasons for why events turn out the way they do and these reasons are often debated. Events and processes are thus multi-faceted at best, and incomprehensible at worst, and psychological considerations are one of several possible explanations, including in this case.[11] That said, the psychological aspects of working in a temporary organization influenced goal pursuit by the Mount Everest expedition leaders. Learning from this disaster, next we offer three tactics for avoiding disastrous goal pursuit and escalating commitment in temporary organizations.

Give Veto Power to a Trusted Person Whose Success is Not Linked to Goal Achievement

As noted earlier, leaders are most often viewed as responsible for achieving the goals of temporary organizations, and therefore, goal pursuit influences their careers. To avoid being too closely associated with the goal, then, there needs to be an organizational culture that allows for failure and where the leaders do not invest everything in one option, such as a specific project. A way of achieving this is to divide the execution of day-to-day operations from the go/no-go decisions of a temporary organization and to keep a close eye on the leader. It is of course delicate to second-guess events, but in the Mount Everest case, Fischer and Hall could have maintained radio contact from base camp, and given a guide at base camp, whose career was not linked to achieving summit success—the final authority in halting summit attempts. This would have left the crucial decision-making to a trusted guide, with a lower stake in the goal attainment. This guide would have been less affected by goal pursuit and escalating commitment, and thus, been better able to halt the expedition.

Monitor the Attainment of Intermediate Goals Along the Path to an Ultimate Goal

Second, leaders of temporary organizations should insert intermediate goals along a given path toward an ultimate goal. If the intermediate goals are not met, the ultimate goal should be reconsidered. An assigned "devil's advocate" (i.e., an person designated to argue against group decisions) should be maintained to help the organization critically scrutinize a chosen path as intermediate goals are not met. At Mount Everest, the goal was clear and physical; to summit and get back alive. The loss of several climbers however, suggests that this singular goal may have been too exclusively followed, and that intermediate goals may have been needed. To avoid this problem, intermediate goals could have been established in relation to timing, for example, climbers needed to be at the Hillary Step (an important, technical part of the final push to the summit) by 6 A.M., and to the summit by noon. When these goals were not met, an assigned guide, perhaps at the base camp, could have helped the teams to reconsider their ultimate goal.

Define the Goal of the Organization as a Long-Term Vision

Thirdly, instead of defining, specifically, what the goal of the organization should be beforehand, leaders of temporary organizations may want to define their goals more vaguely and relate them to a long-term vision. Although such a vision may become clearer over time, it will still be negotiable during the lifetime of the organization. The negotiation about this vision should involve, not only those at the top of the organization, but those at lower levels. These individuals may be better able to offer interpretations of the vision based on experiences in the day-to-day operations of the organization. At Mount Everest, leaders could have emphasized the process of climbing the world's tallest mountain as the vision and goal of the organization, rather than achieving the summit itself. This would have left the summit as an option and not a distinct target. Comments such as "we´ve got the Big E figured out"[12] by Fischer and Hall, for example, emphasized the target rather than the process of getting there, and should have been avoided.

Conclusion

This reading has used the ill-fated 1996 Mount Everest climbing disaster to describe how temporary organizations may lead to processes of single-minded goal pursuit and disastrous escalation of commitment in decision-making. Because these processes are outcomes of the very nature of temporary organizations, it is critical that leaders of such organizations be aware of the signs of goal pursuit and escalation of commitment, and design processes and structures to minimize them. In particular, leaders should be careful about pursuing a single goal that is strongly linked to their own personal and career success, should monitor the achievement of intermediate goals, and should resist defining end goals too specifically at the start of an endeavor, as this limits later negotiation of the ultimate goal.

Endnotes

1. Aegerter Alvarez, J. F. & Pustina, A. & Hällgren, M. (2011). Escalating commitment in the death zone: New insights from the 1996 Mount Everest disaster. *International Journal of Project Management, 29*(8), 971–985.

2. Staw, B. M. (1976). Knee-deep in the big muddy: a study of escalating commitment to a chosen course of action. *Organizational Behavior and Human Performance, 16*(1), 27–44.

3. Mähring, M. & Holmström, J., Keil, M. & Montealegre, R. (2004). Trojan actor-networks and swift translation. *Information Technology & People, 17*(2), 210–238.

4. Hällgren, M. (2010). Groupthink in Temporary organizations. *International Journal of Project Management in Business, 3*(1), 94–110.

5. Lundin, R. A. & Söderholm, A. (1995). A theory of the temporary organization. *Scandinavian Journal of Management, 11*(4), 437–455.

6. Bechky, B. A. (2006). Gaffers, Gofer, and Grips: Role-based Coordination in Temporary Organizations. *Organization Science, 17*(1), 3—21.

7. Compare Kaplan, S. (2010) Framing contests: Strategy making under uncertainty. *Organization Science, 19* (5), 729–752.

8. Engwall, M. (2002). *The futile dream of the perfect goal*. IN Sahlin - Andersson, K. & Söderholm, A. (Eds.). *Beyond project management*. Malmö, Liber.

9. Krakauer, J. (1997). *Into thin air, 234*. London, Pan Macmillan.

9 Groups and Teams

Topic Summary Learning Objectives

1. Recognize the difference between a group and a team.

2. Explain factors that lead to effective groups.

3. Describe group norms and their development including the 5-stage and the 2-stage model of development.

4. Describe group decision-making processes.

5. Describe barriers to effective group decision making.

6. Apply content on groups and teams to organizations.

Key Terms

brainstorming, p. 314

common knowledge effect, p. 315

Delphi technique, p. 314

free-rider effect, p. 315

group, p. 308

group development, p. 311

groupthink, p. 315

heterogeneous group, p. 310

homogeneous group, p. 310

knowledge, skills, and abilities (KSAs), p. 310

maintenance norms, p. 311

nominal group technique, p. 314

norms, p. 311

peer pressure, p. 315

polarization effect, p. 315

psychological safety, p. 316

punctuated equilibrium model, p. 312

roles, p. 310

social loafing, p. 315

task norms, p. 311

team, p. 308

virtual teams, p. 316

1 Recognize the difference between a group and a team.

Introduction to Groups and Teams

Groups and teams are the basic unit by which organizations accomplish goals and co-ordinate work. They are often used to accomplish tasks that cannot be accomplished effectively by one individual. Most researchers make a distinction between groups and teams. **Groups** refer to a collection of individuals who may interact, but do not share similar goals or interdependence. Group processes involve interpersonal, social, and psychological dynamics that arise during human interactions. A group of people may gather together in the office break room each day and discuss sports or the latest TV show, but this group does not necessarily constitute a team. Members of a **team**, a specific type of group, hold interdependent roles and goals—in other words, members of a team depend on each other, must work together, and hold shared responsibility for specific outcomes. Many people know about teamwork from participation in sports teams, musical groups, or in a job. In a classroom, teams of individual are responsible for completing a class project, where each member of the team receives the same grade for the finished class project. Unlike a group, a team also typically fits within a wider organizational structure where all members report to the same manager, share a common identity, and hold relatively stable membership.[1]

Despite the many differences between groups and teams, both involve complex emotional dynamics. Membership creates ambiguity and often results in anxiety as members struggle to answer questions like the following:

- What role should I play?
- What is an appropriate level of commitment to the task?
- What is an appropriate level of intimacy between members?
- What tension exists over what members are thinking and feeling about me as a person and about my performance in this group?[2]

2 Explain factors that lead to effective groups.

In groups, three sets of factors relate to effectiveness: 1) purpose and type, 2) context and composition, and 3) internal factors (see Figure 9.1). The discussion begins with a look at the different types and purposes of groups.

Figure 9.1 Factors for Effective Groups

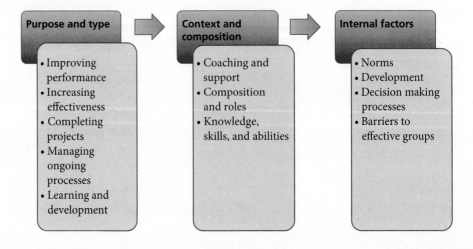

Purpose and type
- Improving performance
- Increasing effectiveness
- Completing projects
- Managing ongoing processes
- Learning and development

Context and composition
- Coaching and support
- Composition and roles
- Knowledge, skills, and abilities

Internal factors
- Norms
- Development
- Decision making processes
- Barriers to effective groups

Purpose and Type

Organizations turn to groups to accomplish tasks that are too time consuming or complicated to be handled by only one person. Organizations rely on groups to achieve several different types of outcomes, such as improving overall performance, increasing effectiveness, completing projects, or managing ongoing processes. Depending on the desired outcome, organizations might rely on and implement a specific type of team. Many types of teams exist: management teams, project teams, and production teams. Following are some examples:

Management teams conduct planning, policy-making, budgeting, staffing, and coordinating activities for organizations. Most management teams also share responsibility for managing subordinates. Executive teams and corporate boards are two common types of management teams.

Project teams, often called *task forces* or *short-term project teams*, share a specific, time bound purpose. Project planning and execution teams usually have narrowly defined goals and are single minded in their pursuit of these goals. An organization might rely on a project team for designing a new product, writing a new software package, filming a movie, or constructing a new building. *Action and performance teams* focus on conducting single performance events, require a higher degree of coordination, and require specialized skills due to the complex nature of the task performed. Cockpit crews, military and geographical expeditions, and professional musicians qualify as action and performance teams.

Production teams focus on production or operations of existing products and typically involve improving performance by increasing effectiveness and efficiency of ongoing operations within production. A similar type of team, called a *service team*, responds to the ongoing needs of customers and may include airline flight crew teams, customer services teams, and maintenance teams.

Some teams may fit multiple descriptions in these examples. In addition, individuals may be members of several different teams simultaneously. For example, organizations form *parallel teams* that work as a *short-term project team* at the same time, or parallel, with membership on a work team, such as the case with advisory committees and quality assurance teams.[3]

The specific purpose of the group will determine what outcomes the organization expects. For example, teams may form in organizations with the sole purpose to improve learning or the development of its members, with little regard to outcomes within the organization. Other times, teams form to help accomplish specific organizational goals.

Context and Composition

Groups almost always operate within a wider organizational context. For example, a student team operates within the context of a classroom; a production team in a factory; or a customer service team operates within the context of the wider business organization. The success of a group often depends on the types of support it receives from external sources within this context, because members themselves usually hold little control over external factors. Coaching and support are two external factors associated with success in groups.

Coaching and Support

Organizations can design systems and supports to improve the work of groups. Coaching, in particular, has achieved increasing popularity. Three major types of coaching exist:

- *Process coaching* improves interpersonal relationships between members.
- *Behavioral coaching* helps to change the behavior and assumptions of the specific members.
- *Developmental coaching* occurs when an intervention is tailored to the needs of a particular developmental stage.

In addition to coaching, groups often rely on other sources of support from their organization. Sources of support include reward systems, such as compensation and recognition programs. Organizations also support groups by increasing the degree of self-management, which is the degree of autonomy that the group has over its task.[4]

Composition and Roles

Composition describes the make-up of the group members. Research shows that when people understand their role in a group, innovation and ability to perform improves.[5] Diversity matters for group performance. Gender, education level, functional specialty, and age are some key characteristics for group diversity. A group can be either **homogenous**, where members are more similar on these key characteristics or **heterogeneous**, where members are characterized by a greater degree of difference.

Roles are another important factor associated with composition. **Roles** refer to the division of labor and skill among members. Roles relate to group composition as they describe the unique activity, competency, knowledge, or preferences that each individual demonstrates. While the list of potential roles that members can take is extensive, generally, roles fulfill either an internal or external purposes. For example, external roles can focus on managing boundaries between the group and its environment and internal roles focus on how the group makes decisions.[6]

Knowledge, Skills, and Abilities

One dimension of composition proves of particular importance: the **knowledge, skills, and abilities, or the KSAs**, of the members. Many organizations expect their employees to work in a group, but may overestimate the ability of individuals to successfully work together. Organizations may believe that effective groups simply emerge naturally, however, research shows that successful groups require members who hold knowledge, skills, and abilities associated with teamwork. In other words, the ability to function as a team member is itself a competency that can be learned.[7] Competencies that individual members can bring to a group include conflict resolution, problem solving, communication, goal-setting, task performance, planning, and task coordination.[8]

Internal Factors

The previous section described composition and context features of a group that may impact its performance. The next section outlines the internal factors that may increase or decrease performance. The focus is on the concept of norms and how these norms develop in a group.

Norms

Norms describe the patterns of interaction within a group, the specific 'rules of the game' to which members must adhere. There are many different types of norms and norms can be difficult to detect because it is often easier to observe individual behavior rather than the deeper patterns associated with group activity. With careful observation, norms can be observed. For example, do members show up on time for meetings or do they show flexibility about when members arrive? Other norms can be more psychological in nature—do members share authority or is there a power struggle within the group? Norms serve an important social and psychological function by setting limits of acceptable or unacceptable behavior, creating predictable environments, setting expectations for members, facilitating the achievement of group goals, forming a common identity, and determining the boundaries of group membership.[9]

Two types of norms exist. Interpersonal norms, often called **maintenance norms**, reflect the interpersonal psychological and emotional aspects of group life such as conflict, emotional awareness, and social interactions. One important interpersonal norm is trust. When team members develop a sense of trust, it becomes easier to bring up new ideas and share in ways that members will follow through with commitments. **Task norms** reflect aspects of group life directed towards work and accomplishing organizational goals. For example, one important task norm is the ability of a group to focus on task issues in a meeting versus engaging in too much interpersonal conflict that distracts from accomplishing the task.[10]

Development of Norms

3 Describe group norms and their development including the 5-stage and the 2-stage model of development.

Norms do not develop sporadically; years of research yield identifiable patterns in how norms are established, how they evolve, and how they impact group performance. Two primary models of norm development exist: the five-stage model and the two-stage model.

Five Stages of Group Development

Groups establish norms early in their life cycle. A predictable pattern of interaction begins to emerge within the first five minutes that a group comes together. Norms, however, change over time. **Group development** describes the life cycle and the process whereby norms develop and change over time in a progressive fashion. Perhaps the most widely known model of how groups develop is Tuckman's five-stage model of group development.[11] Groups and also, specifically, teams need to progress through stages of development to perform at their best. Development involves a relatively predictable sequence of changes in group norms. Each stage presents the group with a challenge. When the group successfully works through each challenge, the group then can move onto a progressively more challenging stage. Note that the following stages must occur in progression from first to last:

1. In the first stage, called the *forming* stage, the group works through issues of dependency and ambiguity. Behavior is polite and conflict is avoided or held to a minimum. Members begin to consider the capabilities and personalities of each group member as individuals search for their place in the group.

2. In the *storming* stage, group members begin negotiating for authority and dealing with conflict. Conflict may become pronounced as members seek an acceptable level of conflict. The storming stage marks an important developmental milestone because as the group successfully moves through storming, the group's members learn to deal with conflict. Some groups may never leave the storming stage, dooming the group to high levels of unresolved conflict.

3. If the group is successful at navigating the storming stage, it progresses to the *norming* stage. In the norming stage, the group begins to lay the groundwork for a productive work environment. Members mutually agree upon work procedures, interpersonal dynamics, and individual roles.

4. During the *performing* stage, which follows the norming stage, the group acquires the ability to take action on the agreed upon goals, begins to improve its working relationships, and can adjust and learn in the face of changes, obstacles, and setbacks. Once a group successfully navigates the first four stages of group development, members will accept individual differences; reserve conflict for tasks rather than emotional issues; reach a consensus through rational discussion rather than an attempt at unanimity; be aware of group dynamics; share acceptable levels of anxiety; and hold greater awareness of expectations and goals of other members.[12]

5. Finally, in the *adjourning* stage, group norms are characterized by the realization that the group itself will come to an end. The group often has a sense of fulfillment, pride, and or even euphoria as members seek to hold positive feelings about the group's experiences.[13]

The five-stage model of group development describes the psychological factors that impact group development and proves to be a helpful model for understanding how groups change over time. The five-stage model describes how psychological norms develop within a group. The five-stage model fails to fully describe the developmental process. One of the limitations of the five-stage model is that group development does not conform to a specified timeline. The two-stage model of group development better describes how group norms develop in relation to deadlines and other project constraints.

Two Stages of Group Development

The **punctuated equilibrium model**, considers how time constraints trigger changes in productivity.[14] The punctuated equilibrium model recognizes two primary stages of group development, which are separated by a midpoint transition (see Figure 9.2).

The first stage is marked by low productivity and the search for direction. During this stage, the members spend their time organizing themselves, working through potential conflict, and establishing work procedures. This stage continues through the entire first half of the project. A midpoint transition separates the first and second stage. The midpoint occurs at the halfway point of the project lifecycle. In this second stage, the group experiences a burst of activity as it redefines its basic process and direction. Behaviors become more task directed and behaviors are focused on achieving a higher level of productivity. This new level of productivity is marked by renewed vigor and inertia towards

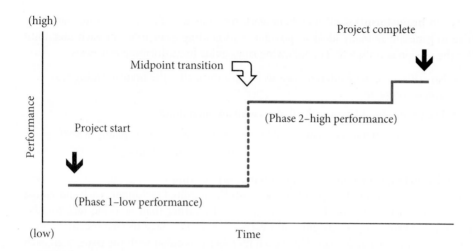

(high)

Project complete

Midpoint transition

Performance

Project start

(Phase 2–high performance)

(Phase 1–low performance)

(low)   Time

Figure 9.2
The Punctuated Equilibrium Model of Group Development

completing the designated task. In the final push towards finishing its project, activity accelerates as the group focuses on meeting external expectations and seeks closure.[15]

Decision-Making Processes

Group decision making involves generating different choices, choosing among these choices, and taking action. Decision making requires the group to coordinate among members to complete work, learn, and accomplish goals. Group decision making can occur face-to-face or virtually, mediated by technology or distance. Three decision-making processes are discussed here: brainstorming, the nominal group technique, and the Delphi technique.

4 Describe group decision-making processes.

Javier Larrea/age fotostock/SuperStock

When **brainstorming**, all members work together in a face-to-face meeting. They strive to generate as many ideas as possible, withholding evaluation for each idea until after the session is complete. The following rules guide brainstorming processes:

- No criticism can be offered towards an idea until after the brainstorming session is complete.
- The group should approach all ideas with an open mind.
- The group generates as many ideas as possible (quantity over quality is key).
- Everyone is encouraged to build upon or improve on each idea.[16]

Similar to brainstorming, in the **nominal group technique**, the group sets out to generate an idea or solution to a problem, but with the nominal technique, each individual member conducts much of the work independently rather than working face-to-face. The nominal group process begins with each member in a face-to-face meeting where they discuss the particular issue. Once each member is familiar with the issue, then each member works independently for 10 to 15 minutes to generate a solution or idea about how to address the issue. After working independently, members return to the collective setting where each individual member, in turn, presents his or her idea aloud to the group as a whole. During this time, the members discuss, refine, and build on each idea. The final step may involve a ranking of each idea before selecting what the group considers the best idea.[17]

The **Delphi technique** provides a more structured alternative to brainstorming than the nominal group technique, requiring more direct involvement from a group leader. The leader collects ideas, distributes the ideas to the group, and collects a response, usually through a formal questionnaire. The Delphi technique works well when membership is geographically dispersed but because the leader serves as the intermediary, the Delphi technique limits direct interaction among members.[18]

5 Describe barriers to effective group decision making.

Barriers to Effective Groups

Certain types of processes and norms foster improved decision making and lead to successful outcomes for groups. Psychological safety, conflict management, and interpersonal understanding help to improve performance, while other types of processes and norms foster poor decision making and serve as barriers to effective groups. Several barriers to effective groups exist. These include groupthink, common-knowledge effect, peer pressure, polarization, and social loafing/free-rider effect.

Groupthink

Irving Janis, a psychologist interested in improving decisions in business and public policy settings, noticed a trend in several disasters.[19] He reviewed decision-making processes in situations like the Space Shuttle Challenger explosion, the U.S. war in Vietnam, and the decision by U.S. President John Kennedy for the U.S. to invade the Bay of Pigs in Cuba. Janis concluded that in these and other cases, the groups advising the policymakers quickly moved toward agreement and consensus. At the same time, critical thinking in the groups disintegrated. Due to both perceived and real pressure from other members of the group, dissenting individuals, those that disagreed with the group as a whole, kept quiet and hesitated from challenging the dominant view point of the group. Janis called this situation, where peer pressure stifles critical thinking and groups move toward consensus, **groupthink**. Groups that fall victim to groupthink share several characteristics:

1. Sharing an illusion that the group is invulnerable. This feeling of invulnerability entices groups to be overconfident and anticipate that all their decisions will be successful.

2. Discrediting of opposing viewpoints without engaging in critical reflection of views counter to their own.

3. Justifying their action on questionable moral principles, such as the ends justify the means.

4. Characterizing all who disagree with their position as evil.

5. Censoring or ostracizing members of the group who do not conform to the dominant viewpoint.

6. Identifying someone in the group who will play the role of 'mind guard'—a person who seeks to isolate the group from opposing opinions.[20]

Common-Knowledge Effect

The **common knowledge effect** interferes with good group decision making. It describes the tendency of group members to share information that is already known by other member of the team rather than share information that is unique. In other words, group member unknowingly hold back information that could contribute to the group, but instead share information that is already known by all members. [21]

Peer Pressure and the Polarization Effect

Groups also tend to make riskier, or more conservative, decisions than individuals working alone—something referred to as the **polarization effect**. The polarization effect describes how peer pressure may encourage decision making that leads to decisions that are either riskier or more conservative than individuals making the decision alone. In a classic study conducted by Solomon Asch, he observed that when an individual group member feels pressured by other members of the group, the individual member of the group was more likely to conform to the group's opinion, even when the opinion appeared obviously wrong. This classic study revealed how **peer pressure** is an important factor associated with group decision making.[22]

Social Loafing and the Free-Rider Effect

Social loafing and the free-rider effect describe a phenomenon where a single individual or subgroup within a group exerts less effort and performs at a lower level than the individual would if he or she were working alone. **Social loafing** occurs when only a few members of the group take responsibility for accomplishing the work of the entire group, thus, certain individuals 'loaf' or exert less effort than others on the group.[23] The **free-rider effect** describes how an individual relies on other group members to do the majority of work, thus taking a "free ride" while other members carry the workload.[24]

Contemporary Issues in Groups and Teams

An emerging factor proving to be quite important for building group performance is **psychological safety**, the shared belief among members that the environment within the group is safe for interpersonal risk taking.[25] When a group has strong norms of psychological safety, the members stand willing to trust and respect each other in the context of the group. In groups and teams with high degrees of psychological safety, team members are more likely to tell other members about mistakes, express ideas that are different from other members, express multiple points of views, and challenge a point of view even if that point of view is held by a powerful person such as a leader or a dominate member of the group.

Globally dispersed groups, the impact of multinational organizations, and cross-cultural membership provide new challenges for the contemporary organization. For example, a group comprised of members from different cultures need to understand how to work together. A better understanding is needed of team learning—those processes by which teams gather, process, share, and take action on information as well as time orientation, how people perceive past, present, and future, varies across cultures.[26] Understanding how learning and time orientation may differ among different members can improve effectiveness of teamwork in a multinational context.[27]

With increasing globalization, a geographically distributed workforce, and unique work arrangements like working from home, organizations increasingly rely on virtual teams to accomplish work. **Virtual teams** use information technology to accomplish work. Not only do contemporary organizations rely on virtual teams to improve work effectiveness, they also contribute to cost savings as organizations can avoid travel and other expenses associated with face-to-face work. The concept of virtual teams has become popular as nearly 60 percent of all professional workers report working in virtual teams.[28]

Virtual teams often encounter problems because members have not met or do not interact on a regular basis. Psychological safety becomes even more important in virtual teams. Some of the problems encountered by virtual teams can be overcome by proper training, keeping a strategic focus, and preparing the team for the unique experience of working virtually.[29]

Conclusion

This topic summary presents three sets of factors that affect groups, including purpose and type of group, context and composition, and internal factors. Groups vary in the purpose that they serve the organization and the duration that they are needed. Various barriers exist that derail a group or team, but teamwork is a competency that can be learned, norms can govern effective behavior, and psychological safety can be developed over time.

OB AT WORK

TEAMWORK SKILLS HELP A TELEVISION NEWS PRODUCER GET THE STORY

Brian Weiss

When Brian Weiss took his first organizational behavior course, he never imagined he would put it to use on the job so quickly. As one of the youngest producers at Bloomberg TV, he produced a program called 'Money and Politics.' In leading his team, he relied on his skills as a news professional to make, gather, and deliver the news. The growing company often relied on young and ambitious college graduates, like Weiss, to lead their productions. At 24 years old, even in his short time as producer, he had mastered the complex technical and logistical side of TV production.

Producing regular television programming required more than just knowledge of the news, however, it required knowledge of how to build and maintain a team. In one case, Weiss pulled together a production team just a few hours before going live at a remote location. He hired a local camera operator, audio specialist and a lighting expert. He faced the challenge of making sure that his on camera reporter stayed dry as it poured down rain. In addition to his local crew, a remote team of technicians and producers sat in a production room in downtown New York City. Building a team quickly across a geographically distributed area and keeping the diverse roles working together proved essential to getting the story.

6 Apply content on groups and teams to organizations.

Weiss realized intuitively how teamwork contributed to getting his story on the air, but learning more about teamwork confirmed his ability to build a team. For example, Weiss knew that in the time critical television news business "there is no time to sugar coat words. I needed to express urgency and be forceful enough to be sure that things happened immediately." At the same time, he always knew not to "shout or make the team members cynical, or make anybody angry." Learning about teamwork in his organizational behavior class only reaffirmed what Weiss understood intuitively: that effective teamwork requires trust among members, especially between the leader and the rest of the team. At the same time, in a live situation, the broadcast culture accepts that "you might frustrate in the moment, but you can apologize later." So even if the team is frustrated in the short term, the team continues to function in working towards its goal of getting the shot onto television sets around the world.

Concepts from research on teamwork helped Weiss understand more clearly that the success of a team relies on two distinct, yet related abilities. First, the team must be able to effectively perform its task. In the case of the television news crew, his team needed to understand the complex technical aspects of live television news. Just as important, the news crew had to coordinate its skills, keep focused in the face of many distractions, and maintain good working relationships in the high stress environment of television news. Concepts from organizational behavior helped Weiss build and maintain stronger teams that lead to getting the story on air successfully.

Source: *Personal interview with Brian Weiss, 2011.*

SPOTLIGHT ON RESEARCH
Do Groups and Teams Share Common Characteristics?

Recent research suggests that groups and teams share some common characteristics. A team of researchers created an experiment where they asked 25 different groups to create an advertisement for a fictional airline. The researchers recorded the 40-minute sessions and then observed the team processes, keeping in mind the two development processes: Tuckman's five-stage model and two-stage model. The researchers paid special attention to statements that reflected task related statements. They found two types of task related statements consistent with the two-stage model, including action statements, such as references to how the team would accomplish their goals, when the team might accomplish a certain aspect of the task, or discussion of specific resources. Other task related statements included content statements about the ads themselves such as references to format of the ad, specific details, or how to present the ad to fictional customers.

The researchers also observed the team's references to various psychological processes consistent with Tuckman's five-stage model of group development. These were references associated with groups such as dependency and counter-dependency, as well as statements that suggested the group members were directly avoiding tasks or aspects of work that were critical of the task. Taken together, the groups made statements about the task, consistent with behavior in teams, but also made statements about psychological factors typically associated with groups.

After complete analysis of the team meetings, the researchers explained that both group and team dynamics exist in teams. The researchers found that, not surprisingly, the teams spent as much as 80 percent of their time on task related activities and far less time on psychological or social dynamics. At most, during any one time, teams spent no more than 25 percent of their time on psychological issues, and in most cases less than 10 percent of their efforts were focused on psychological issues. None the less, the researchers observed that many of the teams did change their patterns of interaction at the midpoint, just as the two-stage model suggested, but the teams spent much of their time before the first half discussing issues like leadership, work allocation, and flow. During the second half, teams focused more on the specific content of the commercial they were developing.

From this evidence, the researchers instructed teams to consider both group elements and team elements when working on a project. Early in the life cycle, the team can establish leadership, identify workflow, and determine process. Addressing the psychological issues up front helps the team develop a strong psychological foundation, which then allows the team to focus more directly on its task in the second half. Groups that fail to deal with the psychological dynamics in the early stages of group life may return to these issues as the project develops, wasting crucial time as the project nears completion.

Questions for Discussion

1. Why do you think it is important for researchers to distinguish between a group and a team? Why or why not do you think people in organizations should distinguish between a group and a team?
2. How might you apply this study to the workplace?

Source: *Based on an article by Chang, A. , Bordia, P. , & Duck, J. (2003). Punctuated equilibrium and linear progression: toward a new understanding of group development.* Academy of Management Journal, 46, 1, 106–117.

Pairing with this Topic Summary

Suggested Expert Contributions

Teamwork from the Inside Out—David Caldwell (Santa Clara University), Deborah Ancona (Massachusetts Institute of Technology), and Henrik Bresman (INSEAD, France)

Making Virtual Teams More Innovative through Effective Communication—Jennifer L. Gibbs (Rutgers University) and Cristina B. Gibson (University of Western Australia)

Teams in Organizations: 10 Team Roles to Foster Team Effectiveness—Troy V. Mumford (Colorado State University), Michael C. Campion (University of South Carolina), and Michael A. Campion (Purdue University)

Suggested Cases

Case 2: "We Are Global or We Are Nothing": Conflict and Cover-Up at ColequarterMaine

Case 3: EMERGENCY! We Need a Better Compensation System

Case 6: NASCAR's Drive for Diversity: Can They Reach the Finish Line?

Case 8: Conflict in Santa's Workshop: Learning to be a Team Player at ToyKing

Suggested Exercises

Exercise 16: Writing a Team Contract

Exercise 18: Team Performance Evaluation

Exercise 31: The Ethics of the Climb

Exercise 32: Mindmapping

Exercise 37: Team Survival Simulation

Exercise 38: FIS Simulation

Endnotes

1. Sundstrom, E. de Meuse, K. P. & Futrell, D. (1990). Work teams: Applications and effectiveness. *American Psychologist, 45,* 2, 120–133.
2. Bennis, W. G. & Shepard, H. A. (1956). A theory of group development. *Human Relations, 9,* 415–437.
3. Sundstrom, et al. (1990).
4. Hackman, J. R. & Wageman, R. (2005). A theory of team coaching. *Academy of Management Review, 30,* 2, 269–287.
5. Swann, W. B., Polzer, J. T., Seyle, D. C. , Ko, S. J. (2004). Finding value in diversity: Verification of personal and social self-views in diverse groups. *Academy of Management Review, 29,* 9–27. Polzer, J. T., Milton, L. P. , Swann, W. B. (2002). Capitalizing on diversity: Interpersonal congruence in small work groups. *Administrative Science Quarterly, 47,* 296–324.
6. Ancona, A. G. (1990). Outward bound: Strategies for team survival in organizations. *Academy of Management Journal, 33,* 2, 334–365.
7. Druskat, V. U., & Wheeler, J. V. (2003). Managing the boundary: The effective leadership of self-managing work teams. *Academy of Management Journal, 4,* 46, 435–457.
8. Stevens, M. J., & Campion, M. A. (1994). The knowledge, skill, and ability requirements for teamwork: Implications for human resource management. *Journal of Management, 2,* 20,

503–530. Stevens, M. J. & Campion, M. A. (1999). Staffing work teams: Development and validation of a selection test for teamwork settings. *Journal of Management, 2,* 25, 207–228.

9. Brown, R. (2000). *Group processes: Dynamics within and between groups.* Malden, MA: Blackwell Publishing.

10. Feldman, D. C. (1984). The development and enforcement of group norms. *Academy of Management Review, 9,* 1, 47–53.

11. Tuckman, B. W. (1965). Developmental sequence in small groups. *Psychological Bulletin, 6,* 63, 384–399.

12. Bennis & Shepard (1956).

13. Tuckman, B. W. & Jensen, M. A. C. (1977). Stages of small-group development revisited. *Group and Organization Management, 2,* 4, 419–427.

14. Gersick, C. J. G. (1991). Revolutionary change theories: A multilevel exploration of the punctuated equilibrium paradigm. *Academy of Management Review, 16,* 1, 10–36.

15. Gersick, C. J. G. (1988). Time and transition in work teams: Toward a new model of group development. *Academy of Management Journal, 31,* 1, 9–41.

16. Sutton, R. I. & Hargadon, A. (1996). Brainstorming groups in context. Effectiveness in a product design firm. *Administrative Science Quarterly, 41,* 685–715.

17. Van de Ven, A. & Delbecq, A. L. (1971). Nominal versus interacting group processes for committee decision-making effectiveness. *Academy of Management Journal, 14,* 2, 203–212.

18. Van de Ven, A. & Delbecq, A. L. (1974). The effectiveness of nominal, Delphi and interacting group decision making processes. *Academy of Management Journal, 17,* 4, 605–621.

19. Janis, I. L. (1972). *Victims of groupthink: A psychological study of foreign-policy decisions and fiascos.* Houghton Mifflin Company.

20. Janis, I. L. (1982). *Groupthink: Psychological studies of policy decisions and fiascoes.* Cengage.

21. Gigone, D. & Hastie, R. (1993). The common knowledge effect: Information sharing and group judgment. *Journal of Personality and Social Psychology, 65,* 5, 959–974.

22. Asch, S. E. (1956). Studies of independence and conformity: A minority of one against a unanimous majority. *Psychological Monographs,* 70, 9, 416. Bond, R. & Smith. P. B. (1996). Culture and conformity: A meta-analysis of studies using Asch's (1952b, 1956) line judgment task. *Psychological Bulletin, 119,* 1, 111–137.

23. George, J. M. (1992). Extrinsic and intrinsic origins of perceived social loafing in organizations. *Academy of Management Journal, 35,* 191–202.

24. Albanese, R. & Van Fleet, D. D. (1985). Rational behavior in groups: The free-riding tendency. *Academy of Management Review, 10,* 244–255.

25. Edmondson, A. (1999). Psychological safety and learning behavior in work teams. *Administrative Science Quarterly, 44,* 2, 350–383.

26. Kayes, A. B., Kayes, D. C., & Kolb, D. A. (2005). Experiential learning in teams. *Simulation and Gaming, 36,* 3, 330–354.

27. Zellmer-Bruhn, M., & Gibson, C. (2006). Multinational organization context: Implications for team learning and performance. *Academy of Management Journal, 49,* 3, 501–518. Rico, F. Sanchez-Manzanares, M., Gil, F. Gibson, C. (2007). Team implicit coordination processes: A team knowledge-based approach. *Academy of Management Review, 33,* 1, 163–184.

28. Martins, L. L., Gilson, L. L. , & Maynard, M. T. (2004). Virtual teams: What do we know and where do we go from here? *Journal of Management, 30,* 6, 805–835.

29. Rosen, B., Furst, S., & Blackburn, R. (2006). Training for virtual teams: An investigation of current practices and future needs. *Human Resource Management, 45,* 2, 229–247.

Teamwork from the Inside Out

David Caldwell
Santa Clara University

Deborah Ancona
Massachusetts Institute of Technology

Henrik Bresman
INSEAD, France

A New Challenge

Customers today are more demanding than in the past as technologies are changing more rapidly than before, and the business environment is now truly global. As a result, organizations are changing just to keep up. Today, it would not be unusual for a European company to have engineers in Silicon Valley and India work together to design a product that will use parts from around the world, be assembled in China, and be sold across the globe. And all of this will need to be done in half the time it would have taken five years ago!

The challenges that organizations are facing today are driven by three broad trends. First, competition is becoming more intense. New information technologies and low communication costs allow small organizations and companies in low-wage countries to compete with traditional, large suppliers in ways they never have been able to in the past. To successfully compete, these organizations need to focus ruthlessly on innovation in products and processes. Second, knowledge is expanding at an ever accelerating rate. Understanding and integrating information about technologies, customers, and competitors in a timely fashion is critical for success. Finally, firms must leverage their existing knowledge and products in new ways. Looking for new uses for existing products and finding synergies is crucial to developing the speed and efficiency necessary to successfully face new competitive challenges.

The upshot of all this is that what might have worked 30 years ago, or even 10 years ago, is not likely to work today. To meet the new challenges, organization structures, and even the look and feel of organizations, are changing. The idea that decisions should flow down through layers of management and a clear set of procedures and structures is sufficient to coordinate complex actions has been replaced with more flexible organization forms designed to enhance productivity and innovation. While executives still usually craft the overall strategy and vision for the organization, mid-level management is being thinned out as the specific decisions necessary to implement the strategy are being made throughout the organization.

One important way organizations have adapted to new challenges is through an increased reliance on teams. Teams are seen as having the potential to expedite decision making, draw information from throughout the organization, and facilitate innovation. Unfortunately, however, what has allowed teams to be successful in the past may not work in the future.

A Good Team Goes Bad[1]

Paul Davidson received funding from Division management to develop the second generation of a successful but aging software product. The new generation had the potential to generate large sales as existing customers upgraded, and also to attract new customers. Once the project was approved, Paul brought in 10 engineers to work on the development. The group vowed to develop a product that contained all the features they believed customers wanted. In addition, Paul had just finished a course in continuous improvement, and he and the team were confident that they could apply the ideas from the course to meet both budgets and schedules—something very few other development teams had done.

The team worked hard to complete the design, develop a prototype, and put together an overall plan, identifying all the tasks and setting achievable delivery dates. The team members were excited about the project and committed to the schedule; they agreed on a clear set of goals, and moved into full-scale implementation.

About a third of the way into the schedule, a senior manager in the company suggested that some new features be incorporated into the product based on customer concerns that had been voiced in a user conference. The firm was committed to the conferences and senior management stressed the importance, at least in part, to show customers that management was listening. Paul and his team, however, were reluctant to make the changes, partly because they were not convinced that the changes were really necessary, but primarily because they did not want to run the risk of failing to meet their schedule and budget targets. The team basically viewed the manager's request as an unwarranted executive power play while the manager saw the team as inflexible and unresponsive.

The team made token modifications to its project and continued developing the product, but within a few months two members of the team were laid off and resentment within the team grew. Paul requested that more people be assigned to the project but the request was denied. Deadlines were missed, morale on the team declined, and two more members of the team resigned. Finally, Paul left the company—feeling that he had no future in such an inhospitable organization. None of the other team members was willing to step into Paul's role, and the project continued its downward spiral.

Why Teams Fail

There is no single reason why teams fail. Textbooks on organization behavior describe a wide array of factors that are necessary for teams to be successful. Teams need a clear goal and the resources necessary to accomplish the goal. Team members need to have the skills and motivation to complete the assignment, and the group needs to develop an effective process for working together. Among other things, this means the team members must communicate effectively with one another, avoid disruptive conflicts, build cohesiveness, and agree on roles and responsibilities for getting the work done. Finally, a team also needs an effective leader who can both provide direction and keep the members satisfied and motivated. Generally, when a team fails, most people—including the authors of books on teams—assume that failure arises from something going on *inside* the team. That is, in some way the group could not work together effectively, and this inability to work together leads to failure.

No doubt, many teams fail because of different dynamics inside the team, but focusing exclusively on these internal factors can limit the ability to fully understand what teams must do to be successful. Think back to Paul's team made up of motivated, talented people. They considered customer needs and were committed to doing something few teams had been able to do. Paul managed to keep the team focused and on schedule. It appears that failure was not due to a breakdown of internal processes or Paul's lack of leadership; rather, the team failed because they were not able to adapt to *external* factors. For all its strengths, the software team built a wall between itself and the outside world—thus preventing the team from understanding how the environment was changing and the relative importance of things they were trying to do. Ultimately, this even led them to question the motives of people who disagreed with them.

Both research and anecdotal evidence demonstrate that successful teams must develop productive interactions with influential outsiders, both inside and outside the parent organization. A team may be cohesive by reducing conflict and meeting the objectives it sets for itself, but still fail if it is unable to obtain information and resources from outside the group and build off support from the group's work—that teams must effectively manage the cultural and strategic contexts in which they operate if they are to succeed.

Looking Beyond the Team

In the last two decades, researchers have begun to understand the importance of a team's building effective relations with outsiders, and to identify some of the specific things a team must do to accomplish this goal. For example, research found that group process has an external dimension as well as the well-established internal dimensions related to task and maintenance activities.[2] In addition to doing things such as sharing information that can help the group accomplish its task or providing support to one another to maintain good relations within the group, group members must also do things such as collecting information from outsiders. Contrary to most previous research, she found that success in dealing with outsiders was related to team performance, but that the teams' internal processes were not. Teams could develop very effective ways of working together and still failed if they were unable to understand the environment in which they are operating and building support from others.

Bringing the Outside In

Ancona and Caldwell expanded on this general idea that how a team interacts with outsiders will contribute to its success.[3] They showed that it is not simply the amount of communication a team has with others that matters, but rather the specific types of interactions team members have with outsiders. They identified three independent sets of activities—Scouting, Ambassadorship, and Task Coordination—that were related to the teams' effectiveness.

Scouting includes those activities that are aimed at developing a broad understanding of the technical, marketing, and political issues the team may be facing. Scouting represents scanning the external environment to identify opportunities or threats, assess customers or competitors, spot trends, and identify the "best practices" of other groups that might aid the team. The overall purpose of Scouting is to develop a broad understanding of what the team is facing. Failure to effectively "scout" the environment can lead the team to miss out on opportunities (for example, not using a new technology) or fail to see a threat (for example, another group is working on the same idea).

Ambassadorship represents how the team builds an effective relationship with the senior level of management in the organization. Some of the most important goals of these ambassadorship activities are to develop a clear picture of the overall strategy of the organization and how the work of the team fits into that strategy, and to obtain the resources the team needs to effectively do its work. If a team fails in these activities, it may spend time on things that are not important, never receive the support it needs, get caught in "political" disputes with other groups, or find its work ignored by others.

Task Coordination activities includes the on-going activities that teams use to manage relations with others, inside and outside the organization. These activities help the team make sure it has the support of others who will be affected by the project. Examples could range from coordinating schedules with other groups, to meeting with customers to fine-tune products, to negotiating with other groups for specific resources. Like Scouting, Task Coordination involves communication with other groups throughout the organization or even outside the organization. However, unlike Scouting, Task Coordination is much more focused; the goal is not simply keeping up with what is going on, but rather collecting specific information or resolving issues related to the team's work.

External Activities and Performance

How do these external activities affect a team's performance? Ancona and Caldwell studied teams that were responsible for developing new products.[4] Like many other types of teams, product development teams have to draw on many different sources of information. They need to coordinate with other groups if their work is going to be useful, and develop a clear understanding of what others expect from the group. And they need to get resources from others.

Ancona and Caldwell found that successful product development teams had a particular pattern of interaction with outsiders. Teams that engaged in large amounts of Ambassadorship and Task Coordination were both more innovative and efficient than teams that engaged in less of these activities. Scouting followed a different pattern. Although Scouting is a key activity for teams, too much Scouting or Scouting that is not combined with Ambassadorship or Task Coordination can actually be detrimental to a team's performance. For example, teams can become so focused on new information that they constantly change what they are trying to accomplish. Some of the teams Ancona and Caldwell studied practically became paralyzed by constantly considering new information. Any rumor about what competitors might be doing led those teams to shift their plans. An article about a new technology might lead these teams to reconsider decisions that had been made long ago. In short, these teams had difficulty making real progress because they were constantly changing decisions they had previously made.

The way these activities affect team performance is somewhat paradoxical and depends on who is doing the rating. When team members were asked to rate their *own* performance, the extent to which the team engaged in these external activities was not related to how the team believed they were doing. Rather, if the group was cohesive and worked well together team members believed they were doing well. However, these external activities were related to *independent* assessments of the teams' performance. This is important, because what it means is that team members tend to *underestimate* how much their performance is affected by the way they interact with others: some teams can believe they are doing well because they have an easy time working together but are setting themselves up for failure by not fully understanding what their project needs to do. They fail because they do not take advantage of market opportunities, they do not align with organizational priorities, they miss out on new technologies or they do not effectively collaborate with other groups within the organization.

Overall, this research and other similar studies lead to a number of conclusions.[5] First, the ways a team engages with people outside the team are related to a team's performance. Second, it is not simply the amount of communication that a team has with outsiders, but the nature of that communication, that helps the team perform well. Third, the optimal pattern of activities for a team can change over time. That is, what works best for a team at one time may not work well at a different time.

Explore, Exploit, Export

There is a pattern of necessary boundary activities that changes over the life of the team.[6] When a team is first starting, the most critical task is to explore—and the goal is discovery. For example, if a team is developing a new product, it must get a clear understanding of customers' needs, the capabilities of different technologies, and what competitors are developing. During this time, the team must appreciate how its product will fit into the company's strategy and how this product will fit into the portfolio of products the company already produces. The team must also make sure it has support from management that will ensure it has the resources it needs. Effectively meeting these challenges requires substantial Scouting and some Ambassadorship.

In order to keep moving forward, the team needs to shift from explore to exploit mode—from seeking information to actually making the decisions that move the project forward. This means that an effective team will reduce Scouting, narrow its search for information, and focus increasingly on fully developing its idea. At this point, acquiring resources and making sure the team's efforts are aligned with the strategic direction of the organization are critical. Although this seems like it should be "automatic," teams often have to devote a great deal of effort to make sure this happens. These Ambassador activities may involve providing detailed progress reports to executives, working to learn how the project is viewed by others, and identifying the things the team will need to get the job done. In addition, the team should begin working with the groups that will ultimately adopt or receive the team's product. This requires some Task Coordination.

Once a design is completed, the challenge for the team is to export its output, successfully transferring it to either customers or those in the organization who will continue to move the project forward. During this time, finalizing specifications, schedules, and new responsibilities is critical as is transferring the knowledge and excitement of the team for the new product or process. This speaks to the need for a high level of Task Coordination. Since the diffusion of the team's output will be easier if it is supported by higher-level management in the organization, some Ambassadorship is also called for.

Building an External Perspective

There are three things that a team leader can do to build an external perspective within the team. First, the leader needs to understand what the team will need from outsiders. Whether it is information, resources, or support, identifying what will be needed is vital. Second, the leader needs to put together a team that has the potential to acquire what is necessary. Finally, the external activities need to be managed successfully. This third step involves both developing a structure for ensuring that external activity takes place, and productively using the information obtained from outside.

Understanding What the Team Needs from Others

The first task for a leader is to develop a sense of what information and resources the team will need from outsiders to complete the job. Although the list of what is needed will change as the project evolves, beginning with an understanding of the outside requirements is important. This involves determining the areas where the team will need information, and identifying specific people who can provide that information for the team. For example, a team that is developing a marketing plan for a new product might identify a person who had worked on the original product design who could provide background that might not otherwise be available. The team might also identify key industry trends, and competitors that need to be monitored. Anticipating how the team's efforts will unfold is important in establishing areas where in-depth Task Coordination will be necessary. In the case of developing a new product marketing plan, the team will need to coordinate its plan with the people producing the product, with the sales force, and with outside advertising agencies.

In addition to making sure the team has the information it needs, the team leader also plays a critical role in structuring the team to diagnose what resources the team may need, any opposition from others in the organization, and who in the hierarchy can provide support for the team. This analysis helps build a plan for Ambassadorship activities.

Composition of the Team

One key way to develop an external perspective is to make sure the team includes members who can easily build links with other important outsiders. Two common ways of doing this are by selecting people who have experience with different functional areas in the organization, and by including people who already have well developed relationships with relevant outsiders.

Building a team of members who come from different functions, regions, or divisions will help the team understand the external challenges it will face. In addition, people from different areas can provide multiple perspectives for assessing the information. Reviews of research on teams suggest that this type of diversity is related to overall performance[7] primarily because of the diversity of knowledge and the potential for easier connections with the range of different groups within the organization. In some cases, of course, it may not be easy to bring people from different functions, regions, or divisions on to a team.

A second approach for managing external interactions is including individuals on the team who have already established connections or relationships with others outside the group. These connections could come from working together in the past, from common experiences in the organization, or simply from personal relationships. When individuals have connections with outsiders, the transfer of knowledge becomes easier.

The types of connections individuals develop with one another vary. Some relationships are strong in that they are characterized by closeness, reciprocation, and substantial time spent together. Other relationships are weaker and are based on more superficial connections in which individuals know one another but do not have a particularly close relationship. In understanding how relationships can help a team develop an external perspective, it is useful to keep three things in mind. First, if there is a strong relationship, people are likely to be willing to extend considerable effort to help each other. When the relationship is weak, people are likely to share information or provide advice, but may not be willing to provide extensive help. Second, since weak relationships require less effort to develop and maintain than strong ones, most individuals will have more weak relationships than strong ones at work. Third, individuals will develop different patterns of relationships. Some people may develop relatively few ties to others. Others may concentrate on developing and maintaining a small number of close relationships. Still others may concentrate on building up a large set of more superficial relationships at work.

Both strong and weak relationships can help a group build an external perspective. When members of a team have extensive relationships with outsiders, the team should be able to locate information and resources throughout the organization that may be useful. Even if the relationships are weak, outsiders can provide advice, identify information sources, and keep the team informed of events. Although these weak relationships can provide extensive information, the motivation of an outsider to actively help the team will be enhanced if a strong relationship with a team member exists.

The key points to remember are that an external perspective is enhanced when team members have extensive contacts inside and outside the organization, even if those relationships are weak, and it is especially helpful for team members to have strong relationships with individuals whose active help may be critical to the group.

Managing External Relationships

After developing an initial roadmap for external interactions and selecting team members, the challenge is managing those interactions across the life of the project. At the very beginning of the project, the major issue for the team leader is to lay the groundwork for developing an effective external perspective. Once the team begins its work, maintaining the external perspective through effective Scouting, Task Coordination, and Ambassadorship becomes critical. Doing this requires actively managing the team members' efforts and ensuring that information the team obtains is included into ongoing decisions.

The pattern of external activities will change as the group does its work. During the early—explore— stage, the key challenge is developing a clear understanding of the specifications for the project. During the middle—exploit— stage, the major task of the team is developing a prototype or initial design. The final—export—stage is oriented toward refining the initial design, finalizing it, and transferring to the end users. Table 1 outlines some of the things team leaders might do to maintain an effective external perspective in their teams.

Table 1 Maintaining an External Perspective

Early Stage: Explore	(Key Task: Developing a clear sense of the specifications)
Scouting	All team members High levels of scouting to understand stakeholder goals, competitive challenges, potential resources, and options for completing the work.
Task	
Coordination	Subset of the team Focus on identifying groups that will need to work with the team in the future or be affected by what the team produces.
Ambassadorship	Team leader and team members with communication skills to interact with top management. Goal is to understand the strategy of the organization and communicate how the team's efforts contribute to that.
Middle Stages: Exploit	**(Key Task: Completing the primary work of the team)**
Scouting	Subset of the team Less scouting than previously; focus on filling in the group's knowledge, testing possible solutions, learning from others who have engaged in similar tasks, and tracking relevant environmental changes
Task	
Coordination	Team leader; individual team members Task coordination is high, to develop shared timelines and negotiate specifications with other groups. Team members draw on networks to do some of this. Leader ensures that external links are developed and shared milestones are reached.
Ambassadorship	Team leader and team members with the communication skills to interact with top management Relatively high levels of ambassadorship to strengthen relationship between the team and top management. Providing top management with team's perspective can help secure resources and support.
Final Stages: Export	**(Key task: Transferring the work of the team to other units)**
Scouting	Little scouting is necessary.
Task	
Coordination	Team members Some task coordination to transfer output. Team members will involve other groups to ensure their support, and use their networks to build enthusiasm for the project.
Ambassadorship	Team leader and team members with the communication skills to interact with top management. Some ambassadorship to maintain top management's support, deal with unexpected problems, and convey enthusiasm for the team's work.

Revisiting a Difficult Team

Looking back at Paul's team, it is clear that much of its failure can be traced to lack of management of external activities. Rather than seeking out information directly from customers, team members relied exclusively on their own assumptions about what customers would want. They were confident enough of their perceptions that they did not see any need to actually check with potential customers.

When team members develop strong ties within the group, they may have a hard time developing relationships with outsiders.[8] In the case of Paul's team, by starting with members who had similar experiences and relatively few connections, and then focusing on building relationships within the group, collecting the critical outside information became more difficult. Paul may also have missed an opportunity to build an external perspective when the team expanded. The new members of the team all came from the same functional area, and Paul did not seem to consider the potential networks and connections they might bring to the group.

Another real failing was in not understanding the strategic priorities for the team. Paul and the team seemed to believe that maintaining the schedule was critical, while the strategy of the organization seemed to be focused on being responsive to customers. It seemed that Paul did not have the kind of interactions with upper management necessary to have a clear understanding of the company's priorities and how his team's efforts could contribute to those priorities. Finally, when the team received information from the outside that challenged their assumptions they became defensive, more inwardly focused, and ultimately suspicious of those providing the information.

Could this outcome have been different? The most likely answer is "yes." Understanding both the organizational environment within which the team operates and the broader external environment are critical for success. Although our focus has been on why a team might fail, there is a positive side to the story. In both our research and consulting, we have seen teams achieve exceptional results by combining an external perspective with good internal processes.[9] This is not always easy, but with effective facilitation and leadership, teams can do it.

Endnotes

1. Adapted from a case described in *X-Teams: How to build teams that lead, innovate, and succeed* by Deborah Ancona and Henrik Bresman. Boston: Harvard Business School Press, 2007. Paul Davidson is a pseudonym.
2. Gladstein, D. (1984). Groups in context: A model of task group effectiveness. *Administrative Science Quarterly, 29*: 433–442.
3. Ancona, D. and Caldwell D. (1992). Bridging the boundary: External activity and performance in organizational teams. *Administrative Science Quarterly, 37*, 634–655.
4. Ancona, D. and Caldwell D. (1992).
5. Bunderson, J. and Sutcliffe, K. (2002). Why some teams emphasize learning more than others: Evidence from business unit management teams. In E. Mannix and H. Sondak, (Eds.), *Research on Managing Groups and Teams,4*, 49–84. New York: Elsevier Science. Cummings, J. (2004). Work groups, structural diversity, and knowledge sharing in a global organization. *Management Science, 50*, 352–364.

6. Ancona, D. and Bresman, H. (2007). *X-Teams: How to build teams that lead, innovate and succeed.* Boston: Harvard Business School Press.
7. Williams, K. and O'Reilly, C. (1998). "Demography and diversity in organizations: A review of 40 years of research." In B. Staw & R. Sutton (Eds.), *Research in Organizational Behavior, 20,* 77–140. Greenwich, CT: JAI Press.
8. Reagans, R. and Zuckerman, E. (2001). Networks, diversity, and productivity: The social capital of corporate R&D teams. *Organization Science, 12,* 502–517.
9. Ancona, D. and Bresman, H. (2007).

Making Virtual Teams More Innovative through Effective Communication

Jennifer L. Gibbs
Rutgers University

Cristina B. Gibson
University of Western Australia

Introduction

Many companies are using virtual teams to bring employees together from different parts of the world. The rise of new information and communication technologies (ICTs) such as email, Skype, instant messaging, smartphones, collaborative software, virtual conferences, and now social media tools like wikis makes it possible for employees to work together across great distances and time zones. Some geographically distributed team members travel periodically so that teams can meet face-to-face while others never meet in person. Virtual teams are used in a variety of industries—they may be sales teams consisting of representatives for different regions or they may be software engineering teams or automotive design teams in charge of developing a new product or process.

Virtual teams are often used to make companies more competitive since they allow for team members in different locations with different skill sets and expertise to work together to innovate. Innovation is the process of sharing ideas and learning from one another by pooling their knowledge to come up with more creative solutions to problems facing the organization. In addition, virtual teams are flexible as they are often set up to work on a particular project and then disband when the project is completed, which means they can respond to organizational needs quickly as they come up. Although virtual teams have many advantages for companies, they also face challenges. Coordinating electronically can be more difficult and it may be harder to sustain interpersonal relationships and trust people one rarely or never sees.[1] Virtual teams may not live up to their creative potential due to interpersonal conflicts, miscommunication, or lack of shared understanding that prevents members from sharing knowledge and ideas. Simply bringing people with the necessary skills and expertise together virtually does not guarantee they will be able to work together to develop new ideas.

Virtuality and Its Influence on Innovation

There are several aspects of virtuality that influence how well team members communicate and how innovative they are as a result: geographical dispersion, electronic dependence, dynamic structure, and national diversity. We have found that these structural features tend to limit team innovation.[2]

Geographical Dispersion

Geographical dispersion refers to team members being located in different places. These locations could be different floors of the same building or different buildings on the same campus, or they could be offices in different cities or countries. We would consider a team whose members are based in the same office but send each other email to avoid a trip up to another floor to be slightly virtual, although much less virtual than a team that operates across several time zones and thousands of miles. Communicating across distances and time zones makes it more difficult to share knowledge and coordinate tasks. Since members are located in different places, they may be less aware of what those in other locations do not know and neglect to share or explain this information. Sharing this contextual or "situated" knowledge—such as information about local holidays, weather, culture, politics, and sports events—is more difficult because members often take it for granted or find it difficult to explain or articulate.[3] For example, a video conference between London and Chicago was delayed for 45 minutes because of a huge snowstorm in Chicago, but the London participants did not know why their remote collaborators were absent until they came in drenched with snow.[4] The lack of common ground among virtual team members in different locations also makes it more difficult to build trust and mutual understanding, as remote collaborators may falsely assume that team members in other locations are simply less reliable or competent rather than attributing their behavior to situational circumstances beyond their control. For example, given they were not aware of the snowstorm in Chicago, the London-based team members likely began guessing what had caused the delay, and may have assumed the members in Chicago were simply rude, lazy, or uninterested! Those assumptions were probably not true, but without information about the local context, people often "fill in" their knowledge gaps, and this can cause misunderstandings.

In addition, there are shorter windows of time for meetings in which all members are participating together when they are spread over different time zones, and meetings may have to be held very late at night or very early in the morning for some members. Team members at remote sites may be inadvertently left out of decision-making, or those joining conference calls at inconvenient times may be less engaged, making the innovation process less efficient and productive. For example, a product development team in the agriculture industry had a core set of members at the same location, but many of its extended team members worked remotely. In addition, the managers of most of the team members were not on-site. Almost all decisions were referred for approval through a complex maze of "hierarchical supervisors" who were located far away from the core. As a result, members of this team felt they were held hostage to slow micro-management, which hindered the spontaneous innovation process. All ideas had to be run past their supervisors and this was time consuming and frustrating, given they were off-site and in different time zones. Requests for support to Europe from North America, for example, were often seen as disappearing into a "black hole."

Electronic Dependence

Electronic dependence refers to team members' reliance on technology to communicate. Virtual team members rely on an ever-growing repertoire of ICTs such as email, teleconferencing and videoconferencing, smartphones, collaborative software such as

Sharepoint, intranets, and new social media tools like wikis and social network sites (such as Yammer and IBM's Beehive, now called Social Blue) to collaborate and share knowledge. Although these new technologies make it possible to communicate and conduct work across distances, if members don't see each other face-to-face in physical meetings or interactions, they may miss subtle gestures, expressions, or other nonverbal cues team members display. For example, in person, a team member can glance at his manager to observe her reaction to a comment made in a meeting, or gesture toward a list of ideas written on a flip chart.[5] These nonverbal signals, through gestures and body language, are absent in much electronic communication, making understanding and interpretation of meaning more difficult. Communicating electronically may also restrict spontaneous and unplanned communication, such as informal information sharing around the water cooler or in serendipitous hallway encounters. This may reduce the amount of improvisation and experimentation that takes place in virtual teams, since the creative synergy needed for innovation is more easily established when team members have the opportunity to meet face-to-face. For example, brainstorming, the process of sharing free-flowing thoughts or ideas immediately as they come to mind without evaluating them or analyzing them in the moment, can be difficult when members are not face-to-face. The difficulty in sparking a creative exchange of ideas using technology such as email, as compared to face-to-face, is illustrated in the following quote from a member of a team in the consulting industry:

> It is really tough working on knowledge creation over the phone and via email. A good example is this project. It is conceptual. We know there is something there, but trying to kick-start a conversation on that is really tough. The way I have done it is that Jack and I have been in the same office with a white board, to at least kick-start it. When you are introducing concepts—that is really hard to do over the phone. How do you motivate people when they aren't in the same room? I think it is so valuable to be there in person.

Dynamic Structure

Dynamic structure refers to how often members leave the team and new ones join it, and to how stable or changeable members' roles are. Rather than having stable membership, many virtual teams are short-term and project-based, or involve frequent member turnover through temporary subcontracting or hiring people to do specific tasks (often called outsourced membership). This poses challenges to innovation due to a lack of a shared work history.[6] Increased turnover among team members also makes it hard to develop strong relationships and trust among members who do not interact frequently. It is difficult to preserve the ideas, information, knowledge and ways of doing things that the team develops as members work together when members are always coming and going! Members may be reluctant to share knowledge with new team members because they are uncertain about their motives. Finally, lack of knowledge of what each member can contribute makes it harder to assign responsibilities and coordinate around novel ideas.[7] For example, relationships weakened by member turnover and conflicts due to changes in reporting structures can be seen among product development teams at a large manufacturing organization, where there was very high turnover. Team members reported that their coworkers sometimes left just as they were starting to understand the complex trade-offs involved in trying to meet the needs of the organization. Several teams had a large number of new hires, and training and mentoring were limited for these new members, creating tension between the experienced members (who had been with the firm a long time) and new members, and reducing innovation.

National Diversity

National diversity refers to the number of different nationalities represented on the team. Virtual teams may consist of members of a single nationality (e.g., a software team split between the U.S. East and West Coasts, but who all share U.S. nationality; or a global team of Germans who are working in different countries, but all share German nationality). Virtual teams often involve multiple nationalities, however, as they often span several countries. For example, Gibbs studied a global software organization headquartered in the United States with software centers in Brazil, China, England, India, Ireland, and Singapore; many of the software development teams were virtual and involved members from multiple countries.[8] National diversity may stifle innovation if not managed properly, as it may lead to conflicts and rifts among team members due to different cultural values, mindsets, and allegiances. Team members from different countries are likely to have different communication styles;[9] for example, Europeans and North Americans tend to be direct and open about their feelings and opinions even if they are negative, while Asians tend to be more indirect and avoid negative or confrontational responses in an attempt to save face and preserve group harmony.[10] Team members from different countries may also have different ideas of a team and how it operates[11] as well as different values regarding the best type of leadership, or what role work should play in one's life. Even norms around knowledge sharing are different in different cultures, which may impede innovation. This is evident in the following quote from a member of a global procurement team in the automotive industry:

> The major issue is probably cultural. In America, knowledge sharing is a lot more promoted. People are very open about sharing knowledge and work in these open cubicles…I'm from Europe, which is a little more competitive in terms of what you know. You feel like if you tell people what you know, then you are at a disadvantage. People are then a little bit more reluctant to share knowledge. They also think that if you share a lot of knowledge, then maybe your job can be taken by somebody else.

Finally, national differences often create subgroups that fragment the team and limit information flow, making it difficult to integrate team knowledge and innovate. For example, a team of Americans, German, and Chinese may split out into three subgroups based on nationality whenever there is an opportunity for free-flowing conversation. This is not necessarily bad. Within the subgroups, people are likely to share the same first language, values, and norms, so sharing ideas or chatting comes naturally and feels comfortable. If the ideas generated in these subgroups are shared in the larger team, this can help the team be more innovative.[12] But if the subgroups become competitive, suspicious or too entrenched, this can be bad for the team as a whole, as new ideas may never be brought to light and the team may find it tough to get anything done.

The Case of the Europe Connect Concept Team

Virtual teams that are highly geographically dispersed, electronically dependent, structurally dynamic, and nationally diverse may struggle to share knowledge and innovate. As an example, consider the Europe Connect Concept Team. It was highly virtual, with nine members from five different countries spread across six firms, four locations, and six subunits (e.g., Human Resources, Research and Development, Technology, Production, etc.). The team was set up among public and private organizations in the information technology sector to develop a new technology prototype for children, funded by the European Economic Commission. The team was a highly complex collaboration and in addition to being highly virtual, the project was loosely defined due to a lack of vision or clear goals. The team was splintered by differences in location, national culture, as well as functional background (researchers versus designers), which led to conflicts and poor communication that ultimately hampered team collaboration and innovation.

A critical episode occurred when the team was designing and testing a touchpad feature to be added to the prototype. The initial project work plan created a clear structure while leaving room for creativity, but each of the partners had different goals and interests regarding the project, and these differences were never discussed openly or explicitly. Early team meetings in the first year of the project were productive and resulted in cross-disciplinary learning and rapid development of numerous creative scenarios, concepts, and a model for structuring future work. Over time, however, the team became more focused on commercially oriented activities (such as developing a working prototype) and excluded other goals such as research and publishing by the academic partners. Concepts were not well developed, and decisions about which concepts to focus on were made without getting input from all of the partners. Team members became more cautious in communicating with one another, which reduced creativity. The team became further polarized into subgroups, and team members who were unable to attend all the meetings felt disenfranchised and left out of decisions made in the meetings. Some members believed that the communication in the meetings was too formal, which stifled open communication and creativity—one member said she felt like she was choking in meetings:

> I think at least there should be a creative atmosphere of openness. I feel... very choked. Because it leaves no room for saying things. Maybe it's because I wasn't there in the beginning and we have had this first year of doing experiments and I just wasn't there. I missed my chance. It seems like everything must be fixed, objective, practical and complete. And when I talk about something more like feeling, or "just try this," or emotions of the users, it's like, "oh no" or "we've done that" or "that's just not what we're into now." So it's this atmosphere where creative thoughts need to be developed. It's missing here.

When asked about discussion in the meetings, another member said, "Yes, there was discussion. But most of the time they were not discussions in which new ideas would come up. It's really two sides and it stays like that." The team ended up dividing the project up into discrete chunks by country location rather than collaborating, and certain usability problems remained unsolved by the end of the project.

Overcoming Virtuality Challenges through Communication

In the previous example, many of the team's problems seemed to stem from the way members communicated. From the start, the lack of initial discussion of goals and vision made it impossible for them to integrate their differing views and develop a shared understanding of how the project could meet the respective interests of the partners. Team members were used to different communication styles, and rather than openly confronting and resolving conflicts arising from such differences, conflicts were suppressed. Poor communication during meetings led to a "groupthink" mentality, in which there was a lack of open discussion, challenge, or feedback. Their communication did not produce the creative energy and debate needed to spark new ideas and innovation. Not all team members were involved in decision making, causing them to feel excluded and resentful. The information technology developed for the project, an Intranet, was quite effective in archiving project data, but it did little to create a shared workspace. Team members used e-mail to communicate with one another, but over time they became more likely to communicate "off the record." The deterioration of the group process, combined with pressure to meet real deadlines, contributed to members focusing on just getting the task done with little collaboration and creative knowledge sharing.

A psychologically safe communication climate can help overcome the negative effects of working virtually and enable teams to be more innovative.[13] We define a *psychologically safe communication climate* as an environment characterized by support, trust, openness, mutual respect, and risk taking. Such a climate fosters innovation because it encourages members to speak up, engage in spontaneous and informal communication, provide unsolicited information, and bridge differences by suspending judgment, being open to different ideas and views, and performing active listening.[14] When members engage in active listening, they provide their full attention to a speaker, nodding, smiling, saying "uh huh" or "yes" or other expressions to show they are listening. Then, they ask questions to clarify anything they don't understand, or ask the speaker to provide more details about their ideas. The listener may even repeat back what they think they heard the speaker say, to check whether they indeed heard them correctly. This reassures the speaker that their message is getting across and that their ideas are respected. It is important to note that the listener does not have to always agree with the speaker! Even if they don't, communicating that they are listening and that the ideas expressed are respected is important. If members feel that they will be heard and respected, they are more likely to share ideas, particularly if these ideas are different, unusual, or risky. Psychological safety has been found to be important for team learning and innovation, as it helps mitigate interpersonal risks and encourages members to admit mistakes, question practices, and ask for help and feedback.[15]

A psychologically safe communication climate is likely to help overcome challenges associated with virtuality by:

- promoting open sharing of information and situated knowledge across geographic locales and contexts.
- increasing informal communication and feedback to overcome problems resulting from reduced face-to-face interaction and lack of social cues in electronic communication.[16]
- making members feel comfortable being more spontaneous and "improvising" rather than being hesitant and restricted by protocol or past routines.

- strengthening relationships in teams with high turnover by building trust[17] and reducing perceptions of risk, as well as providing incentives to build a shared history, contributing to work flow.

- providing a psychologically safe communication climate that can help bridge national differences,[18] as team members who communicate supportively are more likely to develop shared understanding and integrate new knowledge to reach new solutions. In these ways, a psychologically safe communication climate can help to reduce innovation challenges due to geographic dispersion, electronic dependence, dynamic structure, and national diversity, by turning these features from challenges into assets.

Ideas in Action

Although virtual teams are often implemented by organizations to increase innovation, they often (ironically) hinder it. Part of the problem may be that managers are unsure of how to design such teams. We have seen that four characteristics associated with new "virtual" team designs (geographic dispersion, electronic dependence, dynamic structure and national diversity) may be problematic for innovation, but that these challenges can be overcome by creating a psychologically safe communication climate. Figure 1 illustrates the relationship among these characteristics. In terms of actions for managers, this suggests that in order to reduce the negative effects of virtuality, a psychologically safe communication climate can help to surface and clarify differences, resolve conflicts, and foster an open environment in which team members feel comfortable asking questions or admitting they don't understand something, and are comfortable voicing their opinions. This can increase innovation by allowing different perspectives and viewpoints to be heard, enabling the merging of ideas, and helping to find middle ground and bridge differences.

How can such a communication climate be created? Managers can engage in specific communication practices such as surfacing differences, testing for understanding, active listening, and clear communication of meaning—all of which help to overcome both national and geographical differences and increase innovation. In light of such a communication climate, potential benefits such as improved decision quality and creativity—due to the richness of ideas, viewpoints, and perspectives, and more concerted focus on understanding others' ideas, meanings, and arguments—can be realized.[19] Surfacing and clarifying contextual differences contributes to coordination, creativity, and garnering of resources for innovation across contexts. Sometimes, surfacing such contextual differences is as simple as sharing when people are normally at work (i.e., typical working hours and holidays)! This differs around the globe and can be a source of frustration and anxiety when members are uncertain where their counterparts are and why they may be absent from work.

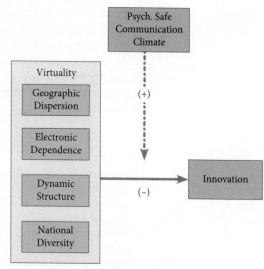

Figure 1 Model of Virtuality, Psychologically Safe Communication Climate, and Innovation

It is also important to understand particular pressures, deadlines, or workflow issues at each site. Resources such as particular skills, tools, or technologies may be abundant in one location and scarce in another—and if it is assumed they are abundant everywhere, this can create conflict and misunderstanding.

Further, the difficulty in sparking a creative exchange of ideas over electronically mediated communication, as compared to face-to-face, can be mitigated through expert use of the technology, which helps to contribute to a psychologically safe communication climate. Establishing clear communication protocols (i.e., rules and routines) with explicit norms for team member interaction, participation, policies, and expectations for communication (how often to communicate, expected response time, which media to use, prioritization of issues, etc.) is likely to improve team performance. New social media tools such as social networking sites, blogs, and wikis may also be used in ways that provide richer cues and facilitate context awareness through the use of status updates or profiles. For example, if each member shares a personal profile, this helps the team understand who each member is at a personal level, what "makes them tick," and what experiences they have had that they can contribute to the team. This personal identity information may also help them find common ground with each other, enhancing knowledge sharing and innovation.

Finally, the disadvantages of dynamic structure for innovation, such as lack of relationship building due to member turnover, can be lessened by clear communication about team norms to ensure they are shared, by holding a team kick-off meeting and periodic social gatherings in order to socialize new members and clarify roles. This can help turn the team's fluid, flexible roles into a source of new ideas and expertise.

Conclusion

We have addressed the sometimes unintended consequences of using virtual team designs for innovation in organizations. These consequences occur because geographic dispersion, electronic dependence, dynamic structure, and national diversity can hinder innovation processes. The unique and varied ways in which each of these characteristics influence innovation can be overcome by creating a psychologically safe communication climate, in which members are able to say what they think, surface problems, feel free to be assertive about their ideas, yet at the same time are considerate of others' feelings. Doing so may be the key to maximizing technology for team-based innovation in today's global organizations.

Endnotes

1. Gibson, C. B., Gibbs, J. L., Stanko, T., Tesluk, P., & Cohen, S. G. (2011). Including the "I" in virtuality and modern job design: Extending the Job Characteristics Model to include the moderating effect of individual experiences of electronic dependence and co-presence. *Organization Science, 22*(6), 1481–1499.
2. Gibson, C. B., & Gibbs, J. L. (2006). Unpacking the concept of virtuality: The effects of geographic dispersion, electronic dependence, dynamic structure, and national diversity on team innovation. *Administrative Science Quarterly, 51*, 451–495.

3. Sole, D., & Edmondson, A. (2002). Situated knowledge and learning in dispersed teams. *British Journal of Management, 13,* 17–34.

4. Olson, G. M. & Olson, J. S. (2000). Distance matters. *Human-Computer Interaction, 15*(2), 139–178.

5. Olson, G. M. & Olson, J. S. (2000).

6. Brown, S., & Eisenhardt, K. (1995). Product development: Past research, present findings, and future directions. *Academy of Management Review, 20*(2), 343–378.

7. Obstfeld, D. (2005). Social networks, the tertius iungens orientation, and involvement in innovation. *Administrative Science Quarterly, 50,* 100–130.

8. Gibbs, J. L. (2009). Dialectics in a global software team: Negotiating tensions across time, space, and culture. *Human Relations, 62*(6), 905–935.

9. Gibson, C. B., & Vermeulen, F. (2003). A healthy divide: Subgroups as a stimulus for team learning. *Administrative Science Quarterly, 48,* 202–239.

10. Adler, N. J., Brahm, R., & Graham, J. L. (1992). Strategy implementation: A comparison of face-to-face negotiations in the People's Republic of China and the United States. *Strategic Management Journal, 13,* 449–466.

11. Gibson, C. B., & Zellmer-Bruhn, M. E. (2001). Metaphors and meaning: An intercultural analysis of the concept of teamwork. *Administrative Science Quarterly, 46,* 274–303.

12. Gibson, C. B., & Vermeulen, F. (2003).

13. Gibson, C. B., & Gibbs, J. L. (2006).

14. Gibson, C.B. (1996). Do you hear what I hear? A framework for reconciling intercultural communication difficulties arising from cognitive styles and cultural values. In M. Erez & P.C. Earley (Eds.). *New Perspectives on International Industrial/Organizational Psychology,* San Francisco, CA: Jossey-Bass.

15. Edmondson, A. C. (1999). Psychological safety and learning behavior in work teams. *Administrative Science Quarterly, 44,* 350–383.

16. Sproull, L., & Kiesler, S. (1986). Reducing social context cues: Electronic mail in organizational communication. *Management Science, 32,* 1492–1512.

17. Jarvenpaa, S. L., & Leidner, D. E. (1999). Communication and trust in global virtual teams. *Organization Science, 10,* 791–815.

18. Maznevski, M. L. (1994). Understanding our differences: Performance in decision-making groups with diverse members. *Human Relations, 47*(5), 531–552.

19. Hambrick, D. C., Davison, S. C., Snell, S., & Snow, C. C. (1998). When groups consist of multiple nationalities: Towards a new understanding of the implications. *Organization Studies, 19*(2), 181–205.

Teams In Organizations: 10 Team Roles to Foster Team Effectiveness

Troy V. Mumford
Colorado State University

Michael C. Campion
University of South Carolina

Michael A. Campion
Purdue University

In modern organizations, work teams have proved to be vital for success. Whether an organization is designing innovative products, improving quality in its manufacturing processes, or creating customer loyalty through great customer service, it needs employees who can effectively collaborate on teams to accomplish work. Functional team roles are clusters of related behaviors that accomplish a particular function within the team[1] and allow the team to integrate the contributions made by individuals to the requirements of the team environment. These functional team roles allow the team to carry out three critical functions in teams, namely the effective execution of the team's work, effective management of the team's relationship with its environment, and preserving the team's ability to work together efficiently through meeting the social needs of members.

High-tech product design teams provide a useful illustration of these functional team roles in action and will be used throughout this article. To be effective, the team must accomplish many things including: define its goals, organize the project, adapt to changes in customer preferences from marketing efforts, integrate the expertise of each team member (and do so without growing to hate each other!). Question: Who does each of these things? Answer: The team members taking various functional team roles. Understanding what these team roles are and when to take them is critical to working effectively in teams.

The goal of this article is to provide managers the 'What' and 'When' of roles in teams. Each role should be defined so managers can enhance their understanding of *what* the team roles are. In addition, the article will define the times and situations *when* these team roles should be taken within a team in order to maximize team effectiveness. Understanding of the situational dependency of individual functional team roles is vital because as a member becomes more skilled at assessing environmental situations and adopting the correct team role, the member increases their value to the team—this ability has been shown to predict the performance of teams.[2]

Team success is driven, in part, by fulfilling ten distinct team roles that fall into three categories: Task roles, socioemotional roles, and boundary-spanning roles. The categories describe how the team role helps the team. Ten team roles represent the specific behaviors that managers should carry out when the team and its circumstances require it, as illustrated in functional categories in Figure 1.

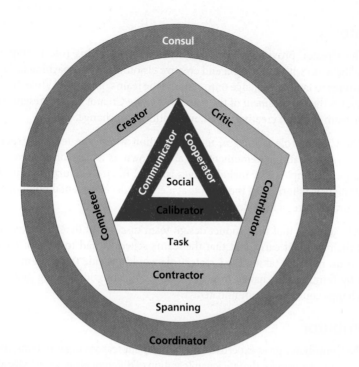

Figure 1 Ten
Functional Team Roles

Task Roles

The first subset is task roles, or the roles pertaining to the accomplishment of work. As team members take on these roles, it enables the team's work to move forward. When team members do not take on these roles, team productivity will falter. There are five primary task roles that team members need to understand and become proficient.

1. Contractor

What: The Contractor gets the team organized. The member taking this role is responsible for a) coordinating, organizing, and assigning tasks within the team, b) providing the team with structure, c) clarifying team member's abilities, resources, and responsibilities, and d) summarizing accomplishments to date.

When: The team needs the contractor role in any environment involving a high level of ambiguity and complexity. Examples of this may include situations where a) team members have little experience working together, b) team members have little experience with a particular task, or c) the tasks are complex and highly interdependent, requiring coordinated assignment according to individual skill-sets.

Illustrated: Let's use the product design team as an example—a team member taking the Contractor role would highlight for the team the deadline when the product was supposed to go into production and help the team articulate the steps in their design process. The Contractor would also likely ensure that certain individuals are individually held accountable for deliverables needed throughout the project.

2. Creator

What: The Creator provides vision. The member taking this role is responsible for providing the team with innovation and creative vision when approaching tasks. This role often functions to facilitate change or to reframe the team's objective. While the contractor role represents the *management* of the team's work, the Creator role represents the *leadership* of the team through creative vision, innovation, and change.

When: The Creator role is integral in any situation where the team is experiencing a loss in creative and strategic momentum, also known as a state of creative and strategic stagnation. Examples may include stages when a) the team's purpose is unclear or its current strategy is faltering, b) the team is at a critical developmental point or transition, or c) the work requires a high degree of creativity.

Illustrated: Suppose that the product design team discovered that their competitor had launched their product early, and that the team's schedule had to be shortened by four weeks. A team member taking the Creator role would provide the team motivation and direction by framing the change in positive terms and providing a big-picture plan for how the change could be accommodated.

3. Contributor

What: The Contributor gives expertise. One of the main reasons organizations utilize teams is to provide a mechanism for the efficient integration of different ideas, knowledge areas, skillsets, and abilities. The Contributor role is defined as the actions taken by the member to ensure that their knowledge, skills, and abilities (KSAs) are known and applied to the team's task. This requires that the individual knows the specific KSAs they have to offer and that they have the ability to determine where they must contribute these attributes to ensure completion of tasks.

When: The role of Contributor is critical specifically in situations where teams are comprised of members with distributed expertise. The Contributor role will become conspicuous in situations where a team is formed of members with different a) areas of expertise, b) levels of authority, and c) backgrounds.

Illustrated: As the product design team works, if one team member has a better understanding of customer preferences, that member would be taking the Contributor role by letting the team know of the expertise and providing the task-related information.

4. Completer

What: The Completer volunteers and follows through. The Completer role contributes to the effectiveness of the team during times when task work has been assigned and work must then be completed by individuals working outside of the team. Examples include: "doing homework" outside of the team, taking responsibility to complete certain tasks for the team, and ensuring that their team commitments are fulfilled.

When: The Completer role is important in most teams, however, the role is particularly prominent in situations where the effectiveness of the team depends on the performance of individuals working alone outside the team setting. These situations are typically when the work has been assigned and is now termed "unitary." This means that the work can no longer be divided among multiple individuals. This role is particularly important as the team approaches its deadline.

Illustrated: While working on the product design, the team discovers that someone needs to prepare a spreadsheet to compare three different configuration alternatives. The individual who volunteers to take on the task and brings it completed to the next meeting has taken the Completer role.

5. Critic

What: The Critic thinks critically. One of the most studied problems in teams is the phenomenon of "groupthink" wherein team members make poor decisions when their cohesiveness leads them to come to decisions through unanimity, or "going with the flow," rather than considering alternative courses of action. This problem brings into light the functional team role of Critic which subjects team decisions to critical evaluation. Often the member in the critic role points out the flaws in a course of action that tends to lead to a more evaluative approach in decision making.

When: The Critic role is most essential when a situation has occurred where there is concurrence without any type of scrutiny. This type of situation refers to a time when a group unanimously decides to move forward with an idea or decision without having considered potential costs or consequences. This role is particularly important in situations where a) there is a high level of trust within the team, b) the task assigned is to make a decision, c) tasks are technically complex, d) the team is highly cohesive and in a stressful work environment.

Illustrated: Suppose a senior member of the product design team suggests that a certain product configuration should be used and that there isn't a need to consider other alternatives. A team member taking the Critic role might point out that the configuration would only work in certain circumstances and decide that the design may not work for the project.

Socioemotional Roles

The second subset of roles is socioemotional roles. These roles enable the team to manage its intra-team relationships and draws upon the team member's interpersonal skills.

Communicator

What: The Communicator makes the team environment pleasant. The communicator role serves to create a social environment that is conducive to trust and collaboration. The member taking this role may exhibit many behaviors that create a social environment that is open, positive, and communicative. This role involves listening to the opinions of others, paying attention to the feelings of others, and communicating effectively.

When: The Communicator is required in almost all situations, however, it is particularly important in situations that are high in social sensitivity. Several examples include: a) when the task is socially complex, b) when ego or emotionally charged issues are involved, c) when the team is diverse either in values or in backgrounds, d) and when the environment is highly stressful.

Illustrated: The product design team may be under a lot of stress due to the schedule change. An individual who remains positive, and thanks a team member for his or her hard work is taking the Communicator role.

Cooperator

What: The Cooperator supports the team's decisions. The Cooperator role serves to sustain the progress of the team by supporting the team's decisions and adhering to leadership and influence attempts within the team. Taking the cooperator role involves being open to feedback and receiving information from others in the team.

When: The Cooperator role is particularly vital in conditions where there is scrutinized consensus, there are high status differentials, and during negotiation tasks. In addition, after a team member has taken the critic role and the concern has been addressed, the Cooperator role allows the team to move forward with its task.

Illustrated: After the product design team has critically evaluated a potential configuration for the potential flaws and tradeoffs, the team member who provided the critique is taking the Cooperator role when he or she agrees to support the team's configuration decision.

Calibrator

What: The Calibrator establishes and promotes healthy team norms. The Calibrator role pays close attention to the social processes within the team. When taking this role, a team member will often make the team aware of how they are communicating with each other and norms for how they treat each other. The Calibrator role plays a critical role in resolving conflict within the team so that social issues don't inhibit task progress.

When: When there is conflict in the team or social interactions in the team are dysfunctional, the Calibrator role becomes essential. These situations are characterized as nonfunctional group processes, including: a) a newly formed team where the individuals are not yet acquainted and used to working together, b) a situation where there is emotional or task-based conflict, c) a situation where there is distrust within the team, and d) when the team context is socially demanding.

Illustrated: If conflict arises within the product design team over the configuration decision, a team member taking the Calibrator role will remind the team of their agreement to always let each team member express their views before making a decision and to depersonalize the decisions.

Boundary Spanning Roles

Teams exist in organizational settings where effectiveness depends upon interfacing with people outside of the team. Team members carrying out these interactions outside the team are displaying the boundary spanning roles.

Consul

What: The Consul promotes the team externally. The consul role involves interactions with people outside the team setting that are in a position of power. The consul seeks to present the team, its goals, and its interests in a favorable light in order to procure resources for the team and gain sponsors for its actions.

When: When the team faces situations involving high dependence on external resources, the consul role becomes vital. Two examples of situations where a team has external dependence include: a) when a team doesn't possess the personnel, money, equipment, or information it needs to perform its task, and b) when the team is new and supervisors need status updates.

Illustrated: After the product design team learns of the change in its deadlines, it may need an additional member to speed up the prototype testing. The team member that approaches management about receiving the additional member is taking the Consul role.

6. Coordinator

What: The Coordinator facilitates inter-team interactions by taking part in interactions outside of the team to coordinate efforts with other teams or parties. This can involve scheduling, information exchange, or feedback solicitation.

When: The coordinator role is vital when times involve external activity interdependence. This occurs, for example, when the activities of the team are interdependent with the activities of other teams, supplies, or customers.

Illustrated: As the product design team accelerates their designs, they will need prototypes created earlier than projected. A team member taking the Coordinator role might interact with the production line to organize the specification delivery and prototype manufacturing schedule.

Team Roles in Action

When managers work both with and within teams, they can enhance both the team's effectiveness and their personal performance by understanding what functional team roles are needed by the team and by knowing when to step up and take each role. Below are five tips that can help managers and leaders put these team roles into action:

Expand Your Role Repertoire: What team roles do you tend to take? Are there some roles you avoid? These functional roles are all needed at various times within teams and you will become a stronger team member as you are able to expand your team role repertoire until you are able to fulfill whichever role the team needs you to take.

Enable your Team's Role Development: Are there members of your team that always assume the same role? The highest performing teams tend to comprise team members who perform multiple roles. Consider providing encouragement and opportunities for team members to take new roles within the team.

Analyze your Team Situation: What is the nature of your team's situation? Do the "when" contingencies discussed here suggest that certain team roles are important? Make sure those roles are being adequately taken within your team.

Be Flexible: Do you ever have conflict in your team over roles? Remember that teams are dynamic and as the task, team members, and situation change, your behavior will need to adjust as well. Be flexible in adjusting the part you play in the team to maximize *team* effectiveness.

To further explore your competence in assigning team roles, test yourself with the quiz in Table 1.

Table 1 Did You Know?

General mental ability has long been a well-known benchmark for its ability to predict employees' performance on the job. However, team role theory has recently been utilized in situational judgment tests to measure how well job applicants are able to work in teams, and research suggests that team role tests can predict performance of an applicant beyond a cognitive ability test alone!

Test Your Knowledge

1. Recently, you have noticed that the ideas and strategies being implemented by your team have led to less than stellar results. Your current strategy does not seem to be working and your team's development has reached a point where it has become stagnant. Which role is needed in this situation?

2. Imagine your team relies heavily on outside sources to remain efficient, which is, the group is characterized as having high external resource dependence. Someone is needed to act outside the team to collect resources and provide information to help the group accomplish its tasks. Which role is needed in this situation?

3. Imagine that all of the tasks have been allocated to each individual in your team and it is now time for everyone to complete the work on an individual-oriented basis. Which role is needed in this situation?

4. Imagine your team has adequately considered every strategy and its possible consequences before coming to a final decision. Which role is needed in this situation?

5. Each member of your team has their specific area of expertise. That is, the team is characterized as having distributed expertise. These areas do not overlap and are all needed to accomplish the team's goals. Which role is needed in this situation?

6. Imagine your team has just received a new project and there is much ambiguity regarding which direction to take and how each member of your group should contribute. The task is highly complex, and your team members are inexperienced. Which role is needed in this situation?

7. Imagine your team is composed of a diverse set of members with different values, levels of communication ability, and attitudes. The team context seems to be emotionally demanding and stressful. One might characterize this team as a socially sensitive one. Which role is needed in this situation?

8. Imagine your team has just been formed—everyone is new and has little experience working with one another. Not enough time has elapsed to allow trusting relationships to form and there seems to be a large amount of conflict within the group. Which role is needed in this situation?

9. Your team has recently been given a task and you have noticed that the strategy and decisions have all been made hastily with little regard for contingencies or consequences. To make matters worse, there seems to be complete agreement about which strategy to implement. In this situation, which role is needed?

10. Imagine that your team worked in an environment where there was a large amount of interaction and reliance on other teams. One might characterize this situation as one with high external activity interdependence. Which role is needed in this situation?

7. Communicator 8. Calibrator 9. Critic 10. Coordinator

1. Creator 2. Consul 3. Completer 4. Cooperator 5. Contributor 6. Contractor

Answer Key

Endnotes

1. Hackman, J. R. (1990). *Groups that work (and those that don't): Creating conditions for effective teamwork*, 1. San Francisco: Jossey-Bass. Mumford, T. V., Campion, M. A., & Morgeson, F. P. (2006). Situational judgment in work teams: A team role typology. In J. Weekley & R. Ployhart (Eds.). *Situational judgment tests*. Mahwah, NJ: Lawrence Earlbaum. Stewart, G. L., Manz, C. C., & Sims, H. P. (1999). *Team Work and Group Dynamics*. New York: John Wiley and Sons.

2. Mumford, T. V., Van Iddekinge, C. H., Morgeson, F. P., & Campion, M. A. (2008). The team role test: Development and validation of a team role knowledge situational judgment test. *Journal of Applied Psychology*, 93, 250–267.

10 Conflict and Negotiation

Topic Summary Learning Objectives

1. Identify the approaches to conflict and the conflict process.

2. Compare and contrast styles of conflict management along the dimensions of assertiveness and cooperativeness.

3. Describe conflict management techniques and their effectiveness.

4. Summarize the process of integrative negotiation.

5. List negotiation strategies.

6. Apply conflict and negotiation concepts to organizations.

Key Terms

accommodating style, p. 352	conflict, p. 349	mediation, p. 358
assertiveness, p. 351	cooperativeness, p. 351	negotiation, p. 354
avoiding style, p. 352	distributive negotiation, p. 354	process conflict, p. 349
BATNA, p. 356	dysfunctional, p. 350	relationship outcome, p. 356
cognitive framing, p. 353	functional, p. 350	substantive outcome, p. 356
collaborating style, p. 352	integrative negotiation, p. 354	task conflict, p. 349
competing style, p. 351	interactionist, p. 349	third-party conflict
compromising style, p. 352	interpersonal conflict, p. 349	resolution, p. 353

Introduction to Conflict and Negotiation

onflict is an ever-present reality in organizational life. This summary will provide you with a better understanding of conflict, help you understand when it is productive and/or counterproductive, and provide you with ideas on how to better react to and influence people's behavior. Negotiation is a decision making process that leads to the resolution of differences involving two or more parties interacting to resolve these differences. A detailed understanding of conflict will lead to better negotiation skills, however negotiation is just one of several ways to resolve conflict. This summary begins with a review of the sources, processes, styles, and strategies associated with conflict. The methods, behaviors, strategies, and processes associated with negotiation are summarized (see Figure 10.1).

Conflict

1 Identify the approaches to conflict and the conflict process.

Most people can easily recall a time when they have experienced conflict. **Conflict** is any disagreement between two parties, although these conflicts vary by type of party, type of issue, and cause. Conflict often arises when one party believes that the actions taken by another party has or will lead to a negative impact on the first party. Conflict occurs at many levels of an organization, and can occur between two people, between different divisions, or between an organization and an external stakeholder, such as a supplier, community group or government entity.

Traditionally, all conflicts in the workplace were thought to be negative and conflict was to be avoided or resolved at all cost. More contemporary approaches to conflict include the **interactionist** approach, which encourages conflict as long as the conflict is functional and leads to productive outcomes. A growing consensus among scholars says that conflict may be necessary to promote change or to increase innovation. The interactionist approach to

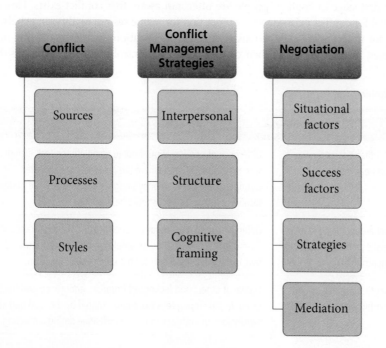

Figure 10.1
Summary of Conflict and Negotiation

conflict argues that too much harmony in a group can decrease productivity. If a group gets along too well and is too peaceful, the group may become complacent and not work as hard towards meeting the goals of the organization. Some level of conflict becomes necessary to spark competition and keep a group focused on achievements. However, some forms of conflict are more productive than others. **Functional** conflicts are, those that encourage achievement. **Dysfunctional** conflict is conflict that detracts from achieving goals and performance.

Sources of Conflict

All conflict is not equal.[2] Conflict can arise from three primary sources: process conflict, task conflict, and interpersonal conflict. **Process conflict** is conflict that affects the work process itself, how work gets done, and has a negative impact on results. Whereas, **task conflict** is conflict around disagreement of specific tasks and how to accomplish those tasks in order to be more productive. Conflict can also arise from relationships. This is called **interpersonal conflict**.[1] Conflict can improve productivity or it can prevent productivity, depending on the type, scope, and parties involved.[3] For example, some productive groups may have low levels of process conflict early on in a project life cycle, but the conflict might increase over time, with low levels of interpersonal conflict and moderate levels of task conflict midway through a project.[4] Table 10.1 outlines some of the different types of conflict found in an organization.

The Conflict Process

Conflict emerges as a five-stage process.[5]

Stage One: Latent

In the first stage of conflict, people are often not aware that conflict exists. However, the potential for conflict exists due to competition for scarce resources, differing goals, and the desire for independence. Functions within the organization, such as marketing or human resources, might want to set their own policies and control budget resources as they seek

Table 10.1 Three Types of Conflict

Type of Conflict	Definition	Example
Process conflict	Conflict that affects the work process negatively	Difference of opinion about how to complete the task including: who is responsible and where the resources are allocated. Example: A project team may disagree about where the budget resources for the project should be allocated.
Task conflict	Conflict around disagreement of specific tasks and how to accomplish them	Difference of opinion about the specifics and the importance of a task. Example: A supervisor and an employee disagree about which work task is the most important for the employee to focus on.
Interpersonal conflict	Conflict that arises from relationships at work	Dislike of others and feelings of irritation, annoyance and frustration. Example: An employee is extremely irritated by the loud and varied expressions of enthusiasm from a colleague during a meeting.

independence to perform their functions. Conflict might arise as tasks within the organization become more interdependent in nature. For example, human resources may want to make sure that a manager's pay is consistent throughout the organization, but the marketing department may want to pay a top performer more than other managers in the organization.

Stage Two: Awareness

In stage two, parties become aware of their disagreements, but differ in what they think are the causes of disagreements. The analysis of the conflict in this stage leads to additional conflict, as people seek to assign blame to the cause. The marketing department may blame poor sales on human resources and their inability to hire and pay top talent for a graphic artist. Human resources may attribute the inability to hire a top graphic artist to the marketing department and reference the department's dysfunctional culture for why the marketing department cannot hire top talent.

Stage Three: Felt

In the third stage, employees internalize stress and anxiety. The conflict is experienced as uncomfortable and cooperation decreases. What began as a small problem or series of problems has escalated into something greater as individuals begin to take the conflict personally and become emotionally involved in defending their own side of the conflict.

Stage Four: Open

The fourth stage of open conflict emerges when the conflict becomes visible by those experiencing the conflict as well as by outside observers. Arguments and visible disagreements become public as people compete for their own interests. Groups that are on either side of an issue may seek retaliation and organizational effectiveness is threatened as conflict diverts attention from the organization's core mission.

Stage Five: Outcome

The final stage involves resolution of the conflict. The conflict becomes resolved when those involved are satisfied by the result or agreement. If the underlying cause of the conflict is not resolved in this stage, however, the conflict will continue to surface. If conflict is not resolved and escalates through the felt stage (stage 3) the relationships may be damaged and trust may suffer.

Conflict Styles

Conflict based behavior can be classified into five different styles that people might prefer and adopt in any given conflict situation.[5] Styles can range from assertive to cooperative as shown in Figure 10.2. **Assertiveness** describes the degree to which a person or group attempts to satisfy his or her own interests. **Cooperativeness** describes to what extent the person or group attempts to satisfy the other party's interests. Five styles result from these dimensions:

2 Compare and contrast styles of conflict management along the dimensions of assertiveness and cooperativeness.

- The **competing** style describes both assertive and uncooperative behavior. This means that the person is pursuing her own interests at the expense of the other party and relying on whatever strategy is necessary for effective achievement of her own interests.

Figure 10.2 The Five Conflict Handling Styles

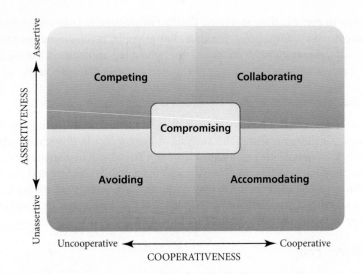

- The **collaborating** style is both assertive and cooperative. The collaborating style reflects a style where an individual will work with another party to satisfy both interests, and both parties work together to achieve a viable solution.
- A **compromising** style of behavior is moderately assertive and cooperative. The style seeks an acceptable solution where self-interest is sacrificed for the sake of resolving the conflict.
- The **avoiding** style is when the issue is never confronted directly. The avoiding style is characterized by a lack of assertiveness and is seen as uncooperative. With the avoiding style, the conflict is not addressed and may be abandoned altogether or put off until the future.
- The **accommodating** is unassertive and cooperative, and is the opposite of the competing style. With the accommodating style, the person may seek to satisfy the interests of the other person at the expense of resolving his or her own concerns.[5]

3 Describe conflict management techniques and their effectiveness.

Conflict Management Strategies

Conflict can be managed in several ways. The use of interpersonal influence techniques, creating an appropriate structure, cognitive framing, and negotiation all represent techniques that can lead to reduced or more productive conflict.

The Use of Interpersonal Techniques

Improved communication, problem solving, and relationship building are common interpersonal techniques to manage conflict.[5] Companies routinely offer conflict management training as part of leadership courses. These courses encourage organizational leaders to resolve conflict productively through quality communication and shared problem solving. Relationship building can range from formal to informal. An informal activity might include two colleagues working on their relationship by having lunch together. Formal activities might include team-building activities, for example, an organization may routinely hold team-building training at an outdoor ropes course with the intention of building

Cultura Limited/SuperStock

stronger relationships and trust among team members. **Third-party conflict resolution** represents a more formal process of relationship building where a neutral person works to help the people involved resolve their differences.[2]

Creating an Appropriate Structure

Organizations also rely on written rules, policies, standard operating procedures, and work redesign as tools for organizations to manage conflict. Some conflicts occur when employees differ in their understanding of how resources are to be utilized and allocated.[2] Lack of clear policies and choices, in the allocation of resources leads to conflict as people with different interests vie for control. These conflicts can be resolved or minimized by clarifying decision rules and resource priorities. Even a simple meeting agenda that sets the rules for what is to be discussed in a meeting can help. Work redesign can also reduce unproductive conflict. Redesigning reporting relationships can also reduce conflict by creating clear lines of decision making authority over allocation of resources.

Cognitive Framing

Cognitive framing is the way a person perceives or frames information.[6] Cognitive frames are mental structures that help individuals organize and take action based on how they perceive a situation. Think of cognitive framing as both a strategy and an interpretive process. As a strategy, a person in an organization may speak about an issue in order to reframe people's perception as a means to resolve conflict. Changing the cognitive frame of either party is a method for resolving conflict.[7] For example, if a project leader frames the intervention of a specific department that is withholding budgetary resources in one of the following ways:

- *supportive of our efforts as they try to prioritize our budgetary needs to complete the implementation* or
- *not supportive of our efforts and want us to fail, and this is why they are withholding budgetary resources.*

Both statements have completely different meanings. In order to resolve interdepartmental conflict, the first frame holds more promise and promotes productive conversation.

Individual differences in how people think and process information during the negotiation process are discussed in the next section. In this way of examining cognitive frames, it is explanatory in how people differ in how they view the same information in the same situation as other people.

4 Summarize the process of integrative negotiation.

Negotiation

Negotiation is a form of resolving conflict that requires a complex understanding of the factors that contribute to its success. **Negotiation** is a decision-making process where two or more individuals agree on how to allocate resources, resolve competing interests, settle an issue, or determine an agreeable position.[8] Negotiation occurs both formally and informally, but even the simplest negotiation can be demanding. Two major approaches to negotiation involve distributive negotiation and integrative negotiation. **Distributive negotiation** is based on the assumption that there is a fixed amount of value that must be divided, and that a negotiation relies on adhering to a rigid position in order to gain as much value as possible.[9] **Integrative negotiation** is often called interest-based negotiation. In contrast to distributive negotiation, values, resources, or positions are not considered fixed. In integrative negotiation, negotiators focus on the interests of each party in order to maximize the value of resources for these parties.[10] Integrative negotiation involves behaviors that seek to 'expand the pie,' rather than fixating on rigid interests where each slice of pie is divided. In the book 'Getting to Yes,' the authors describe a popular integrative approach to negotiation.[16] This approach involves:

1. Separating the people from the problem
2. Focusing on interests rather than on positions
3. Remaining open to options that provide mutual gain
4. Utilizing objective rather than subjective criteria

Separating the people from the problem points to the importance of maintaining a relationship among negotiators, even when interests differ. Thus, any negotiation involves two elements: 1) the content of the negotiation, or the substance, and 2) the relationship among parties. Collaboration, when parties are equally focused on maintaining a relationship as well as the content of the negotiation, yields a fairer distribution of resources.[11]

Prior to any negotiation, negotiators representing all parties should clarify their interests, understand their position on each issue, and establish their priorities. Table 10.2 outlines interests, issues, and positions—elements of all negotiations.

Situational Factors Influencing Negotiation

Situational and individual factors can also impact negotiation and the results that are achieved. Situational factors include the context in which the negotiation takes place, the available information surrounding the negotiation,[13] the power differences between negotiators,[14] and the timeframe for negotiations.[15] Information is critical to the success of any negotiation, but essential and necessary information may not always be available. For example, a new graduate who is negotiating a starting salary may not have complete

Table 10.2 Interests, Issues, and Positions of Negotiation

Interests	An underlying qualitative motivation, need, or desire. This is more of a general goal and not a specific position with an intended outcome. Some examples: • A chance to learn new skills or gain expertise • Serve the community or society at large • Improve one's standard of living • Achieve status and fame
Issues	Items on the negotiating table which are important to meeting one or more of your interests or your opponent's interests. Some examples: • Monetary items like salary, price, or bonus • Benefit terms • Branding terms • Creative decision-making rights
Positions	Each issue on the negotiating table has specific terms or outcomes. These opening or bottom line positions are presented during the negotiation process. Some examples: • $100,000 starting salary • Exclusive branding rights • Final say in creative decisions • A bonus if a project is completed early

information about what a company historically pays for starting salaries or how much the company pays new college graduates for relocation expenses. Unless a job applicant has another job offer, the applicant may have no negotiating power to request a higher starting salary. Time becomes an issue as well as the job applicant may receive an offer with only a window of 48 hours to accept or reject the offer.

Individual factors such as age, gender,[11] race, emotional expressiveness, overconfidence, personality, values, and cognitive framing[6] can also play a role in negotiation. Individual values define what people believe is important, how the world should behave, and what rights people have.[12] These values are barriers to negotiation, especially during ideologically based negotiations.[19] An ideologically based negotiation might include a negotiation for something like workers' rights, or the impact of technology on global warming. Many negotiations, such as the price of a car, are not considered ideologically based negotiation, but are negotiations based on the exchange of economic resources.

As discussed earlier, cognitive framing differs among individuals and shapes how an issue is perceived, the best way to solve problems, and what is important. Cognitive framing impacts how an individual crafts a message in order to build a desired interpretation of a situation.[10] Oftentimes, situational and individual factors are outside the control of negotiators, but some factors are often easier to control than others. It is easier to control the time of the negotiation and how emotions are expressed during the process of negotiation. It may be more difficult to change organizational status or personality of the negotiators. Predetermined factors in negotiations often include the environment surrounding the negotiation, the issues in the negotiation, and the people involved in the negotiation. The process of how decisions are made is not predetermined. This means that effective negotiators focus on the right behaviors that impact results, and the choice of strategy, rather than situational and individual differences.

Successful Negotiations

Interests can be complimentary, even when positions are not; the best negotiators seek mutual gains, where both parties benefit. Certain barriers to successful negotiation exist. Negotiators often define resources as fixed and this leads them to take rigid positions. They lose flexibility and no longer focus on resolving the problem. When negotiators rigidly adhere to positions, they fail to problem solve or look at complimentary solutions. Negotiators may make a judgment too early in the negotiation process—they may fail to consider more than one option, or fail to consider options that benefit all parties. Time pressure causes this early judgment, and when the pressure of time is removed, parties tend to expand beyond a single option, and expand to mutually beneficial options.

The process of negotiation often includes biased, subjective criteria.[17] Avoid e-mail and electronic communication when negotiating. Face-to-face development of objective criteria improves the likelihood that criteria will be fair, objective, and shared by all parties. Negotiators often overestimate their probability of success. This subjective assessment of the situation leads to less successful outcomes and lower resolution rates.[18]

When negotiators fail to secure the results that they want, there is an alternative that helps to anchor negotiations. If parties cannot agree during the negotiation process, the **Best Alternative to a Negotiated Agreement (BATNA)** describes another option that a negotiator might take. For example, if you cannot obtain the price for a used car that you want during the negotiation process, your BATNA would be to continues the search and continue to drive your old car instead. Research shows that negotiators, who have developed a good BATNA, were better at negotiation.[15]

5 List negotiation strategies.

Strategies in Negotiation

A strategy in negotiation is the action plan that the negotiator follows to reach desired goals. Some researchers have argued that all strategies require bolstering the perceived power base of the negotiator in order to be more effective. Perceived power is the interpretation of a party's power in the negotiation relationship. Power includes access and control of resources, access to powerful people, ability to punish, special knowledge, authority, or ability to impact a party's feelings or self-esteem. The level of dependency between parties impacts the degree of power each person has in the negotiation. This power is imbedded in the action plan, or strategy and the tactics deployed. The choice of strategy impacts the negotiation process and the outcome of negotiation. The strategy and the subsequent tactics that are appropriate depend on the outcomes sought. A negotiator has a choice of outcomes and can choose between substantive and/or relationship outcomes. **Substantive outcomes** focus on the content of the negotiation while **relationship outcomes** focus on preserving the relationship between or among negotiating parties. Table 10.3 outlines these goals. The combination of importance of each factor is described in Figure 10.3.[20]

Table 10.3 Strategy, Outcomes, and Tactics in Negotiation

Strategy	Outcomes Sought	Appropriate Tactics
1. Collaboration	Substantive, Relationship	• seek to conduct negotiations on neutral ground • free exchange of agenda items • consider opponent's demands • alternate discussion of requests and demands • respond with moderate offers/demands • indicate reasons for demands, ask for opponent's reasons • seek equitable exchange of concessions • delete, add, or yield items for mutual benefit • honestly assess opponent's concessions • seek mutually beneficial outcomes in accepting or conceding concessions
2. Competitive	Substantive only	• seek to conduct negotiations on own ground • demand discussion of opponent's agenda items while concealing own agenda items • ignore or discount opponent's demands • insist opponent make initial offer • respond with low offers and high demands • commit to each item and exaggerate own position while discounting opponent's position • demand opponent make concessions and threaten consequences if concessions not made • delete, yield, or add only on low-interest items • magnify degree of own concessions, downplay degree of opponent's concessions • seek large concessions from opponent • concede minimally on high-interest items • use concessions on low-interest items as bargaining chips
3. Subordinative	Relationship only	• seek to conduct negotiations on opponent's ground • elicit opponent's agenda items and downplay own • concede to opponent's demands and requests • make initial offers on all opponent's agenda items • make high offers and low demands • accept opponent's commitments to items, explain own commitments • concede to opponent's demands • delete, add, or yield to any of opponent's items • acknowledge opponent's concessions, downplay own • yield to opponent's preferences by accepting low offers and making low demands
4. Avoidance	Neither Relationship or Substantive	• delegate negotiation responsibility • forego negotiation and resort to standard operating procedures for decision making[20]

Figure 10.3 Choice
of Outcome

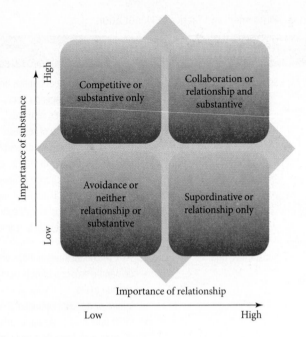

Importance of substance

High

Low

Competitive or
substantive only

Collaboration or
relationship and
substantive

Avoidance or
neither
relationship or
substantive

Supordinative or
relationship only

Importance of relationship

Low   High

Mediation as a Solution to Negotiation

A negotiation may result in a stalemate where parties cannot agree, even when the best
negotiation strategies are in place. When a stalemate occurs, the individuals might turn
to mediation as a solution. **Mediation** involves a neutral third party who listens to both
sides of a negotiation and then crafts an agreement. Mediators can modify the frames,
redefine what is important, and then select the right negotiation strategy. For example,
mediators can find common ground among parties by changing the language that is used
in the negotiation from aggressive to positive. Mediators help to satisfy multiple parties
in the negotiation. The mediator can change the frames used in negotiation by changing:

1. how the parties describe and interpret the issues in the situation
2. how the parties interpret and describe themselves, others, and the relationships
   in the situation
3. the interactions among the parties in the situation and the meaning that is
   placed on the interactions[6]

Conclusion

Conflict and the process of negotiating conflict is a common feature of behavior in organizations. Conflict arises for many reasons and occurs in different stages. Individuals
navigate this conflict using different styles. Organizations have a variety of methods to
manage conflict, including negotiations. There are two different approaches to negotiations, but each approach involves consideration of interests, issues, and positions.
Selection of strategies in negotiation generally focuses on the importance of maintaining
relationships or the importance of substance. The ability to negotiate differences is a key
skill in organizational behavior that allows people to increase their impact.

OB AT WORK

THE NEW RECRUIT: CARL'S CONFIDENCE IN KEN PAYS OFF

Carl Leonard

6 Apply conflict and negotiation concepts to organizations.

Carl Leonard, then a managing partner for the law firm Morrison-Foerster, traveled to interview students for summer intern positions. At that time, Morrison-Foerster, based in San Francisco, had 175 lawyers in offices in Los Angeles, Denver, Washington, D.C., and London. Today, the firm has 950 lawyers and 19 offices, including offices throughout Asia. Even in the early days, the firm had a strategic interest in Asia, especially China and Japan, attracting recent graduates like Ken Siegel to sign up for an interview.

Having interviewed literally hundreds of students at all the top schools, Carl had learned that it is very difficult to figure out in a 30-minute interview whether the person sitting before you would ultimately become a strong partner at the firm, let alone make a serious difference in the success of the firm. But deciding to offer Ken a summer internship was an easy decision. He was a bright, personable, poised young man with excellent academic credentials, a passionate interest in international business, and—Carl would soon discover—skills at negotiating results when it mattered most. What Carl did not know all those years ago is the incredible impact Ken would make on the direction of the international practice.

Ken did very well in his summer internship at the firm, so Carl and the partners gave him an offer to join the firm after graduation. Carl called Ken numerous times at his home in Chicago during his final months in school. Ken, it seemed to Carl, intentionally tried to evade acceptance of this once-in-a-lifetime offer. In one of the calls, however, Carl began to understand Ken's position. What Ken really wanted was to take a year-long course in Japanese at Stanford's language program in Tokyo. Ken was engaged to a Japanese national. Carl knew that even a prime offer could not compete with young love. He quickly decided to make Ken an offer he couldn't refuse: the firm would pay his tuition and living expenses in Tokyo if he would commit now to join the firm on completion of the course. "I think this caught him off-guard," Carl remembered, "because when I said, 'So, do we have a deal?' he simply said, 'OK.'"

By September, the firm opened its first Tokyo office with one partner and one associate—Ken Siegel. Something the firm had learned from their other international office experiences was that it was one thing for an employee to have good grades and have an interest in living abroad, but it is another thing for the new employee to survive in a foreign environment. The only way to find out if Ken would be successful was to put him on the ground overseas and hope for the best.

Two months later, Carl saw Ken's negotiation skills in action. By now, Carl had become the Chairman of the firm and was present for the official opening of the Tokyo office. The reception was followed by a weekend where the Pac-Ten Conference held its annual overseas football game at the Tokyo Bowl, so the firm decided to make the game part of

(continued)

its opening celebration. They invited over 130 Japanese business clients and friends to the game, but had not planned on how cold it can get in Tokyo in the fall, and were in a state of panic. Over 130 Japanese clients and friends failed the prospect of sitting for over three hours in the freezing cold watching a game they knew almost nothing about.

Ken went to work, using his newly acquired skill in Japanese, and negotiated a solution—130 blankets. "To this day I don't know where he found them!" Carl recalls in amazement. Then, there was the problem of getting 130 blankets to the stadium. By now Carl and the other visiting partners had left for the Tokyo Bowl to greet the guests. When they arrived, a long line of taxis pulled up in front of the stadium. Ken jumped out of the lead taxi and began the process of unloading piles of wool blankets from each taxi as it pulled up. He then arranged the distribution of the blankets to the guests with perfectly gracious Japanese introductions complete with low bows. Carl's faith and trust in Ken was sealed. "It was then that I knew our Tokyo venture was in good hands," he says. The Tokyo office of Morrison & Foerster celebrated its twentieth anniversary in September 2007. The office now has over 90 lawyers, one of the largest law offices in Japan. Who is the managing partner of the office? Ken!

Source: Personal interview with Carl Leonard.

SPOTLIGHT ON RESEARCH
Are There Gender Differences in Beliefs about Requests for More Money?

Research around salary negotiations often points to the differences between men and women and their requests for different amounts. One study explored the connection between men's and women's beliefs and how these beliefs impact their specific salary requests in negotiations. Salary differences in organizations between men and women can be tracked back to the original salary negotiations that occurred prior to organizational entry. These differences in original salary negotiations can follow an employee for many years. Some studies suggests that gender differences in salary negotiations are based on the employee's familiarity or comfort with negotiation, confidence in negotiating, context of the negotiation, and even perceptions of entitlement around pay level. To understand the negotiation differences between men and women, and what variables best impact behavior, a group of MBA students were studied in their negotiations with a hiring manager. These simulated salary negotiations were structured to be as realistic a hiring situation as possible, and participants were interviewed both before and after the simulation to ensure that it 'felt' real.

The students involved in the negotiation were offered a job for a starting salary of $61,000 and a bonus of $5,000. The salary offer was strategically selected to be slightly below market value for the industry, the market conditions, and similar jobs that MBA students had earned after graduation from this university. The results from the simulation showed that the men's salary requests were significantly higher than the women's salary requests. The men and women did not differ based on age, past salary, GPA, experience in negotiations, or even expectations of salary upon graduation.

After interviewing the students post-negotiation, specific themes explained their behavior:

1. I know my worth.
2. I am unsure of my worth.
3. I am worth more than others.
4. I am worth the same as others.
5. I need to prove myself in the negotiation.
6. I need to prove myself on the job.

These categories differed for men and women in the negotiation around worth, entitlement, and the need to prove competence at work and in the negotiation. This study indicated that men and women often operate from different beliefs when negotiating salary, and that men make larger salary requests than women. Belief systems impact behaviors when negotiating something as important as starting salary. The study suggests that students' initial salary requests impact their final offers, and that their beliefs drive their requests. Training around belief systems and negotiation behavior may be a solution to help offset the differences in initial salary offers between men and women.

Questions for Discussion

1. How do you think training might help people in the negotiation process?

2. Why do you think there might be gender differences in entitlement relative to salary?

3. What would you like to explore if you were a researcher working on a similar study?

Source: *Based on the article by Barron, L. A. (2003). Ask and you shall receive? Gender Differences in Negotiators' Beliefs about Requests for a Higher Salary.* Human Relations, (56)6, 635–662.

Pairing with this Topic Summary

Suggested Expert Contributions

Trust—Roy J. Lewicki (The Ohio State University)

The Essentiality of "Justice" in Organizations: A Justice-as-Negotiation Perspective —Debra L. Shapiro (University of Maryland)

Negotiation Traps—Kimberly D. Elsbach (University of California, Davis)

Suggested Cases

Case 1: The Case of Apple iPhone 4

Case 3: EMERGENCY! We Need a Better Compensation System

Case 4: Face Time at TechPoint Software, Inc.

Case 6: NASCAR's Drive for Diversity: Can They Reach the Finish Line?

Case 8: Conflict in Santa's Workshop: Learning to Be a Team Player at ToyKing

Suggested Exercises

Exercise 6: Develop Your Career—Leadership Development in Action

Exercise 15: Building My Network—Individual

Exercise 27: Develop Your Professional Code

Exercise 28: Communication Breakdown

Exercise 35: Who Do I Fire?

Exercise 38: FIS Simulation

Endnotes

1. Pinkley, R. (1990). Dimensions of the conflict frame: Disputant interpretations of conflict. *Journal of Applied Psychology, 75(2):* 117–128.
2. Pondy, L. (1992). Reflections on organizational conflict. *Journal of Organizational Behavior, 13(3):* 257–261.
3. Jehn, K., & Mannix, E. (2001). The Dynamic Nature of Conflict: A Longitudinal Study of Intragroup Conflict and Group Performance. *Academy of Management Journal, 44(2):* 238–251.
4. Jehn, K., & Shah, P. (1997). Interpersonal relationships and task performance: An examination of mediating processes in friendship and acquaintance groups. *Journal of Personality and Social Psychology, 72(4):* 775–790.
5. Thomas, K. (1976). In Marvin Dunnette (Ed.). *Conflict and Conflict Management in the Handbook of Industrial and Organizational Psychology.* Chicago: Rand MacNally.
6. Dewulf, A., Gray, B., Putnam, L., Lewicki, R., Aarts, N., Bouwen, R., & Van Woerkum, C. (2009). Disentangling approaches to framing in conflict and negotiation research: A meta-paradigmatic perspective. *Human Relations, 62(2):* 155–193.
7. Yusko, K. P., & Goldsteing, H. W. (2004). A cognitive mapping approach to understanding choice of negotiation strategy. *Academy of Management Proceedings,* C1–C6.
8. Brett, J., Shapiro, D., & Lytle, A. (1998). Breaking the bonds of reciprocity in negotiation. *Academy of Management Journal, 41(4):* 410–424.
9. Neale, M. A., & Bazerman, M. H. (1985). The effects of framing and negotiator overconfidence on bargaining behaviors and outcomes. *Academy of Management Journal, 28(1):* 34–49.
10. Neale, M. A., & Bazerman, M. (1992). Negotiating rationally: the power and impact of the negotiator's frame. *Academy of Management Executive, 6(3):* 42–51. See also Raiffa, H. (*1982*). *The art and science of negotiation.* Cambridge, MA: Harvard University Press.
11. Barron, L. A. (2003). Ask and you shall Receive? Gender Differences in Negotiators' Beliefs about Requests for a Higher Salary. *Human Relations, 56(6):* 635–662.
12. Kray, L. J. (2007). Leading through Negotiation: Harnessing the power of gender stereotypes. *California Management Review,* 50(1): 159–173.
13. Carsten, C. K. W., De Dreu, Van Kleef, G. A. (2004). The influence of power on the information search, impression formation, and demands in negotiation. *Journal of Experimental Social Psychology,* 40(3): 303–319.
14. Kim, P. H., Pinkley, R. L., & Fragale, A. R. (2005). Power dynamics in negotiation. *Academy Of Management Review,* 30(4): 799–822.
15. Thompson, L., & Leonardelli, G. J. (2004). The big bang: The evolution of negotiation research. *Academy of Management Executive, 18(3):* 113–117.

16. Fisher, R., & Ury, W. *(1981)*. Getting to yes: Negotiating agreement without giving in. New York: Penguin Books.

17. Gelfand, M. J., Major, V., Raver, J. L., Nishii, L. H., & O'Brien, K. (2006). Negotiating relationally: The dynamics of the relational self in negotiations. *Academy of Management Review, 31*(2): 427–451.

18. Muir, C. (2007). Tapping the Subjective Values Present in Negotiations: Face, Feelings, and Friendships. *Academy of Management Perspectives, 21*(1): 72–74.

19. Wade-Benzoni, K. A., Hoffman, A. J., Thompson, L. L., Moore, D. A., Gillespie, J. J., & Bazerman, M. H. (2002). Barriers to resolution in ideologically based negotiations: The role of values and institutions. *Academy of Management Review, 27*(1): 41–57.

20. Savage, G. T., Blair, J. D., & Sorenson, R. L. (1989). Consider both relationships and substance when negotiating strategically. *Academy of Management Executive, 3*(1): 37–47.

Trust*

Roy J. Lewicki

The Ohio State University

Introduction

It wasn't supposed to be a day different from any others—Jim expected it to start normally and without any hassles. But then it started.

Jim was getting dressed when his 12-year-old son Aaron popped his head through the bedroom door. "Dad, I need a note for school," said Aaron.

"What for?"

"My science teacher said I didn't turn in the required homework and she is going to give me a zero if I don't turn it in today with a note from my parents. But I did turn it in and she must have lost it. So I did another homework set last night. Can you sign a note saying I did turn it in when it was due?"

Jim looked at Aaron skeptically. "Are you SURE you turned it in? Are you telling me the truth?"

"Honest, Dad, I turned it in!" Aaron looked at his dad with big pleading eyes.

Jim signed the form and watched his son head out the door, wondering if Aaron was really telling him the whole story.

Jim went down to breakfast. Over breakfast, his wife, Debbie, asked him when he was going to get around to cleaning up the basement. All summer, Jim had been dumping books, files and boxes in his basement 'office,' but never seemed to find the time to put things away or throw out boxes of stuff that had been accumulating for years. Debbie was in charge of their church's rummage sale, had been cleaning out closets and the attic all summer, and really wanted Jim to clean up his mess. Jim would much rather play golf than clean up his office, and had been trying to convince Debbie that he would clean it up once the golf season was over. But clearly, she didn't want to wait that long! Jim promised he would clean up his messy office 'soon,' but he could tell from the look on her face that she really didn't believe him.

On the way to work, Jim stopped at the computer repair store to see if his laptop had been fixed. Jim's other son, Michael, had dropped his dad's laptop while playing video games on it; Michael and Aaron were horsing around and had knocked the computer off the coffee table. The computer was still under warranty, and Jim was afraid that if he told the store that it had been carelessly dropped, the warranty wouldn't cover the repair. So he had told the repair shop that 'it had just stopped working.' Jim was hoping that they could fix it and wouldn't figure out that it had been dropped so that he wouldn't have to pay the charges. Jim also noticed that the repair shop had a 'Grand Opening' sign in the window, and he wondered who these repair techs were and whether they really had the experience to complete his repair order satisfactorily.

---

*The author wishes to thank Jacqueline Swanson for her assistance in preparing this chapter.

Jim's experiences reveal the dynamics of two critical themes that are common to all interpersonal relationships: trust, and trust in the context of managing conflict and using influence to resolve differences. And as we will point out, trust is critical to effective negotiation and conflict resolution processes. So let's examine trust dynamics more closely.

Trust is essential to all interpersonal relationships. With trust, relationships run smoothly, almost effortlessly. We can be confident that people will keep their word; do as they say they are going to do; be reliable and predictable. Team members can coordinate their efforts and achieve amazing results with remarkably little friction or mishap. And in organizations with high trust, employees enjoy coming to work and enthusiastically work together to help the organization succeed. Conversely, the results of low trust are also obvious: relationships are strained, communication is incomplete and ineffective, leadership is doubted and questioned, and volumes of rules, policies, and procedures attempt to substitute for the effortless synchronization that high trust can produce.

It is easy to create the case for trust, but more difficult to actually create and sustain the trust necessary for sound and effective working relationships. In this article, we will

- define what we mean by trust, and its accompanying concept, distrust;
- explore two kinds of trust that impact our work relationships, particularly in negotiation and conflict situations;
- explain what can be done to create and maintain trust in business and personal relationships.

A Definition of Trust

Because trust is a psychological phenomenon that we can't observe directly, many authors have defined trust differently. In this chapter, we adopt the definition of trust as "an individual's belief in, and willingness to act on the basis of the words, actions, and decisions of another."[1] In general, an individual's trust judgment is composed of three elements: a trustor's general disposition to be trusting (often part of his personality); situational factors such as the way that the parties have to work together to get a job done, and the parties' past relationship experience with each other.

Two Types of Trust

There are different types of relationships and it cannot necessarily be assumed that the nature of trust and its development are not the same in all the types. The trust that a husband and wife may have for each other after 20 years of marriage might be different than the trust a new patient might have for a dentist who is just opening his practice, or the trust a sports car owner might have when he has to turn his vintage auto over to an inexperienced mechanic. In this chapter, we discuss two basic types of trust: trust in professional and personal relationships. The former is a task-oriented relationship in which the parties' activities are primarily directed toward the achievement of specific, tangible goals, while the latter is a relationship laden with emotion and personal history, where the parties' major goal is simply to sustain or enhance the value of the relationship for each other. We shall refer to these as calculus-based and relationship-based trust.

Calculus-Based Trust

The first form of trust is called calculus-based trust (CBT). This kind of trust is the trust that occurs as people engage in simple (or perhaps not-so-simple) 'transactions' with each other. It is called 'calculus-based' because the trustor is engaged in a mental calculation, considering the benefits to be gained from trusting the other party against the possible costs of being wrong in that judgment or having the trust broken and violated. When Jim takes his laptop computer to the repair shop to be fixed, he expects that the repair person is competent to fix the computer, that he will have the computer returned in a reasonable period of time, and that the cost for repairing the computer will not be excessive. Interestingly, people often make these complex judgments with very little certainty that the trust is warranted. Jim may make the judgment to drop off his laptop computer at this shop because the repair shop is new and appears to be neat and clean, because the repair person 'looks like' someone who could fix a computer, and because there is some form of price schedule hanging on the wall indicating charges for parts and labor, there are lots of computers sitting around with repair tags on them, and the store has printed business cards, etc. Jim doesn't even ask any questions to determine whether his trust is warranted—i.e., how does he know whether the repair tech has the appropriate skills, what parts are needed and how much they will cost, what is a fair price to repair a computer, or even whether they are running a legitimate business?

Parties accept or comply with another's calculus-based trust because the rewards of being trustworthy are seen as valuable (i.e., if the repair shop performs a quick, effective, and inexpensive repair, it gains a good reputation in the community) and because of the "threat" that if trust is violated, that same reputation can be hurt (word will get around that the repair shop is inefficient, overpriced, and does sloppy work). Even if you are not an honest person, having a reputation for honesty (or trustworthiness) is a valuable asset that most people want to maintain. So even if there are opportunities to be untrustworthy, any short-term gains from untrustworthy acts must be balanced, in a calculus-based way, against the long-term benefits of maintaining a good reputation. If the computer store fixes Jim's computer but seriously overcharges him for it, Jim would never return to the store and tell his friends not to shop there either.

While a calculus-based trust decision involves paying attention to both the benefits of trust (How can I gain if I trust the other?) and the risks of trusting (How could I lose if I trust the other?), in general, trustors are more likely to focus on the risk of trusting (What will I lose if I am wrong in my judgment?), while those being trusted are more likely to focus on the benefits to be gained from being trusted ("Look what good things are happening because of the other's trust!) Thus, when Jim drops off his computer, he is probably more worried about the possibility of losses if his computer isn't fixed properly, or that the store does further damage to it, while the store is probably more focused on the fact that it has gained another new customer. So, while trustors will focus on downside risk and may be more likely to initiate trusting actions that do not risk extending high (but potentially unreciprocated) rewards to the other, the trusted will focus on benefits, and may be more likely to reciprocate (and create joint gain for the parties) when the reward level is high.[2] Moreover, trusted parties can enhance their image of trustworthiness by demonstrating the ability to deliver on commitments by acting benevolently and being 'nice' to the trustor, and by acting with integrity so that promises are kept and one's word is one's bond.[3]

Relationship-Based or Identification-Based Trust

CBT is the most common kind of trust that occurs in 'basic' business transactions (sales, purchases and other 'arms-length' exchanges of information, goods, and services). CBT is also common in the early stages of any personal relationship when the parties are simply exchanging information, becoming acquainted, and 'sharing' their time together in common activities. But as parties get to know each other well and develop personal attraction to each other by strengthening their relationship, trust fundamentally changes in character to a second form of trust, identification-based trust. This trust is grounded in each party's emotional attraction to and "identification" with the other person's desires and intentions. Identification-based trust (IBT) develops because the parties grow to effectively understand and appreciate each other's wants and needs and believe that they are working together toward a common goal—either a specific tangible outcome, or simply the goal of sustaining a mutually positive relationship. This shared and common understanding of each other is developed to the point that each person can effectively 'think like' and/or act for the other. Thus, strong IBT allows each party to act as the other's agent and substitute for the other in interpersonal transactions.[4] Each trustor comes to know the other so well that she can make decisions which are in the best interests of the other party, and/or protect the other party from harm so that little or no ongoing surveillance or monitoring of one another is necessary. This might be as simple as buying food one knows the other will like while at the supermarket or redecorating a room in the furniture and color scheme the other will appreciate. A true affirmation of the strength of IBT between parties can be found when one party acts for the other even more zealously than the other might demonstrate, such as when a good friend dramatically defends you against a minor insult, even when you are not present.

Certain types of activities strengthen IBT. Parties take on a collective identity that defines them as a 'couple' or 'partnership' (e.g. a joint name, title, uniforms or logo). Parties agree to share common living or working space together. Parties create joint products or goals (a new product line, a common goal or mission statement, or a detailed plan for how they will live and work together in the future). Finally, parties high in IBT might commit to commonly shared values (such that the parties are actually committed to the same objectives and so can substitute for each other in external transactions). Parties with a strong IBT for each other can work together in what may seem to others to be a seamless chemistry.[5] As noted by one author, "Music is a suitable metaphor for IBT, like the harmonizing of a barbershop quartet. The parties learn to make music together in a harmony that is integrated and complex. Each knows the others' vocal range and pitch; each singer knows when to lead and follow; and each knows how to work with the others to maximize their strengths, compensate for their weaknesses, and create a joint product that is much greater than the sum of its parts. The unverbalized, synchronous chemistry of string quartets, cohesive work groups, or championship basketball teams are also excellent examples of this kind of trust in action."[6]

This form of trust can develop in working relationships if the parties come to know each other very well, but it is most likely to occur in intimate, personal relationships. Moreover, this form of trust stabilizes relationships during periods of conflict and negativity. Thus, when high-trusting parties engage in conflict, they tend to see the best in their partner' motives because they make different attributions about the conflict than do low-trusting parties. The determinant of whether relationships maintain or dissolve in a conflict may be due to the attributions parties make about the other's motives, determined by the existing level of trust.[7] Going back to our opening example of the conversations between Jim and his wife while disagreeing about the importance of cleaning up his study, both trust each other. Their strong relationship allows Debbie to believe that while Jim really hates to clean up his study, the mess will be dealt with eventually; similarly, Jim knows that he has to fulfill his promise to Debbie for their relationship to remain healthy. Similarly, while Jim has some good reason to doubt Aaron's story about turning in the homework paper, he knows that Aaron is fundamentally trustworthy and that one small white lie will not damage the fundamental trust and respect that each has for the other. However, a series of lies—or a major untruth—may cause serious and permanent damage to the relationship that will not be quick or easy to repair.

For a summary of actions that will help to build CBT and IBT, see Table 1.

Table 1   Strategies to Build and Manage Trust

Strategies to build and manage calculus-based trust with another party:

1. Act in a manner that is consistent and predictable. If the other party views you as behaving consistently, they will be able to predict your behavior more accurately and be more likely to trust you.
2. Tell the truth. Be honest about what you intend to do or what is 'true'. Even if the news or consequences are bad, your credibility will be enhanced if you are honest about the bad news.
3. Follow through. Keep your word. If you make promises, keep them. If you commit to a deadline, deliver by the deadline. Do what you say you will do. Agree on expectations as to what will be done and how it will be done.
4. Agree on procedures for resolving difficulties and miscommunications along the way.
5. Express positive emotions. Demonstrate and verbalize happiness, enthusiasm, and appreciation for the other.

Strategies to build and manage identification-based trust with another party:

1. Spend time with the other sharing personal viewpoints, perceptions, priorities, and values, Even in personal relationships, time should be set aside to explicitly focus on these activities. Mutuality is critical—share your own views and make sure to attend closely to the other's views.
2. Identify areas where you and the other have common interests, goals, or priorities. Spend time focusing on these commonalities and engage in activities, which help you come to know and understand the other better.
3. Create unique activities, products, events, representations, etc. that make you and the other distinctive and different, and use these as symbols of your commitment to the relationship.
4. Openly talk about areas where you and the other are uniquely different in tastes, preferences, beliefs, values, etc. and indicate that you appreciate and respect the other for expressing and espousing those differences. Strong relationships are built when we both share strong commonalities with another but also tolerate, respect and appreciate each other's uniqueness.

Summary

Trust is an incredibly important element in both business and personal relationships. With trust, parties can communicate openly, share information easily, not worry that personal vulnerabilities will be taken advantage of, and complete transactions with a minimum of hassle and fear of vulnerability. Trust is thus at the heart of effective negotiation and conflict resolution. Conversely, when trust is absent or broken, all of these processes become more difficult and complex. Parties' communication becomes guarded and strained; the parties have to take extensive time to verify information, and transactions require complex authorization and verification.

In this reading, we noted that there were two fundamental kinds of trust: a more calculus-based trust, which is at the heart of more formal transactions between parties, and an identification-based trust, a more intimate and personal kind of trust that binds strong personal and professional relationships together. Being effective in an organization requires knowing how to develop and cultivate both forms of trust so as to have productive business and personal relationships.

Endnotes

1. McAllister, D. J. (1995). Affect-and cognition-based trust as foundations for interpersonal cooperation in organizations. *Academy of Management Journal.* 38, 24–59. Lewicki, R. J., McAllister, D. J., & Bies, R. J. (1998). Trust and distrust: New relationships and realities. *Academy of Management Review*, 23, 438–458.

2. Malhotra, D. (2004). Trust and reciprocity decisions: The differing perspectives of trustors and trusted parties. *Organizational Behavior and Human Decision Processes.* 94, 61–73. Weber, J. M., Malhotra, D. & Murnighan, J. K. (2006). Normal acts of irrational trust: Motivated attributions and the trust development process. In Staw, B. M. & Kramer, R. *Research in Organizational Behavior*, Stanford, CT: JAI. 26, 75–101.

3. Mayer, R. C., Davis, J. H., & Schoorman, F. D. (1995). An integrative model of organizational trust. *Academy of Management Review, 20:* 709–734.

4. Deutsch, M. (1949). A theory of cooperation and competition. *Human Relations*, 2, 129–151.

5. Shapiro, D., Sheppard, B. H., & Cheraskin, L. (1992). Business on a handshake. *Negotiation Journal*, 8, 365–377. Lewicki, R. J. & Bunker, B. B. (1995). Trust in relationships: A model of trust development and decline. In B. B. Bunker & J. Z. Rubin (Eds.). *Conflict, Cooperation, and Justice: Essays Inspired by the Work of Morton Deutsch.* San Francisco: Jossey-Bass. Lewicki, R. J., & Bunker, B. B. (1996). Developing and maintaining trust in work relationships. In R. Kramer and T. R. Tyler (Eds.). *Trust in Organizations: Frontiers of Theory and Research.* Thousand Oaks, Calif.: Sage. Lewicki, R. J. & Stevenson, M. A. (1998). Trust development in negotiation: Proposed actions and a research agenda. *Business and Professional Ethics Journal*, 16, 99–132.

6. Lewicki, R. J. (2006). Trust, trust development and trust repair. In Deutsch, M., Coleman, P. & Marcus, E. (Eds.). *The Handbook of Conflict Resolution.* San Francisco: John Wiley, 92–119.

7. Miller, P. J. & Rempel, J. K. (2004). Trust and partner-enhancing attributions in close relationships. *Personality and Social Psychology Bulletin*, 30, 6, 695–705.

The Essentiality of "Justice" in Organizations: A Justice-as-Negotiation Perspective

Debra L. Shapiro

University of Maryland

"That's not fair" is heard, at least in Western nations where voice is typically valued and used to express discontent[1, 2] whenever people perceive themselves or others to be victims of unwanted circumstances. When spoken, or merely privately thought, "*That's not fair*" is typically accompanied by negative feelings, such as anger,[3, 4, 5] a desire to engage in revenge[6, 7] and resistance;[8] and these negative emotions are typically associated with uncooperative behaviors that threaten positive functioning on the part of individuals and/or their organizations.[9] This likely negative chain of events is among the main reasons why management researchers have urged managers to treat employees fairly[10, 11] or at a minimum to appear like they do.[12] Additional reasons include the moral, or ethical, rightness in doing so.[13, 14]

To heed the latter advice (to be or appear fair) requires understanding of the circumstances when employees are more than likely to perceive organizational justice (i.e., a sense that an organization has treated them fairly). This reading's first purpose is to describe actions likely to enhance perceived organizational justice, guided by research findings pertaining to this. A second purpose is to make clear that actions intended to create the appearance of justice may *not* always work; and as such, employees (at all levels, including managers) must also negotiate a correction of perceived injustice—that is, persuade others to perceive fairness where this is initially not seen. This reading's third purpose is to identify strategies for negotiating a correction of organizational injustice, guided by research that has occurred more broadly on the topic of managing conflict. This reading, therefore, integrates the justice and conflict management literatures (which are typically isolated from each other) and in so doing, illuminates a "*justice-as-negotiation/conflict management perspective.*" An implication of this perspective, which this reading concludes with, is that organizational justice perceptions are more dynamic and fluid in nature than is suggested by traditional (typically unidirectional top-down) descriptions of justice-managing dynamics. As such, future justice-related interventions and/or studies need to consider who all the potential "managers" of perceived justice may (or may not) be. The remainder of this reading delivers substance relating to its three purposes, in the order noted above.

Actions Likely to Enhance Perceived Organizational Justice

Several reviews of the organizational justice literature have summarized actions that have been theorized and found to generally enhance the justice, or fairness, that employees see.[15, 16, 17] The actions that have been theorized and found to generally enhance perceptions of organizational justice generally fall into three categories as shown in Table 1. Although there has been debate among researchers regarding whether to subdivide

Table 1 Definitions of Justice Perceptions and "Minimalist" Justice-Enhancing Strategies

Distributive Injustice

Definition: The perception that there has been an unfair distribution of valued resources (e.g., bonuses, fringe benefits, job opportunities including paid education-related trips, job promotions, and salary raises, etc.); greater levels of this perception correspond to greater levels of perceived unfairness regarding a valued resource's distribution.

Distributive Justice-Enhancing Strategy: Allocate valued resources fairly and make salient to others (via verbal strategies such as explanations) that the resource's distribution is fair.

Example: Giving equal rewards to all members of a group that achieves a goal.

Procedural Injustice

Definition: The perception that there have been unfair (e.g., biased, incomplete, or logically flawed) procedures and/or criteria used for determining valued resource distributions; greater levels of this perception correspond to greater levels of perceived unfairness regarding the procedure and/or criteria used to determine the manner in which valued resources get distributed.

Procedural Justice-Enhancing Strategy: Use fair criteria and/or procedures to guide the allocation of valued resources, and make salient to others (via verbal strategies such as explanations) why the criteria and/or procedural aspects are free of bias, complete, and/or logically sound.

Example: Follow a mutually developed and agreed-upon process for distributing rewards.

Interactional/Interpersonal Injustice

Definition: The perception that the interpersonal treatment (e.g., degree of interpersonal respect and/or sensitivity) shown by those who enact or explain the procedures used to determine resource-related decisions is unfair; greater levels of this perception correspond to greater levels of perceived unfairness regarding the (lack of) interpersonal respect and sensitivity shown toward receivers of valued resource distributions.

Interactional Justice-Enhancing Strategy: When enacting a procedure and/or explaining criteria used to guide a decision regarding the allocation of valued resources, do so by interpersonally treating participants in ways that demonstrate sensitivity and respectfulness.

Example: Be respectful in interactions with people affected by decisions. Consider local customs and norms.

"interpersonal forms of justice" into informational- and relational-elements,[18, 19] the three categories of injustice perceptions in Table 1 reflect the dominant consensus[20] due in part to the rarity with which survey respondents distinguish informational versus relational aspects of justice.[21] The qualities of the three types of perceptions of organizational justice perceptions, and the actions generally associated with strengthening these, are discussed next, each in turn.

Distributive Justice

As seen in Table 1, "distributive justice" regards the extent to which an allocation of valued resources is perceived as fair. Conversely, then, a lower level of distributive justice—or, equivalently, a greater level of "distributive injustice"— is perceived when a resource allocation is perceived as unfair. Situations involving students that illustrate greater levels of distributive injustice is when the grades given by an instructor at the end of the semester seem unfair, as might occur if students perceive that they deserved the grade of "A" but were denied. Other situations illustrating greater levels of distributive injustice include those where people (usually employees, but sometimes traffic court attendees)[22] reported as unfair: *not receiving resources/decisions they had requested;*[23, 24] *not being fairly paid;*[25] *not being allowed to retain valued resources, such as their jobs;*[26] and *not* being allowed to retain the freedom to smoke at work.[27] Actions likely to enhance distributive justice include, at a minimum, allocating a fair amount of valued resources to recipients and/or avoiding actions that will prevent this (such as denying resource requests, underpaying employees, implementing layoffs, or instituting new policies that ban previously accepted employee behaviors). The reasons being partly because avoiding the latter actions is not always feasible for organizations to justify what researchers recognized years ago as the practical need to consider other (non-distributive) strategies for heightening perceptions of a resource allocation's fairness. Such strategies are related to the other types of perceived justice, discussed next.

Procedural Justice

As seen in Table 1, "procedural justice" regards the extent to which the procedure or criteria used to determine the allocation of valued resources is perceived as fair. Conversely, then, a lower level of procedural justice—or, equivalently, a greater level of "procedural injustice"—is perceived when the procedure or criteria used to determine a resource-allocation is perceived as unfair. A situation involving students that illustrate greater levels of procedural injustice is when the grades given by an instructor at the end of the semester seem unfair *because the instructor failed to consider students' level of class-contribution despite the syllabus naming this criterion as one that would carry substantial weight in determining class grades.* Other situations illustrating greater levels of procedural injustice include those where people (again, usually employees)[28] have perceived the procedures and/or criteria used to guide organizational leaders' or bosses' decisions as inadequate due to seeming illogical, hard to understand, vague, and driven by personal, hence arbitrary, goals and points of view.[29] The actions likely to enhance procedural justice include, at a minimum, making resource recipients aware of the fairness associated with the procedural elements and/or criteria used to determine the amount of their resource allocation by avoiding actions that will prevent this (such as utilizing procedures and/or criteria that are inadequate in the ways described previously). The reason the provision of fair procedures and/or criteria are minimally needed to heighten perceptions of procedural justice is that these perceptions are influenced, too, by the interpersonal manner in which the procedures are enacted and/or resource decisions' criteria are explained. The fact that procedural participants and/or explanation receivers care about how respectfully they are treated by those who are providing the procedures/explanations is evident to anyone who views the U.S. Justice System as fair yet the bullying antics of some of its judges or lawyers when questioning witnesses as unfair. Indeed, the creation of "interactional justice,"[30, 31, 32, 33, 34] later termed "interpersonal justice,"[35] was borne out of the recognition that people care about *interpersonal* elements of decision making procedures—in addition to their structural elements, such as whether they allow participants' viewpoints to be heard (via themselves directly or via a representative, such as a lawyer).[36, 37]

Interpersonal Justice

As seen in Table 1, "interpersonal justice" regards the extent to which people (usually employees),[38] perceive the quality of interpersonal treatment they are receiving when participating in a decision-making procedure, such as when receiving a performance appraisal[39] and/or when being provided a decision's explanation. Conversely, then, a lower level of interpersonal justice—or, equivalently, a greater level of interpersonal injustice—is perceived when the interpersonal treatment administered to decision recipients seems to deprive them of their dignity and respect. Situations involving students that illustrate greater levels of interpersonal injustice is when an instructor, while explaining why a student did not receive an "A" grade, treats the student in a manner that harms the student's self-esteem (e.g., yells at, ridicules, or insults the student with derogatory remarks, especially in a public domain)—that is, treats the student abusively.[40] In work situations, interpersonal injustice is vividly illustrated when layoff victims are publicly "pink-slipped" and immediately required to pack up their personal belongings, return office keys, and escorted outside of the work premises.[41] So prevalent is the latter scenario during layoffs that employees have been found to post concerns about being interpersonally humiliated this way when they learn that layoffs in their organization are impending.[42] It logically follows that the actions likely to enhance interpersonal justice include, at a minimum, respectfully treating employees when administering procedures or when giving explanations associated with decisions of importance to them, and/or avoiding doing anything that will prevent employees from feeling dignity, such as "abusive" behaviors like yelling at them, publicly criticizing them, or doing anything else that will likely harm their self-esteem. The reason why giving employees interpersonal treatment of high quality, also termed "respect" by Tom Tyler and Steven Blader,[43] is minimally needed to heighten perceptions of interpersonal justice is that these perceptions are influenced, too, by the strength with which employees perceive the other types of justice (described above and shown in Table 1). For example, employees who learn that they have been treated with negative bias during a performance appraisal (and are thus victims of procedural injustice) and/or that they have received a lower pay raise than their peers (and are thus victims of distributive injustice) are likely to feel devalued; this in turn is likely to constrain the extent to which interpersonal expressions of appreciation (such as "we value you here") can enable these employees to perceive sincere levels of interpersonal justice. Such a challenge illustrates why Kathryn Roloff, Joel Brockner, and Batia Wiesenfeld[44] have recently noted the need for justice-enhancing actions to be perceived as "authentic" if they are to actually achieve justice-enhancing effects.

In summary, the three types of perceived justice shown in Table 1 and described above carry clear implications for the actions needed, at least minimally, in order to enhance the degree to which justice is perceived. The three types of justice perceptions *interactively* influence how much justice people do or do not see.[45] By definition, this means that the greatest amount of justice will probably be perceived when those assessing this have experienced actions relating to *all three types of justice*; and that a lesser degree of justice will probably be perceived when fewer actions than all of these are taken, explaining why the justice-enhancing actions associated with each type of justice perception have been described as needed "at a minimum" and named "minimalist strategies" in Table 1.

"Justice-Enhancing Actions" Do *Not* Always Enhance Justice

It is a well-known fact that justice-enhancing communications do *not* always enhance perceived justice. In particular, justice is less likely to be perceived when: (1) the *communicator* is distrusted; (2) the *message* lacks logical soundness; and (3) other *"audience members"* convince the receiver that the communicator and/or the message lacks trustworthiness.

These three outcomes are tied intricately to some of the dimensions people use to assess "justice," shown in Table 1. For example, a communicator's degree of trustworthiness is directly related to how concerned the communicator seems to be about receivers' wellbeing,[51] which is typically deemed higher when communicators show interpersonal concern, sensitivity, and consideration—all indicators of interpersonal justice.[52] As another example, the logical soundness of a communicator's message is directly related to the perceived adequacy and fairness of the criteria and procedural elements used to determine decision outcomes—and therefore, to procedural justice.

The third element—the extent to which the communication receives support from audience members—depends *on the expressed (in)justice of others in the workplace,* such as other employees who express concerns about an impending layoff,[54] team members,[55] members of work organizations' networks,[56] and/or members of employees' social networks outside as well as inside the workplace.[57] These multiple sources for (in)justice-related communications mean that control over the justice-enhancing message is increasingly less in the hands of one person. The growing multiplicity of employees' informational sources due to technology,[59] including digital bulletin boards,[60] also means there is a greater chance more than ever for the efforts of any communicator attempting to enhance justice to fail.

For these reasons, a *justice-as-negotiation* perspective during which people attempt to correct others' perceptions of injustice into perceptions of justice seems appropriate. Viewed this way, it becomes necessary for people attempting to get others to perceive justice to understand fundamental strategies of negotiation—that is, strategies by which people who initially disagree can come to agree with each other.

Strategies for Negotiating a Correction of Perceived Injustice

Whether one is attempting to get others to agree on a price, an attitude, or a perception (e.g., how fairly an organizational member has behaved), one is trying to change others' opposing views; such attempts are generally more successful when those attempting to influence others *are trusted* by their recipients. People tend to more willingly cooperate with those they trust rather than distrust.[63] Not surprisingly, then, negotiation researchers have long advised negotiators aiming to gain cooperation, or concessions, to engage in *behaviors that generally earn trust and to avoid behaviors likely to damage trust.*

Extrapolating from this, it seems likely that, when someone in the organization claims that another person (say, "P") has behaved unjustly, and this perception is disputed by the accused party (P), P's ability to potentially get her accuser to correct her perception of injustice will be greater if P can earn the accuser's trust. This is easier said than done since the accusation itself is likely to potentially harm P's legitimacy, and as a result cause P to suffer angst and anger about what she believes is undeserved slander. However, if a collaborative relationship is to ensue, then P needs to do the following:

1. Approach the discrepancy between one's view and that of one's accuser by asking: "What actions have led you to perceive injustice?" *and to listen open-mindedly* to this query's response, then use the data provided in the answer to either express an apology for doing something that created perceived injustice or to point out (utilizing the strategies shown in Table 1) how her actions were, in actuality, fair or fair-minded.

2. If these efforts fail to reverse negative perceptions, the dialogue is at risk of becoming a "conflict-spiral." To break conflict spirals, one or both parties need to point out the mutual damage likely to occur if they fail to reconcile *and* the mutual benefits that accrue if they, instead, can reconcile (with emphasis on the latter positive message). Doing this combines collaborative messages with threatening messages in a manner that makes clear that the communicator's preferred course of action is collaborative, or help-oriented, in nature.[65]

3. If both of the above efforts fail, then a third party who is trusted by both parties—which is possible only if the third party is neutral and unbiased[66]—needs to help reconcile these parties' differences. Since negotiated agreements typically require concessions from both sides, the latter dialogue is most likely to end with agreed-upon perceptions of justice when both sides concede *something*. In the context of negotiating "justice," this may mean both parties' agreeing—with or without the help of a neutral third party—that P's initial actions may have *appeared* unfair from the vantage point of the other party, and that P's actions can here forward be *made more fair* with requested changes to the decision, procedure, and/or interpersonal actions taken by P towards the other party. Such a dialogue would likely influence not only how fair P's most recent or current actions are, but also how fair P's future actions are. This is because, as noted before, agreement on fair procedures tend to enhance the perceived fairness of those procedures' (later) outcomes.

Implications of Justice-As-Negotiation Perspective

What are the implications of recognizing organizational (in)justice as a negotiated dynamic? First and foremost, a *justice-as-negotiation* perspective suggests that the typical top-down descriptions given to justice-enhancing strategies[67, 68] needs to be revised to reflect the role that communication *receivers* play in determining the outcome of any message-giving.[69] Second, and relatedly, those who wish to enhance the fairness with which others view their actions need to become skilled at negotiating and managing conflict; that is, they need to be *perceived as trustworthy messengers*.

Endnotes

1. Brockner, J. (et al.). (2001). Culture and procedural justice: The moderating influence of power distance on reactions to voice. *Journal of Experimental Social Psychology, 37,* 300–315.
2. Shao, R., Rupp, D. E., Skarlicki, D. P., Jones, K. S. (2013). Managing justice across cultures: A meta-analytic review, a management framework, and a crosscultural research agenda. *Journal of Management, 39,* 263–301.

3. Cropanzano, R. (et al.). (2008). How regulatory focus impacts the process-by-outcome interaction for perceived fairness and emotions. *Organizational Behavior and Human Decision Processes*, 105, 36–51.

4. Shapiro, D. L. & Bies, R. J. (1994). Threats, bluffs, and disclaimers in negotiation. *Organizational Behavior and Human Decision Processes*, 60: 14–35.

5. Spencer, S., & Rupp, D. E. (2009). Angry, guilty, and conflicted: Injustice toward coworkers heightens emotional labor through cognitive and emotional mechanisms. *Journal of Applied Psychology*, 94, 429–444.

6. Bies, R. J. & Tripp, T. (in press). Negotiating the peace in the face of modern distrust: Dealing with anger and revenge in the 21st century workplace. In B. Goldman & D. L. Shapiro, (Eds.). *The psychology of negotiation in the 21st century workplace: New challenges and new solutions. Frontiers Series of the Society for Industrial and Organizational Psychology.* New York: The Psychology Press/Routledge.

7. Skarlicki, D. P., Folger, R., & Tesluk, P. (1999). Personality as a moderator in the relationship between fairness and retaliation. *Academy of Management Journal*, 42(1): 100–108.

8. Kirkman, B. L. & Shapiro, D. L. (2001). The impact of cultural values on job satisfaction and organizational commitment in self-managing work teams: The mediating role of employee resistance. *Academy of Management Journal*, 44(3), 557–569.

9. Conlon, D. E. & Ross, W. (in press). The effect of perceived/felt (in)justice on cooperativeness: Implications for negotiators as "justice-enhancing communicators" in an era of social networking. In B. Goldman & D. L. Shapiro, (Eds.). *The psychology of negotiation in the 21st century workplace: New challenges and new solutions. Frontiers Series of the Society for Industrial and Organizational Psychology.* New York: The Psychology Press/Routledge.

10. Bies, R. J. (1987). The predicament of injustice: The management of moral outrage. In L.L. Cummings & B.M. Staw (Eds.). *Research in organizational behavior.* Greenwich, CT: JAI Press 9: 289–319.

11. Shapiro, D. L., Lewicki, R. J., & Devine, P. (1995). When do employees choose deceptive tactics to stop unwanted organizational change?: A relational perspective. In R. J. Lewicki, B. H. Sheppard, & R. Bies (Eds.). *Research on negotiation in organizations.* Greenwich, CT: JAI Press, Inc 5, 155–183.

12. Greenberg, J. (1990a). Looking versus being fair: Managing impreesions of organizational justice. In B. M. Staw & L. L. Cummings (Eds.). *Research in organizational behavior.* Greenwich, CT: JAI Press 12, 111–157.

13. Cropanzano, R., Goldman, B., & Folger, R. (2003). Deontic justice: the role of moral principles in workplace fairness. *Journal of Organizational Behavior*, 24: 1019–1024.

14. Rupp, D. E., & Bell, C. M. (2010). Extending the deontic model of justice: Moral self regulation in third-party responses to injustice. *Business Ethics Quarterly*, 20, 89–106.

15. Conlon & Ross (in press).

16. Greenberg (1990a).

17. Shapiro, D. L. & Brett, J. M. (2005). What is the role of control in organizational justice? In J. Greenberg & J. Colquitt (Eds.). *Handbook of organizational justice.* NJ: Lawrence Erlbaum, Inc., 155–177.

18. Colquitt, J. A. (2001). On the dimensionality of organizational justice: A construct validation of a measure. *Journal of Applied Psychology*, 86, 386–400.

19. Greenberg (1990a).

20. Shapiro, D. L. & Brett, J. M. (2005). What is the role of control in organizational justice? In J. Greenberg & J. Colquitt (Eds.). *Handbook of organizational justice.* NJ: Lawrence Erlbaum, Inc., 155–177.

21. Colquitt (2001).

22. Shapiro & Brett (2005).

23. Bies, R. J. & Shapiro, D. L. (1987). Interactional justice: The influence of causal accounts. *Social Justice Research*, 1: 199–218.

24. Bies, R. J. & Shapiro, D. L. (1988). Voice and justification: Their influence on procedural fairness judgments. *Academy of Management Journal*, 31(3): 676–685.

25. Greenberg, J. (1990b). Employee theft as a reaction to underpayment inequity: The hidden cost of paycuts. *Journal of Applied Psychology*, 75(5): 561–568.

26. Brockner, J., DeWitt, R. L., Grover, S., & Reed, T. (1990). When it is especially important to explain why: Factors affecting the relationship between managers' explanations of a layoff and survivors' reactions to the layoff. *Journal of Experimental Social Psychology*, 26(5): 389–407.

27. Greenberg, J. (1994). Using socially fair treatment to promote acceptance of a work site smoking ban. *Journal of Applied Psychology*, 79(2): 288–297.

28. Shapiro & Brett (2005).

29. Shapiro, D.L., Buttner, E. H., & Barry, B. (1994). Explanations: What factors enhance their perceived adequacy? *Organizational Behavior & Human Decision Processes*, 58(3): 346–368.

30. Bies, R. J. (1987). The predicament of injustice: The management of moral outrage. In L.L. Cummings & B.M. Staw (Eds.). *Research in organizational behavior*. Greenwich, CT: JAI Press, 289–319.

31. Bies, R. J. (2001). Interactional (in)justice: The sacred and the profane. In J. Greenberg & R. Cropanzano (Eds.). *Advances in organizational justice*. Palo Alto: Stanford University Press, 89–118.

32. Bies, R. J., & Moag, J. S. (1986). Interactional justice: Communication criteria for fairness. In B. H. Sheppard (Ed.). *Research on negotiation in organizations*, vol. 1. Greenwich, CT: JAI Press, 43–44.

33. Bies & Shapiro (1987).

34. Bies & Shapiro (1988).

35. Greenberg (1990a).

36. Folger, R., & Greenberg, J. (1985). Procedural justice: An interpretive analysis of personnel systems. In K. Rowland & G. Ferris (Eds.). *Research in personnel and human resources management*. Greenwich, CT: JAI Press, 141–183.

37. Thibaut, J. & Walker, L. (1975). *Procedural justice: A psychological analysis*. Hillsdale, NJ: Erlbaum.

38. Shapiro & Brett (2005).

39. Folger & Greenberg (1985).

40. Tepper, B. J. (2000). Consequences of abusive supervision. *Academy of Management Journal*, 43(2): 178–190.

41. Brockner et al. (1990).

42. Conlon, D. E. & Shapiro, D. L. (2002). Employee postings and company responses to downsizing inquiries: Implications for managing, and reacting to, organizational change. In J. Wagner III., J. Bartunek, & K. Elsbach (Eds.). *Advances in Qualitative Research*. Greenwich, CT: JAI Press, 4: 39–67.

43. Tyler, T. R. & Blader, S. L. (2000). *Cooperation in groups*. Philadelphia, PA: Psychology Press.

44. Roloff, K., Brockner, J., & Wiesenfeld, B. (in press). The role of process fairness authenticity in negotiations and its challenges for 21st century-negotiators. In B. Goldman & D.L. Shapiro, (Eds.). *The psychology of negotiation in the 21st century workplace: New challenges and new solutions. Frontiers Series of the Society for Industrial and Organizational Psychology.* New York: The Psychology Press/Routledge.

45. Goldman, B. M. (et al.). (2008). The role of ideology in mediated disputes at work: A justice perspective. *International Journal of Conflict Management*, 19(3): 210–233.

46. Petty, R. E. & Cacioppo, J. T. (1981). *Attitudes and persuasion: Classic and contemporary approaches*. Dubuque, Iowa: William C. Brown Company Publishers, Inc.

47. For research findings supporting this, see Goldman, B. M., Cropanzano, R., Stein, J. H., Shapiro, D. L., Thatcher, S. & Ko, J. (2008). The role of ideology in mediated disputes at work: A justice perspective. *International Journal of Conflict Management*, 19(3): 210–233.
48. Petty & Cacioppo (1981).
49. Shapiro, D. L., Brass, D., & Labianca, J. (2008). Examining justice from a social network perspective. In S. W. Gilliland, D.D. Steiner, & D.P. Skarlicki (Eds.). *Justice, morality, and social responsibility: Research in social issues in management*. Charlotte, NC: Information Age Publishing, 201–226.
50. Roloff et al (in press).
51. Deutsch, M. (1958). Trust and suspicion. *Journal of Conflict Resolution*, 2(4): 265–279.
52. Shapiro & Brett (2005).
53. Tyler & Blader (2000).
54. Conlon & Shapiro (2002).
55. Roberson, Q. M. & Colquitt, J. A. (2005). Shared and configural justice: A social network model of justice in teams. *Academy of Management Review*, 30(3): 595–607.
56. Shapiro et al. (2008).
57. Conlon & Ross (in press).
58. Shapiro and Brett (2005).
59. Conlon & Ross (in press).
60. Conlon & Shapiro (2002).
61. See a review of the negotiation literature by Neale, M. A. & Northcraft, G. B. (1991). Behavioral negotiation theory: A framework for conceptualizing dyadic bargaining. In B. Staw & L. L. Cummings (Eds.). *Research in organizational behavior*, 13: 147–190.
62. See a review of the negotiation and conflict management literature by Shapiro, D. L. & Kulik, C. (2004). Disputing with faceless opponents: New challenges for conflict management research. In M. J. Gelfand & J. M. Brett (Eds.). *Handbook of negotiation and culture*. Palo Alto, CA: Stanford University Press, 177–192.
63. Shapiro, D. L., Sheppard, B. H., & Cheraskin, L. (1992). Business on a handshake. *The Negotiation Journal*, 8(4): 365–377.
64. Brett, J.M., Shapiro, D.L., & Lytle, A. (1998). Breaking the bonds of reciprocity in negotiations. *Academy of Management Journal*, 41(4): 410–424.
65. Brett et al. (1998).
66. Shapiro, D. L. & Brett, J. M. (1993). Comparing three processes underlying judgments of procedural justice: A field study of mediation and arbitration. *Journal of Personality and Social Psychology*, 65(6): 1167–1177.
67. A description of these top-down justice-enhancing communications was first offered by Bies, 1987; see Endnote #30 for this complete reference.
68. Greenberg (1990a).
69. Conlon & Shapiro (2002).
70. Von Glinow, M. A., Shapiro, D. L., & Brett, J. M. (2004). Can we *talk*, and should we?: Managing emotional conflict in multicultural teams. *The Academy of Management Review*, 29(4): 578–592.
71. Brett, Shapiro, & Lytle (1998).
72. Schei, V., Rognes, J., & Shapiro, D. L. (2011). Can individualists and cooperators play together?: The effects of mixed social motives in negotiations. *Journal of Experimental Social Psychology*, 47(2): 371–377.
73. Conlon & Ross (in press).
74. Roberson & Colquitt (2005).
75. Shapiro et al. (2008).
76. Shapiro & Brett (2005).

Negotiation Traps

Kimberly D. Elsbach

University of California, Davis

Negotiation can be a complex undertaking. There are interests of multiple parties to understand, concessions and trade-offs to consider, and constraints based on past agreements and prior expectations to appreciate. Add to this time limitations and incomplete information, and you have got a recipe for frustration and impasse. It is no wonder that so many negotiations fail to produce satisfactory settlements.

Yet, despite the enormity of all of these obstacles, none of them represent the most common reason that negotiations fail: mental error. Mental errors—which typically involve simplified or non-rational thinking—are the bane of the effective negotiator because such mental errors are often made unconsciously. In essence, these mental errors represent negotiation traps—hidden pitfalls that are just waiting to snare us.

In this article, I will outline some of the most common negotiation traps that result from mental errors. In detail in Table 1, I summarize these traps and explain how to avoid them.

Table 1 Common Negotiation Traps and How to Avoid Them

Name of Trap	How It Works	How to Avoid It
Anchoring	• initial offers anchor negotiators' view of what is reasonable; higher initial offers lead to higher ultimate settlements	• know what is reasonable and do not respond to unreasonable initial offers; use pre-emptive initial offers to anchor the other party
Overconfidence	• unreasonable estimation of the correctness of one's judgments leads negotiators to make fewer concessions and to undervalue alternatives	• be aware that overconfidence is highly likely; consider why your judgment might be wrong; approach negotiations in serious mood
Framing	• negotiators are risk-seeking when offers are presented in terms of avoiding potential losses • negotiators are risk-averse when offers are presented in terms of obtaining potential gains	• re-frame offers in terms of potential gains to avoid taking undue risks or rejecting reasonable trade-offs and concessions
Irrational Escalation	• negotiators continue a previously selected course of action beyond what is rational because they want to appear "consistent" and because they want to justify prior decisions to affirm their competence	• set limits for settlements prior to the negotiation and stick with them • never agree to a deal that is worse than your BATNA • explain to others and yourself why you no longer back a prior decision to demonstrate learning

Negotiation Traps

As noted earlier, negotiation traps typically involve non-rational or simplified thinking. While such thinking can reduce our mental load in everyday situations, they can also cause us to make very poor choices during negotiations. In the following sections, I describe four common mental traps in negotiations and provide some useful tactics for avoiding them.

Anchoring in Initial Offers

Anchoring involves the perception that an initially considered option is reasonable and all subsequent negotiation should relate to this initial option. For example, if I place a house on the market with a list price of $500,000 and a different buyer makes an offer based on this price (even if the offer is below the list price) then that buyer has considered the initial list price as reasonable (reasonable enough to make an offer). Subsequently, if the buyer eventually purchases the house, he or she will end up paying more for the house than if the original list price was $400,000. Why? Because the initial list price of $500,000 anchors the buyer in terms of what is reasonable, and all subsequent negotiation will be based on that anchor. If the initial list price is lower, by contrast, the initial anchor will be lower, and all subsequent negotiation will be based on this lower anchor.

Such anchoring effects have been demonstrated by research on real estate markets[2] and routinely influence negotiation outcomes based on an initial offer. That is, *the* initial offer—given by one negotiating party and responded to by another negotiating party—anchors the negotiation and influences the ending settlement. Such anchors need not be only related to price. For example, if I'm negotiating with my boss about how large my new office should be, and I suggest that my office should be 300 square feet (which is larger than her current office), she may balk, and counter with a smaller-sized office. Yet, because I've anchored her at the high end of the spectrum, she is likely to agree to an office size that is larger than what she would have if my initial proposal were for a 100 square foot office. The fact that she considered my initial offer of 300 square feet and responded to it anchored her at a larger office size.

Notice that in all of examples the person receiving the initial offer has considered it and responded to it. This is essential for an anchor to work in an initial offer. For an anchor to be "set" it must be reasonable enough for the receiving party to consider and counter it. If an initial offer is completely unreasonable, the other party may walk away, or ask for a new initial offer, thus removing the anchor.

This theory suggests a strategy for avoiding being anchored by an unreasonable initial offer; that is, knowing what is reasonable and walking away from an unreasonable initial offer (or asking for a new, more reasonable initial offer) protects you from being anchored in an unreasonable way. What if you're not sure what is reasonable? You can pre-empt an unreasonable anchor by setting one yourself. Make an initial offer that you know is within your reach, and see if the other party responds.

Overconfidence in Constructing Settlement Packages

Overconfidence is an unreasonable estimation of the correctness of one's judgments and is shown to be a common human bias affecting individuals in all walks of life and is most likely to occur when facing difficult or complex judgments.[3] Examples of overconfidence in daily life include overestimations of the likelihood that one will reap gains in personal investments, win in games of chance, and answer questions correctly on exams. Even if we know that the average chance of a correct judgment is 50 percent, most of us predict that our own odds of a correct judgment are much higher (65 to 70 percent).[4] As a result, overconfidence has been blamed for such famous disasters as the decision to launch the space shuttle Challenger (decision makers were overconfident that low temperatures would not affect the launch) and unpreparedness for the Chernobyl nuclear plant accident (administrators were overconfident that an accident would not happen at Chernobyl).[5]

Overconfidence in negotiation often leads negotiators to be unrealistically optimistic that an opposing party will accept their offers or settlement packages. This is because overconfident negotiators perceive that their arguments will be accepted by others, without question, as valid.[6] As a result, overconfidence often leads negotiators to undervalue their opponent's position and not consider why opponents might not want to accept their offers. Negotiators with higher confidence are less likely to make concessions to opponents and to fail to reach agreements when mutually acceptable outcomes are possible.[7]

To counter the negative impact of overconfidence in negotiation, researchers have found that an effective strategy is merely making negotiators aware of the propensity for overconfidence. Thus, in an experimental negotiation, those who were told (versus not told) that negotiators often overestimate their likelihood of success were more likely to make concessions to opposing parties and obtain superior settlements in the negotiation.[8] Another effective tactic for avoiding overconfidence is to stop and consider why your judgment might be wrong. It turns out that merely listing reasons why one's judgments could be wrong substantially reduces unrealistic overconfidence.[9] Finally, because overconfidence is exacerbated by positive moods (because those in positive moods are more likely to perceive that their own intuition is correct),[10] negotiators may reduce the chances of overconfidence by keeping a serious tone during negotiation and avoiding activities during negotiations (e.g., eating, socializing) that are shown to lead to happy moods.

Framing When Considering Alternatives and Accepting Concessions

Framing in negotiation typically refers to whether an alternative is presented in terms of obtaining potential gains (i.e., if you take my offer, these good things will happen) vs. avoiding potential losses (i.e., if you don't take my offer, these bad things will happen).[11] People are shown to be "risk-averse" (i.e., less likely to take risks) when considering potential gains, but "risk-seeking" (i.e., more likely to take risks) when considering potential losses.[12] Thus, if you say, "You could make a large amount of money by investing in this new internet company," I will be risk-averse and be very careful about my decision to invest because you've framed the option in terms of potential gains (i.e., the money I could make). By contrast, if you say to me, "if you don't invest in this new internet company, you will lose an opportunity to make a lot of money," I will be risk-seeking and be less careful about my decision to invest because you've framed the option in terms of potential losses (i.e., the opportunity I could lose).

Such framing of alternatives has been seen frequently as an explanation for the approval of risky ventures. For example, in early 2003, during the U.S. Congress discussion about going to war with Iraq, politicians often argued for going to war by claiming that, "If we don't invade Iraq, Saddam Hussein will develop weapons of mass destruction." These statements framed "going to war with Iraq" in terms of avoiding potential costs (if we don't go to war, bad things will happen). It appears this type of framing led those in Congress to be risk-seeking, as they approved the invasion of Iraq in March 2003. Would this approval have been as likely if the option of "going to war with Iraq" had, instead, been framed in terms of obtaining potential gains (i.e., "if we invade Iraq we can extend democracy to the Iraqi people")? Because this option is framed in terms of obtaining potential gains, members of Congress would likely have been risk-averse in evaluating the option of "going to war with Iraq" and may have been less willing to approve of this option.

In negotiations, framing can similarly affect negotiators and lead them to agree to risky offers that they would not normally accept. For example, if I present a highly sought-after job candidate with a job offer, I might increase her chances of accepting my offer (which is a risk, because she is likely giving up other potential offers) by presenting it in terms of avoiding potential losses (e.g., if you don't accept this offer in one week, we will have to consider other candidates). This tactic, called an "exploding offer" (i.e., an offer that expires at a specific time), is often used to get negotiators to view taking a risky offer as the only way to avoid potential losses.

In other cases, accepting an offer (rather than not accepting the offer) may be portrayed as a potential loss to be avoided. That is, I could approach a job candidate who has a job offer from a competing firm with the pitch that "if you take the other job, you will miss out on this once-in-a-lifetime opportunity to work at our firm." To avoid this potential loss of opportunity, the candidate may decline the other firm's offer.

A third way that framing affects negotiators is in their willingness to accept concessions and make trade-offs (e.g., I'll accept a lower price if you deliver the product faster).[13] Because rejecting concessions and trade-offs is often a risky strategy because it can lead to the loss of a deal, negotiators who view rejecting concessions in terms of avoiding potential losses are more likely to take the risky option. Thus, if I perceive that rejecting a concession would help me to avoid losing out on profit, then I may be likely to reject that concession (and not make a deal). In this way, a loss-avoidance frame on concessions often leads negotiators to walk away from potential deals.

There are, however, ways to avoid these traps of framing. First, to avoid taking risky offers without careful consideration, negotiators should be wary of offers framed in terms of loss avoidance. Thus, an effective tactic is to re-frame any offer one is presented with in terms of obtaining potential gains. If someone frames an offer as, "If you don't take this offer, these bad things will happen", you should ask yourself, "What good is likely to happen if I do accept this offer?" If these gains are not enough to get you to say yes, you should probably think twice about agreeing to the offer. Second, to avoid walking away from a potential deal because you want to avoid potential losses that would result from making concessions, you should re-frame the option of taking concessions in terms of potential gains. Thus, if you find yourself thinking, "If I agree to these concessions, these losses will occur," you should ask yourself, "What good things will I gain if I accept these concessions?" If these gains seem reasonable, then you should probably consider saying yes to the concessions.

Irrational Escalation and Pursuit of Outcomes

Irrational escalation occurs when people fixate on pursuing a course of action or achieving a stated goal, even when there is substantial evidence that such a course or goal is unproductive.[14] Famous examples of irrational escalation come from politics and business. For example, the U.S. escalation of military operations in Vietnam during the 1960s and 1970s has often been blamed on escalating commitment to the pursuit of "winning" the war against communism. This stance made an end to the Vietnam war an admission of losing, regardless of the costs incurred. As Barry Staw wrote in his seminal paper on irrational escalation:[15]

> At an early stage of the U.S. involvement in the Vietnam War, George Ball, then Undersecretary of State, wrote the following in a memo to President Johnson: "The decision you face now is crucial. Once large numbers of U.S. troops are committed to direct combat, they will begin to take heavy casualties in a war they are ill equipped to fight in a non-cooperative if not downright hostile countryside. Once we suffer large casualties, we will have started a well-nigh irreversible process. Our involvement will be so great that we cannot—without national humiliation—stop short of achieving our complete objectives. Of the two possibilities, I think humiliation would be more likely than the achievement of our objectives—even after we have paid terrible costs." *[Sheehan & Kenworthy, 1971, memo dated July 1, 1965]*

In negotiations, the early commitment to a course of action (i.e., winning a contract) can lead negotiators to continue to pursue those actions beyond any reasonable benefit that they may have. For example, if a salesperson for a publishing company brags to his colleagues that he is going to win a large contract from the State Department of Education for one of the firm's textbooks, he has made a public commitment to achieving that goal. If, then, during negotiations with the State Department of Education, he finds that they will not agree to a pricing scheme that covers the firms' costs, he will find it difficult to pull out of the negotiation because he has committed to winning the contract. Instead of pulling out, he may continue to pursue a deal with the State, including lowering the sales price, so that he can act consistently with his previous commitment. Further, he may agree to other requests (e.g., an expensive re-write of the text) to affirm that the original decision to pursue the contract with the State was correct.

This example illustrates two of the underlying reasons that irrational escalation occurs in negotiation: (1) the need to act consistently with public commitments, and (2) the need to justify previous decisions as correct.[16] First, the need to act consistently with public commitments causes irrational escalation because there exists a strong norm, common in the United States and other western cultures, that equates consistency with integrity. By contrast, those that display inconsistency—even if their inconsistency is warranted because new information suggests that old commitments are no longer valid—are perceived as "wishy-washy" or "flip-floppers." In instances where one's prior commitments were made of free will and publicly, there is a widely held belief that one should honor those commitments if one has integrity.

Second, the need to justify prior decisions as correct is a strong pressure that many in positions of leadership feel because justifying past decisions validates their competence to make decisions. Thus, leaders often perceive that if one of their past decisions is not justified, then all of their past decisions will become suspect. To avoid creating doubt in their ability to make good decisions, then, leaders may continue to defend past decisions by continuing to pursue and escalate an established course of action.

To avoid these problems associated with irrational escalation, negotiators should set clear guidelines for pulling out of a negotiation *before* they enter it. For example, before entering talks, negotiators should establish specific limits for quantitative issues (i.e., "we will not offer more than $100,000 for this service") and determine when they need to pull back and seek more information on qualitative issues (i.e., if they change the technology, we will stop negotiating until we can get input from our technical experts). Negotiators should also keep in mind their BATNA (i.e., their Best Alternative to a Negotiated Agreement)—which is their best option to pursue if the current deal falls through. If a negotiator has other options to pursue, then she should always compare a possible settlement to the best of these options before making a deal. Further, she should never agree to a settlement that is worse than her BATNA. Finally, if it is necessary to change course from a previous decision (i.e., before we pursued a strategy of low cost, but now we are pursuing a strategy of high quality), negotiators should explain to themselves and others why they are doing so (i.e., we are doing this because new research shows us that quality is more important than costs). This type of explanation should help both the negotiations and their audiences to value their ability to *learn* over their need to justify past decisions.

Conclusion

Negotiation is a tough undertaking, fraught with complexities and potential pitfalls. The last thing a negotiator needs is to hamstring him or herself by adding mental errors to the mix. In this reading, you have been introduced to a few of the most common mental errors that can trap negotiators and prevent them from achieving positive outcomes. By understanding these errors and how to avoid them, you should be better prepared to face your next negotiation with confidence.

Endnotes

1. See Gilovich, T., Griffin, D. W., & Kahneman, D. (2002). *Heuristics and Biases: The Psychology of Intuitive Judgment*. Cambridge University Press.
2. See Northcraft, G. & Neal, M. (1987). Amateurs, experts, and real estate: An anchoring-and-adjustment perspective on property pricing decisions, *Organizational Behavior and Human Decision Processes*, 84–97.
3. Griffin, D., & Tversky, A. (2002). The weighing of evidence and the determinants of confidence. In T. Gilovich, D. W. Griffin, & D. Kahneman (Eds.). *Heuristics and Biases: The Psychology of Intuitive Judgment*. Cambridge University Press. 230–249.
4. Plous, S. (1993). *The Psychology of Judgment and Decision Making*. New York: McGraw-Hill.
5. Ibid.
6. Neale, M. A. & Bazerman, M. H. (1985). The effects of framing and negotiator overconfidence on bargaining behaviors and outcomes. *Academy of Management Journal*, 28, 34–49.
7. Ibid.

8. Ibid.

9. Plous, S. (1993). *The Psychology of Judgment and Decision Making*. New York: McGraw-Hill.

10. Elsbach, K. & Barr, P. (1999). The effects of mood on individuals' use of structured decision protocols. *Organization Science*, 10, 181–198.

11. Neale, M. A. & Bazerman, M. H. (1985). The effects of framing and negotiator overconfidence on bargaining behaviors and outcomes. *Academy of Management Journal*, 28, 34–49.

12. Tversky, A., & Kahneman, D. (1981). The framing of decisions and the psychology of choice. *Science*, 211, 453–463.

13. Neale, M. A. & Bazerman, M. H. (1985). The effects of framing and negotiator overconfidence on bargaining behaviors and outcomes. *Academy of Management Journal*, 28, 34–49.

14. Staw, B. M. (1991). The escalation of commitment to a course of action. *Academy of Management Review*, 6, 577–587.

15. Ibid, 577–578.

16. Ibid.

11 Diversity and Communication

Topic Summary Learning Objectives

1. Discuss why diversity is important to organizations.

2. Describe and provide examples of different types of diversity.

3. Present three approaches to communication: the sender–receiver model, the co-orienting model, and the conversational learning model.

4. List the challenges of communication and the importance of information literacy.

5. Outline the process for developing a targeted message and how storytelling can be an effective form of communication.

6. Apply concepts of diversity and communication to organizations.

Key terms

Baby-Boomers, p. 389
benefits of diversity, p. 387
"big data," p. 392
co-orienting, p. 392
communication style, p. 391
conversational learning model of communication, p. 392

diversity, p. 387
generational diversity, p. 389
Generation-X, p. 390
Generation-Y, p. 390
information literacy, p. 392

Millennials, p. 390
parochialism, p. 392
role diversity, p. 388
sender–receiver model of communication, p. 391
storytelling, p. 394

Introduction to Diversity and Communication

This topic summary explains two interrelated organizational topics: diversity and communication. The first section provides a definition of diversity and describes the benefits of diversity for organizations. Two facets of diversity are discussed in detail: generational diversity and gender diversity. The second section focuses on communication. Communication is linked to diversity because effective communication requires understanding how differences among people are associated with the communication process. The discussion of communication begins with a review of the contemporary communication context and the importance of information literacy. Effective communication requires targeting a message in different ways, depending on the particular audience. Figure 11.1 provides an overview of the subtopics in this topic summary.

Diversity

1 Discuss why diversity is important to organizations.

Diversity describes similarities and differences among people. In the context of organizations, diversity involves the processes of valuing differences in experience, background, and perspective. By valuing diversity in these areas, organizations are better equipped to: 1) respond to dynamic change because the organization increases its ability to adapt, 2) consider a wider range of perspectives when making decisions, and 3) promote a culture of fairness. As organizations become more global, diversity in thought, background, experience, and values becomes imperative to organizational success.

Benefits of Diversity

The **benefits of diversity** are experienced in at least three ways.

- *Diversity improves how well organizations learn and change.* Diversity helps organizations improve learning and adapting to change because diversity integrates new and broader perspectives into the organizational decision-making processes. Diversity efforts are often aimed at bringing out multiple perspectives, this in turn helps the organization develop new and better ways to function.

- *Diversity creates access to and legitimacy for organizations among different stakeholders.* The access-legitimacy benefit to diversity shows how having a diverse workforce helps an organization represent itself to stakeholders. Here,

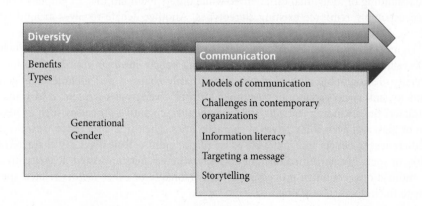

Figure 11.1
Diversity and Communication Subtopics

the organization benefits because a diverse workforce helps the organization's image or market position. The access-legitimacy benefit occurs when a diverse workforce helps the organization to gain access to a broader set of stakeholder groups, and this in turn increases the legitimacy of the organization in the eyes of these stakeholders. For example, having a sales force comprised of Caucasian males might be less effective at selling to customers with certain ethnic backgrounds. A more effective way to sell to a diverse customer base might include hiring a sales force that includes representatives from a diverse set of ethnic backgrounds.

- *Diversity promotes fairness to underrepresented groups.* The third benefit to having a diverse workforce is that it creates fairness. Many diversity efforts are based on the ethical and moral necessity to address patterns based on historical events. Certain groups hold less access to positions of power and have traditionally been underrepresented within the organizational power hierarchy. Diversity efforts help people within these traditionally underrepresented groups gain access to organizations and help gain access to positions of power within organizations. For example, until the early 1990s, no female had headed a *Fortune* 500 company and the number of women in executive positions was noticeably lower than men. With more women in the workforce, the balance of power between men and women changed so that by 2014, the number of female CEOs in *Fortune* 500 companies had grown to 24.[1]

Diversity efforts bring diverse perspectives, backgrounds, sources of information, and networks together to solve problems. A more diverse workforce means more information, which ultimately leads to more creative problem solving. Evidence shows that diverse work groups make better decisions as long as the group members feel that they are valued and respected, share a viewpoint that their work is significant, and hold strong interpersonal relationships.[2]

2 Describe and provide examples of different types of diversity.

Types of Diversity

Considerable debate exists as to whether or not diversity efforts should even focus on differences among individuals. Some believe that diversity efforts should be based on an understanding of individual differences, while others maintain that an emphasis on differences simply reinforce existing stereotypes. Another debate revolves around which specific dimensions of diversity matter most.

Figure 11.2 provides a way to understand different forms of diversity that includes observable and unobservable differences among people in organizations. One form of diversity, demographic characteristics, is not easily changed and includes age, gender, ethnicity, and socio-economics.[3] Another form of diversity is represented in traits and characteristics including learning style, personality, cognitive processes such as perception or bias, and even some physical characteristics. The third category to view diversity is differences in beliefs and values based on role or culture. **Role diversity** characterizes a public or socially determined form of diversity, whereas person-related diversity involves the motivations, cognitive processing style, personality or other factors related specifically to the individual or group.

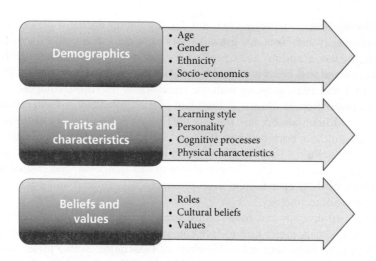

Figure 11.2 Types of Diversity

Two forms of diversity—generational diversity and communication style between genders—are explored in depth.

Generational Diversity

Generational diversity focuses on differences among generations and focuses on the environmental forces that influence individual values, beliefs, and behaviors. Similar cultural influences or shared experiences shape an individual's experiences. For example, U.S. citizens who fought in or were young adults during World War II and those who grew up during the recovery from the Great Depression were shaped by the movement to suburbs from cities and hold common beliefs about civic duty. In contrast, **Baby-Boomers**,

Comstock/Exactostock/SuperStock

those individuals born between 1943 and 1960, grew up during a period of unprecedented prosperity and economic growth. They were shaped by political events such as Watergate, the moon landing, and a prolonged economic recession. For this cohort, economic success and well-being is a top priority. Another group, **Generation-X**, those born between 1961 and 1981, grew up with the rise of cable television, computers, and saw eight years under Ronald Reagan as President of the United States. **Generation-Y**, also known as the **Millennials**, because they are the first generation to come of age in the new millennium, are those born between 1982 and 2005. This generation grew up after the events of 9/11, a world where technology such as the Internet, smartphones, and social media are part of everyday life. The prevalence of this technology has created a generation that is particularly open to new ideas, promotes cross-cultural understanding, and is adept at the use of technology.[4]

Generational diversity can have a considerable impact on communication. For example, Baby-Boomers prefer face-to-face communication and generally hold the belief that fairness is an important value. Members of Generation X also prefer face-to-face communication. They value being mentored by those older than themselves. They prefer informal communication and focus on values when communicating. In contrast, Millennials generally prefer to communicate through technology, expect positive feedback, are not impressed by hierarchical rank within an organization, and often ignore formal organizational protocol.[5] Table 11.1 compares some of the work preferences of four different generations.

Communication Style and Gender

Dr. Debra Tannen, an anthropologist, linguist, and professor who studies communication, explained why understanding gender differences is important for effective communication. People communicate differently, and differences in the way people communicate

Table 11.1 Generational Diversity and Work Preferences

Cohort Name	Born...	Work Preferences
Millennials	1982–2005	Value feedback and praise Prefer to know the rules Strong team workers and collaborators Seek low-risk jobs Focus on individual goals when communicating
Generation X	Between 1961 and 1981	Value mentoring Want engaging work but willing to sacrifice family and leisure time for a price Focus on values when communicating
Baby Boomers	Between 1943–1960	Value fairness Dedicated to their employers See a connection between work and higher values Focus on fairness when communicating

Table 11.2 Communication Style Preference Between Men and Women

Men	Women
Use pronoun "I"	Use pronoun "we"
Display confidence in own ideas	Downplay confidence in own ideas
Make statements	Ask questions
Challenge others	Apologize to others
Focus on achievements	Avoid talking about own achievements
Direct	Indirect
Offer criticism	Offer compliments

can be traced, in part, to demographic differences. Women, for example, have a different **communication style** than men.[6] A communication style is a culturally learned set of signals that people use to communicate meaning. Communication style also serves as a filter that individuals use to evaluate one another's meaning. Table 11.2 outlines a few communication style differences between men and women according to Dr. Tannen.

These style differences in communication can show up in the workplace in areas such as job or promotion interviews, salary negotiations, project work, and performance evaluation. The next section provides more details on how to communicate more effectively in organizations.

Communication in Organizations

Effective communication in organizations is essential. Communication is central for solving problems and offering solutions, making decisions, delivering bad news, prompting action, informing, influencing, motivating, and educating. The next section explores three models of communication. The first model characterizes communication as a simple process of sending, receiving, and responding to information. A more complex explanation that describes communication as a meaning making process is also presented. Finally, communication through conversation is also explored.

Models of Communication

The three-step process model of communication is called the **sender–receiver model**. This model describes how facts and simple information are communicated. The sender–receiver model promotes the idea that effective communication occurs when a sender clearly communicates a message and the receiver correctly receives the message as intended by the sender. As long as the message is clearly communicated and the receiver of the message is attentive, the message should be communicated clearly. Unfortunately,

3 Present three approaches to communication: the sender–receiver model, the co-orienting model, and the conversational learning model.

a variety of factors can interfere with this communication process. The result is that the sender and the receiver hold different interpretations of a message.

A more realistic view of communication describes a process where two or more people create meaning. Communication then, is a complex process involving many variables. Rather than simply describing communication as a process of moving facts or information from one person to another, the co-orienting model describes communication as a process of creating and interpreting messages. Messages contain verbal and non-verbal cues, history and past experiences. Communication is a process of **co-orienting** or understanding intended messages and how these may be interpreted differently. Co-orienting means that both communicators and receivers must move beyond their immediate viewpoint and understand the experiences and perceptions of others.

A third explanation for communication is the **conversational learning** approach. This approach explains how people use conversation to improve understanding of differences. Conversational learning helps resolve another problem with communication, the problem of **parochialism**. Parochialism occurs when a person views another as though they are the same as oneself, that they have the same experiences as others, rather than taking account of another person's uniqueness.[7] Conversational learning focuses on understanding another's viewpoint or experience and withholding judgment until the unique perspective is understood and accepted.

4 List the challenges of communication and the importance of information literacy.

Communication in the Age of 'Big Data': Challenges for Organizations

A challenge for communicating in contemporary organizations is that the vast amount of information available makes communication more difficult as people attempt to sort through what is relevant while maintaining meaning. The amount and types of information people view, process, and disseminate has increased at a rate of about 2.6 percent per year. Between 1980 and 2008, the amount of information a person consumed per day outside of work went from just over 7 hours to almost 12 hours per day. A study revealed that on average, U.S. citizens read about 100,000 words a day of media, the equivalent of a long novel. Non-work related media includes video games, newspapers, and information from the Internet—about 60 percent of this media consumption is through TV and radio.[8] Consider also, that every second, 12,000 new ads are posted on Craigslist, 600 new videos are posted on YouTube, and nearly 700,000 status updates occur on Facebook.[9] Some have called the proliferation of data the age of **big data**.

Improving Information Literacy

Communication can be improved in the age of big data by improving **information literacy**. Information literacy is the ability to properly collect, evaluate, and present information. It emphasizes the process of improving one's knowledge about how to accurately assess and present information. Information literacy involves more than knowing where and how to access information. More importantly, it involves understanding the forms of information, how information is organized, and how to critically evaluate information.

Improving Information Literacy

The Association for College and Research Libraries suggests that information literacy involves key competencies, including the ability to recognize:

- ✔ How information is produced, organized, and disseminated
- ✔ How knowledge is organized into disciplines which influences how data is interpreted
- ✔ That differences in formats may impact how data is interpreted
- ✔ How differences in purpose and audience, including differences in potential consumers and producers of resources influence interpretation of data, for example, popular vs. scholarly, current vs. historical
- ✔ How to differentiate between primary and secondary sources and how specific disciplines or domains rely on primary or secondary sources
- ✔ How secondary sources are constructed from raw data, drawing on primary sources[10]

Improving information literacy is important as people learn to evaluate and utilize information more effectively. Further, by understanding how different disciplines and constituencies evaluate data, we improve our understanding of what types of information are appropriate for an intended audience. The next section provides a more detailed method for developing and targeting a core message.

Developing and Targeting a Core Message

In order to improve communication, developing a specific plan that includes a target for the message is important. A targeted message is particularly important when trying to communicate to a large and diverse group. In Figure 11.3, five steps to constructing a message are outlined.

5 Outline the process for developing a targeted message and how storytelling can be an effective form of communication.

Figure 11.3
Developing a Targeted Message

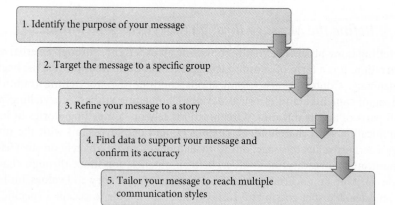

1. Identify the purpose of your message
2. Target the message to a specific group
3. Refine your message to a story
4. Find data to support your message and confirm its accuracy
5. Tailor your message to reach multiple communication styles

Step 1: Identifying the Purpose of a Message

Carefully consider the purpose of the message. In organizations, messages often point towards a specific purpose such as:

- *Presenting a solution* to a problem, like changing a widely criticized policy or offering a flexible work schedule on days with bad weather
- *Announcing a new decision* like buying a new company, announcing a new product launch, or deciding how to improve production
- *Delivering bad news* such as a plant closing or layoff of employees
- *Encouraging action* such as motivating employees to work longer hours or motivating customers to purchase a product

Step 2: Targeting the Message to a Specific Group Within the Organization

In addition to identifying the main purpose of the message, the message should be targeted towards a specific audience within the organization. Within an organization, at least five different messages must be managed:

- *Organizational structure and hierarchy*—who is in charge within the organization, who will make decisions, and how will these decision be made?
- *Organizational results*—what is the purpose of the organization and how will these results be achieved?
- *The role of leadership*—what is leadership's role in the communication process and how will it make decisions?
- *The organization's values and culture*—what are the key beliefs of the company and how does the organization see itself relative to others in the industry?
- *Time management*—how should members of the organization spend their time and how long should various things take to accomplish?[11]

Step 3: Refine the Message through Storytelling Techniques

Storytelling is the process of vividly conveying an experience through a verbal or written narration. It is a form of communication that has been around since the beginning of organizing. Contemporary organizations continue the storytelling tradition and spend significant time and effort to develop compelling stories. Storytelling permeates all parts of an organization. Organizations rely on compelling stories to improve communication with shareholders, customers, and employees, all with the intent to convey a certain value, message, or call to action. Organizations rely on storytelling to communicate an organization's values, help an organization move through change, or provide clarity in an uncertain situation. Stories convey history and values, build credibility, motivate, dispel gossip and rumors, and lead people to accept a specific vision

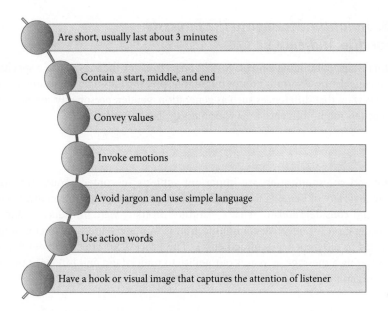

Figure 11.4
Elements of Effective
Storytelling

of the organization. All stories are different, but most good stories share a few common characteristics[12] as outlined in Figure 11.4.

Storytelling serves to structure the desired message with a beginning, middle, and end. Stories often contain components that help to sequence the message in familiar ways. Figure 11.5 outlines a common way to sequence a story.

Step 4: Find Data to Support and Verify the Message

Including data helps to support the message. Many efforts at communicating a message begin with data collection and analysis. In other cases, data serves a secondary purpose to support a message. Whether data is used to generate a message or simply to reinforce a point, data will help provide credibility and show that the sender has done background research.

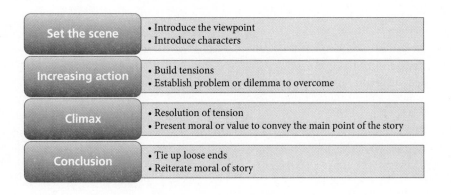

Figure 11.5 An
Example of How to
Sequence a Story

Step 5: Tailor the Message to the Interests of a Specific Audience

In the final stage of building a message, take steps to tailor the message to a specific audience and consider how various groups might interpret the message. For example, consider the various ways that differences such as generation, gender, personality, learning style, or cultural beliefs might influence how your message is interpreted.

Conclusion

Diversity and communication are important subjects in contemporary organizations. There are a variety of benefits for organizations that actively value diversity. Several approaches and considerations of what constitutes diversity were introduced. One important consideration for effective communication is to understand how to craft a message that appeals to different types of audiences. The process for effectively developing and communicating a message increases our ability to understand and influence people's behavior in organizations.

OB AT WORK

DR. JAYE GOOSBY-SMITH DIVERSITY CONSULTANT

Jaye Goosby-Smith

As a researcher, professor, organizational consultant and "sandwich generation" caregiver, Dr. Jaye Goosby-Smith understands the importance of diversity in organizations and practices these concepts in her research and work. In addition to championing diversity, Dr. Goosby-Smith advocates even more strongly for "inclusion,"

"Using an airplane as a metaphor, diversity represents the variety of properly vetted passengers on the plane. Inclusion represents the quality of the ride. Is the ride smooth or excessively turbulent? Are passengers getting sick, bumped around or bruised? Do they trust each other? The pilot? Have they bought into their common destination? Have they had any voice into it? How do they treat each other? If given the choice, would they take that flight again?"

6 Apply concepts of diversity and communication to organizations.

Without a diverse workforce that values individual differences and mirrors the customer base, organizations cannot reach their full potential. However, the synergistic value of this diversity remains unrealized if the organization is not in a sustainable inclusive state: a state which facilitates all employees being willing, able, and valued for bringing their relevant knowledge, skills, and abilities to the table in service of meeting organizational goals.

What does inclusion look like? Organizational stakeholders facilitate "buy in" to team and organizational goals by stakeholders having appropriate voices during goal formation and implementation phases. Organizational design[i] also supports inclusion. In many organizations, managers of certain identity groups are expected to do "double-duty" by mentoring new employees sharing their group membership. In inclusive organizations, managers are rewarded in some way for such mentoring.

There are also generally accepted organizational practices for seeking and appreciating the feedback of *all* organizational members involved in the value chain of production or service delivery processes. The input of delivery people may be sought in the planning process for rolling out a new product, or trainers may be consulted about curriculum changes made by a corporate education department.

In inclusive organizations, equity—not equality—prevails. The "fairest" way to treat employees may not involve identical treatment, as it is more equitable to reward a working parent with a paid day off and another employee with $500 tickets to a professional sports game. The rewards are not equal, but they are equitable.

As a fellow at the U.S. Department of Defense's Defense Equal Opportunity Management Institute (DEOMI), Goosby-Smith analyzed inclusion in the U.S. military. She examined issues impacting the inclusion of Latino and Latina service members.[ii]

---

[i] Galbraith, J. R. (2002). *Designing dynamic organizations: A hands-on guide for leaders at all levels.* Amacom.
[ii] Smith, J. G. (forthcoming). *No laughing matter: Interracial and Intra-ethnic patterns in "off color jokes."* (Technical Report). Patrick AFB, FL: Defense Equal Employment Management Institute.

(continued)

Previously, she proposed recommendations regarding inclusion and sexual orientation in the military following the repeal of "Don't Ask, Don't Tell."[iii] Civilian organizations would do well to understand what the Department of Defense already knows: diversity and inclusion aren't just "nice things to pursue"—they are proven significant contributors to operational excellence and mission readiness.

Source: Personal Interview

[iii] Smith, J. G., Miller, K. A., McBain, M. (2011). LGB and possible challenges that will happen now that "Don't Ask Don't Tell" has been repealed. In *Managing Diversity in the Military: The value of inclusion in a culture of uniformity.* Daniel P. McDonald and Kizzy Parks (Eds). Routledge Publishers.

SPOTLIGHT ON RESEARCH
Merit Based Cultures Can Lead to Discrimination

Studies show that most people around the world believe that merit-based cultures are desirable in organizations. A merit-based culture rewards performance and talent rather than other factors such as likability, internal politics, or social characteristics such as gender, nationality, social class, or ethnicity. In fact, people consistently believe that organizations not only value merit, but they act in a manner that rewards performance. Another important reason that organizations adopt merit-based performance systems relates to diversity. Merit-based systems reward individuals for their performance; so merit-based systems are considered more fair and just so that individuals do not face discrimination. Despite the popularity of merit-based cultures, some argue that merit-based cultures are just that, cultures that value merit; however, merit is an espoused valued, not a practice. In other words, organizations do not necessarily practice rewarding merit and talent. Organizations espouse the value of merit-based performance, not because it is the best practice, but because it creates an image of fairness and equity.

Evidence points to the fact that merit-based cultures fail to deliver what they promise (objective, performance or talent-based rewards for employees) even when applied consistently across employees regardless of gender, ethnicity, or other differences. In some cases, merit-based cultures actually encourage discriminatory practices because they induce biases. For example, one study showed that minorities and women received lower salaries even though they received the same performance rankings as others in the organization. Why should bias persist, despite the adaptation of a culture that values fairness, merit, and pay for performance?

One line of research showed the more unbiased, fair, and objective people thought they were, the more biases they actually demonstrated. In other words, when a culture claims to be unbiased, this belief in one's own objectivity actually results in greater bias. A group of researches wanted to see if a culture that values merit could actually lead to greater bias towards certain groups of employees, especially towards women.

The researchers then turned to a group of MBA students to test their ideas. Each student in the study read a description of a fictitious company and was asked to serve as a manager in this company. Students were then assigned to one of two groups, either a merit-based culture or a non-merit-based culture. The merit-based culture involves value statements like "all employees are to be rewarded fairly," a raise is determined by performance, promotions are given when performance shows it is deserved, and our goal as an organization is to reward equitably. The non-merit-based organization emphasized regular evaluation and autonomy but requested that the manager make decisions and placed the decisions for merit increases at the manager's discretion with no consideration for fairness or equity.

Study participants in each of these 'organizations' then reviewed performance reviews for three employees. The performance reviewers of two employees achieved identical numerical evaluation, but differed by gender of the candidate. The male candidate was named Michael and the female was named Patricia. The researchers changed the qualitative comments on each of the two performance reviews so participants wouldn't become suspicious that the purpose of the study was gender difference and performance reviews. Both Michael and Patricia's evaluations had positive and negative comments on their performance review. Participants also reviewed a third employee, Robert, a low-performing candidate who served mainly as a decoy. Participants were then given $1,000 to distribute among the three employees Robert, Patricia and Michael.

The results would make any manager question the value of a merit-based pay culture. In a merit-based culture, Michael received an average bonus that was $51 higher. In contrast, in the non-merit-based culture, Patricia received a bonus that was $46 higher. In summary, men held an advantage in the merit-based culture but women held the advantage in the non-merit based culture.

Researchers then conducted two additional studies, with different words and phrases in the performance review to eliminate possible gender bias. A total of 445 MBAs participated in the study. The final results showed that the disadvantage to men in non-merit-based culture diminished, but that the advantage to men remained in a merit based culture. Ultimately, in a merit-based culture, women seem to be discriminated against, even when performance (e.g., merit) is comparable to men.

Why would a culture that espouses merit be less likely to apply merit-based practices? Research suggests that reliance on a merit-based culture actually allows individual prejudice to emerge because individual managers can effectively 'hide' under the umbrella of the greater culture. Contributing to the problem is the notion that individual prejudice is more likely to emerge when individuals aren't accountable for their prejudice.

Research also suggests that espoused organizational values are not always passed down to employees. Second, espoused organizational values may not be put into practice when not followed up with organizational accountability. Further, some cultural values can actually have the opposite impact on organizational action than intended.

Based on the article by:

Castilla, E. J., & Benard, S. (2010). The paradox of meritocracy in organizations. *Administrative Science Quarterly,* 55(4): 543–576.

Questions for Discussion

1. What is your preference for a merit-based culture or a non-merit-based culture? Why do you think this?

2. How would you apply this study to behavior in organizations in which you have worked?

Pairing with this Topic Summary

Suggested Expert Contributions

How to Turn an Engaging Conversation into a Creative Collaboration
—Kimberly D. Elsbach (University of California, Davis)

Communication and Diversity—Luciara Nardon (Carleton University)

Diversity Ideologies in Action: Energizing Renewal and Excellence in Healthcare
—Valerie L. Myers (University of Michigan)

Suggested Cases

Case 2: "We Are Global or We Are Nothing": Conflict and Cover-Up at ColequarterMaine

Case 5: Whatever Happened to One of the "100 Best Companies to Work For"?: A Case Study of Hewlett-Packard

Case 6: NASCAR's Drive for Diversity: Can They Reach the Finish Line?

Case 8: Conflict in Santa's Workshop: Learning to Be a Team Player at ToyKing

Suggested Exercises

Exercise 3: My Expat Assignment

Exercise 4: How Leaders Effect You

Exercise 9: Being Positive

Exercise 15: Building my Network—Individual

Exercise 16: Writing a Team Contract

Exercise 21: OD Techniques at Work

Exercise 28: Communication Breakdown

Exercise 29: Diversity Rocks

Exercise 30: You Can't Handle the Truth

Exercise 38: FIS Simulation

Endnotes

1. Ely, R. J., & Thomas, D. A. (2001). Cultural diversity at work: The effects of diversity perspectives on work processes and outcomes. *Administrative Science Quarterly, 46*(2): 229–273.
2. Goosby Smith, J., & Lindsay, J. B. (2014). *Beyond inclusion: Worklife interconnectedness, energy, and resilience in organizations.* New York: Palgrave Macmillan.
3. Model based on Kayes, D. C., & Kayes, A. B. (2006). *Learning style composition in teams: Implications for assessment.* In Ronald R. Sims and Serbrenia J. Sims (Eds.). *Learning styles and learning: A key to meeting accountability demands in education.* New York: Nova Science Publishers. Based on research from Harrison, D. A., Price, K. H., & Bell, M. P. (1998). Beyond relational demography: Time and the effects of surface-and deep-level diversity on work group cohesion. *Academy of Management Journal, 41*(1): 96–107 and Pelled, L. H., Eisenhardt, K. M., & Xin, X. R. (1999). Exploring the blackbox: An analysis of work group diversity, conflict and performance. *Administrative Science Quarterly, 44(1):* 1–28. See also Maznevski, M. L. (1994). Understanding our differences: Performance in decision making groups with diverse members. *Human Relations, 47*(5): 531–551.

4. Howe, N., & Strauss, W. (1992). *Generations*. New York: Quill and Lancaster, L. C., & Stillman, D. (2002). *When generations collide*. New York: HarperCollins. See also Howe, N., & Nadler, R. (2010). *Millennials in the workplace. Human Resource Strategies for a new generation*. Lifecourse Associates.

5. See www.lifecourse.com.

6. Tannen, D. (1995). The power of talk: Who gets heard and why. *Harvard Business Review, 73*(5): 138–147.

7. Clampitt, P. G. (2010). *Communicating for managerial effectiveness* (4th Ed.). Thousand Oaks, CA: Sage.

8. Bohn, R. E., & Short, J. E. (2009). How much information? 2009 Report on American Consumers. *Global Information Industry Center, University of California, San Diego*. www.hmi.ucsd.edu/pdf/HMI_2009_ConsumerReport_Dec9_2009.

9. Available for download at: http://www.businessinsider.com/incredible-things-that-happen-every-60-seconds-on-the-internet-2011-12?utm_source=twbutton&utm_medium=social&utm_campaign=sai

10. The American Library Association (2002). The Association for Information Literacy Competency Standards for Higher Education. *Information Literacy Competency Standards for Higher Education*. Chicago, IL. Available for download at http://www.ala.org/acrl/ilcomstan.html and http://www.ala.org/acrl/standards/informationliteracycompetency and *Information Literacy Competency Standards for Higher Education*.

11. Adopted from Hamm, J. (2006). The five messages leaders must manage. *Harvard Business Review, 84*(5): 114–123.

12. For more on how to create and present a good story see, Elsbach, K. (2003). How to pitch a brilliant idea. *Harvard Business Review, 81*(9): 117–123. Fryer, B. (2003). Storytelling that moves people: A conversation with screenwriting coach Robert McKee. *Harvard Business Review, 81*(6): 51–55. Conger, J. (1998). The necessary art of persuasion. *Harvard Business Review, 76*(3): 84–95.

How to Turn an Engaging Conversation into a Creative Collaboration

Kimberly D. Elsbach
University of California, Davis

Have you ever had a really engaging conversation with someone that resulted in creative collaboration? Think back to that conversation. What do you remember about it? You probably remember being completely drawn into a story or discussion about something that really interested you, or maybe you remember feeling excited or passionate about what you were saying, and reacting with emotion to what the other person was saying. You probably lost track of time. You may have argued with the person, but also built on that person's ideas and perhaps added some of your own ideas to the project. In the end, you probably ended up thinking of yourself as a collaborative partner with the other person.

All of these feelings and attitudes—being drawn into a conversation, reacting with emotion, and perceiving a conversation partner as a collaborator—are signs that an engaging conversation has turned into a creative collaboration. Based on over 15 years of studying creative workers, I have found that creative success often depends on having such a transformation take place during an engaging conversation.[1] Further, using this research, as well as related work by psychologists and organizational scholars, I have developed a framework describing how one might use both behavior and language to turn engaging conversations into creative collaborations. I summarize these processes in Figure 1 and describe them in detail in the following sections.

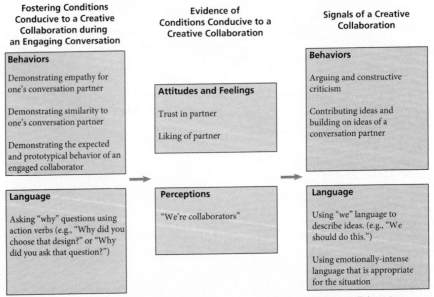

Figure 1 A Framework for Turning and Engaging Conversation Into a Creative Collaboration

Conditions Conducive to Creative Collaborations

It turns out that getting another person engaged in a creative collaboration is made easier by several interpersonal feelings and perceptions. Specifically, you need to get that person to trust and like you, and then to get that person to think of you as an engaged collaborator. These conditions are shown as the middle set of boxes in Figure 1. There are several reasons that these conditions promote creative collaborations.

First, Trust in Another Person Leads to Idea Sharing with That Person

Trust is defined as a willingness to rely on others, especially in situations where one is vulnerable.[2] Thus, trust may be thought of as an attitude or belief about another person or persons.[3] In professional work environments, trust is either based on an understanding of another's values and objectives (i.e., what's called values-based trust), or their expertise and knowledge (what's called knowledge-based trust).[4] In either case, the increased understanding that comes with trust is likely to lead one to feel comfortable giving one's opinions and ideas to others in a creative conversation. In line with this reasoning, trust within work groups has been shown to lead to greater openness in communication and information sharing, especially when group members were motivated by a common goal.[5] Further, under conditions of high trust, researchers have found that task conflicts that often accompany idea sharing (i.e., arguments about an idea or problem solution) are likely to be interpreted positively and not to lead to destructive, relationship conflict (i.e., arguments that arise over personal characteristics, traits, or styles).[6]

Second, Liking of Another Person Leads to Responsiveness and Cooperation with That Person

Psychologists have found that liking may lead us to be responsive to the requests of others because we feel obligated and motivated to please those that we like.[7] As a result, many studies have shown that liking is a common influence tactic used to get others to go along with our suggestions, and even say "yes" to risky ventures.[8] In fact, researchers have shown that liking for a product seller is more than twice as likely as liking for the product itself to lead people to purchase a product.[9] In a similar manner, liking for a conversation partner may lead us to be more open in sharing our thoughts and ideas when asked during an engaging conversation.

Third, Perceiving That One is Engaged in a Collaborative Relationship with Another Person Leads to Collaborative Role Engagement with That Person

That is, perceiving oneself as an engaged collaborator with one's conversation partner (vs. an uninterested listener) may lead one to engage in role-consistent behaviors and engage in collaborative acts. For example, in a study of Hollywood screenwriters, I found that when producers perceived that they were collaborating with a screenwriter (as opposed to merely listening to their idea pitches), they were more engaged in conversations with these screenwriters, and ultimately, offered more of their own ideas during the pitch meeting.[10]

Summary

In sum, getting others to engage in a creative conversation with us appears to depend on getting them to like and trust us, as well as perceive us as engaged collaborators. Given the apparent importance of these conditions conducive to creative conversation, a relevant question is "How do we promote liking, trust, and perceptions of similarity and collaboration with conversation partners?" That is, "How do we foster the conditions conducive to creative collaboration?"

Fostering Conditions Conducive to Creative Collaboration

Psychological and organizational research suggests four actions that may create the conditions that are conducive to a creative collaboration. These actions should take place during an already engaging conversation, and include: (1) demonstrating empathy for a conversation partner, (2) demonstrating similarity to a conversation partner, (3) demonstrating expected and prototypical behavior associated with being a "collaborator," and (4) asking "why" questions of conversation partners, using action verbs. As shown in the left-most set of boxes in Figure 1, the first three of these actions involve behaviors, while the fourth involves language choices, which we discuss in more detail next.

Demonstrating Empathy for a Conversation Partner

Demonstrating empathy involves showing concern, understanding, and appreciation for another person's perspective. My own research on acceptance of explanations for negative events has shown that demonstrating appreciation and understanding of the needs and concerns of others is critical to feeling that one has been treated fairly, and that one can trust another.[11] Further, this research suggests that showing such appreciation and understanding for others' concerns can be achieved by referring to norms, values and ideals that may be widely shared by these others. For example, in an examination of explanations used to quell consumer food safety concerns about beef (e.g., the use of hormones in cattle feed), I found that the explanations that both acknowledged consumers' questions and described food safety as a shared ideal were most effective in producing trust in consumers.[12] In a similar manner, discussing creative ideas with a conversation partner in a manner that acknowledges and appreciates his or her own concerns and needs (e.g., saying, "I understand that you want this product to reflect your unique, artistic style, but we need to make that work within our budget.) may lead to greater trust by that partner.

Demonstrating Similarity to a Conversation Partner

In a comparable manner, psychologists have found that we are more apt to like those we perceive as similar to ourselves—regardless if that similarity comes in the form of appearance, attitudes, traits, background, or lifestyle.[13] For example, research on therapists has shown that being perceived as similar in attitudes and experiences to one's clients, including having similarly "human failings" (e.g., anxieties, self-centeredness, jealousies), enhances clients' liking for their therapists.[14]

Psychologists call this general preference for and liking of everything having to do with the self as "implicit egotism."[15] Implicit egotism explains why women are more likely to marry men with the same first letter of their pre-marriage last name, and why people are more likely to live in cities that contain their first name (i.e., people named Louis are more likely to live in St. Louis than others without that first name, while people named Helen are more likely to live in St. Helen than others without that first name). According to these psychologists, peoples' self-worth and identities are affirmed by such choices. Thus, it seems likely that engaging and sharing ideas with others similar to oneself would also be affirming and enhancing to peoples' self-worth.

Demonstrating Expected and Prototypical Behavior of a "Collaborator"

Another behavior that motivates engagement with conversation partners is the demonstration of expected and prototypical behavior of a "collaborator" (versus an "uninterested listener" or a "lecturing expert"). Role theorists suggest that acting in accordance with a well-known role type is likely to lead an interaction partner to think and act according to complimentary role types.[16] In this manner, engaging in actions perceived to be consistent with the role of "creative collaborator" (e.g., sharing ideas, asking questions, building on others' comments) may lead a conversation partner to categorize him or herself in a complimentary role (i.e., another "creative collaborator"), and thus, begin to act as a collaborator as well. As mentioned earlier, my own research on reacting to idea "pitches" in Hollywood, showed that when "pitchers" (i.e., screenwriters) fulfilled the expected requirements of a collaborator role, the "catchers" (i.e., producers listening to the pitches) were likely to take on and perform corresponding roles as collaborators during those interactions.[17]

Asking "Why" Questions Using Action Verbs

In addition to the interpersonal behaviors described above, there are linguistic choices that may foster the conditions conducive to creative collaboration. One of these linguistic choices is how one asks questions during engaging conversations. In particular, asking "Why?" questions (as compared to "What?" or "How?" questions) may provide information about a conversation partner's underlying motives and desires. For example, answering the question "Why did you put an accountant on each project team?" may reveal your concerns about the cost of a project or your needs to tightly control the budget on a project. As a result, such "Why?" questions enhance trust by a conversation partner, because the sincere concern for the well-being of others, including considering their needs and concerns in decisions and actions, are primary signals of the trust component called **benevolence**.[18]

In addition, researchers of social communication have found that asking "Why?" questions that include more concrete "action" verbs (e.g., verbs such as "do" or "say") may further enhance perceptions of benevolence in a conversation partner. This is because more concrete action verbs lead to answers that reveal something about the subject of the question, while more abstract "state" verbs (e.g., verbs such as "like" or "want") result in answers that reveal something about the object of the question.[19] Thus, if I ask the question "Why do you <u>like</u> dogs?" (which includes the state verb of "like"), I will get answers that tell you something about *dogs* (e.g., dogs are nice, dogs are good companions). By contrast, if I ask the question "Why did you buy a dog?" (which includes the action verb of "buy"), I will get answers that tell you something about *you* (e.g., "I love dogs" or "I always wanted a dog"). As a result, these latter types of questions show an interest in the concerns and needs of your conversation partner, rather than an interest in dogs.

Summary

In sum, demonstrating empathy, similarity, and in-role behaviors consistent with a creative collaborator, as well as asking "Why?" questions using action verbs all lead to the perceptual and feeling states that are conducive to creative collaboration. Once these states are achieved, an engaging conversation is more likely to become a creative collaboration. But how do you know if your conversation is on the right track? That is, how do you know your engaging conversation is actually becoming a creative collaboration?

Creative Collaboration as an Outcome of Engaging Conversations

Once engaged in a conversation, there are several behavioral and language signals that indicate that a creative collaboration is, in fact, taking place. Two signals I will discuss are evident in the behaviors of a conversation partner: arguing and contributing ideas. Two other signals are evident in the language of a conversation partner: using "we" language, and using similarly "intense" language. These signals indicate that the conversation is on the right track toward a productive collaboration.

Arguing

It is not uncommon to mistakenly perceive arguing and criticism from a conversation partner as signs that he or she doesn't like your ideas and wants you to give up on them. Yet, often, such behavior means just the opposite—that a conversation partner is intrigued or interested in your ideas and wants to explore them further. According to communication researcher Deborah Tannen, many people (and men, especially) use arguing and criticism as a form of "ritual opposition" that is used to explore an idea further and to test it for weaknesses. [20]

In addition, arguing and offering criticism can be a signal that a conversation partner is taking ownership of the idea and wants to understand it fully. In particular, participating in an argument about an idea may signal to a person that he or she is, at least partially, responsible for that idea. Psychologists have found that owning or possessing something, including ideas, can increase the attractiveness and value of that thing to the owner.[21] This, "mere ownership" effect may occur because once something belongs to a person, it begins to take on many of the positive traits that the person associates with him or herself.[22] Thus, participating in an argument about an idea may lead to both perceived ownership and increased liking of an idea that may further motivate engagement in a collaboration regarding the idea.

Contributing Ideas

A second, and more obvious signal that an engaging conversation is becoming a creative collaboration is seeing a conversation partner contribute ideas, or build on your ideas. These behaviors signal to observers that a conversation partner is invested in the creative process. Further, these behaviors may signal such investment to the conversation partner, him or herself. In this vein, proponents of "self-perception theory"[23] have found that actors often infer beliefs and attitudes by observing their own behavior (e.g., "If I'm contributing ideas, I must be a collaborator on this project."). More recent research in this area has shown that these inferences may occur even if one's attempts at a specific behavior fail (e.g., "If I try to offer an idea, but can't get heard, I may still see myself as a collaborator.").[24] Adding to these effects, psychologists have found that behavioral mimicry in interactions (i.e., behaviors that copy those of an interaction partner) often occur spontaneously (i.e., unconsciously) in work tasks.[25] Thus, interaction partners may be unaware that they are copying collaborative behavior from others (e.g., contributing ideas and voicing opinions), and in turn, may begin to perceive themselves as engaged collaborators when they notice themselves enacting these behaviors.

Using "We" Language to Describe Ideas

In addition to behavior, language is an important indicator that creative collaborations are taking place. In particular, ownership of and investment in ideas under discussion can be clearly signaled through language. For example, referring to ideas under discussion as "our" ideas, or suggestions that "we should do this" provide strong signals that the partner has taken co-ownership of those ideas. Such "we" language is important because it explicitly communicates shared ownership, rather than non-ownership (signaled by "you" language), or singular ownership (signaled by "I" language). Further, it signals that the conversation partner perceives that he or she is part of a group working toward a common goal (even if this group is just two people).

In addition, social identity theory suggests that such perceptions of inclusion in groups may be important to a person's self-definition, and may lead individual members to perceive their group in more positive ways (i.e., it leads them to show an "in-group" favorability bias).[26] More recent research on self-expansion (i.e., the notion that a person may define him or herself to include close others, such as spouses or close colleagues), also suggests that we are less threatened and more affirmed by the actions of others who are close to us.[27] Together, these notions suggest that "we" language may not only signal to a conversation partner that he or she is invested in a collaborative process, but may also motivate him or her to work harder on behalf of the collaborating group.

Using Similarly "Intense" Language as a Conversation Partner

A second language cue that may indicate that creative collaboration is taking place is the use of high-intensity language by a conversation partner (i.e., language, including descriptive and emotional words, that indicate strong attitudes versus neutrality toward a subject) that is similar in intensity to the language you are using.[28] As an example of high-intensity language, a statement about the potential impact of an invention may read: "On an exciting note, the potential market for this invention is enormous!" By contrast, a similar statement using low-intensity language might read: "On a positive note, the potential market for this invention is large." Research on language intensity[29] has shown that high-intensity language can lead to positive perceptions of a speaker and greater engagement in a conversation *if* such intense language is normal for the situation (as it may be in a creative collaboration), and if it matches the intensity of a conversation partner.* These findings may occur because they lead conversation partners to feel emotions that are consonant with the emotional language expressed. For example, psychological research on "priming effects" of language has widely shown that using words such as "angry," "frustrated," and "joyful" in conversations can prime corresponding emotions in listeners.[30]

Thus, in a creative, collaborative context, high-intensity language may indicate that a speaker has a strong interest in an idea, and may promote similar feelings in a conversation partner. Such language is most commonly seen when conversation partners have investment in the ideas under discussion and are motivated to both fully understand those ideas, and to perfect them.[31] For example, in my study of Hollywood pitching, I found that intense language (such as claims of extremely high potential and expressions of passionate support, e.g., "I absolutely love this idea!"), were perceived as a signal that a conversation partner was passionate about an idea, and often led conversation partners to become equally passionate about pushing it forward.

Summary

In sum, the behaviors of arguing and contributing ideas, along with the use of "we" language and appropriate, high-intensity language are strong cues that an engaging conversation is moving toward becoming a creative collaboration. If these cues are salient, one should continue to nurture and support the direction of the conversation. If they are absent, one should attempt to create a more collaborative environment by engaging in the antecedent behaviors discussed above (i.e., demonstrating empathy and similarity, demonstrating the prototypical and expected behavior of an engaged collaborator, and asking "why" questions of one's conversation partner using action verbs).

Conclusion

Counter-intuitively coming up with creative ideas is often the easiest part of a creative project. Getting other people to buy into those ideas, support those ideas, and join in collaboration on those ideas (all important steps to bringing an idea to fruition) are much more difficult tasks. These desired outcomes require that one can persuade a conversation partner not only that one's idea is good, but that the conversation partner, him or herself, is invested in that idea and its success.

Fortunately, extensive research in psychology and organizations (including my own research on creative workers) provides us with many clues about how to produce this transformative outcome. The framework outlined in this paper provides an outline of some of the more common behavioral and linguistic tools at one's disposal. Using these tools, creators may increase their chances of turning an engaging conversation into a creative collaboration.

---

*It should be noted, however, that inappropriate, high-intensity language (language that is more intense than is normal for the situation) may lead conversation partners to disengage from collaboration.

Endnotes

1. Elsbach, K. D. (2003). How to pitch a brilliant idea. *Harvard Business Review, 81,* 117–123.
2. Mayer, R. C., Davis, J. H., & Schoorman, F. D. (1995). An integrative model of organizational trust. *Academy of Management Review, 20,* 709–734.
3. Dirks, K., & Ferrin, D. L. (2001). The role of trust in organizational settings. *Organization Science, 12,* 450–467.
4. Lewicki, R. J., & Benedict Bunker, B. (1996). Developing and maintaining trust in work relationships, in R. M. Kramer and T. R.Tyler (Eds.). *Trust in organizations: Frontiers of theory and research,* 114–139. Thousand Oaks, CA: Sage.
5. Butler, J. K. (1999). Trust expectations, information sharing, climate of trust, and negotiation effectiveness and efficiency. *Group & Organization Management, 24,* 217–239.
6. Simons, T., & Peterson, R. (2000). Task conflict and relationship conflict in top management teams: The pivotal role of intra-group trust. *Journal of Applied Psychology, 85,* 102–111.
7. Cialdini, R. B. (1993). *Influence: Science and practice,* (3rd Ed.). New York: HarperCollins.
8. Ibid.
9. Frenzen, J.R., & Davis, H.L., 1990. Purchasing behavior in embedded markets. *Journal of Consumer Research, 17,* 1–12.
10. Elsbach, K. D. (2003). How to Pitch a Brilliant Idea. *Harvard Business Review, 81,* 117–123.
11. Elsbach, K. D. (2001). The architecture of legitimacy: Constructing accounts of organizational controversies, In John T. Jost and Brenda Major (Eds.). *The psychology of legitimacy: emerging perspectives on ideology, justice, and intergroup relation*s, 391–415. Cambridge, UK: Cambridge University Press.
12. Elsbach, K. D. (1994). Managing organizational legitimacy in the California cattle industry: The construction and effectiveness of verbal accounts. *Administrative Science Quarterly, 39*(1), 57–88.
13. Cialdini, R. B. (1993). *Influence: Science and practice,* (3rd Ed.). New York: HarperCollins.
14. Lundeen, E. J., & Schuldt, W. J. (1989). Effects of therapist's self-disclosure and a physical barrier on subject's perceptions of the therapist: An analogue study. *Psychological Reports, 64,* 715–720.
15. Pelham, B. W., Mirenberg, M. C., & Jones, T. T. (2002). Why Susie sells seashells by the seashore: Implicit egotism and major life decisions. *Journal of Personality and Social Psychology, 82,* 469–487.
16. Lynch, K. D. (2007). Modeling role enactment: Linking role theory and social cognition. *Journal for the Theory of Social Behavior, 37,* 379–399.
17. Elsbach, K. D. (2003). How to pitch a brilliant idea. *Harvard Business Review, 81,* 117–123.
18. Mayer, R. C., Davis, J. H., & Schoorman, F. D. (1995). An integrative model of organizational trust, *Academy of Management Review, 20,* 709–734.
19. Semin, G.R. (2000). Language as a cognitive and behavioral structuring resource: Question-answer exchanges. In W. Stroebe & M. Hewstone (Eds.). *European Review of Social Psychology,* 75–104. Chichester: Wiley.
20. Tannen, D. (1995). *Talking from 9 to 5: Women and men at work.* New York: Harper.
21. De Dreu, C. K. W. & van Knippenberg, D. (2005). The possessive self as a barrier to conflict resolution: Effects of mere ownership, process accountability, and self-concept clarity on competitive cognitions and behavior. *Journal of Personality and Social Psychology, 89,* 345–357.

22. Gawronski, B., Bodenhausen, G, V., & Becker, Andrew P. (2007). I like it, because I like myself: Associative self-anchoring and post-decisional change of implicit evaluations. *Journal of Experimental Social Psychology, 43*, 221–232.

23. Bem, D.J. (1967). Self-perception: An alternative interpretation of cognitive dissonance phenomena. *Psychological Review, 74*, 183–200.

24. Dolinksi, D. (2000). On interring one's beliefs from one's attempt and consequences for subsequent compliance. *Journal of Personality and Social Psychology, 78*, 260–272.

25. Chartran, T. L., & Bargh, J. A. (1999). The chameleon effect: The perception-behavior link and social interaction. *Journal of Personality and Social Psychology, 76*, 893–910.

26. Abrams, D., & Hogg, M. A. (1999). *Social identity and social cognition*. Oxford, UK: Blackwell.

27. Gardner, W. L., Gabriel, S., & Hoschild, L. (2002). When you and I are "we," you are not threatening: The role of self-expansion in social comparison. *Journal of Personality and Social Psychology, 82*, 239–251.

28. Buller, D. B., Borland, R., & Burgoon, M. (1998). Impact of behavioral intention on effectiveness of message features: Evidence from the Family Sun Safety Project. *Human Communication Research, 24*, 433–453.

29. Aune, K., & Kikuchi, T. (1993). Effects of language intensity similarity on perceptions of credibility, relational attributions, and persuasion. *Journal of Language and Social Psychology, 12*, 224–237.

30. Fazio, R. H., Sanbonmatsu, D., Powell, M., & Kardes, F. (1986). On the automatic activation of attitudes. *Journal of Personality and Social Psychology, 50*, 229–238.

31. Tannen, D. (1995). *Talking from 9 to 5: Women and men at work,* New York: Harper.

Communication and Diversity[1]

Luciara Nardon

Carleton University

Introduction

When asked to identify their most serious challenge in the field, managers often respond: "Communicating effectively across cultures." Why? Because communication is the principal vehicle through which people reach out to others to exchange ideas and commodities, develop and dissolve relationships, and conduct business. However, simple and often unintended words and behaviors, signs and symbols, can lead to misunderstandings, embarrassment, conflict, and even lost business opportunities.

Consider the case of a British professor of poetry, sitting relaxed during one of his lectures at the prestigious Ain Shams University in Cairo. He got so comfortable that he inadvertently leaned back in his chair and crossed his legs, thereby revealing the sole of one of his shoes to his students. In much of the Muslim world, this is an insult. The following morning, the Cairo newspapers carried banner headlines about the student demonstrations that resulted. They denounced what they saw as British arrogance and demanded that the professor be sent home immediately.[1] His unconscious and unintended behavior was interpreted as arrogance and disrespect by his students.

As this example illustrates, our frames of reference and personal experiences can work to filter message transmission and reception by screening in or out what we will likely attend to by attaching meanings to how messages are interpreted and dealt with. For example, financial analysts tend to pick up threads of conversation involving money, while sales managers pick up on market opportunities. But consider, while communication can often be problematic *within* one culture—particularly across occupations, age groups, geographic regions, and gender—these problems pale in comparison with the challenges of communicating *across* cultures. In this reading, we will look at the communication process to better understand why miscommunications—such as with the professor—happen, and most importantly, how to avoid them.

Cultural Screens on Interpersonal Communication

At its core, communication is all about conveying meaning to others—not just words. Messages are only effective to the extent that recipients are both paying attention to them and capable of processing the information in ways that facilitate common meaning. Throughout this process, numerous factors in the communication environment can

---

[1] This chapter draws heavily on Nardon, L., Steers, R. Sanchez-Runde, C. (2011). Seeking Common Ground: Strategies for Enhancing Multicultural Communication, *Organizational Dynamics*, 40: 85–95.

Figure 1 Cultural
Screens as Mediators
of Interpersonal
Communication

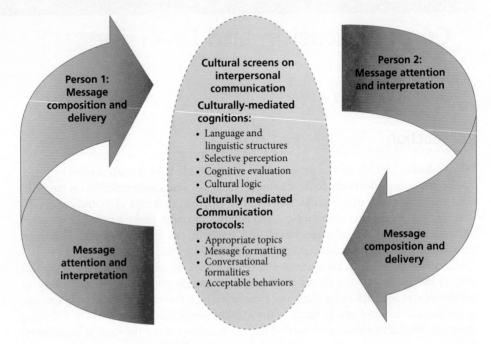

serve to reinforce, attract, or distract attention towards, or away, from the message at the expense of others and influence message interpretation and analysis, as well as message construction and delivery mechanisms.

We will also focus on two interrelated cultural screens, or lenses, that can affect both interpersonal interactions, in general, and multicultural communications, in particular (Figure 1). The first screen involves cultural influences on individual cognitions surrounding communication episodes; that is, how people and messages are often evaluated and processed in the minds of both senders and receivers. The second involves cultural influences on communication protocols, or required behaviors.

Culturally Mediated Cognitions

Patterns of thinking often differ systematically across borders. Cultural patterns and belief structures frequently influence what people see, think, and do. There is something in how people from different cultures attempt to make sense of reality that can easily interfere with their understanding of what is going on, as well as with any possible collaboration across cultures. Four of these cognitive processes are particularly noteworthy: language and linguistic structures, selective perception, cognitive evaluation, and cultural logic.

Language and Linguistic Structures

Language is central to human communication. It plays an important role in initiating conversations and conducting most aspects of human affairs. Language and linguistic structures—the manner in which words, grammar, syntax, and the meaning of words are organized and used—are intricately intertwined with the processes of attention and interpretation to messages.

Languages provide subtle, yet powerful, cues on what to account for in our dealings with other people. Through differences in how verb tenses are used, how gender is or not assigned to things, and how spatial relations are conveyed, people must attend to different aspects of the conversation. For example, in Thai, there are many equivalents to the pronoun "I" in English, depending on differences in gender, age, politeness, status or relationship between speaker and listener.

Language also influences the way individuals interact when communicating. A study of bilingual (Cantonese–English) workers in Hong Kong found that the language in use influenced how topics were managed: when meetings were conducted in English, the discussion followed a sequential and linear pattern, while meetings conducted in Cantonese followed a more spiral or circular pattern,[2] suggesting that language and culture are highly intertwined.

Selective Perception: The Eye of the Beholder

Since people cannot simultaneously focus on all of the events surrounding them at a given time, they make mental choices about what is important, useful, or threatening, and focus their mental powers on these particular issues. These mental choices may differ across cultures. For example, the importance of the context of communication varies by culture. Hall and Hall[3] refer to these differences as high- and low-context cultures. In low-context cultures, such as Germany, Scandinavia, and the United States, the context surrounding the message is far less important than the message itself. By contrast, in high-context cultures such as those found in many parts of Asia, the context in which the message is conveyed (e.g., a formal meeting versus an informal conversation) is often as important as the message itself. Indeed, the way something is said can even be more important in communicating a message than the actual words that are used. As a result, people in high-context cultures tend to infer more to a message than what was said, or maybe intended.

As an example, consider the case of a Korean manufacturer contracted to produce model trains for a United States distributor. After receiving the first shipment, the American distributor sent the Korean manufacturer a long list of discrepancies, including manufacturing and modeling errors. The Korean manufacturer, using a high-context communication logic, inferred that the communication was an attempt to solicit a reduction in price. He then focused his efforts in cutting costs and did nothing to address the discrepancies. The partnership ended soon after.[4]

Cognitive Evaluation: Interpreting Words and Actions

When people see or hear something, they have a tendency to categorize the information so they can make judgments about its authenticity, accuracy, or utility. They try to relate it to other events and actions so they can make sense out of it and know how to respond. This process is called cognitive evaluation, and culture can play a major role. When people face the possibility of alternative interpretations of specific events, they will almost uniformly choose the interpretation that is most consistent with their own cultural outlook. For example, managers from highly individualistic cultures (e.g., the United States) will typically attribute team success to the team leader's skills and efforts, while managers from more collectivistic cultures (e.g., Japan) will typically attribute it to the skills and efforts of the entire team.

Cultural Logic: Assumptions about Shared Meanings

Interpersonal communication is an interactive process, requiring two or more people to exchange thoughts, ideas, and emotions in an effort to find common ground. Research suggests that individuals make assumptions about shared knowledge between themselves and receivers of their messages and construct messages based on common knowledge.[5] Cultural logic is the process of using one's own assumptions to interpret the messages and actions of others, thereby hypothesizing about their motives and intentions.[6] People often rely on this logic to facilitate communication and decrease what needs to be said to a manageable level, since it is often too difficult and time consuming for people to express all of their thoughts and assumptions behind everything they say. A shared cultural logic helps people fill the gaps left by what is unsaid, thereby facilitating the process of creating a shared meaning.

For example, Americans have often been described as "cheerful" and tend to use exclamations and superlatives such as "This is fabulous!" and "Great!" to refer to usual or mundane situations, as well as brag about themselves and their achievements. In a conversation between Americans, this excitement is naturally discounted and a statement about "a fantastic project" is reinterpreted as "a project that worked out alright." In contrast, many Europeans prefer to refer to situations with a light understatement and are more likely to say, "The project was not bad." In a cross-cultural communication episode, the American statement may be taken literally by the European counterpart and cause later disappointment (or the individual making the statement may be perceived as lacking judgment) and the European statement may be interpreted by an American as worse than intended.

Cultural logic is the process of making assumptions about shared knowledge in order to communicate as such is influenced by one's cultural background and assumptions, but also by his or her knowledge of the other's culture and individual. As individuals get to know each other and learn about each other's culture, a clearer understanding about what is shared and what needs to be explained is likely to emerge.

Culture and Communication Protocols

All cultures and subcultures foster socio-normative beliefs and values that guide members' thoughts and actions. These beliefs include what members can't, or shouldn't do, as well as what they can, must, or should do. Not surprisingly, these norms and values influence how we choose to converse with both members of our own culture and others. Included here are a variety of expected communication protocols, or behaviors, including appropriate topics for discussion, message formatting, conversational formalities, and acceptable behaviors. Each of these is likely to influence what people attend to in a message, how they interpret it, and how they respond.

Appropriate Topics for Discussion

Acceptable topics for discussion vary widely across cultures, as many experienced managers know. For example, in most South American countries it is considered polite to inquire about how the family is doing, but in many Middle Eastern countries it is not. Equally important here is the ordering or sequencing of conversational topics. While many Western managers believe in avoiding "small talk" and getting right down to business, managers in South America and East and Southeast Asia typically believe that conversations must first be warmed up with broad or general discussions on topics other than business.

Message Formatting

Experienced managers also understand that how a message is constructed can have a profound impact on how it is received. Should a message be explicit and direct or subtle and indirect? To what degree should messages be communicated through verbal or non-verbal mechanisms? How should the message be delivered: Through the chain of command, or through close associates or friends?

Conversational Formalities

Conversational formalities encompass formal or implicit guidelines and rules governing what constitutes acceptable or preferred formal conversational etiquette. Such formalities include the use of titles, the manner in which ideas or proposals are presented, and the role of apologies.

For example, formal apologies are used throughout much of East and Southeast Asia to restore harmony after an unpleasant incident or crisis. They demonstrate empathy and acceptance of responsibility. By contrast, apologies in many Western countries are often used to admit guilt and, as a result, are used sporadically.

Acceptable Behaviors

Finally, cultures often place constraints and expectations on what is considered acceptable behaviors that accompany interpersonal interactions. For example, is it acceptable to be assertive and initiate conversations, or should one remain silent until invited to speak? When is it appropriate to interrupt another? How much silence is considered acceptable in between speakers? Is it acceptable to display emotions or should one maintain a "cooler" outlook. When and how is it appropriate to disagree, praise, or provide feedback?

Strategies for Enhancing Multicultural Communication

With an increasing need to communicate with people from different cultures, developing the abilities and skills to communicate effectively is fundamental to all managers. As the previous discussion suggests, a lot can go wrong when communicating across cultures. We now come to the issue of what managers can do to reduce or minimize such impediments to clear communication (Figure 2).

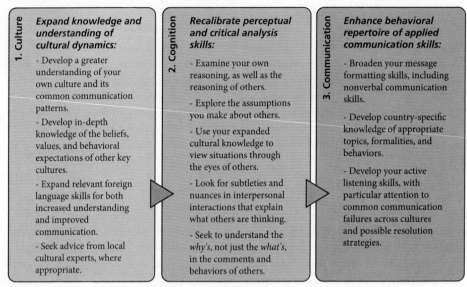

Figure 2   Strategies for Improving Multicultural Communication

Strategy #1: Expand Your Knowledge and Understanding of Cultural Dynamics

Managers can and should invest the time and energy required to learn more about how the workplace often differs across cultures. Of particular importance here is knowledge of how local beliefs, values, and behavioral expectations can differ across cultures and how managers can prepare themselves for such differences. Much of this learning can be accomplished though independent reading and study, sponsored programs on cross-cultural issues, discussions with foreign nationals, and focused observations of what others are doing. Multicultural learning can also be facilitated by language study. Understanding the language of one's counterparts can go a long way toward capturing the essence of cultural differences, an important factor in working successfully across borders.

In expanding cultural knowledge, it is important not to forget one's own culture. Frequently, managers take their own culture for granted and fail to realize that their own social environment creates its own screens that affect communication. Self-awareness about one's culture can serve as a useful point of departure for better understanding others. It can also serve to enhance one's understanding on how others view us.

Strategy #2: Recalibrate Your Perceptual and Critical Analysis Skills

Based on newly acquired multicultural awareness and understanding, managers should be in a position to use somewhat modified cognitive templates or frames of reference when trying to understand why people with different cultural backgrounds do, or say what they do. Recent research has shown that experienced managers often exhibit an ability to look behind external appearances or behaviors and try to understand the why's, not just the what's. They work to understand interpersonal interactions through the eyes and ears of others. They look for subtleties and nuances in social interactions that may help explain what others are thinking.

At the same time, successful global managers seek to understand their own beliefs and values, assumptions, biases, and perceptions. Stepping outside of one's comfort zone allows managers to take a fresh look at situations that confront them. Are their assumptions about certain situations correct, or are there alternative assumptions that are equally valid? The point for managers to understand is that they may be "right" with respect to something, but in a cross-cultural environment, what is right is relative. Arriving at a common meaning requires an ability to tolerate uncertainty and ambiguity in order to seek a deeper understanding of what one's counterparts are trying to say or do.

Strategy #3: Enhance Your Behavioral Repertoire of Applied Communication Skills

On a very practical level, managers can improve their knowledge of various communication protocols that can vary from culture to culture. In addition to knowing where or when certain languages are preferred or required, developing message formatting skills can be critical to successful communication, especially as it relates to the use of non-verbal communication techniques, such as reading facial expressions and other forms of body language.

For example, knowing what topics may be required or forbidden in certain conversations or messages, what formalities are required or preferred in various contexts, and what behaviors are acceptable or unacceptable, may be helpful in facilitating communication across cultures.

Finally, developing active listening skills has long been recommended for managers facing ambiguous situations. This is particularly important in cross-cultural settings when communication failures can be commonplace. Recognizing such failures—not always an easy task—and finding a remedy can be a key to saving a conversation and possible business deal.

Conclusion

This reading began by pointing out that multicultural communication is frequently cited as one of the most serious challenges facing global managers. In closing, we should observe that cross-cultural communication is also one of the most important sources of business opportunity. It is through communication that relationships are formed, conflicts are resolved, and innovative ideas are created and shared. While the perils of poor cross-cultural communication may appear daunting upon first glance, we should understand that increased awareness of the ways in which cultural differences can affect how meaning is constructed in interpersonal interactions is an important first step towards improved communication. We should further note that in order to succeed, managers must be willing to make the effort and risk some initial missteps, and perhaps embarrassment. In the end, effective multicultural communication is a matter of personal commitment and a willingness to learn. Above all, however, it is a willingness to listen. As the Venetian explorer Marco Polo observed long ago, "It is not the voice that commands the story; it is the ear".[7]

Endnotes

1. Ferraro, G. (2006). *The cultural dimensions of international business.* Upper Saddle River, NJ: Pearson/Prentice Hall.
2. Du-Babcock, B. (2006). An analysis of topic management strategies and turn-taking behavior in the Hong Kong bilingual environment. *Journal of Business Communication, 43*(1), 21–42.
3. Hall, E. T., & Hall, M. R. (1990). *Understanding cultural differences: Germans, French and Americans.* Yarmouth, Maine: Intecultural Press, Inc.
4. Haworth, D. A., & Savage, G. T. (1989). A channel-ratio model of intercultural communication: The trains won't sell, fix them please. *The Journal of Business Communication, 26*(3), 231–254.
5. Clark, H. H., & Marshall, C. E. (1981). Definite reference and mutual knowledge. In A. K. Joshi, I. Sag, & B. Webber (Eds.), *Elements of discourse understanding,* 10–63. Cambridge, UK: Cambridge University Press.
6. Enfield, N. J. (2000). The theory of cultural logic. *Cultural Dynamics, 12*(1), 35–64.
7. Bergreen, L. (2007). *Marco Polo: From Venice to Xanadu.* New York, NY: Vintage Books, i.

Diversity Ideologies in Action: Energizing Renewal and Excellence in Healthcare

Valerie L. Myers

University of Michigan

Diversity—it's who we are.

> —*Yvonne Tisdel,*
> *Corporate Vice President of Human*
> *Resources and System Diversity*
> *SSM Health Care System*

A strong culture can be an asset that enhances performance, a liability that limits effectiveness, or a meaningless memory that has no effect. SSM Health Care System (SSM) is an organization that has historically relied upon its strong culture to energize and sustain excellent performance. As Ms. Tisdel's quote indicates, diversity is central to SSM's cultural ideology.

SSM is a private, not-for-profit healthcare system that operates in four states: Wisconsin, Illinois, Missouri and Oklahoma. It employs nearly 24,000 people in its 20 hospitals and numerous other health care facilities (e.g., nursing homes, home care, and hospice). It is the tenth largest Catholic healthcare system in the nation. In 2010, SSM reported $4.2 billion in total assets and $3.0 billion in operating revenues—90 percent of which is derived from hospital care. They also provided $115 million in charity care. SSM has earned national and industry-specific awards for exceptional patient care and diversity management practices.

In this article, we will examine SSM's culture, particularly its diversity culture, to understand the vital role of organizational ideology throughout an organization's lifecycle and its potential to influence mission fulfillment, growth, maturation, renewal and greater effectiveness. SSM illustrates ways that new and mature organizations can similarly leverage and reframe diversity to advance strategic goals.

Background

Organizational Lifecycle

An organization's lifecycle is characterized by different phases of development, conveniently summarized here as birth, growth, maturation, and decline. Crisis is often the catalyst for advancement through each lifecycle phase, each characterized by varying levels of effectiveness and cohesiveness.[1] At birth, the entrepreneurial phase, both cohesiveness and effectiveness, are relatively low. As effectiveness increases, it fosters greater cohesiveness and collective action that results in growth. As the organization matures, it formalizes and institutionalizes practices to achieve greater efficiency. However, standardization and potential hyper-cohesiveness can also become liabilities that foster complacency, inattentiveness to the environment, organizational inertia, and decline (and threats to patient safety in the case of a healthcare organization).[2] Decline is not inevitable, however; renewal is possible depending upon the degree to which characteristics of an open system[3] (e.g., environmental scanning, responsiveness and learning) are embedded in the organization's culture.

Organizational Culture

Organizational culture is established as founding members seek ways to identify themselves as a collective, coordinate their work, and cope with demands of the external environment. Externally, culture distinguishes an organization from its competitor's vis-à-vis values, target markets, human resource management, and core competencies.[4] The underlying components of culture form the organization's DNA and determine: how decisions are made; how facts are determined; beliefs about human nature; how people should related to each other; the right thing to do; and members' orientation toward the past, present, or future.[5] The culture is perpetuated and reinforced as it is taught to new members. Once established, cultural ideologies and practices guide members' approach to mission fulfillment—and to diversity management.

Diversity Paradigms

During the past decades, the focus of diversity management programs has shifted, resulting in three distinct paradigms: 1) discrimination and fairness, 2) access and legitimacy, and 3) learning and effectiveness.[6] Although not developed explicitly for healthcare, each paradigm is essential to manage diverse patients and healthcare providers. Unlike other industries, failure to effectively manage diversity in healthcare can be life threatening.

The *discrimination and fairness* paradigm is based upon a moral imperative to remedy social inequalities. For patients, this means eliminating well documented racial and economic disparities in the care delivery process.[7] For healthcare providers, this translates into improving racial and gender equality in admissions to clinical and managerial educational programs so that women and people or color are no longer underrepresented in clinical and professional roles.[8] However, increasing equity is only a beginning.

The *access and legitimacy* paradigm is based upon the notion that demographic similarity between firm employees and their customers results in greater sensitivity to consumer preferences, and therefore greater customer satisfaction and an increased share of diverse markets. In healthcare, access and legitimacy is evident in initiatives to increase racial concordance between healthcare providers and the communities that they serve, now required by the nation's Culturally and Linguistically Appropriate Standards (CLAS).[9] Research shows that a patient's race predicts physician perceptions and the quality of care that they provide,[10] as well as the degree to which patients comply with medical instructions and are satisfied with their care.[11] Therefore, racial concordance between healthcare providers and recipients is viewed as an antidote to racial disparities in care and a prescription for greater legitimacy in the local community.

Conversely, other studies show that an organization's patient mix (e.g., income, race), rather than provide demographics, predicts disparities in the quality of patient care.

Hence, some organizations simply provide better (or worse) care for everyone—regardless of race.[12] These findings suggest that although increasing access for minority patients and providers is a partial solution, additional steps are needed to insure that all clinicians provide comparable high-quality care across healthcare organizations.

The third paradigm, *learning and effectiveness,* emphasizes ways that diversity enhances overall performance. The benefits of diversity accrue when the CEO of a firm casts a vision and embeds diversity in the organization's strategy; diffuses and integrates it throughout the operating system; and encourages employees at all levels to fully engage in achieving work goals.[13] A well-managed diverse workforce adds value by enhancing the organization's ability to learn, adapt, innovate and solve complex problems.[14] In this manner, a diverse workforce is advantageous to healthcare organizations' clinical operations, and can also improve system-wide performance (e.g., financial, technical, human resources, etc.). The benefits of diversity are only realized however, through the enactment of supportive policies and practices, as well as the informal strategic actions of "tempered radicals"[15]—employees who take calculated risks to change the status quo.

Healthcare organizations must manage all three diversity paradigms in order to achieve the Institute of Medicine's aims to provide safe, efficient, effective, timely, equitable, and patient-centered care.[16]

Lifecycle, Culture and Diversity at SSM Healthcare System

Diversity was woven into the cultural DNA of SSM at its founding, when the Sisters of St. Mary migrated to St. Louis in 1872 and began their healthcare ministry. As the hospital evolved into a multi-state health care system in 1986, it confronted predictable challenges of maturation in the organizational lifecycle—inertia and incremental decline. However, SSM's leaders proactively sought ways to forestall decline and promote renewal, in part, by considering the strategic importance of diversity to achieve results. Diversity was not a new initiative for SSM in 1990, but a renewed focus on core values and practices that were embedded in its cultural ideology.

Throughout its lifecycle, SSM operated using all three diversity paradigms, to varying degrees, to support their mission, enact their values, and refine work practices. These values and practices were not just spiritual, despite the organization's religious affiliation. SSM's values and practices were socially responsible, technically and financially pragmatic, and empirically sound. Their diversity ideologies were evident in their approach to patients, the workforce, their enterprise, the healthcare industry, and external relationships. SSM's diversity ideologies and practices predated the frameworks and research used to describe them here.

Birth 1872–1933: Activist Entrepreneurs on a Healthcare Mission

Five nuns, known as the Sisters of St. Mary, fled Germany in pursuit of religious freedom and to do God's work. They arrived in St. Louis, Missouri during a smallpox epidemic and launched their compassionate mission by caring for sick people in their homes; they also cared for orphans, and housed unwed pregnant mothers. Soon after, the Sisters cared for people in hospitals, expanding their mission to provide healthcare to everyone,

Figure 1 Cultural
DNA of SSM

regardless of race, color, or ability to pay (approximately 60 percent were unable to pay). Originally, they worked in an urban area with a large African American population. In 1877, the Sisters of St. Mary borrowed $16,000 to establish St. Louis Infirmary.

The community of nuns grew, and in 1894, the Sisters split into two factions; six left to start Sisters of St. Francis, which provided access to health care in rural Maryville, Missouri. At one of those hospitals, night shift nurses surreptitiously conducted a radical, quasi-social experiment by integrating black and white babies in the nursery—despite segregation laws. Their actions were both political and pragmatic, given limited staffing. The result: no ill effects on the babies.

When the St. Louis infirmary was re-dedicated in 1933, it became the first Catholic hospital for African American patients in the nation. However, segregation laws prohibited African Americans professionals from working in the majority of institutions. Through SSM's pioneering acts, the organization advanced a social justice agenda to eliminate racial barriers by providing employment opportunities for African American physicians and nurses. This groundbreaking human resource initiative increased racial concordance between healthcare providers and patients, decades before CLAS standards were established in 2001.

SSM's ideologies of social justice, compassion, and inclusiveness were firmly established as core values that defined their key constituents and relationship norms. Similarly, through their activism, risk taking, resourcefulness with an eye toward clinical outcomes, and proactively engaging the environment, they communicated the "right way" to fulfill the mission. As shown in Figure 1, the confluence of those ideologies comprised the underlying components of culture that influenced SSM's evolution and how it interacted with patients, the workforce, and the larger environment.

Growth and Maturation 1934–1989: Continuing the Journey, Expanding the Territory

Hospitals affiliated with Sisters of St. Mary and Sisters of St. Francis proliferated in urban and rural areas, independently fulfilling their mission to provide healthcare for vulnerable populations.

In 1962, SSM supported the political participation of Sister Antona Ebo, an African American graduate of their nursing program, to participate in an interfaith group that marched for Civil Rights in Selma, Alabama. In 1967, Sister Ebo was appointed administrator of St. Clare Hospital & Health Services in Baraboo, Wisconsin—the first African American woman to lead a religious hospital. These actions were a testament to SSM's enduring ideologies of social justice, activism, risk taking, and inclusiveness.

By the early 1980s, inflection points across the institutional environment led the Sisters of St. Mary and Sisters of St. Francis hospitals to contemplate a different and more collaborative future. Foremost, managed care gained momentum in the 1980s, shifting the focus away from government funded healthcare that increased access for vulnerable populations (e.g., Medicare and Medicaid) to a market model of managed care that promoted efficiency, cost containment and increased competition for privately insured patients.[17] Despite SSM's unwavering charitable care mission, they recognized that changes in reimbursements would impose financial constraints throughout the healthcare industry. In order to fulfill their charitable and business missions, SSM needed to maintain healthy operating margins that could best be achieved with greater efficiency, effectiveness and patient volume. The shift toward efficient healthcare occurred in tandem with trends in manufacturing and other industries.

Business and political leaders realized that poor quality was eroding the nation's economic strength and competitive position in an increasingly global market, most notably in the automotive industry. As a result, the Malcolm Baldrige National Quality Improvement Act of 1987 was signed into law. In conjunction with the act, criteria were established to measure quality improvements and reward excellent performance. During that era, U.S. manufacturers strategically embraced quality improvement tactics to gain competitive advantages over international rivals (e.g., Japanese automakers).[18] However, the quality conversation and metrics had not yet permeated healthcare—although there was increasing awareness of the need to define and measure quality, and to prevent medical errors.[19]

In the socio-political environment, the Civil Rights Movement morphed into Equal Rights legislation and initiatives for women, people of color, and later people with disabilities and Affirmative Action. Landmark social movements radically changed the face of modern workplaces, and not without attendant challenges. The emergent field of diversity scholarship sought to ameliorate those challenges by advancing the diversity conversation beyond remedying inequality and increasing access to articulating a business case for inclusiveness and valuing difference.[20]

Individual hospital leaders detected the confluence of institutional pressures in the course of routine environmental scanning (Figure 2). Results of their analysis signaled the need for disparate hospitals to reflect upon their historic culture and vision for the future; to refine daily work practices to achieve greater efficiency; and to formalize processes that enhanced stability and sustainability, lest they fall prey to the perils of mature organizations. Institutional pressures and transformative crises are typical during the maturation phase of an organization's lifecycle.[21] If organizations fail to adapt, they can drift toward inertia, ineffectiveness, and ultimately obsolescence. Conversely, leaders can pursue a path of renewal by critically analyzing the organization's strengths, deficits, and the extent to which their culture enables or undermines their ability to adapt and survive.

Health Care Industry
Managed Care
Reimbursement Rates
Quality Concerns

Scholarship
Diversity Management
Quality Measurement
Institute of Medicine

Manufacturing Industry
Total Quality Management
Diversity Management

SSM

Perceptions
Patients
Workforce

Performance Data
Financial
Clinical/Medical Errors

Figure 2

Transformative Institutional Pressures

Figure 3 Core Ideologies for Renewal at SSM

In 1986, disparate hospitals affiliated with the Sisters of St. Mary and Sisters of St. Francis coalesced to form the SSM Health Care System. SSM's leaders actively sought to revitalize their culture and renew their vision with respect to its historic mission and contemporary realities:

> *"Through our participation in the healing ministry of Jesus Christ, communities, especially those that are economically, physically and socially marginalized, will experience improved health in mind, body, spirit and environment within the financial limits of the system."*

Preventing Decline, Promoting Renewal: 1990–2005 and Beyond

SSM confronted common challenges in the healthcare industry such as shrinking reimbursements, growing deficits, staff turnover, patient (dis)satisfaction, post-operative infections, and lack of standardization in basic processes (e.g., blood pressure measurement).[22] Under the leadership of Sister Mary Jean Ryan, the system's first CEO, the leadership team engaged in rigorous reflection and analysis as they embarked upon a strategic planning process. As shown in Figure 3, the new strategic plan inextricably linked quality improvement and diversity management, supported by their ideological strengths.

Renewal through CQI

In response to business challenges, leaders reviewed research and found that the Continuous Quality Improvement (CQI) principles of industry (i.e., a management philosophy that focuses on constantly improving the way work is done) were aligned with SSM's core values and vision, so they considered ways to implement process improvements throughout the organization. Reflecting upon that time, Eunice Halverson, now the Corporate VP of Patient Safety and Quality Center, remembered the lack of rigor in healthcare industry accreditation standards.

> *"If you look at our accreditation, which all of our hospitals are accredited through the joint commission [JCAHO]—they don't really care about strategic plans. You have to have it. If you have one, they check it off the list. You're good right? They don't look at the budget. You have to have one right? So anything on the financial side, the growth and satisfaction of your physicians, your employees, your customers, you have to have a process for some of those things but for the most part it's all patient care and safety, which is very good. Now obviously our greatest focus is on patient care and safety, but the Baldridge criteria forces you to look at all of your organizations starting with leadership. They grade you moving into strategy, then your customers, then your information systems, then your knowledge sharing, then your staff, your HR, your volunteers and then, oh by the way, your processes and then the results. How are you doing then?[23]*

In pursuit of excellence, SSM took the risk of voluntarily subjecting itself to the rigor and public scrutiny of applying for the Baldrige Quality Award. They chose to use Baldrige performance criteria as a guiding framework because it is more comprehensive and rigorous than standards established by the Joint Commission on Accreditation of Healthcare Organizations (JCAHO). SSM leaders applied the Baldrige criteria across departments, making everyone in the organization aware of the need to focus on data, while encouraging people to innovate and empowering them to creatively solve problems in response to the data. For example, Halverson recalled that a group of environmental services workers were concerned about patient satisfaction data related to room cleanliness.

> *"They implemented some changes in their process—they standardized their cleaning process—they had a wheel which anybody, no matter what their literacy level was, would be able to use [that wheel] to go through the steps of cleaning a room. They called themselves the 'Clean Sweep Team'. They got their satisfaction scores up to 100%. Were they 100% all the time? No, but they stayed extremely high."[24]*

Clinically, Dr. Filippo Ferrigni applied knowledge he acquired from a medical journal to administer intravenous insulin to reduce infections that are associated with high glucose levels.[25] The experiment was so successful with intensive care patients that he encouraged similar testing and treatment of all patients' glucose levels, resulting in a 40 percent decrease in intensive care death rates and a 28 percent reduction in overall deaths.

To promote learning and greater effectiveness throughout the system, they began to "steal shamelessly—when a nun tells you to do it, it's ok," said Halverson. "We have a 'Steal Shamelessly Series' now the fourth Friday of every month. We have something on our webinar that's broadcast across our whole system that people are expected to steal and implement. That's how we improve." SSM has also institutionalized the "Showcase for Sharing" where staff share best practices as part of an annual leadership conference. In sum, CQI metrics and the Baldrige criteria were used to improve every aspect of the organization, including human resources and diversity.

Renewal through Diversity Management

Despite its strong culture and diversity ideologies, a staff person at corporate headquarters noticed that SSM was not "walking their talk." Her comment about the suboptimal number of women and people of color in leadership challenged leaders to reconcile dissonance between their social justice history and current work practices. Was diversity a relic of the past or a resource for the future?

To revitalize SSM's diversity culture, leaders created a diversity executive role that they filled after an external search. In 1997, Yvonne Tisdel, an African American former Navy officer with corporate experience, was hired and promoted to Corporate Vice President of Human Resources and System Diversity. Tisdel leveraged SSM's existing ideologies (e.g., social justice, innovation, inclusiveness) to inspire a new approach to diversity. She launched several change management initiatives, starting with a concerted communication strategy that reframed the diversity mission as both social justice and the pursuit of excellence.[26] Her message: "*Diversity in all areas of SSM Health Care is not only part of our past, it is key to our success in the future. At SSM, we realize that workplace diversity is essential to be competitive.*" That message was reinforced through various media, including their video "Diversity Brings Us Together and Sets Us Apart."

Tisdel, congruent with the data driven CQI approach, went in search of more rigorous diversity standards. We too discovered that healthcare standards lag other industries.

"We were looking for benchmarks because these people [SSM leaders] eat data! So when you stand before them, you can't just say we're the best. They'll say–how do you know that we're the best? Sis. Mary Jean was there and she said, "how do we know it." "They want to be the best." "We were doing Diversity Inc. before any healthcare organization was doing it. I talked to Barbara Frankel a long time ago about, why don't you do healthcare benchmarks? She said "No, no no," because it was for the for-profits. But now, they realize that healthcare—this is a big industry!"[27]

In the interim, Tisdel developed metrics to monitor progress in five strategically important areas: minority employee recruitment, selection, hiring, retention, and promotion to leadership positions.[28] In addition, SSM institutionalized a diversity scorecard to monitor and accelerate strategic goal attainment. Steve Barney, Senior Vice President of Human Resources explained the diversity scorecard and the diversity–quality connection this way:

"SSM needed a tool that was as robust as our objectives are challenging. We needed something that measured our success with diversity as a system of issues, including social justice, strategic differentiation, workforce satisfaction and customer service."

Practical steps used to achieve diversity goals included mandatory training for all employees and a mentoring program that paired executives with minority employees to cultivate future leaders. "When I came here, there was no one like me here. Now there are two others in senior leadership that I can collaborate with," said Tisdel. Focused efforts enabled SSM to realize a 27 percent increase in minorities in professional and managerial positions within 5 years. Similarly, the Vision of Individual Commitment to Excellence (VOICE) boosted staff retention by 24 percent.

Achieving Results: The CQI–Diversity Connection

After several tries, SSM was again at the vanguard as the first health care organization to earn the Baldrige Award in 2002.[29] Both CQI and diversity executives recognize the complementary relationship between their respective functions in achieving this milestone.

Halverson said that the Baldrige criteria helped SSM employees focus and continuously improve key work processes; they still use it for that purpose today. Consequently, SSM has been more successful at implementing CQI than many other large institutions.[30] Halverson also sees a connection between diversity and CQI. "Diversity is something that really is kind of woven into everything that we do." she said.

"You might think of diversity as the role or the discipline where someone comes from. We do consider those who may be, or would be, included on teams because they are in the—I don't know how to say this—they are in a lower paid position. But yet they might be the person who is closest to the process that we're trying to improve or closest to the patient care. And so in that way, we try to include them whenever we can and we look at the make-up of the teams—just knowing that people come from different areas—different parts of the country—different religions—whatever, they bring diverse ideas with them. Because they have different ways of thinking, they just bring that information to the table. And so it opens up horizons—the possibilities for performance improvement.[31]

Tisdel also reflected upon diversity and the Baldrige Award:

"Diversity was already in the criteria. Our early work just positioned us to be ahead of the game. We were leading the pack and I think that gave us an edge. People needed to see the operational connection. How is this going to get me more revenue? Now, they see that we have to be able to serve all people. Things are changing every day, every month in health care. I think people see the operational connection now. But it's still a hard thing to do; people don't want to talk about it."[32]

Tisdel exclaimed that she is glad that "…JCAHO has finally caught on. It [diversity] will be part of the assessment starting next year. It validated what we've been doing all along. We were so far ahead of the curve. Staff was saying 'why is corporate asking us to do this?' But now that JCAHO's doing this and the Baldrige, it has kind of validated what we've been doing and that we've been doing the right thing." In addition, at Tisdel's urging, Diversity Inc. magazine recently established diversity rankings for the healthcare industry. SSM excelled in communication and supplier relations but didn't earn top distinction, in part because SSM has achieved comparable results on the strength of their culture, rather than institutional mandates. Nevertheless, SSM has won numerous diversity awards, routinely outranking American Hospital Association peers.

After 25 years, Sister Ryan transferred the CEO reigns to Bill Thompson, a former Chief Strategist and COO at SSM. "He gets it," said Tisdel. "He's very committed to diversity. It's not a soft skill for him. He's Caucasian. He's a lay person. He's a numbers person. Anyone who can yield results, he wants them on the team," she said. Thompson's promotion, along with other leaders, highlights the fact that SSM's focus is not just on the face of diversity, but also the heart of diversity at all levels of leadership. "They're not doing diversity because it's the right thing to do. They're doing things in their personal lives," said Tisdel.

With regard to quality, the CQI team has turned its attention to refining processes to monitor and eliminate racial disparities in patient care.

Conclusion

SSM's strong culture has been vital to its success and renewal for more than a century. As shown in Figure 4, diversity is central to that culture, the ideological strands of which were woven into SSM's approach to patient care, the workforce, the healthcare industry and the macro environment since its inception. SSM embodied a commitment to diversity management in their social justice mission, inclusive work environment, tactics to develop diverse talent, as well as social activism within the healthcare industry and beyond. Although the menu of activities changed over time, the organization consistently took risks and pursued learning to be on the leading edge.

In each phase of the lifecycle, SSM expanded and enriched their diversity ideology in service of their mission, strategic objective, and to advance broader social change. During formative years, SSM hospitals operated primarily from the discrimination and fairness paradigm, insuring that disadvantaged patients were treated with compassion and dignity, and advancing social justice by integrating the nursery. Evidence of the *access and legitimacy paradigm* was apparent in SSM providing access to healthcare in urban and rural areas, training and hiring African American clinicians, and establishing the first hospital for African Americans in the nation.

PATIENTS	WORKFORCE	ENTERPRISE & INDUSTRY	ENVIRONMENT
Social Justice Mission	Inclusive Talent Development	Innovation Risk Takers Excellence	Boundary Scanning Activism Alliances

Figure 4 DNA of SSM's Organizational Culture

As the organization matured, their social justice focus turned to the Civil Rights movement and Equal Rights for Women, which led them to support Sister Ebo in her march on Selma Alabama, and to subsequently promote her to a senior leadership position, well ahead of the healthcare industry. However, access to leadership positions for other people of color did not keep pace. As the organization matured, it drifted toward inertia and decline. In similar circumstances, many organizations conform to industry norms to promote renewal, survival, and avert crisis.[33] Instead, SSM used shifts across the institutional landscape as an opportunity for reflection and radical action. Although they experienced some decline, SSM's proactive approach and environmental scanning led them to push boundaries, invite scrutiny, encourage innovation, and engage all employees in a culture overhaul that capitalized upon the confluence of diversity and continuous quality improvement—the *learning and effectiveness* paradigm.

Toward that end, SSM relied upon its strong culture of social justice, innovation and activism, which was enriched by continuous learning, data analysis, and diversity management tactics that promoted inclusive teamwork. Toward that end, they implemented targeted plans (e.g., training, mentoring) to develop, retain, and promote diverse talent to achieve strategic goals—not just change the face of the organization. Building upon its diversity culture and using the Baldrige criteria as a benchmark, SSM combined diversity management and CQI to achieve extraordinary performance in all areas of the business—leadership, strategic planning, financial performance, human resources, and patient care. They operated within the learning and effectiveness paradigm long before diversity research supported their approach.

SSM illustrates how organizations can and must manage challenges related to their cultural legacies and lifecycle stages. They did this by honoring their strengths, asking difficult questions, then intentionally and aggressively addressing their deficits, which enabled them to adapt to and influence a changing environment. By adhering to core values that support diversity, learning, and continuous improvement, they remain harbingers of excellence in the healthcare industry.

Endnotes

1. Quinn, R. E. & Cameron, K. (1983). Organizational life cycles and shifting criteria of effectiveness: Some preliminary evidence. *Management Science, 29*(1): 33–51.

2. Quinn, R. E. & Cameron, K. (1983). Organizational life cycles and shifting criteria of effectiveness: Some preliminary evidence. *Management Science, 29*(1): 33–51. Weick, K. (1993). Collective mind in organizations: Heedful interrelating on flight decks. *Administrative Science Quarterly, 38*(3) 357–381.Weick, K. E., Sutcliffe, K. M., & Obstfeld, D. (1999). Organizing for high reliability: Processes of collective mindfulness. In R. Sutton & B. Staw (Eds.). *Research in Organizational Behavior,* 81–124. Greenwich, CT: JAI.

3. Scott, W. R., & Davis, G. F. (2006). *Organizations and organizing: rational, natural, and open systems perspectives.* Prentice Hall: Upper Saddle River, NJ.

4. Schein, E. H. (2004). *Organizational culture and leadership,* (3rd Ed.). San Francisco: Jossey Bass.

5. ibid.

6. Thomas, D. A. & Ely, R. J. (1996). Making differences matter: A new paradigm for managing diversity. *Harvard Business Review,* September-October: 79–90.

7. Smedley, B., Stith, A. Y., Nelson, A. R. (2002). *Unequal treatment: Confronting racial and ethnic disparities in health care,* Washington, DC: The National Academies Press. Committee on Quality of Health Care in America, 2001, *Crossing the quality chasm: A new health system for the 21st century,* Washington, DC: The National Academies Press.

8. Weil, P. A. & Mattis, M. C. (2001). Narrowing the gender gap in healthcare management. *Healthcare Executive*: 357–362.

9. U.S. Department of Health and Human Services, OPHS Office of Minority Health (2001). National Standards for Culturally and Linguistically Appropriate Services in Health Care. See http://minorityhealth.hhs.gov/templates/browse.aspx?lvl=2&lvlID=15 and http://www.omhrc.gov/templates/browse.aspx?lvl=2&lvlID=15.

10. M. van Ryn & J. Burke (2000). The effect of patient race and socio-economic status on physician perceptions of patients. *Social Science & Medicine,* 50: 813–828. Smedley, B., Stith, A. Y., Nelson, A. R. (2002). *Unequal treatment: Confronting racial and ethnic disparities in health care,* Washington, DC: The National Academies Press. Committee on Quality of Health Care in America, 2001, *Crossing the quality chasm: A new health system for the 21st century,* Washington, DC: The National Academies Press.

11. Street, R. L., O'Malley, K. J., Cooper, L. A., Haidet, P. (2008). Understanding concordance in patient-physician relationships: personal and ethnic dimensions of shared identity. *Annals of Family Medicine, 6*(3): 198–205.

12. Rhoads, K. F., Ackerson, L. K., Jha, A.K. & Dudley, R. A. (2008). Quality of colon cancer outcomes in hospitals with a high percentage of medicaid patients. *American Journal of the College of Surgeons, 207*(2): 197–204. Breslin, T. M., Morris, A.M., Gu, N., Wong, S. L., Finlayson, E. V., Banerjee, M., Birkmeyer, J. D. (2009). Hospital factors and racial disparities in mortality after surgery for breast and colon cancer. *Journal of Clinical Oncology, 27*(24): 3945–3950.

13. DeLong, T. J. & Vijayaraghavan, V. (2003). Let's hear it for B players. *Harvard Business Review* (June) R0306F:3–8. Gilbert, J. A. & Ivancevich, J. M. (2000). Valuing diversity: A tale of two organizations. *Academy of Management Executive, 14*(1), 93–105. Myers, V. L. & Wooten, L. P. (2009). The transformational power of a mission-driven strategy: Extraordinary diversity management practices and quality of care. *Organizational Dynamics, 38*(4):297–304. Thomas, D. A. & Ely, R. J. (1996). Making differences matter: A new paradigm for managing diversity. *Harvard Business Review,* September-October: 79–90.

14. Brett, J. Behfar, K. & Kern, M. (2006). Managing multi-cultural teams. *Harvard Business Review*, (June) R0611:1–10.
Page, S. E. (2007). *The difference: How the power of diversity creates better groups, firms, schools, and societies. Princeton* University Press: New Jersey.
Richards, O. C. (2000). Racial diversity, business strategy and firm performance: A resource-based view. *Academy of Management Journal*, 43(2) 164–177.

15. Meyerson, D. (2001). *Tempered radicals: How people use difference to inspire change at work.* Boston: Harvard Business School Press.

16. Institute of Medicine. (2001). *Crossing the quality chasm.* Washington, DC: National Academy Press.

17. Scott, W. R., Ruef, M., Mendel, P. J. & Caronna, C. A. (2000). *Institutional change and health care organizations: From professional dominance to managed care.* The University of Chicago Press: Chicago, IL.

18. Walton, M. & Deming, E. (1986). *The deming management method.* New York: Perigee Books.

19. Donabedian, Avedis. (1980). Explorations in quality assessment and monitoring: The definition of quality and approaches to its assessment, vol 1. *Health Administration Press:* Ann Arbor, MI.

20. Cox, T. (1994). *Cultural diversity in organizations: Theory, research and practice.* San Francisco: Berrett-Koehler Publishers.

21. Quinn, R. E. & Cameron, K. (1983). Organizational life cycles and shifting criteria of effectiveness: Some preliminary evidence. *Management Science, 29* (1): 33–51.

22. Gabor, A. (2004). How to run a hospital like a factory, in a good way. *New York Times*, February 22.

23. Halverson, E. (2011). Telephone interview with the author July 13th, 2011.

24. Ibid.

25. Gabor, A. (2004). How to run a hospital like a factory, in a good way. *New York Times,* February 22.

26. Myers, V. L. & Wooten, L. P. (2009). The transformational power of a mission-driven strategy: Extraordinary diversity management practices and quality of care. *Organizational Dynamics,* 38(4):297–304.

27. Tisdel, Y. (2011) Telephone interview with the author June 30th, 2011.

28. Myers, V. L. & Wooten, L. P. (2009). The transformational power of a mission-driven strategy: Extraordinary diversity management practices and quality of care. *Organizational Dynamics,* 38(4):297–304.

29. SSM Health Care System Organizational Profile, Malcolm Baldrige National Quality Award. http://www.quality.nist.gov/PDF_files/SSM_Application_Summary.pdf

30. Gabor, A. (2004). How to run a hospital like a factory, in a good way. *New York Times,* February 22.

31. Halverson, E. (2011). Telephone interview with the author July 13th, 2011.

32. Tisdel, Y. (2011) Telephone interview with the author June 30th, 2011.

33. DiMaggio, P. J. & Powell, W. W. (1983). The iron cage revisited: Institutional isomorphism and collective rationality in organizational fields. *American Sociological Review, 48*: 147–160.
Quinn, R. E. & Cameron, K. (1983). Organizational life cycles and shifting criteria of effectiveness: Some preliminary evidence. *Management Science, 29*(1): 33–51.

12 Culture

Topic Summary Learning Objectives

1. Recognize the three dimensions of culture.

2. Describe the iceberg approach to organizational culture, competing values framework of organizational cultures, and subcultures.

3. Differentiate between national and organizational culture.

4. Describe the process of socialization and the transmission of culture.

5. Evaluate an organizational culture and organizational strategy.

6. Apply concepts of culture to organizations.

Key Terms

adaptation, p. 440

adhocracy culture, p. 436

artifacts, p. 432

basic assumptions, p. 433

behavioral artifacts, p. 432

clan culture, p. 436

competing values framework, p. 435

dominant culture, p. 437

espoused values, p. 432

executive subculture, p. 437

hierarchical culture, p. 436

iceberg metaphor of culture, p. 434

market-driven culture, p. 437

national culture, p. 437

operational subculture, p. 437

organizational culture, p. 432

professional subculture, p. 437

socialization, p. 439

subculture, p. 437

verbal artifacts, p. 432

1 Recognize the three dimensions of culture.

Introduction to Culture

Organizational culture describes underlying values, beliefs, and assumptions that are shared by people within an organization. Organizational culture is important because it determines the behavior that occurs, and does not occur, in organizations. As shown in Figure 12.1, this topic summary describes four important aspects of culture: 1) dimensions of organizational culture, 2) competing values framework and organizational subcultures, 3) differences between national and organizational culture, and 4) transmitting culture and links between culture and strategy.

Aspects of Organizational Culture

Organizational cultures emerge over time and can often be traced to the organization's origins or attributed to the organization's founders. For example, there is a story that employees at the technology company Hewlett Packard are told when they join the company. The story recounts how David Packard and Tom Hewlett founded the company in a garage and this garage is often referenced in internal and external communications about the company. **Organizational culture** is the patterns of shared beliefs, values, and behaviors within an organization and cannot be accounted for by traditional organizational factors such as organizational reporting systems, structures, and policies. Culture shapes how individuals perceive, think, and feel. Cultures create the rituals, myths, and stories of the organization and provide a means for individuals and organizations to identify with and interpret symbols and events.[1]

Three Dimensions of Culture

The understanding of organizational culture is informed by many disciplines, including anthropology, social science, and psychology, among others. Schein's model of culture, for example, emerged from the intersection of anthropology and psychology. As presented in Figure 12.2, Schein's model describes three dimensions of culture: artifacts, espoused values, and basic assumptions.[2] Culture reveals itself most clearly in **artifacts**. Artifacts represent the objects that can be readily observed in organizations. Physical artifacts are easy to identify and include art, buildings, décor, dress, and other material objects. Day-to-day behaviors are also artifacts. **Behavioral artifacts** include ceremonies, rituals, traditions, and customs. **Verbal artifacts** include jargon, nicknames, stories, myths, villains, and metaphors.[3]

Espoused values are the second dimension of culture. Espoused values describe what the members of the culture say they believe. Notice these values are only

Figure 12.1

Four Aspects of Organizational Culture

Dimensions of organizational culture

Competing values framework and subcultures

National Versus organizational culture

Transmitting culture and links to strategy

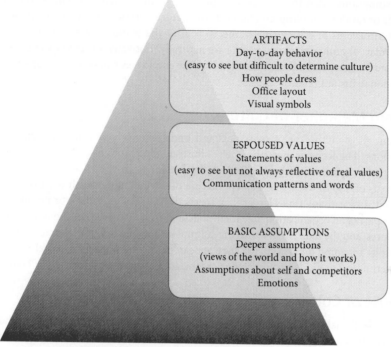

Figure 12.2
Three Levels of
Organizational Culture

'espoused'—meaning the values are expressed, but because they are only espoused, they are not always practiced in reality. **Basic assumptions**, the third dimension, are the foundation of culture. Basic assumptions are the most revealing dimension of culture. Basic assumptions are the accepted, taken for granted, unquestioned beliefs and assumptions shared by the members of the culture. Identifying basic assumptions is central to understanding culture because basic assumptions shape decisions and beliefs as described in Table 12.1.

Table 12.1 Assumptions Associated with Culture

Assumptions	Examples
Reality	• Rational and fair or random and unpredictable
Time	• Short-term or long-term
Space	• The world is vast and diverse or • The world is small and similar
Human nature	• People are naturally motivated or • People need incentives to work hard
Interpersonal relationships	• Fellow employees can be friends or • Fellow employees should be held at a distance

Assumptions often include beliefs about: 1) reality—such as events can be rational and fair or random and unpredictable; 2) the nature of time—the focus of attention is on short-term events or a long timeframe; 3) space—the world is vast and diverse or small and similar; 4) human nature—people are naturally motivated or need incentives to work hard; and 5) interpersonal relationships—fellow employees can be friends or should be in professional, distant relationships.[4]

Iceberg Metaphor of Culture

2 Describe the iceberg approach to organizational culture, competing values framework of organizational cultures, and subcultures.

The concept of culture helps us understand underlying or often hidden elements of organizations. The **iceberg metaphor** helps illustrate the nature of culture in organizations. Above the waterline, an iceberg appears to be a small piece of ice, perhaps so small that it even floats on top of the water. Perceptions are deceiving, underneath what is visible lies a large body of ice, many times larger than meets the eye. The metaphor brings into focus an obvious part of an organization, like their policies, formal structures, espoused values, work procedures, and the like. However, as the cultural iceberg metaphor illustrates, other important things are going on as well, but they appear 'below the water line.' What occurs below the waterline, often hidden from view, is organizational culture as depicted in Figure 12.3.

Purpose of Culture

Cultures, both national and organizational, serve a number of important psychological and social functions. Cultures establish limits of acceptable behavior and define what is legitimate and illegitimate behavior. Culture also sets the ground rules for what constitutes appropriate punishment when rules are broken and what kinds of rewards are given when

Figure 12.3 The Iceberg Model of Organizational Culture

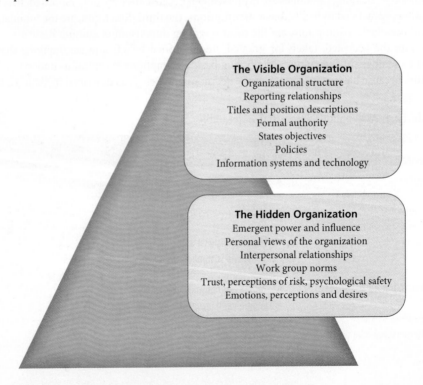

The Visible Organization
Organizational structure
Reporting relationships
Titles and position descriptions
Formal authority
States objectives
Policies
Information systems and technology

The Hidden Organization
Emergent power and influence
Personal views of the organization
Interpersonal relationships
Work group norms
Trust, perceptions of risk, psychological safety
Emotions, perceptions and desires

people follow the rules. From an organizational perspective, culture helps guide the selection and training of employees who will be a good organizational fit. Culture motivates people by providing a shared identity among organizational members and fulfills a human need for belonging and identity. In some cases, culture can support organizational strategy and effectiveness. Culture helps an organization understand what goals to set, which behaviors are important, what standards are acceptable, and how to allocate resources.[5]

Competing Values Framework: A Model of Organizational Culture

The competing values framework of culture is one of many cultural typologies that provides a framework for understanding different types of organizational culture.[6] The **competing values framework** describes how organizations must choose between different cultural values along two dimensions. The *control dimension* involves the degree to which a culture values flexibility versus rigidity. An organization that ranks high on the flexibility dimension often has unclear work roles. Work roles, shared beliefs, and work procedures are in constant flux and changing. An organization that measures high on rigidity would be represented by clear and rigid shared beliefs that leave little discretion to employees. The second dimension considers *organizational focus*. Organizations vary to the degree that they value internal affairs versus external affairs. An organization that values its internal workings and history is characterized by phrases like "This is the way we do things here." An externally focused culture is characterized by a concern with activities outside the organization and might be characterized by a phrase such as "That's not how they do things at company x." The competing values framework identifies four types of organizational cultures, as depicted in Figure 12.4.

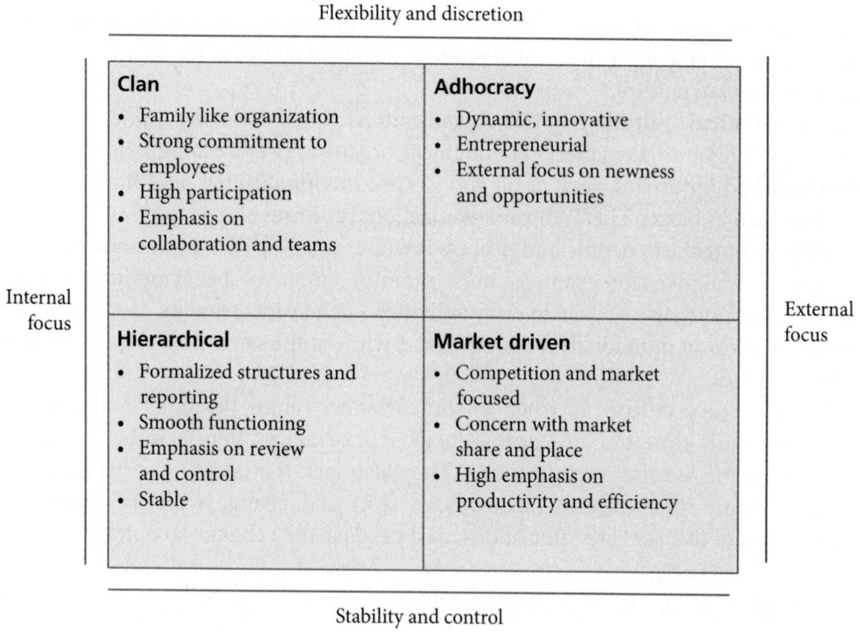

Flexibility and discretion

Clan
- Family like organization
- Strong commitment to employees
- High participation
- Emphasis on collaboration and teams

Adhocracy
- Dynamic, innovative
- Entrepreneurial
- External focus on newness and opportunities

Internal focus

External focus

Hierarchical
- Formalized structures and reporting
- Smooth functioning
- Emphasis on review and control
- Stable

Market driven
- Competition and market focused
- Concern with market share and place
- High emphasis on productivity and efficiency

Stability and control

Figure 12.4
Quinn's Competing Values Framework of Culture

Cusp/SuperStock

The **clan culture** is when an organization has internal focus while maintaining flexibility and discretion. Typically, in a clan culture, values are shared among individuals and behavior that threatens these values is sanctioned. Research shows that employees in a clan culture report high degrees of employee satisfaction with their organization. Clan cultures often develop loyal employees. The downside of the clan culture is that it is often slow to respond to market changes and may lack controls for overseeing or monitoring certain types of behavior. Professional cultures such as law firms and hospitals are often described as a clan culture.

A **hierarchical culture** is when organizations place a strong value on stability, control, and on internal matters. Hierarchical organizations are found in government, well-established industries, such as oil and gas production, utilities, and highly regulated industries such as banks. Hierarchical organizational cultures allow organizations to apply and enforce controls on people and processes while engaging in complex and sometimes risky activities. Banks, for example, must monitor employee behavior for compliance with rules, but must also engage in risky activities, such as investments. It is important to monitor behavior of individuals for compliance, while at the same time engage employees in risky activities.

The **adhocracy culture** is when an organization values flexibility and discretion, while at the same time has an external focus. Adhocracies often lack the controls and consistent norms of other organizations. They also lack the bureaucracy and hierarchy that stifles many organizations. Adhocracies shift and change with the marketplace. Organizations of this sort are often short-lived because they change so quickly.

Market-driven culture is when organizations place a strong value on stability and control but focus on external matters. Market-driven cultures tend to flourish in consumer and industrial products areas where markets shift and new markets emerge. Market-driven cultures help organizations maintain internal controls, for example, to maintain product quality during manufacturing processes, but to respond to environmental changes at the same time.

Subcultures

The artifacts, espoused values, and basic assumption shared by most, or sometimes all, individuals in an organization constitute a **dominant culture**; however, within an organization, many **subcultures** also exist. A subculture is a culture within a culture. Subcultures are just as important as dominant cultures in understanding behavior in the workplace. A subculture is composed of a subset of members within the organization who share similar values and who define their work in similar ways. Edgar Schein identified three primary subcultures associated with contemporary business organizations.[7] The **operational subculture** values local knowledge and skills of those doing the work. The operational culture emphasizes the capacity of the individual to deal with problems within the organization. A second subculture is the **professional subculture**, which is defined by a group of individuals within the organization who share a set of practices within a particular occupation and exercise control over how work is done or how to interpret situations based on this allegiance. In contrast to the operational culture, where people's focus is within a specific organization, the professional culture values technical knowledge that is transferable and general so that it can apply across different organizations. Members of the organization that belong to a professional culture are often trained or certified outside the organization itself. This includes attorneys, Certified Public Accounts, physicians, or engineers whose credentials are certified by external organizations such as the American Bar Association (in the case of attorneys), or the American Medical Association (in the case of physicians). People who belong to a strong professional culture value autonomy and share similar values with others who belong to their profession outside the organization.

The third type of subculture is the **executive subculture**. Executives, often those at the top of the company's hierarchy, share a concern over the organization's measurable financial success. The executive subculture values control and accountability for those in the organization and works to see that others share the same goals.[8]

National Culture

National culture effects behavior in the workplace as it is another lens to understand how people identify with culture. **National culture** describes the shared values, beliefs, and behaviors within a country or culture. Employees bring these values, beliefs, and behaviors into the workplace. Geert Hofstede, a researcher on international culture, offers a model that classifies different cultures along five fundamental dimensions, as depicted in Figure 12.5.[9]

3 Differentiate between national and organizational culture.

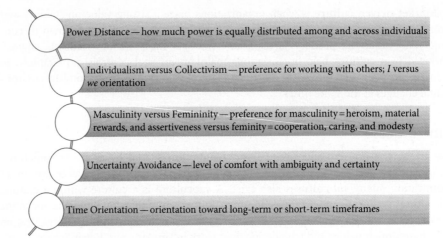

Figure 12.5 Hofstede's Five Dimensions of Organizational Culture

- **Power distance** describes differences in power among individuals, in other words, how much power the culture places in one group at the expense of another. A culture high in power distance means the culture accepts large differences in power between the most powerful and the least powerful.
- **Individualism and Collectivism** explain values that support and reward efforts. Cultures high on individualism tend to focus on individual contribution, where collectivism cultures value close relationships, reward group effort, and hold strong loyalties to groups such as family, organization, or other groups to which you belong.
- **Masculinity and Femininity** describes how cultures differ in regards to gender roles. For example, male gender roles involve assertiveness and competitiveness and female gender roles involve caring, modesty, and nurturing. The masculinity dimension measure the degree of difference between these roles in the culture. A low masculinity dimension means that there is not a lot of difference in male and female gender roles.
- **Uncertainty avoidance** is the culture's value of novelty and structure. In a high uncertainty avoidance culture, ambiguity and lack of clear rules, roles, and appropriate behaviors are not easily tolerated. Cultures that favor low uncertainty avoidance reflect values where rules are largely unwritten and individuals can explore new ways of doing things, including the creation of new cultural norms.
- **Time orientation** is the degree to which a culture focuses on long-term time orientation versus a short-term time orientation. Long-term oriented cultures value perseverance, future orientation, and frugality while short-term oriented cultures value face-saving behavior and conforming to expectations.

Fons Trompenaars and Charles Hampden-Turner offer seven dimensions of culture.[10] They bring a socio–political angle on understanding culture and describe a set of dilemmas that each culture must resolve, as depicted in Table 12.2.

Table 12.2 Seven Dimensions of National Culture

Dimension	Definition
Universalism versus particularism	In a universal culture, people value rules, regulations and general principles of behavior. In particularistic cultures, people value relationships such as friendship and closeness.
Individualism versus communitarianism	In individualistic cultures, people value individual effort. In communitarian cultures, collective work and teamwork are valued.
Specific versus diffuse	A specific culture values looking at individual parts—each element is scrutinized—while diffuse cultures value looking at the big picture.
Affective versus neutral	Affective cultures are likely to openly display emotions, while neutral cultures are likely to hide or keep feelings secret.
Achievement versus ascription status	In achieved status cultures, people in the culture value accomplishments that are proven by effort, work, and creativity. Ascribed status cultures favor birth, longevity, gender, or other hierarchy.
Sequential time versus synchronic time	Cultures that believe in sequential time focus on time as linear and value either the future or the past. Synchronic time focuses on the immediate present and may even see time as revolving.
Inner versus outer directed	Inner-directed cultures believe in control over the environment or that nature can be controlled, and that ultimately people shape events. Outer-directed cultures believe the environment and natural forces shape events.

Transmitting Culture

4 Describe the process of socialization and the transmission of culture.

Once a culture has been created, it must be maintained. **Socialization** is the process by which new members become indoctrinated into the culture. Socialization can occur in all types of organizations. Effectively socializing members can result in committed employees, but there are also downsides of socialization. When members are socialized into a culture, they share common assumptions and similar beliefs that may not be productive or helpful. Socialization involves several actions:

1. **Defining what is important**
   - An organization carefully selects new members by looking for candidates that possess traits or characteristics valued by the organization.

2. **Reframing what is important**
   - The organization will force the newcomer into experiences that cause newcomers to question their previous behavior or choices.
   - The organization will create and tell stories about the organization that reinforce its values. These might involve tales of the founder, stories of how the organization overcame difficult periods, or tales that reinforce the quality of its employees.

3. **Rewarding and punishing what is important**
   - The organization will put the new member into a situation where he or she experiences anxiety and ambiguity and lacks clear guidelines for action. However, the organization will expect the new member to choose the right action. The organization will reward the new member when he or she acts in the proper way.
   - By rewarding good behavior (and perhaps punishing poor behavior), the organization will reinforce its core values.

4. **Showing the way**
   - Organizations will identify role models and use them as a model of the company's values.[11]

Adapting to a New Culture

When a person has been socialized, he or she has adapted to the new culture. Living and working in a new culture often creates uncertainty, stress, and anxiety. Over time, individuals will adapt to the new culture, choose to leave the culture, or continue to experience the stresses associated with the new culture. The process of **adaptation** occurs as a person accepts the new culture. Accepting the new culture is demonstrated as the person learns to successfully work in the new culture. A person can adapt in many different ways.

Linking Organizational Culture and Strategy

5 Evaluate an organizational culture and organizational strategy.

Culture emerged several decades ago as an important concept in understanding organizations. The book *In Search of Excellence* by Tom Peters and Robert Waterman argued that organizational culture was directly linked to an organization's strategy and that certain cultures could lead to organizational effectiveness.[12] The book touted several examples of 'excellent' organizational culture, including examples using General Motors. The book became popular, in part, because it responded to a growing concern among U.S. managers that Japanese management practices had surpassed U.S. management practices in terms of fostering innovation and productivity. Japanese business culture valued loyalty, hard work, sacrifice, and quality. Peters' and Watermen's book showed how U.S. business cultures could also be successful by focusing on customers, innovation, and technological developments. *In Search of Excellence* went on to be one of the best-selling business books of all times. The importance of culture continues to be trumpeted in popular management books like *Good to Great*, by Jim Collins, who makes the same link among organizational culture, strategy, and success.[13]

Henry Mintzberg, a management professor and consultant, developed a model that links an organization's culture to strategy. Organizations struggle to balance seven distinct organizational sub-cultures.[14] When a single sub-culture predominates, the sub-culture begins to influence the organization's overall strategy.

1. The entrepreneurial culture predominates in start-ups, turnarounds, new ventures, and other situations where strong vision and strong direction are needed. The dominant cultural force directs the future position of the organization even if the organization has not currently proven itself.

2. The machine culture predominates in production plants and manufacturing and service organizations such as banks, which require clear procedures to maximize efficiency. The dominant value is efficiency—how the organization achieves its direction by focusing on controlling costs and benefits, creating economies of scale, building in standardized practices, and other formal procedures that contain costs.

3. The proficiency culture relies on the knowledge, skills, and training of the organization's members and is likely to flourish in hospitals, accounting firms, and other professional service firms. The dominant value is professionalism, which covets autonomy so individual professionals are required to exercise independent judgments.

4. The concentration culture values the ability to serve particular markets, customers, or constituencies. The primary value is diversification so specific markets (such as consumer products that develop specific products for hair care, soaps, etc.) can be served.

5. The innovation culture values the ability to discover new ways of doing things, adapt to change, and discover better ways of achieving goals. The primary value in the innovation culture is adhocracy or a culture that values temporary groups that get together to complete short-term projects focused on short-term goals and to develop new solutions.

6. The cooperation culture values the pulling together of ideology—building strong cultures, norms, beliefs, and sharing common values. The main value is ideology, as demonstrated by religious groups, an ideological or political campaign, or not-for-profit organizations.

7. The competition culture describes a culture that has difficulty maintaining internal cohesion within the organization. Power is distributed throughout the organization rather than centralized. Politics, or the fight for power, is the predominant value since there is no central direction and little agreement or desire to compromise among members of the organization.

Conclusion

A better understanding of culture is achieved by examining the dimensions of culture, differentiating between organizational and national culture, reviewing the purpose of a culture, and exploring how a culture is built and sustained. Our understanding of culture is informed by many disciplines, and these disciplines provide insight into the three dimensions of culture: artifacts, espoused values, and basic assumptions. Cultures, both national and organizational, serve a number of important functions through establishing rules and defining what is legitimate and illegitimate behavior. Other organizational applications of culture include rewards, punishments, selection, training, motivation, and organizational strategy.

OB AT WORK
A TAIWANESE STUDENT LEARNS TO ADAPT

Crystal Han-Huei Tsay

As a native of Taiwan, first studying in the United Kingdom and then later in the United States, Crystal Han-Huei Tsay used her knowledge of organizational behavior concepts to adapt to new cultures. Crystal was 23 when she arrived in London. Despite her lifelong fascination with European cultures, she had not anticipated some of the challenges she was about to face. Differences in how professors manage their classroom became clear early on. In Crystal's native Taiwan, professors spend the entire class lecturing. As a student, she spent her time listening to the professor and taking notes and would then quietly absorb the lecture and recite the material back during the exam. The transition to learning in a classroom in the UK proved a challenge. For example, Crystal observed, "I was astonished by the fact that so many European students actively discussed concepts and were not afraid to confront the professor in the classroom."

In the United States, she needed to be an active participant, ask questions, and engage during the class. Crystal began to see that the two cultures were different from what she was familiar with. She knew she needed to adapt to be successful.

6 Apply concepts of culture to organizations.

She wanted to be involved, but was unsure of how. At first, she simply observed the other students. She thought, What are good questions and what if the questions I ask are not good ones? She listened to the class and it reminded her of a Chinese saying she learned in Taiwan. "It's like a duck listening to a thunderstorm: you can hear it but you don't understand it." In Taiwanese, they used this proverb "鴨子聽雷 (a duck listens to thunders)" to describe that when it rains, "Ducks happily swim in the pond because they don't know the thunders are threatening and can be harmful," she says.

With this in mind, she set out to develop a better understanding of this new culture and improve her engagement as a student. She practiced the questions she wanted to ask or the points she wanted to make during class discussion. This both clarified her questions and improved her spoken English. She turned to her dictionary to understand key concepts. She also joined a public speaking club where participants presented speeches and conducted impromptu dialogues.

In order to improve her understanding of the differences between Taiwanese and Western cultures, she turned to concepts she learned in her classes like organizational behavior, psychology, and sociology. She began to use comparative analysis used in anthropology and other fields to understand differences between cultures. She studied Hofstede's cultural dimensions to help her understand some of the differences between Western and Taiwanese cultures, which in turn helped her understand some of the differences between her approach to learning and classroom behavior and the approaches of other students. For example, U.S. citizens, British, and other Westerners appeared to be more confident than the Taiwanese she observed. She observed that one reason for the difference is that in the United States in particular, children are taught to be optimistic and their achievements and talents are recognized early on in their childhoods. In Taiwan,

(continued)

children are focused on hard work and they are not encouraged to stand out from the crowd. Another difference is that Westerners are less afraid of conflict and confront each other on a regular basis. By contrast, in Taiwan, two people who share different opinions are more likely to find similarities in their viewpoints than they are to argue differences.

Public speaking was also more important in her newly adopted culture than in Taiwan. In the United States, she noted, "Communications skills matter a lot. The ability to make a great speech, communicate clearly, and make yourself valuable to an organization means that you will earn a high position. In Taiwan, the ability to persuade and communicate well is not emphasized."

Understanding the culture, improving her language skills, and building confidence were only part of her plan. She also studied the challenges associated with adapting to a new culture and learned that a new culture is a complex psychological process. In addition to building her confidence, she found sources of social support through friends and other students. She also learned that stress was a natural part of adapting to a new culture, so she accepted that stress comes with uncertainty.

Over time, Crystal built confidence in her ability to perform in the new culture. She even decided to pursue a doctoral degree in organizational behavior. Her topic of interest: how people adapt to new cultures.

Source: Personal interview.

SPOTLIGHT ON RESEARCH
Strong Cultures Do More than Engage Employees, They Engage Customers and the Community as Well

What do companies like Apple computer, Harley-Davidson, and Google tell us about the importance of organizational culture? One team of researchers wanted to find out. Not only do these organizations have strong cultures they have strong followings of loyal customers who also share the culture. Companies that have a strong culture offer a compelling message and use their organizational culture to build loyalty in their stakeholders. Companies rely on many different techniques to communicate their culture. Owners of the Volkswagen bug are known to wave when they pass each other. Followers of Apple eagerly watch and wait for the next bit of innovation from the company. Harley-Davidson riders wear distinctive clothing, often labeled with the name of the company. Each of these is part of an organization's cultural 'tool-kit', used to build a sense of connection between the company's culture and outside enthusiasts.

Researchers studied a company that designs, manufactures, and sells mountain climbing gear. The researchers do not name the company directly, they refer to the company simply as 'Alpinista'. The researchers used interviews with company members and customers and observed the company employees. They also relied on archival data, which included reviewing nearly 10 years of the company's mail order catalogs, their websites, and product displays.

(continued)

Alpinista, researchers observed, has a strong customer following due to the unique culture of the company. Like many companies with a strong culture, Alpinista's culture is strongly tied to its founder's ideals. As a mountain climber himself, the company founder became concerned about the impact that climbers have on the environment. Early in his career he noticed that many of his favorite climbing routes were becoming cluttered with climbing gear. Climbers left unwanted gear or gear that was difficult to retrieve. The company founder began advocating a process of 'clean climbing' where climbers rely mainly on the natural formations of the mountain and rocks. This would prevent the climbers from hammering in pins and other aids that left permanent damage to the mountain.

The company culture can be seen in the way it hires employees. To be sure, candidate resumes are screened for job qualifications, but Alpinista also looks for passion for outdoor activities. In fact, passion for the outdoors and activities like skiing, hiking, and climbing may be just as important. One top-level skier felt that he might be rejected for a job because he had worn a suit and tie for the interview and could not convince his interviewer, who was wearing khakis, that he was really an avid skier.

The company's seasonal catalog featured pictures of and short articles about customers, some of whom were well-known outdoor enthusiasts. This showed the connection between the company culture and customers. Researchers noted that the company catalogs did not simply promote the products; in fact, they noted that Alpinista catalogs contained scores of articles that featured people engaging in fun activities. The articles never mentioned the company's products.

The researchers used examples like this one to show the connection between the internal organizational culture and those outside the organization. It was not enough to be qualified, you really had to live the values and lifestyle of the company's culture.

The key point of the research: A strong organizational culture reaches beyond the boundaries of the company and engages stakeholders.

Questions for Discussion

1. What are some advantages of a strong company culture? What might be some disadvantages? Why do you think this?

2. How might you apply this research to your organization?

Source: Based on Spencer H. Harrison and Kevin G. Corley (2011). Clean climbing, carabineers, and cultural cultivation: Developing an open systems perspective of culture. Organization Science, March–April, 22, 2, 391–412.

Pairing with this Topic Summary

Suggested Expert Contributions

Team Learning Culture—Amy Edmondson (Harvard Business School)

Organizational Culture—Richard O. Mason (Southern Methodist University)

The Competitive Advantage of Corporate Cultures—Daniel Denison (IMD, Switzerland), Levi Nieminen (Wayne State University), Lindsey Kotrba (Denison Consulting)

Suggested Cases

Case 1: The Case of Apple iPhone 4

Case 3: EMERGENCY! We Need a Better Compensation System

Case 4: Face Time at TechPoint Software, Inc.

Case 5: Whatever Happened to One of the "100 Best Companies to Work For"?: A Case Study of Hewlett-Packard

Case 6: NASCAR's Drive for Diversity: Can They Reach the Finish Line?

Suggested Exercises

Exercise 3: My Expat Assignment

Exercise 12: Well-Being at Work

Exercise 16: Writing a Team Contract

Exercise 22: A Clash of Cultures

Exercise 23: What's Your University's Culture?

Exercise 24: Find the Artifacts

Exercise 34: Sustainability Practices at Work

Endnotes

1. Trice, H. M. & Beyer, J. M.. (1993). *The cultures of work organizations*. Englewood Cliffs, NY: Prentice Hall; Deal, T. E., & Kennedy, A.A. (1982). *Corporate cultures: The rites and rituals of corporate life*. Reading, MA: Addison-Wesley; Smircich, L. (1983). Concepts of culture and organizational analysis. *Administrative Science Quarterly, 28*(3): 339–358.

2. Schein, E. H. (1996). Culture: The missing concept in organization studies. *Administrative Science Quarterly, 41*(2): 229–240.

3. Hatch, M. (1993). The dynamics of organizational culture. *Academy of Management Review, 18*(4): 657–693.

4. Kluckhohn, F. R. & Strodtbeck, F. L. (1961). *Variations in value orientations*. Evanston, IL: Row, Peterson.

5. Beach, L. R. (1993). *Making the right decision: Organizational culture, vision, and planning*. Englewood Cliffs, NJ: Prentice Hall.

6. Cameron, K. S. & Quinn, R. E. (1999). *Diagnosing and changing organizational culture: Based on the competing values framework*. Reading, MA: Addison-Wesley. See also Quinn, R. E., & J. Rohrbaugh, J. (1983). A spatial model of effectiveness criteria: Towards a competing values approach to organizational analysis. *Management Science, 29*(3): 363–377.

7. Schein, E. H. (1996). Three cultures of management: The key to organizational learning. *Sloan Management Review, 38*(1): 9–20.

8. Abbot, A. (1988). *The system of professions: An essay on the division of expert labor*. Chicago: University of Chicago Press; Freidson, E. (2001). *Professionalism: The third logic*. Chicago: University of Chicago Press.

9. Hofstede, G. & Hofstede, G. J. (2004). *Cultures and organizations: Software of the Mind*. New York: McGraw-Hill; Geert Hofstede. (2001). *Culture's consequences: Comparing values, behaviors, institutions and organizations across nations*. Thousand Oaks, CA: Sage Publications.

10. Trompennars, F. & Hampden-Turner, C. (1998). *Riding the waves of culture: Understanding diversity in global business*. McGraw-Hill.

11. Pascale, R. T. (1985). The Paradox of 'corporate culture': Reconciling ourselves to socialization. *California Management Review, 27*(2): 26–41.

12. Peters, T. J. & Waterman, R. H. Jr. (2004). *In search of excellence*. New York: Harper Paperbacks.

13. Collins, C. (2001). *Good to Great*. New York: Harper Collins.

14. Mintzberg, H. (1991). The effective organization: Forces and forms. *Sloan Management Review, 32*(2): 54–67.

Team Learning Culture

Amy C. Edmondson

Harvard Business School

Introduction

Most of us pay little direct attention to the interpersonal risks we face at work, and yet we manage them every day, if mostly automatically. Even if we love our work, we still face subtle risks that come from being formally and informally evaluated as we engage in a variety of interpersonal behaviors that have the potential to harm our image in the eyes of others. Whether consciously or not, most people skillfully avoid doing and saying things that they believe will lead others to think less of them. In knowledge-intensive industries, interpersonal risks are especially salient because so many of the actions and procedures in knowledge work are not standardized, and the results are uncertain. The goal of this article is to explore interpersonal risk, how it inhibits learning and collaboration, and explain what leaders can do to alter these dynamics and even to speed up the learning process.

After 20 years of studying workplace teams, I began to use the term *teaming* to emphasize the activities, rather than the structures of teamwork.[1] Unlike the traditional concept of a team, *teaming* is a process. Our interest in teaming is driven by a dramatic increase in organizations with more flexible and fluid teams. Stable teams of people who have learned over time to work well together are powerful tools.[2] The speed of change, intensity of market competition, and unpredictability of customer needs in many industries means that building stable teams to work together over long periods is often infeasible. Instead, employees from various groups may come together to work on something for a while, only to disband when they've achieved their goal or when a new opportunity arises. More people in nearly every industry and type of company are working on multiple teams that vary in duration, comprise shifting membership, and pursue moving targets.[3] Product design, patient care, strategy development, pharmaceutical research, and rescue operations are just a few of the domains in which fast-paced teaming is essential.

Learning and teaming go hand in hand. Teaming is how new products and processes are developed, and often how complex services are delivered, by increasingly diverse groups of experts. Teaming to execute novel or complex work is inherently a learning process because no two collaborations unfold the same way. But concern about what others may think of you inhibits the essential behaviors of learning and teaming. The easiest way to manage this concern, of course, is to keep your head down and stay silent! Silence can be crippling in almost any organization. A fast food worker who fails to speak up about cleanliness problems may have a ringside seat to an e coli outbreak. A nurse participating in cardiac surgery who fails to point out an oversight to the surgeon may face a lifetime of regret. An engineer whose doesn't raise a concern may contribute to a tragic accident. For this reason, I have sought to understand the conditions that make it psychologically safe for people to speak up and to contribute as much as they can to the shared enterprise.

INSIGHT 1

PSYCHOLOGICAL RISK ASSESSMENT: WHAT WOULD YOU DO?

On January 16, 2003, the Space Shuttle Columbia was successfully launched from the Kennedy Space Center on a 16-day research mission. The next day, shuttle engineer Rodney Rocha reviewed a launch video and became deeply concerned about the size and position of a chunk of insulating foam that appeared to have fallen off the shuttle's external tank and struck its left wing. The video images were grainy and it was impossible to be sure what had happened. To determine whether damage had occurred, Rocha hoped to obtain photographic images of the Shuttle's wing from satellites. Although the photos would have to be authorized by the Air Force, the request would require neither a technical nor financial miracle. It did mean that NASA would have to ask for help from the Department of Defense.

Rocha initially expressed the need for the images in an email to his immediate superior, emphasizing the urgency by using bold-faced type. When he learned that his request was unlikely to be honored, Rocha wrote a scathing e-mail that stated, "Remember the NASA safety poster everywhere around, stating, 'If it's not safe, say so?' Yes, it's that serious." He didn't send the email to the Mission Manager, however, only shared it with fellow engineers. Later, he explained, "Engineers were often told not to send messages much higher than their own rung in the ladder."

Discouraged by his early efforts to gain attention to the foam-strike issue and convinced that voicing concerns was career limiting at NASA, Rocha refrained from sharing his anxiety in a critical mission management team meeting, eight days into the flight. He fervently hoped others with more clout might offer their concerns. The opportunity passed, however, and the issue was never formally revisited in a mission management team meeting. Just eight days after this lost opportunity to speak up, the shuttle burned up upon re-entry into the Earth's atmosphere, resulting in the deaths of seven astronauts. Much later, asked in a television interview why he didn't speak up with his doubts about the safety of the shuttle in that mission management team meeting, Rocha replied, "I just couldn't do it. I'm too low down...and she [Mission Management Team Leader Linda Ham] is way up here," gesturing with his hand held above his head.

Psychological Safety and Interpersonal Risk

The construct of psychological safety has roots in early research on organizational change, when Schein and Bennis[4] discussed the need to create psychological safety to make people feel secure and capable of changing. Later, Schein[5] argued that psychological safety helps people overcome the defensiveness, or "learning anxiety," that occurs when they are presented with data that contradicts their expectations or hopes. With psychological safety, he reasoned, individuals are free to focus on collective goals and problem prevention rather than on self-protection. In more recent research, Kahn found that psychological safety affects people's willingness to fully engage at work—to "employ or express themselves physically, cognitively, and emotionally during role performances," rather than disengage, or "withdraw and defend their personal selves."[6]

Conducting research on teams, I became intrigued by the small interpersonal risks people face when interacting with others, especially in uncertain or ambiguous situations.

Table 1 Managing Interpersonal Risk

Looks to avoid	Easy ways to manage risk
Ignorant	Don't ask questions
Incompetent	Don't ask for help
Intrusive	Don't give feedback
Negative	Don't challenge the status quo

Specifically, when people want to ask questions, seek help, experiment with unproven actions, or get feedback, they often hesitate. Engaging in such behaviors carries the risk of being seen as ignorant, incompetent, intrusive, or just plain negative. (See Table 1). Yet, it's hard to learn and innovate without such actions.[7] In many organizations, hierarchy engenders fear, making people reluctant to engage in behaviors that could threaten their image and the trust of their superiors. In some cases, speaking up the hierarchical ladder can feel nearly impossible to those on a lower rung.

Most people feel a need to manage interpersonal risk to minimize harm to their image, especially in the workplace and in the presence of those who formally evaluate them. This is both instrumental (promotions and other valued rewards may be dependent on impressions held by bosses and others) and socio-emotional (we prefer others' approval rather than disapproval).

While it's easy enough to reduce interpersonal risk through strategic silence, it is a poor solution for two reasons. First, it inhibits organizational learning. Second, people have been genuinely pained and frustrated by their own silence in the workplace. For the most part, the people studied are not failing to provide ideas or input because they've "checked out" or don't care, but because of a subtle but pervasive fear of the possible consequences. Facing a decision about whether or not to speak, one might quickly consider, "Should I say something, in this moment, about this, to my boss?" In this process, one weighs the potential gain against the potential loss, as in, "If I do this, will I be hurt, embarrassed, or criticized?" Concluding that the answer is no indicates a sense of psychological safety and allows one to proceed. In a sense, proceeding means being authentic. It means expressing the work-relevant thoughts and feelings on one's mind without excessive self-censorship. This is why admitting a mistake or asking for help is readily doable in one situation, even though it may be unthinkable in another.

INSIGHT 2

INTERPERSONAL RISK: WHAT WOULD YOU DO?

Instances where people are reluctant to voice concerns or engage in behaviors that could threaten their image occur within a wide spectrum of industries and organizations. While keeping silent about mistakes when little is at stake, errors can be deadly. Consider a nurse momentarily pondering, but then dismissing, the possibility that the medication dosage for an ER patient seems high. As the thought crosses her mind to call the doctor, by then fast asleep at home, she recalls his disparaging comments the last time she called. In that brief moment of opportunity to voice concern, her brain exaggerates the importance of the doctor's scorn and minimizes the chance of harm to the patient.

Or, a young pilot in a training flight believes that the senior pilot may have made a crucial misjudgment, but lets the moment go by without pointing it out. The young pilot is not only of lower rank, but is also formally evaluated on every flight. The prospect of speaking up to the superior officer brings significant emotional costs, even though the pilots are interdependent members of a cockpit team. Unlike the nurse, the pilot may actually be choosing silence over preservation of his own life. Here again, his mind, against reason, discounts the chances that not speaking up will lead to a fatal crash and exaggerates the importance of his discomfort at being chastised or ignored.

Even those at the top of the hierarchy are not exempt from the fear of speaking up. Consider a senior executive, recently hired by a successful consumer products company, who has grave reservations about a planned takeover. New to the top management team, and conscious of his status as an outsider, he remains silent because other executives seem uniformly enthusiastic. Many months later, when the takeover has failed, the team gathers to review what happened. Aided by a consultant, each executive muses on what he or she might have done to contribute to or avert the failure. The silent executive, now less of an outsider, reveals his prior concerns. Openly apologetic about his past silence, he explains that the others' enthusiasm left him afraid to be "the skunk at the picnic."

What these vignettes have in common is the degree to which interpersonal fear can dominate modern work life and thwart the collaboration that is desperately needed in the knowledge-intensive organizations that dominate today's economy. Interpersonal fear—the fear associated with personal interaction and social risks—is at the root of many of these failures. The problem is widespread. In corporations, hospitals, and government agencies, my research has found that interpersonal fear frequently gives rise to poor decisions and incomplete execution. Yet, in some organizations, a culture of psychological safety makes it easier for people to speak up with their tentative thoughts.

Benefits of Psychological Safety

Research has identified psychological safety as a group-level construct, showing that psychological safety typically characterizes a team as a unit rather than being an attribute of individual employees.[8] Across many organizations and industries, I found that perceptions of psychological safety were similar among people who work closely together. This is because people working together tend to have the same set of contextual influences and their perceptions develop out of important shared experiences. For example, people will conclude that making a mistake doesn't lead to scorn or ridicule when they've had experiences in which appreciation and interest were expressed when discussing mistakes. In some organizations, psychological safety varies greatly from department to department and work group to work group.[9] This means that psychological safety is not a personality difference, but rather a feature of the workplace that leaders can and must work to build.

Psychological safety helps to facilitate the learning and teaming needed to accomplish many challenging goals. When psychological safety is high, the relationship between a goal and the behaviors needed to achieve it is likely to be strong. Without psychological safety, the motivating effects of goals are inhibited; despite a desire to learn, the perceived interpersonal risk can inhibit the necessary behaviors. We have identified seven benefits of psychological safety at work.[10] First, and perhaps most importantly, psychological safety encourages *speaking up* by alleviating concern about the reactions of others to behaviors or actions with uncertain outcomes. *Clarity of thought* is enabled when fear is eliminated; constant risk calculation uses valuable neural processing power that could be used for exploration, design, or analysis. Psychological safety also *supports productive conflict*, allowing self-expression, productive discussion, and the thoughtful handling of conflict. Because it makes it easier to report and discuss errors, an atmosphere of psychological safety *mitigates failure*. Removing the fear of speaking up allows people to suggest the novel ideas and possibilities integral to developing innovative products and services, thereby inspiring and *promoting innovation*. By allowing individuals to focus on achieving goals rather than on self-protection, psychological safety *removes obstacles to pursuing goals*. Finally, psychological safety *increases accountability* by providing support when people take the interpersonal risks necessary to pursue high standards and achieve goals.

Leadership and Psychological Safety

The behavior of leaders in a given work group is a key determinant of psychological safety.[11] The more inclusive leaders are, the higher the psychological safety.[12] Research on leader behavior and psychological safety shows similar results across a variety of settings, including insurance companies,[13] technology firms,[14] and restaurants.[15]

A leader's influence on psychological safety stems from specific psychological mechanisms. First, people are particularly attentive to leaders' behavior.[16] Autocratic behavior, inaccessibility, or a failure to acknowledge vulnerability all can contribute to team members' reluctance to incur the interpersonal risks of learning behavior.[17] When team leaders are selected solely on the basis of technical expertise, such as skill and knowledge about a topic, they may lack the interpersonal skills needed to seek others' input, invite ideas and feedback, and create a climate in which others are willing to speak up with ideas and concerns.

Second, leaders demonstrate failure tolerance when they acknowledge their own fallibility, or limits, or when they scrupulously avoid punishing others for well-intentioned risks that backfire. Self-disclosure by team leaders is one way to demonstrate fallibility.[18] For example, one surgeon I studied repeatedly told his operating room team: "I need to hear from you, because I'm likely to miss things." The repetition of this phrase was as important as the meaning: people tend not to hear—or not to believe—a message that contradicts old norms when they hear it only once. Soliciting feedback suggests to others that their opinion is respected; it may also contribute to establishing a norm of active participation.

Third, leaders can communicate that they respect others by acknowledging their expertise and skills. By actively inviting others to participate, leaders also create an environment of psychological safety. In contrast, autocratic behavior, inaccessibility, or failure to acknowledge vulnerability all can contribute to team members' reluctance to share ideas or examine mistakes. In prior work,[19] we identified eight specific leadership behaviors that promote a climate of psychological safety (See Table 2)

Table 2 Leadership that Promotes Psychological Safety

Behavior	Explanation
Be accessible and approachable	Leaders encourage team members to learn together by being accessible and personally involved
Acknowledge the limits of current knowledge	By clarifying that the state of knowledge is incomplete, leaders encourage others to take risks together in developing new knowledge and practices
Display fallibility	Leaders demonstrate a tolerance of failure by acknowledging their own fallibility, contributing to psychological safety
Invite participation	When people believe leaders value their input, they will be more engaged and responsive
Highlight failures as learning opportunities	Instead of punishing people for well-intentioned risks that backfire, leaders encourage team members to embrace error and deal with failure in a productive manner
Use direct language	Using direct, actionable language instigates the type of straightforward, blunt discussion that enables learning
Set boundaries	When leaders are as clear as possible about what is acceptable, people feel more psychologically safe than when boundaries are vague or unpredictable
Hold people accountable for transgressions	When people cross boundaries set in advance and fail to perform up to set standards, leaders must hold them accountable in a fair and consistent way

Accelerating Learning through Better Teaming

It takes time for individuals and teams to become proficient at new tasks or processes. The question of how to speed up the learning process is an increasingly important one in today's fast-paced work environment.[20] Innovating products and services and implementing new processes as quickly as possible are crucial sources of competitive advantage.[21]

To illustrate, consider a cardiac surgery team learning a new procedure. Cardiac surgery is one of medicine's modern miracles, a testament to medical technology, but also to incredible teamwork. A cardiac surgical team includes an array of specialists who need to work in close cooperation for the operation to succeed. A single error, miscommunication, or slow response can have disastrous consequences. Understandably, learning a new routine when a new technology is introduced can be fraught with challenge. Several years ago, my colleagues and I studied cardiac surgery teams implementing a new technology at sixteen hospitals. We found that teams with psychological safety learned faster than those without it. Psychological safety allowed them to freely express themselves, their questions, their observations, and their concerns.

The teams that learned faster talked openly about what was going well and not going well, with respect to team communication. Interestingly, they did this *in-action*, not in after-action reviews. This real-time learning yielded insights that might have been lost had they waited for a formal review session. During a hospital procedure, for instance, a nurse spontaneously suggested solving a surgical problem with a long-discarded type of clamp affectionately known as the "iron intern." The procedure was successful, and the use of the nearly forgotten medical device immediately became part of that team's permanent routine.

Although formal training provided by the company that developed the technique emphasized the need for everyone on the team to speak up with observations, concerns, or questions, it didn't happen consistently across teams. We found that it depended greatly on the quality of the surgeon's leadership.[22] One team member even reported being upbraided for pointing out what he believed to be a life-threatening situation. More typical was the comment of one nurse: "If you observe something that might be a problem, you are obligated to speak up, but you choose your time. I will work around the surgeon and go through his PA [physician's assistant] if there is a problem." Consider this in contrast to another hospital, one in which a surgeon told team members that they had been selected because of their skills and because of the input they could provide on the process. Here, everyone reported feeling absolutely confident in their ability to speak up and be heard.

Organizations in every industry encounter challenges analogous to those faced by our surgical teams. Adopting new technologies or new business processes is highly disruptive in any industry. Like the surgical teams, businesses that use new technologies for the first time also must deal with a learning curve. The key point is that the learning is not just technical; it is also interpersonal. Some of the barriers that must be confronted directly include status and patterns of communication and behavior and implementing new information technology, for example, involves the technical work in setting operational parameters and ensuring that software runs properly. But more difficult for many companies is not the technical challenge, but the ways that the technology changes interpersonal dynamics and routines.

Conclusion

Teaming doesn't just happen—it takes time for teams to learn how decisions should be made and who should talk to whom and when. Sometimes it takes even longer; in fact, it is nearly impossible if people are afraid to speak up. Managing interpersonal risk the wrong way—through silence—something most of us do routinely in some situations—can be an obstacle to successful teaming. Leaders can take practical steps to create psychologically safe environments that enable the clarity of thought, engagement, experimentation, and flexibility that teaming requires.

Endnotes

1. Edmondson, A. C. (2012). *Teaming: How organizations learn, innovate, and compete in the knowledge economy.* San Francisco: Jossey-Bass.
2. Hackman, J. R. (1990). *New directions in crew-oriented flight training.* Paper presented at The ICAO Human Factors Seminar, Leningrad.

3. O'Leary, M., Mortensen, M, & Woolley, A. (2011). Multiple team membership: A theoretical model of its effects on productivity and learning for individuals and teams. *Academy of Management Review, 36*(3), 461–478. Huckman, R. S. & Staats, B. R. (2011). Fluid tasks and fluid teams: the impact of diversity in experience and team familiarity on team performance. *Manufacturing and Service Operations Management, 13*(3), 310–328. Valentine, M. & Edmondson, A. C. (2012). Team scaffolds: How minimal in-group structures support fast-paced teaming. Harvard Business School Working Paper No. 12-062.

4. Bennis, W., Schein, E. (1965). *Personal and Organizational Change through Group Methods.* New York: Wiley & Sons.

5. Schein, E. (1985). *Organizational Culture and Leadership* (1st Ed.). Jossey-Bass Publishers.

6. Kahn, W. (1990). Psychological conditions of personal engagement and disengagement at work. *Academy of Management, 33*(4), 692–724.

7. Edmondson, A. (1999). Psychological safety and learning behavior in work teams. *Administrative Science Quarterly, 44*, 350–383. West, M. A. (2000). Reflexivity, revolution, and innovation in work teams. In M. M. Beyerlein, D. A. Johnson, & S. T. Beyerlein (Eds.). *Advances in Interdisciplinary Studies of Work Teams*, 5, 1–29. Greenwich: JAI Press.

8. Edmondson, A. (1999). Edmondson, A. C., Bohmer, R., & Pisano, G. P. (2001). Disrupted Routines: Team Learning and New Technology Adaptation. *Administrative Science Quarterly, 46*, 685–716.

9. Edmondson, A. (1999).

10. Edmondson, A. C. (2012).

11. Detert, J. R. & Ethan, A. B. (2007). Leadership Behavior and Employee Voice: is the Door really Open? *Academy of Management, 50*(4), 869–884. Edmondson, A. (1996). Learning from mistakes is easier said than done: group and organizational influences on the detection and correction of human error. *Journal of Applied Behavioral Sciences, 32*(1), 5–32.

12. Edmondson, A. (1996). Nembhard, I. M., & Edmondson A. C. (2006). Making it safe: The effects of leader inclusiveness and professional status on psychological safety and improvement efforts in health care teams. *Journal of Organizational Behavior, 27*(7), 941–966.

13. May, D. R., Gilson, R. L. and Harter, L. M. (2004), The psychological conditions of meaningfulness, safety and availability and the engagement of the human spirit at work. Journal of Occupational and Organizational Psychology, 77: 11–37.

14. Detert, J. R., Trevino, Klebe, L. (2010). Speaking up to higher ups: How Supervisors and Skip-level leader influence employee voice. *Organization Science, 21*(1), 249–270.

15. Detert, J. R. & Ethan, A. B. (2007).

16. Tyler, T. R. & Lind, E. A. (1992). A relational model of authority in groups. *Advances in Experimental Psychology, 25*, 115–191.

17. Edmondson, A. (1996). Edmondson, A. C., Bohmer, R., & Pisano, G. P. (2001).

18. Gabarro, J. J. (1987). *The dynamics of taking charge.* Boston: Harvard Business Press.

19. Edmondson, A. C. (2012).

20. Edmondson, A. C., Bohmer, R., & Pisano, G. P. (2001).

21. Edmondson, A. C. (2008). The competitive imperative of learning. *Harvard Business Review* (July/August), 60–67.

22. Edmondson, A. C., Bohmer, R., & Pisano, G. P. (2001).

Organizational Culture

Richard O. Mason

Southern Methodist University

Every organization has a culture. Like one's personality, Philip Slater observes, culture "is merely a pattern, an arrangement of universal but dissonant elements. In a given time and place one arrangement may be more convenient than another, but every culture makes selections maximizing the fulfillment of some human needs and neglecting others.... Social [and organizational] change is merely a rearrangement of elements, the expression of a preference for one kind of inconsistency over another."[1]

An organization's culture shapes the way its members interact with each other, guides their social interactions, and influences how they set and act on priorities. Culture reflects the sum total of its members' *shared* values, attitudes, beliefs, norms, expectations, assumptions, and rituals. Much of an organization's culture lies below the level of conscious awareness. It is primarily tacit, not tangible. Cultural affects are real and meaningful—one can experience it, but it is difficult to describe it adequately in words. Rituals play a crucial role in perpetuating an organization's culture.

John Gutfreund, chairman of the vaunted investment bank Salomon Brothers (*Business Week* once called him "The King of Wall Street"), frequently visited the trading floor to keep in touch with what was going on by constantly asking the traders questions. Each Q&A session nearly always ended with his challenging them to a game of chance and bluffing called "Liar's Poker." At Salomon, as at other trading firms, traders sharpened their skills by playing this game. It is played as follows: two or more participants take a dollar bill from their wallet, hide its serial number, and then commence to make bids on the best poker hand that can be made using the numbers on all of the bills. (For example, nine 4s is possible but the bidder only knows the 8 digits on his own bill.) Typically, the dollar itself is each player's stake. Following the final bid, the numbers on all of the bills are revealed. If they equal or exceed the last bid, then the final bidder takes the pot. If not, he pays each of the other players a dollar.

One day, Gutfreund upped the ante considerably. [2]He headed straight for the firm's leading trader, the legendary John Meriwether, and threw down a gauntlet: "One hand, one million dollars, no tears." "The code of the Liar's Poker player," Lewis continues, "was something like the code of the gunslinger. It required a trader to accept all challenges." This was the code and culture Meriwether lived by. So, he was on the spot. If he won he risked alienating his formidable boss; if he lost, well, he was out a cool million. Meriwether was quite wealthy and could afford it. Nevertheless, it was a dumb bet. Meriwether had built his entire illustrious career on avoiding dumb bets. So, he countered. "No, John," he said, "if we're going to play for those kind of numbers, I'd rather play for real money. *Ten million dollars*. No tears." Gutfreund backed down. "You're crazy," he said, and sauntered off. "No," thought Meriwether, "just very, very good." [3]

In banking circles, it is generally believed that good Liar's Poker players make good traders, and vice versa. Consequently, the game served as a ritual to hone traders' instincts and test their character. Playing Liar's Poker served to inculcate shared values, attitudes, norms, and modes of thinking and more predictable ways of acting, It became a centerpiece around which the trading culture was built. Moreover, the Gutfreund/Meriwether episode became a widely retold myth that perpetuated the trader's culture.

MIT professor Edgar H. Schein argues that managing the dynamic processes of creating and directing a culture is essential to effective leadership. For him, organizational culture is: "A pattern of shared basic assumptions that a group has learned as it solved problems of external adaptation and internal integration, that has worked well enough to be considered valid and, therefore, to be taught to new members as the correct way to perceive, think, and feel in relation to those problems." [4] Other authors have also contributed to our understanding of organizational culture.

Gareth Morgan, a prominent researcher, takes a related tack. For him organizational culture is the "set of beliefs, values, and norms together with symbols like dramatized events and personalities, that represents the unique character of an organization, and provides the context for action in it and by it." [5]

Three authors classify organizational cultures by means of slightly different two-by-two models. Deal and Kennedy in an influential book[6] describe culture as "the way things get done around here," and propose a four-fold classification model based on how the organization responds to external factors. Plotted on one axis is how quickly or slowly an organization receives feedback and rewards. On the other axis is how much risk the organization is willing to take: high or low. Gutfreund's organization was a high-risk and rapid-feedback culture. Consequently, it required, according to the authors' model, a "tough-guy macho culture." Their three other cultures are "work hard, play hard" (low risk, rapid feedback), "process culture" (low risk, slow feedback) and "bet-the-company" (high risk, slow feedback). Deal and Kennedy emphasize the importance of building a *positive* culture and its role in implementing strategic change. Other authors point out that a culture can be built on a lie or immoral premise and can lead to *negative*, socially or economically undesirable results.

Quinn and Cameron classify organizational cultures according to their internal versus external orientation on one axis, and their flexibility versus stability or control on the other.[7] A friendly establishment, in which leaders act like father figures, is a Clan Culture (internal focus and flexible), a dynamic, innovative workplace is an Adhocracy Culture (external focus, flexible), a competitive workplace led by hard-driving managers is a Market Culture (external focus, controlled), and a well-structured, bureaucratic, and formalized workplace is a Hierarchy Culture (internal focus, controlled.)

Charles Handy's model draws on Greek mythology.[8] Organizational cultures are classified according to the power wielded by the roles its members assume and the functions they discharge within the organization. His four archetypes are: a Power Culture (a culture which concentrates power in a selected few and is patterned after the god Zeus), a Role Culture (a hierarchy, Apollo), a Task Culture (problem-solving teams, Athens), and a Person-based or Existential Culture (individuals are superior to the organization, Dionysius).

Table 1, below, summarizes the culture theories of the above authors.

Table 1 Summary of Organizational Culture Theories

Author	Concept
Slater	Pattern, an arrangement of universal but dissonant elements
Schein	Pattern of shared basic assumptions, worked well enough to be considered valid, correct way to address problems
Morgan	Set of beliefs, values, and norms that provides a context for action
Deal and Kennedy	The way things get done around here Classified by speed of feedback versus level of risk
Quinn and Cameron	Orientation (external, internal) versus degree of control (flexible, controlled)
Handy	Doing orientation (Athena, Zeus) versus Being orientation (Dionysian, Apollo)

All of these authors' views are helpful in assessing and understanding an organization's culture. Each emphasizes unique elements, yet is for the most part consistent with Schein's definition. There are at least two important reasons to assess an organization's culture:

1. As a guide to organizational change. By determining the gap between where an organization currently is and where one wants it to be, the needed direction and context of change can be determined.

2. Retrospective analysis, as a means of explaining why an organization acted the way it did. It turns out that many efforts to retrace why an operation went wrong end up fingering culture as a crucial though often distal cause. In spy-speak, this is called "walking back the cat." [9]

Most organizational problems can be traced back to culture. Indeed, a dysfunctional culture can be lethal as the following summary of NASA and *Columbia's* flight disaster shows. [10]

On February 1, 2003, *Columbia*, speeding on its way to its landing site in Florida, suddenly exploded in the skies of East Texas. All seven crewmembers were killed. A $2 billion ship was lost. Why?

NASA policy requires that an *internal* investigation team of six ex-officio members be formed. Retired admiral Harold Gehman Jr., who previously served as NATO supreme allied commander and was a veteran chair of military investigations, was appointed chairman. Gehman immediately broadened the membership to include *external* members and enlarged the scope of inquiry to include the agency's culture, organization, and history.

That Gehman expanded the charge angered NASA's administrator, Sean O'Keefe. O'Keefe, a cost and budget man, wanted to confine the inquiry to just the narrow limits of the technical issues. Gehman persisted. Experience told him that a broader scope of information would be learned about what happened and why. He appointed six additional *external* members who were chosen to represent a broader set of relevant constituencies.

In addition to the chair, the 13-member Board now included three other military aviation experts, a former astronaut (Sally Ride), a top NASA official, a retired corporate executive, several senior civil accident investigators, and two distinguished engineering professors.

The Board's staff met with over 400 NASA engineers, examined more that 30,000 documents, conducted over 200 formal interviews, heard testimony from dozens of expert witnesses and reviewed thousands of comments from the general public. On Tuesday, August 26, 2003, the 248-page report of the *Columbia* Accident Board was released. Its conclusion was startling:

> the primary, underlying cause of the disaster was NASA's *organizational culture and its history.* [11]

At first, the "cause" of the disaster was presumed to be "a chunk of foam" that had dislodged from the craft's "bipod ramp" and struck a heat shield tile on the left wing. According to the Board report, "During re-entry this breach in the Thermal Protection System allowed superheated air to penetrate through the leading edge insulation and progressively melt the aluminum structure of the left wing, resulting in a weakening of the structure until increasing aerodynamic forces caused loss of control, failure of the wing, and breakup of the Orbiter. This breakup occurred in a flight regime in which, given the current design of the Orbiter, there was no possibility for the crew to survive."

This was *sufficient* to cause the *Columbia* disaster but it did not explain *why* it happened.

Why was the ship was launched in the first place, given an acknowledged vulnerability in its design? "What was the context?" That is, what were the other general, necessary conditions that allowed the foam to separate, and, when it was learned that it had separated during the flight, kept NASA from actively trying to understand what damage had resulted and how the astronauts might be saved? It was the culture.

"The bitter bottom line,... comes down to this: NASA never absorbed the lessons of the *Challenger* explosion in 1986, and four successive American presidents never decided where America's space program should head after the cold war—and what it would cost in dollars and risk to human life to get there." [12]

NASA's current culture was largely to blame because it stifled dissenting views and bred complacency over persistent and dangerous risks. The press seized on phrases such as "NASA's culture of complacency," "deeply flawed culture", and "a broken safety culture." Gehman described some flaws in NASA's culture [13]:

"They claim that the culture in Houston is a 'badgeless society,' meaning it doesn't matter what you have on your badge—you're concerned about shuttle safety together. Well, that's all nice, but the truth is that it does matter what badge you're wearing. Look, if you really do have an organization that has free communication and open doors and all that kind of stuff, it takes a special kind of management to make it work. And we just don't see that management here. Oh, they say all the right things. 'We have open doors and e-mails, and anybody who sees a problem can raise his hand, blow a whistle, and stop the whole process.' But then when you look at how it really works, it's an incestuous, hierarchical system, with invisible rankings and a very strict informal chain of command. They all know that. So even though they've got all of the trappings of communication, you don't actually find communication. It's very complex. But if a person brings an issue up, what caste he's in makes all the difference. Now, again, NASA will deny this, but if you talk to people, if you really listen to people, all the time you hear 'Well, I was afraid to speak up.' Boy, it comes across loud and clear. You listen to the meetings: 'Anybody got anything to say?' There are thirty people in the room, and slam! There's nothing. We have plenty of witness statements saying 'If I had spoken up, it would have been at the cost of my job.' And if you're in the engineering department, you're a nobody." [14]

The Board report tells a tale of two cultures. From its founding in 1958, a *culture of excellence* emerged heavily influenced by Marshall Space Flight Center director Wernher von Braun, the German rocketry wizard and aerospace legend. NASA was widely respected then for its strong technical and management culture. Sociologist Diane Vaughan observes that NASA arose "out of a military heritage that made discipline a core cultural element."[15] Under von Braun's leadership, a team of some 120 German rocket engineers recreated the strong precision/verification research culture that was their scientific heritage. Transparent, all-channels, horizontal communications were established. Everybody's view counted. Stringent technical standards were set. The application of superior knowledge and expertise was required. It was mandated that all operations involve all relevant parties. Projects were conducted by a "hands-on strategy." Importantly, risks were taken very, very seriously. There was a fierce dedication to safety. The agency's early missions almost always succeeded, some spectacularly so. NASA deservedly got a reputation as having a "Can Do!" culture.

That changed. In the early 1970s, President Nixon announced the United States's new direction for exploring space. "This system will center on a space vehicle," he boasted, "that can shuttle repeatedly from Earth to orbit and back. *It will revolutionize transportation into near space, by routinizing it.*" (Italics added in the Board Report.) Driven by a need to cut costs, this commitment to reusable vehicles and routine operations set the agency on a very different course. NASA began transitioning toward a *culture of production*—a hierarchical managerial culture that stressed efficiency over safety and emphasized effective reproducibility (routinization) over creative problem solving. The von Braun dedication to flawless performance and its well-honed management of risk was de-emphasized. A primary function of a culture is to cope with the external risks an organization faces. A great achievement of von Braun's NASA was its ability to identify and defend against an enormous number of novel risks associated with space flight. The agency became effective at identifying and correcting incipient problems *before* they occurred. In fact, NASA had delayed launching many times whenever any of its rigorous criteria was not satisfied.

Following the 1972 decision, NASA's managers began to "fiddle" with their standards. They lowered the threshold of what was "acceptable." The agency became complacent and relied routinely on less rigorous concepts such as "acceptable risk" and "acceptable erosion."

A hierarchical organizational structure replaced the flat one with freer flowing communications. Leaders with managerial, rather than scientific backgrounds, were appointed and imprinted the new culture. Many managers were lulled into believing that NASA's early successes were due to the agency's—and perhaps their own—invulnerability, a misplaced belief in omnipotence. This is a very dangerous attitude for dealing with a complex, unruly, ultimately unpredictable technology used to launch ships into space. It is especially hazardous when fundamental cultural norms of questioning and inquiry have been replaced by norms of silence, self-protection, and managerial efficiency.

In 1992, Dan Goldin was appointed head and NASA's cultural moved further away from scientific excellence. His mantra was "Faster, better, cheaper." Former astronaut Sally Ride recounts its effects when she pointed out that it is virtually impossible to develop something faster, better, and cheaper. She speculated that you could have one or two of those categories, but not all three. Ride also thought it was important to emphasize safety, and was concerned that management's emphasis on costs and schedules gave the impression that schedule and budget were more important than safety.

Sean O'Keefe was appointed director in 2001. He had a reputation as a quintessential government "bean counter" and an implementer of cost controls. A former deputy at the federal Office of Management and Budget with a degree in public administration, O'Keefe was not deeply imbued with the scientific, technological, and safety values that had characterized the von Braun culture. This was the leader and the culture under which *Columbia* was launched.

It was also the culture that the Board implicated. They found that for well over a decade, the agency's culture had not been robust enough in its dedication to safety. As a result, important warning signs were ignored and opportunities to take remedial action were often missed.

Schein's theory suggests that NASA's new emphasis of cost cutting and efficiency raised new fears and anxieties that required new internal integration and adaptation. The result was more compliance, less horizontal communication and a de-emphasis on safety. It also resulted in serious warning signs being ignored.

Ride observed how with Columbia there were multiple incidents where foam would dislodge when the shuttle would launch. The foam shedding was identified as a problem, but even though it was identified as a problem, there was never any action taken to try to troubleshoot or analyze the root cause of the problem. Because there was no disaster the first, second, or third time the foam detached, the foam problem was normalized.[16]

One incident during *Columbia's* flight reveals how the production culture failed the astronauts. Five days after the foam had broken loose, some 30 engineers and contractors met to assess the potential damage. Virtually all agreed that the space agency should immediately get satellite and telescope images of the impacted area. Rodney Rocha, a highly respected engineer, was elected to convey a request to the shuttle mission managers. Rocha tried at least six times to get the managers to make the requests. Similar efforts were made by other engineers. All were stalled. One manager told Rocha that he refused to be a "Chicken Little." *Columbia's* ground flight director wrote an abrupt e-mail message stating, "I consider it [the foam strike] to be a dead issue."[17]

In the old NASA culture, managers would have been eager to listen and would have taken some action. In the culture of production, not being absolutely convinced that a problem existed, they took no action.

Summary

There are at least four advantages to using a cultural approach to understanding organizations and their behavior:

1. It focuses management attention on the *human* side of organizational life.
2. It reinforces the view that an organization's basic *assumptions* reflect its history and relationship with its environment.

3. It stresses the importance of creating appropriate systems of *shared meaning* to help people work together toward desired common outcomes.

4. It requires the organization's members—especially its leaders—to acknowledge that their behavior has *impacts* on the organization's culture and the culture also affects them.

"We choose and operate in environmental domains according to how we construct conceptions of who we are and what we are trying to do.... And we act in relation to those domains through the definitions we impose on them.... The beliefs and ideas that organizations hold about who they are, what they are trying to do, and what their environment is like have a much greater tendency to realize themselves than is usually believed.[18]

Endnotes

1. Slater, Philip (1974). *Earthwalk.* Garden City, NY: Anchor, 3.
2. Lewis, M. (1989). *Liar's Poker: Rising Through the Wreckage on Wall Street.* New York: Penguin Books.
3. Lewis, M. (1989). 17.
4. Schein, Edgar (1992). *Organizational Culture and Leadership.* San Francisco, CA: Jossey-Bass, 12.
5. Morgan, Gareth (1997). *Images of Organization.* Thousand Oaks, CA: Sage Publications, 129.
6. Deal, T. E. & Kennedy, A A. (2000). *Corporate Cultures: The Rites and Rituals of Corporate Life.* New York: Basic Books.
7. Cameron, K. S. & Quinn, R. E. (2006). Diagnosing and Changing Organizational Culture (Revised Edition). San Francisco, CA: Jossey-Bass.
8. Handy, C. B. (1996). *The Gods of Management.* New York: Oxford University Press.
9. Littell, R. (1996). *Walking Back the Cat.* New York: Penguin.
10. Mason, Richard O. (2004). "Lessons in Organizational Ethics from the *Columbia* Disaster." *Organizational Dynamics* (33)2, 128–144.
11. Gehman, H.,et al. (2003). *Columbia Accident Investigation Board Report,* U.S. Government document, Volume 1, August 2003.
12. Sanger, David (2003). "Report on Loss of Shuttle Focuses on NASA Blunders and Issues Somber Warnings." *New York Times,* Wednesday, August 27.
13. Gehman, H., et al. (2003).
14. Langewiesch, W. (2003). "*Columbia's* Last Flight," *The Atlantic Monthly,* November 2003.
15. Vaughan, Diane. (1996). *The Challenger Launch Decision, Risky Technology, Culture, and Deviance at NASA.* Chicago: Chicago University Press, 15.
16. Dreifus, C. (2003). "A Conversation with Sally Ride." *The New York Times,* Tuesday, August 26.
17. Dreifus, C. (2003).
18. Glang, J.& Schwart, J. (2003). "Dogged Engineer's Effort to Access Shuttle Damage." *The New York Times,* Friday, September 27.

The Competitive Advantage of Corporate Cultures

Daniel Denison
IMD Business School

Levi Nieminen
Denison Consulting

Lindsey Kotrba
Denison Consulting

What is Corporate Culture?

At the climax of the annual holiday party in one rapidly growing American company, hundreds of balloons are released from the ceiling. Inside each balloon is a crisp new $100 bill and whoever scrambles the hardest, gets the most money! The lesson is simple, fun, and more powerful than all the personnel policy handbooks in the world. It helps capture the essence of some of the key definitions of corporate culture: Culture is "the way we do things around here," and "what we do when we think no one is looking."[1]

Most scholars further describe culture in terms of two important definitional features, 1) culture has multiple layers or levels, and 2) culture is learned. Schein's classic approach divides culture into three levels.[2] He argues that basic, underlying assumptions lie at the root of culture and are "unconscious, taken-for-granted beliefs, perceptions, thoughts, and feelings." Espoused values are derived from basic underlying assumptions and are the "espoused justifications of strategies, goals and philosophies." Finally, at the top level are "artifacts," that are defined as "visible, yet hard to decipher organizational structures and processes." Like the iceberg presented in Figure 1, only about 10 percent of an organization's culture is visible, whereas 90 percent is below the surface. However, it is the part of the culture that we *can't* see—the fundamental beliefs and assumptions—that often sinks the ship.

Figure 2 reminds us that culture is learned—it includes "the lessons that we have learned that are important enough to pass on to the next generation."[3] The lessons from

Artifacts, behaviors, and norms are visible and tangible.

Personal values and attitudes are less visible, but can be talked about.

Underlying beliefs and assumptions are subconscious, invisible, and rarely questioned.

James Steidl/Fotolia

Figure 1 Schein's Three Layers of Organizational Culture

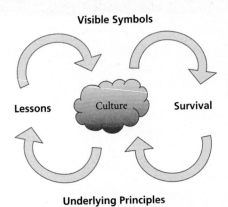

Figure 2 Diagram of Culture as Learned

the past shape our survival strategies for the future. Over time, the cultural values that are important are reflected in the visible symbols that surround us, which further reinforce and shape our culture into the future, and so on. Winston Churchill made a similar point about architecture, stating that, "We shape our buildings; thereafter they shape us."[4] Returning to our discussion from above, it is almost always easier to change the buildings than it is to modify the cultural values that guided their construction. In other words, the stuff that resides below the surface of an organization's culture—the fundamental beliefs and assumptions—is the core of what is learned over time and what comes to guide behaviors and visible structures and processes.

Why is Corporate Culture Important?

Many top executives attest that shaping and managing their organization's culture is one of their most important challenges. As Wells Fargo Bank CEO John Stumpf said, "It's about the culture. I could leave our strategy on an airplane seat and have a competitor read it and it would not make any difference."[5] When asked to name the top two or three challenges facing Daniel Akerson in his new role as CEO following the 2009 bail out of General Motors corporation, he listed *culture* first [after indicating, "I worry about everything…"].[6] Former IBM Chairman Lou Gerstner made a similar point: "culture isn't just one aspect of the game—it IS the game. In the end, an organization is no more than the collective capacity of its people to create value."[7] And the list could go on and on from here…But, why do leaders typically view harnessing culture as the key to unleashing business performance? And what does research have to say about the role of corporate culture in business performance?

The importance of corporate culture has a lot to do with the alignment of stated values with the actual behaviors of leaders and followers on a day-to-day basis. Bank of America's website lists "Doing the right thing," as one of their core values. They elaborate: "We have the responsibility to do the right thing for our customers, shareholders, communities, and one another."[8] Nonetheless, recent media reports have argued that in practice, BoA appears to resist efforts to modify delinquent loans because of the fee income associated with late payments and foreclosures.[9] These and many other examples from the recent past[10] illustrate how a corporation's stated values or mission can sometimes bear little resemblance to what happens on the ground.

Beyond what is advertised, what ultimately drives the organization's performance is the collective capability of its people to deliver on its objectives. As stated by one influential organizational scholar (B. Schneider), "The people make the place."[11] *People* create the organization and its structures and processes, gather the necessary funding, develop the markets, and implement the strategies. An organization's culture is inextricably intertwined with its people, past and present. Going forward, it provides the social context that guides people's actions. As with the above examples, people can choose to the do the "right" or "wrong" thing, and the culture not only shapes how deviations will be handled, but also what actions should be regarded as the appropriate ones—for example, because certain actions worked in the past or because they reinforce a commonly held belief or value. Is it better to act in a way that maximizes profit in the short term or works to ensure a lesser, but safer, return over the long haul? Should decision power be held by the most experienced and qualified few at the top or distributed equally throughout? Who is accountable for getting the work done—leaders, individual contributors, or teams? The people on the ground doing the organization's work face these questions and numerous others on a daily basis. Culture shapes the answers to these questions and helps to explain why some organizations tend to prefer short-term payoffs, decision-making from the top, and individual accountability, whereas others tend to prefer long-term strategies, distributed decision-making, and team accountability.

Given that organizational cultures can reinforce different behaviors in people, scholars have long been interested in studying culture's impact on performance outcomes, including financial metrics such as profitability, sales growth, and market value, as well as non-financial metrics such as safety, employee satisfaction, quality, and innovation. Today, the research evidence that has accumulated suggests that culture does affect organizational performance across a range of the metrics noted above, but that the nature of the relationship can take several forms.[12] The most straightforward is a *direct effect*, whereby certain cultures (or cultural configurations) tend to promote higher performance. For example, research indicates that organizations with stronger *externally oriented cultures*—or which focus on anticipating and responding effectively to the marketplace and the customer's needs—tend to outperform organizations with weaker external orientations.

More complex relationships have also been observed, although the research evidence in support of these is preliminary. A *moderated effect* suggests that organizational culture may impact performance differently within certain industries or geo-political regions. For example, proponents of this perspective might suggest that an external orientation is somewhat less important in industries where the marketplace has remained highly stable over many years. Finally, a *non-linear effect* suggests that the direction of the culture-performance relationship changes at a certain point, such as the inverse u-shaped trend. Proponents of this relationship might suggest, for example, that increasing the external focus of a culture is beneficial only up to a certain point, beyond which further increase might actually harm performance. Although there are a handful of studies that show a moderated or non-linear pattern, the bulk of research evidence points to certain cultural characteristics as being generally associated with higher organizational performance.

What Aspects of Corporate Culture Are Worth Paying Attention to?

Although corporate culture underlies many aspects of the workplace, research has pointed to four main ways that culture impacts business performance: through an organization's sense of *mission*; through its level of *adaptability*; through the *involvement* of its people; and through the *consistency* provided by the foundation of beliefs and core values.[13] Each is defined in greater detail in Table 1. To illustrate how central these four traits are to real-world business success, let's now consider four well-known examples: IKEA, Apple, Domino's, and Toyota.

IKEA: Mission Grows Out of Core Beliefs and Assumptions

IKEA founder Ingwar Kamprad became an entrepreneur at an early age. By 1976, he was well established in the Swedish furniture business and summarized his key principles for

Table 1 Four Key Cultural Traits Related to Organizational Performance

1. Mission. Successful organizations have a clear sense of purpose and direction that allows them to define organizational goals and strategies and to create a compelling vision of the organization's future. Leaders play a critical role in defining the mission, but for this to have a positive impact it must be well understood top to bottom. Three aspects of mission are particularly important and are illustrated in the business case of IKEA: *strategic direction and intent*, *goals and objectives*, and *vision*.

2. Adaptability. A strong sense of purpose and direction must be complemented by a high degree of flexibility and responsiveness to the business environment. Organizations with a strong sense of purpose and direction can often be the ones that are the least adaptive and the most difficult to change. Adaptable organizations quickly translate the demands of the organizational environment into action. Three aspects of adaptability are particularly important and are illustrated in the business case of Apple. *creating change*, *customer focus*, and *organizational learning*.

3. Involvement. Effective organizations empower and engage their people, build their organization around teams, and develop human capability at all levels. Organizational members are highly committed to their work and feel a strong sense of engagement and ownership. People at all levels feel that they have input into the decisions that affect their work and feel that their work is directly connected to the goals of the organization. Three aspects of involvement are particularly important and are illustrated in the business case of Domino's: *empowerment*, *team orientation*, and *capability development*.

4. Consistency. Organizations are most effective when they are consistent and well integrated. Behavior must be rooted in a set of core values and people must be skilled at putting these values into action by reaching an agreement while incorporating diverse points of view. These organizations have highly committed employees, a distinct method of doing business, a tendency to promote from within, and a clear set of "do's" and "don'ts." This type of consistency is a powerful source of stability and internal integration. Three aspects of consistency are particularly important and are illustrated in the business case of Toyota; *core values*, *agreement*, and *coordination and integration*.

So, how should this organization use the survey results to drive positive change? Where are the strengths and weaknesses in the current culture? When the executive team looked at their results, there was a long silence—the un-freezing process was beginning. The President, who had spent his career in operations, said, "Well, I'm not a visionary or a strategist—I'm the guy who makes the trains run on time." When they focused on the results for consistency, they agreed that their emphasis on internal control made it difficult to react to the marketplace. They agreed that they had strong core values, but also questioned whether they were appropriate for the future. Finally, when they looked at their results on team orientation, one of them concluded, "We're a team alright—we're going down together!"

IKEA in a manuscript titled, "A furniture dealer's testament."[14] Like most great organizations, his company did not just produce profits, but rather was designed to serve a higher purpose in society. IKEA brought style, value, and a better life to many. Their products were designed for the global everyman, combining frugality, innovation, and style. Kamprad also expressed strong beliefs about how IKEA should operate, stressing simplicity and self-reliance as the main guiding principles:

> Bureaucracy complicates and paralyzes! Exaggerated planning is the most common cause of corporate death. We do not need fancy cars, posh titles, tailor made uniforms or other status symbols. We rely on our strength and our will.[15]

IKEA is a terrific example of how a global business strategy can grow from the core beliefs and assumptions of the founder. Consider just one key element of the system, the "flatpack." Where did this brilliant strategic innovation come from? In 1952, one of IKEA's first employees, Gillis Lundgren, had a problem. He was trying to load a table in his Volvo to deliver to a customer. It didn't fit. Gillis thought, "God, what a lot of space that takes up! Let's take the legs off and put them under the table top."[16] Voilà! Global strategy. The rest is just implementation. By 1956, this practice was standardized and has been an essential part of the IKEA experience ever since. The current system has continued to build upon these key principles established in the early days.

IKEA's strong sense of mission and powerful corporate culture is not without its limitations. Growth has been steady, but relatively slow, especially given the dramatic enthusiasm of their customer. IKEA has never made much of an impact in the office furniture market, mostly since very few corporations want to assemble their own office furniture. Expanding to countries that are further away from their Swedish homeland has also presented some challenges. Overall, "The IKEA Way" has been a central part of the 50-year journey of an entrepreneur's dream to a global icon.

Apple: <u>Adaptability</u> Leads the Marketplace Into the Future

Since its founding in 1976 in a garage in Cupertino, California, Apple has built their success around an unparalleled understanding of their customer's needs. It is a fascinating example of the competitive advantage created by adaptability. Time and again, they have developed new products that their customers didn't really know they needed until they found out that they couldn't live without them.

Building on their spectacular success with iPod and iTunes, Apple set about developing the hardware and software to create another new market that didn't exist before: the smartphone and the "App" Store (for purchasing software Applications for the smartphone). The iPhone turned an iPod into a touchscreen cellphone with Internet access. People would no longer need to carry a phone and an iPod and still find themselves in need of access to the Internet to look up movie times or restaurant locations. And it was a big bet that the future of cellphones would be differentiated not by "radios and antennas and things like that," but instead by software.[17] The bet paid off handsomely—by the fourth quarter of 2008 Apple surpassed Blackberry to become the world's third largest phone maker after Nokia and Samsung.

At first, developers created their own unsanctioned apps for the iPhone. But in March 2008, Apple released a Software Development Kit to help developers create their own apps. They also created a radical set of rules for the App Store[18] which would cost developers $99 to submit an app and they could charge whatever they wanted for downloads. Apple would retain 30 percent of the sale price for administration. The remaining 70 percent would go to the developer. If the app was offered for free, Apple would take no commission. Apple itself would maintain the App Store, control the approval process, and support the whole thing through iTunes. In July 2008, the App Store was launched with 500 apps to coincide with the global launch of the 3G iPhone in 22 countries. Just over one year later, there were nearly 100,000 apps with 2 billion downloads to over 20 million iPhones worldwide.

Apple's approach to innovation is deeply rooted in their DNA. It has always been informed by a unique mindset that focuses on the *ecosystem* that surrounds their customers. Their innovations combine hardware and software with developers and consumers in ways that create revolutionary markets. The App Store connects the creativity of the developers with consumers' endless demand for software solutions, starting at a price point of $.99 or less—with Apple as the intermediary!

Domino's Pizza: <u>Involvement</u> Builds Your Ability to Deliver

Domino's Pizza was founded in 1960 by two brothers, Tom and Jim Monaghan, who each kicked in $500 to buy a pizza shop. Before long, Jim wanted out, so he traded his half of the store to Tom in exchange for Tom's well-used Volkswagen Beetle. In his 39 years of leading the company, Tom Monaghan transformed his pizza delivery shop into one of the world's top brands. In 1999, with 6,000 stores and over $3 billion in revenues, Monaghan sold 93 percent of the company to Bain Capital, who soon brought in David Brandon as CEO.[19]

How do you go about creating competitive advantage in the pizza delivery business? The new CEO and his team made the decision to focus squarely on their *people,* as reflected by the "People First" guiding principle that was put in place. In his first week on the job, Brandon learned that the annual staff turnover was 158 percent. He soon realized that with 150,000 employees, sustaining a necessary workforce would require hiring nearly a quarter of a million people each year! What stunned Brandon more was Human Resources' acceptance of the status quo. Brandon quickly recruited a new HR Executive, Patti Wilmot, who was ready for the challenge. New hiring procedures placed more emphasis on employee attitudes because they felt that the skills needed could be taught. Drug testing for delivery drivers and a ban on hiring former employees were implemented to further improve the quality of the workforce. A "pipeline" that defined hiring criteria, developmental targets and investments, advanced opportunities, and exit plans was created for all segments of the employee population.

Domino's performance steadily improved. After their 2004 IPO, Bain Capital noted that Domino's was one of the best private equity deals that they had ever done, returning over 500 percent on their investment. Involvement, capability, and teamwork were the hallmarks of their success.

Toyota: <u>Consistency</u> is the Foundation for Quality

In 1937, Toyota was created by the Toyoda Automatic Loom Works to produce automobiles. Their early history was a difficult struggle which required them to take advantage of every opportunity to reduce waste and use resources efficiently. Toyota's culture grew organically for many years before they attracted much attention. But by the 1980s, their world-class quality and conspicuous success led many to try to capture their essence and understand the huge leaps in competitive advantage that Toyota had made within the manufacturing world. Today, the *Toyota Way* is one of the most clearly articulated management philosophies into the world. To quote former President Fujio Cho:

> The key to the Toyota Way and what makes Toyota stand out is not any of the individual elements. But what is important is having all the elements together as a system. It must be practiced every day in a very consistent manner, not in spurts.[20]

There are fourteen elements to the Toyota Way that have been clearly articulated in many different sources. A few that have enabled Toyota to build a culture of consistency include:

- build a culture of stopping to fix problems, to get quality right the first time;
- standardized tasks are the foundation for continuous improvement and employee empowerment;
- base your management decisions on a long-term philosophy, even at the expense of short-term goals;
- grow leaders who thoroughly understand the work, live the philosophy, and teach it to others.

Each of these principles is significant in its own right and is a required part of the overall system. Perhaps the most difficult part of the Toyota Way is to understand its emphasis on process thinking and production flow. It is a system created to manage complexity in an efficient and predictable way through nearly flawless lateral coordination. Toyota has successfully transplanted the logic and culture of their production system all over the world. This evolving philosophy has led Toyota from a struggling automaker in pre-war Japan to the largest and most profitable automotive company in the world.

How Can Organizations Change their Cultures?

These examples are success stories that depict how culture can contribute positively to business performance. But what happens when a culture change is needed? Can organizations effectively manage and change their cultures for the better? Doing so requires that organizations have a clear understanding of their current culture and the culture that is ultimately desired. Without this knowledge, the organization may move in the wrong direction or fail to understand where the critical needs are. Once organizations understand where to focus their efforts, they can begin the arduous task of *un-freezing* the ways things operate, taking the actions necessary to *transition* toward the desired culture, and then *re-freezing* to ensure that the new culture takes hold in daily organizational life.[21]

A number of tools are available to practitioners as they embark on a culture change. One of the most powerful tools is the diagnostic culture assessment. The approach involves administering surveys to employees to gather their perceptions of the values and behavioral norms that are reflected in the organization's current culture. The results of the survey are then organized into a diagnostic report that shows the organizations strengths and weaknesses. The results can be *benchmarked* relative to other organizations, as well as over time so that progress can be tracked throughout the change process.

Conclusion

All organizations develop a culture over time as the people in the organization struggle as a group to adapt, compete, and survive in the marketplace. Sometimes the cultural values that develop serve as a potent source of competitive advantage (e.g., IKEA, Apple, Domino's, Toyota), whereas in other cases, they can be maladaptive and even contribute to—or fail to dissuade—unethical corporate behavior and misconduct. Because the most deeply held elements of culture reside well below the surface, it can be difficult to recognize if and how they impact what happens on a daily basis. However, closer inspection reveals that culture is manifested in the values and behavioral norms that guide actions of people in their day-to-day work. Collectively, those actions determine whether an organization sinks or swims in the increasingly competitive global marketplace.

This chapter described four characteristics of corporate cultures that have been linked in research to organizations' bottom-line financial performance: mission, adaptability, involvement, and consistency. Although culture change is a difficult and complex process, assessment of these specific factors can provide a useful starting point for unfreezing the current culture, targeting key areas for development, and moving the needle in a positive direction. Of course, having a road map for where things are headed is crucial. The four mini-case studies illustrated the *competitive advantage* that can follow when organizations foster a strong mission, a great deal of flexibility and responsiveness to the customer, high levels of employee involvement, and great care toward core values and consistent delivery of results.[22]

Endnotes

1. Acknowledgements for definitions:
   Peters, T. J., & Waterman, R. H., Jr. "The way we do things…" *In Search of Excellence: Lessons from America's Best Run Companies.* New York: Warner Books, 1982.
   Adkins, B. "What we do when…" *Personal communication,* 2008.
2. Schein, E. (1992). *Organizational Culture and Leadership* (2nd Ed). San Francisco, CA: Jossey-Bass.
3. Schein, E. H. (2010). *Organizational Culture and Leadership.* San Francisco: Jossey-Bass.
4. Churchill, Winston. *House of Commons* (meeting in the House of Lords). October 28, 1943. http://www.winstonchurchill.org/learn/speeches/quotations
5. Guerrera, F. "Wells Fargo cracks the whip." *Financial Times,* August 24, 2008.
6. For more on Daniel Akerson's address to the Economic Club of Washington on December 10, 2010, visit http://www.c-spanvideo.org/program/GeneralMot
7. Gerstner, Louis V., Jr. *Who says Elephants Can't Dance?* New York: HarperCollins Publishers, 2002.
8. Bank of America Corporation. (2009). *Code of Ethics.* (June), 2. <http://phx.corporate-ir.net/External.File?item=UGFyZW50SUQ9NzcyM3xDaGlsZElEPS0xfFR5cGU9Mw==&t=1>
9. Goodman, Peter S. (2009). "Lucrative fees may deter efforts to alter loans," *New York Times,* July 29, 2009.
10. As one additional example, consider that Enron's stated corporate values prior to the well-documented and widespread corporate scandal included: *communication, respect, integrity,* and *excellence.*
11. Schneider, B. (1987). "The people make the place." *Personnel Psychology*: 40, 437–453.
12. Sackmann, S. A. (2011). Culture and performance. In Ashkanasy, N., Wilderom, C., & Peterson, M. (Eds.), *The Handbook of Organizational Culture and Climate* (2nd ed). Thousand Oaks, CA: Sage Publications, 188–224.
13. Denison, D. R. *Corporate Culture and Organizational Effectiveness.* New York: John Wiley & Sons, 1990.

14. Kamprad, Ingvar. *The Testament of a Furniture Dealer. A Little IKEA Dictionary.* Inter IKEA Systems B.V., 2007 http://www.emu.dk/erhverv/merkantil_caseeksamen/doc/ikea/english_testament_2007.pdf

15. Kamprad, 7

16. Kamprad, 14

17. Wingfield, N. "IPhone Software Sales Take Off: Apple's Jobs." *Wall Street Journal,* 11 August 2008:B1

18. Krazit, Tom. "Apple Developers Mark a Year of iPhone Apps." *CNET News,* 5 March 2009. http://news.cnet.com

19. Bourdet, Dorothy. "Domino effect: David Brandon has pizza chain shaking and baking. *Detroit News,* December 9, 2006:1

20. Liker, Jeffrey. *The Toyota Way.* New York: McGraw-Hill, 2004

21. Weick, K. E., & Quinn, R. E. (1999). Organizational Change and Development, *Annual Review of Psychology,* 50, 361–386.

22. This reading follows in part from the opening chapter from a book by D. Denison and colleagues. Interested readers are referred to: Denison, D., Hooijberg, R., Lane, N, and Leif, C. (2012) *Leading culture change in global organizations.* San Francisco, CA: Jossey-Bass.

13 Change, Innovation, and Stress

Topic Summary Learning Objectives

1. Identify three tensions of organizational change.

2. Describe and contrast the approaches to change proposed by Lewin and Kotter.

3. Describe the factors that support organizational innovation.

4. Outline the process of creativity, how it relates to innovation, and the elements that support creativity in organizations.

5. Identify different types of stress and methods for stress management.

6. Apply concepts of change, innovation, creativity, and stress to organizations.

Key Terms

Appreciative Inquiry (AI), p. 475

change management, p. 472

competing commitments model of change, p. 475

creativity, p. 477

diffusion of innovation, p. 476

disruptive innovation, p. 476

hindrance and challenge stress, p. 477

incremental change, p. 471

innovation, p. 476

force field model of change, p. 472

organizational change, p. 471

planned change, p. 471

rapid change, p. 471

resistance to change, p. 475

stress, p. 477

stressors, p. 477

Type A and Type B, p. 478

unplanned change, p. 471

Introduction to Change, Innovation, and Stress

This topic summary reviews three interrelated topics: change, innovation, and stress. The topic summary begins with a review of change and outlines several tensions inherent in the change process. Innovation and creativity and their role in organizational change are presented. Finally, stress is described as an inevitable, although often limiting, consequence of change in organizations. Figure 13.1 outlines the aspects of change, innovation, and stress presented in this summary.

Organizational Change

1 Identify three tensions of organizational change.

Organizational change is any modification, planned or unplanned, that alters a structure, process, or outcome in an organization. Change in organizations occurs for many reasons. Figure 13.2 presents a multi-dimensional picture of change. The model of change presents tensions that emerge within the change process: the tensions between internally versus externally driven change, planned versus reactive change, and incremental versus rapid change. Organizations themselves often prompt change by establishing new goals or instituting new procedures. When organizations initiate change, the change is said to be an internally driven change. Change can also be unexpected, caused by external forces. Changes in the regulatory environment, shifts in market or customer trends, or emergence of technologies serve as some of the external changes that force change on organizations.

Organizations deal with change by either planning or responding to change. **Planned change** is intentional change and instituted within the organization. **Unplanned change** arises when organizations fail to plan or are caught off guard by unanticipated events. The third tension of change involves the timeframe of the change. The change can occur as either an incremental change or a rapid change. **Incremental change** occurs slowly and unfolds over time. It often involves shifts in thinking and challenges the basic assumptions of the organization's culture. **Rapid change** is more likely to involve quick surface level changes to policies, procedures, or resolutions to immediate problems, but can also eventually result in incremental change.

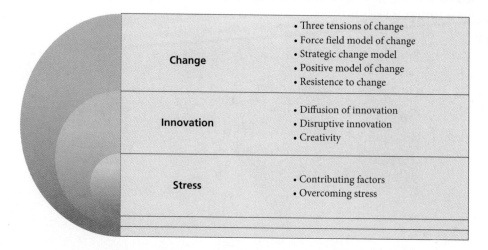

Change	• Three tensions of change • Force field model of change • Strategic change model • Positive model of change • Resistence to change
Innovation	• Diffusion of innovation • Disruptive innovation • Creativity
Stress	• Contributing factors • Overcoming stress

Figure 13.1
Aspects of Change, Innovation, and Stress

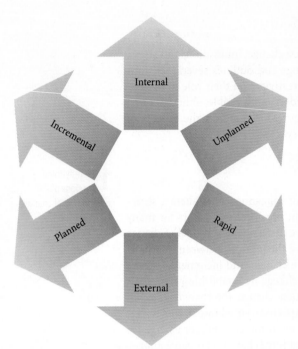

Figure 13.2 Tensions in the Change Process

2 Describe and contrast the approaches to change proposed by Lewin and Kotter.

Models of Change

Organizational change is a continuous process. Many different and distinct models have emerged to describe how and why organizations change. These models have been developed in order to better explain the change process and to improve the effectiveness of change efforts. Each model is based on a different set of assumptions about the nature of change and where in the organization change is initiated. All models of change describe change as a constant process and that managing change increases effectiveness. This section explores commonly cited models of change including the force field model, the strategic change model, and the positive change model. All models of change promote **change management**—the process of moving from the current state in an organization to a future state guided by active management of the change process.

Force Field Model of Change

Psychologist Kurt Lewin suggested a force field model that has been widely used in organizational change efforts. The **force field model of change** is a model that considers variables that promote change and variables that prevent change. Lewin believed that in order to implement change, an organization needed to identify the existing forces that are driving change, such as new customer demands and competitors, and to also identify constraining forces, such as organizational culture, poor leadership, or financial constraints, as shown in Figure 13.3. Most of the factors that both drive change and constrain change are psychological and cultural based. Fear of change, lack of clarity about new roles associated with change, and concerns about losing resources are factors that may constrain change. On the other hand, drivers of change often include dissatisfaction with the status quo. When driving forces were more powerful than restraining forces, change is likely to occur.

Figure 13.3
Lewin's Force Field Model of Change

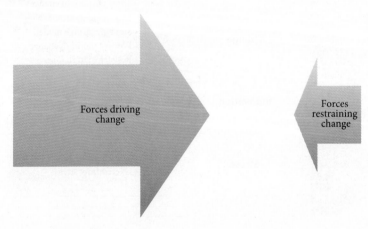

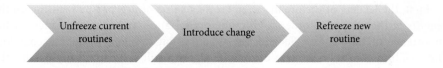

Figure 13.4
Lewin's Three-Step
Model of Change

Lewin's model has been widely accepted because of its simplicity and explanatory value. For Lewin, organizations first need to identify the factors that drive or restrain the change. Lewin suggested that change involves a three-step process: unfreezing, change, and refreezing, as illustrated in Figure 13.4.[1]

In the first step, current routines and knowledge become unfrozen. To unfreeze, the organization needs to identify the forces that restrain the change and seek to eliminate these forces as much as possible. Also during the unfreezing phase, the organization needs to enhance the forces that might lead to change. Only after current routines are unfrozen can change be introduced. The change should seek to improve the organization and move it to a higher level of functioning. More desirable ways of doing things would be introduced, and thus new routines would develop. The new routines would then need to be 're-frozen'. The final phase of refreezing ensures that the newly implemented changes will continue and that the organization would not transgress to its former routines. Some observers add a fourth step to Lewin's change process. This fourth step involves diagnosing the barriers to change at both the organizational and the individual level.

Kotter's Strategic Change

John Kotter considers the strategic positioning of a change as depicted in Figure 13.5.[2] Where Lewin was concerned with the psychological and cultural aspects of change, Kotter describes change efforts that are managed by leaders in an organization, thus, his eight steps to strategic change offers a checklist for planning, communicating, and implementing change. In addition, Kotter's model provides those leading change with mechanisms to manage potential resistance to change. Eight steps are involved in this strategic change model.

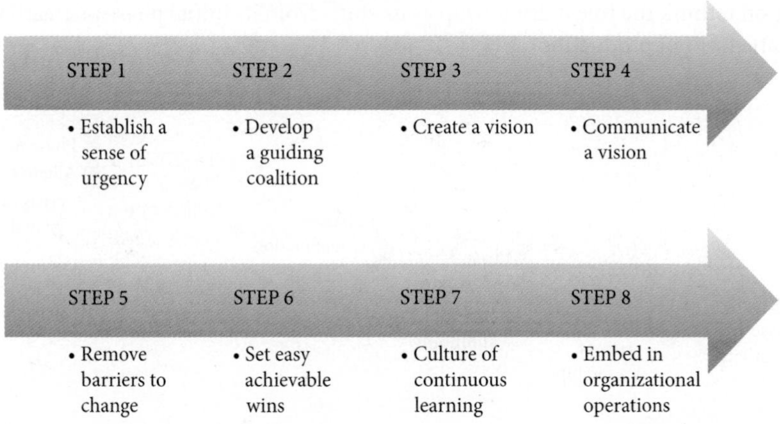

Figure 13.5
Kotter's Steps to
Strategic Change

STEP 1	STEP 2	STEP 3	STEP 4
• Establish a sense of urgency	• Develop a guiding coalition	• Create a vision	• Communicate a vision

STEP 5	STEP 6	STEP 7	STEP 8
• Remove barriers to change	• Set easy achievable wins	• Culture of continuous learning	• Embed in organizational operations

First, the leaders of the organization create a sense of urgency by focusing on the benefits of the change in order to rally the organization and build awareness of the importance of the change. Second, the organization develops a guiding coalition. The coalition consists of a team of individuals who will serve as champions for the change and work to spread the message throughout the organization. The members of the guiding coalition will serve as the emotional, symbolic, and personal supporters of the change. The coalition will build support for the change by further enlisting others to champion the changes—in doing this—the initial guiding coalition will grow to include other members who subsequently become guiding coalition members themselves.

Third, the leaders set a direction for the change by creating a vision. The vision will establish the underlying values that guide the change and outline the specific steps involved with implementing the change. By establishing a clear vision, those individuals within the organization can see the road map for change that lies ahead. Fourth, the leaders of the organization communicate a vision for the change. The communication should occur often and appear in multiple mediums such as newsletters, internal and external social media, and through frequent meetings and 'town hall' type events.

Fifth, the organizational leaders remove barriers to change. Sixth, the organization establishes a few easily achievable goals so that the organization can begin to see the benefits of the changes and the members of the guiding coalition should seek to identify potential sources of resistance. Seventh, the organizational leaders establish a culture of continuous learning and change so that the organization can begin to understand that change is not a one-time event, but a continual process of learning and improvement. Finally, the change becomes embedded in the culture by telling stories, recruiting, selecting, and promoting people who embrace change, and highlighting continual change as a valuable part of operations.

Organizations may experience change due to natural growth patterns. As an organization grows and expands, it goes through a series of inevitable changes, as depicted in Figure 13.6 (Phases of Organizational Growth and Change). The figure depicts six phases of growth where moving through each phase of growth requires an organization to deal with distinct challenges. Each transition can result in crisis. For example, in phase 2 of an organization's development, the organization must deal with moving in a new direction after it has achieved a level of early success. The new direction often requires that the organization rethink the role of leadership as its shifts from its initial phase of creativity to a systematic form of production.[3]

Figure 13.6 Phases of Organizational Growth and Change

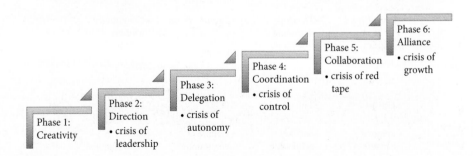

Phase 1: Creativity

Phase 2: Direction
• crisis of leadership

Phase 3: Delegation
• crisis of autonomy

Phase 4: Coordination
• crisis of control

Phase 5: Collaboration
• crisis of red tape

Phase 6: Alliance
• crisis of growth

Positive Approaches to Change

Current approaches to organizational change tend to view change from a negative perspective. For example, change efforts are driven by the belief that change is needed because something within an organization is not working or change is necessary because the organization can no longer remain competitive. An alternative approach looks at the positive aspects of an organization and plans change around those positive aspects. **Appreciative Inquiry (AI),** for example, seeks to identify sources of change that build on past successes and core organizational values. Appreciative Inquiry seeks to identify positive attributes and sources of pride within the organization rather than identifying problems or challenges.[4] Rather than focusing on the organization's limitations or its future goals, AI works to ensure the most enduring and energizing aspects of an organization. Said another way, AI attempts to reinvigorate an organization by identifying future possibilities and opportunities rather than viewing the organization as a problem. Change efforts no longer become efforts to change from something that is deficient, but rather to improve what is already great and enduring about the organization. Appreciative Inquiry involves four steps. Step one involves appreciating the organization for what it is and identifying what gives life to the organization. Step two involves the process of envisioning an even brighter future by dreaming about the possibilities of the future. Step three involves designing the ideal organization. Step four involves sustaining the organization by empowering, learning, and adjusting the organization for the future.

Why Change Efforts Meet with Resistance

The models of change described above guide organizations through managed change. Still many in organizations, especially those who are not part of the guiding coalition, often experience negative emotions during change efforts. These negative emotions often result in resistance to change. **Resistance to change** refers to the process whereby individuals fail to recognize the value of a change and thus cling to old routines, habits, or ways of thinking rather than embrace the changes. Resistance often leads those in organizations to display behaviors that prevent the change from happening. Research confirms that individuals may resist change, even when a change effort is managed systematically. Resistance to change is only one reason that change efforts may fail. Change efforts can fail because those in the organization may not have the skills necessary to deal with the new demands that arise during and after change efforts. Individuals may hold values that are counter to the change, or individuals may simply lack motivation or understanding of the change. Change also increases uncertainty and stress, which may further add to resistance. Ultimately, change is a process rooted in psychology and many organizational change efforts fail because systematic change efforts do not account for these psychological processes.

Harvard University Professor Robert Kegan has taken an alternative approach to creating successful change efforts by addressing the psychological aspects of change. Kegan offers the **competing commitments model of change** which can be summed up in the following way: It is not that people resist change because they are unable to act in the face of change, but it is because they hold two competing commitments. One competing commitment is to the old way of doing things and the second competing commitment is to the new way of doing things. In order to encourage change, Kegan suggests that organizations need to understand these competing commitments and help individuals realize how the old commitments are limiting to both the individual and to the organization. Each of the models and approaches suggest that organizations should promote change, despite the resistance that might emerge.[5]

3 Describe the factors that support organizational innovation.

Innovation

One way to institute change in and around organizations is through innovation. **Innovation** refers to the process of developing, implementing, and marketing a new or novel approach to a project or service. Innovation involves three steps: introducing or creating a new product or idea, transforming the product or idea into a product, and adopting of the product or idea into the marketplace. **Diffusion of innovation,** often considers a fourth step, and occurs when a product or idea spreads and becomes widely adopted, as displayed in Figure 13.7.[6] Several factors in an organization are associated with the diffusion of innovation as the innovation becomes adopted. A culture that supports innovation is key, but for the innovation to be successful, the innovation must be developed within a legal and institutional environment that supports innovation. This includes a legal system that defends copyright and patent ownership and a system of finance and banking to support the development of new ideas and assume the risk associated with potential failures. Further, a marketplace that supports the adoption of new products and ideas is also essential to successful innovation.

When an innovation, or a set of innovations, changes the existing technology and transforms an industry, it is referred to as a **disruptive innovation.** The innovation is considered disruptive because it challenges existing ways of doing things. In most cases, this disruption occurs when a new technology takes hold in the marketplace. Examples of disruptive technology include the switch from film-based technology to digital photography or the movement from purchasing products in stores to purchasing products through on-line retailing.[7] Another example includes Apple's development of iTunes. The iTunes format sought to replace traditional CD formats and changed the way consumers identify, purchase, and store music and other media.

Organizations differ in how they innovate. Some organizations innovate by forming specialized innovation teams within the organization while other organizations

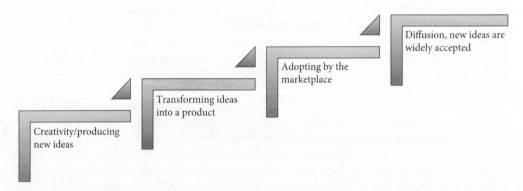

Figure 13.7 Four Steps to Innovation and Diffusion

encourage innovations throughout the company. Other organizations look for innovations that are occurring outside the organization and then seek to acquire the innovation rather than develop the innovation from within.

Creativity

4 Outline the process of creativity, how it relates to innovation, and the elements that support creativity in organizations.

The first, and one of the most important steps in the innovation process is creativity. **Creativity** is the process whereby new ideas emerge and grow within a specific domain. Creativity, then, is not a general attribute of a person or organization, but rather a process of discovery that occurs through trial and error. Creativity emerges from two sets of factors: Individual factors and work-related factors. Individual factors include expertise within a specialized area such as business, music, or science. Individual factors also include creative thinking skills and intrinsic motivation. Work-related factors that promote creativity involve a culture that promotes autonomy, encourages risk taking, and promotes reward and recognition for creative behaviors. Factors that stifle creativity include politics and internal disputes, focusing on the status quo, and time pressure.

Creative efforts do not necessary result in innovation, because creativity does not always result in the transfer of the creative effort into something new that is adopted by the organization. Another distinction between innovation and creativity is that creativity is often associated with individual efforts while innovation is the result of a more comprehensive organized effort.[8]

Stress

5 Identify different types of stress and methods for stress management.

Increasingly, stress has become an important issue in organizations. Stress costs organizations billions of dollars a year in terms of healthcare costs, missed work, and lower productivity. Certain types of stress have also been linked to decreased learning, increased resistance to change, and lack of innovation. **Stress** occurs when a situation poses challenges that exceed an individual's ability to deal with the challenges.

Factors that Contribute to Stress

Factors that contribute to stress are called **stressors.** Life changes, such as taking a new job, moving to a new location, and gaining more responsibility can lead to stress. Certain jobs create higher levels of stress. For example, two job classifications, firefighting and President of the United States, consistently top the list of most stressful jobs. In contrast, florists and librarians ranked among low stress jobs.[9] Working in certain industries and in certain types of organizations can also increase stress, as can the complexity of a job and workload. The leadership or management style of supervisors can also increase stress. Job insecurity, the fear of being fired or losing a job, is also a stressor.[10]

Fancy Collection/SuperStock

People experience stress in two distinct ways. **Hindrance stress** is experienced as stress that limits the ability to perform. On the other hand, **challenge stress** actually improves a person's ability to learn, grow, and perform.[11] While a person might want to experience challenge stress more than hindrance stress in the short term, over the long term, too much stress of either kind can lead to exhaustion. Certain individuals are also more likely to experience stress. Students, for example, often refer to **Type A and Type B** personalities. Individuals who demonstrate Type A behavioral patterns seek situations that require high degrees of achievement, are more competitive, and have a greater sense of urgency than Type B individuals. Type A individuals also tend to be more irritable at work and when dealing with others. People who demonstrate Type A behaviors may be more likely to experience stress than those with other behavioral patterns. Although references to Type A and Type B personalities are common, the differences have yet to be confirmed by research.[12]

Overcoming Stress

Several factors help to overcome stress. Social support can help minimize the effects of stress. Research has identified four types of social support that may help reduce stress: *Instrumental support* involves helping people solve problems or developing skills necessary to deal with stressful tasks and situations. *Emotional support* involves caring for and understanding others' unique situation and helping understand the emotions of anxiety and discomfort that may be associated with stress. *Informational support* involves providing knowledge and direct feedback that may help minimize stress as a result of uncertainty or ambiguity; *appraisal support* boosts self-esteem and confidence so that individuals may develop stronger resistance to stressors and experience less stress inducing self-doubt.[13]

Conclusion

Organizational change can be planned or unplanned, rapid or incremental, and involves a modification to structures, processes, or outcomes in an organization. Change stems from a variety of causes and is explained through various models. Although the models of change vary in assumptions about where change occurs, and the nature of change, the models provide guidance for effectively managing change. Resistance to change is a common challenge in organizations. Innovation, in general, promotes change in organizations, but the method of innovation differs from one organization to the next. Creativity effects innovation and change, and emerges from individual and work-related factors. Stress is often experienced during change and innovation and can be minimized through both individual and organizational factors.

OB AT WORK

BRIAN ROGERS LEADS T. ROWE PRICE
THROUGH CHANGE AND CONTINUITY

Brian Rogers

When **Brian Rogers interviewed** for a job at T. Rowe Price in 1982, the entire company sat on three floors of an office building in downtown Baltimore. Fresh out of business school, he took a job as a portfolio management trainee and became one of 350 people working for the investment firm. Three and a half years later, he was running the T. Rowe Price Equity Income Fund.

During the last three decades, Rogers has performed as one of the industry's top portfolio managers and has managed significant changes in T. Rowe Price, in the financial services industry, and in the business world at large. Today, as Chairman and Chief Investment Officer of T. Rowe Price Group, Brian oversees $550 billion U.S. dollars in assets and remains the portfolio manager for the Equity Income Fund, which has grown to $24 billion in assets under his direction. The company itself has grown to 5,300 employees and has locations in 13 different countries. Brian actively works with other members of the organization's management committee to run these businesses.

6 Apply concepts of change, innovation, creativity, and stress to organizations.

As one of the first U.S.-based investment firms to recognize international opportunities, T. Rowe Price began investing overseas as early as 1979. Still, few could have predicted the importance of investing outside the United States. Some of the changes he has observed include a growing interest in investing in equities by companies in emerging market companies and greater acceptance by investors in bonds issued by foreign governments. These practices were largely unheard of three decades ago. Rogers observes that future economic growth in emerging markets will continue to outpace the United States, and other changes in the financial services industry will continue. Recognizing that change is constant, he notes, "Our predecessors deserve the credit for these early moves. We've just continued to execute the strategy."

Brian learned formal theories of change and innovation nearly 30 years ago while he was an MBA student at Harvard Business School. While he was there, he studied under professors like John Kotter, whose eight-step approach to strategic change remains a well-established approach to change. "The ideas of Kotter and others I learned about in graduate school are models that keep coming back. For example, "During the crisis of 2008," he observed, "it became extremely important for leadership to be visible and accessible within the organization." In a typical year, Brian might communicate directly with all employees two to four times, but during the crisis he increased his communications to 8 to 10 times in a six-month period. "During a time of crisis and uncertainty, you must be heard," he adds. Brian remained optimistic, even as other investment firms began failing, and he spread this optimism throughout his company, "The world doesn't end often," he remarks, "so I was confident it wouldn't end in 2008."

(continued)

In order to manage these and other changes, Brian and his colleagues on the T. Rowe Price management committee rely on a number of change management strategies. One of the most important sources of change management is selecting and retaining top-notch employees who can work effectively in ambiguity and uncertainty. "When you are dealing with markets, you have to function with levels of uncertainty, perfect information doesn't exist," he explains. Another important characteristic for successful change: an ability to understand one's own limits. "You make a lot of mistakes investing and you become more at peace with yourself when you learn from mistakes. People who have a fixation with perfection don't do well in the investment industry because you must be able to make decisions despite imperfect information. No one has all the answers," he says. Another important characteristic of successfully dealing with change is the ability to be open to the opinion and viewpoint of others. "I learned early on to acknowledge how much I don't know. In the investment world, people are right and wrong on a daily basis. It's important to recognize that you don't know as much as you think you do."

Another process Brian engages at T. Rowe Prices is to build continuity into the system. T. Rowe Price has developed a stable workforce where turnover is low, and employees are genuinely committed to the success of the company. This provides an environment where individual members feel comfortable making suggestions and providing input. At the same time, this level of continuity helps build a culture where good decision-making is valued, but measured risk is taken in order to enhance motivation.

Source: Personal interview, Brian Rogers. (2012)

SPOTLIGHT ON RESEARCH
Does Resistance to Change Matter or Are There Better Ways to Characterize Why People Don't Change in Organizations?

Resistance to change is a common occurrence. Several explanations exist for why individuals seem to resist change in organizations. Ultimately, resistance is a problem in many change efforts because individual resistance results in lack of commitment to the organizational change initiative and may lead to the failure of the change effort.

Many researchers believe that resistance to change is a natural part of the change process. For example, in Lewin's force field model of change, organizational members resist change because it is difficult to unfreeze old routines. Newly acquired behaviors that occur due to the change are not natural and must be learned. Others believe that people may resist change because many changes go against the self-interest of the individual and because an individual may not see how the organizational change will benefit them personally. Such resistance arises because change tends to benefit those higher in the organization or those leading change efforts—not those undergoing the change itself.

Researcher Rex Foster proposed a slightly different approach to understanding individual resistance to change. In his view, past understanding of resistance to change was too simplistic. People didn't resist change for only one reason, but many factors come in to play when people experience organizational change. Foster's view was that one factor in particular had been largely overlooked: people's perception of justice and the change. In his view, the more people saw a change effort as unjust, the more likely they would lack commitment and resist the change. Similarly, the more that people saw the change as just, the more they would be likely to support the organizational change effort. He developed hypotheses with this in mind and went about to test them. He identified three companies undergoing an organizational change and invited members, through email, to respond to a series of questions about the change. In all, he had 218 respondents. Using various statistical techniques to analyze his data, Foster's hypotheses were largely supported. He found that perceptions of organizational justice were much stronger predictors of commitment to change than resistance to change. In particular, he found that affective or emotional commitment to the change was the most highly related to perceptions of justice among employees facing an organizational change. In addition, there was a strong relationship between perceived justice and normative commitment to the change. Normative commitment means that the individual did not have an emotional commitment to the change, but nonetheless, still believed that the change was "the right thing to do." Interestingly, resistance to change had almost no impact on an individual employee's commitment to the change. The result was surprising because it challenges the conventional belief that resistance to change by organizational members may impact the success of the change. Further, resistance to change was not related to perceptions of organizational justice. This implies that perceptions of justice do not seem to influence resistance.

The study was not without limitation, but it does bring up an important question when studying the concept of organizational change. According to the author, the study suggests that when employees perceive a change process is fair and just, they are more likely to support the change. In particular, employees value procedural justice in the change process. In addition to other factors already associated with change, those implementing change efforts should identify and build support for change efforts by building a process that is perceived to be just and fair.

Questions for Discussion

1. What is the relationship between justice and resistance to change? How is this similar or different to your own experiences?

2. What actions would you take in a workplace that was undergoing change based on this research?

---

*Based on the article by Rex D. Foster, Resistance, Justice, and Commitment to Change. *Human Resource Development Quarterly, 21*, 1, 3–39.

Pairing with this Topic Summary

Suggested Expert Contributions

Decision Making by Design—Deone Zell (California State University, Northridge), Alan M. Glassman (California State University, Northridge), and Shari Duron (Consultant)

Work and Working in the Era of Globalization—Rabi S. Bhagat (University of Memphis)

Organization Change—W. Warner Burke (Teachers College, Columbia University)

Suggested Cases

Case 1: The Case of Apple iPhone 4

Case 2: "We Are Global or We Are Nothing": Conflict and Cover-Up at ColequarterMaine

Case 3: EMERGENCY! We Need a Better Compensation System

Case 4: Face Time at TechPoint Software, Inc.

Suggested Exercises

Exercise 11: Force Field Analysis

Exercise 12: Well-Being at Work

Exercise 13: What Stresses You Out?

Exercise 14: Laughter Is the Best Medicine

Exercise 17: Design Your Technology

Exercise 19: Overcoming Resistance

Exercise 24: OD Techniques at Work

Exercise 25: Back-to-Back Change

Endnotes

1. Lewin, K. (1951). *Field theory in social science.* New York: Harper & Row.
2. Kotter, J. P. (2007). Leading change. *Harvard Business Review, 85*(1): 96–103 and Kotter, J. P. (1995). Leading change: Why transformation efforts fail, *Harvard Business Review, 73*(2): 59–67.
3. Greiner, L. (1998). Evolution and revolution as organizations grow. *Harvard Business Review, 76*(3): 55–68.
4. Fry, R., Barrett, F., Seiling J., & Whitney, D. (Eds.). *Appreciative inquiry and organizational transformation: Reports from the field.* Westport, CT: Quorum.
5. Kegan, R. (1994). *In over our heads.* Cambridge, MA: Harvard University Press.
6. Rogers, E. M. (2003). *Diffusion of innovations* (5th Ed.). New York, NY: Free Press.
7. Christensen, C. M. (1997). *The innovator's dilemma.* Cambridge, MA: Harvard Business School Press.
8. Amabile, T. M. (1988). A model of creativity and innovation in organizations. In B. M. Staw & L. L. Cummings (Eds.). *Research in organizational behavior,* 10. Greenwich, CT: JAI Press.
9. Krantz, L. (2002). *Jobs rated almanac* (6th Ed.) Fort Lee, NJ: Barricade Books.
10. Cooper, C. L., Dewe. P. J., & O'Driscoll, M. P. (2001). *Organizational stress.* Thousand Oaks, CA: Sage.
11. Le Pine, J. A., Le Pine, M. A., & Jackson, C. L. (2004). Challenge and hindrance stress: Relationships with exhaustion, motivation to learn and learning performance. *Journal of Applied Psychology, 89*(5): 883–891.
12. Friedman, M. (1996). *Type A behavior: Its diagnosis and treatment.* Springer. See also Wilson, S. (2009). Type A and B personalities. *The Guardian.* (March 6). Available for download at http://www.theguardian.com/lifeandstyle/2009/mar/07/personality-type-a-type-b.
13. House, J. (1981). *Work stress and social support.* Reading, MA: Addison-Wesley.

Decision Making by Design: A Blueprint for Balancing Execution and Innovation

Deone Zell
California State University, Northridge

Alan M. Glassman
California State University, Northridge

Shari Duron
Consultant

The announced merger of U.S.-based Company X and Company Y, two industry giants, drew immediate worldwide headlines. Collectively, these media reports highlighted the joint market share, potential cost savings, and expanded complimentary product pipeline, portraying a dominant force in an increasingly turbulent, competitive environment. Yet, several months after the merger received final shareholder and government approval, the combined company had serious challenges.[1] Duplicate processes—often based on very different overall philosophical and tactical beliefs—in such areas as marketing and human resources, had created internal struggles on how best to integrate their systems. Moreover, no major decisions had been made on (a) choosing which of the two extremely different Information Technology (IT) systems would be adopted as the platform for all internal operations, and (b) setting a joint strategic direction, perceived as an absolute necessity to invent new products on tight timelines in order to stay competitive in the marketplace. As summarized by one senior executive:

> There were thousands of decisions that had to be made in a matter of weeks. We didn't know how to do that. We got caught up in the complexity of the situation. That became a spiral that led to us not making decisions, instead of us making better decisions…In other instances, attempting to hit market windows [put forth by the west coast firm] demanded the creation of new products on very tight timelines. We learned that these folks were very reluctant to standardize the creative process and to innovate on a schedule.

Another executive noted that while many high-powered teams were created to make the necessary decisions, they often seemed overwhelmed by the magnitude of the merger—frequently referred to as "merger fatigue"—and consequently fell victim to *analysis paralysis*—gathering mountains of data but never making decisions.[2] In the end, morale suffered, redundancies remained, and the breadth of successful products never materialized, causing severe customer dissatisfaction and leaving the company vigorously searching for answers.

What Went Wrong

This reading, an amalgam of real examples, illustrates that this company had stumbled in a key process—decision making. Situations like this are not unique, as more and more evidence indicates that many executives are struggling with taking action in an increasingly turbulent, competitive business environment.[3] Simply stated, decision makers are being asked to make critical choices with limited information. Thus, while time pressures demand rapid decisions, the lack of information simultaneously raises the risk of making a serious error. The combined company had become much more risk adverse than either company prior to the merger.

Ironically, the decision-making process itself is simple and straightforward. Open any management textbook and you will find a version of the following sequential steps: (a) analyze the situation and the accompanying problems to be resolved, (b) establish decision-making criteria, (c) generate information and search for alternative solutions, (d) evaluate choices against the decision criteria, and (e) make a decision. While this certainly sounds easy enough, research indicates that with increasing frequency, under complex conditions the process fails, and in some cases, goes horribly wrong.

At the combined company, hindsight revealed that the myriad of decisions needing resolution were made more difficult by (a) the complexity of group decision making involving people who didn't know each other and felt the need to preserve/defend their previous approach, (b) ambiguity about when to stop generating alternatives and start deciding between them—in other words, when to shift from divergence to convergence in decision making, and (c) decision makers' inability to separate their emotions from rational decision making. Had the company realized that not all decisions are the same—and that different decisions require different contexts—it is possible that many of these problems could have been avoided.

Decision Making by Design

Due to the difficulty of decision making, companies today often outsource management of the process to experts who offer what is often called *decision acceleration services*. These facilitators are specifically trained not in the subject being decided upon, but in the process of making decisions. They are, in essence, taskmasters who march participants through a structured process and demand focus, which is no small feat given the tendency of many executives to be connected 24/7. One facilitator described the importance of her "outsider" role in demanding attention:

> We tell executives that if it is important enough for you to be here, you need to unplug. They don't like that, but we insist. Often that means asking executives to hand over their cell phones. That's something most employees wouldn't want to ask of someone at that level. But that's the kind of thing we have to do.

Most importantly, decision acceleration facilitators provide fundamentally different processes depending on whether the decision type is rational (execution) or creative (innovation).

Figure 1 summarizes the design elements of each decision type as revealed in companies' use of decision acceleration services to tackle both problems of innovation and

Design Element	Execution	Innovation
Problem-solving style	Rational	Creative
Environment	Austere, bare-bones	Resource rich
Participants' focus	Tasks	Relationships and tasks
Relationship between participants	Hierarchical	Egalitarian
Levels represented	Senior levels	All levels
Idea generation	Immediate convergence	Divergence followed by convergence
Decision-making process	Majority rule	Consensus
Conversation style	Constrained discussion	Dialogue
Desired level of change	Compliance behaviors	New understanding

Figure 1 Designing for Innovation Versus Execution

execution over the course of several years. In the sections below, we describe what these elements look like in practice. Our research, as described, shows mixing and matching erroneously can spell disaster, while "decision making by design" can spell success.

Designing for Execution

As one facilitator explained to us, strategy execution is about the output, not the experience—the goal is convergence of ideas with minimal divergence. Consequently, the decision-making process is extremely streamlined:

- The meeting space, regardless of the level of the participants, is often sparsely furnished with serviceable tables and chairs to prevent people from becoming too comfortable. Upon arrival, participants briefly introduce themselves and immediately begin work—no time is allocated for socializing. Therefore, meeting space and participant design is targeted at immediate and focused outcomes.

- Ground rules for the decision-making session(s) are clearly posted, emphasizing the need to (a) move fast and be mindful of time, and (b) ask clarifying questions only, avoiding the introduction of tangential ideas and processes. When someone does digress from a rule, the facilitator simply cuts him or her off with a statement such as "that's not relevant to this discussion" or "a novel idea, but not today" or "talking about that possibility would not be a very good use of our time."

- Participants are presented with pre-determined alternatives for decision making and then ushered through a structured process designed to analyze these choices based on criteria such as goal alignment and cost reduction. Discussion must stay within the existing parameters and constraints posed by the alternatives.
- Hierarchical rules apply throughout the discussion, meaning opinions aired by senior managers carry more weight than subordinate participants, because, as all participants are told, the ultimate decision making responsibility resides with the group's titular leader.
- While the goal of the discussion is to reach consensus, time and/or date constraints on reaching decisions often precludes this occurrence. When disagreements arise, a vote is taken and the majority wins. The minority is expected to "live with" the decision so the team can move on.

This rigid process works because the goal of execution decision making is to reach a practical, immediate agreement, rather than a deeper, long-term commitment. Moreover, participants know that if they cannot make a decision, the leader tasked with the outcome will make it for them. This efficiency oriented, cut-throat mentality pervades the decision execution process—which, according to one facilitator, has "no room for sympathy." Elaborating, she asserted, "We deal with hard-core decisions that involve little creativity. For instance, if we need to cut $1.5 million out of operating expenses, and doing so requires making painful decisions, that's what we do. It's just part of the territory." From our perspective, it had all the trappings of a military operation.

Designing for Innovation

In contrast to execution decision making, companies adopt innovative decision making for problems whose alternatives are unknown. As stated by a senior manager:

> We'd use the execution process when a group comes in with a big, hairy problem that needs resolution quickly. We'd embrace the innovation process when a group comes in saying, "We have some possible future business space and we want to explore whether there's an opportunity out there."

Another manager put it this way: "The goal of the execution process is to get people working in the box, while that of innovation is to get people working out of the box."

With the emergence of success stories at many of the world's leading companies— such as Apple with its elegant product design and service through "genius bars," Wal-Mart with its supply chain excellence, Facebook with its social network revolution, and Dell with its business model that altered its business sector—instilling innovation into the decision-making process has become an imperative within many organizations. Simply stated, companies wishing to become innovative should not leave the process to chance, but need to integrate innovation through organizational design and accompanying decision making.

The process of innovative decision making looks and feels far different from that of execution:[4]

- Environments designed for innovative decision making are often flush with sensory stimulation and flexibility. In one room, for instance, we observed fresh flowers, posters and paintings, bean bag chairs, colorful furniture, tables on wheels, curved portable walls and whiteboards, children's toys, games, costumes, hats, puzzles, magazines and books on topics from business to photography. Music ranging from soft jazz to heart-pounding rock can be used to evoke the desired mood and energy level. The goal, according to a facilitator, is to get people in a *state of flow* and stimulate divergent and visionary thinking with a "smorgasbord of sensory experiences."

- This luxuriously designed setting—particularly when compared to the backdrop for execution decision making—is based on research that demonstrates that creativity requires a distinct mental zone in which the mind can combine unrelated thoughts, recognize an insight, and articulate imaginative solutions. Creative thought is stimulated by factors such as interaction with others, mood, energy level, natural light, and games and social activities designed to stimulate mind activity. So important are these design elements to the production of creativity that, in the words of one facilitator, "the soft stuff is the hard stuff."

- While innovative decision making sessions are customized for the specific group (e.g., engineers, product teams, regional sales representatives), nearly all sessions begin with icebreakers and team-building activities designed to build rapport and trust. Socializing and mingling is encouraged through numerous breaks and even catered lunches. A facilitator explained, "You can't just say, 'Let's have a brainstorming session and come up with brilliant ideas—you have to warm folks up first.'"

- During the innovation decision-making process, there is no hierarchy–egalitarianism rules. The basic rule is to listen closely and take everyone's ideas seriously, regardless of organizational rank. As proudly stated by one facilitator overseeing an innovation decision-making lab, "If the administrative assistant in the corner raises her hand, we'll make sure she gets heard, and gets just as much time to talk as a VP. If anyone tries to cut her off, we'll make sure that doesn't happen!"

- The actual decision-making process aims to iterate between divergent and convergent thinking. To encourage divergence, participants are expected to deconstruct the current situation and to suspend disbelief about what can and cannot be done; indeed, radical thinking is reinforced. During this process, folks accustomed to rational choice processes may find it difficult, the facilitators become educators, teaching the participants how to ask appreciative questions and engage in exploratory dialogues aimed at reaching new understandings. The approach abandons a conventional discussion that would simply broaden perspectives.

- Brainstorming serves as the pivotal activity throughout the sessions to generate alternatives. Facilitators insist that everyone actively offers input, not allowing silence or "bobblehead" behavior (i.e., simply nodding or shaking your head in tacit agreement). Once the search for new ideas is complete, convergence is achieved through techniques such as the Nominal Group Technique and "affinitizing," a process whereby participants categorize all ideas generated and then prioritize them with each participant having an equal voice. The remaining alternatives are then investigated using tools such as contingency and scenario planning.

- Actual innovative decision making requires a consensus rather than mere behavioral compliance with the chosen path—in order to reach the deep philosophical commitment needed to implement a new idea or direction. Team building and change management techniques are used to further build and align the teams, encourage team collaboration, and the adoption of group decision making.

When we observed the innovative decision-making sessions, they had the feel of a well thought-out "three-ring circus." Participants were often engaged in multiple activities, for instance, some brainstorming a possible solution to an issue, others reconfiguring the infrastructure for a major product area, and still others critiquing a recent client event—all separate, but interrelated. Within any group of participants, some might be playing with a toy or shooting baskets. At other times, the participants came together for important consensus building activities. In addition, there were support staff recording discussions and outcomes, providing personal coaching, and mapping emergent areas and potential large-scale changes for further areas for analysis and decision making. Some sessions were even filmed (with participant knowledge) behind a one-way control room. Throughout, the facilitator played the role of Ringmaster.

A Concluding Note on the Balancing Act

We highlighted the characteristics of both execution and innovation decision-making processes, noting that they serve very different company purposes. At critical times, companies can mix and match these approaches inappropriately. They may digress into creative conversations when disciplined executor-type processes are required, or they may demand short, time-measured problem solving when creative methods and outcomes are needed. While it may seem easy to differentiate when each should be used, noted scholar James March, who underscored the difficulty when he framed the choice as a war between "exploitation" and "exploration." Exploitation is characterized by refinement, choice, production, efficiency, and implementation, while exploration is typified by play, dream scenarios, experimentation, flexibility, discovery, and risk.[5] Like two sides of the brain, each functions differently and is uncomfortable in the other's territory. However, neither can act as a unified whole without the other. As a senior executive who had experienced both the Executor and the Innovator astutely noted:

> When you're in execution mode, all the innovation packaging seems like fluff. But when we get into the creative phase of things, that fluff becomes important—and then the Executor feels constraining and not as useful. So, it's a cycle; but you need both.

The paradoxical key, therefore, is not only to recognize which approach to decision making is needed, but to be disciplined in applying that approach and to simultaneously be aware that the complexities of a major issue may require the use of both along the way; you may need to shift from one approach to the other and back again. It is an iterative process.

Endnotes

1. This hypothetical case is based on several real cases observed by the authors over a number of years and should not be construed as accurate representations of any given company since certain facts have been embellished or re-arranged to illustrate a point.
2. For more on typical problems such as "analysis paralysis", personality clashes, unproductive conflict, and excess socializing that often plague the decision-making process, see G. Huber, *The Necessary Nature of Future Firms* (Thousand Oaks: Sage Publications, 2003).

3. For more books and articles on the notion of environmental turbulence and the need for accelerated strategic management, see B. Chakravarthy, "A New Strategy Framework for Coping with Turbulence," *Sloan Management Review, 38*(2):69–82; S. Brown & K. Eisenhardt, *Competing on the Edge: Strategy as Structured Chaos* (Boston, Harvard Business School Publishing, 1999); R. D'Aveni & R. Gunther, *Hypercompetition: Managing the Dynamics of Strategic Maneuvering* (Free Press, 1994).

4. It is sometimes argued that innovation requires the absence of a deadline. This isn't necessarily true. Research has shown that pressure can spawn creativity as long as individuals feel that they are on a "mission" rather than a "treadmill." When on a treadmill, individuals are pressured by time and wonder about the importance of their decisions; when on a "mission" they feel meaningful urgency. The discussion of the innovative decision making process assumes the latter. For more on this topic, see pioneering research suggesting that creativity is not necessarily incompatible with time pressure can be found in T. Amabile, C. Hadley, and S. Kramer, "Creativity Under the Gun," *Harvard Business Review, 80* (August) (8): 52–61.

5. James March's description of the dichotomy between exploration (innovation) and exploitation (execution) appeared in his seminal article, "Exploration and Exploitation in Organizational Learning" published in *Organization Science, 2*(1), February 1991, 71–87.

Work and Working in the Era of Globalization

Rabi S. Bhagat

University of Memphis

Meet Robert Smith. With an attractive offer from a global investment firm on Wall Street, he and his wife, Ruth, moved from their hometown in Las Cruces, New Mexico to New York City. He was excited about his new assignment as the investment manager of a select global equities fund. A lot was expected of him because of the superior performance he showed with an investment bank in Dallas, Texas. He was willing to exert his best effort in improving the performance of the firm that he was in charge of managing. However, what he and his wife didn't expect was the early morning telephone calls to his apartment near Wall Street. Most of these calls came from important overseas clients of the investment firm inquiring about the performance of the various accounts that he was in charge of. After six months, Robert started complaining of serious migraine headaches that could not be cured by visits to his physician. His physician recommended that he needed more uninterrupted sleep—which he suspected led to the development of migraine headaches. Robert continues to undergo treatment while his wife is fed up with the fast-paced life in New York City and is urging Robert to return to their idyllic and low-pressure life in Las Cruces.

What Robert experienced was severe symptoms of the work overload that many managers experience in the current era of globalization—especially when there is strong pressure to remain connected with clients and colleagues of the company in overseas contexts. Another incident comes to mind: In 2001, a dear friend of ours was coordinating the activities of globally distributed members of a software development team for Texas Instruments. Unfortunately, his wife died from a car accident before Christmas Eve. During periods of mourning and taking care of his two young children, he still answered emails from colleagues in India, Ireland, and Singapore on various technical issues associated with the software development that he was managing. This example illustrates how the expectation that managers be available round the clock, no matter the circumstances, becomes especially daunting in a global work environment.

What's Different about Work and Working in the Current Era of Globalization?

Since 2000, the term "globalization" has become a commonplace term for describing work that involves connections and coordination across nations and cultures. All of us are aware of growing relationships and economic interdependence among companies and people across dissimilar nations and cultures. It is a process whereby worldwide interconnections in virtually each sphere of business activities are growing. Global interconnections and relationships that result with increased interdependence of companies and countries across dissimilar nations and borders are rapidly reshaping the context for many organizational activities. One of the major consequences of globalization is blurred boundaries within and between organizations, nations, and global economic interests, such as the ones upheld by the Davos Group in Zurich, Switzerland, the World Trade Organization, the International Monetary Fund, and the World Bank.

The primary, organizational consequences of rapid globalization are as follows:

1. Phenomenal rate of growth in mergers and acquisitions between firms
2. Complexities in coordinating worldwide operations
3. Relentless pressures to innovate
4. Adjusting to new workplace realities and organizational structures
5. Evolution of new managerial roles
6. Changing patterns in employee attitudes
7. New challenges in managing work–life balance

We discuss each of these consequences next.

Phenomenal Rate of Growth in Mergers and Acquisitions

Since the early 1980s, the rate of international mergers and acquisitions of firms has increased. These mergers and acquisitions have led to routine waves of downsizing (i.e., the new merged firm requires fewer total employees) and business process reengineering (designed to allow work to continue with fewer employees) have led to a workforce that is largely suspicious and cynical. It has been well documented over the last 20 years that senior managers in the *Fortune* 1000 reported their primary worry and anxiety was the fear of losing their job to a merger or acquisition as mergers or acquisitions almost always take a major toll on the psychological well-being of both the managers and employees involved.[1]

Complexities in Coordinating Worldwide Operations

In the U.S., the early 1990s were characterized by an economic slowdown that led to plant closings, budget reductions, and layoffs of both blue-collar and white-collar workers. As a result, today's U.S. organizations have become 'leaner' and 'meaner' as they compete globally and face unprecedented challenges of coordinating worldwide operations.[2] New types of work arrangements, including globally distributed work teams in different countries, are becoming commonplace in high technology and financial services organizations. These new work arrangements have fostered the growth of a 24/7-work culture in both U.S. and East Asian organizations. It is precisely these kinds of work arrangements that create work stresses for managers like Robert Smith and our friend at Texas Instruments.

Relentless Pressures to Innovate

Despite recent economic downturns in the U.S. and Europe, some *Fortune* 500 U.S. global corporations are thriving. IBM, Coca Cola, Pepsico, Google, Microsoft, Apple, Intel, FedEx, and Caterpillar are all succeeding in the current era. The strategy they share for success has become the benchmark in their industries. The legendary Jack Welch, former CEO of General Electric, explained the rationale on CNBC in September 2010. He noted that after years of bumping around innovative technologies that improved efficiencies and reduced the need for labor, American corporations, especially in the high-tech sector, have been able to produce technological growth and innovation on an ongoing basis. The result is that while the companies are becoming more innovative, they are also shedding jobs and lowering their payroll obligations and related medical and retirement benefits. This consequence of globalization, (i.e. the relentless pressure to innovate), has produced companies where both indigenous and external resource-based knowledge are making dramatic improvements in operational management. But in the process of doing so, unemployment is a natural byproduct. And we know from previous research studies that unemployment is a stressful experience that can have major psychological and behavioral consequences for employees who are laid off or terminated.

Dealing with New Organizational Structures

As a result of rapid innovations in technologies and global competition, modern workplaces in the United States and other countries are being transformed in terms of emphasizing globally distributed work teams, network organizations, and an integration of research activities on a worldwide scale. It might appear to most of us that these new forms of working are becoming common in high-tech organizations like Microsoft, Siemens, Apple, and Tata Consultancy Services from India. However, on a closer examination, we also see the emergence of these new forms of workplace realities in emergent economies, including Brazil, Russia, India, and China—the so called "BRIC" countries which are considered the new players in the global economic scene. As a result of these new organizational structures, work stresses in the form of increased time and performance pressures, work overload, ambiguities in understanding the nature of working relationships, interpersonal conflicts, and work family issues have increased significantly.

Evolution of New Managerial Roles

The pressures of adjusting to and dealing with global workplace demands has also led to the new types of managerial roles. In a recent survey of managerial work in Western Europe, one researcher found that the sheer number of new demands being placed on both junior and senior level managers are increasing over time.[3] In addition, a majority of them had minimal training to cope with such changes and pressures. Eighty two percent of the managers felt that they were suffering from excessive amounts of information overload due to reliance on computer-mediated forms of communication, email, Internet, teleconferencing, and videoconferencing. All in all, the reality of managerial work described by noted management scholar, Henry Mintzberg, has gone through a major transformation since 1973.[4] Sixty percent of managers surveyed thought that their jobs were becoming increasingly fragmented and that they had much less uninterrupted time on the job to concentrate on and complete a given task with sufficient attention to speed, detail, and quality.

Changing Patterns of Psychological Contract and Employee Attitudes

U.S. businesses are navigating this new world of technological change and globalization. Capital and technology are mobile; labor is not. One major reason why domestic unemployment is on the rise since 2008 is because of the unwillingness of large U.S. multinational and global organizations to hire workers from the U.S., which has the highest wages in the world. As a result, there has been a significant growth in contingent, short-term, and part-time work contracts. The nature of the psychological work contract (i.e. the beliefs that individuals hold regarding promises made, accepted, and held between themselves and the work organization) is undergoing considerable transformation due to the growth of these alternative forms of work arrangements. Although research has shown the psychological contract to be critical in sustaining work motivation and long-term well being,[5] modern organizations competing for a larger share of the global market do not appear to value such implicit guarantees with their workers.

Managing Work–Life Balance

Increasing globalization is reflected in the increasing number of hours that individuals work. Time studies have shown that working hours have been increasing steadily since 1980s, not only in the Western countries, but also in the context of East and South-East Asian countries. Americans work the most number of hours (1,949 hours and rising every year) followed by the Japanese. The more globalized the country and work organizations are, the longer the work days become. Longer work days lead to the development of work–family conflict, and may contribute to major consequences for family life and personal life satisfaction. Research centers focusing on work–family studies are being established in leading universities (i.e. the State University of New Jersey, in New Brunswick, IESE in Barcelona Spain), and managers of multinational and global corporations are taking lessons on how to manage the conflicting expectations of work and non-work related demands. There are major consequences of increasing the importance of work in relation to personal life, which typically increases as one moves up the corporate ladder. A total of 65 percent of managers think that the amount of work they do has an adverse effect on their psychological and physical health. Over 70 percent report that spending long hours on the job leads to poor relationships with their spouses, significant others, and children. In more individualistic countries like the United States and Sweden, the divorce rate is over 50 percent—primarily due to relentless pressures to manage the interface between work and family.

Managing Work Stresses in Western and Non-Western Countries

Research over the past 20 years has shown that factors that create stress in the workplace and the processes associated with the experience of psychological strain tend to be similar in both western and non-western contexts. In general, workers experience stress when confronted with a work-related situation or event that is *demanding*, causes *uncertainties* and is of long *duration*.[6] For example, dealing with an unexpected increase in workload that might arise from the challenge of meeting unexpected demands from an important international client can be quite stressful for managers. This stress can be relatively less troublesome if the demand is of short duration, not when it is going to last for a relatively long period of time and is full with uncertainties regarding how to meet the demand and how best to satisfy the needs of the clients.

In dealing with such stresses, the type of coping skills and resources (including various types of social support) that workers have is greatly dependent on their cultural background. Members of collectivistic countries (e.g. Japan, China, India, South Korea, Brazil) are more likely to receive considerable social support from their coworkers and supervisors. In addition, they also receive significant socio-emotional support from their families. With the exception of Japan and South Eastern part of China, most collectivistic countries are not as affluent as the individualistic countries of the west (e.g. United States, Canada, UK, France, Sweden, the Netherlands, Australia, and New Zealand). However, the kind of social support that members of organizations in collectivistic countries receive from their superiors, families, and in-group members are very helpful in dealing with the pressures and stresses of work, and working in the current era of globalization.[7] Stress management mechanisms that are emphasized in collectivistic countries are focused on making the best use of resources in their family and social networks. Reliance on one's religion, religious rituals, and culturally sanctioned use of diversions and holistic medicine (such as Ayurvedic practices in India, Taoism-based medicines in rural China) are emphasized.

At the same time, employee assistance programs and seeing a professional counselor or therapist on a regular basis to manage work stress and symptoms of distress or psychological strain is not a culturally viable option in most collectivist cultures. The cost of providing western methods of dealing with psychological strains and discomforts is simply prohibitive in developing countries and emerging economies with collectivist cultures.[8] In addition, individuals risk losing their reputations if it becomes known in their communities that they are seeing a counselor appointed by the company for stress-related symptoms. Social stigmas can be associated when seeking help from certified psychological counselors and make it extremely difficult for collectivists in developing countries and emerging economies to receive proper guidance and medication for coping with symptoms and manifestations of work stress.

Where Do We Go from Here? The Experience of Positive Stress

The lion's share of existing research on how globalization-related pressures create new types of stresses focus primarily on the determinants of stresses, their prevention, and resolution. Western organizational scholars and health professionals have been focusing on prevention and management of distress. The emphasis has been on the pervasiveness of negative experiences that individuals have as they seek meaning and balance in their work and non-work lives in the current era of globalization. However, there is a growing movement in organizations in terms of identifying the presence of positive forms of stress that are associated with positive arousal, good health, and peak performances.

Consider the case of the late Steven Jobs (2011). Despite receiving a terminal diagnosis of pancreatic cancer, he continued to inspire his associates in creating innovative products like iPods, iPhones, iPads etc. His lifestyle and his ways of coping with work-related challenges continued from the days when he and his Apple co-founder Steve Wozniack started producing Macintosh machines from their garage in 1978. The type of continuous arousal and excitement that Steve Jobs experienced throughout his lifespan is called "being in the zone" or "in the flow". Time feels suspended and there is only pure joy and pleasure from immersing into a productive activity in the context of one's work-role. Research on the effects of positive work stress energize an individual to perform at a peak level while at the same time manage the growing demands of life at home. There are many instances where some individuals are likely to appraise a situation or event as beneficial or as providing positive enhancement of their well being. Feelings of intrinsic accomplishments coupled with extrinsic rewards and recognition from one's work organization and professional societies can greatly enhance positive stress or "eustress". Positive affect, meaningfulness, manageability, and hope are also good indicators of eustress.[9] Researchers working in the positive organizational scholarship[10] tradition have been emphasizing the role of positive behaviors in the workplace and that highlighting the positive aspects of work–life is likely to enhance the experience of eustress. More experiences of eustress will certainly go a long way to offset the dysfunctional consequences of working in the current era of globalization.

Endnotes

1. Robert Half International. (1991). Mossholder, et al., 2000.
2. Heckscher (1996). *White collar blues: Management loyalties in an age of corporate restructuring.*
3. Cooper, D. & O'Driscoll. (2001).
4. Mintzberg, H. (1973). *The nature of managerial work.* New York: Harper & Row.
5. Rosseau, D. M. (1995). *Psychological contracts in organizations: understanding written and unwritten agreements.* Thousand Oaks, CA: Sage Publishing.
6. Beehr, T. A., & Bhagat, R. S. 1985. *Human stress and cognition in organizations: an integrated perspective.* New York: John Wiley & Sons.
7. Bhagat, R. S., Segovis, J. C., & Nelson, T. A. (2011). *Work stress and coping in the era of globalization.* New York: Routledge Press/Taylor and Francis (in press).
8. Bhagat, R. S., Sterverson, P. K., & Segovis, J. C. (2007). *Cultural variations in employee assistance programs in the era of globalization.* In Dianna L. Stone, & Eugene F. Stone-Romero (eds.). *The influence of culture on human resource management processes and practices.* New York: LEA Publishing: 207–234.
9. Simmons, B. L., Nelson, D. L., & Neal, L. J. (2001). "A comparison of the positive and negative work attitudes of home healthcare and hospital nurses." *Health Care Management* Review. 26: 64–75.
10. Cameron, K. S., Dutton, J. E., & Quinn, R. E. (2003). *Positive Organizational Scholarship: Foundations of a new discipline.* San Francisco: Berrett Koehler Publishers.

Organization Change

W. Warner Burke

Teacher's College, Columbia University

Change has joined the legendary givens of death and taxes. Change, especially in organizations, is ubiquitous, occurring everyday. Most change in organizations is unplanned and it is likely that insufficient planning contributes to the high rate of failure in change efforts. Around 70 percent of organizational change efforts fail to accomplish their stated goals,[1] while the rate is even higher for mergers and acquisitions—which have greater than a 75 percent failure rate.[2] Although lack of planning is a significant contributing factor, an even greater cause of failure is lack of sustainment. When problems with a change effort arise and matters seem chaotic, organizational members tend to think negatively and give up, for example, "I knew this crazy idea of changing the organization wasn't going to work."

But even *planned* change does not have a high rate of success. To increase the probability of success, organizations need to rethink the way they consider and deal with the need for change. The typical approach to planned change is to think in terms of steps, stages, or phases. The classic and original contribution to this way of thinking and acting was provided many years ago by Kurt Lewin—who argued that organizational change is a three-step process of unfreezing, changing, and refreezing. Unfreezing is a matter of demonstrating the need for change by creating a sense of urgency. Next comes implementing change processes. Finally, in refreezing organizations put reinforcements into place to sustain the change brought about during implementation.

While this linear way of planning change seems logical, how organization change actually occurs is anything but linear. Change rarely occurs according to plan—unanticipated events and reactions happen.[3] When we implement a change in a system, referred to as an *intervention*, people react to it, some positively, some negatively. Often organizational members we thought would be supportive end up not being, and some of those we thought would resist the change end up supporting it. In other cases, the new software package that the organization was counting on to facilitate the whole change process does not work, or the new reward system undermines the hoped-for change.[4] What we must anticipate is that the plan may not go as planned, and if we do not deal with these unplanned-for-occurrences quickly, the change process will bog down, with organizational members tending to give up on making it all work.

To more effectively deal with the unexpected we need to understand the following aspects of organizational change:

- Levels of organization change
- Resistance to change
- The importance of data to organizational change
- The importance of organizational culture to change
- The importance of leadership to change

Based on these factors, we present an overall model of organizational change that may help managers to develop change efforts most likely to succeed.

Levels of Organization Change

Change differs at different levels in the organization—meaning that what and how we change will depend on whether we are focusing on individuals, units, or groups—or the larger system. Change at the individual level means that we are concerning ourselves with recruitment, selection, replacement, or displacement, and our methods often involve training and development, coaching, mentoring, and career counseling. If working at the group level, we are focusing on teamwork and team building, self-directed groups, and intergroup relations, (e.g., managing conflict). If at the larger-system level, we are concerned with the organization's vision, mission, leadership, and culture, and our methods are large-group interventions, town meetings, survey feedback, and multi-rater feedback systems. If at the interorganizational level, we are dealing with such matters as mergers, acquisitions, strategic alliances, joint ventures, partnerships, and consortia.

Resistance to Change

Resistance to change is real, for sure, but does not always occur. Some people may embrace change, especially if they believe the outcome will be positive for them. What needs to be made clear is that people do not always resist the change itself. More universal in terms of resistance is when change is *imposed*—when people believe they have no choice then resistance is likely.

Two additional points regarding resistance should be considered. First, what may look like resistance may not be as such, but instead, ambivalence. People can be skeptical, uncertain, and perhaps somewhat worried about the consequences of change, but with more information and assurance, can be persuaded that the change may be worth it. The contribution by Piderit is an elaboration of this distinction between resistance and ambivalence.[5]

Second, what is worse than resistance is apathy. It is difficult, if not impossible, to manage apathy. If people simply do not care, the whole process means nothing to them, then as a leader of change, one has little to work with. With resistance, there is energy. People care about something. The change leader has something to work with so it is a matter of attempting to redirect the energy that underlies resistance.

The Importance of Data to Organization Change

Collecting data over time via surveys, multi-rater feedback systems, work unit climate, and questionnaires that are brief with quick turnaround feedback, and performance outcomes are all important indices for tracking progress regarding a change effort. Conducting a survey based on a framework, such as the Burke-Litwin model, helps to focus on where the change is working and where it may need more emphasis. The point is this: how can you tell if any progress is being made with a change effort if measurements are ignored?

The Importance of Organizational Culture to Change

It may be that the greatest impediment to organization change is the organization's culture, "The way we do things here." Moreover, there is considerable evidence today that the external environment is more complex and changes more rapidly than organizations can adapt to. Organization's cultures get locked-in over time. But you do not change organizational culture by trying to change the culture itself—its history, norms, and values. You must start with *behavior,* not values or norms. Thus, identifying the behaviors that will lead to the desired culture is the first thing that is necessary when cultures clash with desired change.

The Importance of Leadership to Change

In a comprehensive study of organizational culture and performance, Kotter and Heskett showed that there was a strong relationship between an organization's culture and its performance.[6] With respect to organization change, they pointed out that a number of factors contributed to success, but the single most important one was leadership. In *Good to Great*, Collins identified a number of factors that contributed to organizations' becoming great, but to his apparent surprise, it seemed that the strongest contributing factor was the leader, what he labeled "Level 5"—one who possessed the two critical qualities of humility and perseverance.[7]

The leader's primary responsibility is to provide the vision for the desired change, then to help identify the key goals that will be needed to achieve the vision and, finally, to persevere for the long journey. At British Airways, the culture change journey took more than five years, but the CEO, Colin Marshall, never wavered. His dedication to change and staying the course was absolutely necessary for the success that was achieved.

Bringing it All Together: An Organizational Model of Change

Given the many factors that affect change efforts, it may be useful to consider these items in an organizational model. An organizational model is a representation of an organization, a framework that can help us to understand more clearly the dimensions of organization performance and change. An organizational model helps us to categorize the many, sometimes overwhelming, pieces and parts of a larger system, thus, making the data we are working with more understandable and manageable. An organizational model can provide a common, shorthand language to use and, finally, a model can help to guide action for change. There are a number of models available but for the purposes of parsimony, we will consider one—the Burke-Litwin model—see Figure 1.

The model was derived from practice, in particular, consulting with British Airways from 1985 to 1990 and was explained for an academic audience.[8] Based on the open-system theory, input is the external environment, output the individual and organizational

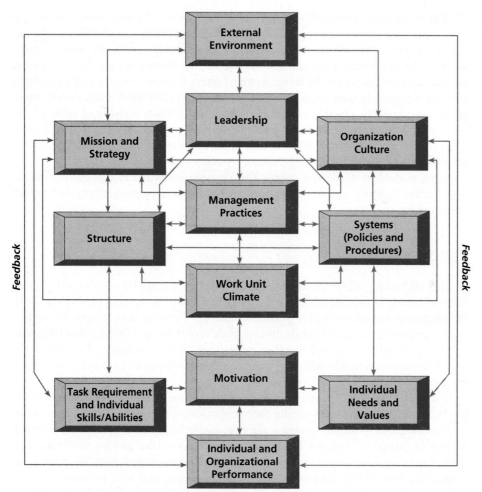

Figure 1 The Burke-Litwin Model of Organizational Performance and Change.

performance, and throughput consists of the remaining areas. The requisite feedback loop is also represented. The display of the model is meant to make a statement about how organization change should occur. It all begins with the external environment, and if the change is on a large scale, the categories most directly affected by the external environment and the ones that carry the most "weight" are mission/strategy, leadership, and culture. Beginning with these "heavier" boxes means that we are attempting revolutionary change. These top boxes are referred to as the *transformational* categories with the remainder as *transactional* categories, meaning they involve evolutionary change. Changing mission, strategy, top leadership, and culture affects the entire organization. Changing such categories as structure, work climate, and information technology may or may not affect the entire organization, thus, they are more transactional.

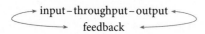

The boxes in the model mean what one would expect—mission is *what*, strategy is *how*, leadership exists throughout the organization but in the model refers to the top executives primarily, culture refers to history and current norms and values, structures is the organization design and accountability system, management practices are day-to-day supervisory behavior, systems refers to those policies and procedures that are designed to help organizational members get their work done (information technology, budgets, reward system, etc.), work unit climate consists of what a local work group's perceptions are about and how they are managed, motivation is aroused energy to tackle and complete tasks, task requirements and individual skills/abilities are essentially the degree of congruence between a person's talents and what the job requires, individual needs and values also concern congruence, especially with the organization's culture, and finally performance is the level of productivity and overall effectiveness.

Conclusion

In baseball, batting .300 is considered quite good. This average for success with organizational change is unacceptable. We need to learn much more about how to deal with the enormous complexities of organization change. Planning is necessary. We need a road map toward the change goals, but we must accept the inevitability that there will be bumps along the way and diverted routes that we did not anticipate. One of the secrets to success is to deal with the "diversions" immediately and get the process back on track.

For the future, then, we must learn more about how to sustain the change once it has been initiated. Also, our learning about organization change has largely been based on loosening tightly coupled systems, for example, reducing bureaucracy, not so much on how to change and improve loosely coupled systems (virtual groups, networks, etc.). And, finally, we have only scratched the surface about leading change. We must learn more about how to help leaders persevere, communicate, deal with resistance, remain upbeat, inspire, support, and remain optimistic, to list only a few needs for learning. If, by the year 2025, the failure rate for organization change has been significantly reduced from 70 percent, we will have succeeded.

Endnotes

1. McKinsey Global Survey Results. (2008). The McKinsey Quarterly survey on organizational transformations, 1–7.
2. Burke, W. W. & Biggart, N. W. (1997). Interorganizational relations. In D. Druckman, J. E., Singer, & H. VanCott (Eds.), *Enhancing organizational performance*, 120–149. Washington, D.C.: National Academy Press.
3. Burke, W. W. (2011). *Organization change: Theory and practice* (3rd Ed). Thousand Oaks, CA: Sage.

4. Kerr, S. (1975). On the folly of rewarding A, while hoping for B. *Academy of Management Journal*, 18, 769–783.
5. Piderit, S. K. (2000). Rethinking resistance and recognizing ambivalence. A multidimensional view of attitudes toward an organizational change. *Academy Management Review*, 25, 783–794.
6. Kotter, J. P., & Heskett, J. L. (1992). *Corporate culture and performance*. New York: Free Press.
7. Collins, J. (2001). *Good to great: Why some companies make the leap and others don't*. New York: Harper Business.
8. Burke, W. W. & Litwin, G. H. (1992). A causal model of organizational performance and change. *Journal of Management*, 18, 532–545.

14 Corporate Social Responsibility, Ethics, and Sustainability

Topic Summary Learning Objectives

1. Describe why corporate social responsibility and sustainability are relevant for organizational behavior.

2. Define the triple bottom line and the environmental and human approaches to sustainability.

3. State the elements of the business case approach and the ethical mandate approach for corporate social responsibility.

4. Compare and contrast the shareholder and stakeholder perspectives.

5. Apply concepts of corporate social responsibility, ethics, and sustainability to organizations.

Key Terms

applied ethics, p. 511	instrumental values, p. 507	stakeholders, p. 510
benefit corporation, p. 510	integrity, p. 508	sustainability, p. 503
corporate social responsibility (CSR), p. 503	morals, p. 506	terminal values, p. 507
	ombudsman, p. 508	triple bottom line, p. 503
corruption, p. 508	organizational ethics, p. 506	values, p. 507
ethics, p. 506	pay-to-play schemes, p. 506	values clarification, p. 507
human sustainability, p. 504	shareholder value, p. 509	values orientation, p. 508

Introduction to Corporate Social Responsibility and Sustainability

1 Describe why corporate social responsibility and sustainability are relevant for organizational behavior.

This topic summary reviews corporate social responsibility, ethics, and sustainability. A better understanding of these topics is important because many organizations, including for-profit enterprises, not-for-profits, as well as governmental organizations are demonstrating an increased awareness of the impact that their activities have on society and the environment. The summary also compares and contrasts the stakeholder versus the shareholder approach to organizations and reviews the importance of values and values orientation for organizational behavior. The summary concludes by discussing some of the challenges in making ethical decisions in organizations (see Figure 14.1).

Corporate Social Responsibility

2 Define the triple bottom line and the environmental and human approaches to sustainability.

Corporate social responsibility (CSR) refers to the expectations that society holds of an organization and how the society chooses to uphold the organization to those expectations. For example, although it is common to say that a company's primary responsibility is to make a profit, there are other expectations for companies in addition to making a profit. Companies have responsibilities to society, the environment, the community in which they operate, and to their employees.[1] The diverse responsibilities are called the **triple bottom line** which includes 1) economic viability, including profits; 2) environmental concern which focuses on minimal impact on the natural environment; and 3) concern for the health of its community, which includes fair treatment of employees.[2] Essentially, calls for greater corporate social responsibility suggest that all organizations, and corporations in particular, have a responsibility to consider the impact they have on society that goes beyond simply following the rule of law.

Sustainability

Sustainability is referred to as the set of voluntary actions that an organization takes to demonstrate its environmental and social responsibilities.[3] Organizations that have a commitment to sustainability seek to minimize their impact on the natural environment

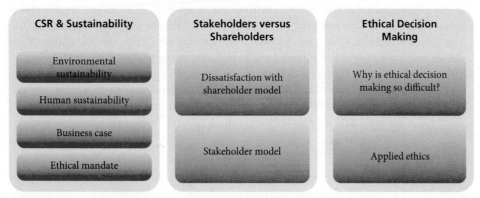

Figure 14.1 Corporate social responsibility, sustainability, and ethics

Tips Images/SuperStock

and take care to insure the long-term maintenance of the environment. Two types of sustainability are reviewed: environmental and human sustainability.

Environmental Sustainability

In 1968, ecologist Garret Hardin published an essay in *Science* magazine[4] that described a situation that has come to symbolize the current state of the environment and the way it has been managed. He described a situation when all cattle owners lived in a small village and shared a common grazing area called 'the commons.' Under these conditions, each owner had an incentive to maximize his number of cattle because he had no restriction on the amount of grass his cattle could consume. But there was a problem. If all the cattle owners took advantage of this incentive, then soon the entire pasture would be overrun with cattle and the common land would no longer be sufficient to sustain the cattle. This scenario, where common resources are shared, but the incentive is to exploit these common resources for individual gain, has become known as the 'tragedy of the commons.'

In the same way as the farmers in the commons, organizations have an incentive to take full advantage of natural resources, without consideration of the impact that consuming these resources has on the environment as a whole. Fortunately, organizations have become more aware of their impact on the environment and have begun to realize how their own actions look similar to the cattle ranchers who try to take advantage of the shared resources. Due to this growing concern about the impact that consumption has on the environment, organizations have begun to demonstrate their concern for preservation of the natural environment. Examples of organizational actions that show responsible use of resources include recycling, use of renewable resources, minimizing use of hazardous chemicals, and water and energy conservation efforts.

Human Sustainability

Another approach to sustainability focuses on a broader concern for human factors such as the need for medical insurance, working conditions, work–life balance, stress management, and equality. **Human sustainability** or (social sustainability) is the voluntary action that an organization takes to focus on the well-being of people within the organization and those who belong to the greater community in which it operates. Organizations can choose to focus on both environmental sustainability and human sustainability or choose to focus on one area over another. For example, Wal-Mart, the largest employer in the United States, has developed a focus on environmental sustainability, while at the same time, pays its employees 15 percent lower than other retailers. In addition, 46 percent of children whose parents work at Wal-Mart remained uninsured.[5]

Advocates of human sustainability are often concerned with unfairness and the concern that many organizations take advantage of workers, suppliers, and customers for the benefit of the company. For example, organizations may charge high fees for certain transactions, engage in lending that overburdens the borrower, or fail to pay health insurance to workers. Other proponents of human sustainability offer that organizations have the knowledge and resources to affect social change in their communities, and should do so. In this instance, an organization operating in a developing country might offer education programs to develop the basic skill set of their workers.

With growing globalization, organizations increasingly have access to new pools of labor in developing countries. Many companies are attracted to these labor pools. Companies can pay these workers a fraction of a worker's wage that they would pay in a developed country like the United States because developing countries do not hold organizations to the same work standards, such as allowing for breaks, time off, and clean working conditions, and because workers are less likely to object to poor working conditions. Others are not as concerned about these practices. Some critics have argued that, in fact, most workers choose to work under certain conditions and that these conditions provide better options than the worker would otherwise have.[6]

Corporate Social Responsibility and Sustainability: A Business Case

Two major arguments have been made for why organizations should adopt CSR and sustainability efforts (see Figure 14.2):

1. The business case approach emphasizes strategy, stability, and survival.
2. The ethical mandate approach emphasizes ethics, values, and integrity.

Organizational Strategy

Some people have argued that greater social responsibility can be a good organizational strategy because it aligns the organization's social efforts with its overall mission. Strategy professor Michael Porter offers a remedy to address the perception that corporate social responsibility is simply a façade. He argues that a corporation's efforts at social responsibility should be aligned with its corporate strategy,[7] for example, when a multinational corporation that does business in Africa also works to solve the AIDS problem as part of its strategy. The strategy works because the corporation has a business case: by lowering the rate of AIDS infections it expands the pool of healthy labor for the corporation and helps create economic and social stability in the geographical area in which it operates.

3 State the elements of the business case approach and the ethical mandate approach for corporate social responsibility.

Figure 14.2

Organizational Stability and Survival

Another perspective that makes a business case for social responsibility in organizations is the organizational stability and survival argument. When organizations fail to pay attention to their impact on the human and natural environment, they can find themselves at risk. There are several examples where ethical lapses have resulted in the total collapse of the organization. For example, Barings Bank in 1995, Britain's oldest commercial bank, collapsed due to the risky behavior of one of its employees. Arthur Anderson, one of the most respected and largest accounting firms in the world, went out of business due to its perceived complicity misrepresenting financial statements at Enron, one of the biggest bankruptcies of all times. Other issues related to organizational survival and stability focus on product safety, health and safety, and environmental concerns.[8]

Corporate Social Responsibility and Sustainability: An Ethical Mandate

A business case perspective is not enough to justify corporate social responsibility in organizations. Many see CSR as an ethical mandate where organizations should be concerned with ethics, values, and integrity, and not solely concerned with a business case.

Ethics

Ethics is the general study of behaviors and judgments, and **organizational ethics** are the standards for behaviors and judgments within the context of an organization. Ethics is an attempt to describe the rationale for engaging in certain behaviors and about the appropriateness of these behaviors. Discussions of ethics often begin when people find their code of prevailing rules to be unsatisfactory for explaining events.[9] Morals, in contrast to ethics, are individual or generally acceptable sets of preferences about right and wrong or good and bad. Morals are often thought of as the 'inner direction of ethics.'[10] **Morals** describe an individual's rule around what is acceptable versus unacceptable.

Discussions of ethics fall into three basic categories:

- *General ethics* seeks to describe general moral standards. Of particular interest are the origins of these standards and what they suggest about the culture that follows them.
- *Normative ethics* is an attempt to find universal principles about what is appropriate and inappropriate behavior to measure right from wrong.
- *Applied ethics* focuses on areas of interest and how to make practical judgments about moral issues where there is either great disagreement about what constitutes right and wrong or where right and wrong are not at all clear.

Concerns about ethics are not with businesses alone. Governments too can be the source of concern. One commonly used tactic seen in government is a so-called **pay-to-play scheme** where an organization pays a government official in order to gain access to influential officials or win a contract with the government. Interest in organizational ethics has increased as the result of globalization. Increased globalization offers organizations the ability to dodge undesirable regulations in one jurisdiction and set up operations in another jurisdiction where they can avoid oversight. Some nations lack the ability to impose regulations that support human rights values, environmental values, or cultural values. Companies can avoid ethical and legal implications of corruption, taxes, or questionable business practices by moving operations to countries that have laws that prove more favorable to business.[11] With the onset of globalization, codes of ethics have become more difficult to enforce, so organizations are left to define and create standards of moral behavior, judgment, and decision making as part of their organizational culture (see Table 14.1).

Values

Values describe beliefs in general and suggest a broad set of priorities around what is important. In contrast, ethics are the standards for behaviors and judgments. Ethics are about following rules, and since ethics can be tied to rules, there are formal approaches to defining ethics and ethics codes. Values focus on the choices that are made about what is important, but usually exist within a set of values, known as values systems. Within the context of an organization, codes of ethics provide rules and guidelines to help an organization maintain its values.

Values Clarification

Values clarification is the process of clarifying or becoming more aware of one's own individual values. Values clarification involves understanding and evaluating one's own values with the goal of increasing self-awareness and confronting inconsistencies or uneasiness with one's own values. The values clarification process is useful to understand person–organizational fit (the compatibility between a person and their organization) and person–job fit (the degree to which someone is compatible with a specific job). If an individual's values are in conflict with the values in the organization, or even the requirements of a job, it may not be an optimal work situation.

The Rokeach values survey lists two sets of values **terminal values**, or values that serve as goals to be achieved, and **instrumental values**, values that serve in the process of achieving those values.[12] Said another way, terminal values describe the outcomes we hope to achieve, and instrumental values describe our internal motives and how we attempt to achieve certain outcomes in life.

Table 14.1 Terminal and Instrumental Values

Terminal Values	Instrumental Values
A comfortable and prosperous life	Ambitious
An exciting, stimulating life	Broad-minded
A sense of accomplishment as a last contribution	Capable
A world at peace, free from war and conflict	Cheerful
A world of beauty, beauty of nature and the arts	Clean
Equality, brotherhood, equal opportunity	Courageous
Salvation, eternal life	Forgiving
True friendship, close companionship	Helpful

Values Orientation

Values orientation describes the systems of values that predominate within a culture and can be summarized along three primary systems: pragmatic, intellectual, and human values as described in Table 14.2.[13]

Organizational Integrity

Organizational corruption occurs when an entire system engages in unethical behavior. Whereas ethical lapses and moral transgressions are often isolated events that can be attributed to the actions of individuals, **corruption** implies the system itself has gone bad and that unethical behavior cannot be attributed solely to the actions of a subset of individuals. Like ethics, what is considered 'corrupt practices' differs across countries and cultures. Corruption often is associated with the illegitimate use of power in organizations. Another challenge with defining corruption is that practices that constitute corruption differ across cultures. Different countries not only have different practices, but also different laws that define and govern corruption.[14]

The idea of integrity has been offered as an alternative to the negative focus on corruption.[15] Organizations that demonstrate **integrity** track and respond to the ethical lapses made by employees, maintain oversight over organizational actions, build a culture of compliance, and have internal reporting systems to capture ethical breaches as they occur. Three criteria exist for an organizational culture of integrity:

1. people in the organization clearly understand what is right and what is wrong;
2. those in the organization act on what they discerned to be right, even at personal cost; and
3. people openly link actions to what they understand as right and wrong.[16]

Many organizations put into place an organizational ombudsman. An **ombudsman** is a person or group of people that employees turn to if they believe they have seen an unethical practice or a practice that is not consistent with the organization's values. The ombudsman is then responsible for following up on the concern and investigating to see

Table 14.2 The Values Categories of Western Culture

Pragmatic	Intellectual	Human
Usefulness and utility of an idea.	Rationalism and strengths of ideas in the abstract.	Specific close personal relationships such as family, friends, and acquaintances. The impact of decisions and resource allocations on close relationships.
Emphasize effort, the desire to maximize output, with a focus on measurement of output and ways to determine relative value across different perspectives.	Emphasize the intellectual value and emphasize perception of reality and a set of concepts that explain it. The intellectual values orientation relies on logical coherence, contextual relevance, meaning, and a well thought out argument.	Emphasize loyalty and consistency as they relate to personal relationships.

if there is a problem. The ombudsman may be an employee of the organization or work outside the organization.

The ombudsman allows the organization to:

- Build awareness of what constitutes ethical and unethical behavior, and understand the ethical implications of decisions
- Clarify values of the employee and the organization
- Develop structural supports, such as an ethical ombudsman who listens to whistleblowers (people who report wrongdoing in their organization), institute clear rules to follow when ethical issues arise
- Foster a culture of openness and trust
- Include strict oversight and compliance by third parties

Shareholder versus Stakeholder

4 Compare and contrast the shareholder and stakeholder perspectives.

Two arguments associated with CSR hold merit in studies of contemporary organizational behavior: the shareholder approach and the stakeholder approach. While the actual causes of ethical lapses in organizations are varied, business schools and their students have not been immune to criticism. Some of the blame for these scandals has been assigned to higher education. Critics have specifically pointed to the fact that coursework in business schools, in particular, ignore the human and environmental concerns and instead focus on profits. Because of this, students have an inadequate understanding of the need for organizations to do more than what is legally mandated. Some observers believe that the values taught by business schools are a primary driver of ethical lapses by organizations. One commonly cited problem thought to encourage unethical behavior is the predominance of the **shareholder value** perspective in education. Perhaps the most commonly cited advocate of shareholder value perspective is economist Milton Friedman. He wrote that:

> "The social responsibility of business is to increase its profits. There is one and only one social responsibility of business—to use its resources and engage in activities designed to increase its profits so long as it stays within the rules of the game, which is to say, engages in open and free competition without deception or fraud."[17]

The predominance of the shareholder approach, according to the critics, focuses on the pursuit of self-interest at the expense of other values. The predominance of shareholder value and its focus on shareholders at the expense of other values shows the influence that economic thought has had on what is taught in business schools. Critics of business education cite a study of 2,000 masters-level business students conducted by the Aspen Institute. The study concluded that the number of students who believed that maximizing shareholder value was the primary responsibility of a corporation increased from the time they entered school to the time the completed their first year. This trend may be changing, however, as more students report that they believe companies should value customers, another stakeholder group, above shareholders.[18] Courses in organizational behavior are beginning to respond to these criticisms by expanding discussions from solely focusing on the business case for CSR to identifying a more complete understanding of an organization's responsibilities. Some universities have responded by encouraging their students to sign a code of ethics or asking students to promise they will do good when they enter the workplace.

Dissatisfaction with the Shareholder Model

The need for a broader definition of an organization's role grows out of dissatisfaction with the narrow definitions of business offered by those like Milton Friedman.[19] The demand for organizations to consider CSR focus on concerns for the environment and the desire for corporations to consider their impact and their potential exploitation of developing countries, and for corporations to consider following higher ethical standards. Some have even questioned the underlying values of capitalism and suggest that capitalism itself should be transformed.

Stakeholder Model

An important alternative to Milton Friedman's shareholder approach can be found in the stakeholder approach. Many groups have a vested interest in the success of an organization and exert pressure on organizations, these are called **stakeholders** and include groups such as the community, employees, regulators, customers, suppliers, as well as shareholders.[20] As interest in alternative forms of corporations arise, many corporations are reevaluating their impact on the environment, communities in which they do business, their employees, and the larger society. One alternative approach is the **benefit corporation,** also known as a flexible purpose corporation or a B corporation, which is a legal entity that holds a corporation legally accountable for a broader set of stakeholders rather than shareholders. Although only a few states recognize the designation of a benefit corporation, there is growing interest in this form of business. Under a benefit corporation charter, company directors must consider not only profits of their businesses, but will consider the company's broader impact as well.[21] Some remain skeptical and argue that organizations' efforts of corporate social responsibility are no more than public relations stunts designed to hide corporate goals which involve an unrelenting pursuit of profits and economic-driven activities.[22]

Why Is Making Ethical Decisions So Difficult?

Ethical decisions are often difficult to make for several reasons. Ethical decision making requires unsatisfactory choices when rational-economic models are not sufficient to solve a problem. Ethical rules are often confusing and ambiguous since we live in a society with multiple competing values systems. A person is said to be in an ethical dilemma when he or she faces a situation where taking an action requires taking into account multiple ethical considerations—a complex situation with two or more competing choices. When a person faces an ethical dilemma, no choice is completely desirable.

Decision making in organizations often requires taking decisive actions in ambiguous situations. Some challenges for making ethical decisions include:

- Aligning multiple stakeholder interests
- Difficulty determining the correct answer

- Viewing what is right by one group is wrong by another
- Solving a problem that requires more than rational-economic models provide
- Confusing and ambiguous potential outcomes
- Living in a world with multiple competing values systems

Applied Ethics

Applied ethics helps people in organizations make decisions when they are faced with an ethical dilemma. Applied ethics guide people as they integrate ethics into their day-to-day behavior and try to determine what is appropriate and inappropriate behavior. Applied ethics offers five distinct 'tests' of a behavior. Each test is a question that a person should ask before or during the ethical decision-making process:

- *New York Times* **test.** Ask yourself: How would I feel if my actions were printed in the front page of the *New York Times* for everyone to read? This question helps to determine how your actions would appear to the general public. If you answer the question, "No, I would not like this on the front page of a major news paper because I would be embarrassed or ashamed," then you should not do the action.

- **The compliance test.** This compliance test asks you: Would my actions break any organizational regulations or written policies? If your actions break regulations or policies, then you should not participate in the activity.

- **The legal test.** The legal test asks a similar question to the compliance test but asks whether or not you are breaking any laws. You should ask: does my action break any laws?

- **The culture test.** The culture test asks: Are my actions consistent with the culture in which I work? What would my peers say? In many cases, your actions may not break a law, a regulation, or a specific company policy, but it may threaten the culture of the organization.

- **The values test.** The values test asks: How does this relate to my values? Will I be able to live with myself if I engage in these actions?

Applied ethics, in addition to asking people to determine how their behavior impacts the workplace, looks at the governance structure of organizations to see if certain types of governance structure compels people to make more or less ethical decisions. The role of corporate governance has been of increasing interest in light of several high-profile ethical challenges by members of boards of directors at major companies.

Conclusion

Organizations have responsibilities to society, to the environment, to the community in which they operate, and to their employees. Ethics and values help us understand people's beliefs and how these beliefs impact behavior. Ethical decision making in organizations is challenging but necessary. An organization's role in increased corporate social responsibility suggests that all organizations, and corporations in particular, have a responsibility to consider their impact on society that goes beyond simply following the law or considering stakeholders, but requires considering the impact of the decision more broadly.

OB AT WORK

MIKE MCLAUGHLIN SHOWS HOW CORPORATE SOCIAL RESPONSIBILITY IS THE BUSINESS OF EVERY EMPLOYEE

Mike McLaughlin

Mike McLaughlin spends time each day considering the health and well being of his customers, his employees, and his community. In the morning, he analyzes the impact a new product may have on the environment. In the afternoon, he speaks with a supplier who might adopt a new farming practice to boost yield, determining how this may affect his company's goal to increase the use of organic ingredients because of the positive impact on the planet. Before he heads home, he sits down with one of his employees to discuss staffing. It turns out that the company is sponsoring the employee to perform volunteer work for the community while still on the company's payroll, and short-term coverage may be needed.

With all the time he spends thinking about human, organization, and environmental sustainability, you might think he is the head of Human Resources, or perhaps even the Chief Corporate Responsibility Officer in his company, but he isn't. He is the Senior Vice President of Food Supply for Clif Bar & Company, a company that manufactures and sells energy bars and other food products.

5 Apply concepts of corporate social responsibility, ethics, and sustainability to organizations.

A key part of Mike's job is to ensure that the raw materials that go into those products come from reliable sources. To ensure that the farmers and other suppliers meet the company's high standards, his company has instituted a rigorous review process. The standards vary by product and in most cases include the use of organic materials and avoiding hormone supplements in animals to boost output, all efforts to minimally impact the environment. Of course, the products must also taste good and meet customer needs. However, perhaps the most important job he has is to ensure product safety. In the food business, he argues for a dedicated focus on food safety and on the long-term health of the business, not simply short-term profits and production. "An ethical business factors day-to-day decisions into the long-term goals of the business," he says.

Mike feels lucky to work for a company that considers social responsibility part of its mission. "I've always been attracted to companies that have a strong culture directed towards more than simply short-term profits," Mike says. He likes to say that the food company is "serious about results, without taking *ourselves* too seriously." This kind of organizational culture provides a great ethic for running an organization, especially a high-growth business. "The company is engaged in an intense effort to do good, do well, and is passionate about its brand," he notes.

Many organizations focus on one bottom line: profits. Some inspired companies may focus on the triple bottom line consisting of profits, community, and the environment. The energy bar company focuses on five bottom lines, what the company calls "The Five Aspirations". These include an aspiration for business, for the brand, for its people, for the planet, and for the community. In fact, each of these five aspirations are measured and factored in when bonus time comes around. "The important thing from a

(continued)

management or leadership perspective," says Mike, "is to confront all five aspirations in every decision I make, but to realize that all aspirations may not necessarily be achieved equally in every decision."

This may seem like a surprising set of goals for a company whose intention is to make money. The company represents a small but growing trend among businesses that see themselves as playing a larger role in society and the environment. The mission moves beyond the simple goal of making profits. Mike's employer has joined with other companies in the region that hold similar values. The collaboration focuses the efforts of more than 20 companies on something of importance that might include cleaning up litter on the ocean coasts or building affordable housing. These companies, and the mindsets of their employees, are representative of a new mindset among businesses that adopt practices of corporate social responsibility.

Whether identifying new suppliers of protein, ensuring the safety of his products, supporting the community through volunteer activities performed on company time, or further considering the impact on the planet, Mike McLaughlin represents a new kind of company leader whose concern goes beyond profits to building a better world.

Source: Personal interview.

SPOTLIGHT ON RESEARCH
Does Goal Setting Lead to Unethical Behavior?

Can people in organizations be so motivated to achieve a goal that the goal encourages them to engage in unethical behavior? Recent research reveals that, under certain circumstances, goals can motivate unethical behavior. A group of researchers noticed a trend in organizations—some organizations were so focused on achieving short-term goals that they set policies that motivated unethical behavior. For example, one case found that Sears's auto repair shops routinely overcharged their customers, conducted unnecessary work, and often delivered less than acceptable work. The motivating force: a $147 per-hour sales goal. It seemed that sales goals overshadowed other factors like customer service, quality, and honesty. But were goals really to blame for this nationwide problem? To find out, the researchers created an experiment in a controlled environment to find out how goals and incentives might motive unethical behavior.

The researchers relied on an anagram task to first determine what was an appropriate performance goal. In the anagram task, study participants were paid to take seven letters and create as many words as they possibly could with the letters they were given. For example, if given the letters a, t, c, m, e, r, o, the participants in the study might create words such as "to, at, me, ..."

For the study, the participants were divided into three groups. Researchers provided each of the groups with different instructions. Group 1 was told simply to 'do your best'. For Group 2, researchers set the goal for each participant to make nine words from the list of 7 letters. Group 3 was given the same goal as Group 2, make nine words, but was

(continued)

given $2 each time they achieved the goal. Each group went through several rounds of anagram tasks. Group 1 and 2 were each paid $10. Group 3 was provided an envelope of $1 bills and told to take out $2 for each word that was done correctly.

At the end of the experiment, each participant recorded his or her own success rate on the task, essentially tallying the number of correct words they produced for each anagram. This is where the researchers identified the unethical behavior, because in some cases, there was a great discrepancy between what the participants reported as their score and what they actually scored. The results appear to be influenced by the type of goal and the rewards.

Group 1, told to "do your best," took their $10 with no goal—they were simply paid to do the work. Group 2, directed to meet the goal of nine words per task, was not given money. Group 3, the group that was instructed to take out $2 for each word that met the goal, returning the remaining money in an envelope.

As confirmed by prior research, the participants instructed to 'do your best' scored the lowest, the goal setting group with no incentive scored second, and the goal setting with an incentive scored the highest on actual production. However, the researchers found no statistical difference between the actual performances among these three groups. For statistical purposes, each group produced about the same number of words. In terms of what members from each group reported, however, there were significant differences from actual production. The table below summarizes the three groups. As can be seen, the group instructed to 'do your best' overstated actual production by about 10 percent, the group with a goal, but no incentive, overstated by about 22 percent, and the group with a goal and a monetary incentive overstated actual production by 30 percent. Research supported the notion that goals and incentives increase unethical behavior, as demonstrated by over-reporting of production. Interestingly, it wasn't only the group that had a financial incentive to misrepresent their production (e.g., Group 3) even the group with no financial incentive, but who had been instructed to meet a high goal (e.g., Group 2), misrepresented their production.

Group	Instructions	Reward	"cheating index" How much the group, on average, overstated actual productivity	Average number of words per round
1	"do your best"	$10 simply for doing the task	10.5%	5.46
2	"set goal of creating nine words per round"	$10 simply for doing the task	22.7%	5.83
3	"set goal of creating nine words per round"	$2 per word	30.2%	6.17

The study revealed something else: People most likely to misrepresent their production were those who missed the mark by just a little. In other words, the closer the person was to accomplishing the goal without reaching it, the more likely they were to misrepresent their production. The study suggests that falling just short of your goal actually increases unethical behavior.

The study has several implications for managers. It suggests that some managerial practices, like goal setting, can actually be harmful to the organization and to fostering an environment of ethical behavior. Also, managers need to consider not just how to motivate employees, but should consider exactly what they hope the motivation will accomplish. This research reveals that managers need to consider more fully the unintended consequences of goal setting and other managerial motivation techniques.

Questions for Discussion

1. What are some problems with goals? Do the benefits of goals offset the problems with goals? Why do you think this?

2. How does this research match your own experience in the workplace?

*Based on the articles: Ordóñez, L.D., Schweitzer, M.E., Galinsky, A.D., & Bazerman, M.H. (2009). Goals Gone Wild: The Systematic Side Effects of Overprescribing Goal Setting, *Academy of Management Perspectives*, 23(1), 6–16; Schweitzer, M., Ordóñez, L. D., & Douma, B. (2004). The Dark Side of Goal Setting: The Role of Goals in Motivating Unethical Behavior. *The Academy of Management Journal, 47*, 422–432.

Pairing with this Topic Summary

Suggested Expert Contributions

The Business of Making a Better World—Philip H. Mirvis (Private Consultant) and Bradley Googins (Boston College)

Ethics—Gary R. Weaver (University of Delaware)

The Psychology of Fairness at Work—Robert Folger (University of Central Florida), Stephen Gilliland (University of Arizona), and David Bowen (Thunderbird School of Global Management)

Suggested Cases

Case 2: "We Are Global or We Are Nothing": Conflict and Cover-Up at ColequarterMaine

Case 3: EMERGENCY! We Need a Better Compensation System

Case 7: Perceptions of Leaders Following Public Failures: A Tale of Two Coaches

Case 8: Conflict in Santa's Workshop: Learning to Be a Team Player at ToyKing

Suggested Exercises

Exercise 2: Creating My Brand

Exercise 23: What's Your University's Culture?

Exercise 27: Develop Your Professional Code

Exercise 30: You Can't Handle the Truth

Exercise 31: The Ethics of the Climb

Exercise 33: Could I Be a Whistleblower?

Exercise 34: Sustainability Practices at Work

Endnotes

1. Carroll, A. B. (1979). A three-dimensional conceptual model of corporate social performance. *Academy of Management Review, 4(4)*: 497–505. p. 500. See also Ireland, P. (2009). Corporate social responsibility. In P. Cane & J. Conaghan (Eds.). *The New Oxford Companion to Law*. Oxford: Oxford University Press; and Campbell, J. L. (2007). An institutional theory of corporate social responsibility." *Academy of Management Review, 32*(3): 946–967.

2. Elkington, J. (1997). *Cannibals with forks: the Triple Bottom line of 21st century business*. Capstone. See also http://www.johnelkington.com/TBL-elkington-chapter.pdf.

3. Marrewijk, M. V. (2003). Concepts and Definitions of CSR and Corporate Sustainability: Between Agency and Communion. *Journal of Business Ethics, 44* (2/3):95–105; and Starik, M., Rands, G., Marcus, A., & Clark, T. (2010). Special issue on sustainability in management education. *Academy of Management Learning and Education,* 9(3): 377–383.

4. Hardin, G. (1968). "The tragedy of the commons. *Science Magazine, 162,* 1243–1248.

5. Pfeffer, J. (2010). Building sustainable organizations: The human factor. *Academy of Management Perspectives,* 24(1) 34–45.

6. Zwolinski. M. (2007). Sweatshops, choice, and exploitation. *Business Ethics Quarterly, 17,* (4): 689–727; and Snyder, J. (2010). Exploitation and sweatshop labor: Perspectives and Issues. *Business Ethics Quarterly, 20*(2): 187–213.

7. Porter, M. E. & Kramer, M. R. (2006). Strategy and society: The link between competitive advantage and corporate social responsibility. *Harvard Business Review, 84(12): 78–92.*

8. See for examples: Hartley, R. F. (2005). *Business ethics: Mistakes and successes.* (1st Ed). New York: John Wiley, & Sons; and Mitroff, I. I. (2004). *Crisis leadership: Planning for the unthinkable.* New York: John Wiley, & Sons.

9. Frankena, W. K. (1973). *Ethics* (2nd Ed.). 13. Prentice Hall, Pearson. Available at www.ditext.com/frankena/ethics.html.

10. Frankena, K. (1973).

11. Scherer, A. G., Palazzo, G., & Matten, D. (2009). Introduction to the special issue: Globalization as a challenge or business responsibility. *Business Ethics Quarterly, 19*(3): 327–347.

12. Rokeach, M. (1973). *The nature of human values.* New York: Free Press.

13. Boyatzis, R., & McKee, A. (2005). *Resonate leadership.* Cambridge, MA: Harvard Business Review Press.

14. For more on difference in definitions of corruption across cultures see: Donaldson, T. (1996). Values in tensions: Ethics away from home. *Harvard Business Review, 74*(5):48–62; Davis J. H., & Ruhe, J. A. (2003). Perceptions of country corruption: Antecedents and outcomes. *Journal of Business Ethics, 43*(4): 275–288.

15. Kayes, C. D., and Nielsen, T. M., and Stirling, D. (2007). Building organizational integrity. *Business Horizons, 50(1):* 61–70; Palanski, M. E. , & Yammarino, F. J. (2007). Integrity and Leadership: Clearing the Conceptual Confusion, *European Management Journal,* 25(3):171–184.

16. Carter, S. L. (1996). *Integrity.* New York: Harper Perennial.

17. Friedman, M. (1993). *Why government is the problem.* Essays in public policy, 39. Stanford, CA: Hoover Institution on War Revolution and Peace, Stanford University.

18. Browing, L. (2003). Ethics lacking in business school curriculum study, students say in survey, *New York Times,* (May 20). See also Center for Business Education (2008). *The Aspen Institute,* www.apsencbe.org. In particular, see document: *A closer look at business education: MBA student attitudes.* (May).

19. Freeman, E. R. (1984). *Strategic Management: A stakeholder approach*. Boston: Pitman.

20. Mitchell, R. K., Agle, B. R., & Wood, D. J. (1997). Toward a theory of stakeholder identification and salience: Defining the principles of who and what really counts. *Academy of Management Review, 22*, 853–886. See also Freeman, E. R., Harrison, J. S., & Wicks, A. C. (2007). *Managing for stakeholders*. New Haven, CT: Yale University Press.

21. The story of Patagonia and its quest for a new corporate status can bee seen at http://www.bloomberg.com/news/2012-01-04/patagonia-road-tests-new-sustainability-legal-status.htmlr. For more on the B-corporations see http://www.bcorporation.net/why.

22. Banerjee, B. S. (2007). *Corporate Social Responsibility: The good, the bad, and the ugly*. Northhampton, MA: Edward Elgar. See also David Henderson, (2001). *Misguided Virtue: False Notions of Corporate Social Responsibility*. London: Institute of Economic Affairs.

The Business of Making a Better World

Philip H. Mirvis

Private Consultant

Bradley Googins

Boston College

General Electric (GE) has made big moves in "green technology" with its ecomagination campaign. Under CEO Jeffrey Immelt, GE is being transformed from the Jack Welch-era finance-based firm back into the innovation-driven company envisioned by its founder, Thomas A. Edison. GE's repurposing has been most visible the past eight years in its doubling of research and development (R&D) spending on environmentally friendly technologies, the hiring of thousands of employees with PhDs, new research projects in the fields of nanotechnology, hydrogen power, photo batteries and such, plus new laboratories in Munich, Shanghai, and Bangalore.

In late 2010, Unilever unveiled its Sustainable Living Plan that positions the company aim to improve the health of 1 billion people, to buy 100 percent of its agricultural raw materials from sustainable sources, and to reduce the environmental impact of everything it sells by one-half, while doubling its revenues. To achieve its aim, the company will have to reach out to its consumers and activate them on sustainability. For instance, to reduce energy by half associated with its soaps, consumers would have to cut their shower time by one minute. If twenty million consumers did so, the emissions reduced would be the equivalent of taking 110,000 cars off the road! Accordingly, Unilever has announced a campaign in the United States for "Turn off the tap", a consumer behavior awareness campaign to encourage people to save water when they shampoo by turning off running water.

> Since 2008, IBM has sent over 1,000 employees on 80 teams to 20 countries on one-month service learning assignments through its Corporate Service Corps. In Tanzania, IBM teams collaborated with KickStart, a nonprofit organization exploring new technologies to fight poverty in Africa by developing modular e-training courses in marketing, sales, and supply chain management for local entrepreneurs. What are IBM's motivations? To bring to life its corporate commitment to "Innovation that Matters—for Our Company and the World."

Over 75 percent of executives worldwide believe that sustainability is important to the financial success of their companies, but, as of 2010, only around 30 to 40 percent are taking serious steps to embed it into their business practices.[1] Why the significant gap? One reason is that many companies do not have a clear, or agreed-upon, view on sustainability. Some define it narrowly with regard to environmental performance—their greenhouse gas emissions, energy use, waste management, and the like. Interestingly, those that take it seriously, typically have a more expansive and integrative perspective that links environmental, societal, and governance responsibilities together into an overall sustainability or corporate social responsibility (CSR) agenda.

Another reason for the gap is that many companies simply don't make a strong commitment to sustainability. As a result, competing priorities intervene; short-term profit pressures supersede good intentions; and sustainability efforts slow down, are marginalized, or are limited to a few "quick wins" with little more to follow. As one executive explained it, "We have lots of initiatives, programs, and such, but sustainability has not been 'interiorized' in our business." At General Electric, Unilever, and IBM, by contrast, a commitment to sustainability beats at the heart of its business and strategy. How can you tell? It is embedded in these companies' vision, mission, and values, and is brought to life in their company cultures and business models.[2]

Research on Company Mission, Vision, Values

Perhaps you have heard about the total quality movement(TQM), where U.S. manufacturers made quality "job #1" in the face of Japanese competition. Or maybe you've read *In Search of Excellence* or *The Fifth Discipline*.[3] If so, the idea that companies should pay attention to vision, mission, and values may seem "old hat" or a "been there, done that" exercise, yet we have found that many of the sustainability leaders (the companies described here, plus Novo Nordisk, Néstle, Interface Carpets, Dow Chemical, Teléfonica, and others) have repurposed themselves by attending to these foundational matters. Take a moment to consider each of these components:

A *vision* articulates a desired future for a company. On paper, of course, this often reduces to sloganeering: "Be the Industry Leader", "#1 or #2 in Our Markets", "Simply the Best", and so on. But in its detailing, a vision provides an intellectual framework for company strategy—it defines a strategic direction and presents a conceptual map of how a company moves from its current reality to a desired future state. A vision is also a motivational driver. Management experts Jim Collins and Jerry Porras, for instance, document how top companies use a BHAG—"big hairy audacious goal"—to make their vision tangible and emotionally energizing.[4]

Mission has to do with the purpose of a company. When Mirvis began working with Ben & Jerry's (B&J's) in the mid-1980s, the company's guiding framework was to "have fun" (Jerry) and "give back to the community" (Ben). While appealing, this frame provided scant guidance of how to respond to quality problems and financial pressures. Nor did it forestall conflicts over the company's image and positioning in select product and social investments ("Peace Pops"). Through a series of retreats, first with members of the Board, then management, all B&J leaders spoke to their personal views of what the company was all about. Employees attended all-staff meetings to provide insight. There was within B&J's a sharp divide over the ice cream maker's communal versus commercial emphasis. One influential Board member drafted a "three-part" statement that detailed the firm's economic, social, and quality missions—all to be considered equally under the rubric of "linked prosperity." This was debated by Board members and managers and eventually adopted as the company's mission. Sustainability thought leader John Elkington, who later conducted B&J's first social audit in 1992, saw this as anticipating the "Triple Bottom Line."

Finally, research points to individual values as a driving force behind personal responsibility; is the same true for corporate values and responsibility? A Booz Allen Hamilton/Aspen Institute survey found that 89 percent of companies surveyed globally possess written values statements.[5] Note, however, that Enron and Lehman Brothers had salutary value statements and engaged in the finagling and fraud that led to financial crises bookending this past decade. Aren't value statements simply a window dressing? Much depends on how the values are developed and lived through a firm. In *SuperCorps*, Rosabeth Moss Kanter finds, "Vanguard companies go beyond the lists of values posted on walls and websites by using their codified set of values and principles as a strategic guidance system."[6]

Pulling these ideas together, professor Peter Senge combines vision, mission, and values into a set of "governing ideas" for a business; we adapt them for companies as follows:

1. Vision is the 'What'—the picture of the future we seek to create.
2. Mission is the 'Why'—the organization's answer to why we exist (purpose).
3. Values are the 'How'—how we act to achieve our vision.

Can these governing ideas extend to sustainability and serve to position, direct, and guide a firm forward along this path? Three hands-on case studies illustrate their potential to do so.

GE's Ecomagination Vision

With ecomagination, GE was making a commitment to "develop solutions for the world's toughest challenges." Immelt explains, "The last twenty five years were about the development of information technology. My belief is that the next twenty five years are going to be about technology and the economics of scarcity. How you get more healthcare into people's hands. How you get more energy into the system." Today, GE is a leader in multiple partnerships to reduce greenhouse gas emissions and improve energy efficiency; they have taken a stand, to the dismay of some of its biggest customers, in favor of carbon trading.

Before launching its green strategy, GE invited its big customers to two-day "dreaming sessions" where they envisioned life in 2015 and what they would want from GE. The combination of high energy prices and expected limits on greenhouse gas emissions, plus booming demand from Asian economies and consumer preferences for cleaner technology, translated into a spectacular business opportunity for GE. GE then expanded its stakeholder engagements from 2006 through 2009 in major cities around the globe and added to its roster "material" issues of concern to society and the business.

It also established an Ecomagination Advisory Council, of 6 to 8 members, from non-governmental organizations (NGOs), think tanks, and academe (e.g., Pew Center on Global Climate Change, Climate Change Capital, World Resources Institute, William McDonough & Partners, MIT, and others). This council provides updates on climate change and environmental conditions and offers input on industry trends, technology developments, and innovative practices. It also reviews GE's environmental performance.

Unilever's Vitality Mission

Unilever's historic commitment to society traces to its founder, William Hesketh Lever, who, in the late 1800s, tackled the challenge posed by workers who had to wash their hands and bodies with products made from acidic lye that burned their skins. His company introduced a safe and affordable soap, later called Lifebuoy. He also created a company village offering housing to workers at reasonable rents and introduced the then-unheard-of eight-hour workday, sickness benefits, holiday pay, and pensions for both male and female employees. The challenge, as another executive put it, was "to take Lever's heritage and move it into the new world."

Unilever had developed a new corporate brand identity that would integrate its home-and-personal-care and food-and-beverage businesses beneath a corporate umbrella. The new corporate mission would be: "To add vitality to life by meeting everyday needs for nutrition, hygiene, and personal care brands that help people feel good, look good, and get more out of life." In recognition of Unilever's historic commitment to and contemporary strengths in its relationships to society, it was proposed that the company reinvent its corporate social responsibility or CSR thrust through its new vitality mission—in messaging and deeds. In a contentious move, the decision was made to put Unilever's new logo on product packaging and let consumers know the corporation behind the brands they selected in the marketplace.

One of the first orders of business was to be more proactive on issues around nutrition. The company had previously introduced a margarine aimed at reducing cholesterol. But with its Vitality mission, nearly twenty thousand recipes were put through a nutrition profile model and subsequently reformulated to reduce trans fat, saturated fats, sugar, and salts—amounting to over thirty thousand tons worth in three years, according to the latest company reports. In addition, Unilever began to put a "Healthy Choices" logo on products to help consumers identify foods that have limited amounts of these ingredients.

One of the most visible of the Unilever's vitality initiatives: the Dove soap "inner beauty" campaign. Company research found that just 12 percent of women are very satisfied with their physical attractiveness; 68 percent strongly agree that the media sets an unrealistic standard of beauty; and 75 percent wish the media did a better job of portraying the diversity of women's physical attractiveness, including size and shape, across all ages. Dove's public message about inner beauty has been conveyed through advertisements showing "real women have curves" and a film that shows how fashion model images are distorted to conform to an idealized but unattainable type. It is carried to schools around the world in a complementary program promoting young women's self-esteem.

IBM: A Matter of Values or 'DNA'

This thrust began with an "online jam" that had tens of thousands of IBMers participate in brainstorming, debate, and follow-up planning on the direction of the company. Two years later, the company held a "values jam" that consisted of seventy-two hours of brainstorming that established three IBM core values: dedication to every client's success; innovation that matters—for the company and the world; and trust and personal responsibility in all relationships. Since then, the company has created a site called ThinkPlace for ongoing e-conversations about its culture and business.

In the 1990s, IBM launched a series of initiatives under its CSR mantle to reinvent education. Building on its experience with applying innovative technology to education, IBM next expanded its attention to other societal challenges like healthcare, transportation, energy use, urban life, and the environment. Then, an insight was born: IBM's social investments could be integrated into its commercial strategy. Explaining this, CEO Sam Palmisano pointed out that, in his eyes, CSR was not something unique or special, or just to apply to "crown jewels" like education; on the contrary, he said: "It's who we are; it's how we do business; it's part of our values; it's in our cultural DNA." In the past several

Company	Mission, Vision, Values	CSR/Sustainability Actions	Strategic Purpose
General Electric	Ecomagination: Solutions for the World's Toughest Challenges	Business models with energy-saving products	Central to future growth strategy
Unilever	Vitality Mission: healthy, eco-friendly products to feel good, look good, and get more out of life	Better and sustainably sourced products; relevant social campaigns	Repositions company and brands in the consumer marketplace
IBM	Innovation that matters: for our company and the world	Smarter Planet, Smarter Cities, Smart Grid	Builds on open sourcing and IBM's global integration

Figure 1   Companies that Want to Make a Better World

years, IBM has melded its innovative technologies like grid computing, social networking, and virtual worlds, and applied them to creating a "smarter planet."

One of IBMs new initiatives, the Corporate Service Corps melds the idealism and spirit of the U.S. Peace Corps with the pragmatism and global business capability of the IT giant. It sends IBM's top talent on service learning assignments involving three months of pre-work, one month abroad, working with nonprofits, government agencies, or small businesses, and then two months in post-service where they harvest insights for themselves and their organization. It is, at once, a leadership development program, a demonstration of IBM's corporate service ethic, and a chance to open new markets and build relationships around the world. Kevin Thompson, who designed IBMs program, tells of how relationships with a host government, developed over the course of a service project, led to a million dollar business contract.

Implications for Next Generation Leaders

1. **Find a job at a mission-driven company.** Increasing numbers of young people in the United States (and worldwide) aspire for "something more" from a job. Surveys by Cone Inc. find that three out of four of the Millennial Generation (born 1978–1998) want to work for a company that "cares about how it impacts and contributes to society." Cone also finds that among those already in the workforce, nearly seven out of ten say that they are aware of their employer's commitment to social and environmental causes and 65 percent say that their employer's actions make them feel loyal to their company.[7] It is important to scour the corporate website, read a company's social and annual report, research the ratings on the Dow Jones Sustainability Index, and ask questions during interviews.

   Still, it behooves you to do your homework about a potential employer's commitment to sustainability—is it in their vision, mission, and values and, importantly, do they practice what they preach? PepsiCo, for instance, says it is all about "profits with purpose." This past year, Pepsi announced that instead of spending $20 million on Super Bowl ads, it would donate those funds to people who had "refreshing ideas to change the world." Applicants could make their pitch on its "refresh everything" website and the public could vote on their ideas. There is no doubt that the many projects proposed by Pepsi supplicants are worthy causes and reaching out to customers is surely relevant to the business. If you ask consumers which issues matter to them about Pepsi (or Coke), items like "junk food," "obesity," "advertising in schools," and "water use" are discussed. So, it raises the question, why doesn't Pepsi solicit and fund ideas from science students on taking the junk out of food?

Getting hired after graduating in a CSR or sustainability function can be difficult; we suggest starting in a marketing job or entry-level business position to learn the operations and figure out where you, and your employer, can make a difference in the workplace.

2. **Do something socially responsible at work—and at school!** On the operational front, more employees today are engaged in sustainable supply chain management, cause-related marketing, and green business initiatives—in effect, doing social responsibility on the job. A recent survey of employers by the Society for Human Resource Management found that 81 percent of organizations reported new green duties have been added to existing positions at their organization. Nearly one quarter (23 percent) reported creating completely new green positions or adding green duties within newly created jobs.[8]

This means that there are a growing number of opportunities to make a difference on the job. If there are not obvious opportunities, take the initiative to start a recycling program, get people to bike to work, use mass transit or carpool, look for ways to reduce energy or water use, and so on. In addition, get involved in corporate volunteer programs to mentor schoolchildren; care for the homeless, elderly, or disadvantaged; participate in disaster relief; build community playgrounds; or join Habitat for Humanity, and so on. Be aware of more skill-based engagement efforts wherein employees use their technical and commercial know-how to address social concerns—like IBM's global effort or the GAP's local community support programs.

One place to practice being a good corporate citizen is on campus. Service learning projects, sustainability initiatives, and volunteering are good for the soul—and also look good on a resumè.

3. **Smarten up about sustainability and CSR.** The *Princeton Review* provides green ratings for 600 colleges after receiving feedback that 63 percent of college applicants surveyed said they would value having information about a college's commitment to the environment and that such data could affect their choice to apply or attend a school. The Aspen Institute offers a *Guide to Socially Responsible MBA Programs*, which evaluates and ranks 130 MBA programs based on their coverage of CSR and sustainability in coursework and extra-curricular activities, as well as faculty research. GreenReportCard.org publishes detailed information on the green and not-so-green aspects of 300 colleges and universities; only 15 received the highest grade, an A-minus, in the last rating. Check out these resources if you're heading toward an MBA and consider the criteria in rating your own school today.

Meanwhile, take courses on sustainability and CSR, learn about social entrepreneurship, and get involved in Net Impact—whose members are current and emerging leaders in CSR and environmental sustainability with chapters on over 200 undergraduate campuses. No chapter at your school? Start one!

Endnotes

1. McKinsey & Co. (2010). *How companies manage sustainability.* May. Accessed at www.Mckinsey.com.

2. For more on these companies and others, see Googins, B, Mirvis, P. H. & Rochlin, S. (2007). *Beyond 'good company': Next generation corporate citizenship.* New York: Palgrave; also Mirvis, P. H., Googins, B., & Kinnicutt, S. (2010). Vision, mission, values: Guideposts to sustainability. *Organization Dynamics, 39,* 316–324.

3. Peters, T. J. & R. H. Waterman, Jr. (1992). *In Search of Excellence.* New York: Harper & Row, 1982; Senge, P. M. (1990). *The Fifth Discipline: The Art and Practice of the Learning Organization.* New York: Doubleday/Currency.

4. Collins, J. & Porras, J. (1994). *Built to Last—Successful Habits of Visionary Companies.* New York: Harper Business Essentials.

5. Van Lee, R., Fabish, L. & McGaw, N. (2005). *Deriving Value from Corporate Values.* Booz Allen Hamilton/Aspen Institute.

6. Kanter, R. M. (2009). *SuperCorp. How Vanguard Companies Create Innovation, Profits, Growth, and Social Good.* New York: Crown Business.

7. Cone, LLC. (2009). *Past. present. future. The 25th anniversary of cause marketing.* Boston, MA., at www.coneinc.com.

8. *Advancing Sustainability: HR's Role.* (2011). A Research Report by the Society for Human Resource Management, BSR and Aurosoorya at www.shrm.org

Ethics

Gary R. Weaver
University of Delaware

On a visit to a financial services company, I observed a meeting between the company's top legal officer and approximately 30 relatively new managers. While waving a copy of the company's conflict-of-interest policy, the legal officer asked the managers if they were familiar with the policy. The company attorney was more than a little surprised when not a single manager indicated familiarity with this important company policy, mostly because every manager had signed his or her name to the policy during new-hire paperwork. This particular ethics policy was important enough to be singled out for signature during new employee orientation, yet in practice it made little, if any, impact on otherwise intelligent, hardworking managers.

This situation isn't too surprising: Enron, WorldCom, AIG, and other recent exemplars of questionable company business practices had codes of ethics or similar policies in place. Obviously some process in the company workflow did not work well in the way organizational ethical practices were conveyed. Perhaps in some cases, management never intended ethics policies to have a real meaning; hopefully, the case of the well-meaning legal officer we observed is more typical: he really expected the company's ethics policies to have an impact. So what supports or undermines company efforts to encourage good business behavior? And why does this matter?

The Case for Organizational Ethics

An early-career manager noted that his newfound knowledge of his organization's poor ethics "...made me a lot tougher. Every time I meet someone new in the company—a new manager or a co-worker—I'm careful....I don't trust people as much as I used to...."[i] It is difficult to manage in an environment of distrust, for example, an executive once informed me that because of employee distrust generated by prior management's unethical behavior, problems would appear in the local newspaper before he would hear about them internally. At breakfast, he checked the morning paper to see what he'd have to deal with at work that day. But an ethically well-managed organization yields positive employee outcomes: better awareness of potential ethical pitfalls, more willingness to seek advice about possible ethical problems, more willingness to report ethical problems, more commitment to the organization, and less unethical behavior.[ii] These are important outcomes. For example, if there's a problem in your business, you want your employees to report it to you early so you can address it and not let the problem fester until it becomes so intolerable that employees report (i.e., "blow the whistle") on a much bigger problem to someone outside the organization.

---

[i]Treviño, L. K. & Weaver, G. R. (2003). *Managing Ethics in Business Organizations: Social Scientific Perspectives.* Stanford, CA: Stanford University Press.

Outcomes like employee commitment, in turn, are important elements of continued competitive advantage for a company, as they are the kinds of intangible assets that can be hard for competing organizations to reproduce.[1] There are other benefits too: the legal system tends to react more gently to organizations caught up in legal problems if those organizations can demonstrate that they made good faith efforts to foster ethical and legal behavior. There can be reputational benefits also: as one bank executive told me, the bank's former chairman never forgot which potential clients the bank should avoid because of problems with their integrity. And in a dynamic business environment, requiring rapid changes in strategies and practices, a strong ethical compass can help keep people focused in a way that prevents dangerously risky decisions. A vice president, for example, spoke proudly to me of his company's dynamic entrepreneurial spirit, but in the next breath noted that this dynamism can produce the proverbial loose cannon. A strong ethical culture can keep the cannons pointed in the right direction.

Yet acting ethically simply for strategic reasons might undermine the goal such action seeks to achieve.[2] If employees, customers, or other interested parties suspect that you're just acting ethically because doing so brings about benefits, the risk is that they will start wondering whether you will continue to act ethically even when there's no obvious benefit from doing so (e.g., when you think you won't be caught). And if that perception spreads, efforts to foster good ethics in an organization can lose the trust they're intended to foster. For example, I've heard more than one employee cynically dismiss management's talk about ethics as purely self-serving, and not to be trusted. When that's what employees think, potentially positive outcomes from efforts to foster ethics are lost.[3] Purely strategic ethics, in short, is high-risk, limited ethics; real management commitment to ethics matters.[4]

Key Influences on Organizational Ethics: Fairness, Integration, and Identity

Many organizations invest substantial resources into programs for fostering ethical employee behavior. These initiatives typically include codes of ethics plus one or more training programs, communication efforts (e.g., ethics newsletters), monitoring or auditing processes (e.g., regular surveys of employee attitudes or knowledge, or audits aimed at catching ethical failures), staff dedicated to handling ethics matters, and performance evaluation in ways relevant to ethics. But as the opening example indicates, such programs and policies might not always connect with employees in ways that actually influence behavior. My own research, and that of others, has probed some of the reasons for this failure, and how to avoid it. Three themes stand out: fairness, integration, and identity.

Fairness Toward Employees

Research in organizational behavior highlights the importance of employees' fairness perceptions in influencing behavioral outcomes.[5] Employees use their perception of fair (or unfair) treatment by an employer as a rough-and-ready guideline, or heuristic, for determining whether it is safe for them to invest themselves in their organizations—by trusting management, by committing themselves to their jobs, and by being good organizational citizens.

Fairness comes in multiple forms: outcome (i.e., distributive) fairness (Did I receive what I deserve?); process (i.e., procedural) fairness (Are procedures and policies applied impartially and consistently?); and interpersonal (i.e., interactional) fairness (Am I treated respectfully?). When employees perceive fairness, they are more willing to support, trust, and give themselves energetically to their organizations. They also are more willing to trust and commit to their organization's ethics policies and practices, resulting in less unethical conduct and also increased behavior supportive of good organizational ethics.[6] This holds not only for employees' perceptions of their organization's overall fairness, but also for the fairness inherent in the workings of organizational ethics policies. So, for example, if a company follows through on its ethics policies—applying policies clearly and consistently—employees will see that ethics effort as embodying procedural fairness (consistently applied policies) and distributive fairness (people receive what they deserve), and more readily will support the organization's ethics goals.

So managers need to realize that the overall climate of fairness (or unfairness) in an organization influences the reception given to ethics initiatives and policies. A climate of unfairness can undermine employees' reception of well-intentioned ethics efforts. More generally, organizational context matters in determining whether efforts to foster good behavior will have significant impacts within an organization, and issues seemingly far removed from an ethics policy can support or undermine that policy. What management might view as a matter unrelated to organizational ethics—e.g., workplace physical characteristics (comfort level), or an outrageously expensive executive dinner—can be important matters of fairness in the eyes of employees, and in turn can affect employees' views of management's talk about, and policies toward, ethics.

Integrated Ethics Policies

Organizational context also matters in making sure that ethics initiatives are connected to the core activities of an organization in meaningful ways. Most of us probably have witnessed some organizational policy or practice that had no impact on the rest of an organization—maybe training sessions that employees mindlessly endured and quickly forgot, or a customer survey the results of which were simply "filed" and forgotten, or a task force whose output was ignored. Ethics policies and programs, no matter how well intentioned, are not immune to this kind of disconnection.

Sometimes, of course, policies are implemented simply as "window dressing"—something to make the organization look good, but only as an external veneer that changes nothing internally. But many times disconnected policies unintentionally develop because their implementers didn't consider how the policies would be influenced by other organizational practices which form the context within which particular policies must function. Many factors besides formal policies can influence employees' ethical behavior—for example, pressures for performance at all costs, behavioral modeling by co-workers ("peer pressure"), and taken-for-granted ways of thinking and seeing (such that problematic assumptions are never challenged, and important perspectives are never noticed).

Ethics outcomes are better when official ethics initiatives are supported by multiple elements of organizational life, so that the organization can be said to have an ethical infrastructure.[7] Organizational cultural norms, leader behaviors, and the way people talk about decisions (i.e., in ways open to or closed to ethical concerns being raised) can help make good ethics a routine part of organizational life. But other contextual factors can undermine ethics. For example, organizations in which unquestioning obedience to authority is expected of employees have higher risks of ethical problems.[8] In short, besides thinking about how fairness concerns will frame the way employees respond to organizational ethical goals, managers also need to consider how other organizational practices and policies might support or undermine those ethical ideals.

Moral Identity in Organizations

Managers need to think about how the organizational setting encourages or discourages employees in developing a strong moral identity, a sense of being someone with a clear, "second nature" commitment to doing what is right. A moral identity is one in which a person's sense of self includes a set of moral traits (such as honesty) as a stable, core element, and in which a person's actions regularly give evidence of those moral traits.[9] Moral identities have clear connections to ethical behaviors, and a strong moral identity provides a core motivation for acting ethically.

Organizational settings provide a variety of influences that can develop or undermine employees' moral identity. Identities are shaped in interaction with other people; the way people interact with you defines the roles they expect you to fulfill, and those roles might or might not include acting ethically. With the wrong kinds of workplace interactions, people can get the sense that their moral identity is irrelevant at work, and they should leave it at home and become a different person, ethically speaking, in the workplace. Behavior patterns also tend to shape and reinforce our sense of who we are, and so moral identities also are strengthened by regular exercise and weakened by lack of opportunity for exercise.

Leading for Ethics

Whether they're at the top of large organizations, or heading small departments or work groups, organizational leaders play crucial roles in developing organizational ethics.[10] Leader commitment is a key factor in fostering an integrated approach to ethics.[11] Yet sometimes leaders are out of touch with ethical realities[12] not realizing, for example, how practices they don't associate with ethics nevertheless look unfair to many employees. Ethically effective leaders instead are good listeners, trustworthy, and interested in employee well-being. They're concerned that ethical standards are upheld, with appropriate rewards and discipline. They set personal examples of ethical behavior, and talk regularly and openly about the importance of ethics.[13] In short, they are fair in multiple ways, they make ethics an integral and legitimate part of organizational life through their decisions and actions, and they're willing to be ethical role models[14] so that their behavioral example helps enhance the salience of employees' moral identity. And by talking openly about their concern for ethics, they present ethics as an aspirational ideal, rather than a legalistic burden; doing this helps frame company ethics policy as supportive of employees (we aspire to do the right thing) rather than suspicious of employees (we're trying to catch you in a violation)[15] Ethically effective leaders have high expectations for others, in effect strengthening employees' moral identity by giving employees' opportunities for ethical success.[16]

Ethically effective leaders also attend to their impact on organizational culture. A global heavy industrial company in which I interviewed a variety of managers impressed me by the extent to which everyone had employee safety foremost in mind. Safety was an ingrained part of the company culture; beliefs about the importance of safety were deeply embedded assumptions, which had behavioral implications. This wasn't surprising; top management regularly talked about and visibly modeled concern for safety. For example, the CEO's policy was that in the event of a workplace fatality anywhere in the world, either the CEO or another top officer from the executive committee would immediately go to the scene of the fatality. Now, the CEO might have known little, if anything, about the particular industrial process involved. But the CEO's presence reinforced the company's cultural norms around safety; making it clear that safety is central to the company's identity. Leaders at every level of an organization have that kind of potential influence on ethics too, in their particular realms of responsibility. But even employees not in positions of authority can help to foster ethical cultural norms by their own behavior and their peer influence on co-workers' moral identity and sense of fairness.

Finally, ethically effective leaders use their influence on organizational practices to see that ethics policies are supported. Hiring processes, for example, need to be integrated with the company ethics goals, so that recruits understand that their prospective employer is committed to ethics, and so that the search process actively looks for people who want to work in a highly ethical environment. Training programs—whether on ethics or other general company policies—need to be for everyone, not just some people, lest employees see those programs as unfair (perhaps because "well-connected" employees are excused from training). And reward systems need to embody ethical goals and criteria alongside typical performance measures, so that it's not just what an employee accomplishes that matters, but also whether those outcomes are achieved in an ethical fashion.

Key influences on organizational ethics....	What leaders can do....
Fairness perceptions • Outcomes • Processes • Interactions	• Listen; be aware of employee concerns • Consistency in practices • View ethics as an aspirational ideal, not just a burdensome requirement
Integration of ethics across the organization	• Use ethics language so that ethical decision making seems normal and important • Use your influence to encourage ethical values in organizational culture • See that organizational routines (hiring, promotion, performance appraisal, etc.) emphasize ethics

Moral identity development	• Affirm and encourage employees' moral identity, by
	  • modeling ethical behavior
	  • talking about ethics
	  • providing employees with opportunities for ethical success

Conclusion: Good Organizational Ethics Can Be Achieved

Creating a strong ethical outlook in your department or business can seem like a difficult task. But if you recognize that an ethical organization involves more than what looks overtly to be about ethics, the task becomes easier. When led with an eye toward fair treatment, ethically supportive organizational practices, and encouragement of moral identity, the task of fostering organizational ethics can be divided into smaller, more tractable practices, many of which you'd have to do anyway (e.g., performance appraisal, hiring, or designing opportunities for subordinates to succeed). And seen as a collection of individually supportive but in many ways ordinary organizational activities, good organizational ethics aren't so hard to achieve after all.

Endnotes

1. Pringle, C. D. & Kroll, M. J. (1997). Why Trafalgar was won before it was fought, Lessons from resource-based theory. *Academy of Management Executive,* 11(4), 73–90; Margolis, J., Walsh, J., & Krehmeyer, D. (2006). The business case for ethics. Charlottesville, VA, Business Roundtable Institute for Corporate Ethics.
2. Quinn, D. P. & Jones, T. M. (1995). An agent morality view of business policy. *Academy of Management Review,* 20, 22–43.
3. Treviño, L. K., Weaver, G. R., Gibson, D. G. & Toffler, B. L. (1999). Managing ethics and legal compliance: What hurts and what works. *California Management Review,* 41(2), 131–151.
4. Weaver, G. R., Treviño, L. K. & Cochran, P.L. (1999). Corporate ethics programs as control systems: Influences of executive commitment and environmental factors. *Academy of Management Journal,* 42, 41–57.
5. Weaver, G. R., & Treviño, L. K. (2001). The role of human resources in ethics/compliance management: A fairness perspective. *Human Resource Management Review,* 11, 113–134.
6. Treviño, L. K. & Weaver, G. R. (2001). Organizational justice and ethics program follow-through: Influences on employees' harmful and helpful behavior. *Business Ethics Quarterly,* 11, 651–671.
7. Tenbrunsel, A. E., Smith-Crowe, K., & Umphress, E. (2003). Building houses on rocks: The role of the ethical infrastructure in organizations. *Social Justice Research,* 16(3), 285–307.
8. Weaver, G. R. Treviño, L. K. & Cochran, P.L. (1999).
9. Aquino, K., & Reed, A. II. (2002). The self-importance of moral identity. *Journal of Personality and Social Psychology,* 83(6), 1423.
10. Weaver, G. R., Treviño, L. K. & Cochran, P.L. (1999).
11. Weaver, G. R., Treviño, L.K., and Cochran, P. L. (1999). Integrated and decoupled corporate social performance: Management values, external pressures, and corporate ethics practices. *Academy of Management Journal,* 42, 539–552.
12. Treviño, L. K., Weaver, G. R. & Brown, M. (2008). It's lovely at the top: Hierarchical levels, identities, and perceptions of organizational ethics. *Business Ethics Quarterly,* 18, 233–253.
13. Brown, M. E. & Treviño L. K. (2006). Ethical Leadership, A Review and Future Directions. *The Leadership Quarterly,* 17, 595–616.
14. Weaver, G. R., Treviño, L. K., & Agle, B. R. (2005). "'Somebody I look up to'" Ethical role modeling in organizations. *Organizational Dynamics,* 34, 313–330.
15. Treviño, L. K. & Weaver, G. R. (2003).
16. Weaver, G. R. (2006). Virtue in organizations: Moral identity as a foundation for moral agency. *Organization Studies,* 27(3), 341–368.

The Psychology of Fairness at Work

Robert Folger
University of Central Florida

Stephen Gilliland
University of Arizona

David Bowen
Thunderbird School of Global Management

You've worked at Acme for about 15 years now. The work's OK. The pay's not great, and right now you can barely get by from paycheck to paycheck (although there are some people in other divisions whose work is easier and who don't seem to work nearly as hard, and yet they get paid the same as you). Actually, you haven't exactly been a ball of fire either. Your boss hasn't said anything about it yet, but you're feeling that maybe you haven't been exactly pulling your weight for a while now. At least you're not trying to take advantage of the old "five-finger discount" of helping yourself to a few of Acme's things every now and then, like some guys you know. The company calls that kind of petty theft "shrinkage" (it runs at about 3 percent), and they build it into their cost structure.

Naturally the economy has also affected Acme, and a vice president in your plant just made the following announcement.

> *It is inevitable in a business like ours that cost-cutting measures are often necessary to make ends meet. Unfortunately, the time has come for us to take such measures here at Acme. I know it won't be easy on anyone, but Bill, our president, has decided that a 15% across-the-board pay cut will be instituted effective Monday. This is largely the result of the fact that we've lost our contracts with Zenox. However, soon we'll be picking up jobs with Damzing, so we're sure the pay cuts will last only 10 weeks. I realize this isn't easy, but such reductions are an unfortunate fact of life in the manufacturing business. On behalf of Bill and myself, we thank you for bearing with us over these rough times. I'll answer one or two questions, but then I have to catch a plane for another meeting.*[1]

What a low blow! Somehow you'll scrape by, but you sure wish you'd gotten time to plan for this. You resent the VP's whole attitude, too: He drops in abruptly, no warning, reads a short note, and then hightails it out of there without allowing time for an adequate explanation of the what's, why's, and wherefore's. The guy seemed pretty insensitive (and insincere) about the whole thing.

Your Justice Portfolio

We made up this example (partly, as we'll explain) to illustrate different kinds of fairness at work: distributive, procedural, interpersonal, and informational justice. The fairness of the outcomes you receive (e.g., the relative size of a paycheck) is a way to think about *distributive* justice. You might also compare your paycheck *outcomes* to your *inputs,* such as productivity (e.g., "not pulling your weight"). Several aspects of a decision-making process can influence *procedural* justice perceptions—such as its *representativeness* and *correctability*, and trying for *accuracy* and *lack of bias.*

Well-designed decision-making procedures can make feelings of distributive unfairness more tolerable a well-established finding called the *fair-process effect,* which is especially likely to occur when people have been given a *voice* in the decision-making process.[2] Even the fairest of procedures can lose that advantage, however, if the decision is communicated poorly. *Interpersonal* justice comes from communicating a genuine interest in treating people with dignity and respect. In our example, the impact was just the opposite because the vice president's announcement made it sound as if the employees were looked down upon. The vice president also violated principles of *informational* justice concerning "why procedures were used in a certain way or why outcomes were distributed in a certain fashion"[3] The information from a decision maker should include reasonable explanations that are thorough, candid, timely, and tailored to the listener's specific needs.[4]

Our example was based on a real company that actually had two plants, reported in a study by Professor Greenberg.[5] The announcement printed above is the *inadequate* explanation, verbatim, from Greenberg's study. Employee theft and turnover at Acme rose significantly during the 10-week period of the pay-cuts, but were much lower in the second plant, where Greenberg recalled the *adequate* explanation given (see Figure 1). Exhibit A presents a partial transcript of this explanation given by the company president, complete with charts and graphs, where he then spent over an hour answering questions from employees. With a fairly small investment in executive time, this company saw a dramatic reduction in employee theft and turnover—a strong demonstration of some of the powers of organizational justice.

Psychologically speaking, fairness—like beauty—is in the eye of the beholder. What seems fair to me might seem unfair to you, or vice versa, whether I decide what you get, you decide what I get, or each of us reacts to what someone else got. Despite all this subjectivity, the scientific study of the psychology of fairness has been remarkably successful and has led to our topic: the study of organizational justice.

The organizational justice literature has now established a broad spectrum of findings across a wide range of contexts. The literature is so voluminous that it has resulted in many review articles and books, as well as a comprehensive handbook addressing a host of justice-related issues.[6] This knowledge helps organizational managers to understand when employees feel fairly or unfairly treated. We know, for example, that perceptions of organizational justice can

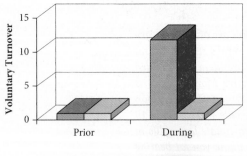

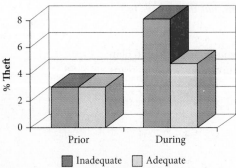

Figure 1 The Impact of Organizational Justice on Theft and Turnover

have effects on variables such as job satisfaction, organizational commitment, employee performance, absenteeism, and turnover.[7] Fair treatment of employees also spills over to customers, as employees who are treated fairly are more likely to treat customers fairly.[8] In short, creating an atmosphere of organizational justice by attending to fairness in management practices can be a source of sustained competitive advantage.

EXHIBIT A

EXAMPLE OF A STRONG INFORMATIONAL AND INTERPERSONAL JUSTICE DURING LAYOFF ANNOUNCEMENT

Something we hate to do here is lay off any of our employees. But, as you probably know, we've lost our key contracts with Zenox, which will make things pretty lean around here for a little while. As a result, we need to cut somewhere, and we've come up with a plan that will get us through these tough times. The plan is simple: Starting Monday, we will each get a 15% cut in pay. This applies to you, to me, to everyone who works here. If we do it this way, there'll be no cut in benefits and no layoffs – just a 15% pay reduction. So, either your hourly wages or your salary will be reduced by 15%. Will it hurt? Of course! But, it will hurt us all alike. We're all in it together. Let me just add that it really hurts me to do this, and the decision didn't come easily. We considered all possible avenues, but nothing was feasible. I think of you all as family, and it hurts me to take away what you've worked so hard for. But, for the next 10 weeks, we'll just have to tough it out. The reason I'm sharing all this information with you is that I want you to understand what is happening here. It's just a temporary problem we're facing, and one that I hope will never happen again.[9]

Question: Can you find examples of distributive, procedural, informational, and interpersonal justice in this speech?

In the remainder of this chapter, we identify the components of organizational justice that make up your justice portfolio, and then discuss ways to build fairness into traditional management activities (e.g., hiring and performance management). For a more thorough discussion of organizational justice in management, we encourage you to read *"The Management of Organizational Justice."*[10]

Four Components of Organizational Justice

Intuitively, it seems like fairness is a single dimension—you can experience fair or unfair treatment, with many shades of grey in between. Good management, however, considers all four elements we mentioned earlier: distributive, procedural, interpersonal, and informational justice (see Table 1).

Distributive Justice: Fairness of the Outcome

People have been writing about justice since Aristotle. We can trace organizational justice more specifically to Adams and his theory of fairness as the *equity of outcomes to inputs*.[11] Adams conceptualized fairness as equivalent rates of return: To get what you deserve

Table 1 Four Components of Organizational Justice

Distributive Justice	Procedural Justice
Key Question: *"Did I receive a fair outcome?"*	Key Question: *"Did I receive a fair process?"*
Concerns:	Concerns:
• Comparable outcomes to those in similar positions • Ratio of outcome to inputs equal to others' outcomes to inputs ratio • Outcomes consistent with expectations	• Voice or representation in decision-making • Consistent treatment with others and across time • Unbiased, accurate evaluations • Opportunity to appeal decision
Informational Justice	**Interpersonal Justice**
Key Question: *"Did I receive adequate explanation?"*	Key Question: *"Was I treated appropriately?"*
Concerns:	Concerns:
• Detailed and candid communication of decisions • Thorough and reasonable explanation of procedures • Timely communication and information	• Treatment with dignity and respect • Polite and interpersonally sensitive interactions • Refraining from improper remarks or comments

at work, for example, you should get out (e.g., pay) what you put in (e.g., productivity) at the same relative rate (the outcomes/inputs proportion) as a co-worker on the same job. Suppose you are person A and your co-worker is person B, with what you get out of work, called Outcomes (O), and what you put into work, called Inputs (I). Proportionally equivalent rates of return from productivity would be $O_A/I_A = O_B/I_B$. By the same algebra, your relative underpayment when you get less than you deserve would be $O_A/I_A < O_B/I_B$, and your relative overpayment would be $O_A/I_A > O_B/I_B$. There are several important implications of these equations:

- The values of inputs and outcomes are subjective and can be anything that A and B receive (e.g., vacation time rather than pay) or contribute as inputs (e.g., you might think education level should be part of what determines your pay).

- The person you compare yourself to ("B") can be another coworker in the same department, a different department, or a different organization. The comparison can also be the rate at which you were paid by the same employer in the past, or it could be what you think you might get if you were working for another employer, and so on.

- The outcomes of A and B do not need to be equal as long as the proportions (rates of return) are equal. It can be completely fair in your eyes for someone to get more than you if they work harder, have a much more dangerous job, and so on; it is fine for their outcomes to be greater than yours because their inputs are equivalently bigger.

- Because fairness is subjective, there are many ways to achieve equity, such as making your perceptions of the situation different rather than actually doing anything about them at all! Imagine you are angry about feeling underpaid—but you can't really do anything about it. You could increase your outcomes *perceptually* (psychologically, subjectively, cognitively), for example, by deciding that your work provides you with more than just your pay, because the work is really enjoyable, provides many friendships, and so on. You could cognitively reduce your inputs by deciding the work was really easier than you had been thinking.

Procedural Justice: Fairness of the Decision-Making Process

Not everyone will be satisfied with their boss, and we can be sure that not everyone will think every decision is fair—because, as we noted, fairness is subject to an individual's own perceptions. Research on *procedural justice* showed that disappointment with outcomes does not necessarily create anger toward the decision maker, however, as long as people can express their opinions about the fair way to do things and what would be considered a fair result.[12] In addition to the fair-process effect of voice from participation in decision making, which we mentioned above, another perspective proposed several other ingredients that influence perceived procedural justice: *consistency, correctability, ethicality, lack of bias,* and *accuracy*.[13] Procedural justice research has the following important managerial implications:

- Seeking input from those affected by the decision creates a sense of involvement and representativeness in decision processes, resulting in more positive reactions to the decision and sustained commitment to the organization.

- Procedural justice is particularly important when the decision is negative or seems suspect to those whom it affects.

- With hiring, promotion, performance evaluations, and layoffs, it is particularly important to ensure consistency, accuracy, and lack of bias in the decision-making process. Offering the opportunity to appeal the decision also enhances the perceptions of procedural fairness.

Informational and Interpersonal Justice: The Importance of What You Say and How You Say it

When MBA graduates were asked what made a recruiting experience particularly fair or unfair, many discussed the ways they were treated interpersonally, rather than solely focusing on decision processes and outcomes. Based on this research, the perceptions of fairness are also shaped by (a) the types of explanations for an outcome, and (b) the degrees of sensitivity and transparency about decision-making processes that lead to that outcome.[14] Greenberg labeled these *interpersonal* justice and *informational* justice.[15]

Interpersonal justice is "the degree to which people are treated with politeness, dignity, and respect by authorities or third parties involved in executing procedures or determining outcomes"; *informational justice* results when "information about why procedures were used in a certain way or why outcomes were distributed in a certain fashion."[16] Together, they have the following implications:

- Although all reasonable and accurate explanations help to foster fairness perceptions, the timeliness of explanations are also important. Post hoc explanations are less effective than thorough communication in advance of decisions.

- Showing sensitivity and respect—even offering an apology for a decision with negative consequences—can go a long way to promote fairness through interpersonal justice. In our litigious environment, legal counsel often warns that an apology can be interpreted as an admission of guilt. Research demonstrates that when people are offered an apology and treated with respect, however, they are less likely to take legal action—even when they feel the decision and process were unfair.

- Collectively, therefore, the different components of organizational justice can compensate for each other—providing informational and interpersonal justice, for example, can partially compensate for a lack of distributive and procedural justice.
- We now offer suggestions about incorporating justice into daily management practices.

Building Organizational Justice into Management Practices

Building organizational justice into management practice can be as easy as walking up to an employee and asking for advice on a managerial problem—simply asking for advice will promote procedural justice, and you may actually get some good suggestions! When facing tough financial times with possible budget cuts and layoffs, communicate, and even over-communicate—tell people what you know and what you don't know. Such examples suggest that all areas of management can benefit from attention to organizational justice; we highlight four in particular (see Table 2).

Table 2 Keys to Building Organizational Justice into Managerial Activities

Managerial Activity	Key Organizational Justice Actions
Recruiting and Hiring	• Hiring process and interview questions that appear to be job-related • Timely feedback on hiring decision and delays in hiring process • Rejection letters that explain who was hired and why *Remember:* Recruiting never ends and interpersonal and informational justice are effective recruiting tools
Performance Management	• Ratings that meet expectations—no surprises—and that mean something because they are tied to raises or promotions • Seek input (self-evaluations and peer feedback) prior to conducting evaluation • Base evaluations on accurate and specific behaviors and results • Timely feedback is more important than annual evaluations *Remember:* Performance management is more about an effective ongoing dialog than an annual appraisal and feedback meeting
Compensation and Rewards	• Compensation and rewards that accurately reflect inputs • Structured, systematic processes for reviewing and adjusting compensation • Explanations to accompany pay increases and lack of increases *Remember:* Open compensation means fair compensation—secrets are only needed to hide underlying unfairness
Terminations and Layoffs	• Decisions based on objective criteria that are consistently applied to everyone • Thorough and timely explanations for why layoff or termination is necessary and what other potential actions were considered *Remember:* Maintain trust, respect and human dignity—layoffs are a difficult process for everyone and interpersonal justice is essential

1. *Recruiting and Hiring.* Applicants want a fair chance to demonstrate their capabilities—a fair opportunity to compete. And if they don't get the job, a phone call, email, or detailed letter can go a long way toward promoting informational and interpersonal justice. Why should we care if we are not hiring them anyway? They might be applicants for future positions. They might be customers. And, their word of mouth recommendations may influence many others.

2. *Performance Management.* Fair managers seek input from employees (and if appropriate, from their coworkers, too) prior to conducting evaluations. Informational justice is used to manage expectations. Interpersonal justice is particularly important when an evaluation is negative—or simply more negative than the person was expecting. Ensuring timely feedback means making the performance management process an ongoing dialog, not a once-a-year event.

3. *Compensation and Rewards.* Too often, compensation reflects salary grades, longevity, or negotiating prowess. Managing compensation fairly means tying compensation and rewards to accurate and objective criteria. A fair compensation structure should be open to public scrutiny—how about posting everyone's compensation levels on the bulletin board? If you would rather not publicly share compensation information, you should ask yourself whether you are trying to hide fundamental unfairness in pay levels.

4. *Terminations and Layoffs.* In many ways, managing in tough times becomes the litmus test for the fair manager. The principles of accurate, consistent, unbiased criteria, along with open, honest information sharing, must be maintained during layoffs to promote organizational justice—not just for the victims of the layoffs, but also for the survivors, who watch and form impressions of the organization and management based on the level of fair treatment of layoff victims.

Concluding Thoughts: Two Sides of the Justice Coin

We have stressed managing fairly to promote a culture of trust and respect. In closing, we want to reinforce the message that organizational justice is a two-sided coin. On one side, when people feel unfairly treated, they will decrease their effort, neglect customers, steal, sabotage, and quit. Unfair treatment can be a powerful motivator of negative behavior. On the other side of the justice coin, fair treatment can motivate people to go above and beyond. Creativity and superior customer service result from an atmosphere of fair treatment. Organizational justice can turn the psychology of fairness into one of the biggest differentiators of effective and ineffective management.

Endnotes

1. Greenberg, J. (1990). Employee theft as a reaction to underpayment inequity: The hidden cost of pay cuts. *Journal of Applied Psychology, 75,* 561–568.
2. Folger, R. (1977). Distributive and procedural justice: Combined impact of "voice" and improvement on experienced inequity. *Journal of Personality and Social Psychology, 35,* 108–119.
3. Colquitt, J. A., Conlon, D. E., Wesson, M. J., Porter, C. O. L. H., & Ng, K. Y. (2001). Justice at the millennium: A meta-analytic review of 25 years of justice research. *Journal of Applied Psychology, 86,* 425–445.

4. Colquitt, J. A. (2001). On the dimensionality of organizational justice: A construct validation of a measure. *Journal of Applied Psychology, 86*, 386–400.

5. Greenberg, J. (1990). Employee theft as a reaction to underpayment inequity: The hidden cost of pay cuts. *Journal of Applied Psychology, 75*, 561–568.

6. Greenberg, J. & Colquitt, J. A. (2005). *Handbook of organizational justice*. Mahwah, NJ: Erlbaum.

7. Colquitt, J. A. (2001). On the dimensionality of organizational justice: A construct validation of a measure. *Journal of Applied Psychology, 86*, 386–400.

8. Ibid.

9. Greenberg, J. (1990). Employee theft as a reaction to underpayment inequity: The hidden cost of pay cuts. *Journal of Applied Psychology, 75*, 561–568.

10. Cropanzano, R., Bowen, D. E., & Gilliland, S. W. (2007). The management of organizational justice. *Academy of Management Perspectives, 21 (4)*, 34–48.

11. Adams, J. S. (1965). Inequity in social exchange. In L. Berkowitz (Ed.). *Advances in experimental social psychology* 2, 267–299. New York: Academic Press.

12. Thibaut, J. & Walker, L. (1975). *Procedural justice: A psychological analysis*. Hillsdale, NJ: Erlbaum.

13. Leventhal, G. S. (1980). What should be done with equity theory? New approaches to the study of fairness in social relationship. In K. J. Gergen, M. S. Greenberg, & R. H. Willis (Eds.). *Social Exchange: Advances in Theory and Research, 27–55*. New York: Plenum.

14. Bies, R. J. & Moag, J. S. (1986). Interactional justice: Communication criteria for fairness. *Research on Negotiation in Organization, 1*, 43–55.

15. Greenberg, J. (1993). The social side of fairness: Interpersonal and informational classes of organizational justice. In R. Cropanzano (Ed.). *Justice in the workplace: Approaching fairness in human resource management*, 79–103. Hillsdale, NJ: Erlbaum.

16. Colquitt, J. A. (2001). On the dimensionality of organizational justice: A construct validation of a measure. *Journal of Applied Psychology, 86*, 386–400.

Section II

CASES

Diego Cervo/Shutterstock

CASES

CASE 1

The Case of Apple iPhone 4

Kimberly D. Elsbach

University of California, Davis

Eric Thayer/Corbis

Over the course of four months in the spring and summer of 2010, the highly respected Apple Corporation dealt with several organizational challenges in relation to its new iPhone 4. In the following sections, I will provide an overview of Apple Inc., and describe the challenges faced by Apple in three parts.

Overview of Apple Inc. (from http://en.wikipedia.org/wiki/Apple_Inc)

At the time of this case study, Apple Inc. was a multinational consumer electronics company headquartered in Cupertino, California (United States). Established in 1976, Apple was a world-wide leader in the production of personal electronics devices, including both laptop and desktop computers (iMacs), personal audio devices (iPods), mobile smartphones (iPhones), and most recently, tablet computer devices (iPads). In the industry, Apple was known as "innovative" in its electronics design and aesthetics,[1] and as a free-spirited "underdog," who took on stuffy corporate giants like IBM and Microsoft.[2] Apple had a history of producing products of "superior quality," and had been named to *Fortune*'s list of the Most Admired Companies in the World in 2009 and 2010. At the same time, Apple had a reputation for "caring about its customers," and had an almost evangelical following of loyal fans.[3] For the past decade, Apple Inc. was embodied by its charismatic CEO, Steve Jobs, who revealed new products in high-tech, multi-media presentations watched by millions worldwide.

Challenge 1: The Lost Prototype

On April 19, 2010, technology Website Gizmodo published photos, videos, and extensive reviews of what it said was the yet-to-be released Apple iPhone 4.[4] Claiming that they had received a prototype of the next generation iPhone from someone who found it in a bar (later revealed to have been true), Gizmodo engineers disassembled the phone to inspect its components and features.[5] Based on their inspection, Gizmodo bloggers believed the prototype to be a genuine Apple product and revealed that the new phone had several very cool new features, including a glass-like ceramic back, improved camera with flash, improved display, and longer-lasting battery.[6] These features and a review of the phone were posted on Gizmodo's Website by blogger Jason Chen.

While these events were mildly embarrassing to Apple, who prided itself on tight control of its research and development,[7] the main challenge these events produced for Apple was managing the excitement that the unanticipated pre-release had inspired in consumers. Much of this excitement was spurred by industry analysts whose first views of the lost iPhone led them to make exciting claims about the new device. For example, one industry writer noted:

> This could be the first phone to bring video telephony to the masses.... [this development] would get people very, very, excited.[8]

In response to this challenge, Apple took a heavy-handed approach to quiet the discussion of its unreleased iPhone. Although the lost iPhone 4 was returned to Apple by Gizmodo immediately after Apple acknowledged that it was their product,[9] officers from the San Mateo, California Police Department and California's Rapid Enforcement Allied Computer Team (REACT) raided the home of Gizmodo writer, Jason Chen, on April 26, 2010—confiscating computers, hard drives, and a new iPad supposedly used in "committing a felony."[10] It was later revealed that Apple Inc. executives sat on REACT's steering committee and had contacted police about potential stolen property in relation to the phone.[11]

Industry writers as well as mainstream media quickly denounced what they saw as oppressive persecution by Apple Inc. against a journalist engaged in free speech. Calling Apple a "behemoth" in a "David and Goliath confrontation," British Web entrepreneur Nick Denton, who was associated with Gizmodo, said he was "shocked" to hear of the raid on Chen's house and was concerned about Apple's apparent role in the raid. As he noted:

> It's extraordinary that one would have a police force that was so aligned with corporate interests.[12]

Other journalists went further, including late night television satirist Jon Stewart who devoted a nine-minute slot to a parody he called "Appholes".[13] In that skit, Stewart complained that Apple was "becoming the Man" (a role that was previously reserved for competitor Microsoft) and pleaded to Jobs to say it wasn't so.

These events appeared to damage Apple's reputation as the free-spirited underdog, and painted the organization as just one more, big corporation. As the *London Times* reported:

> *It will be hard for Apple, who recently posted record profits of $3.07 billion, to maintain its image as a company staffed by free-thinking technology buffs who prefer t-shirts and chinos to corporate suits and ties.*[14]

Challenge 2: Unveiling the iPhone 4

Three weeks after the raid on Jason Chen's home, Apple introduced the new iPhone 4 through a press release and press conference on June 7, 2010. In the press release, Steve Jobs described the features of the new phone as follows:

> *FaceTime video calling sets a new standard for mobile communication, and our new Retina display is the highest resolution display ever in a phone, with text looking like it does on a fine printed page. We have been dreaming about both of these breakthroughs for decades.*[15]

Jobs also demonstrated the new FaceTime video-calling feature in a press conference at Apple's Worldwide Developer's Conference in San Francisco. Wowing the crowd, Jobs affirmed his geek identity and Apple's reputation for coolness by saying:

> *I grew up with The Jetsons and Star Trek just dreaming about video calls. And it's real now.*[16]

Jobs even showed some humor, and finally responded to the Gizmodo leak of the iPhone prototype in his introduction by joking, "Stop me if you've already seen this."[17]

The entertaining and uber-cool unveiling by Jobs was a hit with industry writers and analysts. Calling the event a "touchdown," *Dallas Morning News* technology writer Jim Rossman said he was likely to buy the new phone because of its new features.[18] Other writers waxed poetic about the complete coolness of the design, calling it "magically great,"[19] and "unprecedentedly slick."[20] These comments reinforced Apple's reputation as an innovator, despite the recent hit to its reputation. As one writer noted:

> *You have to respect a company that iterates and innovates when what was presently in-market seemed more than above average.*[21]

Clearly, the unveiling was a huge success and enhanced Apple's reputation for innovation. Yet, the event also created a challenge for Apple (i.e., how to make the most of the positive press regarding its newest iPhone but not disappoint consumers by creating unrealistic expectations). This challenge required Apple to decide which features of the new phone they would highlight.

There were many features of the new phone that Apple could have touted. Some of them were frame-breaking, like the video-calling feature, while others were more incremental, like their perfected cut and paste feature and updated operating system. In regard to these more incremental features, technology writers claimed that the iPhone was known to be the most rigorously tested and honed system out there, which was a primary reason to buy the phone.

In the end, Apple chose to focus mostly on its breakthroughs in video calling and high-resolution display. Further, Apple created extremely high expectations about its new iPhone for consumers. In fact, in a letter to Apple consumers on June 7, 2010, Steve Jobs was quoted as saying: "iPhone 4 is the biggest leap since the original iPhone."[22]

Challenge 3: "Antenna-Gate" and the "Death Grip"

On June 24, 2010, the first iPhone 4s were finally delivered to the Apple faithful. Almost immediately, there were complaints from customers about dropped calls related to Apple's new external antenna. Apparently, holding the new iPhone in one's left hand—with one's thumb on one side and fingers wrapped around the other side (what came to be known as the "death grip"—could cause the two antennae, that were embedded in the external case, to bridge and result in loss of signal strength—and ultimately dropped phone calls.[23]

In response to these complaints, Steve Jobs' appeared to blame the antenna problem on consumers rather than on Apple. As several blogs noted, when one customer emailed Jobs about the antennae issue and asked if this was a design flaw, Jobs emailed back something along the lines of: "No. Just don't hold it that way." Later, another consumer got the following, similar response from Jobs:

> *Gripping the phone will result in some attenuation of its antenna*
> *performance, with certain places being worse than others*
> *depending on the placement of the antennas. This is a fact of*
> *life for every wireless phone. If you ever experience this on your*
> *iPhone 4, avoid gripping it in the lower left corner in a way that*
> *covers both sides of the black strip in the metal band, or simply*
> *use one of the many available cases.[24]*

Unsurprisingly, this "blaming the victim" approach of responding to consumer concerns was not met with enthusiasm. Further, Apple showed no evidence that they considered users' concerns or views when they designed the antenna or when they responded to complaints about its faults. This lack of responsiveness regarding the apparently faulty antenna became known as "antenna-gate."

Further complicating matters were reports by antenna experts who claimed that the problem arose from placing the antenna on the bottom of the phone (where people naturally hold it) as a means of reducing the radio wave emissions close to a person's head when he or she is on the phone.[25] While other reporters claimed that the antenna issues resulted from the lack of left-handed testers on Apple's design teams.[26] Finally, rival electronics firms Nokia and Motorola ran print and Web advertisements that poked fun at Apple by claiming that a person could hold their phones any way they wanted and that it shouldn't be a problem to hold one's mobile phone like, well, like a phone.[27]

In the days that followed, dozens of Websites and media outlets printed comments from angry consumers who complained that Apple should have known about the problem before it released the phone.[28] Further, consumers were upset that they would have to purchase a $30 case to resolve the signal problem. These problems appeared to threaten Apple's reputations for superior quality and customer care. As one blogger wrote:

> The [iPhone 4] has a major design flaw that threatens Apple's reputation of producing higher quality devices that justify the high costs. Usually a company of this magnitude would issue a recall, but not Apple, they blamed the issue on not holding the phone correctly. They even went so far as to make a commercial that showed everyone holding the phone "correctly".[29]

In response to the increasing bad press, Apple issued a press release on July 2, 2010 about the iPhone 4. In it, Apple claimed that after looking into the cause of the dropped calls reported by some iPhone users, they were "stunned" to find out that the formula they used to calculate signal strength (i.e., number of bars) was "totally wrong" and had been since the original iPhone was released in 2007.[30] As a result, Apple claimed users perceived that they were losing signal strength, when in fact, they had no signal strength to begin with. Apple claimed to have fixed the problem with the help of AT&T and said it was issuing a free software update that would eliminate the problem for consumers.

This response, which essentially denied the existence of an antenna problem, did not improve things for Apple. Users continued to claim that the antenna was faulty,[31] and bloggers continued to sound the death knell of Apple's reputation for high quality and customer care.[32] Things got even worse on July 12, 2010, when the highly respected magazine *Consumer Reports* verified that the antenna problem was legitimate, stating that "none of the [other phones tested] had the signal-loss problems of the iPhone 4".[33] In the end, *Consumer Reports* declined to recommend the iPhone 4—the first time the magazine had failed to recommend an iPhone.

In response to this continued public outcry, Jobs held a press conference on July 16, 2010, to once and for all respond to consumer complaints about the iPhone 4 (watch the video at: http://events.apple.com). He began the press conference by stating, "we're not perfect" and "phones aren't perfect"—appearing to balance the blame for the reception problems on both the company and on the state of wireless communication.

Yet, throughout the presentation, Jobs emphasized that the signal loss issue was not unique to the iPhone 4, placing most of the blame on the Wi-Fi environment, and excusing Apple from responsibility. Jobs demonstrated, through video, how phones from Blackberry, HTC, and Samsung could be made to lose signal strength by holding them in the same way as the iPhone 4. He then excused the problem as "life in the smartphone world" and claimed that "every phone has weak spots." These excuses appeared to blame the antenna problems on unforeseeable environmental issues that Apple should not be held responsible for. In the end, Jobs reported that Apple would give a free bumper case to all iPhone 4 purchasers and would offer full refunds to all buyers who requested them. He promised that Apple would work hard to solve the underlying problem with the antenna and vowed that he wanted all of Apple's users to be happy.

Based on media reports, Apple's "antenna-gate" press conference was viewed as a draw. Consumers received a free fix for their reception problems and recognition from Apple that their concerns were valid. Further, Apple provided a reasonable excuse for the antenna problems (it's the wireless signal environment). Yet, Apple refused to apologize for blaming users for holding the phone the wrong way and didn't respond to the *Consumer Reports* issue. As a result, many industry experts remained critical of Apple's response to the antenna problems, calling Apple's reaction high-handed and dismissive. It appeared that Apple, which was typically so good at public relations, had created a PR disaster by its own actions.

Challenge Scorecard: Late July, 2010

By late July, 2010, the four-month iPhone 4 saga appeared to be more of a loss than a gain for Apple. First, Apple's reputation as the scrappy underdog was, perhaps, irretrievably undermined. As Queen's University (Kingston, Ontario) Professor of Internet Marketing, John Pliniussen, noted:

> People tend to view Apple as being "the angels, the cool guys, the nerds who have done well and kicked the ass of the big companies.... But now they're big themselves and they're turning into the 'big guys' and sort of being scammy. [34]

In addition, Apple's reputations for superior quality and customer care had both taken a major hit. As columnist Berkow, reported:

> When an iPhone 4 ended up in the hands of Jason Chen.... Apple called the police... When problems first arose with the design of the iPhone 4 antenna...Steve Jobs...initially blamed the problem on his own customers...[and later] pushed the blame on to AT&T...Even after Consumer Reports *confirmed there was a hardware problem caused by a design flaw in the phone's antennae, Steve Jobs still refused to apologize and admit that Apple erred.... Those kinds of actions make the company look cold and arrogant, tarnishing its hard-fought image as warm and understanding.* [35]

Still, the iPhone 4's cool new features led Apple to sell over 1.7 million devices in the first weekend of its release, and caused one of its faithful fans to produce a

YouTube video defending Apple against all attacks (watch it at: http://www.youtube.com/watch?v=VKIcaejkpD4). Apparently, the company's reputation for innovation had weathered the storm.

*Optional Discussion Questions (Answer questions that correspond to the topic area you are illustrating with this case.)

Topic Area	Question
Innovation/Change	Was the introduction of the iPhone 4 a disruptive innovation? Did Apple discount or ignore any steps in the strategic change process when releasing the iPhone 4 and then by not responding to customer complaints?
Motivation	How did Apple's leader, Steve Jobs, motivate innovation?
Culture	What about Apple makes it an innovative company? How did Apple's innovative culture lead to the antenna problems it encountered? How was Apple's innovative culture responsible for how it responded to the challenges in this case?
Influence/Impression Management	What could Apple have done differently to protect its reputation in responding to the challenges? How could Jobs have used Influence and Perception Management tactics to improve how he came across in his press conference on July 2, 2010?
Leadership	How was Job's leadership responsible for how Apple responded to the challenges in this case?
Decision Making	How did Apple go about deciding how to respond to the initial antenna problems?
Justice	If you were an iPhone 4 purchaser, would you have felt satisfied following Steve Jobs press conference on July 2, 2010? Why or why not? Do you think that Apple's initial response to the antenna problems was fair? Why or why not?

Endnotes

1. Joel, M. (2010). One device to rule them all. *The Montreal Gazette,* June 10, B5.
2. Berkow, J. (2010). Worm in Apple's reputation. *National Post* (Canada), July 17, FP5.
3. Corrigan, T. (2010). Will fans risk another bit of the Apple? *The London Daily Telegraph,* July 17, 22.
4. Heining, A. (2010). Found 'iPhone' a rare breach of Apple secrecy. *The Christian Science Monitor,* April 19.
5. Peck, T. (2010). Apple worker leaves 'prototype of top-secret 4G iPhone' in bar. *The London Independent,* April 20, 16.

6. Ibid.
7. Heining, A. (2010). Found 'iPhone' a rare breach of Apple secrecy. *The Christian Science Monitor,* April 19.
8. Gelles, J. (2010). Apple keeps the buzz buzzing. *The Philadelphia Inquirer,* April 22, C1.
9. Arthur, C. & Kiss, J. (2010). Apple demands return of iPhone 4G prototype. *The London Guardian,* April 21, 7.
10. Heining, A. (2010). Police raid home of Gizmodo writer over iPhone prototype. *The Christian Science Monitor,* April 26.
11. Harris, M., & Tobin, D. (2010). Apple peels off its nice-guy mask. *The London Sunday Times,* May 9, 32–33.
12. Pilkington, E. (2010). Media: Taking a bite out of Apple. *The London Guardian,* May 3, 1.
13. Ibid.
14. Ibid.
15. Apple Inc. (2010). Apple Presents iPhone 4. https://www.apple.com/pr/library/2010/06/07Apple-Presents-iPhone-4.htmlwww.apple.com, June 7.
16. Sarno, D. (2010). Video calling takes center stage; Apple's next iPhone hits shelves June 24. *Los Angeles Times,* June 8, B1.
17. Ibid.
18. Godinez, V. (2010). Apple raises its game. *The Dallas Morning News,* June 8, D1.
19. Joel, M. (2010). One device to rule them all. *The Montreal Gazette,* June 10, B5.
20. Lim, C. (2010). Looking beyond the specs; The iPhone 4's hardware is its least interesting aspect. *The Business Times Singapore,* June 14.
21. Joel, M. (2010). One device to rule them all. *The Montreal Gazette,* June 10, B5.
22. Apple Inc. (2010). Apple Presents iPhone 4. https://www.apple.com/pr/library/2010/06/07Apple-Presents-iPhone-4.htmlwww.apple.com, June 7.
23. Silverman, D. (2010). Are you seeing these iPhone issues? *TechBlog, Houston Chronicle,* June 24.
24. Ibid.
25. Gaj-It.com. "iPhone 4 Antenna Woes Explained by a Man in the Know," June 25, 2010.
26. Hamilton, J. (2010). Apple's 'lost its 4G grip'. *The Sun* (England), June 26, 14.
27. Bertrand. (2010). "Nokio Pokes Fun at Apple, Tells Users to Hold Their Phones Any Way They Like," Erictric (Blog), June 28.
28. Arthur, C. (2010). Irate iPhone owners resort to nail polish to fix £499 gadget. *The London Guardian,* June 26, 9.
29. Electronic Urban Report. (2010). "The Gadget Guy: iPhone 4: The Good, the Bad, and the Just Plain Wrong" (Blog). July 1.
30. Apple Inc. (2010). "Letter from Apple regarding iPhone 4." https://www.apple.com/pr/library/2010/07/02Letter-from-Apple-Regarding-iPhone-4.htmlwww.apple.com, July 2.
31. Martin, M. (2010). "Law firms suing Apple not impressed with explanation of reception issues." TUAW (Blog), July 3.
32. Smith, S. (2010). "Are Apple's happy days over? Minyanville" (Blog). July 2.
33. Burrows, P., & Guglielmo, C. (2010). Apple engineer told Jobs iPhone antenna might cut calls. *Bloomberg News,* July 15.
34. Berkow, J. (2010). Worm in Apple's reputation. *National Post* (Canada), July 17, FP5.
35. Ibid

CASE 2

"We Are Global or We Are Nothing": Conflict and Cover-Up at ColequarterMaine[1]

Samantha Fairclough

University of Mississippi

Christopher Kolaczan/Shutterstock

G ordon Eberle sighed as he read the email message. "Not again" he thought. Another Canadian analyst on the Gotham oil sands project team was request-ing a transfer back to Calgary, complaining that there was a "negative working environment" at the team base in Caracas, as well as a "constant state of friction" amongst the team members. As the ColequarterMaine (CqM) partner responsible for client ser-vices to Gotham Oil Corporation, Gordon's role was to ensure that everyone on the oil sands project team was happy. From his office on the 15th Floor of the Colefax Building in downtown Calgary, he could see Gotham's Canadian offices, and was a frequent visitor to its headquarters in San Antonio, Texas. Gotham was an important, and lucrative, client

---

[1]This fictional case is based on the author's extensive experience researching the so-called "Big Four" professional service firms. ColequarterMaine is an amalgam of some of the characteris-tics of these firms. Any resemblance between the events in this case and actual events is purely coincidental.

of CqM, and its consistent flow of work into the Calgary office alone was worth almost $5 million per year. For CqM, on a global scale, Gotham was included on its "Elite25" roster of clients. Gordon knew it was his responsibility to make sure that Gotham received the very best service from CqM, wherever in the world it was delivered.

As a fellow Canadian, Gordon was sympathetic to the young analyst's emailed pleas. The lead partner on the oil sands project was Dustin Jenner, a U.S. partner and Texas-native, whose arrogance and insensitivity to the personal lives of his junior team members was becoming evident. "Some of these U.S. guys really are cut from a different cloth than us Canucks," thought Gordon. Men like Dustin are demanding, ambitious, and incredibly successful, but their brute force mentality is not always good for cohesion and morale amongst project teams, nor, for that matter, CqM's clients. A multi-national team of six consultants was in Venezuela working on a communications strategy for Gotham's expansion of its oil sands operations in South America, ahead of a new joint venture with the Venezuelan government to extract so-called "heavy oil" from the Carabobo region of the Orinoco Valley. Two senior analysts from the CqM's Calgary office had been sent to work with Jenner in Caracas. Calgary had worked with Gotham on numerous projects in the oil sands region of Northern Alberta, including the development of a similar public-relations strategy to address the concerns of indigenous people, environmental, and wildlife groups, who were becoming an increasingly vocal and persistent force in their attempts to disrupt extraction of the so-called "world's dirtiest oil". Keeping journalists and groups like Greenpeace from attacking the reputation of companies like Gotham was vital if the oil giant's operations were to continue. It was an ongoing propaganda war.

The Venezuelan project team had been beset by problems from the start. In his own mind, Gordon saw the team as a "perfect storm" of cultural and personality clashes. Not only was Dustin Jenner in charge, but the mix of hard-driven Americans, measured Canadians, and laid-back South Americans was, in hindsight, a recipe for antagonism. He had already lost two Canadians from the team. In their own way, the Canadians were just as assertive as their U.S. colleagues, given that they were not prepared to spend week-ends and 20 hour days on a project with an uncompromising team leader. The other team members were Venezuelans, whose English skills were basic at best, were often slow, and had an inflexible attitude to deadlines, which riled Dustin and only added to the tensions within the team. "A cultural thing in South America," Gordon thought. It was becoming increasingly difficult to hide the team's problems from Gotham's managers.

Gotham's CEO, Alex Remski, was in town for the Canadian Oil Industry annual con-ference, and Gordon was due to meet him for lunch at *Les Trois Magots* restaurant tomor-row. He was not looking forward to the meeting. "We are supposed to be a global firm," he thought, "an integrated whole working together across borders to provide exceptional client service". That was what the mission statement said. At that moment, Gordon felt like he, and CqM, were anything but exceptional.

Background on ColequarterMaine

Structure and Services

ColequarterMaine is a member of the so-called "Big Four" group of audit and profes-sional service firms who provide accounting services to the majority of the world's pub-licly traded companies. They have also diversified to provide a range of knowledge-based services that include tax, financial, and management consulting advice. The Big Four emerged from a series of mergers of the Big Eight, as well as the demise of the firm Arthur Andersen after the Enron scandal in 2002. CqM is the result of a merger between Maine Hopkins and Colequarter which occurred in 1998. The firm operates in more than 100 countries and employs almost 120,000 people. However, CqM is not a single firm, but a network of more than 60 member firms, most of which practice in one country and are structured to comply with their own domestic laws and regulations. Although each member firm is owned and managed independently (usually as a partnership), and collects its own revenues, each has entered into an agreement with the other members of the network to share a common name, brand, methodologies, and quality standards. This form of organization is designed to protect each member from liability, which otherwise could put the whole network at risk. Clients of the firm, however, see only CqM's global brand name, and assume flawless integration between its various units. As Alan Cogliano, managing partner of the Calgary office, explained to the CqM Canada's management board, "We want our clients to think that it's all one seamless enterprise"

CqM's range of professional services are targeted at the world's largest international corporations, as well as smaller, local clients; but in both cases, the firm strives to customize its services by deploying teams of experts with both professional and industry knowledge, wherever in the network they are located. Global clients often prefer to hire a single, integrated firm to provide professional services in all of its locations, and believe that a firm like CqM can leverage its global resources to fulfill their every need.

Reciprocal Relations and Mission Statement

Given that CqM's member firms are financially independent, they use a set of formulas to calculate the distribution of profits generated when project teams are made up of members from different firms. These formulas accommodate the hourly rate of the various participants so that team members are not inhibited by financial concerns from collaborating across firms, and member firms who "lend" their people to teams based in other offices will get revenues to cover their costs. More importantly, CqM encourages a culture of cooperation between member firms, encapsulated in its "Accord" mission statement, which emphasizes the practical benefits and rewards of collaboration across practices and countries. Emblazoned across the firm's publications, pens, mouse pads, and other corporate communications, the Accord philosophy encourages and supports unity around the CqM brand, a borderless network, and the rhetoric of "One World, One Voice".

Specifically, the statement talks about member firms cooperating across borders to deliver high-quality, consistent service to demanding global clients. These collaborations, it says, create benefits for the whole firm and its international brand, which will have positive and long-term practical and financial consequences for national and local practices. As Alan Cogliano told this year's intake of graduate recruits,

> *"We are global or we are nothing, so we have to work to be global, and in practical terms that means supporting, and being supported by, other countries."*

Putting the Team Together

Gordon first began putting the pieces of the Venezuelan team in place three weeks ago after receiving a call from Miroslav Smid, Gotham's Latvian-born head of field operations in South America. The project seemed to be straightforward, a five-week window to prepare and implement a communications strategy on environmental issues. He anticipated that a team of six would be needed to research competitor strategies, local and international regulations, relevant stakeholders, media interest, possible ecological impacts, and the potential effect of environmental and wildlife groups. As Gotham's Global Client Service Partner (GCSP), Gordon's role was to identify the competencies and individuals required for the project, and to "negotiate" with partners and member firms to secure their availability and commitment. As he explained to one of the new analysts recruited into the Energy group,

> *"The project team is built systematically by looking at the skills that are required, the backgrounds of the people. Who are the people who run the major projects? Who are the people who can handle this type of integration? As a lead partner, I pull a team together from the hundreds of people I know, or I reach out to the service line guys or the subject matter experts to pull in the kinds of skill sets you need."*

Although he was a Canadian partner, Gordon had been appointed as GCSP to Gotham—a U.S.-based corporation—three years ago, having worked with them extensively on projects in the Alberta oil sands. He had also been seconded to CqM's Houston office when he was a senior analyst in the late 1990s, and there was little that he did not know about the oil industry.

Dustin Jenner was the automatic choice to be project leader. He was available for the five weeks of the engagement, and had just completed a project advising Gotham in their negotiations with the Venezuelan government to secure extraction rights in the Orinoco Valley. Made a partner only three months ago, Dustin was a rising star in the U.S. firm, having led a number of oil industry projects, including some for Gotham in Utah. He was known as a prickly character, but the annual revenues brought in for the firm were incredible, and he had demonstrated a consistent ability to bring projects in under budget and on time.

Gordon was able to identify two analysts in the Calgary and Vancouver offices who knew Gotham's business and had oil sands experience. Their experience would be a valuable resource in formulating an environmental communications strategy for the Orinoco Valley oil sands project. He also used his contacts in Toronto to find individuals in Venezuela with the right skills; in particular, he called Rafael Torres, a consultant in the Primary Industries group, for suggestions on who to bring in. Rafael had spent three months in CqM's Caracas office, and could vouch for the abilities of two senior analysts he had worked with on an oil industry project last year.

The revenues from the consulting project in Venezuela would be distributed between the Calgary, San Antonio, and Caracas offices, according to CqM's globally agreed internal financial formulas.

Venting Frustrations

Gordon picked up the telephone and called Carol Sutter, a partner in the Energy group of CqM's management consulting practice in Vancouver. "Hey Carol," he said, "would you have anyone free to go down to Caracas for a few weeks to work on the Gotham team? We've got a hole that needs filling with a junior. Jenner needs fresh meat." Carol's hesitation revealed her reluctance to assign one of her young consultants to a team headed by Dustin Jenner. With a sigh she replied, "I'll have to take a look at my guys' schedules, and let you know if I can spare anyone. Things are pretty busy at the moment. Can I call you back in an hour?" "OK, that's fine," said Gordon. "Thanks Carol. I'll put a call in to Wayne in Edmonton and see if he's got anybody" he added. His frustration was building, and he felt the need to vent. "You know what it's like with some of these U.S. projects," he said. "It all comes back to me when they pull the trigger and shunt someone out the door. I'm ultimately responsible for keeping the Gotham guys happy. They see no problem with demanding consistent fifteen, twenty-hour days from our people with little or no regard for individual needs, individual priorities, or the fact that team members may have other things they need to do as opposed to sitting for five, six hours in meetings late at night to satisfy a partner's agenda."

"Listen, I sympathize, I really do", said Carol. "Believe me, I've seen it many times before. I think a lot of the U.S. practice is driven by a big city, New York, do-it-at-all costs mentality. The fact is that we don't have the luxury of, you know, a limitless pool of MBAs strolling the streets of Vancouver. We can't just fire one and pick up another. Look, I'll have a word with Alan and with Human Resources, and let's see what we can do."

Today: Lunch at *Les Trois Magots* Bistro

The grilled salmon had been delicious, but as the dessert arrived Gordon began to feel his appetite waning. He could sense that Alex Remski had something important to get off his chest, and so was unsurprised when Alex turned the conversation to Gotham's activities down in Venezuela. "It's been a challenge down there," said Alex. "Because the product has such a high sulphur content it's difficult to meet international environmental standards. We're throwing money at the problem and hoping our engineers come up with a solution. We need your guys to be on their game in helping us put the story out on our green credentials." "Absolutely," said Gordon, "and Dustin and his team are the best we've got."

"But I'll be frank," Alex responded, "I've heard from Miro that your team has been having some problems with turnover, meeting deadlines, and working with our guys. You need to get your South Americans out of their siestas and mañana attitude, and get the others to stop squabbling. This is a massively important project for us and we need CqM to bring their A game. The stakes are even higher now, because we've just found traces of solvent in the Orinoco river from our test drillings, and some dead fish—a rare species of piranha I think—downstream of the spill. Greenpeace and the others will be down our throats if they find out. We need you to help us keep it quiet."

Gordon's appetite for the remainder of his crème brulée quickly disappeared. He liked and respected Alex, and had enjoyed a professional relationship with him lasting more than 10 years, but today his responsibilities to CqM and to Gotham seemed to weigh very heavily. What was he to do about Jenner and his toxic team? The lack of urgency displayed by the Venezuelans? And now he felt pressure to assist Gotham in their efforts to hide illegal behavior from the Venezuelan authorities. He felt a knot twist in his stomach.

*Optional Discussion Questions (Answer questions that correspond to the topic area you are illustrating with this case).

Topic Area	Question
Teams	What should Gordon do to fix the team dynamics in Venezuela? What should he do about Dustin Jenner? How can the Venezuelan team members be made to work faster?
Motivation	What was motivating Dustin Jenner to work hard on this project? Is his motivation different to that of Gordon Eberle? Do you think the analysts who have requested transfers back to Canada were worried about how their move could impact their career prospects? How can Eberle use research on happiness and trustworthiness to improve the work climate in Venezuela?
Ethics	What should Gordon do about Alex's request to help cover up the toxic spill? What pressure is Gordon under to comply with the request?
Communication/ Diversity	What does Alex mean when he asks Gordon to "*get your South Americans out of their siestas and manana attitude*"? How does Gordon interpret this demand?
Perception	How does ColequarterMaine's external image differ from its internal one? What problems might this create?
Stress	How might the stress of 15–20 hour work days have affected the consultants on the Gotham project? What changes could Gordon make that might alleviate these stresses or help his consultants to better cope with these stresses?

CASE 3

EMERGENCY! We Need a Better Compensation System[1]

Kimberly D. Elsbach

University of California, Davis

Jan Kees Elsbach

CEP America

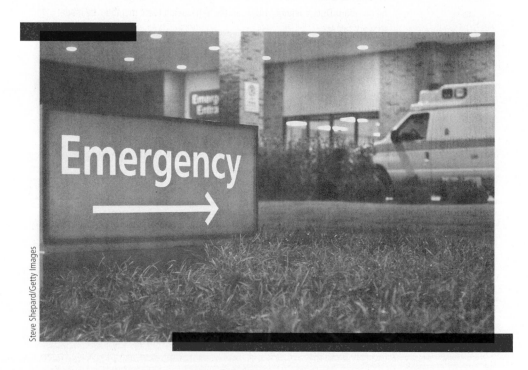

Steve Shepard/Getty Images

D r. Padma Singh, Director of Emergency Medicine at Westlake Hospital, collapsed into her desk chair with a sigh, being careful to avoid spreading the blood stain on her shirt to the chair fabric. Finally, another 10-hour emergency room (ER) shift in the books. Only a few notes left to write, and she would be out of hospital and on her way home to bed and six solid hours of sleep before she had to be back to lead tomorrow's staff meeting. Then she remembered the agenda—review the compensation and bonus system for the ER physicians and get their approval on a new plan. That wasn't going to be easy. The ER doctors were sharply divided in their preferences for a compensation system. Some wanted a system that kept a communal atmosphere in the group, where everyone worked equally hard and was paid accordingly. Others felt like they were

---

[1]This fictional case is based on the second author's 20-plus years of experience working in actual emergency rooms in five large cities throughout the United States.

carrying more of the load and should be compensated for that. It was clear from looking at monthly records that some doctors routinely treated more patients than others. Dr. Singh wanted the system to motivate the group rather than add dissatisfaction.

Padma groaned and buried her head in her hands. She now doubted that she'd be getting a good night's sleep after all. She had three alternative plans to present to the physicians in the morning, and she wondered if they would accept any of them.

Background on Westlake Hospital and the Emergency Physicians of Sacramento Group

Westlake Hospital is a privately owned, 162 bed, full-service hospital located in Sacramento, California. Westlake serves a mostly working-class patient population who rely on government insurance such as MediCal or Medicare. The hospital staffs its 29-room ER with doctors from a privately owned, physicians group called Emergency Physicians of Sacramento, or EPS. EPS has 20 physician members who staff their sister hospital, Eastlake, in addition to Westlake. Thus, EPS is a service provider for Westlake Hospital, and Padma Singh and the other 19 EPS physicians are not employees of Westlake Hospital, but employees of EPS.

Working in the ER at Westlake

When ER doctors work at Westlake Hospital, they work in teams of two. One doctor is the "triage doctor," who sees all patients in a "triage room" shortly after they arrive, and the second doctor is the "follow-up doctor" who sees patients, who are deemed in need of a higher level of care, in actual ER treatment rooms.

The triage doctor interviews and briefly interacts (approximately three minutes) with all new patients after they have checked into the ER. If the triage doctor determines that the patient needs to be seen by the follow-up doctor, he or she will pre-order tests or treatments (e.g., blood tests, urine tests, X-rays, or scans) that are likely to be needed by the follow-up doctor. This pre-ordering of tests saves time for the patient because the follow-up doctor will have the test results sooner and will be able to diagnose the patient sooner. Because the triage doctor has limited information about the patient when he or she orders the tests, however, this doctor may "over order" to cover all likely tests that might be needed. In about half the cases, the triage doctor may determine that the patient doesn't need to be seen by the follow-up doctor, and may send him or her to the "Fast Track" clinic that is attached to the ER and staffed by physician's assistants (PAs) and nurse practitioners (NPs). The triage doctor will see an average of 80 patients during a 10-hour shift. But the triage doctor gets "credit" (explained later as "charge points") only for those patients that he or she sends to the Fast Track (about 40 patients per shift). These patients also tend to have milder issues, and typically have lower charge levels (also explained below). Patients that go to the follow-up doctor are credited to that doctor.

The triage shift is a high-intensity job that is emotionally and mentally draining, and least preferred by most doctors. As a result, more of these less desirable shifts are disproportionally filled by more "junior" physicians. The triage shift was added about a year ago in response to an ER audit that showed that patients were waiting too long (sometimes several hours) before being seen by a physician. It was clear from feedback forms that the issue of long waiting times was most responsible for patient dissatisfaction.

By contrast, the follow-up doctor performs a more traditional role in the ER. The follow-up doctor examines patients in examination rooms, based on the order of arrival, unless immediate attention is needed. The follow-up doctor performs a more thorough physical exam of the patient and may order more tests if necessary. Patients seeing the follow-up doctor have, typically, two final outcomes: ER treatment and release, or ER treatment and admission to the hospital. In a typical 10-hour shift, the follow-up doctor will see 25–30 patients, and will get credit for all of these patients.

Physician Compensation at EPS

Levels of Charge and "Charge Points"

EPS collects fees for its doctors' services directly from insurance companies based on a five-level formula—the higher the level, the greater the fee. The five levels of charges for an ER visit are defined as follows: Level 1 = minor first aid, Level 2 = minor illness requiring some evaluation, such as a sore throat, Level 3 = moderately serious illness or injury requiring more tests or procedures, like stitches, Level 4 = serious illness or injury that often leads to hospital admission, and Level 5 = very serious illness or injury that requires immediate surgery or transfer to intensive care.

Greater detail on a patient chart allows for a higher charge level. For example, if a chart simply says, "patient has abdominal pain," a Level 2 charge may be given. If, by contrast, a chart says, "patient has abdominal pain, worse when lying down (moderating factor), started after eating spicy food (precipitating factor), and lasting 3 days (duration)" then a Level 4 charge may be given. In addition, there are certain triggering factors that lead a charge to automatically receive a Level 4 or 5. For example, if a physician spends more than 30 minutes at the patient's bedside (i.e., what's called "critical care time"), the visit is automatically charged a Level 5. As another example, if more than five tests are performed on a given patient, a Level 4 charge is automatically triggered. The necessity for any test or treatment is a relatively subjective decision, and doctors sometimes differ greatly in how they treat and charge any individual patient case. In theory, a physician could always aggressively order tests for every patient, and thus, increase the overall fees that may be charged to the insurance companies.

For each level of charge, physicians receive a corresponding number of "charge points" (i.e., a Level 5 charge leads to five charge points). These charge points are totaled each month for each physician. Then, a physician's "average charge points per hour" (ACPH) is calculated each month (i.e., ACPH = total charge points for the month divided by the number of scheduled hours worked for the month). For example, if a Dr. Singh had a charge points total of 1,640 for the month of July, and she worked sixteen, 10-hour shifts that month (i.e., 160 hours), she would have an ACPH = 1,640/160, or 10.25. For each charge point, EPS is paid about $50. So, Dr. Singh would have generated 1640 × $50 = $82,000 for EPS in the month of July.

Compensation Formula

Currently, doctors at EPS are paid on the basis of an *hourly wage* + *monthly individual bonus* + *year-end bonus*. **The hourly wage** is a flat rate of $100 per hour, and is paid based on the number of 10-hour shifts each doctor works. So, if Dr. Singh worked sixteen 10-hour shifts in July, her hourly pay would be 160 hours x $100/hr = $16,000 for that month. Doctors often work an hour or two past the end of their scheduled shifts in an attempt to complete treatment for all of the patients that they saw during their shift, but they are not paid for this extra time worked.

The **monthly individual bonus** is based on the ACPH earned by each doctor. Any doctor with an ACPH > 10 for the month receives a bonus based on the formula: [(ACPH above 10) × (hours worked per month) x ($100 revenue per charge point)]. So, if Dr. Singh had an ACPH of 10.25 and worked 160 hours for the month, she would receive a bonus of [(.25) × (160) × ($100)] = $4,000. This would bring her monthly compensation to $20,000. The individual monthly bonus was instituted about a year ago to motivate doctors to work more efficiently and to more carefully document their procedures and tests, to protect them from malpractice lawsuits. It should be noted, however, that it is difficult for doctors to achieve an ACPH > 10, and currently, less than half of the ER doctors at Westlake make this bonus standard each month.

Finally, there is a **year-end bonus** for all physicians. The money that EPS earns that is not paid out in hourly wages and bonuses is used to pay administrative and insurance costs. If any revenue remains at the end of the year, after these costs are paid, it is divided among all physicians proportional to the number of hours they worked over the year. This payment is typically around $10,000 per physician.

Problems with the Current Compensation System

Dr. Singh was aware of at least three problems that resulted from the current compensation system. First, doctors who worked in triage often had lower ACPH's than follow-up doctors. This is because even though triage doctors averaged more credited patients per shift than follow-up doctors (40 versus 25–30), the triage patients were typically charged at a lower level than the follow-up patients (Level 1 or 2 versus Level 3 or higher), making the total ACPH lower for the triage doctors. As result, scheduling was becoming contentious as no one wanted to take on the triage shifts. Some doctors had threatened to quit if the equity in assigning triage shifts was not improved. In addition, Dr. Singh was worried that triage doctors might send patients to the Fast Track when they actually needed more extensive care (because those patients would be credited to the triage doctor and not the follow-up doctor).

Second, the monthly bonus system was seen as unfair, because doctors who achieved an ACPH just below 10 completely missed out on any bonus. In addition, pressure to meet the hurdle of an ACPH above 10 might encourage unnecessary tests or falsely embellished documentation by follow-up doctors who wanted to gain charge points. While Dr. Singh had no documented proof that this was happening, she was aware that some doctors consistently had more Level 4 and Level 5 charges than others, making her wonder if they were "working the system" (and committing insurance fraud) to get their individual bonuses. Ordering unnecessary tests and procedures (such as CT scans) were not without risk to patients, as well. CT scans exposed patients to unhealthy radiation, and even a simple blood draw posed a risk to the patient health due to the possibility of infection.

Finally, the system led to wide variance in the time spent with patients. Dr. Singh had heard from patient feedback forms that some doctors were spending very little time with patients. Dr. Singh wondered if the monthly bonus system might also be encouraging physicians to see more patients per hour (and thus, spend less time with each patient) as a means of achieving a higher bonus. Dr. Singh worried that this could endanger patient safety. Further, some doctors had complained that they weren't getting to do the fulfilling job they trained for (i.e., treating and interacting with patients) because they were so rushed that they did little more than order tests and prescribe medication.

Dr. Singh was less worried about the year-end bonus system leading to the above behaviors, because that bonus was so far removed from daily work activities, and individual benefit from over-charging would be diluted when the revenues from all doctors were pooled. She was not 100 percent sure, however, that the year-end bonus was not motivating any unwanted behavior.

Possible Alternatives to the Current Compensation System

In thinking about these problems, Dr. Singh had consulted her friend, Dr. Fred Taylor, who worked in Los Angeles for a similar ER physicians group. Dr. Taylor suggested three possible alternatives based on his experience, in all cases the year-end bonus would continue to be paid. These options included: (1) pay doctors a straight hourly wage (possibly at a higher rate than the current $100/hr) with no monthly bonus, (2) pay doctors completely based on a percentage of the revenue generated by their personal charge points (i.e., 25% of the revenue generated by their charge points per month) with no hourly pay, or (3) pay doctors an hourly wage plus a monthly *group*-level bonus based on the entire group's charge points (i.e., if the entire group's average charge points per hour was above 10, the entire bonus would be divided up among all the doctors, in proportion to the number of hours they worked per month).

Dr. Singh realized that there were pros and cons to each of these alternatives. She also knew that she would have to help the physicians to balance these pros and cons, if she had any chance of getting them to agree on a plan.

*Optional Discussion Questions (answer questions that correspond to the topic area you are illustrating with this case).

Topic Area	Questions
Motivation	What behaviors would each of Dr. Singh's alternatives motivate? Explain how and why. Which alternative do you think is best? Would you suggest a fourth alternative that is better than any of those suggested by Dr. Taylor?
Culture	What values and assumptions are underlying the current compensation system at EPS? What do these values say about the organizational culture at EPS? How would each of the proposed alternatives affect the culture at Westlake?
Negotiation	How can Dr. Singh increase the chances that the doctors feel they will be treated fairly by the compensation system? What dimensions of justice/fairness should Dr. Singh consider and attend to?
Ethics	What ethical issues should Dr. Singh consider in developing the compensation plans? What ethical problems may arise from each of the three proposed compensation plans? Is there an alternative plan that is more ethical than the three that are proposed?
Innovation and Change	What process could Dr. Singh use to come up with a completely innovative and new compensation system? What are some factors that might be considered in a more innovative decision process?

CASE 4

Face Time at TechPoint Software, Inc.[1]

Kimberly D. Elsbach

University of California, Davis

Steve Prezant/Corbis

It was 8 p.m. on a Tuesday night and Jay Robinson was still hard at work in his office at TechPoint Software Inc. Jay often stayed into the evening, as did several of the managers, software engineers, and designers at TechPoint's San Ramon, California offices. It was part of the culture at TechPoint to be in the office late at night, early in the morning, and even on the weekends. It was even more important to work these extra hours if you were a junior colleague and were hoping to move up the ladder. Hard work, or at least the appearance of hard work, seemed to matter at TechPoint. And that was part of the problem that Jay Robinson was currently facing.

As he looked over the progress report summarizing the performance of one of his sharpest young software engineers, Julie Abdula, Jay was uncertain about what he should recommend to the promotion committee at tomorrow morning's 10 A.M. meeting. This meeting was essential to moving Julie from a probationary status (that all new engineers went through) to a secure, full-time position. Sure, Julie was bright, graduating at the top

---

[1] This fictional case is based on the author's field research on "face time" (i.e., merely being seen at work) across a number of corporate contexts. Any resemblance between events in this case and actual events is purely coincidental.

of her engineering class at California Polytechnic State University in San Luis Obispo (one of the top engineering schools in the United States). She was also very productive, completing all of her assigned tasks on time, and even finishing an extra project on a new software application that would allow mobile smartphones to access local television channels. Lastly, she was well-liked by most of her teammates. A couple of them had even commented to Jay that they appreciated her creativity and her ability to solve problems quickly.

But Julie never came in early, worked late, or volunteered to come in on the weekend. And she didn't seem to care that everyone else was putting in extra hours either. One of her less admiring teammates, Allison, had causally mentioned Julie's absence at last week's weekend file cleaning extravaganza (the once-a-year event where all team members come in and clean up online and paper files, scanning in documents that need to be saved, and erasing or shredding those that should be deleted). Allison had commented at the following Monday's staff meeting, "Julie, we missed you this weekend at the file clean up." This was Allison's way of giving the not-so-subtle hint that Julie should have been there. But Julie didn't seem to take the hint, and simply replied, "Yeah, it sounds like you had a full day." Jay had stressed that the file clean-up was voluntary, and didn't pressure anyone to come, but he assumed that everyone knew that this was an annual "bonding experience" and all of the junior staff members were expected to show up. Julie had joined the team just last Spring. Jay wondered if she could have somehow missed that element of TechPoint's culture.

In fact, as Jay reflected on Julie's performance, he wondered what else she might have missed about Tech Point's culture. In looking at Julie's team, it occurred to Jay that Julie was the only member who had not been a summer intern at TechPoint prior to getting her job. She was a star student, and had made such a positive impression in her interview, that Jay and the other managers had made an exception to their unwritten rule of "only hiring our tried and tested interns." But perhaps Julie had missed much more in skipping the internship than Jay had thought.

The summer internship for undergraduates at TechPoint was renown in the industry as one of the toughest "bootcamps for engineers" that existed. Interns worked 12-hour days on real projects and met with actual clients on a weekly basis. Interns were expected to jump right in and work side-by-side with seasoned employees and to be involved in all aspects of their work projects. For example, last summer, Julie's teammate Allison, along with two other new hires, Juan and Mirabel, worked on a project to allow educators to easily create customized online "textbooks" that combined readings, videos, interactive simulations, and cases—all bundled in an online packet that students accessed with a password. The customer was the State of California—a very important client, with more than 10,000 public schools as potential adopters.

During this project, Allison, Juan, and Mirabel learned early on that they would not be given any slack because they were inexperienced or young. They were expected to get "up to speed" immediately, even if it required coming in early and staying late everyday. They were also expected to do a lot of "grunt work"—such as copy editing, fact-checking, and other clerical tasks. This work was often done on the weekend, as that was the only time available when the interns did not have more pressing tasks to do.

These weekend work shifts also allowed the three to bond over their mutual suffering, and to become experts at learning all of the quirks of the TechPoint managers through shared stories. Anytime one of them heard a story about a famous "incident" or quirky behavior by a TechPoint manager, he or she would jot it down, and report back to the other three during the weekend. This way, Allison learned not just how best to divide work with Juan and Mirabel (e.g., Juan was a fast typist, and Mirabel was a diva with Internet search engines), but also how best to interact with the TechPoint managers. For example, they all learned that Steve Barber, one of the Software Engineering Managers, was compulsive about the format of presentations, and all presentations to his group should follow a specific sequence involving the presentation of background material first, then unanswered questions, new data collection, and research findings, and finally, preliminary recommendations. They also learned that another manager in Software Design, Tom Cahill, was an early morning person, who always had coffee in the cafeteria at 7 a.m. Tom was a goldmine of information about competitor trends, so meeting him for coffee was more than just a social requirement for interns, it became an essential part of their training.

As Jay thought about what Julie had missed by not meeting Tom Cahill, he suddenly recalled some things that Cahill had said recently. Just last week, Tom had mentioned to Jay that he didn't know who this "Julie-person" was, who was going to be evaluated in the promotion meeting. He added, "I know most of the junior software engineers because we have early morning coffee down in the cafeteria. But I've never seen Julie there. Is there a problem for her coming in when everyone else does?" Jay had said that there wasn't a problem that he knew of, and replied that Julie didn't seem to be a "morning person"—as a way of explaining her absence. But that comment had stuck in Jay's mind ever since. He wondered what other managers were thinking, and he was sure that they had also noticed Julie's absence at late-evening Chinese Food runs and trips to Vendo-Land in the basement. These were opportunities for managers to check up on who was there and who wasn't, and Jay was sure that most of the senior managers took advantage of them.

Finally, there was last Friday's team brainstorming meeting for the new project on educational software for home-schooling programs. Julie, Allison, Juan, and Mirabel were supposed to meet with Jay to brainstorm some ideas for developing an online mentoring and idea exchange program for home-schooling parents. Very quickly, however, the meeting turned into an argument with Allison, Juan, and Mirabel discounting and rejecting any ideas that Julie put forward. They complained that all of her ideas rested too heavily on her personal expertise in programming, and would exclude input from others. At first, Jay tried to understand the logic of these arguments, but as the meeting wore on, he began to wonder if the three engineers were merely contradicting Julie's ideas because they didn't like her, and didn't want to help her to succeed. The outcome of the meeting was that the group could not agree on a set of next steps—which was not a positive outcome—and would not help any of the team members to pass their upcoming promotion evaluations.

Jay needed to make a decision about Julie, but he wondered how much of Julie's performance and interaction with others was the result of his lack of supervision, or was due to her personality (something that could make it hard for her to succeed in the long term at TechPoint). He also wondered if it should matter that Julie did not bond with her colleagues, and if that should be a requirement for promotion.

Optional Discussion Questions (answer questions that correspond to the topic area you are illustrating with this case).

Topic Area	Question
Justice/Motivation	If Jay were to use procedural justice to make a decision about Julie, how would he go about it? If he were to follow ideas from interactional justice in his decision making, how would he go about it?
Perception	What perceptual biases are people using to evaluate Julie? What evidence is there of these biases? How should Jay go about making his decision to minimize these biases?
Learning	If Jay took a "Learning-Directed" approach to leadership in making this decision, how might he approach it?
Culture	How would you define the culture at TechPoint? What underlying assumptions define this culture? What evidence is there of these underlying assumptions? How are Julie's actions in concert or conflict with the assumptions that guide TechPoint's culture? Does Tech Point have a culture of "psychological safety"? How might Jay change the culture at Tech Point?
Teams	What team roles might Julie be a good fit for? Why?

CASE 5

Whatever Happened to One of the "100 Best Companies to Work For"? A Case Study of Hewlett-Packard

Kimberly D. Elsbach

University of California, Davis

Corbis

O n January 12, 1998, *Fortune* published its first-ever ranking of the "100 Best Companies to Work for in America."[1] This ranking was designed to measure employees' trust in a company based on the five dimensions of employee trust developed by the *Great Places to Work Institute*.[2] These five dimensions include credibility, respect, fairness, pride, and camaraderie.

In the inaugural ranking, the top 10 were dominated by technology firms including SAS (#3), Microsoft (#8), and Hewlett-Packard (#10). The following year, SAS was still #3, Hewlett Packard remained at #10, and Microsoft was at #27. Yet, by the fourth ranking, in 2002, Hewlett-Packard had completely dropped off the list, while SAS and Microsoft remained (at #3 and # 28 respectively). Worse, Hewlett-Packard never returned to the list in the following nine years (while both SAS and Microsoft stayed on the list throughout this time period). In fact, by late 2010, Hewlett-Packard was described as a company with "undermined and frayed" values, and one in which employee trust had been severely, if not irretrievably damaged.[3]

What happened to Hewlett-Packard? How did one of the "100 Best Companies to Work for in America" in 1998 completely fall off the list by 2002? In particular, what happened to employee trust in the company? Since employee trust was the basis for the "100 Best Companies to Work for in America" ranking, understanding how employee trust was affected during HP's downfall seems essential to unlocking the answer to this reputation puzzle.

In this case study, we examine the story of employee trust at Hewlett-Packard (called HP hereafter), through public documents,[4] from 1995 (prior to the first *Fortune* survey), through 2002 (when HP fell off the survey for good). We begin with some background on HP and its historical values.

Background: Hewlett-Packard and the "HP Way"[5]

At the time of this case study, Hewlett-Packard was a multi-national, high-tech company specializing in developing and manufacturing information technology, including personal computers, industry servers, storage devices, networking products, imaging and printing devices, and software. The company was headquartered in Palo California in the United States, and had offices in more than 170 countries on six continents. HP was ranked as one of the top two IT companies worldwide in revenues, and maintained over 324,000 employees.

The company—called the "godfather of Silicon Valley"—was started by two Stanford Engineering graduates, Bill Hewlett and David Packard, in a one-car garage in Palo Alto. When HP went public in 1957, Packard wrote down the management beliefs he and Hewlett shared, including a respect of and trust in employees, an environment that fostered creativity, and a flat management hierarchy. These ideals became known as the "HP Way" and served as a model for company culture in the emerging Silicon Valley. Over time, the HP Way became synonymous with a culture that embraced flexible work hours, creative freedom, great employee benefits, and a sense that layoffs would be used as only a 'last resort.' In return for this positive culture, employees gave their all to the company, even taking pay cuts to avoid layoffs, and remaining loyal when other job offers came their way. By the mid 1990s, the HP Way was known worldwide as a model for entrepreneurial corporate culture.

Hewlett-Packard 1995–1999

From 1995 to 1998, popular press stories about HP revealed much about its values and leadership. For instance, in a pair of stories accompanying the announcement that HP had received a Distinguished Partner in Progress Award for its operations in Singapore, several employees reported that the company's leaders gave them the freedom to decide how to do their own work. As the reporter noted on June 17, 1995:

> *Mrs. Anne Lim… has a particular liking for the way her employer, Hewlett-Packard, tells staff what to achieve but leaves the how-to-do-it to them…. "It's the belief in people, that they want to work hard and do their best, and then recognition will be forthcoming."*[6]

This "belief in people" was claimed as the reason that 47 of the original 62 employees at HP Singapore had remained since starting their jobs 25 years ago. As the reporter noted in a second story, also published on June 17, 1995:

> Mr Soo Kok-Leng, 43, HP's director of human resources (Southeast Asia)... explains, "There's no feeling of hierarchy here; everyone can talk like colleagues and not feel threatened.... Overall job goals are made known, but employees are left to achieve them as best they can." As Mr. Soo put it, "We provide the resources and environment, then let them loose, with no fixed rules."[7]

Numerous other stories highlighted the many programs designed by HP to give employees flexibility in work schedules. For example, one story in November, 1997, reported on a new program that was promoted by HP top management:

> Hewlett-Packard Ireland Sales has introduced a program allowing up to 40 percent of the 100 strong staff at its Blackrock, Co Dublin offices to work from home or other non-office locations ... "I hope that it gives employees more choice and more flexibility. It makes us an employer of choice and should help us retain people and keep them happier," says Managing Director Mr. Brian Kennan, ".... this is not about the company getting a return on these [policies]. It is about giving people more choice."

In addition, HP was portrayed as "a close knit family," and "a second home" to many employees.[8] This camaraderie was made even more evident in a new television advertising campaign that debuted in early 1997. As was reported in the *New York Times* on January 3, 1997:

> Hewlett-Packard gently pokes fun at its own engineers in an effort to make its technology seem more accessible. The ads... propose wacky uses for Hewlett-Packard printers and bear the slogan 'Built by engineers, used by normal people.'

Finally, HP was portrayed as committed to the values of work–life balance.[9] These values were noted by *Fortune* in its first ranking of the "100 Best Companies to Work for in America," published in January of 1998. In describing HP (#10 on the list), the magazine called the company "a trailblazer in people practices" and noted:

> [HP] recently added domestic-partner benefits and nursing-home-care insurance for spouses, parents, and grandparents to an already lush benefits package. "They walk the talk" when they say their people are the most important asset, one worker told us.[10]

In sum, in years leading up to HP's #10 ranking in *Fortune's* "100 Best Companies to Work for in America" survey, the popular media revealed extensive actions by the company and its leaders that showed respect for employees, fostered camaraderie among employees, and were viewed by employees as credible. Given these strong signals, it is not surprising that employee trust was high at this time (reflected in the high ranking in the *Fortune* survey). By mid-1999, however, all of this was about to change.

1999–2001

On July 19, 1999, HP announced that it was appointing a new Chief Executive Ofiicer (CEO) to replace then-retiring Chairman, Lewis Platt, who had led the company for seven years. In a move that surprised most industry analysts, HP appointed an outsider, Carly Fiorina—former director of Lucent Technology's Global Services business unit—as the new CEO. HP had rarely appointed outsiders, especially in top management positions, and Fiorina was known for being highly competitive and results oriented. Notably, in an interview immediately following her appointment, Fiorina claimed that HP needed to be "reinvented". Specifically, she noted:

> I think in general, the people of HP would agree that we need to increase our sense of urgency, reinvigorate our competitive spirit and focus on speed.[11]

Similarly, in a keynote speech at the high-tech Comdex conference later that Fall, Fiorina also talked about "reinventing" HP by taking more risks and moving more quickly.[12]

Industry experts and observers took note of Fiorina's comments and predicted the end to the HP Way, including its long-standing traditions of employee respect and camaraderie among engineers and other creative types. As one observer at the annual Comdex conference (a large computer and high-tech conference) noted in December, 1999:

> Fiorina...talked about a company culture that balances radical ideas and inventiveness with traditional approaches. Sentamentalist that I am, the words I heard were these: The legendary HP way is dead. As carved out by the founders, the old ways of careful deliberation, conservatism and tradition are part of history, along with the famous one-car garage that was HP's first home.[13]

Technology consultant Mark Anderson went further, saying earlier that year: "Picking her [Fiorina] is not about technology or strategy. It's about culture."[14]

On January 10, 2000, HP fell to #43 on *Fortune's* annual survey of the "100 Best Companies to Work for in America. Perhaps, sensing nervousness among HP employees about the company's impending "reinvention", *Fortune* reported:

> New CEO Carly Fiorina promised that the new, streamlined HP.... would remain true to the culture of integrity and respect known as the HP Way.[15]

Yet, Fiorina's actions continued to suggest that the old HP ways would not last. Thus, later that summer, Fiorina launched a new global advertising campaign designed around the theme "Invent" featuring the new CEO as narrator. This new campaign was the first time that HP had produced an all-encompassing brand message for its products (versus having a number of campaigns produced by individual business units). In this way, the ad campaign mirrored Fiorina's goal of centralizing control over HP's business units and removing the tradition of entrepreneurship previously enjoyed by these divisions. As was noted in an article published on June 1, 2000:

> *Hewlett-Packard's advertising had mirrored its decentralized, entrepreneurial structure. The printer group had its own advertising, the PC division sponsored its work and the e-services unit ran its own campaign.* Just as the company suffered from what seemed a lack of focus, H-P's fragmented advertising had difficulty building brand strength.... *"The difference you'll see from HP now and in the foreseeable future is that this is an integrated campaign"* says Allison Johnson, *head of communications.*[16]

Yet, despite these actions, in the next ranking of "100 Best Companies to Work For" list, published on January 8, 2001,[17] HP's ranking fell to #63.

2001–2002

A few months into 2001, on April 19, HP reported that their earnings were severely down and pay bonuses and raises would be suspended and managerial staff would be cut.[18] Then, in July, employees were asked to take voluntary pay cuts to fend off further layoffs,[19] which were eventually taken anyway (i.e. 6,000 were laid off in late July, 2001).[20] Sensing concern from stockholders and employees, HP's board of directors took the unprecedented step of issuing a statement declaring their unwavering support for Fiorina. On August 20, 2001, the press reported:

> *Directors of Hewlett-Packard Inc. broke a tradition of silence yesterday to declare their 100% support for Carly Fiorina, the embattled chief executive, despite the company's weak financial performance over the past nine months.... They also gave their wholehearted support to Ms. Fiorina's changes to HP's operations and culture.*[21]

This vote of confidence was important, because just two weeks later, on September 4, 2001, HP announced that it was seeking to merge with Houston-based Compaq Computer Corporation, to form the world's largest personal computer (PC) maker.[22] Early reports indicated that the merger would result in at least 15,000 lost jobs and the new culture at HP that would focus on sales and services, rather than engineering innovation.[23] Spokespersons also indicated that HP was looking to become an "alternative to IBM"—suggesting an identity change from a more specialized producer of computing products to a large corporate force in information technology.[24]

Observers, analysts, and especially employees immediately protested what they saw as an end to the HP Way. As one commentator reported on September 17, 2001:

> *I suspect electrical engineers will take more than their share of the proposed [job] cuts of 15,000 if HP's acquisition of Compaq*

> goes forward.... Fiorina implies she wants to build the next IBM,
> but I doubt she has the taste for the engineering costs. Maybe
> she really is poised to reverse HP's three-year slide in R&D
> expenditures as a percentage of sales, but the move to acquire a
> company that spends even less on engineering speaks otherwise.
> Fiorina once courted PriceWaterhouseCoopers. I think that shows
> where her heart lies. If the rice flies at this wedding, engineers
> had better duck.[25]

A tenacious proxy fight then ensued when David Packard, eldest son of one of the founders of HP, sent a statement to shareholders on November 11, 2001, opposing the merger on the grounds that it would destroy the culture at HP and that its accompanying loss of 15,000 jobs was in stark opposition to the founders' values.[26] As one reporter noted:

> David W. Packard has slammed Carly Fiorina, HP's CEO, for a
> 'weakest link' style of management. "My father and Bill Hewlett
> managed a company in a way that is was never necessary to tell
> people, 'sorry, business is not so good right now. Goodbye.' "

These statements by Mr. Packard showed an alliance with employees and a distancing of the founding families from the current CEO.

HP then launched a series of attacks on Mr. Packard—who was eventually joined by all members of the Hewlett and Packard families in opposing the merger—through company news releases. These news releases focused on the theme of change and the notion that if HP stands still, it will be overtaken by the competition.[27] Terms like "bold steps", "withstanding challenges", and "charging ahead" were used in these news releases to describe the merger.[28] By contrast, opposing the merger was described as "retreating into the past", "incremental approach," and "attempting in vain to preserve the status quo."[29]

While there were advocates on both sides of the merger debate, most comments from employees appeared negative. Many of these comments equated the merger with layoffs, and like David Packard, suggested that making a deal that required layoffs was not the HP Way. As one news story reported, on December 17, 2000:

> [Employee] Judy Anderson won't hesitate for a moment. Her 500
> shares aren't that much, she knows, but she'll pledge them all
> against the effort to join with Compaq Computer . . . she opposes
> any such merger solely because it's not the HP Way. . . . For many
> HP employees and shareholders like Ms. Anderson, . . . the vote is
> about much more than the bottom line: It's about the soul of one
> of America's most storied businesses—the original Silicon Valley
> start-up. . . . Laying off 15,000 employees is not my idea of the HP
> Way, agrees Ms. Anderson. . . . "If that merger goes through, the
> HP Way is dead."

It was not surprising, then, that HP fell completely off the 2002 list of the "100 Best Companies to Work For," published on February 4, 2002.[30] Similarly, it was not surprising that, at the pivotal shareholder meeting in which the merger was voted on, Bill Hewlett received a standing ovation, while Carly Fiorina received boos.

Yet, the merger did pass by the slimmest of margins, meaning that the layoffs would happen, and that Fiorina would have to soldier on with a new company, all the while knowing that a great many of the remaining employees voted against the merger. As one reporter put it: "With so many of HP's shareholders having voted against the union, her seat will remain distinctly hot....It will be hard to motivate Hewlettites to give their best for the new firm. Some are sure to leave."[31]

*Optional Discussion Questions (answer questions that correspond to the topic area you are illustrating with this case).

Topic Area	Question
Intro to OB	What skills did Fiorina need in order to be successful at the reinvention of HP? What Tactics could Fiorina have used to improve her chances of successfully reinventing HP?
Indiv. Characteristics	What personality dimensions might define Fiorina? How might introverts react to her personality? How well does Fiorina manage emotions in the workplace?
Leadership	How would you describe the leadership style of HP's founders and leaders prior to Fiorina? How would you describe Fiorina's leadership style? How did the different leadership styles affect employees?
Perception	What were the social identities of HP employees when Fiorina came on board? How did Fiorina's actions affect these social identities?
Culture	What values were underlying the HP Way? How did this culture change after Fiorina? Why?
Communication	How did the language and labels used by Fiorina affect employees? Did Fiorina develop a creative collaboration with employees in her efforts to "reinvent" HP?

Endnotes

1. Levering, R. & Moskowitz, M. "The 100 best companies to work for in america" January 12, 1998, *Fortune*, 137, Issue 1, 84–95. This survey was later named simply, "The 100 best companies to work for".
2. Great Places to Work Employee Survey at: http://www.greatplacetowork.com/what_we_do/employee_survey.php
3. *The Washington Post*, August 15, 2010.
4. Sources used include major world newspapers, magazines, and newsletters (indexed in databases Lexis-Nexis, and BusinessSource) as well as company news releases posted on the Hewlett-Packard website.
5. http://www.hp.com/hpinfo/newsroom/

6. Koh Buck Song. (1995). "Why they stay on" *The Straits Times* (Singapore), June 17, L2.

7. Koh Buck Song. (1995). "Keeping employees just a matter of style" *The Straits Times* (Singapore), June 17, L1.

8. Koh Buck Song. (1995). "Why they stay on" *The Straits Times* (Singapore), June 17, L2.

9. Kaufman, L. (1999). "Battling burnout: Some companies are insisting that employees cut their workloads." *The Gazette* (Montreal), May 10, 1999, F1.

10. Levering, R. & Moskowitz, M. (1998). "The 100 best companies to work for in america" January 12, 1998, *Fortune, 137,* Issue 1, 84–95.

11. Paul Kangas & Jeff Yastine. (1999). "Hewlett-Packard—CEO; Outgoing Chairman—Interview on Nightly Business Report." *The Nightly Business Report,* National Public Radio, July 19.

12. Runyon, S. "The HP way is dead, long live the HP way," *Electronic Engineering Times,* December 20, 1999, 62.

13. Runyon, S. "The HP way is dead, long live the HP way," *Electronic Engineering Times,* December 20, 1999, 62.

14. Naughton, J. (1999). "Observer Profile: Carly Fiorina: HP's Sauce; Forget Hillary Clinton, this is the most powerful woman in the U.S. Last week corporate America was reeling as she rocketed to the top of Hewlett Packard with the mission of dragging the staid electronics giant into the age of the Net." *The Observer,* July 25, 25.

15. Levering, R. Moskowitz, M. Garcia, F. & Vella-Zarb, K. (2000). "The 100 Best Companies to Work For" *Fortune,* 2000, 141(1),,82–93.

16. See Farrell, G. (2000). And then there was one HP. New ads aim to unify image of Hewlett-Packard. *USA Today,* June 1, p. 5B.

17. Levering, R. Moscowitz, M., Schlosser, J., & Sung, J. "The 100 best companies to work for" *Fortune,* January 8, 143, 148–168.

18. Gaither, C. (2001). "Hew2001), lett-Packard warns of dismal earnings and job cuts." *New York Times,* April 19, C4.

19. Avery, S. "Many HP employees accept pay cuts" *Wall Street Journal,* July 2, B8.

20. Staff, "Hewlett-Packard to let go another 6000 employees" (2001). *Irish Independent,* July 27, C5.

21. Kehoe, L. (2001). "Fiorina not facing axe: board" *National Post* (Canada), August 20, 2001, p. C1.

22. Creed, A. (2001), "HP to swallow Compaq for $25 Billion" Newsbytes, September 4.

23. Creed, A. & Kelsey, D. (2001). "CEO calls HP-Compaq merger a 'big damn deal' – update," *Newsbytes,* September 4.

24. Richtel, M. "Wall St. remains cool to Hewlett-Compaq Merger," *New York Times,* September 6, C4.

25. Boyd Merrit, R. (2001). "The new HP way" *Electronic Engineering Times,* September 17, 56.

26. Lohr, S. "A growing group of disgruntled relatives may seal the fate of Hewlett-Packard and Compaq," *New York Times,* November 8, 2001, p. C6.

27. Ginn, S. "Letter to the Editor, Hewlett-Packard's Way" December 2, 2001 *New York Times,* Section 4, p 14.

28. Lohr S. & Gaither, C. "A family struggle, A company's fate, " *New York Times,* December 2, 2001, Section 3, p. 1.

29. Lohr, S. Gaither, L. "A family struggle, A company's fate, "*New York Times,* December 2, Section 3,1. HP News Release, HP Issues Statement and Sends Latest Letter to Shareowners on Compaq Merger PALO ALTO, Calif., February. 11, 2002.

30. Levering, R., Moskowitz, M., Munoz, L. Hjelt, P. & Wheat, A. "The 100 best companies to work For" *Fortune,* February 4, 2002, Volume 145, Issue 3, pp.72-83.

31. Gaenor Lipson, "Hewlett-Packard beats about the bush" (2002). *Sunday Times* (South Africa), March p. E1.

CASE 6

NASCAR's Drive for Diversity: Can They Reach the Finish Line?[1]

Sonya Jewell
University of California, Davis

Kimberly D. Elsbach
University of California, Davis

Jill Toyoshiba/MCT/Newscom

I t's Sunday morning. You slowly wake up to the first sounds of life outside the walls of your camper and open the door to a sea of RVs and tents. Beer cans, beaded necklaces, and smoking fire pits remind you of the Mardi Gras-like partying that ended only a few hours ago. As more fans awake and gather themselves, eggs and beer cans are cracked open in perfect harmony. The familiar smells of barbeque and burning rubber remind you what's happening today . . . it's race day!

From your seat in the grandstand at the Bristol Motor Speedway you can feel the anticipation building. The smell of sweat and exhaust fills your senses. The grand marshal takes the stand and 170,000 fans catch their breath as they await those famous words.

---

[1]This case was prepared to stimulate class discussion. It is not intended as a policy statement or recommendation.

"Gentlemen, start your engines" signals the roar of engines, and with the drop of a flag, the race begins. Welcome to NASCAR.

Deeply rooted in Southern tradition, NASCAR (or the National Association for Stock Car Auto Racing) is one of America's most popular and well-attended sports. Many of the values embraced by NASCAR define much of contemporary American culture, including small-town and rural values, working-class ideals, and a deep respect for patriotism and the military.[1] NASCAR's affiliation with the military is especially notable, and extends from team sponsorships (e.g., the Army and the National Guard both sponsor race cars), to military color guards and flyovers at every Sprint Cup event, to a large presence of military personnel in the stands. Because the military is so diverse in its membership, NASCAR's strong affiliation with it has increased the diversity of fans in the stands. Yet, in the last decade, NASCAR has been criticized for its lack of diversity on the track.[2] In fact, it has been almost 50 years since the only African-American to ever win a NASCAR Cup Series race claimed his victory.[3]

In 2004, executives at NASCAR launched *Drive for Diversity*, a program aimed at attracting minority and female drivers and crew members to the sport of professional stock car racing. NASCAR said that the program was designed to bring drivers from underrepresented minority groups to the top echelons of the sport. Yet, by 2012 (the time of this case study), they had failed to bring in one such driver to their Cup Series.

So why was a program labeled "NASCAR's top corporate initiative" having such difficulty producing results? What follows is an in-depth look at the implementation of the Drive for Diversity program and the role of diversity in NASCAR's culture.

NASCAR[4]

At the time of this case study, NASCAR was a family-owned and operated business, founded in 1947, that sanctioned and governed multiple auto racing sports events, including the elite Sprint Cup Series, as well as the mid-level Nationwide Series and Camping World Truck Series. Annually, NASCAR sanctioned over 1,500 races at over 100 tracks in 39 states, and Canada. NASCAR was officially headquartered in Daytona Beach, Florida, but also maintained offices in four cities in North Carolina: Charlotte, Mooresville, Concord, and Conover. Due to its southern roots, all but a handful of NASCAR teams were still based in North Carolina, especially near Charlotte.

NASCAR was one of the most-watched professional sports in the United States. In fact, in the year 2012, professional football was the only sport in the United States to hold more television viewers. Also, at that time, NASCAR held 17 of the top 20 attended single-day sporting events in the world, and claimed 75 million fans who purchase over $3 billion in annual licensed products. *Fortune 500* companies sponsored NASCAR teams and drivers, and were instrumental in making it a $3 billion (in annual revenue) sport.

Overview of Drive for Diversity Program

According the program's website, in 2012:

> "Drive for Diversity is the industry's leading development program
> for minority and female drivers and crew members. The Drive
> for Diversity (D4D) program currently supports drivers in two of
> NASCAR's introductory level racing series—the NASCAR K&N

> *Pro Series and the NASCAR Whelen All-American Series (both regional stockcar racing series). D4D also supports crew member candidates through a year-long pit crew training program."*

Much like Major League Baseball's minor league system, D4D was attempting to recruit and develop new racing talent that could be moved through the circuit with the hopes of attracting new fans and sponsors to the sport.

According to the NASCAR's diversity website (nascardiversity.com), the mission of the D4D program was to "To engage women and people of diverse, ethnic and racial backgrounds in all facets of the NASCAR industry."[5] The program was also designed to further diversify NASCAR's participant and audience base."[6] In this manner, NASCAR's D4D program was positioned as the path to a more inclusive culture, a way to reinforce their commitment to diversity. NASCAR suggested that this move was not only the right thing to do, but made good business sense as well. Widening their audience would bring more people to the races and to their television sets on weekends.

In line with the D4D program, NASCAR had attempted to remove controversial symbols from official NASCAR venues. For example, they decided not to display the Confederate flag at the NASCAR Hall of Fame, which opened in 2009, despite the flag's role in the sport's heritage. As Winston Kelley, executive director of the Hall of Fame and a longtime pit reporter for MRN (Motor Racing Network) Radio, said, in May of 2010: "The Rebel flag means different things to different people. Since it is offensive to some, that is the reason we don't want it in there [the Hall of Fame]."[7]

Struggles in the D4D Program

Despite the above claims and efforts, NASCAR's D4D program had struggled to produce results. In its first year, 2004, the Drive for Diversity program invited four African-American drivers, including Joe Henderson, and one female driver to try their hand at NASCAR's weekly short track circuit. These drivers were selected based on their resume of experience and performance record as well as their minority status. By 2012, D4D drivers competed in nearly 200 events at NASCAR Home Tracks across the country each year."[8] Since its inception, 31 drivers had competed under the Drive for Diversity banner, winning 34 races combine.

Yet, by 2010, no D4D driver had ever made it to the Promised Land, NASCAR's big three: Sprint Cup Series, the Nationwide Series, and the Camping World Truck Series. Promises made to the young talent brought into the program remained unfulfilled. D4D drivers, like Henderson, recruited in 2004, were still waiting for their 15 minutes of fame. According to a *New York Times* article, Henderson was under contract from 2005 to 2006 and was used for publicity for NASCAR diversity efforts but was given poor equipment in 2005, and was not provided a racecar in 2006." "It's a sham," Joe Henderson Jr. said in a telephone interview...The program is not designed to be successful because, No. 1, it's not properly funded. They claim that it's a pipeline. Well, nobody came out the pipe."[9]

Some critics suggested that these problems stemmed from mixed signals that NASCAR sent about its commitment to diversity—including both racial and gender diversity. For example, in one of its first moves after starting D4D, NASCAR gave responsibility for creating, managing, and promoting the D4D program to an outside marketing agency and brought in, not a race car driver, but a basketball legend (Magic

Johnson) to help drum minority support. NASCAR also did not link their developmental program, Fueling Dreams, or D4D to their main website, creating a symbolic disconnection between the two. Finally, in one of the most-often quoted statements in recent years, NASCAR Vice President, Robin Pemberton—in telling reporters that NASCAR was going to stop policing drivers so strictly—said, "Boys, have at it and have a good time."[10] That statement, more than anything else, affirmed that NASCAR drivers were male.

At the same time, other critics suggested that D4D struggled because NASCAR never put in the necessary resources for success. Joe Gibbs, owner of Joe Gibbs Racing, for example, was heard commenting about the lack of funding for the program. Similarly executives from automakers as well as journalists for stock car racing routinely discussed the need for more funding in the D4D program. It appeared that these commentators liked the idea of the D4D program, but thought its initial rate of funding was not enough to help it take off.

Finally, some argued that NASCAR would never have minority drivers in a sport that was perceived to appeal most widely to white audiences. Specifically, they argued that sponsors, who drove the sport, were wary of investing in minority drivers, when minority fans were not prevalent. As Kurt Roehring, of Roehring Engineering (a former team sponsor) mentioned:

> In marketing products, if you're selling the product to primarily
> a black demographic group, well, blacks aren't really in the stands
> right now in NASCAR. There are possibly other sporting events
> or sports marketing that you could do that could target a black
> demographic better than stock car racing.[11]

Moving Diversity Forward—Can D4D Succeed at NASCAR?

By 2012, the question that remained for NASCAR and its leaders was "What will it take for the D4D program to succeed in placing more minority and women drivers into NASCAR's top competitive levels?"

Some, like team owner Joe Gibbs, said it would take the next Tiger Woods. As Gibbs noted, "I think that's what we need [i.e., another Tiger Woods]. The reality is, I don't care who finds the person, how you get him involved, I think the sport needs it. Once you open those doors up, I think there's going to be a benefit for every team out there, not just the team that finds him."

Others suggested that NASCAR must change its deeply rooted traditions and culture to achieve success in its diversity programs. Further, they noted that traditions and cultures aren't made in a day. In fact, according to researchers, most organizational cultures are grounded in long-held and continually reinforced values.[12] As sociologist and NASCAR enthusiast Jim Wright notes, "race is not something that is talked about" as a current issue in NASCAR.[13]

At the same time, there were hints that diversity may, yet, thrive on the track at NASCAR. First, diversity seemed consistent with NASCAR's core values of Freedom and Individualism. As Wright also pointed out:

> The values of the NASCAR subculture are best described as
> the traditional American virtues. . . . Individualism, freedom,
> community, mobility—these are NASCAR values, important
> values, the things we stand for as a nation.[14]

Further, there was evidence of recent strides in diversity at NASCAR, albeit, not in relation with the D4D program. Following the 2012 Daytona 500, for example, one blogger wrote:

> *This year at Daytona, youth, diversity and social media all took turns in the spotlight—in the end, a good weekend for NASCAR.... two Brazilians and a woman earned top starting spots in the Truck Series and Nationwide Series races at Daytona. Brazilians Miguel Paludo and Nelson Piquet Jr. took the pole and outside pole for the Truck race Friday night, while Danica Patrick took the limelight to a new level when she became the second woman to win a pole in NASCAR's top three series with the Nationwide Series pole. Paludo, in his second full-time season in the Truck Series, and Piquet Jr., son of three-time Formula One champ Nelson Piquet, both drive for Turner Motorsports. Patrick, in her first full-time season in the Nationwide Series, was the first woman to win a pole since March 1994, when Shawna Robinson won the pole at Atlanta.[15]*

Faced with these facts, some had wondered if NASCAR should continue its D4D program and support it more strongly, or discontinue the program and just allow diversity to increase on its own.

Optional Discussion Questions (answer questions that correspond to the topic area you are illustrating with this case).

Topic Area	Question
Decision Making	In deciding to keep or discontinue their D4D program, how would NASCAR use a "rational" approach to decision making? What heuristics and biases might decision makers be prone to? How can decision makers cultivate constructive conflict while building consensus for their decisions?
Learning	How can NASCAR officials learn from the D4D struggles so far? What should they do to ensure that they learn the most from this experience? How can they build on this experience to improve the future of D4D?
Perception	How might one's social identity as a NASCAR fan be influencing peoples' perception of the D4D program?
Culture	How would you describe the culture of NASCAR? What are the values that underlie this culture? How are those values reinforced in daily activities and behaviors? How is the culture symbolized?
Diversity	What diversity management practices and methods might help the D4D program? What communication practices might be used to communicate better the goals of the D4D program?

Endnotes

1. Wright, J. (2002). *Fixin' to git. one Fan's love affair with NASCAR's Winston Cup*. Durham, NC: Duke University Press.
2. Livingstone, S. (2007). "NASCAR seeks diversity but find the going slow." *USA Today*, April 27, http://www.usatoday.com/sports/motor/nascar/2007-04-26-diversity-cover_N.htm
3. Fielden, G., (2009). *NASCAR: The complete history*. Lincolnwood, IL: Publications International.
4. http://en.wikipedia.org/wiki/NASCAR
5. http://www.nascardiversity.com/about/about_mission.aspx
6. http://www.fuelingdreams.com/page/overview-1
7. http://www.aolnews.com/2010/05/12/what-the-nascar-hall-of-fame-has-and-what-it-doesnt-have/
8. http://drivefordiversity.info/content/?page_id=62
9. http://www.regalma g.com/critics-nascar-diversity-priority-a-335.html
10. Posted on http://nascar.speedtv.com/article/cup-nascar-boys-have-at-it-one-last-time
11. Ibid.
12. Christensen, C. M. (2006). "What is an organization's culture?" *Harvard Business Review*, August 2. Boston, MA: Harvard Business School Press.
13. Jim Wright. (2002). "Fixin' to Git. One Fan's Love Affair with NASCAR's Winston Cup." Durham, NC: Duke University Press.
14. Wright, J. (2002). *Fixin' to git. One fan's love affair with NASCAR's Winston Cup*, 162–163. Durham, NC: Duke University Press.
15. Thompson, P. (2012). One Fan's Perspective: Youth, Diversity, Social Media Served at 2012 Speedweeks, Yahoo! Contributor Network, Posted Feb 29, 8:34 pm EST, http://sports.yahoo.com/nascar/news?slug=ycn-11034316.

CASE 7

Perceptions of Leaders Following Public Failures: A Tale of Two Coaches

Kimberly D. Elsbach

University of California, Davis

More than any other group of individuals, we scrutinize leaders—especially leaders who fail. In this case study, I describe two leaders (both college football coaches) who were involved in public failures. Although both failures were damaging to public perceptions of these leaders, one leader was fired, while the second was retained. This "Tale of Two Coaches" illustrates some of the high expectations placed on leaders, as well as the difficulty leaders may have in living up to those expectations.

The Case of Coach Mike Leach

By December of 2009, Mike Leach, head football coach at Texas Tech University, in Lubbock, Texas, had been through a tough, but successful year. Early in the year, Leach had negotiated a lucrative new coaching contract that included a sizeable bonus for staying on as head coach for the next season. Leach had then led his "Red Raider" football team to an 8–4 record for the season, placing them third in the Big 12 Conference which led them to be selected to play in the Valero Alamo Bowl, scheduled for January 2, 2010.[1] By all accounts, things were going well for the coach, but that was about to change.

Background

Long considered an outsider to the game (having never played college football), Leach had become known as an adept strategist with a sometimes quirky personality (he apparently loved pirates and was known to lecture his team on the history of Caribbean pirates in the past). Leach's atypical pedigree included a J.D. from the Pepperdine University School of Law and a Master of Sports Science/Coaching from the United States Sports Academy.

Before coming to Texas Tech in 2000, Leach served as the offensive coordinator under legendary coach Bob Stoops at Oklahoma, and as the offensive coordinator at the University of Kentucky under head coach Hal Mumme. Early in his coaching career, Leach's "spread offense" helped college superstars like Tim Couch (Kentucky) and Josh Huepel (Oklahoma) to become top NFL draft picks. Leach's success continued at Texas Tech, where, as head coach, he produced nine-win seasons in 2002, 2005, and 2007, and an eleven-win season in 2008. In 2008, Texas Tech defeated then #1 ranked Texas, and that year Leach was chosen as the Big 12 Coach of the Year and Associated Press Coach of the Year. On November 21, 2009, Leach became the all-time winningest coach in Texas Tech history with a victory over Oklahoma. Later that month, Texas Tech was invited to play in the Alamo Bowl against Michigan State University.[2]

The Event

On December 16, 2009, football player Adam James—son of former NFL player and ESPN football commentator Craig James—suffered a concussion during practice. According to accounts printed in the *Lubbock Avalanche Journal*,[3] Adam James was diagnosed with a concussion by team physician, Dr. Michael Phy, who told him sit out of practices for the coming week. The next day, James came to observe practice—as is the custom for injured players— in street clothes and sunglasses, and began walking around the practice field in a slow and nonchalant manner. When asked about his sunglasses, James said that he was told to wear them by the team physician to help deal with his headaches and light sensitivity, both after-effects of the concussion. Reports indicate that coach Leach was angry about James' behavior and apparel and thought James was faking the concussion.[4] Later reports revealed that coach Leach already believed that Adam James was lazy and had a poor attitude based on his efforts during practice.[5] Further, Leach appeared to have become weary of what he claimed was meddling by Adam James' celebrity father to garner Adam more playing time[6].

Sworn affidavits given by doctor Phy and athletic trainer, Steve Pincock[7] describe the actions then taken by coach Leach. According to these affidavits, coach Leach told Pincock to lock James in a dark training shed. Pincock also noted:

> *Leach further told me to have him stand in the dark during the entire practice. He did not want James on the field, and he did not want James in the training facility. He did not want to see James. He wanted James to be uncomfortable.*[8]

The affidavits then state that James was taken to the sports medicine/athletic training shed and objects were removed so James could not sit or lie down, in keeping with Leach's orders. Pincock said that when practice ended approximately two to three hours later, he let James out of the shed and apologized, noting that he was following the instructions of Coach Leach.

Two days later, on December 19, 2009, James came to practice again. According to Pincock, Coach Leach instructed him again to place James in a dark shed. Because the team was now practicing at the stadium and not the practice field, James was put in the media room and anything that a person might sit on was removed, except for two tractor tires. Also, according to Pincock, a student trainer monitored James to make sure he was standing the entire practice.

Regarding these two incidents, Dr. Phy's sworn affidavit notes that:

> In spite of the fact that James may not have been harmed by these actions, I consider this practice inappropriate and a deviation from the medical standard of care.[9]

Similarly, Pincock claimed that the treatment was atypical and inappropriate. As he noted:

> [I don't know of any other Tech players] ever being placed in a darkened shed or room similar to James.... Other players who have sustained concussions in the past were sometimes placed in the physician's examination room with the lights dimmed, or in the weight room or athletic training room.... I feel that Leach's treatment of James was inappropriate, and I did not agree with it. However, I felt I had to follow the instructions of the head coach.[10]

The next day, December 20, 2009, James' parents filed a complaint with the university about the treatment of their son following his concussion. The university president and athletic director then met with coach Leach and discussed the allegations. They also asked him to sign an apology to Adam James and to agree to a set of specific guidelines regarding his treatment of players. Leach refused to sign the document, and was suspended on December 28, 2009, five days before his team was to play in the Alamo Bowl.

Reaction to the Event

Immediately following the suspension of the 2008 "AP Coach of the Year" the popular press picked up the story of Mike Leach and Adam James. In numerous accounts published in major U.S. newspapers, as well as in commentary and interviews on national television, reporters gave their assessment of Leach's alleged offenses. In many of these accounts, Leach was called "brilliant,"[11] "smart,"[12] and "revered".[13] Yet, at the same time, his alleged actions were called the result of "arrogance" and "disdain" for player health and well-being.[14] As one reporter noted:

> [Leach].... sent a message.... to the rest of his players. Concussions may be the most underreported injuries in athletics, which makes them all the more dangerous. When a coach, in effect, tells his players this is how he deals with head injuries, it hardly encourages them to say they might have a problem.[15]

In response, Leach flatly denied any wrong-doing. Further, he claimed that his suspension was due to the influence of ESPN analyst Craig James and the university's desire to get out of paying him his expected bonus.[16] Finally, he criticized Adam James and downplayed his injury. Through his lawyer, Ted Liggett, Leach claimed that Adam James was a "disgruntled student athlete that like many were not happy with their playing time" and called his injury a "mild concussion"—suggesting that it was somehow not a true concussion.[17]

Yet, statements by the press made it clear that Leach's actions could not be so easily excused. As one reporter noted:

> Adam James was diagnosed with a concussion. His coach
> mocked the prescribed treatment. Other than that, you can
> believe all the scenarios and conspiracy theory you like, and
> it won't make any difference. Even if Tech officials did hold
> a grudge against Leach over past sins and his ugly contract
> negotiations, he'd deserve this suspension. Even if Adam James'
> father were not an ESPN commentator and former college
> football star, Leach would deserve it. Even if Leach were not
> such an entertaining character whom I enjoy interviewing, he'd
> deserve it.[18]

Leach responded to the negative press by filing a court motion that would have allowed him to coach the Alamo Bowl. But just before the motion could be heard on December 30, 2009, Texas Tech fired Mike Leach.[19] A statement released by Texas Tech University, gave the following explanation for Leach's firing:

> The coach's termination was precipitated by his treatment of a
> player after the player was diagnosed with a concussion. The
> player was put at risk for additional injury. After the university
> was apprised of the treatment, Coach Leach was contacted by
> the administration of the university in an attempt to resolve
> the problem. In a defiant act of insubordination, Coach Leach
> continually refused to cooperate in a meaningful way to help
> resolve the complaint. He also refused to obey a suspension
> order and instead sued Texas Tech University. Further, his
> contemporaneous statements make it clear that the coach's actions
> against the player were meant to demean, humiliate and punish
> the player rather than to serve the team's best interest. This action,
> along with his continuous acts of insubordination, resulted in
> irreconcilable differences that make it impossible for coach Leach
> to remain at Texas Tech.[20]

Two days after his firing, Mike Leach did a live interview on ESPN where he attempted to give his side of the story. In this interview with ESPN analyst Rece Davis on January 1, 2010, Leach continued to criticize Adam James, calling him "lazy" and saying he had a "sense of entitlement." Further, he claimed to have no regrets for his handling of the situation and couldn't think of much that he would do differently, if given the chance.

Immediately following the interview, ESPN commentator Trevor Matich claimed on the air that Leach was "radioactive" in terms of his attractiveness to colleges, while analyst Rob Parker said, "coaches go out of their way to take responsibility, but he's trying to weasel his way out of this." Parker went on to call Leach a "stubborn, arrogant, vain man." In his column, Dick Weiss of the *New York Daily News* echoed these comments, complaining that Leach "didn't sound like he cared about the implications of his words" and said he came across as "less concerned about a player's health when he is no longer useful to the team." [21] Finally, *New York Times* columnist George Vecsey chastised Leach for his comments and lectured that "football does not exist in some ethical vacuum". [22]

The Case of Coach Gary Barnett

Gary Barnett's University of Colorado football team had been in trouble before. In complaints dating back to 2001, football players had been accused of sexual assault and providing alcohol to minors during off-campus recruiting visits. [23] In these cases, the players in question were dismissed from the team and/or charged with felonies when the evidence supported such charges. There was, however, little evidence that head coach Barnett was knowingly involved in such acts, and he denied any wrong-doing. But this time was different. This time coach Gary Barnett opened his mouth.

Background

Gary Barnett was a successful high school head coach and college assistant coach for 20 years before becoming the head football coach at Northwestern University in 1992. In 1999, he left Northwestern after turning the team—which was perennially at the bottom of the Big Ten Conference—into a consistent winning team who made it to the Rose Bowl in 1995. After leaving Northwestern in 1999, Barnett became the head football coach at the University of Colorado, taking over the program from former coach Rick Neuheisel, whose tenure at Colorado had been plagued by NCAA recruiting violations resulting in the loss of 25 scholarships in his final year as head coach. Colorado was looking to Barnett to repair the tarnished reputation of its football team and athletic department. [24]

The Event

On February 18, 2004, SI.com (the online version of *Sports Illustrated* magazine) published an interview of former Colorado place kicker, Katie Hnida. In the article, Hnida claimed that, while a member of the Colorado football team in 2000, she endured verbal harassment, groping in the huddle, other players exposing themselves to her, and finally, a rape by a teammate. She also said that, at the time, she didn't report the harassment and assault to coach Barnett, because she was afraid he would kick her off the team.

She claimed, "He didn't want me on the team in the first place. I thought for sure he'd kick me off." Finally, she said that she did not report the assault to the police, in part, because she was scared that would anger Barnett. In addition, Hnida's father claimed in the article that, at the time, he told both Coach Barnett, as well as Athletic Director Dick Tharp, about the sexual harassment of his daughter (he did not know about the rape at the time), and said he 'got nowhere' talking with them. The article also reported Barnett's and Tharp's denials of any knowledge of the sexual harassment or assault of Katie Hnida. Barnett was quoted as saying "Not one time did I ever see or hear about anybody treating her wrong." [25]

The next day, February 19, 2004, coach Barnett's response to media questions about the Hnida story were published. When asked about the allegations of sexual harassment and assault leveled by Hnida, Barnett responded:

> There isn't a shred of evidence [to back up Hnida's rape allegation]. [26]

Further, he inexplicably commented on Hnida's playing ability, claiming that Hnida was an "awful" player who couldn't compete in a "guy's sport." As he put it:

> Katie was a girl. Not only was she a girl, she was terrible. There was no other way to say it. She could not kick the ball through the uprights.... It's a guy's sport, and [the male players] felt like Katie was forced on them. It was obvious Katie was not very good." [27]

These remarks motivated University of Colorado President Elizabeth Hoffman to put Coach Barnett on paid leave. [28] Although president Hoffman said she was "reserving judgment on what Barnett knew [about the Hnida case]," [29] she was angered by his remarks about Hnida's playing ability. As quoted in a *USA Today* report,

> "I have told him [Barnett] in no uncertain terms that was an unacceptable remark." Hoffman told the Associated Press. "You have a rape allegation here. That's a very serious criminal allegation. It's simply inappropriate to essentially blame the victim, which is what he did." [30]

Now it was the media's turn to judge Barnett.

Reaction to the Event

In the eyes of many newspaper reporters and concerned observers, there was plenty of blame to go around for the apparent sorry state of the University of Colorado football program. In several articles, reporters blamed the institution, including the University of Colorado President and Athletic Director, for creating a culture in which the transgressions of football players went unnoticed and unreported. [31] Yet, across all accounts, reporters refrained from directly accusing Coach Barnett of deliberate wrong-doing. Instead, they continually called the coach incompetent.

For example,[i] *Washington Post* writer Tom Knott asserted:

> *Barnett was sent to his home, with pay, following his asinine*
> *comments. . . . If the man [Barnett] had one active brain cell, he*
> *might have shown some compassion to Hnida. . . . He is dumber*
> *than dirt, that is for sure, and he should be thankful that the*
> *school president, a woman, no less, is still allowing a paycheck to*
> *be dispatched his way.*[32]

Even president Hoffman was surprised by Barnett's lack of understanding, as she noted:

> *It was my feeling . . . that he did not understand the seriousness of*
> *the comments he had made the day before.*[33]

On the evening of February 19, 2004, Coach Barnett apologized for his earlier remarks in a live television interview with CNN's Larry King about criticizing Hnida's kicking ability. In response to King's question, "What did [comments about Hnida's kicking ability] have to do with her charges of being raped?" Barnett was quoted as saying:

> *I said the wrong thing about Katie. . . . And I was trying to*
> *communicate that we cared about Katie.*[34]

Yet, several reporters continue to complain that Barnett's actions could endanger the well-being of others. As one commentator reported:

> *The attitude toward women and sex at Colorado and in much*
> *of college football is archaic, dangerously so. What's needed at*
> *that university, and a few others besides, is a head coach with*
> *a more modern notion of what a real man is, so he can teach it*
> *properly to his players. . . . But a portrait is emerging of Barnett*
> *as a coach so out of touch that he firmly disciplined lateness or*
> *dressing out of uniform, but failed to report an alleged rape to*
> *authorities. . . . What a good modern football coach ought to be*
> *interested in creating is not a virile man, but simply a grown man,*
> *an adult who is in command of himself and his impulses. Clearly,*
> *Gary Barnett is not the man for that job.*[35]

Barnett defended himself by saying that he had done everything he could to prevent sexual harassment by his players. As he told King:

> *When I came to Colorado in 1999, I made a decision to change*
> *the culture there, around academics and around recruiting. I*
> *introduced a 124-page manual that talked about behavioral and*
> *character expectations including. . . . sexual harassment, alcohol*
> *abuse, and specifically date rape. You know, we brought in*
> *speakers, nationally-known speakers on sexual harassment and*

> diversity. We bring in every night during our summer camp for
> three weeks from 9:00–10:00 at night, we go through every single
> section of that book with our players.

Further defenses of Barnett came from former players, as one ex-player noted:

> He [Barnett] has faithfully directed the participants in this
> program to the highest level of integrity and moral discipline.[36]

Even legendary Florida State University football coach, Bobby Bowden (no stranger to recruiting violations himself) came out in defense of Barnett's character, saying:

> I know this. You can't get many men much better than ol' Gary
> Barnett. Talk about a good man. And I know he's got good
> morals.[37]

In response, observers seemed to consider the fact that Barnett had put in place policies and educational programs to prevent recruiting abuses when evaluating him. For example, one president Hoffman reported:

> [U]nder Barnett, Colorado had substantial guidelines about
> monitoring high school recruits' visits to campus.[38]

Hoffman went on to say:

> On paper, we had a stricter recruiting program than most
> universities. We want to make sure that now we have a nationally
> respected recruiting program.[39]

These assessments were further substantiated in May, 2004, when the independent commission reported that:

> There is no clear evidence that university officials knowingly
> sanctioned [the use of sex, alcohol, and drugs as recruiting tools]
> or had direct involvement.[40]

In the end, the panel did chastise Barnett for providing "insufficient supervision of recruits," but they did not find him to have deliberately sanctioned improper recruiting practices. Further, the panel seemed to perceive that, over time, the coach might improve in this area. As one member of the Board of Regents remarked:

> Certainly Gary said some dumb things, things he wished he
> wouldn't have said. I'm not saying he did everything right…. but
> the report, though it shows a certain insensitivity on Gary
> Barnett's part, does not rise to the level of dismissal.[41]

On May 27, 2004, President Hoffman officially reinstated Coach Gary Barnett as head football coach at the University of Colorado.[42, 43]

***Optional Discussion Questions** (answer questions that correspond to the topic area you are illustrating with this case).

Topic Area	Question
Indiv. Characteristics	How might audiences' emotional reactions to the Coaches' failures affect how they are viewed? How might these emotional frames affect perceptions of the coaches' trustworthiness? Do either of the coaches display components of the Narcissistic Personality?
Perception	How was Coach Leach perceived by the public? How was Coach Barnett perceived? How were the coaches' self-perceptions consistent or inconsistent with those of the general public? Why do you think inconsistencies arose?
Leadership	How could have the two coaches more effectively managed their individual crises?
Persuasion, Influence Impression Management	What tactics could each of the coaches have used to improve their impressions with the public? How could they have impressed their superiors? How could they have improved their images of trustworthiness?
Ethics	Why was one coach fired, while the other one was retained?

Endnotes

1. Red Raider Football Season Review. (2010, January 8). Retrieved from http://www.texastech.com/auto_pdf/p_hotos/s_chools/text/sports/m-footbl/auto_pdf/2009-football-season-review, posted.

2. Mike Leach (American Football Coach) Retrieved from http://en.wikipedia.org/wiki/Mike_Leach_(American_football_coach)

3. Williams, D. (2010, January 3). Doctor, Trainer say Leach Mistreated James. *Lubbock Avalanche-Journal*. Retrieved from www.lubbockonline.come/stories/010310/loc_542285074.shtml

4. Staff Reports (2009, December 29). Tech Suspends Leach after Complaint. *Lubbock Avalanche-Journal*. Retrieved from www.lubbockonline.come/stories/122909/spo_540556326.shtml

5. Evans, T. & Thamel, P. (2009, December 31). Leach is Fired Over Treatment of Player. *New York Times*, B11.

6. Ibid.

7. Williams (2010, January 3). op. cit.

8. Ibid.

9. Ibid.

10. Ibid.

11. Sherr, J. (2009, December 29). Suspension of Texas Tech's Mike Leach Well-Deserved. DallasNews.com. Retrieved from www.dallasnews.com/sharedcontent/dws/spt/stories/12290 9dnsposherrjamesqt.2724b12b.html

12. Schad, J. (2009, December 28). Leach Suspended After Player Complaint. ESPN.com. Retrieved from sports.espn.go.com/espn/print?id=477684&type=HeadlineNews&ImagesPrint=off

13. Staff Reports (2009, December 29). Shocking Suspension of Tech's Leach Sparks Debate. *Wall Street Journal*, online at: blogs.wsj.com/dailyfix/2009/12/29/shocking-suspension-of-techs-leach-sparks-debate/tab/print

14. Sherr (December 29, 2009). op. cit.

15. Ibid.

16. Knott, T. (2009, December 30). "Power Keeps College Football Coaches in the Dark," *Washington Times*, C1.

17. Associated Press. (2009, December 28). TTU Suspends Leach Indefinitely. SI.com. Retrieved from http://sportsillustrated.cnn.com/2009/football/ncaa/12/28/ttu-leach.ap/index.html

18. Sherr (2009, December 29). op. cit.

19. Blaney, B. (2009, December 31). Leach Fired by Texas Tech. *Boston Globe*, S7.

20. Red Raider Football Season Review (January 8, 2010). op. cit.

21. Weiss, D. (2010, January 3). NCAA Looking for Kinder, Gentler Head Coaches. *New York Daily News*, p. S64.

22. Vecsey, G. (2010, January 5). Football Culture Keeps Some in the Dark. *New York Times*, B11.

23. Knott, T. (2004, February 20). Get this Guy Out of Here. *The Washington Times*, C1.

24. Gary Barnett. Retrieved from http://en.wikipedia.org/wiki/Gary_Barnett

25. Reilly, R. (2004, February 18). Another Victim at Colorado. SI.com, at: http://sportsillustrated.cnn.com/2004/writers/rick_reilly/02/16/hnida

26. O'Keefe, M. & Siemaszko, C. (2004, February 19). Coach Rips Lady Kicker, Slams Rape Story. *New York Daily News*, 6.

27. Ibid.

28. Johnson, K. (2004, February 20). Boulder Rattled by Charges Against Football Team. *New York Times*, A12.

29. O'Driscoll, P. & Brady, E. (2004, February 19). NCAA Shaken by Charges that Sex, Booze, are used in Recruiting. *USA Today*, 1A.

30. Ibid.

31. Araton, H. (2004, February 20). Team Player Prolongs Colorado's Woes. *New York Times*, D1. Also see Editorial Staff (2004, February 20). More than College Football. *New York Times*, A24.

32. Ibid.

33. Jenkins, S. (2004, February 20). Boys Will Be – How About Men? *The Washington Post*, D1.

34. Quoted from *Larry King Live*, airdate: February 19, 2004. Retrieved from http://transcripts.cnn.com/TRANSCRIPTS/0402/19/lkl.00.html

35. Jenkins (February 20, 2004), op. cit.

36. Hutchinson, B. (2004, February 20). Colorado U. Socked with New Rape Claim. *New York Daily News*, 30.

37. Staff Reports. (2004, March 3). Bowden Defends Character of Colorado Coach. *Wire Reports*, C7.

38. Drape, J. (2004, March 6). To Clean Up its Program, Colorado Sets Stringent Recruiting Rules. *New York Times*, S29.

39. Ibid.

40. Sink, M. (2004, May 19). A Commission at Colorado Lays the Blame on Officials. *New York Times*, D5.

41. Kenworthy, T. & Whiteside, K. (2004, May 19). D.A.: Colorado Report Validates Comments. *USA Today*, 9C.

42. Ibid.

43. Brennan, C. (2004, May 27). Colorado Punts Instead of Changing Football Climate. *USA Today*, 11C.

CASE 8

Conflict in Santa's Workshop: Learning to Be a Team Player at ToyKing[1]

Kimberly D. Elsbach

University of California, Davis

Fourmy Mario/Newscom

K aren Washington was fuming as she marched back to her workspace. "How could that arrogant, so-and-so do that to me!" she thought. She had just come from the presentation of her new toy concept to the executives of New Product Development and Marketing at ToyKing's Design Studio. It wasn't that the presentation went poorly—quite the opposite had happened, in fact. Both Max Carroll (the head of New Product Development) and Sherry Greenberg (the head of Marketing) loved Karen's idea and prototype for a new interactive toy city where children were able to assign names and personalities to programmable character pieces. Sherry called it a "frame-breaking" concept that would revolutionize their ToyCity line of products. Even more exciting, Max had said that the toy concept was a front runner to be featured in ToyKing's exhibit at next years' American International Toy Fair, the largest and most prestigious trade show in the toy business.

---

[1]This fictional case is based on the author's extensive experience researching creative workers, including toy designers. Any resemblance between the events in this case and actual events is purely coincidental.

What was bothering Karen was that senior designer, Jeff Chang, had taken over the presentation, without Karen's permission, and had basically claimed credit for the toy concept. As the senior designer on the project team, Jeff was, technically, in charge of all design projects. Yet, the culture at ToyKing allowed junior designers to take the lead on projects they had conceived. Further, these designers were often allowed to take control of formal presentations on their ideas, and to guide revisions to the designs following meetings with New Product Development and Marketing.

Karen had assumed that she would be allowed to present the idea to Max and Sherry, and had developed a Power Point presentation for the meeting at Jeff's request. After Jeff saw it, said it was great, and that he would like to "introduce" the new design to Max and Sherry at the meeting using the Power Point. Karen thought that Jeff meant that he would merely start the presentation, and then hand it over to her following a brief introduction. But Jeff didn't do that. He made the entire presentation, using Karen's Power Point, and only referred to her briefly in his remarks and during the Q&A. In Karen's mind, Jeff had stolen credit for her idea, and used her own Power Point to do it!

Background on Toy King

What Was it Like to Work at Toy King?

ToyKing was a large, U.S.-based toy design and manufacturing company that specialized in educational toys and games. The company headquarters were located in Torrance, CA, and included a large Design Studio department that housed over 60 toy designers, along with another 20 technicians and fabricators. The Design Studio had a very flat organizational hierarchy with just two ranks: junior designers and senior designers. Senior Designers made up about 15 of the total designers (the remaining 45 were junior designers), and were typically long-time employees (10 years or longer at ToyKing). Senior designers had supervisory responsibilities for all the projects that were underway in the Design Studio, but junior designers could (and often would) be seen as the "creative lead" on design projects that they spearheaded.

ToyKing produced about 200 new toy concepts per year. These toy concepts ranged from minor modifications to the design of a toy car, or to a completely new toy system (such as a new toy system involving inter-locking toy bricks). Of these 200 new concepts, about 50 of these would be put into pilot programs, and about 20 would ultimately be produced for retail sale. For each of the 50 pilot programs, a senior designer would construct a team of 3–5 members, including junior designers, technicians, and fabricators.

What Were ToyKing's Best Sellers?

ToyKing's most successful product line was ToyCity. The ToyCity line included packaged sets of interlocking and customizable toy houses, stores, streets, parks, and other structures that kids could construct to make an entire working city. Kids could also add people, pets, cars, trucks, and construction machinery to the city. Although the packages came with suggested construction ideas, kids could modify these designs and construct completely original designs for the structures in their one-of-a-kind cities. This feature was what made ToyCity so popular that they won several awards at the American International Toy Fair.

ToyCity was considered the crown jewel of the ToyKing product line, and there was fierce competition among designers to design components for this line. Working on the ToyCity line was seen as one of the best ways to win design awards and move up from junior to senior design.

Background on Karen's Toy Concept

The events occurring over the previous three months during the development of Karen's toy concept are important in understanding what happened in the presentation. The concept was born during a lunchtime conversation between Karen and two other junior designers on her team.

Three Months Ago: Lunch at Mo's

Karen, and two other junior designers, Sam Gupta and Cassie Wu, were having their weekly lunch out at Mo's, a hip diner in Santa Monica that attracted more unknown artists and musicians than celebrity television and movie actors. While waiting for their triple espresso's to arrive, Karen decided to tell Sam and Cassie about a "wild-brained" idea she had for an interactive spin on ToyKing's popular ToyCity line of toys. As Karen explained,

> *"The ToyCity line is a huge hit with kids ages 4–9 because it allows them to make their own "city" and continue to add on to it as they acquire more pieces. The customizability of the line is what kids love."*

Karen went on,

> *"What would be even cooler, is if kids could program some of the play pieces (e.g., the people and pets) so that they had their own personalities and would remember past interaction with other play pieces."*

In Karen's concept, kids would be able to provide the people and pet pieces with personalities, ages, voices, and genders through a simple program installed in each play piece. Then, these programmed play pieces could interact with other play pieces based on these personalities and their actual past, play experiences. For example, a play piece resembling a dog could be named "spot" and given a super-energetic personality. This play piece would then ask all other play pieces who greeted it to play ball or go for a run. If it interacted with another play piece (resembling a child, for example) that it had played with before, it would remember that instance and talk about it with the "child" play piece.

Both Sam and Cassie thought this was a very cool idea, indeed. They hashed out the details with Karen over the next hour and a half, making notes on napkins and coasters. By the end of lunch, Karen, Sam and Cassie felt they had an idea worthy of the American International Toy Fair. Sam and Cassie both encouraged Karen to pursue it with their Senior Designer, Jeff Chang, at that week's staff meeting. Sam also mentioned that Karen should make the cars, trucks, and machines programmable, because a recent focus group with kids had revealed that they liked to give these objects personalities. Karen was inspired by their enthusiasm and promised to include them in the design team.

Staff Meeting with Jeff Chang

Later that week, Karen followed up on Sam and Cassie's suggestion and presented a more polished version of her idea to the entire work group and their Senior Designer, Jeff Chang. Jeff thought the idea had merit, but wondered about the cost and the difficulty that kids might have programming their play pieces. He gave Karen permission to pursue the idea and a small budget with which to develop some prototypes. At her suggestion, Jeff put Karen on a team with Sam and Cassie, along with a technician and fabricator. He said he'd look at the idea in prototype in six weeks.

Six Weeks Later: Prototype Presentation

After six weeks of late nights and constant tinkering, Karen—with the help of a technician and fabricator—had built prototypes of several programmable play pieces for the ToyCity line. She hated to admit it, but working with technician, Andy Sprague, and fabricator, Mike Camacho, had been really productive. In fact, these two lowly staff members had helped Karen not only to produce the prototypes, but had come up with some cool new features for the play pieces. For instance, Mike, a former welder and electrician, had suggested that they use waterproof, underwater welding materials to encase the computer chips, so that even if kids threw them in the bathtub, they would still work. In fact, they would work with ToyCity's new DiveCity—an underwater research vessel with scuba divers that could be used in the tub or a swimming pool. In addition, Andy, a computer designer and rendering specialist helped Karen to design a hand-held programming device that play pieces would be "seated" in and then easily programmed through a simple menu of commands.

Working with Andy and Mike had been so easy and productive, in fact, that Karen had avoided meeting with her junior designer teammates, Sam and Cassie, during the past six weeks. She really felt that she owned this project and should be given latitude to make all the decisions, because it was her original idea. As technicians and fabricators, Andy and Mike would not challenge her ideas and not be upset if she vetoed their suggestions. By contrast, Karen knew that the other junior designers on her team (Sam and Cassie) would want to change some of her ideas, and she did not want to give them the chance to do that. She knew that their ideas would not be as good as her own, and they would really slow down the design process. She thought if she waited until right before the prototype presentation to fill them in, it would be too late to make changes to the design. So that's what she did, and now she was about to reveal her prototypes to the team.

The presentation took place in the 3rd Floor Conference Room, with a view of the Pacific Ocean. Karen opened the presentation by thanking Jeff Chang for the opportunity to pursue her idea for the ToyCity line. She then brought out the prototypes and hand-held programmer, and demonstrated how the pieces would work. Her teammates were surprised that she had moved so far in the design process without consulting them, and had many questions about the design. In particular, Sam asked why she had programmed just the people and pets in her prototypes, and why she hadn't made the cars, machines, and other structures programmable. As he noted, "Karen, I thought we had talked about allowing the cars and trucks and machines to have personalities? You know that was something our kids' focus group showed to be important. Why did you leave that feature out?"

Karen brushed off this comment, and said, "Well, we never agreed to that. And it's too late to make that change anyway." Karen quickly finished up the presentation to avoid any other suggestions from Sam and Cassie, and thanked everyone for coming. Noticeably, she didn't mention the contributions of Andy or Mike during the presentation, even thought they were sitting right there in the front row. She also didn't mention that she had bypassed Sam and Cassie in her design work.

As everyone filed out of the conference room, Jeff Chang stopped Karen and said, "Karen, I really like the concept, and I'm ready to move this project forward to the next stage. I want to include it in my presentation to the Heads of New Product Development and Marketing in six weeks. Do you think you can have a full line of play pieces, and some marketing ideas ready by then?"

Karen was surprised but delighted, "Of course I can!" she said. Then Jeff went on to say, "Just make sure you keep me up to date on your progress. I want to meet with you once a week between now and then so that I can make sure this thing is ready. I know what these honchos want, and I want to make sure I'm ready for them." Karen, said, "Sure, no problem. I'll schedule the meetings right away."

As Karen walked away, she couldn't help but smile. This was better than she had expected. She was on her way to an award at the American International Toy Fair for sure. Buried in her own thoughts, Karen didn't notice Sam and Cassie shaking their heads as she walked by. Further, she didn't hear their conversation about how she had taken over the project and left them out completely. As Cassie complained to Sam, "I can't believe Karen. We helped hash out the original idea, and even gave her the confidence to pursue it further. But she totally dissed us in that meeting. And she didn't even follow through on your suggestion about the cars and trucks. Well, I for one am done helping her on this project. If she wants it, she can have it!" Sam shook his head in agreement and added, "Karen has no idea how to work in a team. She never has."

Today's Presentation

Six weeks later, and the big presentation was about to begin. Karen had gone over the presentation in detail with Jeff Chang the previous week. Jeff had added several of his own edits to the final power point slides, and had convinced Karen that he should take the lead on "introducing" the presentation because he "understood what these corporate honchos wanted to hear." Jeff mentioned that he would call on Karen when he needed her, but that he had a good idea about how to position the concept so that it got the green light for further development. Karen really wanted to make the presentation, but she wanted more for the project to be approved. So she agreed to let Jeff introduce the presentation.

Jeff began the presentation with some witty banter with Max Carroll and Sherry Greenberg, and then moved into the financial summaries of last years' best sellers. After a half an hour of financial reviews, Karen was getting impatient. When was Jeff going to talk about her idea? Why was he spending so much time talking about the profit margins on ToyCity and DiveCity from last year?

Finally, Jeff got to the new toy concepts. He said he would present three ideas. He began with two rather lackluster improvements on the ToyCity toddler line. These were not hit ideas, and Karen did not understand why he was even presenting them. He then presented Karen's idea for the "Programmable ToyCity Line." Jeff was really good, Karen had to admit. He showed Max and Sherry clips of kids' focus groups, and highlighted the kids saying they wanted their toys to have personalities and to be "their friends." He also showed Max and Sherry how much kids loved the underwater DiveCity line. Then he brought out the prototypes for Karen's toy concept. He showed Max and Sherry how the play pieces could be programmed to have personalities and become friends with each other and with the kids. He also showed them how the play pieces could even be used with the DiveCity line due to their waterproof welding feature. Throughout the presentation, Karen was tempted to speak up and offer more information, but Jeff never gave her the chance. In fact, other than pointing out that she was the junior designer who had come up with the concept during the Q&A, Jeff never said one word to or about Karen the entire time.

Max and Sherry loved the idea and congratulated Jeff on another winning concept. They both said that they looked forward to seeing the full line at next years' American International Toy Fair, and patted Jeff on the back as they left. Jeff hustled after them and asked if they could go to coffee to talk about a few other things. Smiling the three left without saying another word to Karen.

Later, back at her desk, Karen was still fuming about the meeting, when Sam and Cassie came by and asked how the presentation went. Karen, practically screaming said, "That jerk Jeff took all the credit and stole my idea. I'd be surprised if my name goes on it at the Toy Fair!" Sam and Cassie could not help but smirk, and Karen barked at them, "What are you two smiling about anyway!" Sam, turned to her and said, "Karen, you need to learn to be a better team player if you're ever going to succeed at ToyKing." Then he and Cassie walked away.

Karen, stunned, thought to herself, "Better team player? But I'm a great team player. I worked really well with Mike and Andy, didn't I? What on earth are they talking about?"

*Optional Discussion Questions (answer questions that correspond to the topic area you are illustrating with this case).

Topic	Question
Groups/Teams	Do you think that Karen was a good team player? Why or why not? Did she work as team with Mike and Andy? What could she have done to be a better team player?
Motivation	What was motivating Karen to work hard on this project? How did ToyKing's promotion system affect Karen's behavior? How could ToyKing use technology to better train employees like Karen to work in teams?
Communication/ Diversity	What did Jeff mean when, talking to Karen after the initial prototype presentation, he said, "*Just make sure you keep me up to date on your progress. I want to meet with you once a week between now and then so that we can make sure this thing is ready. I know what these honchos want, and I want to make sure I'm ready for them.*"? How did Karen interpret this statement? What issues in communication and gender could account for their differences in interpretation?
Indiv. Characteristics	What personality characteristics do you think define Karen? How might Karen's personality affect her work in teams?
Negotiation	How might Karen negotiate with Jeff to allow her to maintain control over the toy concept going forward? How can Karen make her proposal appear fair to Jeff? What negotiation traps should Karen be aware of and avoid?

Section III

EXERCISES

EXERCISES

Exercise 1 Big Five Celebrity Spotlight

Exercise Overview

The Big Five Personality refers to the five dimensions of personality described by psychologists. These five dimensions can be described as either 'high' or 'low'. Personality characteristics influence people's behavior in the workplace.

Working Through

 AS AN INDIVIDUAL

1. Refer to the chart below to brainstorm ideas of celebrities, real and fictional, living and deceased that you think represent high and low levels of this personality dimension. Several examples are provided for you.

Example Chart:

LOW	BIG 5 DIMENSION	HIGH
	OPENNESS	SPONGE BOB
	CONSCIENTIOUSNESS	
	EXTRAVERSION	LADY GAGA
DONALD TRUMP	AGREEABLENESS	OPRAH
SQUIDWARD	EMOTIONAL STABILITY	JAMES BOND

 **AS A CLASS**

1. Plot your individual ideas on the dimensions chart that your instructor has designed on the board.

2. Discuss:
   a. What do you consider a really good example of a celebrity for one of the personality dimensions? Why do you think this person best depicts this dimension?
   b. Are there any examples that you do not see the connection? What connection did the person who designed this example make between the characteristics of the dimension and the celebrity?
   c. What is the benefit of identifying personality characteristics in the workplace through observation? What is the potential problem with identifying personality characteristics of others through observation?

Exercise 2 Creating My Brand

Exercise Overview

For this exercise you are to design a 'leadership brand' and a slogan to accompany the brand. A leadership brand represents the reputation of a leader throughout an organization; it is what stakeholders can count on relative to your leadership in your organization. For example, at Wal-Mart, the organization is known for low prices and leaders in the organization are known for being cost conscious. At Apple, the organization is known for being innovative. Leaders in this organization are known for development of products that are creative and stand out in the industry.

Working Through

👤 AS AN INDIVIDUAL

1. Write a three-sentence declaration of leadership. These few sentences should explain what personal reputation you aspire to have and what you want to be known for as a leader. The three sentences can include what you value and what you stand for. Example: I want to be known for _____ so that I can _____. I value _____, _____, _____. I will reinforce these values by _____.

2. What actions will you take in your organization that will enforce your brand? What will you avoid that would detract from your brand?

3. Is this brand something that I am proud of? Could I share this with others? Is it authentic?

4. Devise a slogan that explains your leadership brand. Here are a few pointers to writing a slogan:
    a. A slogan should be simple and memorable and should not exceed a sentence.
    b. A slogan should also be honest, referring to you as the best leader in the world, will probably not be believable.
    c. There should be a clear connection between what you wish to stand for as a leader and your slogan.

👥 AS A GROUP

1. What differences existed among group member's leadership brands and slogans? What similarities?

2. How would a leadership 'brand' be useful in an interview? What are some other organizational applications where you might share a leadership brand?

3. What are some potential problems with having a leadership 'brand' and/or a leadership slogan?

4. How would you judge the effectiveness of a leadership brand? What criteria would you use to determine if a brand met the needs of various stakeholders?

Exercise 3 My Expat Assignment

Exercise Overview

For this exercise you will simulate the experience that occurs when someone from one culture must work in a different culture and the learning and adaptation that must occur. One volunteer from your group will identify himself/herself as a project manager from a different country of origin. The 'project manager' has been sent to your organization to lead a successful launch of a software upgrade for your business. The project manager must quickly learn and adapt to your new cultural context if he/she will be successful. *Custom* means the cultural rules and etiquette that organizational members follow and in which they must engage at work. As a group, minus the volunteer, decide on three customs that you must follow at work and do not tell the volunteer what they are. An example is provided below. These customs are ultimately critical to the success of the project and unknown to the project manager.

Working Through

STEP ONE

Select a volunteer as a project manager and ask them to leave the group for five minutes.

Group Instructions

Complete with just the group (volunteer is removed to an area of the classroom where they cannot hear the group). Decide on three customs that will be displayed in your meeting that are important in your culture. The customs should not necessarily be easy to figure out.

Example:

Secret Custom Known Only to Your Group
1. If a question is asked, each group member must clear their throat
2. Everyone must cross their arms in meetings
3. Everyone unties their shoes

Volunteer Instructions

Volunteer complete before rejoining the group

1. What will you discuss with the group when you join them to plan for the software upgrade?

2. How will you make sure that you are successful in a different culture?

STEP TWO

Group and Volunteer Instructions

The volunteer rejoins the group and 'leads' a meeting to discuss the software. The volunteer tries to guess and copy the protocols that the group identified.

Take 10 minutes for the project manager to discuss with your group how to plan its work to be successful. During this period of time, you are to engage in your three agreed-upon customs without verbally explaining what you are doing. The project manager will need to figure out what these three important customs are without directly asking and will need to identify them and engage in the same behavior.

3. How many customs did your project manager guess and engage in within the 10 minutes?

STEP THREE

 ## AS A GROUP

1. What happened during the meeting that the project manager led? How much progress was made on identifying objectives for the software upgrade project?

2. Explain why the customs were identified or missed.

3. What are some of the problems with working in a different cultural context?

4. Debate the notion that someone going to another culture should adapt to that culture. What is the other side to this argument?

Exercise 4 How Leaders Effect You

Exercise Overview

Think of a 'leader' that has influenced you the most. This leader might be from your work, family, or childhood. The leader might be a public or historical figure. This leader could be 'inspirational' or an example of someone who you consider 'toxic'. Once you have selected your leader, complete the chart below in your notes. It is helpful to think of specific examples in order to complete the questions.

Working Through

 ### AS AN INDIVIDUAL

1. What stands out about this leader? For example, did they take certain actions, posses certain qualities, or express certain values? List up to four things that stand out.

2. What did *you* learn from this leader? For example, what did you do differently because of this leader? How did you think differently because of this leader? List up to four things that you learned.

3. What impact did this leader have on *others*? Who were the followers associated with this leader? How did they change as a result of the leader? List several other followers and the impact achieved on these people.

 ### AS A GROUP

1. What similarities and differences are there in our group's selection and description of our leader example? Be specific.

2. Draw a picture that summarizes the relationship between the leader and the follower. Include the similarities that you identified in question #1.

3. Do you believe that leaders will always have a lasting impact on followers? Why or why not?

Exercise 5 My Best and Worst Learning Experiences

Exercise Overview

This exercise provides you with an opportunity to reflect on different types of learning experiences that are important in professional and personal situations.

Working Through

 **AS AN INDIVIDUAL**

1. As an individual, think about a time where you learned something new. This could be a new hobby, a new sport, a new technology, a new concept, or even a new skill.

    a. What did you learn?
    b. How did you feel when you anticipated learning something new?
    c. How did you feel during the learning process?
    d. How did you feel after you learned something new?
    e. What was the environment in which you were learning like?
    f. Did you learn something new by yourself or were others around to help you?
    g. Could you teach what you learned to someone else? Why or why not?

AS A GROUP

2. In a small group, compare your learning experiences. Are there similarities or differences in what you learned or how you felt? How about any of the other questions that you thought about above?

3. Discuss as a group:

    a. Can learning be 'fun'?
    b. What conditions or circumstances create some of the best learning experiences?
    c. What conditions or circumstances prevent the best learning experiences?
    d. What types of practices can we use in the workplace to encourage learning?

Exercise 6 Developing Your Career— Leadership Development in Action

Exercise Overview

Leaders in organizations have a diversity of backgrounds, including educational experiences, work experiences, training, personality, and other differences. Not one path is identical from one leader to the next. This exercise involves having a conversation with someone who you admire as a leader and bringing the information from your conversation to class in order to compare similarities and differences.

Working Through

 AS AN INDIVIDUAL (OUT OF CLASS)

Identify and approach a leader who you would like to learn more about. Think about who you would consider a 'leader'. Leaders are not necessarily in formal managerial roles in an organization and come from a variety of workplaces and contexts. A leader, for example, can be a parent, a teacher, the dining hall supervisor, a security guard on campus, a coach, or a student club or association leader. Request a 15-minute conversation and ask the following:

1. What experiences shaped you as a leader?

2. Where did you learn the most about leadership?

3. How do leaders use *negotiation* skills? What other skills do you think are important?

4. What experiences, specialized training, or education would you still like to participate in? Why?

5. What other information do you wish I had asked you about?

AS A GROUP

1. Take turns discussing the out of class conversations that you had.

2. What similarities do you notice? What differences do you notice? What surprised you in your discussions or in your classmates' choice of leader?

AS A CLASS

1. What interesting insights came out of your group discussions?

2. What conclusions did you make about development of leadership?

3. What types of experiences or training and education seem to be useful?

Exercise 7 Development While in College

Exercise Overview

Learning different leadership knowledge and skills can be accomplished in many different situations. Some of the most valuable experiences can occur out of a traditional workplace setting. This exercise allows you to explore the many different opportunities there are to learn leadership.

Working Through

 ### AS A GROUP

1. As a group, brainstorm ways that you can learn leadership while still in school. Consider all types of situations, such as religious organizations, volunteer work, internships, family, etc.

 ### AS AN INDIVIDUAL

2. Each individual should select one skill that you would like to learn that would help you be an effective future leader. These skills are reported as the most desired skills from the perspective of employers in a recent Gallup Poll.

   - Team building
   - Quantitative skills
   - Oral communication
   - Written communication
   - Strategic planning
   - Decision making

3. Each individual should match the skill that was selected in #2 above with one situation from #1 where this skill might be learned. For example, team skills could be matched with volunteer work.

AS A CLASS

   a. What skills did your class members select and why?
   b. Where will your class members learn these skills?
   c. How will they know if they have improved?
   d. What skills would you have expected to see on this list that you did not?

Exercise 8 Facts and Opinions

Exercise Overview

This exercise provides you with an opportunity to critically reflect on your beliefs and classify them as facts or classify them as opinions.

Working Through

👤 AS AN INDIVIDUAL

1. As an individual, generate a list and write what you think about the following topics:

    - Public displays of affection
    - Employers monitoring Internet usage of employees in the workplace
    - The health value of drinking water versus drinking an energy drink
    - Children's use of caffeine
    - Country music
    - Canceling a date with someone when you have a chance of a 'better' date for the same evening
    - The use of profanity by public officials

👥 AS A GROUP

2. Compare what each person wrote down as individuals.

3. Together, decide which statements of group members are based on facts and which statements are based on opinions. Designate an 'F' next to the factual statement and an 'O' next to the opinion based statement.

4. What criteria did you use to assign an 'F' or an 'O' for the statements?

5. Discuss:

    a. What are three examples where you have experienced people passing off opinions as facts in the workplace?
    b. How can you minimize other people's bias when they do this?
    c. How can you minimize your own bias when you do this?

Exercise 9 Being Positive

Exercise Overview

This exercise provides you with an opportunity to understand the use of positive attitudes and emotions and how they impact people's behavior in the workplace.

Working Through

 AS A GROUP

1. In your group take turns sharing a story about a really bad day that was experienced.

2. Take turns and write down a couple of sentences that are descriptive of the worst part of that day.

3. For each description, add a sentence to the description to generate positive emotions about what was learned from that experience.

Example:

My alarm didn't go off and I missed my job interview. (original sentence) I have learned better time management because of this experience. (new sentence).

4. Discuss:
   a. How do the words that we use make us and others feel?
   b. How can we use more positive language in our workplace? How can I be more positive at work?
   c. How can we seek out other positive people at work?

Exercise 10 Force Field Analysis

Exercise Overview

This exercise illustrates that there are different variables in an organization that impact the success or failure of organizational change.

Working Through

👤 AS AN INDIVIDUAL

1. Read about Force Field Analysis.

   A tool that many find useful to use when analyzing an organizational situation is to use a tool call a 'force field'. A force field has both promoting and resisting variables that will prevent or enable a change. Consider the use of the force field analysis in the example below and then you can select your own.

   Change situation: A recreational softball league is deciding whether or not to change their uniform adoption.

Force Field Analysis:

+ Variables that are promoting the change	− Variables that are resisting the change
Uniforms are a dingy mustard yellow	Long tradition of this color
New members joining the softball team expressed an interest in a wicking fabric like an Under Armour® style	More expensive to get high tech fabric—the sponsor unwilling to pay the extra cost
New color and style might attract better players and get the team more visibility	Core group of players have been with the team for many years and do not like any sort of change
The players often go out to local restaurants and bars after a game and are very visible in the community at large; more attractive uniforms would help their image	Same color as the sponsor's business
Rival team teases them for their ugly uniforms; compares the players skill level to the level of their uniform	

AS A GROUP

2. As a group, discuss:

   a. In your opinion, is the softball team likely to change their uniform? Why or why not?

   b. Are there any other variables that are not listed that you would have liked information on? Why these variables?

3. Select a change that is going to occur in one of your group member's workplace. Use the force field analysis tool to analyze the variables that are promoting the change and the variables that might prevent the change.

Force Field Analysis for a Change at Work

+ Variables that are promoting the change	− Variables that are resisting the change

4. As a group, discuss:

   a. In your opinion, is the change likely to happen smoothly? Why or why not?

   b. Are there any other variables that are not listed that you would have liked information on? Why these variables?

   c. How might this tool be a useful framework to think more systematically about changes in organizations?

Exercise 11 Bias and Decision Making

Exercise Overview

People are subject to a variety of biases and errors in decision making. This exercise provides an opportunity to identify several areas by which you have experienced bias, and then plan for strategies to minimize your own bias in judgment.

Working Through

 ### AS AN INDIVIDUAL

Listed on the table below are some common biases. For the five decision biases described, generate your own example where you were biased, you experienced bias, or you observed bias. As a group, you will plan strategies to minimize bias.

- **Framing:** Deliberate presentation of a situation to impact your decision
- **Bias blind spot**: Underestimating your own bias and overestimating the bias of others
- **Confirmation bias:** Evaluate new information in order to confirm existing beliefs and decisions
- **Escalation of commitment:** Once committed to a decision, difficult to change your mind because of the sunk costs with pursuing the decision
- **Hindsight bias:** Remembering events as if we already predicted them

 ### AS A GROUP

1. Compare examples in your group. Were any bias examples easier or more frequently identified than others?

2. Brainstorm a list of strategies to minimize bias in decision making for each of the six categories of bias.

Example:

Bias	Strategies to minimize this bias
Framing	
Bias blind spot	
Confirmation bias	
Escalation of commitment	
Hindsight bias	

Exercise 12 Well-Being at Work

Exercise Overview

Research has continually shown a connection between regular physical activity and improved physical and mental states. This means that exercise and physical activity promotes well-being and decreases depression, anxiety, and stress. This exercise will encourage you to plan how you can incorporate the benefits of physical activity into the workplace. The President's Council on Physical Fitness and Sports estimates that only thirty percent of Americans get the level of physical activity that they need (http://health.usnews.com/health-conditions/heart-health/information-on-fitness).

Working Through

 AS A CLASS

1. Brainstorm suggestions for how employees can promote physical activity at work. For example: Encourage employees to take the stairs to meetings.

2. Evaluate the suggestions. Which of these are easier to implement than others? Why do you think so?

3. How as students can we incorporate physical fitness into our daily routine?

Exercise 13 What Stresses You Out?

Exercise Overview

There are many different sources of stress, but not all stress has the same effect on people in the workplace. This exercise allows you to reflect on these differences.

Working Through

 **AS AN INDIVIDUAL**

Identify some common items that cause you stress in each of the categories below.

1. Emotional stressors (e.g., a recent failed relationship):

2. Family stressors (e.g., family drama):

3. Social stressors (e.g., pressure to attend club activities):

4. Change stressors (e.g., just transferred majors):

5. Chemical stressors (e.g., too much coffee):

6. Work stressors (e.g., increased hours at part-time job):

7. Decision stressors (e.g., pressure to select a career track):

8. Fear stressors (e.g., afraid of public speaking):

9. Physical stressors (e.g., have a bad cold):

10. Environmental stressors (e.g., this room is too hot):

AS A CLASS

1. Is the role of a college student very stressful? Why or why not?

2. What are some common areas that cause students a lot of stress?

3. How can students plan for these stress factors and minimize their impact?

Exercise 14 Laughter Is the Best Medicine

Exercise Overview

Laughter yoga has become an increasingly mainstream method to bring people together to laugh in order to experience positive emotions. First started in the mid-1990s, it has spread to over 75 countries. Its supporter's claim reduced stress and positive psychological and physical benefits. Laughter yoga clubs and independent practitioners have spread around the world and most major cities offer a laughter yoga chapter that anyone with an interest can join. Videos on YouTube offer a glimpse at laughter yoga used in the business world and what a typical session involves. Laughter yoga relies on 'emotional contagion' where one person can influence another, until the entire group starts laughing. Advocates even say to 'fake it until you make it', or start with fake laughter, and eventually it spreads to real laughter. This exercise provides you with an opportunity to experience how emotion can impact attitude and behavior.

Working Through

 **AS AN INDIVIDUAL**

Answer the following questions:

1. Under what circumstances would I be involved in a laughter yoga club?

2. Other than laughter yoga, how can I incorporate humor into my daily life?

3. What specifically has made me laugh out loud in the past week?

 **AS A GROUP**

Discuss:

1. Compare and contrast your group member's ideas around laughter yoga.

2. Look each other in the eye and try to make your group members laugh. If no one is laughing, 'fake it until you make it', by starting with fake laughter.

3. What attempts were successful? How did people feel after they laughed?

Sources:

Sala Horowitz. *Effect of Positive Emotions on Health: Hope and Humor; Alternative and Complementary Therapies.* August 2009, 15(4): 196–202. doi:10.1089/act.2009.15706.
http://www.youtube.com/watch?v=ZKNB0OTrXKw
http://www.nytimes.com/video/2010/08/20/nyregion/1247468644525/in-the-city-serious-laughter.html

Exercise 15 Building My Network—Individual

Exercise Overview

Learning how to apply the basics of networking skills helps to increase your communication and influence skills. Your network is not just the people that you know that can help you find a job, but includes anyone that you know with which you interact. Networks can be considered by depth—how well do people know you? and by breadth—how many people do you know?

Working Through

 ### AS AN INDIVIDUAL

Make a list of everyone that you know and with which you interact. Divide this list by the depth of your relationship. For the people that know you well, and which you interact frequently, place them in the middle of the circle. For those that you interact with, but do not know you that well, place in the outside of the circle. The third circle includes people that you plan to approach and get to know.

Example:

AS A GROUP

1. Compare your network diagrams.

2. How do your interactions differ with those in your network? Do you resolve conflict differently with those who you interact more frequently?

3. Who had the most complete diagram? What strategies does this person use to build their network?

4. What strategies can a college student use to build their network? Should a student be building depth or breadth of relationships? Why do you think so?

Exercise 16 Writing a Team Contract

Exercise Overview

The action of writing a contract together allows for attention to all of the components that a team will need to plan for its success. This exercise provides you with an opportunity to write a team contract. A contract is a formal agreement that the team discusses and writes with all of the team members signing to symbolize their agreement. The terms of the contract usually include the following components:

1. *Goals:* What goals do we plan on accomplishing as a team?

2. *Roles:* Who occupies specific roles necessary for our team to be successful and when will we rotate these roles?

3. *Confidence:* How will we know when we have mastered specific tasks? How will we celebrate small and large successes?

4. *Interpersonal understanding:* How will we identify and utilize our team members' strengths? How will we cover for each other in an unforeseen circumstance?

5. *Psychological safety:* What are the rules around what is appropriate behavior on our team? What is respectful behavior and what is disrespectful behavior?

6. *Coordination:* How will we coordinate and share our knowledge and our resources? How will we allocate work and when will we check in on each other to view our progress?

7. *Continuous Improvement:* What is our timeframe to re-evaluate our contract, the goals of the team, the roles, and other items that are important?

8. *Adapting:* When will we seek outside help or expertise? When and how will we evaluate our need to change as a team?

Working Through

 ### AS A GROUP

1. Select a member of your group to write down the contract of the team.

2. Decide on a team name. Your team name can represent your team values, it might be an acronym of its member's names or it might symbolize who you are and what the class can expect from you.

3. Review the eight components of a successful team contract. For each of the eight components, write down the steps that you would take and the timeframe by which you would accomplish these steps.

4. Review the entire document that has been drafted as a team. If you are in agreement, sign the document and determine where it will be stored so that you can access it during your time together as a team.

👤 AS AN INDIVIDUAL

1. What concerns do I have about working on a team that this process helps with?

2. What remaining concerns do I have about working on a team?

3. What can I do to work on my concerns with this team?

4. How is the process of writing a contract going to help us be successful?

👥 AS A CLASS

1. Compare your contracts and how you addressed each of the eight components of a successful contract.

2. What might you change as a team after hearing the other contracts?

3. How will this process of discussion and planning of your team's work and process help you to be successful?

Exercise 17 Design Your Technology

Exercise Overview

This exercise allows you an opportunity to apply your creativity at designing an innovation that is both novel but also solves a pragmatic challenge.

Working Through

AS AN INDIVIDUAL

1. Think of a frustration that you have as a student that could be solved with the right technology that does not currently exist in the form in which you need it. Brainstorm a list of three frustrations that you are prepared to share with your group.

AS A GROUP

2. Discuss your ideas in a group and note common themes.

3. Considering your common themes as a group, design a piece of technology that does not currently exist. The new technology should improve your lives as students.

   a. What specific purpose would this new technology be used for?
   b. What features would you like this technology to have?
   c. Who would be the audience for the technology?
   d. Sketch out a rough model of your design on a piece of paper.
   e. What would you name your new product?
   f. How does designing something innovative relate to motivation in the workplace?

4. Each group should share their new 'product' design with the class.

AS A CLASS

   a. What similarities and differences did you notice as a class with the resulting new 'products'?
   b. Describe the similarities and differences with the process by which you designed your new 'products.' (e.g., Did you revise your idea many times? Did everyone in the group participate in the same way? Did you have many ideas that you generated or just one?)
   c. What part of this exercise was the most 'energizing' for each group? What are ways that this same type of creative 'energy' could be captured in the workplace? How does creative energy relate to people's motivation at work?

Exercise 18 Team Performance Evaluation

Exercise Overview

Drafting behavioral expectations that can be evaluated by the team is a helpful way to make sure that each individual on the team understands his or her role in building a successful team experience. This exercise will allow for you to first, individually reflect on what behaviors contribute to a positive or negative team experience, and second, agree as a team what behaviors will be expected and evaluated for successful participation on this team.

Working Through

 AS AN INDIVIDUAL

Answer the following questions:

1. What positive experiences have I had previously on a team? What performance expectations do I have of myself and others based on my previous positive experience?

2. What negative experiences have I had previously on a team? What performance expectations do I have of myself and others based on my previous negative experience?

3. What behaviors would I like to evaluate on a team based on my experience? (e.g. attendance at team meetings, making a serious effort at work before the meetings, fulfillment of team responsibilities during and between meetings, demonstration of respectful communication, demonstration of cooperation with the team, communication between meetings, etc.)

 AS A GROUP

Discuss:

4. Compare and contrast your experiences and ideas around the behavioral expectations for successful participation on this team.

5. Agree on 5–10 behavioral expectations that you will evaluate yourself and on others while participating on this team.

6. Agree on a behavior rating scale that you will use. Here is a sample:

    a. Excellent—Consistently exceeded expectations on the team
    b. Very good—Consistently met expectations on the team
    c. Ordinary—Often met expectations
    d. Deficient—Often failed to show up and complete quality work on time
    e. No show—No participation in the team

7. Draft a document that includes your behavioral expectations, your rating scale with a description of each scale item and at least two future dates that you will evaluate yourself and your team members.

 ## AS A CLASS

1. Compare your documents with other group. What similar or different approaches did each group devise?

2. Would your group change your document now that you have heard from other groups?

Exercise 19 Overcoming Resistance

Exercise Overview

One of the sources of frustration during organizational change is the perception of resistance to that change. This exercise allows you to apply the concept of resistance to change.

Working Through

 AS AN INDIVIDUAL

Read the scenario of an organization going through a major change effort. Identify resistance to change behavior and sources of the resistance to change that you find in the scenario.

Scenario

An IT executive, Gerta, has implemented changes to the insurance reimbursement and billing system. She met with her executive team and explained thoroughly the cost savings that would result from this change. However, one leader, Bill, did not share the information that was provided, because he thought it would draw attention to the bad news of changing computer systems and workflow. Bill also speculated that sharing the information would undermine his authority—his employees might see Gerta as having more power and influence than him, since he had already bragged about his influence in the organization. Employees even speculated that with the improved efficiency, there would be lay-offs. The project team assigned to make the software changes consistently overestimated how long it would take them to complete the changes. In reality, they could be finished in a week, but publically, they stated that the software changes would take six months. This team had a culture of not being too responsive to management. Otherwise, they reasoned they would have more work to do. Gina, an employee in the billing department, has decided to call in sick to avoid the project implementation. Her co-worker, Raj, decided to pretend that he does not understand the new process of insurance reimbursement, in particular the paperwork approval. He continues to follow the old process, and submits paperwork for approval to three different levels of management.

Example:

Source of resistance to change	Resistance to change behavior

 ## AS A GROUP

1. Compare your results.

2. Make a table that lists each resistance to change behavior and specific strategies that you would recommend in order to resolve this behavior and overcome resistance to change.

 ## AS A CLASS

3. Compare your table with other group members. What similar or different approaches did each group devise?

4. What did you learn about change and resistance to change?

Exercise 20 Employment Branding

Exercise Overview

Employment branding is managing the impressions that are produced by an organization in order to convince the marketplace that the organization is an excellent place to work. This form of managing perceptions in the marketplace encompasses a wide variety of techniques and strategies.

Working Through

 ### AS A GROUP

1. Select an organization that has been having difficulties lately. For example, Ford Motors had a period of economic turmoil, as did many in the auto industry.

2. Write phrases and words that describe this organization, and what you think its employees and customers think of this organization. These phrases and words can contain negative or positive images.

3. Compile a list of three of the most negative words or phrases. As a group, discuss how you would transform these three words/phrases to convey a positive image that matches what you know about the company.

4. Brainstorm strategies an organization could use that would encourage employees and the marketplace to connect the three positive words/phrases with their company. Ford Motor Company uses the slogan 'Go Further' to connect to both internal and external company stakeholders. Employees have the message to work harder, to not settle for anything than the very best. Customers receive the message that the Ford vehicle 'goes further' because of its quality.

 ### AS A CLASS

1. Compare the final results of the employment branding exercise.

2. What strategies do you think will be the most effective? Least effective? Why do you think so?

Exercise 21 OD Techniques at Work

Exercise Overview

Organizational development consists of one or more planned techniques designed to increase effectiveness in an organization. Some common techniques are listed below:

- Team building
- Conflict resolution
- Process redesign
- Reward and performance systems
- Downsizing
- Organizational redesign
- Third party interventions
- Assessment and analysis
- Coaching and mentoring
- Stress and wellness interventions
- Leadership training

Working Through

 AS A GROUP

1. Discuss how you would use organizational development techniques and which techniques you would use to resolve the following situations:

   a. A difficult roommate keeps arguing about his lack of personal hygiene.
   b. There is a faction of students in a student club that want to overthrow the elected student leader.
   c. There are two students on your organizational behavior project team who do not show up to team meetings.
   d. Your workgroup has been under extreme stress ever since your workload changed post layoff; you have two extra hours of tasks to do after the close of business.
   e. There are widespread rumors about your colleague that he is involved in an inappropriate relationship with another worker; new stories and speculation grows each day.

AS A CLASS

1. Compare and contrast the techniques used to resolve each situation.

2. Under what circumstances in organizations can organizational development interventions help? Are their circumstances where organizational development interventions might cause harm? Why do you think so?

Exercise 22 A Clash of Cultures

Exercise Overview

This exercise provides you with an opportunity to experience the differences in organizational cultures during an organizational merger and the challenges that arise.

Working Through

 AS A CLASS

Instructions:

1. Divide the class into two groups—Group A and Group B. Group members can wear sticky notes to label people with their group designation.

2. Read a description of your organization. Group A members can discuss among themselves what it is like to work in their company's culture. Group B can discuss among themselves what it is like to work in their company's culture.

3. Merger occurs. The class is divided into subgroups with half of each subgroup from the original Group A and half of each subgroup from the original Group B.

4. The subgroups are part of the 'change task force' and they have to come up with a plan for the new organization. The plan should include how your newly merged organization should handle dress code, flexible work arrangements, and expense accounts.

5. Each subgroup should present their recommendations to the class.

6. Complete discussion questions.

Background for Organization A

Your company has just announced a merger. You are a middle manager at your organization and you really like things just the way they are. You hope that nothing significant will change with this merger, you are still a bit shocked at the news as this was a complete surprise. Your workplace is full of easygoing, creative people and it is common to smile and greet people as you walk through the hallways, even if you do not know them. The dress code has always been somewhat relaxed; it is ok to wear flip-flops as long as you do your work. When people break for lunch, there are friendly and noisy groups of people in the cafeteria; rank and position is not important; lunch groups easily are a mix of different departments and position levels within your company. The big 'boss' is always accessible and you readily share your ideas with her, you feel that your company has an entrepreneurial culture. You love that you are able to bring your adopted greyhound dog with you to your office—the 'pets allowed' policy at work has been very successful. Your company is a bit more conservative with spending, you do not have the biggest expense account, but it is a nice change of pace to hold a meeting down the street at the local deli over sandwiches when they offer a coupon. The flexible work arrangement that is common practice allows employees to work a portion of their day from their home office, virtually. This flexibility with scheduling means that you get to avoid morning rush hour. Life is good; now back to the business of the merger...

Background for Organization B

Your company has just announced a merger. You are a middle manager at your organization and you hope nothing really changes after the merger, you like your work, your colleagues and your company just the way it is, you are still a bit shocked at the news as this was a complete surprise. You look around and you notice that everyone is polished and professional, your normal choice of work attire is a dark business suit. When you enter a room, people recognize your position, and your authority. If you pass someone in the hallway, they know who you are and do not speak to you, they are impressed with your status and they know their place. Just how you like it. Even the cafeteria is separated, which you enjoy. You do not have to be bothered with employees pestering you at lunch, managers have a separate eating area, and you wouldn't want to be friendly with the employees, because everyone has a job to do. Each week you received a pricy fruit basket (fresh mango and imported Asian pears), and fresh flowers for your office. Your expense account is rarely scrutinized and you enjoy these perks. After all, how many mangers get to dine at five-star restaurants when they conduct business? You do love lobster! You know exactly where to find your employees, your company does not indulge those ridiculous flexible work arrangements where people work from home that you heard other less successful companies use. Life is good; now back to the business of the merger...

The Merger Occurs: Here Comes the Change...

You just found out that your department is moving, you will now be in a department consisting of about half of employees from the 'other' company with which you recently merged. To make matters worse, you have been placed on the 'Change Task Force' and have been handed a mandate from the vice president, seems you are some expert on change because of your background in organizational behavior. This task force will consist of a mix of employees from both of the companies that merged, all of equal status and position in the new organization. You have to make some decisions at your first meeting, according to the letter from your vice president:

Dear Change Task Force Committee Member

Congratulations on your selection to this important team! As a team you need to decide on a few important items: 1) preliminary draft of the new dress code, 2) policy around expense accounts including what is appropriate to list as a business expense and what type of approval is granted for these accounts, 3) whether or not we have flexible work arrangements, and 4) the best way to communicate these changes. I expect that your team will present a step-by-step plan of how to minimize employees' resistance to these changes. I look forward to your results.

AS A GROUP

A Few Useful Tips

1. Take note of who in your newly formed task force is from Organization A and who in your team is from Organization B.

2. Discuss and decide as a task force on critical changes to your new organization's practices.

3. Use flip chart paper or the board in the class to summarize your decisions; here is a sample template:

Items to Decide On	Adoption of Organization A 's Practice?	Adoption of Organization B's Practice?	Adoption of a Hybrid or New Practice?	Explanation of Your Decision
Dress Code				
Flexible Work Arrangements				
Expense Accounts				

4. Be prepared to discuss your decision process for the new recommendations.

AS A CLASS

Discussion Questions:

1. In what ways were the cultures of these two organizations incompatible?

2. What are some approaches that organizations can take to ensure that cultures mesh versus clash during a merger?

3. How can managers create a culture that supports change?

Exercise 23 What's Your University's Culture?

Exercise Overview

An organization's culture describes people's behavior and the meaning that people make out of these patterns. It can be understood at three levels—artifacts, values, and basic assumptions. The artifacts are visible, tangible symbols that tell us about how people behave and what they believe in an organization, can include physical structure, stories, style of dress, ceremonies, etc. Values tell us what is important and are informed by assumptions. Assumptions are more difficult to identify as they are deeply held beliefs that impact values.

Working Through

 ### AS A GROUP

Describe your university's culture, using artifacts, values, and basic assumptions as the categories for analysis.

1. What are my university's artifacts? (e.g., graduation ceremony)

2. What are the values of my university? (e.g., 'we value excellence in teaching')

3. What are the assumptions of my university? (e.g., 'students are the most important resource we have')

 ### AS A CLASS

Your instructor will provide a chart on the board listing the general categories of: 1) artifacts, 2) values, and 3) assumptions.

1. Write the words and phrases that your group agreed upon.

Discuss:

    a. What patterns do we notice in how we describe our university's culture?

    b. How did we learn what the culture of our university is? How will other stakeholders that are new to the university learn the culture?

    c. Why is culture important?

Exercise 24 Find the Artifacts

Exercise Overview

Artifacts—visible and tangible symbols in an organization's internal environment—provide clues to outside observers what the underlying assumptions and values of an organization are and what the overall 'feel' is like.

Working Through

 ### AS AN INDIVIDUAL

1. Think of an organization that you visited for a tour, an interview, an internship, or other purpose.

2. List as many items that you recall from your visit to this organization.

3. What conclusions might you make based on the artifacts that you observed about this workplace?

4. Read the passage below. What examples of artifacts do you find in this passage? What conclusions would you make about this organization based on these artifacts?

Example:

I saw that the grounds were well kept and flowers had been freshly planted. I was excited for my interview. When I walked inside, however, the carpet was old and stained. The restroom in the waiting area had not been cleaned, and I noticed that someone had written rude messages in pencil on one of the bathroom stalls. The receptionist did not have a computer at his desk, nor did he have a plant or any personal items. He had stacks of corporate promotional materials shoved under his desk. The only pictures on the walls of the waiting room were stock posters urging 'teamwork'. There was no music, but occasionally an annoyed voice could be heard over the loudspeaker summing an employee to the Human Resources office.

AS A CLASS

1. What artifacts did you identify from your own experiences? What conclusions did you make based upon these artifacts in your experience?

2. What artifacts did you identify from the example? What conclusions did you make about this organization?

3. Under what circumstances do you find identification and interpretation of an organization's culture useful? Under what circumstances would you foresee a problem with this approach to understanding an organization's culture?

Exercise 25 Back-to-Back Change

Exercise Overview

Change in organizations can occur incrementally or rapidly. The changes that occur can be small or large scale transformation efforts. Many examples of organizational change include large-scale organizational transformation, such as a change in strategy, values, or corporate identity, but change can also be change of a small process, implementation of a single idea within a department, or a single line item budget adjustment.

Working Through

 ### AS A GROUP

1. For one minute, stand up and observe the other people in your group. Take note of how they are dressed and what accessories they have.

2. Turn back to back. Each person should change two things that others might not notice (e.g., take out an earring).

3. Face each other again, observe the others in your group and try to guess what was changed.

 ### AS A CLASS

1. How many of you were able to guess everything that was changed? What are some examples of changes that students made?

2. How many were not able to figure out what was changed? Why do you think you were not able to figure this out?

3. How does this exercise relate to change in organizations?

Exercise 26 Social Media Dilemma

Exercise Overview

This exercise provides you with an opportunity to experience the competing demands that new employees experience around information, impression management, decision-making, and ethics.

Working Through

 AS A GROUP

Many companies engage creative ways to check references, character, and employment background of potential employees. One method involves asking a potential employee for an interview and surprises them at the interview with a request to browse their Facebook, MySpace, email, or other social media account during the interview. Someone's 'digital footprint' is the record that someone leaves behind including social media interactions; email records; voicemail recordings; news stories; blogs; or any other digital trail. Employers can routinely check this digital footprint with a few simple searches on someone they are considering hiring or they can be more invasive into someone's personal information by requesting passwords to log on to these accounts and look at photos and other information.

One student recently reported not being hired because of private pictures she had posted on her Facebook account showing her during Spring Break celebrating excessively. Her future employer stated that her behavior would be embarrassing and even compromising in a conservative corporate culture where employees undergo rigorous security clearance and background checks.

Discuss

1. Has this situation occurred with any of the members in your group? What happened? What was the result?

2. Would you or wouldn't you allow a prospective employer access to your social media account? Your private email account? Your personal photos? Where would you draw the line as to what you would allow your prospective employer to view about you?

3. What factors would influence your decision?

4. Is this information useful to an employer? Why and why not? What impact might occur if you refused access to your potential employer?

👤 AS AN INDIVIDUAL

1. What accounts do I need to review to see if they would pass the scrutiny of a future employer?

2. What is my 'digital footprint'? What do I need to change? Should I be concerned?

👥 AS A CLASS

1. How concerned are you that employers might make an important decision about you based on your 'digital footprint'?

2. How accurate are these records? Do the private pictures you have posted represent who you might be as an employee?

Exercise 27 Develop Your Professional Code

Exercise Overview

Various career Websites and business trade publications encourage employees to 'be professional', to demonstrate their 'professional code', or to engage in 'professionalism'. In fact in many workplaces, the designation that someone is 'professional' is used as a compliment to highlight a positive cluster of behaviors, attitudes, and skills. But, what is professionalism? This exercise allows for you to think about the definition of what code governs your professionalism in an organization. Compare your code to others in the class.

Working Through

 ### AS AN INDIVIDUAL

1. Brainstorm a list of behaviors, attitudes, and skills that represent 'professionalism' (e.g., professionalism is the skill of being a good listener or the attitude of having an open mind).

Professionalism is...

Behavior	Attitude	Skill

2. Next, rank order your list of behaviors, attitudes, and skills, and select your three most important.
3. For the three most important categories that you identified, provide an example of when you demonstrated these.
4. Are there any conditions at work where you would *not* need to demonstrate professionalism? (e.g., a conflict with a peer, a boss yells at you, a subordinate is chronically late?)? Why do you think so?

 ### AS A CLASS

1. Generate a class list compiled from the three most important behaviors, attitudes, and skills.
2. What patterns do you notice in the class list?
3. How can the concept of professionalism lead to a better organizational climate?
4. What actions can organizations take to promote professionalism in employees?
5. When if at all does professionalism hold employees back from their best work?

Exercise 28 Communication Breakdown

Exercise Overview

Good communication is necessary for effective decision making, learning, leading, working together, and coordinating ideas. The process of effectively communicating to others is a skill that can be practiced. This exercise allows you to think about what causes the breakdown of communication and practice specific skills necessary for listening and giving feedback.

Working Through

AS A CLASS

1. What causes communication to breakdown?

2. As a class, brainstorm a list of rules that show good listening skills. (e.g., be patient and do not interrupt the speaker)

3. Differentiate between active listening and passive hearing.

4. Brainstorm a list of what constitutes effective feedback.

AS A GROUP

1. You are to divide up three roles and each take a role: 1) *Observer* to give feedback, 2) *Active Listener*, and 3) *Communicator*.

2. Take five minutes for the Communicator to provide to the Active Listener (follow the rules of active listening!) what they think on one of the topics listed below:

    * Whether political views should be shared at work or not.
    * The sharing of music or video files, when illegal.
    * Why I would or would not want to be a senior level manager.
    * My views on dating in the workplace.

3. After five minutes, the Active Listener will communicate back what she heard. the Observer, (following the rules of effective feedback!) will comment on the process.

4. Switch roles until everyone has had a turn playing all three roles.

5. Discuss:
    a. What did we learn about communication?
    b. What was it like to give feedback in this situation?
    c. How can this be applied in an organization?

Exercise 29 Diversity Rocks

Exercise Overview

This exercise provides you with an opportunity to explore surface and deep level diversity assumptions.

Working Through

 AS AN INDIVIDUAL

Complete a sticky note and fill in your favorite music category listed below. Stick the sticky note on yourself

Choices:
World music
Dance
Hip-hop
Classic
Singer songwriter
Soundtracks
Rock
Reggae
Pop
Latino
Jazz
Christian
Country
Alternative
Blues

 AS A CLASS

1. Find others with the same musical preference. Have each person gather into one group by musical preference.

 AS A GROUP

Discuss

1. Do the members of my group surprise me? Was anyone by himself or herself? Could I have guessed who I would be grouped with in advance? Why? Why not?

2. Observe one of the other groups. What do you think their favorite music choice is? What perception do you have of people with different taste in music than you? Why do you think this?

3. How does this exercise relate to surface and deep level diversity?

Exercise 30 You Can't Handle the Truth

Exercise Overview

Many examples exist of organizational leaders who were caught not telling the truth. In addition, there are examples of leaders engaged in 'insincere' apologies, which are not blatant lies, but feel false to the listener. This exercise allows you an opportunity to explore under what conditions people in organizations should and should not tell the truth. Potential consequences for this decision are explored.

Working Through

AS AN INDIVIDUAL

1. Brainstorm a list of specific instances that people in the workplace should and should not tell the truth.

Example

Should	Should Not
Interviewed during an internal investigation	Might make your boss angry

AS A GROUP

1. Compare your lists. What do you agree or disagree with?

2. Provide an example from your experience where someone told the truth and what the consequence was. Also, provide an example where someone did not tell the truth, and what the consequence was.

3. What are some potential consequences for truth and untruth?

4. What personal and situational factors should be considered when an employee decides whether or not to tell the truth?

AS A CLASS

1. What did each group conclude on telling the truth in the workplace?

2. (Optional). Draw a class decision tree that includes situational factors for truth telling choice and potential consequences.

Exercise 31 The Ethics of the Climb

Exercise Overview

Leading an expedition to climb a large mountain or facing a difficult, changing, and ambiguous situation requires ethical decision-making skills. This exercise allows you to engage in critical-thinking skills, think about and discuss a decision with competing and equally important goals, make a decision, and be able to explain how you arrived at the decision. This encourages a connection between personal values and choices that are made in difficult situations.

Working Through

👤 **AS AN INDIVIDUAL**

1. Read the passage below.

   You are leading a mountain climbing expedition with a team of climbers who are relatively inexperienced in summiting high-altitude situations. You are paid to make sure they have a good experience, reach the top of the mountain, and make it back down. There is a narrow window of opportunity to be successful in the climb, as weather can be somewhat unpredictable at this altitude and in this part of the world. You have just arrived at the top of the mountain. Your team that you are leading is in trouble. On the way back down the mountain, a terrible storm covers the mountain with blinding snow and wind. Even seeing your hands is virtually impossible. At around 24,000 feet, one of the climbers on your team has collapsed from the conditions. The other two climbers cannot carry the collapsed team member, and decide to continue down the mountain. You cannot be rescued at this high level of elevation—helicopters cannot fly above 18,000 feet. Your decision is to continue down the mountain with the other two team members and leave the exhausted third member to die alone on the mountain, or to stay with him, and you would also probably die.

2. Would you remain with your teammate on the mountain or descend the mountain and let him die?

3. Prepare a justification including the elements listed below in the example:

    a. What are the problems and benefits with each of the two choices?
    b. What are the underlying values associated with each of the two choices?
    c. What values do you have that influenced your final decision in this scenario?
    d. What prior experience or information helped you make your decision?
    e. How does this relate to difficult situations that are made in the workplace (e.g., let someone fail in a meeting on his or her own, or help them out, and be blamed with them for a failure)?

 ## AS A GROUP

1. Compare your individual reactions and resolution to the scenario.

2. What was similar and different in your ethical reasoning?

Based on actual events described in: *Into thin air: A personal account of the Mt. Everest Climbing Disaster* (1997) by Jon Krakaur, New York: Villard.

Exercise 32 Mindmapping

Exercise Overview

A mindmap is a visual tool to capture ideas and pictures. The mindmap starts with a circle, which contains the central idea or question and contains branches that stem from the center. Each branch contains additional ideas. This is a tool to help with group problem solving, fostering creativity, or promoting innovation.

Working Through

 ### AS A GROUP

1. In your group, your instructor will select an organizational behavior topic for you to create a mindmap.

2. Start with the central topic that your instructor assigned by placing it in the middle of a circle. Draw a picture to represent this topic.

3. As a group, work together to create sub-topics as primary branches that flow from the central idea. Use symbols and pictures to represent these ideas.

4. Continue this process by creating secondary branches that attach to the primary branches. These secondary branches can contain examples or other subtopics that the group identifies as important.

5. When complete, post your mindmaps on the board.

 ### AS A CLASS

1. Observe the different mindmaps created by classroom groups.

2. How did this process of mindmapping help students to think more deeply about an idea?

3. How do you see this process utilized in the workplace? In what types of situations do you think a mindmap could be applied?

OPTIONAL WEB SUPPLEMENT

Research different images and examples of mindmapping used in organizations. Google 'images' provide a variety of pictures that show partial and finished mindmaps. These maps utilize a variety of colors and images in order to convey ideas in interesting and novel ways.

Exercise 33 Could I Be a Whistleblower?

Exercise Overview

A whistleblower is *someone who points out wrongdoing in an organization in order to stop it*. There is even attention given to these acts through the *National Character Week*. The United States Senate passed this act in 2011 to highlight the work that whistleblowers have accomplished in making the world a more ethical place. There are a number of character traits often attributed to heroic whistleblowers. These character traits include trustworthiness, fairness and honesty, not to mention strong core ethical values that they are willing to act on. However, there is often a downside to the act of whistleblowing, it takes a lot of risk. Even though there are laws that protect the act of whistleblowing, many still report negative consequences. Whistleblowers report losing their own reputation, having their honesty and loyalty questioned, and even losing their jobs. One example was the case of Bunny Greenhouse, former chief contracting officer of the United States Army Corps of Engineers and the highest-ranking civilian in the Corps of Engineers. She testified in June 2005 before a Democratic Party public committee against a government contractor, Halliburton, of waste, fraud, and other abuses in its operations during the Iraq War. After she pointed out this alleged wrongdoing, she was described as a 'nuisance' and reported being demoted and removed from her position.

Working Through

 ### AS AN INDIVIDUAL

1. Under what circumstances would I become a 'whistleblower'? How important is it to me to point out wrongdoing in the workplace? Am I willing to suffer any personal consequences as a result?

2. Would I describe myself as a risk taker? Why or why not? In what areas of my life do I take risks and in what areas am I more cautious? Personal? Professional? How does risk-taking orientation connect with whistleblowing?

3. Under what circumstances would I encourage someone else to become a 'whistleblower'? What argument would I make to encourage or discourage a colleague who might suffer personal consequences?

 ### AS A GROUP

1. Compare your reflections to the questions you completed as individuals.

2. Would your answers differ if you had a group of colleagues who were willing to point out wrongdoing? Would it be easier or less risk as a group to engage in whistleblowing? or easier and less risk as an individual? Why do you think this?

3. What organizational consequences exist if employees are afraid to voice concerns over wrongdoing? How could these consequences be minimized? What are some suggestions that organizations could incorporate to open up communication around wrongdoing?

References for 'Could I be a Whistleblower?'

http://whistlewatch.org/National Character Week. Retrieved: January 2012.

http://www.vanityfair.com/politics/features/2005/04/shnayerson200504. Retrieved January 2012.

Emily Kern, "Whistle-blower Greenhouse: Integrity not matter of choice", *The Advocate*, December 7, 2005, 01B.

Exercise 34 Sustainability Practice at Work

Exercise Overview

Your team has just been hired as sustainability consultants for an organization named ADSTRATEGY Inc. that specializes in advertising and graphic design. The CEO of the company has a particular interest in devising a strategy to integrate sustainability practices into the organization. She wants to demonstrate to her clients that the firm is committed to the environment and to social issues in the community. Your team is a bright group of new university graduates that specialize in applying organizational behavior concepts to the workplace in novel and creative ways. Your first and immediate deliverable for AD-STRATEGY Inc. is to brainstorm a list of activities, programs, or actions that the company could take in the areas of economic and social sustainability. The company has considerable resource constraints and wants a list that includes low cost or no cost ideas. You wonder if this is possible, so your team meets to brainstorm...

Several of your group members have brought examples of sustainability practices that other industries adopted that you hope might spark your creative juices:

Examples for Environmental Sustainability

- A company offers bicycles to its employees in an effort to reduce congestion and pollution for their commute to work.

- A consulting firm offers flexible work hours for employees to avoid rush hour traffic and balance work and life responsibilities.

- A city planning office reset all printers and copiers to automatically produce double-sided copies in an effort to reduce paper waste.

- A university installed sensors in all classrooms to shut down lights and heat/air when not in use.

- A designer designs all of her new line of men's shirts out of recycled tires. She mandates that employees at her design firm only wear recycled clothing and accessories.

Examples for Social Sustainability

- A manufacturing company offers free language and basic math classes to employees and their families after business hours to develop their skills.

- A multinational company establishes online social support networks for people who use their products.

- A company gives its employees two paid days off a year to volunteer for their favorite local charity.

- A catering company donates all day-old bread to a local shelter and actively hires people living in transitional housing.

Working Through

 ## AS A GROUP

1. Devise a list of 10 ideas for how an organization can practice sustainability in the area of environmental sustainability.

2. Devise a list of 10 ideas for how an organization can practice sustainability in the area of social sustainability.

3. Sort your lists by 'resource intensive', 'moderate resource needs', 'low resource needs.' These categories are based on your initial guess as to how many resources it would take to implement. Think of resources including time, effort, cost, etc.

4. Present to the class your ideas. Was it difficult to find solutions that were low cost? Were there similar solutions across class groups?

Exercise 35 Who Do I Fire?

Exercise Overview

Decision making in organizations is sometimes a complex process. This exercise allows you to explore some of the challenges associated with decision making and the preconceived ideas and experiences that people hold onto when making decisions.

Working Through

 ### AS A GROUP

Instructions for exercise: Below you will find profiles and the relevant employment background of two employees. Your group has been tasked with making a decision as to which employee to fire. As a group, discuss the two candidates, Tom and Janelle, and reach a decision on which employee should be fired.

Background on the situation: Times are tough at your organization. Every conceivable method of cutting the budget has been carried out. The organization's leadership has decided to reduce employees to lower costs and your team is responsible for firing one person because both Tom and Janelle basically perform the same job.

Your company's employee handbook stipulates that your employees can be let go at any time for any reason and there is no protection for employees based on seniority or performance.

	Tom	Janelle
Time with company	Six years	Four and a half years
Performance evaluations	Tom has been a very consistent performer. He usually received comments such as "positive attitude" and "team player". Tom's latest success as a project team member was reported in last year's performance evaluation and he is ranked "above average" and "excellent" in interpersonal and team skills. Areas for improvement on his performance evaluation usually mention something about his technical skill level, as he is average to below average in these areas. Tom has won the Employee of the Month award once and earned a fruit basket for the honor.	Janelle is a very hard worker and a consistent performer. She received comments on her performance evaluations such as " workhorse", and even "technical genius". In the technical skill level section, she is usually ranked "above average" or "excellent". Janelle tends to select projects as an individual contributor and her areas for improvement section on her evaluation mention that she needs to work on her team skills. Janelle has won the Employee of the Month award once and earned a free parking space for the honor.

(continued)

	Tom	Janelle
Ability/Skill	Tom's supervisor advocates that his ability is greater than his current skill level. He needs to improve his technical skills but has very strong interpersonal and team skills.	Janelle's supervisor advocates that her ability and her current skill level are the same. She has outstanding technical skills and holds an engineering degree. Her interpersonal and team skills are average.
Other information	Tom usually is at every after-hours event at work (plays on the company softball league) and performs a comedy routine at the annual company holiday event. Tom's cousin works at the company in a sales position.	Janelle can be seen working weekends and late hours. She is often the last to leave work and the first to arrive. She is very quiet and keeps to herself at company events. Janelle spent her vacation time volunteering with a local school.

Action to take: Your group must decide which employee to fire. Then, each group must provide justification and reasoning for the decision. Be prepared to answer the following questions:

1. What was the basis of your decision?

2. How did prior knowledge or experience influence your decision?

3. What specific criteria, if any, did you use to evaluate the candidates?

4. Can you ever be sure your decision was the correct one? How will you know if you made the correct decision?

🧑 AS AN INDIVIDUAL

Analysis of your decision-making style: People who work in organizations rely on many tools and decision-making models to help them make decisions. Organizations may rely on a combination of experience, personal values, and rational/criteria based approaches to decision making.

Review the decision you made. Which of the following decision making categories best describes your decision making style?

Experience based	Opinion based	Criteria based
I made my decision based on my personal and professional experiences.	I made my decision based on my opinions and values.	I assigned a set of criteria to my decision and based it on these variables.

 **AS A CLASS**

Discuss:

What were some similarities in the way that class members made a decision? What were some differences?

    a. What other types of decisions that you make could you use the classification experience, opinion, and criteria based? How is it useful to use this type of classification?

    b. Would you change your decision as a group now that you have heard from the entire class? Why? Why not?

    (This exercise is based on King and Kitchener's model of Reflective Judgment)

Exercise 36 What Are My Values?

Exercise Overview

Values are an important part of what governs people's actions and decisions. These can be used to help us understand how we are different and similar from others, why people behave the way they do, and how they match or mismatch with our work. Consider the two primary ways that values can be sorted—by desired objectives and by what will get me to my desired objectives.

Values that *are* my desired objective	Values that *will get me to my* desired objective
Friendship	Cheerfulness
Love	Ambition
Self-Respect	Love
Happiness	Cleanliness
Inner Peace	Self-Control
Equality	Capability
Freedom	Courage
Pleasure	Politeness
Social Recognition	Honesty
Wisdom	Imagination
Redemption	Independence
Family Security	Intellect
National Security	Open-Mindedness
A Sense of Accomplishment	Logic
A World of Beauty	Obedience
A World at Peace	Helpfulness
A Comfortable Life	Responsibility
An Exciting Life	Forgiveness

Source: Rokeach, M. (1973). "The nature of human values." New York: FreePress.

Working Through

 **AS AN INDIVIDUAL**

1. Review both lists above. Select your top five values from each list and rank order them in terms of priority.

2. What experiences have you had that you think impacts the order of your values? Do you hold similar values to your family? To your friends? Colleagues? How do you know what other people value?

3. How will you connect your job with your values? How important is this?

4. How will you select your workplace based on a match between your values and the organization's values? How can you know what an organization values before you work there?

AS A GROUP

1. Compare your value ranking with each member of this group. What similarities or differences do you note?

2. Discuss how your values have changed or remained the same over time. What degree of change have you seen in your values? Was this based on a specific experience? Why?

3. Compare your priorities around matching values with job and workplace. What similarities or differences do you note?

AS A CLASS

1. Why are values so important to understand in the workplace?

2. How can you know what an organization values? How is this different as an outsider to the organization, such as a job applicant as opposed to an employee inside the organization?

Exercise 37 Team Survival Simulation

Exercise Overview

You and your team have just survived the crash of a small plane that was taking you to a workplace conference in Canada. The pilot is injured and the plane is damaged and cannot fly. It is the middle of February where the daily temperature is 30 degrees below zero, with the nighttime temperature around 40 below zero. There is snow and ice on the ground; there are woods, and small frozen bodies of water. The nearest civilization is a town 20 miles away. At least you think this is correct, this was the last announcement that the pilot team made before the descent. You are all dressed in clothes appropriate for a business casual business meeting, but most of you are wearing dress shoes. Your team of survivors managed to salvage the following odd items from people's luggage and the wreckage:

Item	Your Rank Order
A ball of steel wool	
A small ax	
A loaded pistol	
Can of shortening	
Newspapers	
Cigarette lighter (without fluid)	
Extra clothing for each survivor	
Large piece of heavy-duty canvas	
A sectional air map made of plastic	
One quart of whiskey	
A compass	
Large chocolate bars	

Working Through

 ## AS AN INDIVIDUAL

You are to rank order the items listed above by the order of importance for your team's survival.

 ## AS A GROUP

You are now to (as a group) list items in order of importance for your survival. List the uses for each. You have to agree as a group on the final list. Eventually you will compare your list with the 'expert's' list and compare your individual lists with the overall group's list.

How to Score Individual and Team Points

1. To award points; look at the ranking numbers that your instructor provides. The lowest score wins.

2. Compare your individual score with the team score.

 ## AS A CLASS

Discuss:

1. Did you have a lower score as a group or as an individual member? Why do you think this happened?

2. What are the benefits of more people when deciding on information?

3. What are some of the problems associated with more people deciding on information?

GLOSSARY

accommodating style A style of conflict behavior that is cooperative yet unassertive; the opposite of *competing style*. With the accommodating style, the person may seek to satisfy the interests of the other person at the expense of resolving his or her own concerns.

action learning A learning technique that guides a team from problem generation through solution implementation.

adaptation A process that occurs as a person learns the new culture in an organization.

adhocracy culture When an organization values flexibility and discretion, while at the same time has an external focus.

applied An applied discipline is one that seeks to improve organizations and make positive impacts on people while solving practical problems that people face in the workplace.

applied ethics A process that utilizes five distinct tests of a behavior to help guide people in organizations make decisions when they are faced with an ethical dilemma.

Appreciative Inquiry (AI) Seeks to identify sources of change that build on past successes and core organizational values, through a process of recognizing positive attributes and sources of pride within the organization rather than problems or challenges.

artifacts Objects that can be readily observed in organizations that reveal the organization's culture.

assertiveness The degree to which a person or group attempts to satisfy his or her own interests.

attitude The summation of a person's beliefs, feelings, and actions usually subject to change based on experience.

attribution Describes how blame or credit is attributed to someone, whether or not they had anything to do with it.

authentic leadership Offers an approach that emphasizes ethics and integrity, while de-emphasizing the importance of power.

authority A tactic, which involves displaying the trappings and behaviors of those in power.

autonomy Involves having independence and discretion over decisions in a particular area.

avoiding style A style of conflict behavior where the issue is never confronted directly, characterized by a lack of assertiveness and cooperation.

availability heuristic The notion that we may think that something is more important or more worthy if we can easily recall similar examples of scarce and valuable things.

baby-boomers Individuals born between 1943 and 1960 and grew up during a period of unprecedented prosperity and economic growth.

basic assumptions Considered the foundation of culture, as the accepted, taken for granted, unquestioned beliefs and assumptions shared by the members of the culture.

behavioral artifacts *Artifacts* that reveal an organization's culture through behavior, rather than *physical artifacts,* such as ceremonies, rituals, traditions, and customs.

benefit corporation A flexible purpose corporation, or a B corporation, defined as a legal entity that holds a corporation legally accountable for a broader set of stakeholders rather than shareholders.

benefits of diversity Benefits felt by organizations that have a diverse workforce which include improved learning and adaptation, access-legitimacy among stakeholders, and increased fairness for underrepresented groups.

Best Alternative to a Negotiated Agreement (BATNA) This describes the option or action plan one would take as an alternative position in a negotiation.

behavior The study of how individuals will behave in a particular context.

behavioral economic-based decision making Focuses on how incentives and psychological biases may interfere with rational decision making and cause decision makers to make less than optimal decisions.

bias blind spot An individual bias that occurs when people underestimate the role that bias plays in their own decisions, but overestimate the role that bias plays in other people's decisions.

big data "The age of big data" denotes a period in which the vast amount of information available makes communication more difficult as people attempt to sort through what is relevant while maintaining meaning.

Big Five personality types Five traits found in individuals that reflect certain outcomes in the work environment, including extraversion, agreeableness, conscientiousness, emotional stability, and openness to experience.

bounded rationality The process where decision makers are forced to act, but must rely on limited information and time constraints when making a decision.

brainstorming A process of idea generation in which all members work together in a face-to-face meeting and strive to generate as many ideas as possible, withholding evaluation for each idea until the session is complete.

bureaucratic leadership A leader who motivates followers by appealing to legitimate authority bestowed by an institution or by appealing to rules and traditions.

certainty The confidence that an event will occur.

change management The process of moving from the current state in an organization to a future state guided by active management of the change process.

challenge stress One of two ways people experience stress, this stress improves a person's ability to learn, grow, and perform. See also *hindrance stress*.

characteristics of contemporary organizations Characteristics that are shared by various contemporary organizations, including pressure to achieve more complex goals, an emphasis on data-driven decisions, greater competition across the organization, the necessity of individual and team performance, and an action orientation in an ever-changing environment.

charisma From the Greek meaning "divinely inspired gift," a personal quality of appeal inspiring interest and regard in followers.

charismatic leadership A view of *charisma* as a behavior or skill that can be learned to gain the attention and loyalty of followers.

clan culture When an organization has internal focus while maintaining flexibility and discretion.

classical conditioning A technique developed by psychologist Ivan Pavlov that involves modification of behavior through associations between triggers and rewards.

cognitive complexity A series of progressive steps where each new step is marked by an increase in the ability to process information in a more complex, and therefore more complete way.

cognitive evaluation theory A theory that intrinsic or internal motivation creates a sense of personal accomplishment and competence while monetary or other incentives are actually less fulfilling and therefore less motivating.

cognitive framing The way a person perceives or frames information. The frame is a mental structure that helps individuals organize perceptions.

collaborating style A style of behavior that is both assertive and cooperative, where an individual will work with another party to satisfy both interests and a viable solution to any conflict.

common knowledge effect Describes the tendency of group members to share information that is already known by other members of the team rather than share information that is unique.

communication style A culturally learned set of signals that people use to communicate meaning, which also serves as a filter that individuals use to evaluate another's meaning.

competencies describe the knowledge, skills, and abilities necessary for performing different jobs, functions, or tasks.

competency models Various models that offer a comprehensive way to identify the groups of employees and their skills within an organization.

competing style A style of conflict behavior that describes both assertive and uncooperative behavior, pursuing one's own interests at the expense of the other party.

competing values framework Describes how organizations must choose between different cultural values along two dimensions.

competing commitments model of change A psychological reaction, or resistance, to change when an individual finds themselves caught between a commitment to the old way of doing things and a commitment to the new way of doing things.

compromising style A style of conflict behavior which is moderately assertive and cooperative, which seeks an acceptable solution where self-interest is sacrificed for the sake of resolving conflict.

conflict Any disagreement between two parties, which vary by type of party, type of issue, and cause.

consensus Occurs when behavior is analyzed as being just like other people's behavior in the same situation or different than all other people's behavior.

consistency Occurs when behavior is analyzed as being similar or dissimilar over time.

conversational learning model of communication An approach that explains how people use conversation to improve understanding of differences.

cooperativeness Describes to what extent the person or group attempts to satisfy the other party's interests.

corporate social responsibility (CSR) Refers to the expectations that society holds of an organization and how the society chooses to hold the organization to those expectations.

corruption Whereas ethical lapses and moral transgressions are often isolated events, corruption implies the system itself has gone bad and the unethical behavior cannot be attributed solely to the actions of a subset of individuals. See also *integrity*.

creativity The process whereby new ideas emerge and grow within a specific domain.

critical reflection A process of managing perceptions by questioning the assumptions that went into the initial observation.

dark side Potential destructive aspects of leadership, which emerge when a leader appeals to fear or prejudice in order to gain followers.

decision making Describes how individuals and organization choose among different alternatives and identify the best solution to a problem.

deliberate practice A concentrated effort to learn a task that is directed or designed by someone with knowledge of the task.

Delphi technique An idea-generating technique where the leader collects ideas, distributes the ideas to the group, and collects a response often though a formal questionnaire.

demagogue Leaders who draw on negative emotions, often espousing a vision that reflects personal need rather than the larger goal.

developmental opportunities Job assignments that provide the basis for learning, improving skills, and growing as a professional.

diffusion of innovation Occurs when a product or idea spreads and becomes widely adopted.

displayed versus felt emotions Displayed emotions are those that are visible, while felt emotions are those that are interior, or real, to the employee.

distinctiveness Occurs when behavior is analyzed as seldom occurring in other situations.

distributive justice Describes fairness in how rewards and resources are distributed across an organization.

distributive negotiation A form of *negotiation* based on the assumption that there is a fixed amount of value that must be divided, and that a negotiation relies on adhering to a rigid position in order to gain as much value as possible.

disruptive innovation When an innovation, or a set of innovations, changes the existing technology and transforms an industry.

diversity Describes similarities and differences among people. In the context of organizations, diversity involves the processes of valuing differences in experience, background, and perspective. See also *generational diversity*.

dominant culture The artifacts, espoused values, and basic assumptions shared by most members in an organization.

dysfunctional conflict Conflict that detracts from achieving goals and performance, unlike *functional conflict*.

efficacy Also called *self-efficacy*, describes the sense of self-determination that emerges as a person observes others, and the sense of confidence that emerges as the person performs the task independently.

emotional contagion The capacity of emotions, mood, and affect to spread in a workplace.

emotional intelligence The capacity to be aware of one's own emotions and the emotions of others, manage emotions, and respond to emotions in an appropriate way.

emotional labor The effort an employee must exert to modify his or her display of emotions as appropriate to the situation or workplace environment.

emotions Strong feelings with a short duration.

equity theory Describes a psychological process where people compare the efforts put into a task and the rewards they receive with others.

espoused values Considered a dimension of culture, they describe what the members of the culture say they believe.

ethics The general study of behaviors and judgments.

executive subculture Led by those at the top of the company's hierarchy, this subculture values control and accountability for those in the organization and work to see that others share the same goals.

existence, relatedness, and growth (ERG) A theory of motivation developed by Clay Alderfer, which posits that all levels of needs can be pursued simultaneously, unlike Maslow's *hierarchy of needs*.

expectancy theory A theory in which expectations serve as an important form of motivation, leading an employee to increase effort to gain a perceived reward.

experience Considered a type of personal power, it provides greater knowledge than that given by theoretical models.

experiential learning Experience-based learning in which learning is a process that occurs primarily through generating new experiences, reflecting on those experiences, placing them in a logical framework, and then acting upon them.

expertise The ability to make good decisions quickly in a particular field, holding greater content knowledge and vocabulary. Can also serve as a form of personal power.

flow Describes the process where a person becomes completely engaged in the activity at hand.

follower attribution A line of thinking that explains the emergence of leaders as a fulfillment of psychological needs in followers.

formal authority Positional power through assigned titles, ranks, privileges, and responsibilities, providing a clear chain of command.

four dimensions of perceived justice The employee's perception of fairness that impacts motivation. The four include *distributive, procedural, interpersonal,* and *informational justice.*

free-rider effect Describes how an individual relies on other group members to do the majority of work, thus taking a "free ride" while other members carry the workload.

functional conflict Conflict that encourages achievement of tasks, unlike *dysfunctional conflict.*

garbage can approach A model that views decision making as irrational process but rather infused with emotions, politics, and other factors.

generational diversity A type of diversity that focuses on differences among generations and the environmental forces that influence values, beliefs, and behaviors.

Generation-X Those born between 1961 and 1981 and grew up with the rise of cable television, computers, and saw eight years under Ronald Reagan's presidency.

Generation-Y Those born between 1982 and 2005, also called the *Millennials,* grew up in the post-9/11 world in which technology such as smart phones and social media are a part of everyday life.

group Refers to a collection of individuals who may interact, but do not share similar goals or interdependence.

group development Describes the life cycle and the process whereby norms develop and change over time in a progressive fashion.

groupthink A situation where peer pressure stifles critical thinking and groups move toward consensus. Often generates a shared illusion of group invulnerability.

halo effect Occurs when a person has one positive characteristic that effects all other perceptions of the person. See also the *horns effect.*

heredity versus environment The heredity perspective states that people are born with a particular set of personality traits, while the environment perspective supports the notion that personality develops over time and is heavily influenced by the environment.

heterogeneous group Characterized by a greater degree of differences among members. See also *homogenous group.*

heuristics Rules by which people make decisions, focusing primarily on making economics-based decisions.

hierarchical culture When organizations place a strong value on stability, control, and on internal matters.

hierarcy of needs A theory developed by Abraham Maslow that explores motivation as a response to a series of progressively higher needs. Lower needs (food, safety) must be met before higher needs (social belonging, self-actualization) can be sought.

hindrance stress One of two ways people experience stress, this stress is experienced as a limitation on the ability to perform. See also *challenge stress.*

hindsight bias Occurs when an individual perceives that the likelihood of an event has increased after the fact, or in hindsight.

homogeneous group Where members of a group are more similar than different on key characteristics such as gender, education level, functional specialty, or age. See also *heterogeneous group.*

horns effect Occurs when a person has one negative characteristic and this effects all other perceptions of the person. See also the *halo effect.*

human sustainability Also called social sustainability, this describes the voluntary action that an organization takes to focus on the well-being of people within the organization and those who belong to the greater community in which it operates.

hygiene factors Elements of short-lived motivation, such as pay, working conditions, quality of supervisor, and organizational policies. One dimension of Herzberg's *two-factor theory.*

iceberg metaphor of culture This metaphor helps illustrate the nature of culture in organizations. Described as an iceberg, underneath the tip of the iceberg that is visible lies a body of ice many times larger than meets the eye, proving that perceptions can be deceiving.

Implicit Associations Test (IAT) A test that measures the unconscious attitudes and beliefs that people hold about different groups.

impression management The process of controlling the influence process in order to impact the ideas that are formed about a person, an idea, or an event.

incremental change Often involving shifts in thinking and challenges the basic assumptions of the organization's culture. Incremental change occurs slowly and unfolds over time. See also *rapid change.*

individual difference The impact of personal characteristics associated with individual processes on what people think, feel, and do.

individual processes Describes individual differences in characteristics, learning, and perception.

informational justice Describes fairness in what information is used and communicated within the organization.

information literacy The ability to properly collect, evaluate, and present information.

in-group favoritism Giving preferential treatment to a member of one's group.

innovation The process of developing, implementing, and marketing a new or novel approach to a project or service.

instrumental values Values that serve in the process of achieving goals, see *terminal values.*

integrative negotiation A form of *negotiation,* often called interest-based negotiation, in which values, resources, or positions are not considered fixed, unlike a *distributive negotiation.*

integrity Seen as the opposite of *corruption,* organizations that demonstrate integrity track and respond to the ethical lapses made by employees, maintain oversight over organizational actions, build a culture of compliance, and have internal reporting systems to capture ethical breaches as they occur.

intelligence A general cognitive ability or intellect, often considered a threshold competency.

interactionist An approach with encourages conflict as long as the conflict is functional and leads to productive outcomes.

interdisciplinary study A study that draws from different disciplines in order to understand organizations from multiple perspectives and viewpoints.

intergroup level attribution Occurs when member or a subgroup of an organization assign credit or blame to another work group within the organization.

interpersonal behaviors Behaviors related to people interacting with others. See also *task behaviors.*

interpersonal conflict Conflict that arises from relationships with others.

interpersonal justice Describes fairness in how people interact and are treated.

interpersonal level attribution A form of *attribution* (blame or credit) placed on another person with whom you interact. See also *intrapersonal level attribution.*

interpersonal processes refer to the pattern of interactions among individuals that includes groups and teams, negotiation, and communication and diversity.

interpretive-based learning An approach to learning that encourages the student to integrate concepts and differentiate among and across ideas.

intrapersonal level attribution A form of *attribution* (blame or credit) assigned to oneself. See also *interpersonal level attribution.*

intuition The process of assessing a situation identifying problems or opportunities, and knowing what action to take, even when the decision maker cannot consciously describe the situation.

job characteristics Elements of work that motivate work behavior, such as skill variety, task identity, task significance, autonomy, and feedback.

knowledge, skills, and abilities (KSAs) Competencies, which are important for individuals and for group composition.

leader–member exchange (LMX) An approach that emphasizes the importance of the relationship among leaders, followers, and the context.

leadership The process whereby a leader enlists others to help achieve a change, vision, or goal.

leadership grid A grid developed by researchers Blake and Mouton describing five *styles of leadership* based on the degree to which a leader shows concern for people or a task.

leading and leadership Processes which explain the factors that impact differences in leadership, motivation, persuasion, influence, impression management, and decision making.

learning The act of gathering, generating, processing, and acting on knowledge.

learning cycle A learning process in which a person engages with the world, which invokes a concrete experience, which involves feelings, emotions, and direct experiences.

learning flexibility The willingness and ability of a person to move from relying on specialized knowledge to a more complex and universal understanding of a situation.

learning goal orientation When an individual focuses on developing or attaining a certain competency.

learning styles Describes a person's preference for learning in one or more of the four learning phases of the *learning cycle*.

levels of organizational behavior Behavior occurs at three levels—individual, team or group, and organization.

Lewin's force field model of change A model that identifies the forces that promote and prevent change in organizations.

liking A form of persuasion that impacts people's beliefs and behaviors, for instance we are more likely to say "yes" to the requests of people we like. See also *reciprocal liking*.

locus of control The extent to which someone believes that they are in control of their environment.

Machiavellianism An attitude toward others as objects to be manipulated, based on the character from the essay *The Prince,* by Niccolo di Bernardo Machiavelli (circa 1500).

maintenance norms Also called interpersonal norms, reflect the interpersonal psychological and emotional rules that govern group life and that impact conflict, emotional awareness, and social interactions.

market-driven culture When organizations place a strong value on stability and control but focus on external matters.

mediation Involves a neutral third party who listens to both sides of a negotiation and then crafts an agreement.

mental accounting A term coined by economist Richard Thaler to refer to the mental tricks that individuals employ when making financial and business decisions.

Millennials Those born between 1982 and 2005, also called the *Generation-Y,* were the first generation to come of age in the new millennium.

modeling The process of learning that occurs through observation and imitation.

mood Distinct from *emotions,* a mood is broader and lasts longer.

morals Describe an individuals rule around what is acceptable versus unacceptable.

motivators Sustained goals such as improving opportunities for advancement, recognition, and self-development. One dimension of Herzberg's *two-factor theory.*

Myers-Briggs Type Indicator A personality test based on psychologist Carl Jung's belief that personality is based on a specific cluster of four different dichotomies: introversion/ extraversion, sensing/intuiting, thinking/feeling, and judging/ perceiving.

multiple intelligences A systematic alternative to traditional measures of intelligence developed by Howard Gardner, including seven forms of intelligence including verbal, mathematical, visual, kinesthetic, musical, interpersonal, and intrapersonal.

national culture Describes the shared values, beliefs, and behaviors within a country or culture.

naturalistic decision making Describes the process where decision makers rely on a quick assessment of a situation and draw on experience and intuition to determine a course of action.

need for affiliation, achievement, and power A theory from psychologist David McClelland which characterizes motivation as a process of fulfilling individual needs, focusing primarily on these three basic psychological needs.

negative organizational outcomes Describes a full range of undesirable behaviors including unethical behavior, sabotage, absenteeism, and incivility.

negotiation A decision-making process where two or more individuals agree on how to allocate resources, resolve competing interests, settle an issue, or determine an agreeable position.

nominal group technique A process by which a group sets out to generate an idea or solution to a problem with individual members conducting much of the work independently rather than face-to-face.

non-programmed decisions Require new methods and procedures, often involving highly complex and non-routine problems.

norms The patterns of interaction within a group, the specific "rules of the game" to which members must adhere.

novelty Describes what is new or different, that influences *perception*.

ombudsman A person or group of people that employees turn to if they believe they have seen an unethical practice, responsible for following up on the concern and investigating it.

operational subculture A *subculture* that values local knowledge and skills, emphasizing the capacity of the individual to deal with problems within the organization.

operant conditioning An adaptation of the stimulus, reward, and response connection in humans developed by psychologist B. F. Skinner through introduction of predetermined positive rewards.

optimal experience An experience of *flow* in which an activity feels effortless and a person feels mastery over the task.

organizational behavior The study of people and what people think, feel, and do within organizations.

organizational change Any modification, planned or unplanned, that alters a structure, process, or outcome in an organization.

organizational culture The patterns of shared beliefs, values, and behaviors within an organization which cannot be accounted for by traditional organizational factors.

organizational ethics The standards for behaviors and judgments within the context of an organization.

organizational level attribution Occurs when members or sub-groups in an organization assign credit or blame to the organization.

organizational politics Any behavior by people in organizations based on social power designed to get one's way.

organizational processes include the ingrained patterns of acting and interacting at the organizational level and cover topics of culture, change, innovation, stress, corporate social responsibility, ethics, and sustainability.

organizational psychology-based decision making Includes the systematic weighing of options, but in addition considers the role of emotions, politics, and practical considerations which impact outcomes.

parochialism Occurs when a person views another as though they are the same as oneself, that they have the same experiences as others, rather than taking account of another person's uniqueness.

path–goal theory Suggests that access to external resources may be more important in determining leadership success than the capability of the individual leader.

pay-to-play schemes Where an organization pays a government official in order to gain access to influential officials or win a contract with the government.

peer pressure When an individual group member feels pressured by other members of the group.

perception Involves selecting a subset of sensory information. By selecting and processing only a limited amount of information, what is perceived as reality also becomes limited.

perfect information When all relevant, necessary, and accurate information is at the disposal of the decision makers.

performance goal orientation Unlike *learning goal orientation,* performance goal orientation focuses on achieving success through goal attainment.

performance-based learning An approach to learning that focuses on the basic concepts, terms, and theories associated with organizations to facilitate a student's performance.

personal attractiveness A type of personal power, including physical attractiveness as well as charisma and likability.

personality A set of individual characteristics that are consistent over time.

persuasion tactics Purposeful techniques to attempt to change people's behavior, sell ideas, gain resources, or shape impressions.

planned change Intentional change instituted within the organization. See also *unplanned change.*

polarization effect A tendency of groups to make riskier, or more conservative, decisions than individuals working alone.

positive organizational outcomes Outcomes such as effectiveness, job satisfaction, organizational commitment, and performance, that an organization seeks to achieve.

practice-based and developmental learning Essentially, the application of concepts through case study and exercises in an effort to experience the concepts firsthand.

probability A mathematical formulation that seeks to predict the *certainty* that an event will occur.

problem framing Explains how a situation is framed, or presented, will impact the choices made by decision makers.

procedural justice Describes fairness in how decisions are reached and how outcomes are determined.

process conflict Conflict that affects the work process itself, how work gets done, and has a negative impact on results.

professional subculture Defined by a group of individuals within the organization who share a set of practices within a particular occupation and exercise control over how work is done or how to interpret situations based on this allegiance.

programmed decisions Characterized by routine decision-making situations where actions have clearly identifiable and often predictable outcomes.

prototype An imagined version of the situation that the decision maker has previously encountered.

psychological safety The shared belief among members of a group that the environment within the group is safe for interpersonal risk taking.

punctuated equilibrium model Considers how time constraints trigger changes in productivity by examining two primary stages of group development, low performance and high performance, separated by a midpoint transition.

qualitative An approach that explores situations and seek a deeper understanding of a situation through the use of detailed methods such as focus groups, interviews, and observation.

quantitative An approach that tries to predict results and identify factors that are universal. Quantitative approaches rely on surveys and other large-scale data collection techniques.

quid pro quo The "something in exchange for something" mentality often found in a *transactional leader.*

rapid change Involves quick surface-level changes to policies, procedures, or resolutions to immediate problems. See also *incremental change.*

rational decision making The systematic weighing of options to maximize desired outcomes by estimating the probabilities of various outcomes.

reciprocal liking A phenomenon further to the persuasion technique of *liking,* when people like those who like them in return.

reciprocity A tactic in which the a persuader does you a favor, and then asks for a specific favor in return.

reinforcement theory The application of *operant conditioning* theory to organizational practices, using rewards for behaviors as incentives.

relationship outcome A strategy of negotiation that focuses on preserving the relationship between or among negotiating parties.

relevance A secondary type of positional power which refers to a person's importance to achieve collective goals.

resistance to change The process whereby individuals fail to recognize the value of a change and thus cling to old routines, habits, or ways of thinking rather than embrace the changes.

role diversity A type of diversity which characterizes a public or socially determined form of diversity associated with a role, rather than a person-related diversity.

roles The division of labor and skill among members of a group or team.

satisficing Making a decision that is not based on perfect information and pure objectivity.

scarcity A tactic used to get people to overvalue and over-desire a specific outcome by portraying it as scarce.

schema A mental image of what an authority figure will look and act like.

selective perception The process where information and its recall becomes consistent with people's values and experiences, while information that disconfirms people's values and experience is ignored.

self-determination theory Describes how individuals have a need for autonomy, competence, and relatedness.

self-efficacy The confidence that someone experiences relative to a particular task.

self-fulfilling prophecy A perceptual limitation that occurs when someone's expectations influence another person to act consistently with those expectations.

self-monitoring The ability of an individual to adjust her behavior based on the environment in which she operates.

self-serving bias A specific form of attribution, where people take credit for personal success but deny responsibility for failure.

sender–receiver model of communication A three-step process model of communication which describes how facts and simple information are communicated.

sensemaking A process of how people gather information, make judgments, and then take action.

shared leadership A perspective which considers what happens when leadership responsibilities are shared among multiple leaders.

shareholder value A perspective which focuses on the pursuit of self-interest at the expense of other values, commonly thought to encourage unethical behavior.

situational approach An approach that suggests that problems or situations need to be evaluated in a particular context in order to find the best tool or ideas to respond.

situational, or contingency, leadership A leadership approach that focuses on how leaders shift their behaviors to address different situations as they arise.

social learning An approach to learning that takes into consideration the function of social circumstances and environment in how meaning is transmitted from one person to another.

social loafing Occurs when only a few members of a group take responsibility for accomplishing the work of the entire group.

social power An individual's ability to influence others, by effectively using persuasion tactics.

socialization The process by which new members become indoctrinated into the culture.

social proof A tactic in which an ambiguous situation where appropriate action is not readily apparent we look to others to tell us what we should do.

stakeholders Individuals or groups that have a vested interest in the success of an organization and exert pressure on an organization.

stereotype Determining that someone holds certain traits based on a category.

storytelling The process of vividly conveying an experience through a verbal or written narration.

stress Occurs when a situation poses challenges that exceed an individual's ability to deal with the challenges.

stressors Factors that contribute to stress.

styles of leadership Described in the *leadership grid,* the five styles include Country Club style, Impoverished style, Authoritarian style, Team Leader style, and Middle of the Road style.

subculture A culture within a culture, composed of a subset of members who share similar values and who define their work in similar ways.

substantive outcome A strategy of negotiation that focuses on the content of the negotiation itself.

sustainability The set of voluntary actions that an organization takes to demonstrate its environmental and social responsibilities.

talent management An approach to motivation in which programs are designed to integrate various human resource and motivational efforts that exist across an organization into a comprehensive organizational strategy.

task behaviors Behaviors associated with performing a particular task. See also *interpersonal behaviors.*

task conflict Conflict around disagreement of specific tasks and how to accomplish those tasks in order to be more productive.

task norms Reflect aspects of group life directed towards work and accomplishing organizational goals.

team A specific type of group which holds interdependent roles and goals, and holds shared responsibility for specific outcomes. See also *virtual teams.*

terminal values Values that serve as goals to be achieved. See also *instrumental values.*

Theory X and Theory Y Developed by Douglas McGregor, a theory that draws a distinction between the assumptions that managers make about employees and how they choose to focus on internal or external rewards with the employees.

third party conflict resolution Represents a formal process of relationship building where a neutral person works to help the people involved resolve their differences.

traits Attributes associated with a leader, such as extraversion, intelligence, cognitive ability, and physical characteristics such as height and weight.

transactional leadership A leader who appeals to the self-interests of the followers, often offering something tangible in exchange for loyalty.

transformational leadership A leader that obtains followers by building trust and a sense of loyalty between the leader and follower.

triple bottom line The diverse responsibilities of an organization, which include economic viability, environmental concern (focusing on minimal impact), and health of the community/fair treatment of employees.

two-factory theory (or motivator–hygiene theory) Developed by Fredrick Herzberg, this approach to motivation relates two dimensions: short-lived *hygiene factors* (such as pay or working conditions) and long-term *motivators* (such as improving opportunities for advancement and recognition).

Type A and Type B personalities Common personality types whereby Type A individuals seek situations that require high degrees of achievement, are more competitive, and have a greater sense of urgency than Type B individuals.

types of contemporary organization Organizations come in an endless variety of types, from a network of shared responsibility, to bureaucratic, to professional, to a community of practice, to a representative democratic organization.

uncertainty Nearly every possible outcome is, to some degree, unknown; a variable in decision making.

universal approach An approach that suggests that one idea or set of tools applies to any situation.

unplanned change Arises when organizations fail or plan or are caught off guard by unanticipated events. See also *planned change*.

values Describe beliefs in general and suggest a broad set of priorities and judgments, usually within a set of values known as values systems.

values clarification The process of clarifying or becoming more aware of one's own individual values.

values orientation The systems of values that predominate within a culture and can be summarized along three primary systems: pragmatic, intellectual, and human values.

verbal artifacts *Artifacts* that reveal an organization's culture through verbal means such as jargon, nicknames, stories, myths, and metaphors.

virtual teams Teams that use information technology to accomplish work, with members in various locations.

INDEX

Page numbers followed by "*f*" and "*t*" indicate figures and tables.